To 'an unknown woman in Minsk'

Acknowledgement

'I have a dream', by Martin Luther King, reprinted by arrangement with The Heirs to the Estate of Martin Luther King, Jr., c/o Writers House, Inc. as agent for the proprietor. Copyright 1963 by Martin Luther King, Jr., copyright renewed by Coretta Scott King.

Preface

I would like to thank Templeton College and the Said Business School at the University of Oxford for facilitating my initial sabbatical terms and for supporting the last two years when I have been the recipient of an Economic and Social Research Council Senior Research Fellowship (No. H52427500197). I would also like to thank many people who have discussed the issues involved with me or kindly read drafts at various stages. Amongst these are the members of Keele University Management Department, especially Martin Parker and Mihaela Kelemen. Additionally I have received much support from Mick Grint, Colonel G. C. Grint, Colonel Mike Harper, Peter Wilson, and Eddie Finn. At a detailed level I would like to thank Kuseni Dlamini for his help on the Anglo-Zulu wars, Knud Rogilds for help with Nelson and the Nore and Spithead mutinies, Steve Tilt for help with the charts, John Gastil at the University of Washington for his constructive advice and patient reading of the entire first draft, Hilary Walford for turning my usual literal mess into something approaching literary English, and David Musson at OUP for support and common sense. Finally I would like to thank Sandra, Katy, Beki, and Kris for their forbearance, particularly when I have told them yet another 'story' from 'the book'.

Contents

List of Figures and Table

Figures

Tables

1

Introduction: The Arts of Leadership

Socratic Thinking about Leadership

In 1986, before I first began to study leadership in a serious manner, my knowledge of it was complete. I knew basically all there was to know and I had already spent over a decade practising it as a senior representative of a trade union in England. I should have stopped then, because ever since that time my understanding has decreased in direct proportion to my increased knowledge: in effect, the more I read, the less I understood. This was partly to do with a Socratic problem: the more I read, the more I realized how ignorant I was. But there was something else at work: the more I read, the more *contradictory* appeared the conclusions I came to. Despite all my best efforts to analyse the data as objectively as possible and to run the numbers past as many sophisticated statistics as I could manipulate, the results refused to regurgitate any significant pattern except one banal truism: successful leaders are successful. In 1997, at the start of the research project in which this book has its origins, I stopped trying to read everything about leadership and began to try and think through the implications of my problem. And at this point, when I had ceased my quest for information, and started my quest for understanding, a light of some form began to emerge. Fig. 1.1 reproduces my efforts at understanding leadership since the beginning of my studies.

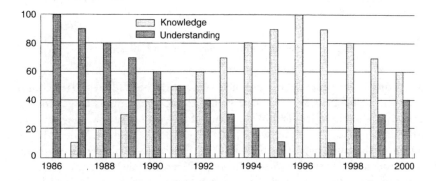

Fig. 1.1. Socrates, information, and leadership

That light was not an answer but a series of questions that undermined whatever faith I had previously had in traditional 'objective' forms of analysis. In general these comprise three approaches that remain popular in the conventional literature: *trait* approaches, *contingency* approaches, and *situational* approaches. The fourth approach, *constitutive*, forms the basis of this book. These are summarized in Fig. 1.2. In the *trait* approach, the 'essence' of the individual leader is critical but the context is not. Thus, providing we select the right leader with the appropriate leadership traits, everything should be plain sailing on our metaphorical journey. In short, a leader is a leader under any circumstances and it is more than likely that such traits are part of the individual's genetic make-up—otherwise the circumstances of the situation that faced the individual at some time in his or her life would have had an influence upon his or her leadership 'traits'. This kind of model implies that organizations should concern themselves with the *selection* of leaders rather than their *development*, though traits can, presumably, be honed, just as one's singing can be improved through training or one's athletic ability can be improved. However, since—in this approach—you cannot 'make a silk purse out of a sow's ear', there is no hope for those of us not born with certain gifts or talents for leadership.

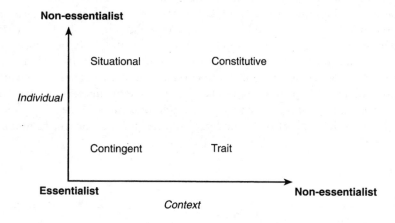

Fig. 1.2. Essentialist and non-essentialist leadership

In the *contingency* approach, both the essence of the individual and the context are knowable and critical. Here one would expect individuals to generate an awareness of their own leadership skills and of the context so that they can compute the degree of alignment between themselves and the context. Where the permutation of the two suggests a high level of alignment—for instance, where a strong leader and a crisis situation coincide—then the leader should step into the breach, only to step out when the situation changes and the context is no longer conducive to his or her vigorous style. Self-awareness and situational analysis are the two developmental areas for such approaches to concentrate upon and, providing these are carried out satisfactorily, we will get to our destination.

The third variant, the *situational* approach, reproduces the essentialist position with regard to the context—certain contexts demand certain kinds of leadership—so we do need to be very clear about where we are. However, in this model the leader may be flexible enough to generate a repertoire of styles to suit the particular situation. In effect, the leader's actions and behaviour change to suit the situation. Consequently, development work is required both in terms of situational analysis and in terms of expanding the variety or versatility of the leader. Here, the leader's methods for getting us from A to B will vary infinitely, but we should still get to B.

The final, and most recent, model here, the *constitutive* approach, questions the significance of the allegedly objective conditions that surround leaders and implies that the 'conditions' are as contested as any other element. For example, contingency models suggest that, under certain conditions, a particular form of leadership is most appropriate—that is, a crisis requires 'firm' leadership. But the problem with this is twofold. First, it is no different from the scientific-management approach pursued by F.W. Taylor at the beginning of the century in which 'the one best way' of organizing production became synonymous with good management—and leadership. But Taylor was never able to prove what this best way was, nor can contingency theory. Secondly, and the probable reason for the problem, what counts as a 'situation' and what counts as the 'appropriate' way of leading in that situation are interpretive and contestable issues, not issues that can be decided by objective criteria. This might sound counter-intuitive—for example, surely in war we know when a crisis exists? Yet one argument for leadership would be that those people who can operate calmly because they do not consider the situation to be critical—while the rest 'lose their heads' because they perceive a catastrophe about to happen—will provide the most successful forms of leadership. Take, for example, an air raid on a group of soldiers: is this not a crisis? Would we not expect the appropriate behaviour of successful leaders to be screaming at the troops to return fire at best or at least to scatter and diving for cover oneself? Yet, when Patton's Third Army was north of Avranches in 1944, a *Luftwaffe* attack sent all of the troops and officers racing for the hedgerows to escape—all except Patton, who 'sat in a deckchair in a nearby field a cigar in his hand . . . The word spread that if Patton was not afraid there was no reason for anyone else to be either' (quoted in D'Este 1996: 636).

Contrarily, those leaders seeking to exercise greater control over their population might construe (imagine/invent) a situation as critical in order to legitimate their action. Under these circumstances it becomes impossible to know what is contingently the best form of leadership, because the information to assess the situation is monopolized by the leaders. Despite this, leadership must still be perceived as 'appropriate', but what that means is an interpretive issue. By implication, leaders must respond to the culture within which they operate, but, like Hitler, they are also capable of changing that culture.

The *constitutive* approach, therefore, is very much a pro-active affair for leaders. It is they who actively shape our interpretation of the environment, the challenges, the goals, the competition, the strategy, and the tactics; they also try and persuade us that their interpretation is both correct—and therefore the truth—and, ironically, not an interpretation but the truth. But because this is essentially an interpretive affair, it casts doubt upon those claiming scientific legitimations for their claims and buttresses an approach to leadership that is firmly within the arts, not the sciences. In effect, I am suggesting here that one of the main reasons that we have so much difficulty in explaining leadership and in trying to enhance the leadership qualities and skills of those who are leaders is that we have adopted a philosophical perspective that obscures rather than illuminates the phenomenon. In other words, the more 'scientific' our methods of analysis become, the less likely we are to understand leadership because it is not accessible to scientific approaches. This would be the equivalent of trying to measure the merit of a picture by reference to a scientific system that evaluates the objective use of colour, form, and definition. Such a measuring system is far less relevant than evaluating the picture on the basis of alternative measures that are non-scientific. For example, we can establish a picture's value by how much we can sell it for, how long the queue is to see it, whether it wins any prizes, whether we like it, whether other artists like it, and a whole variety of other ways, none of which is scientific or objective.

While natural science is generally held to progress through experimentation, in which all variables except one are held constant to establish the significance of that variable, such experimentation is extremely rare in social science in general and leadership research in particular. There have been experimental forms of leadership research, but either they have been very limited in their numbers and replicability, or, while replicable, the results have been less than compelling (Sherif 1967). As a result, most leadership research has tended to be either a review of successful leaders or grounded in survey approaches. Either way, the results are often informative but not definitive. The major problem seems to me to be the very complexity of the subject. There are so many potentially significant variables in establishing what counts as successful leadership that it is practically impossible to construct an effective experiment that might generate conclusive evidence on the topic. Let us take, as a simple example, the role of football managers in the English Premier League. Surely these individuals are 'leaders' and to take the actions of football clubs in appointing and sacking managers at face value we should assume that these leaders make a difference. We should, therefore, be able to establish what makes a great football leader and then replicate that greatness—or at least know what we are looking for when we are trying to replicate it. Fig. 1.3 concerns the fate of Everton Football Club under various managers since the 1984–5 season.

It is clear that the club is anything but consistent in its performance but that inconsistency also extends to the managers. Thus, for example, although the club did well under Howard Kendall initially, his returns to the club did not produce

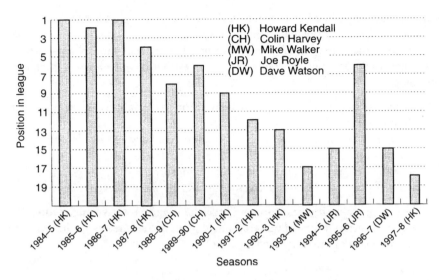

Fig. 1.3. Everton FC: does leadership matter?

the same success and his departures imply that the club held him responsible—both for the successes and for the failures. But should they? To what extent is a football manager in control over—and therefore responsible for- the myriad things that determine a club's success? This is an impossible question to answer—but it does not stop clubs holding their managers/leaders responsible. There is a double irony here. In the first place, the success or failure of a football team rests squarely upon the shoulders of the footballers on the pitch—but ironically we hold the manager solely responsible for their efforts. Secondly, I have lost count of the number of times a football manager has been given the 'kiss of death' by the board of directors publicly stating their absolute faith in the manager. Almost by definition this means the sack within twenty-four hours and thus the irony.

It is also important to note here the limits of leadership, in particular the capacity of leaders to make mistakes. In effect, for organizations to succeed, the followers must play their part and cannot rely upon the leader or leaders to secure success alone, both because that success is a social not an individual achievement and because followers carry the responsibility of compensating for leaders' errors. It is this mirroring of followers' responsibilities that Heifetz (1994) concentrates upon as the proper role of leadership and the motivation and mobilization of this responsibility distinguish the successful from the unsuccessful leaders.

That, surely, is one of the greatest ironies of leadership, for, while we traditionally look to leaders to solve our problems, it would seem that leaders are most likely to be successful when they reflect the problems straight back to where they have to be solved—at the feet of the followers.

If, then, leadership is an art—or rather an array of arts—more than a science, then that might account for the four paradoxes that have bedevilled its understanding:

- it appears to have more to do with invention that analysis, despite claims to the contrary;
- it appears to operate on the basis of indeterminacy whilst claiming to be deterministic;
- it appears to be rooted in irony, rather than truth;
- it usually rests on a constructed identity but claims a reflective identity.

Let me explore these four paradoxes a little and suggest how we might adopt the metaphors of art as a way of understanding them better, first by beginning with that most elusive of questions: *who* are we?

The Who Question: Constructing Identity and the Construction of Truth

Leadership is not simply about leaders. Leadership is an essentially social phenomenon: without followers there are no leaders. What leaders must do, therefore, is construct an imaginary community that followers can feel part of. In this case the imagination of the followers is critical, because few will ever know their fellow community members well enough really to know whether they have anything in common either with them or their putative leader (Anderson 1991: 6). We can probably take this further to suggest—ironically—that imaginary communities may well be considerably stronger than 'real' communities. By this I mean, for example, that we may feel we have more in common with a community that we do not know intimately than with one that we do. Take, for instance, the problem of moving house: if I think about moving locally—within my 'real' community—I know that I should avoid living in 'that' part of town or down 'this' particular street or next door to 'them' because I *know* what kind of people live there. But if I intend to move a hundred or a thousand miles away, I am quite happy to live near anyone because I *don't know* what they are like. Thus, in my imagination, I construct my unknown destination rather more generously than I do my known destination. Paradoxically, then, when I am called to defend my national community against 'foreigners' (who have allegedly invaded a country that I had not heard of until the invasion), I again have to imagine that I have more in common with my fellow nationals than with 'the enemy'—even if my lifestyle, chances, and culture are actually much closer to those in the 'enemy' camp than in my own. It was precisely this 'objective' reality across social classes that persuaded Marx to believe that the unity between the same social classes across national boundaries was stronger than the solidarity between different social classes in the same country. Marx was wrong, and he was wrong partly because solidarity is constructed in the imagination and does not mechanically reflect the material similarity of conditions. As Anderson (1991: 7) suggests, 'regardless of the actual inequality and exploitation that may prevail in each, the nation is always conceived as a deep, horizontal comradeship'.

Leaders, then, must spend at least some of their time constructing not just followers, but a *community* of followers. Whether that community is held together by love of the leader or of the community, by hate of the 'other', by greed, or by honour is less relevant than that identity is an issue that successful leaders address. Yet few people will ever really know their leader, least of all those at a national level. As Machiavelli (1981: 56) pointed out: 'Men in general judge by their eyes rather than their hands; because everyone is in a position to watch, few are in a position to come in close touch with you. Everyone sees what you appear to be, few experience what you really are. And those few dare not gainsay the many who are backed by the majesty of the state.'

The significance of this can be seen in the public reaction to the death of Diana, Princess of Wales, in 1997. Literally millions of people around the world were touched by the events of the death and the funeral, but there cannot have been more than a few hundred people who knew her personally and only a handful would have been able to experience what she 'really' was. Her mourners had to imagine themselves into a community that knew her. Here the double meaning of 'imagined' is especially pertinent. On the one hand, the British public did indeed seem to unite in grief and the national media duly recorded—that is, *revealed*—that collective grief; through a collective leap of imagination, Britain's social, cultural, and political divisions were stripped away to reveal the bedrock consensus that holds Britain together. On the other hand, the unity also appears imaginary in the sense that the media *constructed*, rather than *revealed*, the national consensus. For example, the British Film Institute's research suggests that half the population was *not* profoundly affected by the death. In fact, 40 per cent thought the media coverage excessive, while many who were affected saw Diana's life and death as a vehicle to analyse their own personal troubles rather than one solely concerned with that of the princess (Willis and Turnock 1998: 8–9).

It is but a short distance from the imaginative construction of a community of followers to the distorting invention of a community of fanatics, and much of that distance is routed directly through the emotional underpinnings of identity and the identity of the 'other'. For example, Adolf Hitler was reluctant to engage in war with the British, not because he was particularly concerned with British military prowess—he was not—but because he regarded the British as second only to the Germans in their 'Aryan' purity. Ironically he usually referred to the British as the English but, amongst all the nationalities making up the British, the English have probably the least claim to a definitive ethnic identity. Indeed, one consequence of the wars in the twentieth century has been that the very idea of a British identity has been cast into doubt as the empire collapsed, Europe arose, and the various elements of the United Kingdom showed clear signs of imminent separation, with Scottish and Welsh devolution and some degree of independence returning to Northern Ireland. But the identity of all these groups has long been a contested arena. Historically, linguistically, and ethnically, the component parts of the 'Celtic fringe' have little in common, other than being 'not-English'. Indeed, S. James (1999) has argued that much of the ancient history of the Celts as a discrete ethnic people is a myth, constructed for political purposes in the early eighteenth century by the Welsh patriot Edward Lhuyd. And Daniel Defoe's albeit satirical *The True-Born Englishman*, with its eighteenth-century account of the ethnically diverse origins of the English—'a mongrel half-bred race', as he describes it—casts doubt upon all those who suggest there was a time when English identity was both clear and ethnically 'pure'. The force of Defoe's dissent draws its vitriol from a denial of clear boundaries between groups, for Sahlins is surely right to suggest that 'National identity, like ethnic or communal identity, is contingent and relational: it is defined by the social and territorial boundaries drawn to distinguish the collective self and its implicit negation, the other' (Sahlins 1989: 271, quoted in Colley 1994: 5–6).

Defoe's point also reminds us that collective identity is imagined, for if to be 'English' implies having a whole raft of things in common with every other English person, then the diversity of people living in Britain needs to be transcended through what Anderson refers to as a collective leap of the imagination. In effect, because the English—or any other population—hardly know each other, they have to imagine the similarities that apparently bind them together. But, to follow Jenkins (1996: 28), to say that something is imagined does not mean that it is imaginary. In effect, identity is constructed not discovered; it is imposed upon a population rather than emerging from one; it does not reflect what is a deep essence within a people but is essentially steeped upon a people. It is not an event but a process, for 'social identities exist and are acquired, claimed and allocated within power relations. Identity is something over which struggles take place and with which strategies are advanced: it is means and end in politics . . . Social identity is a practical accomplishment, a process' (Jenkins 1996: 25). Because of this, identities tend to become relatively stable in and through conflicts over boundaries (Douglas 1966)—that is to say, they are doubly 'forged'. First, in the sense that conflict generates heat and violence, identities are often 'forged' through war—as, for instance, British and French identities were forged through their interminable wars with each other, especially in the late eighteenth and early nineteenth centuries (Colley 1994; Pears 1997).

War is a particularly powerful crucible for identity construction because it often denudes the possibilities of difference; it makes us choose between them and us, between being for us or against us. As Jabri (1996: 5) reminds us: 'To be a dissenting voice is to be an outsider . . . what would previously have been blurred social boundaries become sharpened primarily through a discursive focus upon features, both symbolic and material, which divide communities.'

A further consequence of this 'forging' is a tendency for the complete stripping of all critical faculties, such that an identity based in a balanced construction of the admirable and distasteful elements of a group becomes rendered down to an infatuation, where the group or nation can do no wrong. In effect, there is a transition from a 'warts-and-all' patriotism to a xenophobic 'engulfment' (Scheff 1994). It is not far from such an engulfment to an assumption that 'the other' is the epitome of evil whose shaming and humiliation of one's own society can be revoked only by the annihilation of that same 'other' (Cooley 1922; Lewis 1971; Elias 1989; Scheff 1994).

Secondly, they are 'forged' in the sense of being 'not a true likeness', in that national identities are superimposed upon a myriad of competing local, regional, class, religious, ethnic, status, and any other identities that pre-exist the national construction. They are also 'forged' in the sense that identities do not exist as 'facts' or as 'things'—that is, independently of people; rather they have to be reproduced by people if they are to survive, though identities, like groups, may survive irrespective of who the particular individuals are that make them persist (Barth 1969). In the latter form we might note how the recent eruptions of violence over ethnic identity (in Rwanda, Turkey, Northern Ireland, and what used to be Yugoslavia, for example) appear in one form to be manifestations of resistance against 'false' identities imposed by 'the other' (Tutsis resisting Hutu identity, Kurds resisting Turkish identity, Nationalists resisting Loyalist identity, and Croats and Bosnians resisting first Yugoslav and then Serbian identity. In 1999 the very identities of the Kosovan Albanians were removed by the destruction of their official papers by the Serbian forces.) Here we have apparently 'true' identities— that is, they reflect *essentially* different ethnic groups with historically legitimate claims to their own culture and land: the 'real' and often 'innate' conditions generate 'real' identities, that then become manifest in national stereotypes. On the other hand, the history that they proclaim is itself littered with ambiguities and imagined times: for before Belgian intervention the Tutsis and Hutus lived relatively harmoniously together; at the same time, Turks and Kurds fought together under the same banner of the Ottoman Empire; while Irish history is a veritable jumble of eras when different groups at various times have either consorted with each other or attempted to eliminate each other (Sadowski 1998). In ex-Yugoslavia, Croat and Serb intermarriage was quite common before the break-up of the federal state, and the power of that state to 'suppress' the 'simmering' pot of ethnic violence appears to have been much exaggerated. Kosovo's territory is as disputed as its ethnic identity, for it has been ruled, in sequence, by Bulgarians, Byzantines, Serbs, Ottomans, Austrians, Serbs, Italians, Germans, Yugoslavians, and latterly, Serbs again (Malcolm 1999). Similarly, it is an open question whether the Soviet Union collapsed *because* it could not hold together the disparate ethnic groups whose identities it had coercively and vigorously repressed or *because*, as a consequence of the USSR falling apart, those left in the ruins were forced to construct new identities for themselves (albeit, often on the basis of previous ones) (Keitner 1997). In other words, the only essential element of identities are that they are essentially contested, and that contestation is the context within which leaders vie to impose their own version of identity upon populations.

This particular approach to identity owes much to constructivism. Constructivism in its most radical formats rejects the notion of essences entirely (see Grint and Woolgar 1997). That is to say, it rejects the idea that we can ever have an objective account of an individual or a situation or a technology—or, in this case, an identity—because all such accounts are derived from linguistic reconstructions; they are not, in effect, transparent reproductions of the truth. Instead the approach suggests that what the identity (or situation or leader or whatever) actually is, is a consequence of various accounts and interpretations, all of which vie for domination. In effect, we know what an identity or leader or situation actually is only because some particular version of it or him or her has secured prominence. The relativism at the heart of the approach does not mean that all interpretations are equal—and that what the leader/context is, is wholly a matter of the whim of the observer—because some interpretations do appear, to misquote Orwell, to be more equal than others. For example, my version of an identity—individual or collective—must fight for dominance along with others. Similarly, my account of a popular individual may be that he or she is an incompetent charlatan, but, if the popularity of this person rests upon the support of more powerful 'voices' (including material resources), then my negative voice will carry little or no weight. The critical issue for this approach, then, is not what the identity or leader or the context 'really' is, but what are the processes by which these phenomena are constructed into successes or failures, crises or periods of calm. For example, when the CEO declares an impending crisis based on information that must remain confidential to prevent the crisis deepening, how are we mere ignorant subordinates to evaluate the claim? When governments declare military 'incidents' to be 'the mother of all victories', how are we to judge the situation? [1] Do we ever really know what happened? When the media represent all the leaders of a particular country or area as villains or heroes, do we really know enough about them to agree or disagree? The point of this approach, therefore, is to suggest that we may never know what the true essence of an identity, a leader, or a situation actually is, and must often base our actions and beliefs on the accounts of others from whom we can (re)constitute our version of events.

Furthermore, even the most powerful leaders are restricted by the social discourses within which they operate. In other words, leaders cannot invent a completely new world or identity but are constrained by the language, the customs, the social mores, the dress codes, and so on with which we all operate. For example, the discourse of marriage is primarily, but not only, a set of words and phrases that encourage those within it to perceive themselves and to act in certain ways: they are 'wives' or 'husbands' or 'spouses' rather than 'partners'; they are 'widows' or 'widowers', 'divorced' or 'separated' or whatever. The marriage discourse does not *force* people to think and act 'appropriately', but it operates as a kind of 'default'—we have to make conscious decisions to step outside it if we want to challenge the status quo. These categories are clearly not 'objectively real' in the sense that husbands or wives can be scientifically proven to look different or act differently from those not involved in marriage, but discourses do appear to take on a life of their own—they reify the world, they make something appear real when it is merely a cultural convention. A gardening example might clarify this better. Trying to define 'weeds' in a scientific way is impossible, because weeds are merely plants that are in the 'wrong' place. To some people poppies are weeds, but I consider them flowers; to encourage consumers, seed-sellers label them 'wild flowers'. The difficulty is that the form of discourse encourages us to consider plants as 'weeds' or 'not weeds', as if they were objectively different; indeed, children are frequently bemused when seeing adults 'weeding' the garden, because it is far from clear what criteria are being employed to differentiate between wanted and unwanted green things. Thus the identity of a green thing cannot be secured against an objective weed-measurer; it is culturally constructed. However, the gardening discourse encourages us to identify plants in this bipolar way—weed/not weed—in precisely the same way that we appear to perceive people as one identity or another.

This would not be the case if we could get to the world, in this case the plant or the person, without first going through language, but we can get to them only through the words that describe them or explain them or categorize them and so on. The implication of this mediated approach to the world is that our assessment of the validity of the account lies not in the world itself but by reference to other words. This is rather like trying to define or explain a word without reference to other words—it simply is not possible. It looks as though we are then forced to conclude that there is no objective way of assessing which account of the world is true or closer to the truth because every account has to be adjudged by other accounts, not by comparison to the world itself. And from this 'relativist' conclusion we may conclude that every account of the world, every definition of a weed, every version of identity is as good as any other. The relativist's dilemma is usually taken to mean that an anarchic free for all exists with no mechanism for establishing truth from falsehood, morality from immorality, weeds from plants, or true identities from false. In some ways this is an accurate (I hesitate to use the word 'true'!) conclusion: there is no objective way to be absolutely and permanently sure of the truth. On the other hand, this does not necessarily mean that any morality is as good as any other or that we must abandon attempts to analyse the world. On the moral problem it simply means that we need to agree a form of morality that we can all live with—and this includes agreeing what to do about those people who refuse to accept this agreement. On the analytic problem the issue is surely not that every account of the world is as good as any other because some accounts are taken to be more reliable and robust than others and thus the issue is: what makes successful accounts successful? For our purposes this means that we do not have to agree, for example, that British versions of the Anglo-Zulu wars are more objective than Zulu or third-party versions, but we might want to investigate why British versions appear to be more *persuasive*. And rather than worrying about whether the British mutineers were 'really' revolutionaries, we might consider why and how one side attempted to persuade the population that this was the case.

It is also important to remember *how* identities are forged not just why they are forged. For instance, the mutineers represented themselves—and were vilified in the press—for flying the 'red flag' from their masts. Thus we should be alert to the way symbols are deployed, perhaps never more so than in Hitler's Nazi parades, but more conventionally in school and corporate uniforms, in company songs, in clothing, and in corporate images. Indeed, A.P. Cohen (1985) has suggested that the symbolic construction of a community is especially relevant where the apparent equality of community has to transcend the inequalities that exist in collective hierarchies. In short, the greater the difference between individuals in a community, the more the symbolic element is likely to be deployed to persuade people that the differences are less relevant than the similarities.

The emergence of the 'true' identity of a character in a play is often constructed through a particular revelation: one's origins are revealed to lie in a 'handbag' or one's true father is revealed as the individual whom you previously murdered and whose wife you married, and so on. In practice, however, the social constitution of identity is more akin to a labour of Sisyphus than Odysseus' quest: there is no 'homecoming' awaiting the completion of the tasks, there is only another task; there is no single final truth, only different interpretations that construct, rather than reflect, the phenomenon. The struggle is to persuade others that your own version of their identity is true, and it is also a struggle to convince them that they have not been convinced—in effect, that it is not through argument that their identity exists, but through revelation of the 'truth'. Thus, for example, whether the mutineers in England were loyal sailors, merely industrial 'strikers' seeking the resolution of legitimate grievances, or whether they were political firebrands seeking to import the heady ideas of the French Revolution, is not something that can be revealed by looking closely at them, but is something that was—and still is—fought over. Their identity is not essentially embodied by their actions and words; it is constructed by themselves and those around and after them. Relatedly, whether the Zulus were bloodthirsty 'savages' bent on expanding their beastly empire, or whether precisely the same description fits better on the shoulders of the British army fighting them, is something that, again, was and remains contested. And whether Nightingale was a heroine and 'her' soldiers were forgotten lambs, or whether she was an interfering busybody and her soldiers were the scum of the earth, has yet to be agreed by all and sundry. More significantly for us, it may well be that whichever leader can most successfully 'construct'—as opposed to 'tap'—the identity of his or her followers in a way that generates maximum effort may also be the most successful leader. For Branson, the youthful, customer-focused, and entrepreneurial Virgin identity remains a critical component of his success; for Laker, the identity or branding was not so much a youthful 'alternative' to the staid corporations but appeared more like a cheap, and second-class, substitute.

To some extent leaders seem to forge not just a community or a common ideology but a parallel practice. For example, many military leaders take personal risks in an attempt to galvanize their troops to do the same. But leaders do not need to resemble their followers to remain as successful leaders. For example, many leaders purposefully adopt clothes or styles of speech that differentiate them from their followers. Even some of the most long-lived leadership systems have not necessarily been rooted in a physical or social alignment between followers and leaders: 'The late British Empire, for example, has not been ruled by an "English" dynasty since the early eleventh century; after that a motley parade of Normans (Plantagenets), Welsh (Tudors), Scots (Stuarts), Dutch (House of Orange) and Germans (Hanoverians) have squatted on the imperial throne' (Anderson1991: 83). Of course, where thought beneficial, the various 'British' ruling families have asserted either that they are descendants of an unbroken ancestral line since whenever, or insisted that they are truly British. But what, precisely, does this mean anyway?[2]

To sum up, the constructivist approach does not necessarily deny the importance of leadership. However, it does assert that an epistemological question mark hangs over all issues, human and non-human, and, particularly for us, the issue of—and literally the invention of—identity. And for this reason we may regard the construction of identity both as a critical element and task of leadership and as one that is appropriately captured by the image of the philosopher's study, for it is in philosophical endeavours that one's identity is considered and constructed and it is through philosophy that we begin to answer that slippery question: *who* are we? But there is more to leadership than answering this question, for, having constructed an answer, we are then forced to consider the *what* question: *what* do we want to be and do?

The What Question: Strategic Vision and the Invention of Leadership

Leadership is an invention. I do not mean that this implies leadership is a trick or is unnecessary or false in some sense—although it might be any or all of these at times; rather, I mean that leadership is primarily rooted in, and a product of, the imagination. Imagination is the 'faculty or action of producing mental images of what is not present or has not been experienced' (*Collins English Dictionary* 1979). To imagine 'what is not present' is to concern oneself both with what may be and what was but is no longer. It is to look at the *what*—the content of the vision—but also to consider *where* this will be achieved, *when* it will be achieved, and *why* it should be achieved. In other words, this aspect of the imagination can look backwards as well as forwards; leaders may rekindle the activities of their followers by recalling some golden age of the past, quite possibly mythical—or imagined—but which nevertheless mobilizes people to move from one situation to a different one. To imagine 'what has not been experienced' is to relay to one's followers the hope of a better future, or again, quite possibly to remind them that a preferable state of affairs did once exist but that such a state has not been experienced by the current generation. In this sense the imagination of the leader is very much locked into notions of utopia—imaginary other worlds that are literally 'no place' at the present but may be in the future. From Plato's *Republic* to More's original *Utopia*, utopian thought has attempted to transcend the present rigidities and construct a better future. And, although many have criticized utopian thought on the grounds that it is impossibly naïve, there are good reasons to suggest it has a kernel of critical importance to leadership; for, if leaders cannot imagine a preferable alternative to the status quo, why should followers follow them? Thus, if we ensure that utopias must be capable of realization—that is, concrete rather than merely abstract—then we can utilize the creative potential of the imagination and not suffer from it or suffer from its absence (see Bloch 1986 and Grint 1995: 90–123).

Most leaders do not actually do a great deal—in the sense that they usually lead the making of parts on the assembly line by sitting at a machine, or they usually lead an army by being at the front, or they usually lead a political party by speaking on the doorstep to voters. Instead, the role of the leader tends to be one where the imagination, not the body, is required to act. They have to dream up new strategies to expand the business, they have to devise plans for the defence of a nation, and they have to imagine a way for their party to take or retain power. Many people in positions of leadership do none of these things for the community they lead. They imagine little and do little, or they imagine ways to siphon off riches from the community to their own bank account, or they imagine ways to remain in power no matter what the consequences may be for the community. These may be poor leaders as far as the community is concerned, but they are still leaders.

The imagination is also crucial in the construction of what may be the most important element of leadership: the community narrative or myth. Again, I do not mean 'myth' in the sense of a false story but rather myth in the sense of a narrative that roots a community in the past, explains its present, and conjures up a preferred future. A leader without a persuasive account of the past, present, and future is unlikely to remain a leader for long. Even overtly corrupt and tyrannical leaders cannot survive on their own; they too must persuade their coterie of gorillas and gangsters that life under them is preferable to life under an imaginary alternative.

The level of leadership is less relevant than the process. A supervisor on the shop floor, a trade-union shop steward, a corporal with a section of soldiers, and a locally elected politician all face the same form of problems: who are we, how did we get here, where do we want to go to, why should we go there, and what do we need to do to get there? These are all problems of the imagination in the first place.

The imagination of followers is also relevant because they have to interpret events, gestures, speeches, texts, and so on to mean something similar to that which the leader implies. There cannot be a way of *ensuring* that followers interpret a leader's actions or words in precisely the same way that the leader intends, but there are methods for trying to limit the discrepancy between the two and it is this discrepancy, this gap of the imagination, upon which leaders need to concentrate.

Naturally, there will be followers who cannot or will not close this gap of imagination to join the community and facilitate its goals. Here the leader may well fail in his or her attempt to mobilize the entire community, but is this critical? Not necessarily, and for several different reasons.

First, there are many examples, some of which will be covered later, where only a limited proportion of the community are ideologically mobilized in line with the leader. Indeed, a majority of followers may be disinterested in the issue, but, providing a sufficient core of people is mobilized, they can persuade or coerce the rest into undertaking the action necessary to achieve the goal. For example, the soldiers at the front may have little idea why they are fighting, but, providing their immediate officers are willing to share the risks of injury, and providing there are sufficient coercive systems to deter desertion and mutiny, they may well be prepared to risk their own lives for a cause that does not interest them. Similarly, shop-floor or office workers may simply disbelieve the vision and mission statements of their employers and take no interest in what the firm is trying to achieve, but, providing the line managers are true believers, the goal may still be achieved (see Abercrombie *et al.* 1980). In this case the imagination of the front-line officers must be mobilized by the top leadership, but it may not be necessary to fire the imagination of all and sundry. In short, a critical mass of subordinate leaders may need 'to believe' but the mass need only obey.

Secondly, self-interest may generate the necessary response on the part of followers without mirroring the interests of the leaders. For instance, office-cleaners may have no real interest in providing the cleanliness that their boss says the cleaning company guarantees—but, if the cleaners' jobs are suddenly on the line then they may make the effort, not because they are concerned for the customer or their boss but for self-interest. But even here the leader must get inside the head of the follower to ascertain what will persuade the follower to undertake the necessary action.

However, even though we may have established that gaps between the imagination of the leader, manifest in the strategic vision, and the action of the followers in pursuit of that vision can be transcended, it is still the case that the most successful leaders appear to be those whose inventiveness is rooted in, rather than separate from, the imagination and lived experience of their followers. By that I mean that leaders are most likely to be followed when their strategic vision is not simply clear but also resonates with the desires of the followers; in effect, that the strategic vision operates within the *Zeitgeist*—literally the time spirit of an age. This is probably best represented by the likes of Horatio Nelson, whose vision of destroying the French fleet coincided with and mirrored the threat felt by many of the British population of a French invasion. Similarly, Hitler's rabid incantations against the shame of Versailles and the November 'stab in the back' resonated with the resentment of many ordinary Germans against the cause and effects of the defeat in the First World War. Furthermore, where the strategic visions of a community or organization become aligned with the personal agenda of the leader—as they were in both the previous cases—then we have the potential for a very seductive message: followers should sacrifice themselves to the requirements of the leader, not because this will fulfil the leader's private ambitions but because it will further the social needs of the collective.

To summarize, the role of invention is so significant that we should perhaps attempt to formalize its role in metaphorical terms. In this sense, not only is leadership an art in general; it is a particular form of the arts, in effect, fine art. Since the fine arts include painting, drawing, and sculpture, we might suggest that this art is most appropriately considered as the one responsible for constructing the strategic vision of an organization—that is, its future destination, its current direction, and its past deployment. It is, in effect, the world of the artist's studio, for here the fine artist/leader must draw or paint or sculpt the future. Moreover, leadership in this context must engage in drawing for the future by drawing on the past and in each case the imaginative use of the paintbrush distinguishes the powerful from the indifferent vision. Furthermore, where the fine artist/leader manages to construct a vision that superimposes his or her own agenda onto the collective agenda—without the superimposition being crudely self-evident—the imaginative vision can be crucial in explaining the success or failure of a leader. But there is more to leadership than constructing an identity and imagining the future—that is, answering the *who* and the *what* questions. To achieve the *what*, leaders need to consider the *how* as well.

The How Question: Organizational Tactics and the Indeterminacy of Leadership

In Shakespeare's *Henry V*, the King is certainly active in envisioning for his troops a memorable victory on the basis of a glorious past. And one of the reasons why Agincourt is regarded as a great English victory is because it was achieved against considerable odds; indeed, a simple stacking-up of the resources on both sides in any objective sense would have *determined* that the English must lose to the French. They did not, and this indeterminacy of leadership, this inability to predict the outcome of events on the basis of objectively analysing the resources available to each side, is a second critical weakness in conventional approaches to leadership.

Indeterminacy concerns the political gap between theory and practice—that is, between the issuing of orders/requests and achieving appropriate action. The orders/requests may appear perfectly logical to the leader but not necessarily to the followers, and even if they do appear logical that is not a sufficient reason to expect them to be carried out. I may understand that completing my task is essential for the success of the organization, but if that also means losing my job once the task is completed then I have a logical reason for not completing the task that is contrary to the logical reasoning of the organizations. In short, the logic of the leader is seldom sufficient to persuade followers to follow.

The suggestion that a gap exists between theory and practice, between dream and reality, and between what you want and what you get is, of course, hardly new. In Shakespeare's *Othello*, Iago is the antagonist to Othello, and political contest between individuals remains the very essence of many narratives, fictional or not. The assumption that political conflicts are an inevitable component of all organizations—and therefore that leaders should take cognizance of their inevitability—is something that many writers seem to have understood—but not many leaders. The assumption that technology is shot through with the same problem is something that few writers have even discussed.

For Clausewitz (1976), for instance, an army commander naturally and normally commanded unswerving obedience from his, or very occasionally her, troops. There was occasionally some 'friction' in any military machine, through the breakdown of weapons, supplies, weather, or even the troops themselves, but these were abnormal issues that could be resolved through the appropriate application of corrective techniques.

For Marx, the corrosion or friction between what workers were paid to do and what they did, between labour power (theory) and labour (practice), ensured that workers' discretion remained an essential element in the so-called labour process, and remains a central element in the 'labour-process' approach to this day (see Marx 1954 and Grint 1998a). Littler (1982), for example, calls this the 'central indeterminacy of capital', while Boreham (1983) applies a related notion of indeterminacy to the professions.

Adopting the original Greek word, *agon*, meaning contest,[3] Foucault suggests that conventional power relations can be classified as 'agonism', a permanent struggle between two sides in which neither side dominates.[4] Further, Foucault (1980: 39) insists that power is not a property but a relationship. That is, power is not something that you can hold or have, but, rather, is a relationship between people: 'it is exercised *within* the social body, rather than above it.' This 'capillary power', then, works through us rather than upon us: we are both held in place by—and responsible for holding in place—power. Another French writer, Latour (1986), has suggested that between the 'principle' of power, or its 'ostensive existence', and the 'practice' of power, or its 'performative existence', lies this same gap. This gap also generates the distinction between power as a *cause* of subordinate action and power as a *consequence* of subordinate action: followers can almost always refuse to carry out the leader's requirements—and suffer the consequences—so whether a leader has power over his or her followers depends upon the action of the followers more than the order of the leader (see Grint 1995). This is critical because it implies that networks of power are the foundations of success. That is to say, only a sufficiently extensive network is strong enough to deter subordinates from resisting superordinates and widening the gap between theory and practice, orders and actions, demands and results. The gap is also one that Strauss (1978) talks of as facilitating 'the negotiated order' of organizational existence.

When we move from the problem of accounting for people's inability to do what they are supposed to do, to the problem of accounting for the equivalent issue in non-human phenomena, such as machines—usually an essential element of any kind of leadership—the same kind of debate recurs. Hence, what a machine is, what it will do, and what its effects will be tend to be more or less indeterminate, the upshot of specific readings of the machine rather than the direct result of the essence of an unmediated or self-explanatory technology. A technology's capacity and capability are never transparently obvious and necessarily require some form of interpretation; technology does not speak for itself but has to be spoken for. Thus our apprehension of technical capacity is the upshot of our interpreting or being persuaded that the technology will do what, for example, its producers say it will do. The crucial role of interpretation and persuasion suggests we need to attend closely to the process of interpretation rather than assuming that we are persuaded by the effectiveness of the technology. Again, this does not mean that any interpretation is as good as any other. Rather, the point is to analyse why some accounts seem more persuasive than others. Very often the most powerful accounts are those rooted in the strongest and most heterogeneous networks.

In sum, all of these writers recount a similar problem: between the order and the execution, between the leader's wishes and the followers' actions, there is a form of political corrosion that undermines leadership, not as an occasional, unusual, or atypical event, but as a systematically recurrent problem. This does not mean that there is no relationship between what leaders want and what actually happens, but it does mean that subordinates may comply with leaders' requests for their own reasons and in pursuit of their own interests. It is this that undermines the direct link between the request and the act; the leader and the led.

Even if we can ensure that followers do what leaders want them to do it may still not secure the wishes of the leader, because the resources available may be inadequate. Conventionally, of course, success tends to be associated with accumulating sufficient power and resources to bludgeon the opposition, competitor, or enemy into submission. For example, when the Nazis entered Poland, the contest was grossly unequal and Hitler simply used his manifestly greater power to destroy the Polish armed forces. In business, this kind of success through dominating the market is achieved by monopolistic firms such that consumers have little choice but to buy the products of the monopoly producer. Beyond the military and business we might consider here how a small number of very rich football clubs dominate the leagues of their country with their extensive purchasing power that buys in the best available players. In effect, their sporting success is premised upon their financial and physical domination of the opposition.

The sporting arena is a useful way of thinking about the different forms of organizational tactics, especially if we adopt the idea of the Martial Arts and its requisite site: the dojo. And at an individual level this approach is captured in karate's traditional reliance upon the development of sufficiently overpowering strength and technique to deliver a single strike to a pressure point of an opponent that will effectively terminate an attack.[5] But not many of us are blessed with the physical strength or technical skill to dominate all others, nor are we leaders of organizations that are resource rich while all others are resource poor. Very often we may find that the competition is just as well equipped and resourced and skilful as we are. Under these circumstances, a 'battle' of attrition is likely, manifest in the trench warfare of the First World War, or the battle for market control by Coca-Cola or Pepsi, or the struggle between two relatively equal political parties that vie for electoral office. In these conditions the victor may well be the side with the marginally superior resources or tenacity or stamina or just better luck, but the tactical aim remains the same—to eliminate or undermine the opponent.

And what happens if we are significantly weaker than the opposition? Well at least two possibilities remain open—beyond submission or retreat—though it is important to note that leadership is critical here too, for the inability to recognize an impending defeat and a determination to struggle on when the costs are unnecessarily high is surely the sign of poor leadership. In other words, that submission or defeat ought to be regarded as a pro-active decision not something forced upon the weaker side if damage limitation is something leaders are concerned with.

Neutralization of the opposition's resources is one such possibility beyond defeat or failure. Here the other's resources are not resisted but rather avoided. Aikido tends to rest upon this tactic of neutralization—the intention is to neutralize the attacker and prevent further attack. There is no first strike and the aim is to return the attacker to a position of stability where no further aggression will occur. It is inherently a reactive system designed solely for personal protection and promotes a version of moral action intended to minimize damage to an attacker. But if we consider aikido as a metaphor for organizational tactics rather than simply a personal self-defence system we can see how applicable it can be in markedly different areas. For example, in business Swatch managed to survive the onslaught of cheaper Asian products by neutralizing the primary resources of the producers—their cheap labour. By redesigning the Swatch product, the company reduced the proportion of costs taken up by labour down to 10 per cent—a point at which quality and fashion aspects became the main selling point, not the costs of the watch.[6] In political terms perhaps a good example of a neutralizing principle in action would be Hitler's acquisition of power. In theory the political opposition in the guise of the Social Democratic Party and the trade unions could have made Hitler's rule untenable—but this was premised upon his *illegitimate* seizure of power, and when Hitler took control legally all their power and resources were neutralized. In short, the determinate power of Hitler's internal opponents was rendered indeterminate.

But it is also possible to consider indeterminacy in which it is not just that the weaker side wins but that the weaker side's victory is premised upon using the strength of the stronger against itself. Take the Battle of Cannae, for example, where Hannibal's smaller and less cohesive Cathaginian army defeated the larger and more cohesive Roman force. To explain this we have to turn to the notion of resource inversion. A conventional assessment would suggest a relatively simple Roman victory, because the Romans had more troops and fought in a way that every Roman soldier would have been familiar with. Hannibal's only hope of success in an open battlefield was to avoid a head-on conventional clash and seek a way of using the greater Roman strength to undermine itself. Whether by luck or stratagem, this is what Hannibal did, as is revealed in Fig. 1.4. In phase (1) 80,000 Roman infantry attacked Hannibal's 45,000 troops, while the latter's

6,500 heavy cavalry on his left under Hasdrubal attacked the Roman cavalry. On Hannibal's right his 4,000 Numidian light cavalry met the Roman cavalry attack. In phase (2) the Carthaginian infantry, which were more numerous in the centre, bowed under the Roman assault, but the wings, composed of African troops, remained firm as the centre, composed of Spanish and Celtic troops, gave ground. Meanwhile both Roman cavalry wings were driven from the battlefield. In phase (3) the Carthaginian heavy cavalry returned to attack the Roman infantry from the rear and the African infantry extended their positions around the flanks of the Romans to complete the encirclement in (4) and (5). In phase 6 a small number of Romans fought their way out of the circle to safety but the rest were caught. About 2,500 Romans surrendered but around 49,000 Romans were killed.

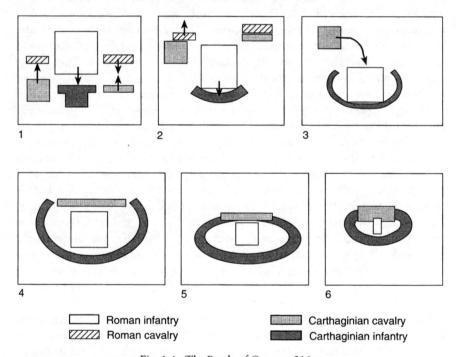

Roman infantry

Roman cavalry

Carthaginian cavalry

Carthaginian infantry

Fig. 1.4. The Battle of Cannae, 216BC

The critical question here concerns the principle by which Hannibal pulled off the victory. Since he could not match the Romans in strength he could have avoided a battle, but this would not have secured him the victory he needed. Instead, he used the Roman strengths—their propensity to fight in solid formation and to depend upon a well-armoured infantry advance—to his advantage. Had the Romans not been so successful in this battle tactic previously they would not have retained it, but that they did enabled Hannibal to make use of their resources to his own advantage. In short, Hannibal enticed the Romans into a trap that only their own strength made possible.

The Trojan Horse has a similar explanation. The Greeks had spent twelve years attempting to break down or through the walls of Troy but to no avail. As is well known, ultimately they devised a stratagem that involved them leaving the city and apparently sailing away leaving only a wooden horse, within which were left several Greek soldiers. Once the horse was dragged inside the city, the hidden Greeks managed to open the city gates and let in the now-returned Greek army. Thus the pitching of Greek force against Trojan walls simply failed because the latter were too strong. But, knowing that the Trojans were confident in their defences, the Greeks used that resource against them: if an entire Greek army could not enter the city, then what harm could this strange wooden statue do? So, when the Greeks inverted the strength of the Trojans, the Greeks succeeded.

At Agincourt the strength of the French army lay in its heavily armoured cavalry and the English could not hope to match them in a traditional contest. Instead, the desire of the French cavalry to close with and eliminate the English led the former to attack in a narrow area that rapidly filled with French dead, cut down by English arrows, to the extent that the size of the French attack made manœuvre impossible amidst the growing body of dead.

Wars abound with similar examples: the impenetrable French Maginot Line that could not be breached by the German army was not breached by it, because the Germans went round it through Belgium. But the consequence of the Maginot Line was that France generated a level of overconfidence in its defences wholly out of keeping with the situation in 1940. The fall of the 'impregnable fortress' of Singapore to the Japanese is a cognate story. The principle of using the opposition's force against it was also clearly demonstrated when the Allies led the Germans to believe that the Pas de Calais was the site of the invasion. This encouraged the Germans to mass their armour around the area, thereby freeing up Normandy for the real invasion. In effect, the strength of German armour was used against itself.

But we do not need to remain in the military world to see the significance of this resource inversion. Take Dell computers, for example. When Michael Dell first began considering the idea, he faced the giants of IBM, Apple, Compaq, and DEC, all of which had a large slice of the market and delivered through conventional shops. There was little hope of Dell meeting this competition head-on because he had no network of shops to sell through and little hope of developing a traditional distribution channel. However, by choosing to market his computers through direct mail he not only avoided a direct clash with the giants—which he probably would not have won—but he ensured that the giants remained stuck with distribution channels that proved increasingly inefficient. In short, the more they used their traditional strengths against him, the more Dell benefited. By March 1999 Dell, then the world's fastest-growing computer manufacturer, and IBM, then the world's biggest computer manufacturer, signed the world's largest information-technology agreement, a $16 billion dollar deal, to develop the next generation of computer technology (Finch 1999). By September 1999 Dell (with 20 per cent of the market) had overtaken Compaq (with 15 per cent) to become the UK's biggest PC seller (IBM had 6 per cent of the UK market) (Doward 1999).

Similarly, Avis-Rent-a-Car developed a whole customer care service and a cultural tradition based on being the *second* largest rental company and therefore having to work much harder to retain its customers than the premier rental company.

It is, then, this resource inversion that appears to explain some of the more remarkable examples of leadership when the resource imbalance is considerable, when the determinate is reversed. Here, the closest martial art is probably something like T'ai Chi, a 'soft' martial art where the aim is to use an opponent's strength to defeat him or her rather than attempting to stop him or her head-on, as in much of karate, or neutralize his or her efforts to continue the attack, as in Aikido. Now that we have established *who* we are, *what* the vision is, and *how* we can overcome opponents, we have still to consider that group without whom there are no leaders: the followers—for *why* should they follow a leader?

The Why Question: Persuasive Communication and the Irony of Leadership

One of the most interesting scenarios in everyday life is the purchase—by which I mean the mechanism and skills with which sales representatives induce us to part with our hard-earned money for the dubious benefits of a timeshare, or a new car, or whatever. Sales representatives do not sell on the basis of the benefits to themselves, in terms of commission or bonus or shifting old stock and so on, and we would be wary of any such approach. Yet the irony is that so often leaders at all levels assume that they can persuade their subordinates to change on the basis of the leader's problems, or rationale, or advantages. So, for example, leaders regularly demand belt-tightening efficiencies or sacrifices on the basis of their own budgetary problems or the needs of the shareholders—and such leaders are just as regularly surprised when their subordinates appear unimpressed by such impeccable business logic or corporate needs. What is so often missing from business leadership, ironically in the circumstances of the context, is any attempt to *persuade* followers to follow, to *sell* them the future.

This brings us to a further element of irony, in which not only must a leader fire the imagination of the followers in their own identity, induce them to seek their future destination, and develop the organizational tactics to get them there, but he or she must also ensure that, within that imaginary alternative, that victory, that sales success, that production target, or whatever, the followers are sufficiently motivated to get there. That motivation is partly constructed through the envisioning of an identity, a strategic vision, and set of organizational tactics that enhance the chances of success and reduce the risks of failure, but it is primarily achieved through the fourth form of leadership art: the performing arts. In this we can include the theatrical performances that leaders must engage in if they are to achieve the necessary mobilization of followers and it is also derived from the skills of rhetoric and the skills of negotiation. Thus having a persuasive message, delivering it effectively, and deploying negotiating skills to achieve movement are also critical elements of leadership. But again, although science and rational argument can be used to support these practices, they are fundamentally rooted in emotional and symbolic grammars, not the language of science. At a very basic level this can be demonstrated by trying to capture the persuasive effects of Martin Luther King's 'Dream Speech' by simply repeating it word for word—it simply does not move people, though clearly the original did. Thus the irony of leadership includes an acknowledgement that persuasive communication is the bedrock of achieving change, but relying on rational logic to move followers seldom works. For example, it may well be that managers and workers will agree with the rational logic that suggests the company must remain efficient and effective—but when that same logic also requires the dismissal of those same people somehow the logic fails to work. Thus, just as a play comes alive only if the script is regarded as good, the actors as persuasive, and the sets appropriate for the context, and the audience are engaged to *believe* in the production, so leaders can be successful only if their followers come to believe in the collective identity, the strategic vision, and the organizational tactics of the leader. For that to happen the skills of the performing arts are crucial. Leadership, therefore, is more a performance than a routine; it is the world of the theatre and it has to be continuously 'brought off' rather than occasionally acted out.

Theatres are about communication—communicating the plot, the characters, the atmosphere, the interpretation, and so on—and it is clear that Hitler relied heavily upon his theatrical rhetoric to construct and recruit to the identity of the new Germany. Theatre is overwhelmingly a rhetorical communication but is not solely rhetorical. That is to say, the focus is usually upon the words and the way that the words persuade the audience to accept the stage and its narrative as 'real', but that 'reality' has to be brought off in the imagination of the audience. As the chorus/narrator in Shakespeare's *Henry V* suggests at the beginning of the play:

> But pardon, gentles
> The flat unraised spirit that hath dar'd
> On this unworthy scaffold to bring forth
> So great an object: can this cockpit hold
> The varsty fields of France? . . .
> On your imaginary forces work.

A performative approach to communication seems a long way from the earliest academic business research where 'how to win friends and influence people' was the order of the day, but actually the two are not that far apart—nor are they especially distant from the initial assumptions and analyses of rhetoric in ancient Greek society. In all three cases the critical issue was how to persuade someone of something. Much of the writing in the field of communication is still locked into the persuasive issue but often premised on quite different axioms from those considered here. In the main, most business research still seems rooted in what has been called the 'transmission' or 'conduit' model, in which the crucial point of communication is to ensure that the message from the origin to the destination, usually from (active) superordinate to (passive) subordinate, is transmitted or carried in as undistorted a fashion as possible. This essentially means that all kinds of organizational problems can be explained away through 'communication failures'—that is, because of distorted or misperceived messages. Hence the solution is to clarify communications as much as possible, to simplify and repeat messages because the subordinates have not understood. That the subordinates have understood the message perfectly well (for example, 'you are our greatest asset'), but may construe it as a blatant lie, is seldom part of this approach.

A second way of considering communication is as a lens or filter, in which the information flying around an organization is of such a great quantity that some form of quality filtering is necessary to make sense of it all (Putnam *et al.* 1996). In this case the filtering may be by the individual receiving the message or it may occur at a higher level in the hierarchy. At its most obvious, this occurs through censorship during war; at its least obvious we may never know whether the communication has been censored. In the latter case this runs into what Marx called the 'dominant ideology', where distorted communications appear undistorted because they reflect what is taken for granted as 'common sense'.

A third way of considering leadership is as a performance. A performance is not just the uttering of words from a script, though these are obviously important. A performance involves the script, the props, the players, the audience, the interpretations, the context, the shared cultures, and so on and so forth. Reading the text of Shakespeare's *Henry V* may give you some idea about leadership, but it is not the same as watching a performance of the play itself. The equivalent for leaders would be to assume that reading this or any other book on leadership will provide you with all you need to know about leadership; it probably will not. Leadership is something to be experienced rather than simply read. Of course, it helps if we know the plot of *Henry V*, and, if we are familiar with the lines and their apparent meanings, then this can enhance our appreciation of the play as it is performed; but the text and the performance are not identical.

However, the error of reducing the performance to the text should not be taken to mean that a clear and significant difference exists between rhetoric and reality. On the contrary, it is only through language, only through rhetoric, that we can experience, nay imagine, what reality really is. For example, to take Machiavelli's point again, since few of us ever met or knew Princess Diana (or any other figurehead or leader for that matter) we can only know her through various forms of language: we are persuaded by TV programmes, or the radio, or the newspapers or magazines, that she was a particular kind of person. These interpretations differ, so we must choose between them or accept that the confusion is an inevitable reflection of the complexity of the case. Either way, our knowledge of the 'reality' is one constituted by the language of others, which we, in turn, interpret.

Sometimes a particular speech by a leader is held to be responsible for a radical change of direction in a community. The Peruvian rebel José de San Martín allegedly achieved this in 1821 by declaring: 'In future the aboriginees shall not be called Indians or natives; they are the children and citizens of Peru and they shall be known as Peruvians' (quoted in Anderson 1991: 193). Similarly, Lincoln's Gettysburg address is regarded by Wills (1994) as another such case where the core of the nation's identity is ruptured and remade through the 272 words that he uses at the memorial service to the dead. But, as we shall see later, the meaning of the words is deeply embedded in the past, present, and future of the USA. It is not simply a series of sentences that anyone can read at any time and expect to reproduce the same experience; it was a performance not merely a speech act. Moreover, the irony is that 'mere' words are as responsible for the 'effects' of the American Civil War as the bullets and cannonballs.

The significance of persuasive rhetoric echoes Foucault's (1998) argument about the relationship between power and knowledge in discourse. Since, for Foucault, power is implicitly encased by knowledge, and vice versa, we cannot secure a true representation of the world that is untainted by power relations. Discourse, then, is not so much a reflection of material reality but a construction of it, a particular way of representing the world through language and practice. As Gergen (1992) argues, the modernist assessment construes 'truth' and language in a reflective relation, such that language acts as a slave to the 'truth'; the more objective the empirical measure of 'reality', the closer is language to the 'truth'. Against this, more sceptical currents prioritize the status of language and representation more generally: what counts as true and false is not determined by the essence of the phenomena themselves, because such phenomena are brought into existence only through representation. In short, the 'truth' is determined by the power of the discourse. In Foucault's (1980: 13) terms: 'Truth isn't outside power . . . each society has its regime of truth, its "general politics" of truth.'

The importance of this issue becomes clear when we try and 'discover' the truth about a leader such as Nightingale. None of the people reading this book will have met her, so we have to rely on the words and accounts, including pictures, artefacts, and so on of others. Even those who fought in the Crimea when Nightingale was there may not have met her personally and few of those that did would have known exactly what she was like or thought or felt. So how does the leadership of someone like Nightingale work? Certainly not through riveting speeches, since, by all accounts, she avoided public speaking wherever possible. But, if we consider Nightingale's leadership as rooted in a 'performance', then we may get a better grip on it. For example, her past 'performances' and doing of good deeds before the Crimea would have played some part—but note again that only a few people would have witnessed these—so others' accounts of these (and her own) would have locked the past into a rhetorically replayable present. Her personal risk taking is alleged to have mobilized her nurses and followers to great personal sacrifice. But few of the soldiers in hospital would have been able to verify this with their own eyes, so again they would have had to rely on the verbal accounts of others to know what happened. Nightingale's leadership reputation would also have been generated through her development of hospital organization, but only her fellow nurses would have been personally privy to these, so, again, her reputation would have had to have been transmitted—by word and print—to others for it to have assumed significance. In effect, therefore, Nightingale's leadership *performance* is inevitably reproduced, expanded, distorted, and reconstructed through rhetoric of one form or another. We need not reduce performance to rhetoric to acknowledge that the reproduction of performance is essentially a rhetorically grounded device.

Similarly, General Patton had a reputation for theatrical leadership, but we should be careful about attributing his actions to a particular cause. For example, Patton was renowned for taking inordinate personal risks, yet, ironically, he was an extremely fatalistic individual who believed himself destined to command a great army across Europe; thus any dangers before this great act were regarded by him as insignificant. On the other hand, Patton was constantly aware that fear stalked every soldier, himself included, and to prove to himself that he was unafraid he would take extreme risks—not because he was brave but to prove to himself that he was not a coward. Whether such actions were interpreted by his subordinates and superiors as bravery, stupidity, or anything else depended more upon their state of mind than his. Hence his performances were not objectively good or bad or brave or stupid but simply performances that were adjudged by others—once communicated—to be one thing or another.

In Patton's case it could be said that his successes were forged. Again I take this to mean two different but related things: forged in the sense of false and forged in the sense of beaten into shape. For example, Patton's success with the illusionary FUSAG (First US Army Group) on D-Day persuaded the Germans that he was about to invade the Pas de Calais with a much larger force than had just landed in Normandy—but this was a blatant 'forgery' because there was no FUSAG. At a different level one might want to question the claims of many leaders to have instigated or led successful change programmes when the 'real' cause of success lay elsewhere. On the other hand, the 'forging' of Patton's Third Army, which did so much damage to the Germans after D-Day, was, allegedly, a direct result of his vigorous—not to say zealous—disciplinary approach to war: his military successes were 'forged' in the heat of battle—or so we are told, since few, if any, of us would have been there.

Patton, like Henry Ford, was a strong believer in reincarnation and certain that he had also fought at Gettysburg, but Gettysburg is remembered not just as the site of major battle in the American Civil War, but as a turning point in the history of that nation. The change of direction, strangely enough, was retrospective and rhetorical—though one might be forgiven for not assuming this if one had heard Lincoln's own assumption of the power of his speech: 'The world will little note, nor long remember what we say here, but it can never forget what they did here.' Seldom can a speaker have been so completely wrong yet achieve precisely what he intended: to bring a nation (back) to life by breathing new words into its shredded lungs. When Lincoln sought to reduce the significance of his speech, in favour of raising the significance of the Union dead, at Gettysburg on

19 November 1863 during the American Civil War, he reproduced a common subordination of the word to the deed. For Mao Tse-Tung the equivalent was to pronounce, in his *Problems of War and Strategy,* that 'political power grows out of the barrel of a gun'. Jonathan Swift, however, in his *Ode to . . . Sancroft,* had a rather different view: for him, language was itself a weapon, for he could unleash 'the artillery of words' to great effect. For others it is represented by the children's phrase:

> Sticks and stones may break my bones
> But words will never hurt me.

Contrast Stephen Spender's retort in the *Express* that:

> My parents kept me from children who were rough
> Who threw words like stones and who wore torn clothes.

And for those of us well past childhood (in age if not sense), it may be the more common retort that 'actions speak louder than words' that rings in our ears— though Ralph Waldo Emerson's *The Poet* thought that 'words are also actions, and actions are a kind of words'. This is why persuasive communications are so important to leadership, for without a persuasive *why* there is little to mobilize followers further than you can push them.

Philosophical, Fine, Martial, and Performing: Leadership Arts

To summarize, therefore, I am suggesting that leadership might better be considered as an art rather than a science, or, more specifically, as an ensemble of arts. Under this approach we might consider how four particular arts mirror four of the central features of leadership: the invention of an identity, the formulation of a strategic vision, the construction of organizational tactics, and the deployment of persuasive mechanisms to ensure followers actually follow. In sum, leadership is critically concerned with establishing and coordinating the relationships between four things: the *who*, the *what*, the *how* and the *why*:

- *Who* are you?—An identity.
- *What* does the organization want to achieve?—A strategic vision.
- *How* will they achieve this?—Organizational tactics.
- *Why* should followers want to embody the identity, pursue the strategic vision, and adopt the organizational tactics?—Persuasive communication.

Science may help the leader and the organization achieve these but fundamentally they are all subjective issues and are better considered as various arts.

- *Identity* is constructed out of the amorphous baggage of myth and the contested resources of history; it is not a reflection of the world but a construction of it. It is rooted in the philosopher's stone not the scientist's microscope.

- *Strategic visions* are designed through the imagination not the experiment, they are the equivalent of the fine arts not physics, for they involve imagination rather than experimentation, they are paintings not photographs.
- *Organizational tactics* are rather better envisaged as martial arts than mathematics, for here the leader must evaluate the organizational forms and manœuvres suitable for the competition and must take account of the likely indeterminacy of outcome.
- *Persuasive communication* can certainly be supplemented by scientific knowledge, but fundamentally this is the world of the performing arts, the theatre of rhetorical skill, of negotiating skills, and of inducing the audience to believe in the world you paint with words and props.

Fig. 1.5 summarizes the four areas of concern.

Outline of the Book

To return to a previous question: how do we know that leaders make any difference? Could it be that leaders are like talismans? That is to say, that everyone has one, that no one really knows whether they are necessary but, just to be on the safe side, we keep them close to our hearts. We can see this principle operating most visibly under war conditions when many soldiers carry lucky mascots, charms, crosses, and—in the case of Black Adder's sidekick, Baldrick, a bullet with his name on it so he could not be killed by it. Such talismanic philosophies are also self-confirming: those soldiers who died did not complain about their flawed amulets or charms, while those that survived—injured or not—could rest assured that their talismans worked; thus lucky charms proved essential; whether they actually worked or not was irrelevant. The same might be said of leaders—we may not actually need them, but, just in case they do act beneficially, we feel obliged to keep them.

Conventional science would resolve the problem by experimental methods in which the variable (talisman) was removed in a controlled environment to establish its significance. We do not have that luxury—or dangerous power— but it might be possible to establish to some extent what significance leadership makes if we can find a series of cases where parallel scenarios are played out with what appears to be marginal differences—except in terms of leadership. This might help us decide whether leadership is itself critical, and, if it is, whether there are resemblances between its formation in different walks of life—in effect, whether leadership is similar in political, social, military, and business environments.

Adopting this approach, the first part of the book focuses upon four instances of 'parallel leadership' to try and establish what difference leadership makes and whether there are particular issues that appear to be more important than others. To this end we begin by looking at two contemporary business leaders whose fortunes appear quite different but where the particular business is almost identical:

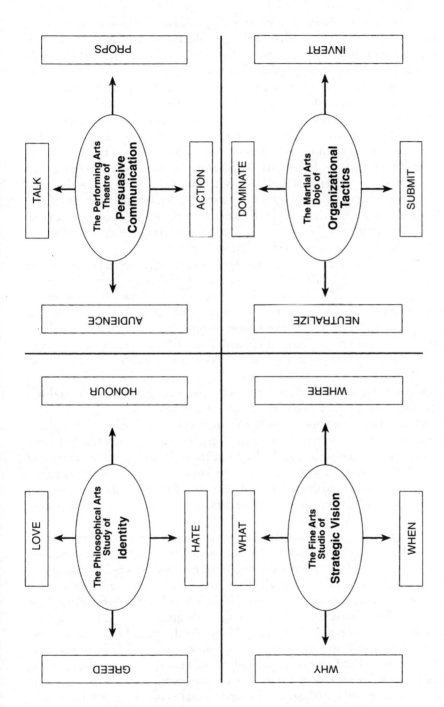

Fig. 1.5. The arts of leadership

Freddie Laker and Richard Branson. The failure of Freddie Laker's Skytrain makes the success of Richard Branson's Virgin Atlantic all the more unusual, because Branson first flew under the licence abandoned by Laker. Moreover, while Laker managed a late and very limited comeback in the late 1990s, Branson went on to become what is probably Britain's best-known—and probably most popular—entrepreneur. This first chapter seeks to explain why the fortunes of these similar individuals should have turned out so radically different.

The next chapter moves from air to the sea, from the politics of business to the business of politics, from the late twentieth to the late eighteenth century, and from the question of livelihoods to the questions of lives. In this chapter, the subject is the naval mutinies that occurred within weeks of each other in England in 1797, one at Spithead off Portsmouth and one at the Nore off Sheerness. The conventional accounts of these mutinies suggest that leadership played a critical role in the success of the former and the failure of the latter and the analysis developed here agrees with the conclusion but not in the apportioning of responsibility for the outcome to the various leaders involved.

Chapter 4 shifts us from the political leaders of the eighteenth century to the social leaders of the nineteenth century in the particular garb of Florence Nightingale. Though the formal leader of only a relatively small and informal organization of nurses in the Crimea, Nightingale had an enormous influence on the public and the politicians in Britain and through her actions managed to lead the management of military hospitals in a radically different direction. However, when she returned to England, determined to set up hospitals for the army's soldiers and the nation's sick, she was markedly less successful. Here, then, we have one leader involved in parallel circumstances—so the question underlying this is what explains the initial success and the ultimate failure?

Chapter 5 moves from 'social' leadership to 'military' leadership at the close of the nineteenth century in southern Africa. Here the parallel cases are the British army's defeat at Isandhlwana at the hands of the Zulu army, and the repulse of the latter by the former, within twenty-four hours, at Rorke's Drift. Since the armies were identical and the tactics for both sides had been firmly established by their respective senior leaders, why did the first go so badly for the British but the second so badly for the Zulus?

Having run through four parallel examples of leadership with relatively clear cases of success and failure in the first part of the book I move from parallel to extreme cases on the assumption that one of the most useful ways to examine an issue is to deploy it against a case where it is most clearly important. To that end Chapter 6 considers the case of Horatio Nelson, where I evaluate the utility of the four arts in explaining the success of England's greatest admiral. Chapter 7 returns to the business world to look at Henry Ford, whose leadership inaugurated a qualitative leap from craft to mass production and gave us the term 'Fordism'. And if Ford gave us mass production, Hitler, the focus of Chapter 8, did more than anyone else to bring the twentieth century to its knees through mass destruction and genocide. Finally, and in sharp contrast, we move to consider Martin Luther King's leadership in the acquisition of civil rights for black Americans in the 1960s.

The final chapter then summarizes the issues and conclusion from across all the previous material and sets out what the analysis has to say to leaders from all forms of organization at the turn of the twentieth century into the new millennium.

Notes

1. Two cases will suffice to demonstrate the point. In August 1964 President Lyndon Johnson authorized air attacks on North Vietnam after 'unprovoked' torpedo attacks upon two US destroyers. There is now considerable doubt as to the veracity of the official claims (Lennon 1999). In June 1994 an RAF Chinook helicopter carrying British military security officers crashed on the Mull of Kintyre killing all twenty-nine passengers and crew after what was officially described as 'pilot error'. Again, there are now doubts as to the veracity of the official report (Millar 1999).
2. See also Colley (1999) for a succinct critique of the 'special relationship' between the USA and the UK.
3. From which we have derived the terms agonist, where one muscle is opposed by another, agony, antagonist, and protagonist.
4. Such domination for Foucault did not imply a power relationship at all (Foucault 1983: 208–26).
5. George A. Dillman (1992) has long regarded pressure-point karate as the most legitimate inheritance from the martial arts.
6. See the original interview with Nicolas Hayek by William Taylor in the *Harvard Business Review* (Mar.–Apr. 1993: 99–110), and a subsequent analysis by Pino (1999).

Part One

Parallel Leadership Situations

2

Crash-Landing and Take-Off:
Business Leadership on Skytrain and Virgin Atlantic

I must hasten away since my baggage has been sent off before me.

(Last words of 'La Rivière' de Bailli, in 1605, after disposing of all his possessions, quoted in Green 1979: 10)

At 08.00 on Friday, 5 February 1982, the receivers were called into Laker Airways. Eight hours before this, Laker had still been engaged in frantic efforts to save his company, but (for) now the self-styled buccaneer of the air was gone. Within three months Braniff had gone the same way. Just over two years after this, on 22 June 1984, Virgin Atlantic's inaugural flight took off using the same licence that Laker had been forced to surrender.

Why did Skytrain become a black hole sucking in and shredding millions of pounds before metaphorically crash-landing, while Virgin Atlantic took off to become a shooting star, not just commercially successful in its own right, but just one part of the ostensibly ever-expanding Virgin universe? At the end of the twentieth century you would be hard pressed to go shopping, read the daily papers, and watch the news, at least in Britain, without coming across a Virgin product of some kind. And the greatest branding icon for Virgin is Branson himself—even if only in self-deprecating mode, warning the consumers of Virgin Clothing, for example, that though 'Giorgio designs, Ralph designs, and Calvin designs, don't worry, Richard [inset in a "suitable" multi-coloured sweater] doesn't' (*Guardian Weekend*, 19 Sept. 1998). The exact opposite is the case with Freddie Laker's business empire: although Laker Airways Incorporated began flying in 1996, it remains a small and lonely plane(t) in a firmament of stars.

This chapter sets out to explain the apparent contradiction that is firmly grounded in the leadership styles of both individuals. Since they are both of the 'adventure-capitalist' or 'buccaneering-entrepreneur' mould, and since they both appear to mobilize their followers in similar fashion, what, precisely, makes the difference between success and failure in business leadership and to what extent are the four arts of leadership capable of explaining this?

Laker's Crash-Landing

In November 1982, at the annual meeting of the International Air Transport Association (IATA)—basically a cartel representing the largest international airlines—the Director-General, Knut Hammarskjöld, told the meeting that collectively they had lost $1.2 billion the previous year. 'We are walking a financial tightrope with the abyss of bankruptcy on the one hand and the slippery slope of subsidization or permanent bondage to the loan market on the other' (quoted in Sampson 1984: 17). As Sampson (1984: 18) notes: 'Laker's ghost stalked through the conference hall.'

Born in 1922, Laker's interest in aircraft was stimulated by the flight of the Hindenburg airship in 1936 and subsequently by a Handley Page biplane flying over Canterbury, his home town. He left school and joined Short brothers in Rochester at the age of 16 as an apprenticed engineer, quickly developing his entrepreneurial skills when tea boy by buying the tea in bulk. During the war he flew with the Air Transport Auxiliary (Laker 1997: 1).

In 1946 the Bermuda Agreement on North Atlantic Air Traffic between the USA and the UK, which sought to regulate—that is, balance—the interests of both countries, was signed and Laker started Aviation Traders Ltd., buying and selling surplus army lorries, then selling garden produce. He borrowed £38,000 from a friend and bought twelve Halton aircraft (converted Halifax bombers) and a mass of spares for the Rolls Royce Merlin engines from BOAC for £42,000.[1] Laker's Haltons then saw continuous service in the 1948–9 Berlin Airlift, though he seems to have made most of his money from the spares and servicing of aircraft engines.

In 1951 the British government began sending troops abroad by plane, rather than sea, and Laker bought up old planes to ferry them. He also began a scheduled cargo service to Berlin, and Laker's Air Charter began cheap flights to the Commonwealth. At the time, the IATA controlled flights outside the Commonwealth and the British government protected BOAC's Commonwealth interest by preventing Laker from operating either first-class service or modern planes. Two years later he formed Channel Air Bridge, selling air transportation of vehicle, passengers, and animals, and bought all BOAC's Avro-Tudor aircraft to do it. In a typical—but at the time relatively novel—publicity stunt he then took journalists to Hamburg on board a Laker Tudor aircraft to publicize its utility.

This habit of buying up a large number of aircraft stayed with him when, in 1956, he bought all the RAF's (252) Percival Prentice trainer aircraft, restored them, and put them up for sale. However, as a foretaste of the disaster that was to strike him a quarter of a century later, his deal of the decade turned out to be a financial catastrophe when only twenty could be sold. Eventually he managed to resolve the financial mess by selling the aircraft company complete with the trainers to train new pilots.

But better times were just around the corner and in 1958 he sold his remaining companies to a group that became British United Airways (BUA) under his tutelage as its first managing director. The Conservative government of the day, under Macmillan, had been concerned at the uncompetitive size of much of the British airline industry and through the 1960 Civil Aviation Act created the Air Transport Licensing Board (ATLB) to regulate civil aviation. The ATLB encouraged the consolidation of small airlines and aircraft manufacturers to enhance British competitiveness and BUA was formed as a result, from Airwork and Hunting Clan. BUA grew to become the largest fleet of non-government aircraft in the UK. Characteristically, Laker ordered VC-10s for BUA in 1961, when they were largely untested, and used the large order to gain leverage on the government to secure routes to West Africa. He then redesigned the VC-10s to take cargo to fill the aircraft, turning loss-making routes into profitable ones.

By 1965 Laker had had enough of BUA and left it to form the largest individually and privately owned airline in the world at the time: Laker Airways Ltd. Starting in 1966, Laker Airways was designed as a low-cost operation dealing exclusively with holiday tour operators. It had just £10,000 of capital; 90 per cent was his and 10 per cent belonged to his (first) wife, Joan. Laker Airways was registered in Jersey, to avoid taxes and to avoid what he regarded as restrictive labour practices in mainland Britain—Laker insisted that his airline would not recognize trade unions. Laker recruited 120 employees in the first wave, and his initial strategy was to ride the expected wave of package holidays by contracting his aircraft exclusively to the holiday operators via his new concept of 'time charter': tour operators would buy flight hours from him.

Then, once again, Laker began buying aircraft at a time when no one else was (so he could achieve a good deal) and of a kind (BAC 1-11) that was largely untried and untested. The BAC 1-11 was in trouble after a couple of test-flight crashes and very few orders. Still, Laker ordered 3 BAC 1-11s at £4 million, putting in £211,500 of his own money and borrowing the rest from Clydesdale Bank. He also bought two ageing Britannias from BOAC while waiting for delivery of the BAC 1-11s and used them to ferry oil to Zambia during the blockade of what was then Rhodesia, which had made a Unilateral Declaration of Independence in 1965 under Ian Smith.

By 1967 Laker had secured his first two major contracts with Lord'Brothers and Wings but he failed to persuade Thomas Cook to enter into an agreement and the holiday market nosedived as the Arab–Israeli War broke out and Britain devalued sterling by 14.7 per cent. Arrowsmith, a holiday company that used Laker Airways, got into financial difficulties in 1967 and Laker bought it. Contrary to most of the market indicators, Lord Brothers predicted a growth in the travel market and contracted with Laker for another aircraft, and Laker duly ordered two new BAC 1-11s. But Lord Brothers soon found themselves in financial trouble and this time Laker benefited from the speculative order and bought them out. However, the British government was still intent on creating larger airlines from the alliance of smaller ones and Laker's independent strategy was about to falter under the first of several hammer blows.

First, in 1969, the Labour government's two-year review committee into the airline industry suggested a second major airline should be created—which led to suggestions of a merger between BUA and BOAC before Caledonian and Laker had time to bid for BUA. After some embarrassment, Caledonian successfully bid for it to create British Caledonian (BCal.). Laker then made a (failed) bid to fly to Australia but, not for the first time, was crushed between the wings of a competitive pincer movement by two rivals, this time a joint BOAC–Quantas appeal against competition, which was accepted by the (Australian) International Civil Aviation Policy (ICAP).

Secondly, in 1971, the regulations designed to limit the impact of competition from charter airlines on national airlines—by insisting that charters could operate only for clubs and were acceptable only for *bona fide* members (that is, those with six months' membership)—were tightened up. Spot checks found that virtually all the charter airlines (including BCal.) appeared to be involved in poor regulation of the *bona fide* club-membership rules. In May, 25 per cent of a Laker flight were asked to leave a plane at Gatwick airport after being found not to have been members of the 'Left Hand Club' for at least six months. Laker's reputation with the American Civil Aviation Board (CAB) was further tarnished when he refused to provide information to them.

Thirdly, widebodied jets, particularly 747 Jumbo (385 seats versus 185 on the Boeing 707) then put increasing pressure on competitors across the Atlantic, as the average potential capacity of the airlines increased by a quarter, while actual loads fell to half. This was further aggravated by a decline in American activity in Vietnam, which, in turn, led to a loss of business for many American airlines who had previously been ferrying troops. In the circumstances, some of the companies were heading for bankruptcy, and, in his usual contra-market-indicator approach, Laker obviously sensed now was the time to secure cheap aeroplanes as the plane-builders began searching desperately for new customers. This was not as crazy as it may seem; after all, his post-war successes had been made on this basis and when he had made speculative purchases that went wrong he had always managed to find a way of resolving his financial problems. In effect, Laker's model of success—take risks and expand when others are shrinking—worked. It should have come as no surprise, then, that Laker bought two DC–10s at this time to launch his most famous product: Skytrain.

Skytrain

In June 1971 the Conservatives under Heath came to power and Laker began to put his dream into effect. Skytrain was to be an air service that would operate like a train in terms of its speed of operation and economy of price and would cater for what he called 'the forgotten man' (*sic*). This turned out to be a semi-skilled/skilled manual worker, of whom Laker estimated that at least 200,000 existed, who would be keen to fly if the price were right—and that could be achieved only if low overheads were incurred.

On the basis of his previous successes, Laker bought two (180-seat) DC-10s from Mitsui at reduced prices after Mitsui's All Nippon airways had been persuaded by the Japanese government to switch from DC-10s to Lockheed Tristars. What could go wrong? He had the idea and he had the necessary technology and staff—but he did not have a licence and he did not have sufficient friends in high places to get him a licence quickly. Nor did he read the situation appropriately: the Civil Aviation Act replaced the ATLB with the Civil Aviation Authority (CAA) to ensure that competition between airlines—which the Conservatives were in favour of—did not compromise air safety or result in airline economic failure. The priority given to safety and economic security over competition is clear from a textual analysis: only once does the word 'compete' appear in the 60,000-word document and 'competition' is not mentioned at all (T. Jackson 1995: 320).

At around this time, in 1972, British Airways (BA) was (re)formed from BEA and BOAC, but the initial objections to Skytrain came from BCal., which complained that Skytrain was taking scheduled traffic away from it. Laker denied this, arguing that Skytrain was generating new traffic—that is, traffic from 'the forgotten man', who—until Skytrain—had not been able to afford to fly. However, the low overheads clearly provided a competitive advantage over the scheduled airlines and Laker's argument about generating a wholly new market that would not undermine the national airlines was treated with considerable suspicion. It was to resolve this problem that Laker made a virtue out of a necessity. He proposed the idea that no reservations would be possible—not to facilitate the system for the passengers but to placate the other scheduled airlines, where business travellers in particular needed to make reservations. As he recalled: 'We had to propose a service that would cater to the genuine quick-ticket man and yet put a sufficient artificial barrier in his way that it would not divert traffic from scheduled services. And this is where the no-reservations idea came from. This is the artificial barrier that we dreamed up' (quoted in Banks 1982: 38).

However, BOAC was well aware that, if Laker's Skytrain ever took off, it would suffer severe difficulties and it applied to the IATA to introduce APEX (advanced purchase fares) to beat off the proposed charter competition across the Atlantic. Through this it hoped both to fill empty seats at marginal prices and to stifle Skytrain at birth. The British Board of Trade eventually agreed a prebooked form of charter fares, the ABC fares (Advanced Booking Charters), but these required a long delay between booking and flying—not the walk-on/walk-off system Laker was hoping to develop on Skytrain.

Laker appealed against the IATA's block on a licence for the Skytrain proposal as it stood, and the new CAA upheld his appeal, giving him a ten-year licence to begin 1 January 1973, subject to certain conditions. In particular, he would have to restrict the capacity of his DC-10s to that of a Boeing 707 during winter and he would have to fly from Stansted not London.

Despite this partial success the omens were not good. Certainly the growth of holiday traffic abroad had been expanding in fits and starts since the 1950s. In

1955, two million Britons had gone abroad on holiday, 25 per cent with charter companies; by 1972, eight and a half million were winging their way out of the country, with 60 per cent on charter flights. This was partly stimulated by the rising affluence of the country, but it was also facilitated by the government gradually removing the inhibition that prevented tour operators selling tickets for less than the cheapest scheduled flight. However, political uncertainties, intensifying competition, and the rapid rise in the cost of oil meant that the entire holiday company began to take a battering after 1971—the peak year for charter passengers across the Atlantic. In 1972 and 1973 the collective industry made substantial losses.

Early in 1973 the British government asked the USA to change the Bermuda Agreement to allow Skytrain to fly from Stansted to New York, but even this silver lining hardly lightened the gathering storm clouds. The US government hesitated; Pan Am and TWA, as well as a host of smaller airlines, were already losing money and Laker's conviction for breaking affinity club rules led the Civil Aeronautics Board (CAB) to fine him $101,000. This was the largest ever fine, though 130 other companies were also convicted, including Japan Air Lines, PanAm, TWA, and BA. As one US senator said of the CAB's actions:

The Board has concentrated its enforcement efforts upon stopping improper low-cost travel; it has done so persistently and not always fairly. The result is public criticism of, and resentment against, the Board's enforcement policy . . . The public wants low-cost travel; several airlines wish to provide low-cost travel; the Board's rules inhibit the provision of low-cost travel; the public is willing to violate those rules.   (quoted in Banks 1982: 42).

But the airlines crisis was yet to reach its nadir. In 1974 OPEC oil prices quadrupled, reducing North Atlantic traffic markedly: scheduled flights dropped by 6 per cent, and charter flights dropped by 30 per cent, making an overall annual reduction of 8.5 per cent. This left huge overcapacity in the airlines; PanAm was in serious financial trouble and BCal. reduced its staff by 15 per cent to cut costs. The consequence for Laker was dire. Between 1969 and 1974 the American CAB had resisted forty-seven requests for new routes and allowed only two, and in June 1974, as expected, the CAB recommended to President Nixon that Laker's application for a licence be rejected, ostensibly because of the affinity club conviction. The US and UK governments, plus TWA, PanAm, BA, and BCal. subsequently agreed to a 20 per cent reduction in air travel across the Atlantic during winter 1974–5. Part of the deal was that Skytrain would not be allowed to run and Laker's US lawyer (Bob Beckman) used the US Freedom of Information Act to get a transcript of the meeting. On hearing it, Laker accused the British civil servants of being 'bums and gangsters'—to the obvious irritation of George Rogers, then the undersecretary at the Board of Trade (quoted in Banks 1982: 44). Laker filed a conspiracy writ for damages against the 'conspirators' for £7 million in damages. The Big Four then rewrote the agreement so that Laker was not specifically excluded, but, just as Laker appeared to be making some headway, on 23 December, BA applied to the CAA to revoke Laker's licence, granted in 1972 (but still not executed), on the grounds of new over-capacity.

On 5 February 1975 the CAA responded to BA through its chair Lord Boyd-Carpenter: 'We are conscious also that the only reason Skytrain services have not already been in operation for the past two years is that the United States' authorities have engaged in unconscionable procrastination . . . In sum, notwithstanding the weighty and well-argued case advanced by BA, we conclude that it would be wrong to revoke the licence' (quoted in Banks 1982: 45). Again it looked as though Laker had at last got the green light for launch. But yet another delay appeared in the guise of Peter Shore, then the British Secretary of State, who told Laker in July that his licence was, after all, being revoked and that all overseas flights would now occur only on either BA or BCal. Laker immediately threatened to go to court and announced that 'Skytrain will be on the books until the day I die' (quoted in Banks 1982: 71). As Banks (1982: 71) notes: 'Laker learned to speak in headlines and would do whatever was necessary to get into the newspapers or on television.' But, even if Laker had got Skytrain into the air, the possibility of making a financial success at this time looked small. Both BCal. and PanAm had already pulled out of the London-Los Angeles route to save money and overall North Atlantic traffic was down a further 5 per cent on 1974.

The House of Commons duly voted in favour of the new White Paper on civil aviation and the Lords concurred but simultaneously called on the government to reinstate Skytrain's licence. This prompted Laker back into action and on 16 March 1976 Laker issued a writ against Peter Shore claiming he had acted beyond his legal powers in revoking the licence. Only now did the tide seem to be turning in Laker's favour, five years after he had first outlined the Skytrain proposal. First, in June, Edmund Dell, who was much more sympathetic to Laker, replaced Shore at the Board of Trade. Secondly, and equally fortuitously, the British government issued notice to revoke the 1946 Bermuda Agreement after it had become clear that US carriers were carrying two-thirds of the North Atlantic traffic compared to Britain's one-third. The UK wanted to have single-destination carriers, not both national airlines to the same place, so this was self-evidently not a pro-Laker move. However, the USA disagreed, insisting on dual carriers. Again, this did nothing for Laker, since BCal. was the second national carrier to BA. But the withdrawal of BCal. from the London–New York route for economic reasons left Laker as the default second carrier—assuming, of course, that he could obtain the necessary licences and operate successfully where BCal. had failed.

The licensing problem began unravelling when, in July 1977, the British courts found in favour of Laker, and against Shore—who was deemed to have acted *ultra vires* (beyond his legal powers). The British government appealed, but in December of the same year the Court of Appeal again found in favour of Laker. An appeal by the government to the House of Lords was considered but ultimately dropped. And, with North Atlantic traffic up 11 per cent on 1975, the scene was beginning to favour Laker—but this was not to last.

Laker's attempts to introduce Skytrain to Australia came to naught after he visited the Australian House of Representative's Select Committee on Tourism, telling them that he would bring more British tourists out to Australia than Australian tourists back to England. He subsequently told the CAA meeting in London on the same issue the precise opposite. The Australians declined to issue a licence.

On the other side of the Atlantic, however, things looked a little brighter. With the pro-deregulating Carter now in the White House, and the guru of deregulation, Alfred Kahn, as head of the American CAB, Laker was given a permit to fly by Kahn on 10 June 1977. Within two weeks a renegotiated Bermuda Agreement (Bermuda 2) increased British access to US airports, switched new US carriers to Gatwick, and, as a consequence, moved Laker from Stansted to Gatwick. As Banks (1982: 57) concludes: 'After six years, three court cases and umpteen appearances at the CAA and CAB, the real battle facing Laker and his Skytrain was about to begin.'

But first Laker had to take on the unions. Laker had always been hostile to trade unions and had made no secret of this, preferring to act as a paternalistic employer to the extent that unions would be unnecessary. But a survey from the Advisory, Conciliation and Arbitration Service (ACAS) found 108 members of the Transport and General Workers Union (TGWU) among the 279 cabin crew. Laker set up a staff association to head off the TGWU, but in September the union asked ACAS to investigate whether it could represent the now 550 cabin crew in Laker Airways. Laker refused to cooperate with the investigation and only twenty-five cabin crew admitted membership of the TGWU, so the union quietly retreated.

With the last hurdle cleared, Laker was now ready for the inaugural flight, and on 26 September 1977 the first Skytrain took off from Gatwick for New York. Various conditions applied to the service: no tickets were to be sold before 04.00 on the day of flight and tickets could be purchased only in the UK from Gatwick airport or Victoria Station. The queues of students and others seeking cheap flights soon turned both venues into what became known as 'Lakerville'. In New York, Kennedy airport refused to sell tickets, because its owners, the New York Port Authority, were worried about a similar image of long lines of 'hippies' queuing in the airport lounge. Eventually the tickets were sold from outside the airport.

The following month President Carter's new deregulation policy became established in a letter to Kahn: 'We should seek international aviation agreements that permit low-fare innovations in scheduled services, expanded and liberalized charter operations, non-stop international service, and competition among multiple US carriers in markets of sufficient size. We should also avoid government restrictions on airline capacity' (quoted in Banks 1982: 65). Bermuda 2, however, primarily covered scheduled services, not charter flights, and the US charter airlines were now in even deeper trouble. Although Skytrain carried 50,000 in the first year, it rarely breached an 80 per cent loading.

Never one to be daunted by the increasing possibility of failure, Laker set about expanding Skytrain, first, through an additional CAA licence to run a London–Los Angeles Skytrain from May 1978, and, secondly, by securing agreement to sell tickets through travel agents. In June of the same year Freddie Laker became Sir Freddie Laker after being awarded a knighthood by Prime Minister Callaghan for his services to aviation, but the honour was about to acquire the mantle of Don Quixote rather than Sir Lancelot. Laker, already with two Boeing 707s, four BAC 1-11s, and four DC-10s to his name (more than sufficient for expected traffic), announced plans to buy fifteen widebodied jets for £380 million: five DC-10-30s for the US routes and ten European Airbuses for European scheduled flights.

The European Airbus was in deep trouble as orders were lost to the rival Boeing 757. British Aerospace (BAe) had dropped out of the European Airbus project as a partner in 1977 but continued to make the wings. Boeing had already asked BAe to join it in developing the Boeing 757, along with Rolls Royce, who wanted the 757 to use its engines, and BA, who wanted to buy it. Since there were more jobs on the line through Rolls Royce engines than Airbus wings, the government decided to pursue the BAe–Boeing link—much to the annoyance of the European governments supporting the Airbus. Even Laker had been previously disinterested in the Airbus, and he was reminded of the fact by a journalist attending the press conference to announce Laker's new deal. After all, had he not said of the Airbus that it would be 'like a horse designed by a committee and would therefore fly like a camel'? (quoted in Banks 1982: 99).

In fact, the Airbus deal was a typical Laker tactic: the project was in trouble, and therefore was in a very weak bargaining position, which consequently put Laker in a very strong bargaining position—providing, of course, that the deal was worth making in the first place. The Airbus deal virtually saved the Airbus project and simultaneously saved Laker about £7 million in financial support— the equivalent of a 10 per cent down payment. However, Laker's decision to buy the planes through borrowed US dollars saddled him with both a huge debt-servicing agreement and a vulnerability to currency swings that would eventually destroy him (M. Brown 1998: 252). Moreover, what was he going to do with all the hardware? It was, as Campbell-Smith (1986: 16) put it: 'Less bold than foolish in the extreme'.

In characteristic fashion Laker announced the purpose of the new fleet of hitherto unnecessary planes: he would develop a world-wide 'Globetrain'. Admittedly, North Atlantic traffic was up 28 per cent on 1977, but this was an astonishingly large investment for a project, the first part of which had already been delayed for five years, and in a market where rapid fluctuations of fortune were the essence of the game. He also needed licences from London to Hong Kong and from Hong Kong to Los Angeles.

Securing other licences proved relatively easy. In 1979 he managed to secure them to Honolulu, Tokyo, and Sharjah without too much difficulty. And on the back of this he bought two more DC-10s, financed by the Japanese government to reduce its trade deficit with the USA. But even with a licence, the London–Los Angeles route—which BCal. and PanAm had already dropped out of—proved a problem, with load factors averaging only one-third in the first year. Four further factors added to his woes. First, Laker's DC-10s were short-range versions; which had to stop at Prestwick to refuel—adding an extra two and half hours to journey time; only the new DC-10-30s would avoid this problem. Secondly, Californians exceeded New Yorkers and Londoners alike in their dislike of the 'Lakerville' image. Thirdly, both BA and TWA introduced cheap flights to lure Skytrain customers away. Fourthly, in May 1978 (the beginning of the main season) an American Airlines DC-10 crashed at Chicago killing all 274 passengers (it was the worst US air crash to date) grounding all DC-10s worldwide for six weeks. Laker spoke publicly in defence of the DC-10—a gesture that McDonnell would remember later—but it was to no avail. Skytrain was cancelled for the duration of the ban and Laker estimated this cost him £13 million in revenue, to leave barely £800,000 post-tax profits for the year. Subsequent analysis showed that virtually all of Laker's profits in tax years 1979/80 and 1980/1 were due to beneficial movements in the exchange rate (Banks 1982: 123). Furthermore, Laker had already taken on a $59 million debt from Mitsui, plus $228 million from US Export-Import Bank (EXIM) for five DC-10s. He was now stuck with a huge overcapacity and he was paying for this in dollars at a time when all his receipts were in sterling and the dollar/sterling ratio was turning disadvantageously.

Laker planned a new Australian route, but his assertions about numbers and the nationality of numbers carried again varied according to the meeting—and he was reminded of the 1977 'confusion'. But not everything was troublesome: a Conservative government under Thatcher (a long-time family friend) was elected in April 1979 and the figures for North Atlantic traffic at the end of the year showed an increase of 15 per cent on 1978.

In 1980 he attempted to get his Globetrain venture off the ground and applied to the CAA for a licence for the London–Hong Kong route, but he was turned down (along with Hong Kong's own carrier Cathay Pacific); BCal.'s application was accepted, along with BA's existing licence. The CAA's decision was subsequently overturned by the Conservative government, but Hong Kong then rejected Laker. Laker was now on the brink of very serious financial trouble. He had, to quote Campbell-Smith (1986: 11), 'decimated the profitability of what, a decade earlier, had been one of the most lucrative as well as one of the most prestigious of BA's routes anywhere round the globe'. Laker had also paid a high price for high market share: the accounts showed the company to be very highly geared, but political support for Laker meant that few questions were asked and no finances were refused. He now had eleven DC-10s and this overcapacity was about to be compounded by the world's economic recession, which lasted until 1981.

In March 1980 he temporarily teamed up with Intasun tour operator to fly the London–Miami route, but, not content with limited expansion in what was a serious financial situation, Laker went for broke and started manœuvring to gain access to Europe. Decrying the pleas for caution by sympathetic politicians, and faced with a solid cartel controlling European flights in favour of national airlines, Laker relied on those same instincts that had served him so well before: when others begin to doubt, an opportunity exists. As he countered to his mentors, 'Trying to do it politically means they won't do anything and it'll come to nothing, like everything else done politically. I want to get a can-opener on Europe . . . but it's taken me thirty years to get to America. I'll be dead before I get a Skytrain into Europe' (quoted in Banks 1982: 86). Laker, confident in his ability to use the courts to undermine cosy cartels and vested political interests, simply asserted that the Treaty of Rome rendered the whole of European air policy redundant. It probably did, but that was no reason to assume he would win.

In 1981 Laker applied to the CAA for 630 routes to and between thirty-seven European cities. At the time, existing policy prohibited a company from a third country taking passengers between two others—that is, interstate traffic. The CAA, as expected by everyone bar Laker, rejected his application. The only route secured was to Switzerland, outside the EU. With North Atlantic traffic up only 1.5 per cent on 1980, the storm clouds looked ominous. In August a report in the *Daily Telegraph* suggested that Laker was having to reschedule his EXIM loan and the weight of the dollar/sterling ratio changed yet further in favour of the dollar, leaving Laker about 25 per cent worse off in his repayment schedule from the original deal. The Bank of England called the Midland Bank to ask it to refinance Laker, who was, as Dennis Kitching, head of Corporate Finance at the Midland, admitted, 'a very popular figure in the public eye' (quoted in Sampson 1984: 152). Then the reorganization began: the two Boeing 707s and four BAC 1-11s were put up for sale, but, as Laker began to cut his costs, North Atlantic traffic slowed even more. In March Laker reversed all his previous strategies and *raised* fares between 11 and 33 per cent. As he rationalized, 'A man who does not change his mind does not think' (quoted in Banks 1982: 124).

Load factors averaging 78 per cent were still being achieved, but the absence of any substantial summer rush left his finances precarious. EXIM, after pressure from the Midland Bank, agreed to defer capital repayment for September providing the interest was repaid and the Airbus financing, subsidized by the Thatcher government, was also rescheduled. The British government then persuaded EXIM to hold back on a claim for capital repayment for October in a second—and final—attempt to resolve Laker's finances and Laker considered selling one of the three airbuses, but, since this would have effectively stopped the government subsidy, it was abandoned. Thatcher even gave Laker (her 'Knight in a shining fuselage') an official endorsement at the Tory party conference that year: 'It is thanks to Freddie Laker that you can cross the Atlantic for so much less than it would have cost in the early 1970s . . . Competition works' (quoted in Banks 1982: 115). But the last two words also spelt the kiss of death for Laker. As Knut Hammarskjöld concluded, 'Laker became the victim of the open market he was preaching himself' (quoted in Sampson 1984: 159).

Laker also reversed another of his strategic intents by establishing a Regency Class (first-class business), which, unlike Skytrain, took Laker into direct competition with the big Airways: TWA, BA, and PanAm, and their response—for they were also in trouble—was immediate and devastating. On 16 October, PanAm (which had just been forced to sell its hotel chain to survive) hit back by cutting up to 59 per cent off its fares. BA, now under Lord King, secured the approval of the government for a similar reduction in its own fares—even though BA called it 'mutual suicide'. Laker, certain that the low fares were an attempt to ruin him, accepted that 'there was no way I could survive if they matched me' (quoted in Sampson 1984: 153). Laker—with transatlantic traffic down 59 per cent in the first two weeks of November and a rail strike making things worse—complained to the CAA that PanAm's fares, now matched by BA and TWA, were too low (Laker was then charging £125 each way London–New York) (Sampson 1984: 153; Campbell-Smith 1986: 16; M. Brown 1998: 451).

But the CAA rejected his richly ironic complaint. On 4 November there was a meeting of all interested parties to reschedule Laker's debts or call for the company's liquidation. German and French parties to the Airbus project failed to see why their governments should bail out a British company, since the British had already deserted the Airbus project and BA was buying Boeings. But General Electric (GE) and McDonnell Douglas agreed to turn debts into preference shares. The Germans were also under pressure from a failed loan to Poland, and from Lufthansa, which had little love for the attempted undermining of the EU cartel.

By Christmas Eve 1981 a final agreement on a rescue package seemed to have been secured, and it was, according to Laker, 'the best Christmas present of all time. We have secured our long-term future. We aren't going to lurch from one crisis to another' (quoted in Banks 1982: 117). However, when news of GE's and McDonnell Douglas's financial stake in, and support for, Laker leaked out, rival airways demanded a retraction. In particular, Sir Adam Thomson, chair of BCal., sent a telex to Brian Rowe, head of GE's aero-engine division—who had been a prime supplier of BCal.—saying: 'BCAL HAS NO FURTHER INTEREST IN MCDONNELL DOUGLAS AIRCRAFT' (quoted in Sampson 1984: 154). Rowe then received another telex from Carlos Van Rafelghem, head of the Belgium airline Sabena, saying: 'SUCH PRACTICES WOULD ADVERSELY AFFECT OUR PRESENT GOOD BUSINESS RELATIONSHIP' (quoted in Sampson 1984: 154).

Other telexes came in from the French airline UTA and from the Dutch airline KLM. Similar messages, or 'nasty-grams' as Sandy McDonnell called them, reached McDonnell Douglas, whose actions were viewed with 'grave apprehension' by SAS, as 'amazing and disappointing' by Sabena, and as of the 'gravest concern' by Swissair; and so the complaints rolled in.

Skytrain's load factor went down to 64 per cent, with the outlook for January 1982 at 55 per cent. In fact, January 1982 produced Skytrain's worst ever load factor at 40 per cent—just at the time it passed its two millionth passenger. Laker sacked twenty-one pilots and demoted ten more to save money; furthermore, all staff were told they must forgo the next two pay rises.

On 2 February the CAA estimated that Laker needed £10 million immediately to survive. But GE withdrew its £1 million offer, leaving only £4 million from McDonnell Douglas on the table. Bizarrely, on the same day, Laker announced to a reporter on his way to New York that McDonnell Douglas had arranged a loan for £36 million and, with additional funds totalling £60 million, all his worries were over. 'In fact, we are in a better position than we have ever been,' he said. 'I'm flying high today and couldn't be more confident about the future' (quoted in Campbell-Smith 1986: 16).

McDonnell Douglas immediately withdrew its £4 million, and on 4 February the Midland Bank withdrew Laker's overdraft facility. The following day Laker made one more effort to raise £5 million but he failed. He called Ian Sproat to ask Mrs Thatcher to help and she called a meeting but was dissuaded from providing further 'open-ended' finance by her treasury officials. At 04.30 on 5 February 1982 Laker admitted defeat and called in the receivers. Later that day BA announced record losses of £144 million—and another loan from the government. In July 1983, the *Sunday Times* carried an article by John Oakley that summarized the position succinctly: 'The Americans think Sir Freddie was mugged in Central Park. Perhaps not. He collapsed in Britain, and it may have been from natural causes' (quoted in Campbell-Smith 1986: 106).

Nine months after the collapse, Bob Beckman, Laker's US lawyer, and Christopher Morris, the liquidator, filed a lawsuit alleging a conspiracy to destroy Laker by the Midland Bank, BA, PanAm, Lufthansa, Swissair, TWA, and BCal. The suit was divided between a civil case for damages and a criminal case alleging price fixing in contravention of the anti-trust laws. BA and BCal. secured an injunction to prevent Morris suing them in the USA, but this was not recognized by the US authorities. McDonnell Douglas wrote off $48 million in 1981 and GE $10 million. Laker's official web-site biography does not explain why the company was 'forced into receivership', only that the $1.5 billion anti-trust action in the USA claiming conspiracy by twelve major airlines to put Laker out of business 'was settled out of court, with all creditors being satisfied and all staff fully compensated' (Laker 1997: 3). But, for Laker, BA was the major culprit; as he said to Richard Branson ten years after the event: 'British Airways put me out of business . . . The bastards stopped my refinancing package with McDonnell Douglas' (quoted in Branson 1998: 364). In fact, the enquiries unearthed evidence that Laker had himself been deeply involved in discussion with his competitors to set particular rates in return for particular guarantees. Laker himself had been caught 'holding the smoking gun' (Campbell-Smith 1986: 175).

Ten years after the collapse, in 1992, Laker Airways (Bahamas) was launched with some of this compensation, operating scheduled flights between various cities in the USA and Grand Bahama. In 1996, fourteen years after winding up Laker Airways with the words, 'We really do want to get the show on the road again', Laker, then aged 74, launched Laker Airways Incorporated. This was a joint venture with Oscar S. Wyatt Jr., to fly from the UK to Florida, a route already served by five major airlines and a host of charter lines. Unlike the first time, he secured the necessary licence quickly, leaving just twelve weeks between the licence and the inaugural flight. Leasing three twenty-year-old revamped DC-10s and with only six weeks to launch, a major problem occurred with the video equipment for the back of each seat on his new Regency service. As Bob Iversen, Company President, said with just one week to go (and a still 'unproved' aeroplane): 'The only item which we have not foreseen is if we have a major mechanical problem with the aircraft. I don't expect that to happen' (quoted in BBC2 1997). It did. On the return 'proving' flight for the CAA, the pilot's windscreen shattered and the plane was delayed by over a week, forcing Laker to find a replacement plane at the last minute. Naturally, this disappointed those passengers who had booked Laker (*a*) because of the Regency service—which did not exist at the time of the inaugural flight anyway—and/or (*b*) because the flight was non-stop—which in the event it was not, because the replacement plane could not make the distance and had to stop over for refuelling. As Laker himself admitted: 'You always need a bit of luck in this world. You can be very clever, you can be a mastermind but you always need a bit of luck' (quoted in BBC2 1997).

On the 'true' inaugural flight of Laker Airways Inc. from the UK, flying from Manchester to Orlando, the ovens failed and there were still no videos (these arrived seven months later). On 5 August 1996 one of the—by now—overused planes (Laker had only two at this stage) broke down—as did the replacement—and the consequential forty-nine-hour delay for passengers led to a near riot at Gatwick—and suitably colourful coverage by the still sceptical press. By the end of 1996, Laker had received his third plane, was achieving 85 per cent capacity, and was 'making a modest profit . . . and back in the market' (quoted in BBC2 1997).

At about the same time a new competitor was launched: Virgin Express, Richard Branson's second airline company, which was modelled in some ways on Laker's Skytrain.

Branson and Virgin: Preparing for Take-Off

Sir George Branson, Richard's grandfather, was a successful high court judge, but Richard's own father, Edward, failed to follow in Sir George's footsteps when he was unsuccessful in his exam to enter Eton. He later joined the army during the Second World War, but then failed to pass his law exams first time, although he succeeded at a second attempt. Richard's mother, Eve Huntley-Flindt, derived from a stockbroking-turned-farming family, and after a short stage career as a dancer had become one of the first of the new 'Star Girls', or Air Hostesses, on British South American Airways just after the war. Richard Branson was born, almost exactly nine months after their wedding, on 18 July 1950, in Shamley Green, near Guildford. He was the first of three children. With Edward's legal career as a junior barrister stumbling along fitfully, Eve made craftwork for Harrods, while Edward's father, Sir George, paid for the children's private education (M. Brown 1998: 13–30).

Encouraged, particularly by his mother, to be independent and confident, Branson's first entrepreneurial scheme began at 12 years of age, when he planted 100 Christmas trees in a plot of land next to the new house the family had moved to, Tanyard Farm. Then his interest switched to breeding budgerigars, but, as with the tree scheme, Richard and his commercial partner, Nik Powell, a long-time friend from their mutual prep school, soon lost interest (M. Brown 1998: 40–1).

Academic enquiry was of marginal concern to Richard Branson: he learned to read only at 8 years old, was interested only in sport (until a knee injury ended this promising career prematurely at the age of 11), and only just managed to scrape into Stowe School, where he failed maths three times, passed six O levels, and left, in 1967, with one A level in Ancient History. Branson's headteacher had predicted, when he left school at 17, that he would 'either go to prison or become a millionaire' (quoted in Denoyelle and Larréché 1995: 1).

He was certainly regarded as a maverick who hated—to quote his mother's injunction—'watching others achieving something', and, although he was frequently in trouble with the school authorities, this was not a consequence of any insubordinate streak. As Tim Albery, a classmate recalled: 'If he got into trouble it wasn't because he was making a radical statement against the system but because he simply wasn't interested in doing what was demanded of him. He was only interested in doing what he wanted to do, and if he could inveigle other people into doing it, so much the better; if he couldn't, too bad' (quoted in M. Brown 1998: 32). In 1968 Branson launched his entrepreneurial career proper, publishing *Student*, a national magazine without any funding: 'I didn't have any money. I was fifteen years old. My parents didn't have any money, either. I had a friend who said you have to fund the magazine by selling advertising space before you actually publish the first edition. It took me a year and a half to do that' (quoted in Callan and Warshaw 1996: 31). Much of the time was spent while still at school writing to all and sundry in *Who's Who?* to secure their contributions— and he was often quite successful. By the summer of 1967 Branson had persuaded his parents to accept that he was leaving school early to concentrate on his real interest: *Student*.

Student never made any money, but even the first copy, in January 1968, demonstrated Branson's uncanny ability to get people to part with their money— in this case £6,000 for advertising space. And, though the magazine carried articles from the likes of James Baldwin, a prominent black activist at the time, it also carried Enoch Powell's 'Rivers of Blood' speech. Branson himself participated in the famous anti-American demonstration in Grosvenor Square on 17 March 1968, but this was the limit of his political radicalism and the left-wing activists who initially associated themselves with *Student* soon left it alone. Branson, however, still managed to corner an array of celebrities to be interviewed. Alice Walker, John-Paul Sartre, and Stephen Spender all appeared in issue three, for example. He also developed a huge talent for invention: he doubled the alleged circulation of the magazine from its probable 50,000 at that time to an improbable 100,000 when selling advertising space. He also arranged for his friends to ring him whenever he was being interviewed by journalists as the new whizz kid. Nik Powell was impressed: 'It really surprised me how easy it was to con people into thinking you had something successful which you quite patently didn't' (quoted in M. Brown 1998: 68). But beyond the invention was a serious skill: not just persuading advertisers to part with their money but persuading his staff to work without any money: to work for what Branson has always believed an essential element of work: fun, but fun oriented towards work, not in and for itself.

The last copy of *Student*, in 1970, carried an advert for Virgin (to mirror his own lack of business experience), a mail-order company inaugurated by Branson to exploit the ending of the Retail Price Maintenance Agreement that kept the price of records at an agreed rate. This had been disposed of in 1964, but the music shops' cartel-like actions ensured that the pricing remained high. In 1971, partly in response to the threatened postal strike that would have destroyed his mail-order business, the first Virgin shop opened in London. T. Jackson (1995: 30–1) relates a tale of Branson's early negotiating skill when a bootlegger rang the mail-order firm with an offer to sell pirated Jimi Hendrix records. Branson told him to meet a man called Zimmerman at the Virgin office. However, when the man arrived, he was made to wait for two hours while being sent on false trails for Zimmerman. Eventually Branson himself turned up and 'innocently' asked what the man wanted—and then at what price he was hoping to sell the records to the still absent Zimmerman. On being told £1 per record Branson offered him 50p and bought the entire stock on the spot, subsequently selling them for £3 each.

With two Virgin shops open and a recording studio in his new manor house at Shipton-on-Cherwell, things may have looked good, but the company was already £60,000 in debt. Branson then found himself in deep water with Customs and Excise after a dubious export scheme fell foul of the inspectors and he spent the night in prison (Brown 1998: 103, 104). But the £53,000 fine forced Branson to rethink his future and there were only two avenues: sell up and pay off the debt or expand the chain of shops as fast as possible and hope the results generated sufficient funds to keep the company afloat. Branson chose the latter and within two years fifteen more Virgin ships had opened around the country with a turnover of £1 million—but still no proper payroll system (M. Brown 1998: 110).

His new adventure into record making soon repaid the £53,000 fine levied on him when he signed up an unknown with a record that every other record company had rejected: Mike Oldfield and Tubular bells. Without any knowledge of music contracts on either side, Oldfield signed to Virgin for ten albums and a 5 per cent royalty—a contract based on that belonging to Sandy Denny, which they had borrowed.

In 1972 Branson married Kirsten Tomassi, an American architecture student, who assisted with Virgin Rags, an early venture into clothing, and the following year Virgin record label, now awash with the profits from Tubular Bells, signed Genesis, Boy George, and Peter Gabriel. As usual, practical jokes were never far from Branson's mind. On one occasion he drove Frank Zappa past the Manor house recording studio and on down the road to an altogether grander mansion. Letting Zappa out at the front door, Branson told him he would park the car and Zappa should ring the bell—which he duly did, only to be informed that the building was not a recording studio but Blenheim Palace (M. Brown 1998: 131)!

Like Laker's companies, this one was registered as the property of an offshore trust in the Channel Islands to minimize tax. It was during this period that Virgin organized company 'weekends' that were, in theory, optional but where no 'work' was done. Rather, the company members spent their time playing tennis, swimming, eating, and drinking in what has become the kind of company where fun rather than rewards were the reason to start and the reason to stay. As Branson admitted: 'I can't face the idea of smiling courses: it's much easier to let them actually *enjoy* it' (quoted in Sampson 1984: 217). Indeed, this aspect is not separated from Branson's commercial sense but a fundamental element of it, because, as he explained his move into the airline business: 'We didn't want to get into the transportation industry. We're still in the entertainment industry—at 25,000 feet' (Branson quoted in Callan and Warshaw 1996: 31).

In 1977 Branson took another calculated risk that paid off, signing the Sex Pistols—though he had also rejected their first single 'Anarchy in the UK' some time previously. The following year the Sex Pistols broke up after Sid Vicious had died of a drugs overdose, but the notoriety acquired by Virgin ensured that other artists regarded Virgin as a label with maximum street credibility (Simple Minds, Human League, Heaven 17, China Crisis, and Japan were quickly signed up.) With the record company now expanding dramatically, Branson ceded direct daily control over the record business to his subordinates and with some of the profits bought a private island in the British Virgin Islands for $300,000.

Branson's next business venture was not so successful. In 1979 he set up Virgin Books with Maxim Jakubowski. Branson said that he was looking for undiscovered talent—the literary equivalent of Mike Oldfield—but the strategy was universal rather than selective and within two years Virgin Books was in trouble and Robert Devereux, his younger sister Vanessa's boyfriend who worked for Macmillan, was brought in to save it. He narrowed the title base to non-fiction books about rock music, sport, and videos, thereby realigning the company towards Virgin's specific image. Devereux later married Branson's sister and became a full member of the Virgin board and was viewed with some suspicion by the other members when he appeared to be attempting to beat Branson at his own games. But, in the words of Simon Draper, 'for all his [Devereux] cerebral qualities . . . he lacked his brother-in-law's uncanny ability to inspire not merely great loyalty but also enormous effort among those who were working for him' (quoted in T. Jackson 1995: 68). A merger with the failing W. H. Allen subsequently lost Virgin a substantial amount of money.

Worse was to come. During the 1980–1 economic recession, 'Virgin teetered on the edge of disaster, seven days a week'.[2] Virgin then comprised a record label, record studios, retail outlets, restaurants, and an island. Twenty-five per cent of the 200 staff were sacked but Branson survived the recession by using his accumulated overseas deposits as security for bank loans (T. Jackson 1995: 60).

The retail side managed by Nik Powell was doing considerably less well than the music side, especially after Boy George was signed in 1981. Powell was gradually distanced from the interests of the rest of the board and his holding of 40 per cent of the shares was bought out for around £1 million; within five years 40 per cent was worth around £96 million (T. Jackson 1995: 60).

It was at this point that Branson began to trail in the wake of Laker's disaster.

Virgin Atlantic Airways

On 5 February 1982 Randolph Fields, a 29-year-old Californian lawyer, American born but with English parents, heard on the radio that Freddie Laker had gone bust. In June, Fields was in the same hotel where Laker had dutifully accepted bankruptcy, to talk to ex-Laker executives about a scheme for a replacement airline. Within two weeks David Tait, Laker's US sales operations manager, and Roy Gardner, Laker's technical manager, agreed to go into business with Fields under the name British Atlantic Airways. Fields's intention was to buy Laker's now unused licence to fly a single jet between Heathrow and JFK New York, flying only business class, but the CAA turned down Fields's application.[3]

Fields appealed against the CAA decision in September 1983 and the CAA decided to allow him to fly between Gatwick and Newark (New York's third airport), providing he could provide proof of sufficient financial support to guarantee not to leave passengers overseas should British Atlantic become bankrupt. Fields realized that a business-class-only route could not operate successfully between these two secondary airports, and that he would have to operate in the same market that Laker had been in, now dominated by People Express, led by Donald Burr. However, Fields decided to differentiate British Atlantic from People Express by carrying business class as well as economy and by providing meals, limited baggage, and entertainment as part of the ticket (unlike People Express). Fields had three months to find the capital backing for the March 1984 formal CAA hearing into his application.

In February, Fields, having failed to find any major banker to support British Atlantic, phoned Branson and a meeting was arranged. Virgin was in the throes of financing the film version of *1984*, which overran on budget almost threefold and failed to live up to either Virgin's or the critics' expectations. Moreover, neither Branson nor anyone else in Virgin had any airline experience, but Branson's failed attempts to get through to the reservation desk at People's Express confirmed that there must be a market there. Draper said it would be 'a total disaster' (quoted in T. Jackson 1995: 86).

. But Branson argued that, at worst, it would cost Virgin £20 million per annum to run but only £2 million to 'cut and run'. Paradoxically, then, Branson's risk was much smaller than Laker's, because a major failure for Branson would injure but not destroy Virgin; for Laker a major failure was terminal. Furthermore, at 70 per cent capacity the airline would break even, and for every percentage point above this Virgin would earn $250,000. Branching into an airline was against the Virgin principle of expanding only into related fields; yet Branson persuaded himself, and then his colleagues (after all, he still held 85 per cent of Virgin's shares), that the airline would carry the same kind of passengers that currently bought their records, books, and films. As Brown (1998: 249) notes, Virgin 'was now in that most eighties of concepts, the *Lifestyle* business'.

Virgin agreed to take a 45 per cent interest in the new airline, while Fields had another 45 per cent, and the balance was to be distributed amongst the employees. Branson wanted to call the airline Virgin *Airways* but Fields insisted it must be Virgin *Atlantic Airways*. By 29 February Virgin Atlantic Airways (VAA) was in existence, but Branson insisted that Fields remained personally liable (unlike Branson) for any financial failure.

At the CAA hearing BCal. insisted that VAA must wait—as it had done—for its first licence. Initially the CAA listened to, but were unpersuaded by, Fields's address; however, Branson's promise to underwrite the airline with £3.5 million from Virgin led the CAA to dismiss BCal.'s claim and VAA was granted a licence conditional on it proving financial reliability. Virgin then guaranteed whatever losses VAA made, and Fields became Chair of VAA without a salary but making £25,000 on the first £1 million made by VAA plus 5 per cent of the profits thereafter. They had just three months to catch the summer holiday traffic. As soon as CAA accepted the proposition, Branson demanded that Virgin take overall control, but initially Fields refused, eventually accepting a minority stake (Virgin took 75 per cent) in return for £200,000 (Jackson 1995: 92). Initially, Fields became the Chair, with day-to-day responsibility, while Branson assumed the more long-term strategic role of President.

The next problem was securing a plane. A second-hand Boeing 747 was leased from a subsidiary of the Chemical Bank of New York, which, in turn, leased it from Barclays Bank, which bought it from Boeing. This enabled VAA to spend $27.8 million rather than $100 million on a new aircraft—a lesson Branson had already learned from Laker's error—as was the agreement that protected VAA from fluctuations in the exchange rate. A clause also allowed Virgin to profit from any increase in the aircraft's value if it surrendered it back to Boeing after a year, but protected Virgin from any drop in value at the same time. It was, said Bob Wilson, who negotiated on behalf of Boeing, 'easier to sell a fleet of aircraft to United Airlines, than to sell one to Virgin' (quoted in M. Brown 1998: 256).

Branson then had lunch with Freddie Laker who confirmed that business-class passengers were essential to profitability. After all, Laker had already demonstrated that concentrating on the cheaper end of the market generated inadequate margins. 'You don't want to be all no-frills economy service . . . that was my mistake. You'll be vulnerable to the simple cost-cutting attack which put me out of business.' However, Laker also warned him that the competition was fierce, especially from BA, which was 'utterly ruthless. My mistake was that I never complained loudly enough' (quoted in Branson 1998: 196). Branson even suggested calling his first plane 'Spirit of Sir Freddie', though Laker was quick to insist that such a name night not be the best omen.[4]

The team from Virgin Games was called in to help create and market the airline and suggested calling economy class 'Riff Raff' and first class 'Upper Class' (the latter at business-class prices). Others objected to the names and Branson, having changed his mind three times, eventually accepted Upper Class but decided on 'Economy' rather than 'Riff Raff' (T. Jackson 1995: 111).

The goal of VAA was 'to provide all classes of travellers with the highest quality travel at the lowest cost' (quoted in Denoyelle and Larréché 1995: 2). Initially, it was aimed at the typical Virgin customer—young—but it moved quickly to a much wider appeal. Virgin managed to combine the appeals to all customers, Upper Class and Economy travellers, to ensure high loading factors, with the premium pricing on Upper Class securing high yields. By 1991 10 per cent of passengers and around 40 per cent of its income came from business (Denoyelle and Larréché 1995: 8).

Branson's approach to flying was quite different from the 'pile 'em high and sell 'em cheap' that Laker had started with. He intended to make flying an experience in itself, rather than just a method of getting from A to B quickly: 'We must be memorable, we are not a bus service. The journeys made by our customers are romantic and exciting and we should do everything we can to make them feel just that. That way they will talk about the most memorable moments long after they leave the airport' (quoted in Denoyelle and Larréché 1995: 6). Concern for customers became immediately apparent when thirty customers were asked to complete questionnaires on each flight; the only major criticism seems to have been about (the lack of) punctuality. VAA also pioneered facilities for children and babies with a children's channel on video, a children's menu, and changing facilities.

Even the motivation to work was novel. VAA hired ex-BA pilots who had just received early retirement. But they also decided to hire some 'virgin' cabin crew. Salaries were not competitive (comparing BA and VAA, pilots and crew of the latter earned around two-thirds of the former), training was rapid, and 'all hands to the telephones' was a frequent request of the aircrew waiting to fly. Branson's appearance at the initial conference in flying gear ensured that advertising would be virtually unnecessary, but this was a step into the unknown for Branson who until this point had not actively sought publicity. But in the absence of an advertising budget such a stunt was deemed necessary by his new publicity guru, Tony Brainsby. From this point onwards, Branson's public persona, hitherto either unknown or socially awkward, was rewritten as the non-exploitive entrepreneur. He became the 'acceptable face' of capitalism, 'the people's businessman' (M. Brown 1998: 3). Denoyelle and Larréché (1995: 3) suggest that, until the launch of Virgin Atlantic, 'while Richard Branson had always befriended rock stars he had otherwise kept a low profile'. But the commercial strength of BA made him change tack: 'I knew that the only way of competing with British Airways and the others was to get out there and use myself to promote it.'

In a striking similarity to Laker's latest venture, the early days of VAA were precariously balanced. Authorization from the American Civil Aeronautical Board to land at Newark was granted only three days before the first flight, due on 22 June, but Virgin had already expected this, since the British government had just done the same to People Express. And, since Virgin was forbidden to advertise in the USA until landing rights were approved, Branson employed sky writers to create a sign around New York sky saying: 'WAIT FOR THE ENGLISH VIRGI . . .'—the 'N' had disappeared behind a cloud (Denoyelle and Larréché 1995: 2).

Still, all was not well. Two of the four engines on the Boeing were rejected as under power and the engines were exchanged and ready to go only two hours before the proving flight organized by the CAA to ensure an operations certificate. One of the engines caught fire during this flight after a bird was sucked into it and only the return of the previously discarded engine, and a helpful *Financial Times* journalist and photographer who omitted the fire in their coverage, managed to save the day (Branson 1998: 204; M. Brown 1998: 264).

In June 1984 *the*, since there was only one, Virgin Atlantic Airways Boeing 747 took off from Gatwick on its inaugural flight to Newark, New Jersey. The maiden voyage of the 'Maiden Voyager', as the plane was baptized by Branson (wearing a First World War leather flying helmet, and accompanied by his 2-year-old daughter), appears to have been one long party. When, on its landing, the representative of the Newark authorities 'asked for the ship's papers he was greeted with roars of laughter' (Branson 1998: 204; M. Brown 1998: 264). On average each passenger had drunk two bottles of champagne (T. Jackson 1995: 114). Branson had forgotten his passport and was only able to step off the plane after some nifty negotiations. Meanwhile Branson mistook the black mayor of New York who led the reception party for one of the caterers and the porcelain dinner plates were only just saved from the bin after an error.

When Branson returned home, he was met by a representative from his bank, Coutts, who informed the Virgin boss that the recent application for a temporary increase in overdraft had been rejected and that any cheque, for as little as £25 over the limit (£4 million), would be 'bounced'. Given that Virgin had made £11 million profit in the previous financial year and was probably worth around £100 million at the time, Branson was understandably distraught (M. Brown 1998: 266, 268).

The reservations system also got into trouble after Air Florida's central reservation computer (which undertook Virgin's computerized system) went down and stranded Virgin. This, and the aftermath, led to a deteriorating relationship between Fields and Branson, and Branson had himself appointed to the board of VAA. At one point Fields—still VAA's Chair—was even denied a flight on board a VAA flight to London. The reservation-system problems persisted through 1984, with some flights being shown as full when they were not and others flying with 300 empty seats. Branson told his reservation staff to overbook the flights significantly and the consequential chaos turned the normally pro-Branson press against him—not for the conventional limited overbooking but for unlimited overbooking.

As winter approached, and the reservations crisis eased, BA (soon followed by PanAm and TWA) reduced its economy prices from £278 to £259—within £1 of VAA's price. 'Predatory pricing'—in which a larger company offers a loss leader to eliminate a smaller competitor—is illegal but difficult to prove or prevent. Branson could hardly complain about the low prices, but he did suggest that the other airlines (now including TWA and PanAm) should cut a similar percentage off all their other prices if they were truly concerned about the customer, rather than driving VAA out of business. As Branson made clear to Nicholas Ridley, then the Secretary of State for Transport, 'we believe in competition but having a bleeding competition with a blood bank isn't fair competition' (M. Brown 1998: 273).

Branson threatened to sue BA—about to be privatized—and in October the government, having failed to secure US approval exempting BA from any legal dispute over the new price war) and fearful that the flotation of BA would fail, refused to accept BA's plans for price reductions. Yet the major airlines soon found a way to reduce their fares, leaving VAA to mirror the drop. At 90 per cent capacity the first six months of VAA managed to return a profit of £250,000 and VAA introduced a short-haul flight to Maastricht for just £19 one way. But, like the flight between Luton and Dublin, the Maastricht journey was short both in the flight time and in terms of how long it lasted. The future was not in short haul but long haul; not cheap seats but quality seats; not economy but service.

The new year began well with Virgin Holidays, another venture for Branson, for whom 'business opportunities are like buses. There's always another coming along' (Branson, quoted in T. Jackson 1995: 66). In February, Branson dressed as Long John Silver to publicize his attempt on board the Virgin *Atlantic Challenger* to break the record by boat across the North Atlantic. A greater challenge was made in spring when the Chemical Bank, worried over the technical legality of its original deal with VAA for the aeroplane, tried to repossess it. At this point the £–$ exchange rate had moved from $1.45 to $1 and VAA needed to find an extra third to stay afloat—it began to look as though VAA was about to be 'Lakerized'. But Branson took a two-month injunction out to prevent repossession, threatened to sue Chemical Bank, and, during the interval, arranged a new leasing deal with Security Pacific. He also arranged a new Chair of VAA, for in May Fields resigned.

By August the record attempt across the Atlantic was ready but just two hours short of reaching England the boat hit some driftwood and sank, leaving the crew to be picked up by a passing freighter. With what one journalist called £5 million of free advertising through the attempt, VAA's ticket sales in the UK (though not in the USA, where VAA and Branson remained relatively unknown) grew rapidly. In Jackson's words: 'The airline's launch had established him in the public mind as a plucky fighter for the interests of the consumer. *Challenger* turned him into a daredevil, and a good sport who behaved well when he lost' (T. Jackson 1995: 136). He may have lost the race but VAA appeared to be saved and in the summer, with VAA finances improving rapidly, Branson leased a second jet and began negotiating for a London–Florida route.

In 1986 the Virgin Group (excluding VAA) was floated and made £13 million profit on £250 million turnover. VAA, in the meanwhile, had doubled in size since its inception, taking £34 million turnover with losses of £775,000 (T. Jackson 1995: 211). In April, six years after Laker had suggested it, but four years too late to save him, the European Court of Justice ruled air transport also subject to Treaty of Rome rules against price fixing.

In a master stroke of timing and publicity, or rather luck, the speedboat Virgin *Atlantic Challenger II* made the fastest-ever sea crossing of the Atlantic with Branson on board and it arrived exactly at half-time during the World Cup final in Mexico, so that pictures of Branson were flashed all around the world. As the boat came into the dock there was a delay whilst another boat was moved and the journalists on the quayside became increasingly restless as their deadlines approached. In the end Branson got his crew to throw him overboard so he 'had' to swim to the land and talk to the journalists (T. Jackson 1995: 142). Branson subsequently appeared with Mrs Thatcher sailing down the Thames: RICHARD THE LIONHEART, the *Daily Express* called him.

In 1987 the market really began to shape up. BA was privatized (it then accounted for 79 per cent of all British-originating international passenger traffic), and price controls on European Airlines were relaxed. VAA was still expanding, having secured the ex-BCal. routes to Boston, Los Angeles, JFK New York, and Tokyo. And the Virgin *Atlantic Flyer*, the largest-ever hot-air balloon, became the first balloon across the Atlantic—again with Branson on board. By the summer, VAA turnover was up to £60 million with post-tax profits of £3.2 million. Eastern Airlines had begun to undercut VAA's prices but not its quality, and it was the latter aspect of VAA that Branson was determined to enhance. 'Branson . . . realized early on that his competitors' pockets were deep enough to drive him out of business if he were to try and compete on price alone. That was the mistake that Freddie Laker had made. To survive in the long term, Virgin must offer a better quality of service' (T. Jackson 1995: 320).

On the inaugural flight to Miami, Branson once again secured enormous free publicity for VAA, dressed as Peter Pan, but VAA still had only two aircraft and this made technical problems a constant source of irritation and delay. The public ownership of the Virgin Group was also a source of irritation to Branson and he bought back all the shares—to avoid being responsible to institutional shareholders and the City, despite their financial support. In the same year VAA turnover increased to £75 million, with post-tax profits of £12 million and Virgin's management started to professionalize under Syd Pennington, a former Marks & Spencer retailer, as the previously flat structure—with all twenty-seven senior managers reporting directly to Branson—became increasingly unmanageable. VAA was already winning several customer-service-related prizes (for example, Executive Travel Airline of the Year Award), but, wanting to keep ahead of the opposition, it introduced in-flight video entertainment. With VAA now flying to Tokyo, the Seibu-Saison group of Japan bought 10 per cent of VAA's shares and provided a £30 million cash injection.

At the start of 1990 everything was going well. He had already married his long-time partner, Joan Templeman, Virgin Atlantic flew to Los Angeles, Branson crossed the Pacific in a balloon, breaking all records, and VAA turnover doubled to £180 million; indeed, in June VAA was voted Airline of the Year in the *Executive Traveller* magazine. But post-tax profits fell from 16 to 3 per cent and in August the Iraqis invaded Kuwait, oil prices rose, and airline traffic began to drop. Notwithstanding the financial problems—3,000 passengers cancelled their flights with Virgin in the first week after the invasion—Branson attempted to play his part in the unfolding drama by organizing a rescue flight for the British women and children initially seized by the Iraqi forces but now deemed suitable for release by Saddam Hussein (Branson 1998: 275). However, the Iraqis denied VAA the right to land and transported the group out of the country by bus (M. Brown 1998: 406). VAA subsequently engaged on several mercy missions for refugees in Jordan and brought back some of the ill hostages from Iraq.

With global air traffic declining under the economic recession and the impact of the Gulf War, the world's collective airlines lost $4 billion. VAA moved its accounting period back so that the current financial year included eighteen months' trading, and sold one of its own aircraft, thus turning a bad financial year into a moderately successful one. Other airlines were not so successful in the circumstances: TWA and PanAm sold their Heathrow slots to American and United Airlines, while VAA secured the right to fly from Heathrow rather than Gatwick in 1991 after, perhaps coincidentally, Mrs Thatcher (a long-time supporter of Lord King) was replaced by Mr Major. Lord King promptly cancelled BA's annual donation of £40,000 to the Conservative party. Heathrow is twenty times busier than Gatwick and the switch enabled Virgin to have higher load factors and better access to first-class passengers, interline airways, and cargo. In effect, the average yield per customer is 15 per cent higher at Heathrow than at Gatwick (M. Brown 1998: 439).

On the morning of the first Heathrow departure in July 1991, Virgin staff painted the BA concord at the entrance to the airport tunnel with a Virgin logo and photographed Branson dressed as a pirate in front of it before security turned up (Denoyelle and Larréché 1995: 4). The joke began to turn sour when VAA employees began to receive anonymous phone calls claiming that Branson was being investigated or that VAA was having to pay for fuel in cash because its credit was worthless. This was the first part of the so-called Dirty Tricks campaign run by BA against VAA and Branson. The campaign included persuading VAA Upper Class ticketholders to switch to BA (both sets of passenger information were held on the same computer). BA's Chief Executive, Sir Colin Marshall, denied any such campaign, but a Thames Television programme in February 1992 suggested otherwise. Within weeks, writs were flying back and forth between BA and VAA, but by December BA had withdrawn its counter-writ against Branson and paid £610,000 in an out-of-court settlement plus £4.5 million in legal costs. Branson's own share of the damages—£500,000—was shared amongst Virgin employees at £166 each, the 'BA Bonus' as it became known

(M. Brown 1998: 459). To add insult to BA's injury, VAA won the Best Business Airline award from the *Business Traveller* magazine for the fourth year running in 1991.[5]

By 1992 global air traffic was increasing by 10 per cent per annum, but large losses were still being made. Branson lost £21 million in the financial year and came under great pressure to sell parts of his empire to reduce his debt burden, but he resisted until he considered the timing was right. Seibu-Saison gave notice of their decision to withdraw from VAA, and VAA agreed to buy back the 10 per cent shares, but, with the economy looking weak, VAA stalled the deal in the hope of overrunning the end of year deadline and renegotiating the deal from scratch—which it did.

Still, VAA needed a capital injection and Virgin Music (then the sixth largest record company) was sold to Thorn EMI for £560 million—what T. Jackson (1995: 5) called 'an astounding price'. The offer of Thorn EMI shares had been on the table and Branson was keen to retain a controlling interest in the music business, but he was more desperate for cash and certain that VAA would fold if he failed to support it immediately. He felt he had only one choice: 'If I took Thorn shares and they fell dramatically in value, I could be powerless to stop the bank moving in. Sir Freddie Laker had reminded me how it happens so fast that it takes your breath away. Rather like Virgin, his airline had fought a long battle against British Airways, and just when he needed their support the banks pulled in their loans' (Branson 1998: 409).

VAA then introduced 'Mid Class' to cater for those Economy passengers who were, in fact, either on business—but not in the First Class range—or the new middle classes, who now had considerably more money to spend than ever before. In April Branson followed a Laker precedent when he ordered four A340s Airbuses for over £30 million. 'We are proud to buy an aircraft which is in large part British built, and on which so many jobs in the UK depend' (quoted in Denoyelle and Larréché 1995: 4).

He bought these at a low point in the economic cycle, thus securing a good price on them, but then began to imitate some of Laker's wilder ideas by suggesting that VAA take the windows out to save weight and fuel costs; fortunately Branson, unlike Laker, was not a one-man band and he was dissuaded by his board. The first A340 Airbus was launched by Diana, Princess of Wales, in one of her last public ceremonies after separating from Prince Charles, once again getting Branson and Virgin onto the front page of global news.

Branson was now keen to keep VAA ahead of the pack by installing seat-back videos that would provide the best in-flight entertainment anywhere. But the cost of $10 million was simply too much. Branson then telephoned Phil Conduit, CEO of Boeing, and asked whether Boeing would provide the seat-back videos for free if Virgin bought ten Boeing 747-400s; the answer was yes, as was the answer to a similar request to Jean Pierson at Airbus. The result was a new fleet of aircraft and leading edge in-flight entertainment systems. As Branson (1998: 434) recalled, 'we discovered that it was easier to get $4 billion credit to buy eighteen new aircraft than it was to get $10 million credit for the seat-back video-sets'.

At the beginning of 1994 the Virgin group was generating revenues of around £1,500 million and VAA won the Best Transatlantic Airline and Best Business Class for the sixth year. In March VAA broke into the duopoly London–Hong Kong route held until then by BA and Cathay Pacific. In a typically Branson piece of publicity, tailors were sent on some Hong Kong-bound flights to take measurements of customers and fax them directly to Hong Kong, so that suits were ready by the time the flight landed. In May VAA broke into the duopoly held by BA–United on the London–San Francisco route. When the inaugural flight touched down in San Francisco, it stopped by a giant tax meter; Branson emerged from the plane, put a huge 'coin' into the meter, and a Virgin Flag promptly appeared; Branson was subsequently 'jailed' in another stunt in Alcatraz Prison. As the new century approached, VAA was once again under pressure from the new rash of global alliances between the major airlines, but it was by no means certain that the man who had escaped from Alcatraz would be brought back to earth by them.

By November 1998 Branson was able to claim that VAA had doubled in size in the previous four years with twenty-four aircraft and 6,400 staff (5,750 at its Crawley headquarters), and it began recruiting a further 1,500 staff, in addition to the extra 250 staff for his Virgin Sun short-haul charter holiday company (*Guardian*, 27 Nov. 1998). VAA and the holiday division of Virgin group increased sales by 20 per cent in the 1997/8 financial year to £942 million—making the Virgin group Britain's largest privately owned business, displacing Littlewoods, with annual group revenues at £2.4 billion, with profits before tax up from £65 million in the previous year to £90 million and employing 15,000 people in twenty-four countries (*Observer*, 4 Oct. 1998; Blackhurst 1998).

From the wreckage left by Laker in 1982 this was some take-off. By the end of the 1998/9 financial year, Virgin Atlantic's profits had increased (by 40 per cent over two years) to £100 million, while BA's had dropped 61 per cent to £225 million (Harper 1999).

Analysis

The Philosophical Arts: Identity

Laker oriented his product around cost—he virtually invented the low-cost airfare that has now become a standard part of air travel—but the initial identification of the 'cheap' rather than the 'good value' ticket allowed Laker's commercial and political enemies to associate his airline and his passengers with the 'cheap' end of the market. And, as long as Laker continued to focus wholly on this sector of the market, the down-market labelling of his product continued. In contrast, and partly as a consequence of what happened to Laker, Branson operated across the various market sectors and chose to position Virgin as a product associated with 'young and fun' rather than 'the forgotten man'.

The second element of this identity was that Laker very much restricted his brand to cheap airline services, while Branson's radical expansion of the Virgin brand has demonstrated just how elastic and powerful a brand identity can be. In effect, Laker, to continue the philosophical analogy, literally imposed upon his airline the oversharp focus that had encouraged him to ignore economic warning signs: the 'knight in a shining fuselage' had become Don Quixote tilting his paltry lance at the windmills of European and global politicians, bureaucrats, and state airlines with as much chance of success as his fabled predecessor. Branson, on the other hand, appeared as Robin Hood, an irreverent buccaneer who allegedly attacked the rich, the staid, and the privileged establishment on behalf of the dynamic, meritocratic, and fun-loving young. Laker had shown how fun could be cheap, Branson had apparently shown how life could be fun.

The Fine Arts: Strategic Vision

To what extent is Branson's superior success rooted in a greater appreciation and application of the fine arts—that is, the use of imagination and utopian thought to create an alternative future? Clearly both leaders are visionaries, Laker in initially imagining a way radically to increase the potential market for flying and Branson for constantly dreaming up schemes to expand his business empire. One could also argue that the difference lies in the timing of the two developments—that is, that it was partly a consequence of Branson managing to learn from the mistakes made by Laker, and thus the greater imagination lies with the first mover, Laker. There is something in this, because it took an interminably long time to get Skytrain off the ground and, by the time it had happened, the economic situation had become very unstable. However, the timing was not simply beyond Laker's control, because on many occasions he took advantage of the timing to secure planes at their very cheapest price. The problem was that the cheap price could not transcend the reason for the cheap price: the market for air travel was shrinking rapidly. We should also note that the timing of his developments led Laker directly into conflicts over the territorial designs of rivals. Competing by generating additional markets was one thing, but, in a business where airspace is regarded as the private possession of state airlines, to attack the élite end of the market spectrum was always a risky venture. And with Laker risk was something not to be weighed but to be taken advantage of. Thus Laker's strategic vision was seldom powerful enough to hold his concentration on the object and he was too easily diverted into focusing upon secondary and often contradictory strategic visions—usually of the 'how-to-make-a-quick-financial-killing' variety and often when this imaginative deal threatened the entire future of the organization.

On the other side, imagination is undoubtedly one of Branson's primary strengths. 'Richard Branson . . . knows that simply thinking differently at the beginning doesn't ensure success. The world is full of business people who had a brilliant idea, but whose businesses have milked the idea dry and then stagnated.

You need to keep on thinking differently' (White *et al*. 1996: 42–3). It is this expansionary vision that keeps Virgin at the leading edge, whether that is in-flight entertainment systems, financial services, or Virgin Clothing (Sage 1997). Laker was an effective innovator at particular times but seems not to have been able to renew this creativity or employ people who could.

Branson's failures are also as important as his successes in explaining the difference between him and Laker. Both are apparently buccaneers—that is, they allegedly take inordinate risks—and the difference, therefore, is that Branson is either better at assessing risk than Laker ever was or simply luckier. In effect, and since the imagination is also involved in assessing risks and rewards, we can suggest that Laker's utopian thought was indeed 'abstract' while Branson's was 'concrete'. Laker was likely to fail and fail badly, while Branson might have failed but it would not have been a catastrophe even if he had. For example, Laker failed when he took on BA, PanAm, and TWA face to face at the top end of the market. The resulting cost-cutting war inevitably cut Laker's reserves quicker than those of any of his competitors. Branson learned from this strategic mistake by competing on quality as well as on price—which the competition found much more difficult to beat him on.[6]

However, a critical issue remains that of risk. Brummer and Cowe, for example, suggest that the dilution of the Virgin brand is a potential disaster for Branson and that

extending a brand will only weaken it unless the new addition brings something to the party. Virgin could bring nothing to computers, which were still born, or vodka, which has effectively been withdrawn, or cola, which is made by the same Canadian company that manufactures cola for retailers such as Sainsbury and has struggled to make an impact . . . The most damage has been done by his attempt to sprinkle some of the magic of the skies on the railways . . . It is surprisingly cheap to create an international airline. But building an international soft drink operation is not cheap, nor is setting up a savings and investment business world-wide. And in both cases Virgin would be competing against some of the world's largest corporations, whether that be Coca-Cola or the Prudential. (Brummer and Cowe 1998: 3)

Here, the analysis is perceived through a marketing lens: Virgin Cola, Virgin Trains, and Virgin Direct personal finance add nothing to the brand and therefore were risks not worth taking. Yet Branson's approach, ironically, is the inverse of the 'high-risk-high-dilution' that paralyses financial and marketing innovations.

Two aspects are critical here. First, and contrary to popular opinion and Brummer and Cowe, the financial risk directly related to establishing a soft drink plant is not high—especially if the manufacturing is virtually outsourced anyway. Thus the financial risk is low not high.[7] Similarly, when Branson first thought about establishing VAA, his thoughts were not simply focused on the amount of profit to be made but on minimizing the loss if necessary: 'If I could lease the plane for one year, and then have the chance to return the plane, we would have a clear escape route if it all failed. It would be embarrassing but we would limit the amount of money we lost' (Branson 1998: 193). When he first broached the idea to his colleagues, they were vehemently opposed, but he persisted: 'The most Virgin would lose would be £2 million . . . Come on . . . Virgin can afford to make this step. The risk is less than a third of this year's profits . . . The beauty of starting up from scratch rather than buying an existing airline was that we could easily retreat if it didn't work' (Branson 1998: 195). These are the words not of a high-risk taker but of a calculated risk-taker with an insurance policy if the risk fails. While Branson's empire came close to financial collapse, it always managed to survive on the basis of a proportionately lower amount of debt than Laker. Branson never generated as much overcapacity by his speculative buying of planes as Laker did, and Laker's insistence on pursuing the cheaper end of the market always left him with marginal pricing, whereas Branson's wooing of the top end of the market allowed him to adopt premium pricing. In short, by being second in time Branson was able to benefit from Laker's mistakes, and a crucial error to avoid was attacking the competition in the spaces they regarded as inviolable and within which they could undermine any competitor. The minimalist approach to risk taking is also evident in the way that the Virgin companies are largely independent of each other, so that a collapse in one remains a local not a collective failure. Thus the spawning of businesses within the Virgin group is not just to ensure localized control and identification but a damage-limitation exercise.

Secondly, the issue of branding identity relates to the issue of language. Does language reflect or construct the world? If we assume language reflects reality, then those worried by the dilution of the Virgin brand have every right to be worried: the brand has a 'real' identity that means something concrete and has an essence that must be protected. But, if we assume that language creates the world, then the identity of the brand is equally created. In other words, Virgin can come to represent whatever its supporters can persuade us to believe is 'essentially' Virgin. If that means personal-finance plans, cola, cinemas, trains, or whatever, then so be it. The world, and the identity of the brand, are there to be created and recreated, not to be embalmed in concrete and deified—though in an attempt to undermine a rival brand a mortician's approach might be very successful.

In sum, both leaders are clearly imaginative but Branson's imagination appears to go further and last longer than Laker's and, as a consequence, Branson's strategic vision is both more concrete and more robust than Laker's. But is the difference limited to the imagination of the fine arts or is there a link to the martial arts as well?

The Martial Arts: Organizational Tactics

The simplest explanation for the comparative failure of Laker was weaker organizational, especially financial, control—that is his organizational tactics were less robust. Banks relates the story of a Whitehall mandarin arriving at Laker's Gatwick HQ to find the finance director on the floor trying to fix the broken photocopier (Banks 1982: 124). There seems to have been few formal accounting methods used. Laker was not self-evidently in trouble until 1981, but the apparent robustness of his loan guarantors meant that few really thought he would go under. After all, he had several governments, several of the world's leading banks, and several of the world's leading corporations supporting his finances: what could go wrong? In this case, the heterogeneity of the banks led to the initial unravelling.

Paradoxically, then, it was Laker's ability to generate substantial political and economic support—despite his detractors—that set up the final denouement, for he adopted the tactic of domination when his resources were simply unable to deliver success. In his own words: 'I thought that forty-three banks couldn't be wrong. The banks were no smarter than anyone else. Why do people think I was stupider than anyone else?' (quoted in Sampson 1984: 159). Banks (1982: 128) concurs that the banks were woefully inadequate to the task of advising Laker: 'It does seem surprising that no banker appeared to be sufficiently concerned about the potential exchange losses at the time these loans were raised to do something about it.'

In this case the very ability of Laker to persuade the world that he would not only survive but actually prosper merely dug the hole he was in even more quickly. But beyond this Laker misread the power of his political enemies—some of whom were as angry at the British government as they were with Laker. Thus his powerful network of allies looked impervious to attack, but it was precisely this disregard for others' interests and resources that stimulated his collapse at the hands of a rival network of interests.

The danger of hubris is always hovering around successful leaders and that inability to appreciate that the future is indeterminate and that your own resources are just potentialities not certainties seems to have encouraged Laker to assume that nothing could go wrong. Here again Laker's apparent arrogance, so often communicated through his love for the media, is another element in explaining his relative failure. In contrast, Branson's bravura performances appear very much the acts of a rather shy person—and this shyness undermines any hint of the hubris that brought Laker down. The conventional meaning of hubris—pride or arrogance linked to the ultimate ruin of the individual—indicates the way the overwhelming strength of an individual is the cause of the weakness. This is substantially different from the claim (by Hunt, for example) that leaders can benefit from a weakness if (a) it demonstrates their frail humanity—they are like us mere mortals after all and we can thus relate to them—and (b) it deflects attention from what might be a more serious weakness (Hunt 1996).

In the case of hubris it is the *strength* of a characteristic that undoes the individual when—and only when—this strength is inverted to a weakness. But the weakness is not an attractive manifestation of common—and insignificant—human failure; rather the weakness is serious and it is Hegelian in its embodiment of opposites. That is to say, the weakness is the other side of the same coin. In Laker's case we can see how his inability to listen to others' warnings, and the way this had previously proved to be a great strength of his, led—like a veritable Greek tragedy—to his downfall. As he himself admitted in 1996: 'I'm a nit picker by nature and I want my way and no other way. It could be that I'm difficult. So be it' (BBC2 1997).

Laker's blustering style also seems to have deterred any employee—and quite possibly any of his bankers—from ever checking his wilder ideas, and he frequently appears to have been only amateurly prepared for the interminable meetings with the CAC and CAA. Indeed, he seems to have made many decisions *ad hoc* and 'on the hoof', with little attempt at full analysis of the issue concerned. As Banks (1982: 127) concludes: 'Constant repetition of the line that he was the man who had revolutionized air travel and beaten governments appeared to make him feel invincible.' He was not, but he developed an organization that effectively silenced all those people who may have been able to save him. As we shall see, Laker was obviously not alone in making errors of judgement—but he was unusual in the extent to which his subordinates were unable to help the organization prevent, or recover from, their leader's mistakes. In contrast, where Laker appears as an arrogant joker, Sampson (1984: 217) suggests that Branson is another Janus-like figure but with a different tactical mask, for Branson 'conceals his shrewd business mind behind a casual bohemian façade'. This might be regarded as an important element of Branson's success rather than a quirk of character. That is, it may be that Branson's *bonhomie* operates to deflect attention from his hard-nosed business intentions by disarming his target. And he clearly has a strong will to succeed. In his own words: 'You can succeed as long as you've got the will and something you really believe in, that you have a passion for' (quoted in Callan and Warshaw 1996: 31).

Staff involvement is one area where Branson and Laker are different. Both prefer to remain paternalistic rather than accede to demands for trade-union representation.[8] But Branson was always less of a control freak and always more willing to allow others to have a say in the way the airline was run. As Branson admitted: 'I want employees in the airline to feel that it is *they* who can make the difference, and influence what passengers get' (quoted in Denoyelle and Larréché 1995: 8). While Laker wanted to remain in control of everything at all times, Branson encouraged his staff to take the initiative and gave everyone his home phone number to ring him with ideas or complaints about service. The idea of serving ice cream during in-flight videos came from a staff suggestion not from customers (Denoyelle and Larréché 1995: 9). Similarly Virgin Bride developed after two flight attendants complained to him about having to shop in six different stores to organize their wedding (Callan and Warshaw 1996: 31). In effect, Branson's subordinates appear to be able to dissuade him from some of his wilder schemes, while Laker's never could.

Branson, in conjunction with Jack Welch of GE and Percy Barnevik of ABB (a Swedish–Swiss engineering group), is considered by Kets de Vries (1996: 487) to be qualitatively different from other leaders in so far as they release creative energy at *all* levels of their organizations, want *all* their employees involved, and have redesigned their organizational architecture to inspire employees wherever they are within the organization. That is, they split the organization into smaller groups whenever it appears to be growing so large that direct personal interaction between all is difficult. What Branson also accepts is mistake making, but this is strongly linked to responsibility.

But Branson's strongest card in the arena of organizational tactics lies in his adoption of the resource inversion beloved of 'soft' martial arts like T'ai Chi, in which the strength of an opponent is used against that same opponent. For example, Branson always tries, and usually succeeds, in achieving the moral high ground in his business ventures. For instance, he takes on the corporate 'fat cats' who appear beyond competitive forces, such as Coca-Cola, BA, the major banks and so on. In each case he is almost guaranteed public support as the 'underdog' and this may be important for publicity purposes, for marketing purposes, or simply in terms of popular support for legal procedures either taken by or against Virgin (Dearlove 1998: 27–33).

Secondly, Branson has developed a tactic of taking advantage of the disparity in resources available to his corporate targets; in effect, he induces them to strike out at him and to make a mistake. Thus, for example, the evident irritation of BA's chair, Lord King, with Branson stimulated King to write what the courts subsequently decided was a libellous letter in the *BA News*. Until this point Branson had been unable to dent BA's confidence. The day BA caved in was, according to Branson, 'one of the happiest moments of my life . . . it had been so unpleasant. It was frightening—they hit us below the belt and tried everything to push us over the cliff. That victory was really the turning point for Virgin. From that day on we climbed over the wall' (quoted in Frew 1998: 9).

Similarly, Branson claimed that Guy Snowden, Chair of GTECH, which runs the British National Lottery, had tried to bribe him to stay away from the competitive tendering to run the scheme. Had Snowden not reacted his reputation might have been under attack but he might still be at GTECH; but he responded by suing Branson—and lost the case and his job.

Mazur (1996) suggests that Branson, this time likened to Bill Gates and Peter Wood (Direct Line), is 'focused, commercially intuitive and innovative . . . obsessed with customer satisfaction and service, and skilfully manag[ing] [a] powerful corporate brand'. Yet, paradoxically, although Branson does seem obsessed with customer satisfaction, this was hardly a novel obsession in the late 1990s. A different way of understanding why Branson has been so successful compared to thousands of other entrepreneurs and large corporations is to consider where his priorities actually lie:

Our priorities are the opposite of our large competitors. Convention dictates that a company looks after it shareholders first, its customers next, and last of all worries about its employees. Virgin does the opposite. For us, our employees matter most. It just seems common sense to me that, if you start off with a happy, well-motivated workforce, you're much more likely to have happy customers. And in due course the resulting profits will make your shareholders happy.   (Branson 1998: 444)

Whether Branson's claim reflects the view of his employees or not, such a philosophy, rooted in an appreciation of the significance of followers, is not new. Dore (1989) suggested that such an inward-looking 'organization-oriented' organization was typical of Japanese approaches, in marked contrast to the 'market-oriented' organizations more familiar in the West. The 'customer-is-everything' approach of the West should also be associated with a similar phenomenon: the 'employee-is-nothing'. For the Japanese and for Virgin an inversion of priorities does not necessarily lead to a dereliction of the customer or the shareholder, but these are indirect beneficiaries of the direct and primary concern for employees.

The Performing Arts: Persuasive Communication

Finally, let us consider the fourth leadership art—the art of performance—for surely Laker and Branson are both adept in this particular field, so to what extent can their relative success and failure be accounted for through the performing arts?

Certainly Laker was always a 'performer' and fond of using the media wherever possible, but he never had the relationship with the press that Branson established and Laker's apparent arrogance always opened him up to journalists eager to bring all such individuals down. Nor was Laker a particularly strategic negotiator. Thus, although he could drive a very good bargain in terms of buying cheap aircraft, he only managed to do this by sinking himself into debt, and the only reason the planes were cheap was because the market was depressed, not because he was a great negotiator. Moreover, while Branson seems to charm more people than he worries, the opposite seems to be the case with Laker. In effect, Laker's performing skills are more akin to a market trader than the dashing entrepreneur ostensibly captured by Branson.

Ironically, despite being a 'natural' in terms of publicity seeking and marketing, Branson is not an especially good public speaker—even if he is a great communicator in other ways. Hollands-Gems, a schoolfriend, describes him as 'incredibly incoherent—impossibly so, as if he had hundreds of things to say, but he didn't know how to say them. It was like a tornado of frustration' (quoted in M. Brown 1998: 33). For T. Jackson (1995: 9), 'Underneath this gregariousness is an insecurity. Richard Branson's lack of verbal fluency was intimately linked to his poor academic record at school . . . For a man who has made his money in industries that are all about communication and people, Branson is sometimes astonishingly inarticulate.' Jonathan Meades, one-time editor of *Event*, Branson's failed competitor to *Time Out*, says of Branson: 'He's impossible to conduct a conversation with because he is inarticulate . . . Branson's very good at making money, but the rest of him hasn't kept up. It's like a form of autism' (quoted in T. Jackson 1995: 65).

But, while Laker was himself a publicity-seeker, he has never achieved the kind of success created by Branson's antics, either on a balloon, in a speedboat, or just dressed in some outrageous outfit. As one journalist said of the advertising value of Branson's ballooning expeditions: 'there aren't enough zeros to do the maths' (quoted in Dearlove 1998: 97). It is just as well, because Virgin has never had the kind of funds that BA and Coca-Cola and Pepsi have for advertising. All of this has been pro-active, seeking out the media rather than being sought by it. As James Murray, head of the press office, said in 1994: 'We are not here just to react to press enquiries. We also try to gain publicity for the airline's products and services and to show how much better we are than the competition' (quoted in Denoyelle and Larréché 1995: 12).

Branson always appears to have been willing to talk directly to reporters and newspaper editors and openly admit to his failings as well as writing constantly in his notebook when anyone says something he regards as important to him. Denoyelle and Larréché (1995: 9–10) suggest there are four reasons why Virgin Atlantic have had such good relations with the press: first, Richard Branson's persona; secondly, the airline's openness in dealing with the press; thirdly, the news value of its innovations; and, fourthly, good management of media relationships. As Denoyelle and Larréché (1995: 13) assert, while BA refused to participate in the BBC programme *Secret Service*, where covert investigation of service standards occurred, VAA showed itself to be much more open. The consequence is that Virgin spends relatively little on advertising (about half the relative corporate norm), though there were many in the business who thought his attempt to introduce Virgin Cola against Coca-Cola and Pepsi-Cola could not succeed without traditional advertising. It has done and it has managed to succeed so far because Virgin is now one of the world's leading brand names. In effect, it is the brand that succeeds rather than the product, hence the diversity of Branson's current portfolio of business and products. Indeed, the Magazine *Marketing* announced Virgin as 'the finest British brand of the late twentieth century' (*Marketing*, 7 Mar. 1996).

Of course, not everything that Branson touches turns to gold. In 1997 Virgin West Coast received £76.8 million in subsidies from the British government but by October 1997 the Office of Passenger Rail franchising reported that Branson's Virgin Trains offered the worst service in the country. More than 25 per cent of its trains to and from Scotland were late (*Guardian*, 18 Oct. 1997; *Observer*, 19 Oct. 1997; *Guardian Weekend*, 14 Nov. 1998). Indeed, by October 1998 at no time had Virgin Trains managed to run more than 90 per cent of its services on time. Yet a poll of over 1,000 Londoners suggested that the runaway winner of any election for London's possible new mayor would be Richard Branson, who took 47 per cent of the eleven-strong election slate (second was Ken Livingstone, with 15 per cent) (*Guardian*, 17 Oct. 1997). By July 1998 the number of passengers complaining about poor trains had increased to 200,000 but the company had, at last, begun to reap a healthy profit at £13.5 million over the previous year's £10.2 million loss (*Observer*, 19 July 1998). Branson's argument has always been that it would take five years to turn the railway around and his confidence is manifest in his announcement in October 1998 of a bid to run a railway in the USA, the Florida Overland Express, as part of a consortium from 2003 (*Guardian*, 5 Oct. 1998).

Conclusion

Branson seems to have consistently outperformed Laker—though this is hardly grounds for assuming Laker is a poor leader, since there are few of us who have achieved as much as Laker and probably none who has achieved as much as Branson. But the critical point remains that Branson has constructed a resilient and vibrant corporate identity, he does embody a vivid and vigorous imagination to envisage alternative futures, he has a skilful knack of wrong-footing much stronger opponents, and he has a charmed relationship with the media rooted in his strong performing abilities. But these arts of leadership are hardly of the form that can be captured and replicated. As Branson (1998: 432) concludes his auto-biography: 'There aren't ingredients and techniques that will guarantee success. Parameters exist that, if followed, will ensure a business can continue, but you cannot clearly define our business success and then bottle it as if it's perfume . . . You certainly can't guarantee it [being successful] just by following someone else's formula.'[9]

Notes

1. British Overseas Airways Corporation (BOAC) was formed in 1939 when the nation-alized British Airways merged with Imperial Airways.
2. Don Cruickshank, consultant brought in to float Virgin, quoted in T. Jackson (1995: 13).
3. Originally, Fields had intended to use the airline to fly between Gatwick and Port Stanley, the capital of the recently 'rescued' Falkland Islands (M. Brown 1998: 247).
4. In May 1990 a Virgin Atlantic B747–123 aircraft was named 'Spirit of Sir Freddie'.
5. In July 1999 BA was fined £4 million by the European Commission for breaching European Commission rules on competition after complaints from Virgin Atlantic about the commission system used by BA to persuade travel agents to book their clients with BA rather than any other airline (Harper and Bates 1999).
6. However, in 1997 Branson introduced Virgin Express, a low-cost airline flying out of Brussels to various European destinations (based on an existing carrier—EuroBelgian Airlines—with 90% of the equity) and threatened to reduce prices to 80% of BA's on certain routes. In late October 1997 BA responded by creating 'Go', a 'no-frills' dis-count subsidiary to compete with Eurostar rail services and airlines like Virgin Express. By the end of the 1989/9 fiscal year it was not clear whether BA's response was viable: operating profit dropped 12% and by July 1999 the expectations of most analysts remained pessimistic, many claiming that the 'multi-ethnic marketing cam-paign' to replace the traditional tailfin colours (abandoned in May 1999) had merely confused the 'otherwise impeccable' image (*Airline Financial News*, 14/28: 1).
7. In April 1999 the Virgin Group invested a further £9.7 million into its Virgin Cola com-pany after severing the production deal with the Canadian company Cott. Virgin Cola's share of the Cola market rose from 3.6 to 4.3% in 1998 (*In Business*, Apr. 1999, 7). In 1997 Virgin Cola made £116,000 profit compared to a pre-tax loss of £7.2 million in 1998 (Lister 1999).

8. There are exceptions: around 80% of the 100 projectionists in Virgin Cinemas are members of the Broadcasting Entertainment Cinematograph and Theatre Union (BECTU).

9. On 20 December 1999 Branson sold a 49% share in VAA to Singapore Airlines for £600 million.

3

The Floating Republics: Political Leadership in the Spithead and Nore Mutinies

For your damn rogues of officers use men so cruel
That a Man-o-War's worse than hell and the devil.
There's the master a swearing, the bosun a growling,
The midshipman's howling 'out-take the full bowline'.
You speak but one word you're a mutinous rascal
With your legs laid in irons and tried by court martial.
Now boys we are pressed from our own habitation,
And we leave wife and children in grief and vexation.
We venture our lives in defence of our nation,
And we get nothing for it but toil and vexation.

('The Spithead Sailor', traditional folk song)

Britain's 'Senior Service', the *Royal* Navy, ironically really came into existence only during the Commonwealth, the republic led by Oliver Cromwell.[1] Admiral Robert Blake, formerly an army commander, established a Navy Board, a set of tactics, and an organization with formal hierarchies, ranks, and rates of pay. The latter had been set in 1653—and they remained at the same rate until the Spithead mutiny in 1797 (S. Pope 1998: 12). One of the long-term consequences of the Commonwealth, and particularly the period when direct military control was enforced over Parliament, was a deep distrust of any standing army by the country's élite (Wheeler 1999). Hence, the navy, and indeed the sailors, never quite received the same level of opprobrium heaped upon the army and its soldiers. Thus, in 1796, rather as in 1940, when Britain stood virtually alone against a continental invader who seemed invincible on land, total reliance, and much confidence, were placed on the Royal Navy to hold the republican French at bay. It was rather like combat between the British whale and the French elephant (Temple Patterson 1968: 3).

However, the French elephant seemed to have the upper hand: not only was the war against France on land going badly almost from the beginning in 1793 (despite the successful sea war); the harvest was poor, food prices had doubled, and the Bank of England had suspended payments in gold. The French had already made (albeit unsuccessful) expeditions to Ireland and Wales and were accumulating another invasion fleet off the Dutch island of Texel. As (British) luck would have it, the Royal Navy was about to star in the prequel to the Battle of Britain. After all, as Pitt, the British Prime Minister, informed the British House of Commons in 1796, 'the fleet was more respectable and more formidable than ever before'. Yet Pitt, no lover of the war, knew that the weather and the local Welsh 'Fencibles'—equivalent of the homeguard—had defeated the French invaders, not the British navy. Moreover, the British public were growing weary of the costs of it all. Now, with the revolutionary Jacobin regime in Paris displaced by what appeared to Pitt to be the much more reasonable officers of the Directorate, the possibilities of peace were hovering around, but the negotiations failed and Britain trembled. Then, on 14 February 1797, Admiral Sir John Jervis, with the help of Admiral Nelson, defeated the Spanish navy off Cape St Vincent. Everything was restored to its 'rightful' place and the Royal Navy once more stood invincibly between France and Britain. Yet within a couple of months Britain faced what a subordinate officer to the Lord of the Admiralty called 'the most awful crisis these Kingdoms ever saw' (quoted in Gilmour 1993: 416).

The crisis was not manifest in a revolutionary tricolour looming over the horizon; instead it was the red flag of mutiny fluttering on Royal Navy ships of the Channel Fleet[2] at the Spithead anchorage off Portsmouth, and on the North Sea Fleet at the Nore anchorage off Sheerness.[3] These mutinies took place within a few weeks of each other and were relatively similar in their leadership, organization, and demands. The Spithead mutiny ended with a pay rise and improved conditions for the mutinous sailors, as well as the expulsion of many unpopular naval officers. On the day the mutiny was called off, Joyce, the mutineers' leader, dined with the Admiral of the Channel Fleet and the mutineers were fêted throughout Portsmouth. But the Nore mutiny ended in disaster for the mutineers: 400 were court-martialled, fifty-nine sentenced to death, and twenty-nine, including Parker, the mutineers' leader, were hanged from the forward yardarm. So politically embarrassing were the mutinies that the *Naval Chronicle*, which operated as a semi-official publication, was extremely reluctant even to admit that something untoward had happened. As Lord Gardner noted: 'To dwell on transactions like these is highly offensive to our feelings . . .' (quoted in Tracy 1998a: 213).[4]

But what accounts for the success of the Spithead mutiny and the failure of the Nore? Was it because of the justifiable and moderate demands of the former and the politically radical demands of the latter? This is certainly the traditional interpretation of events, but a close scrutiny of these suggests that there was precious little to choose between the two sets of demands. Was it because the Spithead mutiny was competently led by Joyce while the Nore mutiny was incompetently led by Parker? Possibly, but again Parker and his cadre of 'Delegates' had followed the pattern established by Joyce and were perplexed and frustrated when their strategy self-evidently failed. A third possible explanation lies not in the mutineers' leaders nor in the events and circumstances of the mutinies but rather in the way the Admiralty switched strategies and tactics after the first mutiny and generated a publicity campaign—the *what* and the *how* of leadership. The switch simultaneously altered the *why* of leadership, because it successfully changed the rules of the game. Finally, the popular interpretation of the mutineers' identity— the *who* of leadership—changed from oppressed but honest and loyal sailors to reprobate and revolutionary scum. This was not simply a question of controlling information and spreading lies to a populace kept ignorant by the authorities. More subtly, it involved the authorities changing their strategic vision from containment to outright victory, and adopting the tactical principle that had just enabled the first mutineers to win: resource inversion. By this I mean that the resources of the opposition were used to defeat them. In the first mutiny the mutineers had control over the fleet and some public sympathy, but these counted for little when contrasted with the resources available to the state. However, the resources of the state were deployed through channels that rested upon notions of legitimacy and they were unable to bring these to bear upon the mutineers in time to defeat them. In the second mutiny, however, the leaders of the mutiny lost the plot, the game, and their lives because they were wrong-footed by the Admiralty and the state that changed the rules. Instead the very resources of the mutineers—their control over the Nore fleet and access to London—were used by the Admiralty to undermine their own claims to loyal and legitimate dissent. It need not have been thus, but the ambiguities that ran through the two mutinies were effectively written out of the situation first by the Admiralty and then by the various authors who have written on the subject. In short, successful leadership involved more than leading in a particular situation in a particular way; it involved persuading others what the situation was and what form of leadership was appropriate. In what follows I outline the background to the events, provide some detail of the mutinies themselves, and then offer my interpretation on the question of leadership.

Background

Britain, or at least England and Wales, had the harshest penal code in Europe at the time of the mutinies. Between 1770 and 1830, 35,000 British subjects were condemned to death, though only around 7,000 were actually executed; over 200 crimes warranted (public) execution, including burglary, sodomy, handkerchief stealing, sheep stealing, forgery, and issuing false coins (Gatrell 1994: 3).[5] Executions in the Royal Navy were rather rarer—it was, after all, a major problem just to recruit enough men, so reducing their numbers further was not an especially productive idea.[6] Mutiny, however, was punishable by death—but it was a rather elastic term to cover a multitude of sins from individual insolence to collective revolt.[7] Mutiny Acts tended to be passed on an annual basis by Parliament—which remained ever suspicious of a standing army—and it was this perceived threat to their control, rather than an immediate and direct concern about naval insurrection, that stimulated the Act.[8] Yet mutinies were not uncommon in the late-eighteenth-century British navy and during the period of the French wars, roughly 1793–1815, over 1,000 occurred—though what counted as a 'mutiny' tended to lie with the captain of the ship rather than being deter-mined by the offence itself. Thus simply 'whispering' amongst the crew or 'refus-ing to show due respect' might well count as mutiny (S. Pope 1998: 73).

When we use the rather more contemporary definition of mutiny as 'the force-ful taking over of a ship by the crew', then in March 1783 the crews at Spithead had threatened to run every ship on shore and destroy them all if they were not immediately given their back pay.[9] Rather more common than mutinies were written complaints to the Admiralty from sailors complaining about the unjusti-fied treatment meted out to them by their officers. In 1795 these arrived from HMS *Weazle* and HMS *Nassau*, prompting Captain Patton, transport officer at Portsmouth, to warn the First Lord of the Admiralty that a general mutiny was possible unless conditions improved (Temple Patterson 1968: 4).[10]

But, if the ultimate deterrent was rarely used, coercion was a normal and every-day occurrence. Recruitment to the Royal Navy had involved some form of com-pulsion and coercion from its very inception. Although the officers and marines were all volunteers, the number of ordinary sailors who were volunteers was probably always a minority. 'Probably' is an important caveat here, because the coercive methods used to recruit, especially in wartime, involved the capturing of likely candidates and giving them the choice of 'volunteering' to serve in the navy—with a valuable bounty, often including several months' advance pay—or being 'pressed' without reward. Few resisted and hence few are marked in the ships' muster books as 'pressed' (D. Pope 1997: 119). Hence the numbers *really* 'volunteering' for service in the navy were probably small and Guttridge (1992: 45) estimates that only 20 per cent were genuine volunteers. It is generally assumed, for example, that only one-third of the crew of the *Victory* at Trafalgar were genuine 'volunteers', while Steve Pope (1998: 47), for example, suggests that on most ships around one-third were pressed.

Press gangs operated only under the law, which required a signed warrant to press, and under the leadership of a pressing officer.[11] Non-seamen were often taken in the confusion and violence that followed a press, but could obtain their release by proving their identity—the navy did not want inexperienced land men manning its ships of war when mistakes cost lives, unless, of course, a war was imminent. Officers were never pressed into service because there was never a shortage of volunteers, but sailors were always pressed because there was always a shortage of them. Thus most pressed men came from the merchant fleet or were local fishermen or sailors.

According to Lavery (1989: 117–18), the pay was worse in the Royal Navy than the merchant fleet,[12] the discipline tighter, and the conditions worse, but the real problem was the length of service required. Members of His Majesty's fleet could be at sea for years at a time, whereas merchant sailors would probably spend a couple of months away at most. Until the end of the seventeenth century, press-ing, though never popular, had usually only meant a period on board of less than a year. But by the eighteenth century a pressed man could look forward to a period at His or Her Majesty's pleasure of perhaps several years—especially if the country was at war, for pressing was usually for the duration of hostilities. In at least one instance a pressed man was 'enrolled' for nine years (Manwaring and Dobrée 1937: 23). Only during international emergencies were the rules of pressing (restricted to experienced seamen) relaxed and the 'Hot Press' used—where people who would normally be protected from pressing would lose their right of protection while each region filled its required quota (Laveny 1989: 122).[13] These quotas, which required each region to deliver a certain number of recruits, derived from the two Quota Acts of 1795: the first required each county to provide a quota of men and the second required each port to provide a quota. And such measures appeared necessary: in 1792 the navy muster was just 16,000, by 1794 it was 85,000, and by 1802 it had risen to 135,000 (Manwaring and Dobrée 1937: 24).

In fact, attempts had been made to improve conditions at sea and to secure better recruitment in a bill in 1777 'for the more easy Manning of the Navy', but the bill was easily defeated, primarily on the grounds of costs and the necessary taxation that would have had to be raised to fund the reforms, so pressing continued (Gilmour 1993: 191). Between 1793 and 1815 the navy cost around £30 million per annum, a sum equivalent to about 15 per cent of government expenditure, but, unlike expenditure on the army, the authorities were usually able to find the necessary costs of maintaining control over the seas (S. Pope 1998: 20).

Yet conditions on board ship were, ironically, often better than on land. Certainly fresh food and water were a luxury, but at least there was, in theory, plenty of food. Scurvy had been theoretically removed by the addition of lemons and limes to naval diets—but it took the Admiralty fifty years to develop a policy for its eradication after Lind had published his cure in 1753.[14] There was also plenty of beer—about eight pints a day—but this was 'small beer'—that is, beer that was only marginally alcoholic, since being drunk was an offence worth twelve lashes, but sufficiently alcoholic to kill most of the germs in the water. In some ways, then, as Neale (1985: 121) suggests, 'A man-of-war was a community of 600 chronic alcoholics'. If they were drunk it would at least have facilitated the earning capacity of the ships' pursers, who were allowed to earn a commission of one-eighth of everything except tobacco and clothing, due to 'rats and leakage'. Pursers were renowned for short-changing the men's rations; so much so that one of the mutineers' demands was for the return of a sixteen-ounce pound, rather than the typical fourteen-ounce pound that the pursers used (D. Pope 1997: 149).[15]

At least some medical assistance, however poor, was available on board, at a time when neither Portsmouth nor Plymouth, the leading two naval bases, had a hospital. As mentioned above, however, pay was abysmal: in the Royal Navy it had not changed since the days of the Protectorate under Cromwell (1653)—though pay in the army had risen in 1795 (Guttridge 1992: 46). Yet merchant sailors' rewards had kept up with inflation to the point where their average wages were three or four times higher than Royal Navy wages. And, since the merchant fleet's conditions were better, their time at sea shorter, and discipline more moderate, it is hardly surprising that the Royal Navy had trouble recruiting and retaining people (Poulsen 1984: 130; Gilmour 1993: 416). Moreover, pay was invariably late, partly to prevent sailors from deserting but also because of organizational chaos and a disinclination on the part of the authorities to concern themselves with the requirements of the sailors. In practice, this could mean that sailors were often unpaid for two years. Indeed, it was claimed at the time of the Nore mutiny that there were ships in that fleet that had not been paid for eight, ten, twelve, and even fifteen years (Manwaring and Dobrée 1937: 27).[16] The consequence of this was clear for all to see: between 1774 and 1780 25 per cent of the navy deserted, and Gilmour (1993: 186) estimates that between 1600 and 1800 fully 50 per cent of the pressed seamen died at sea. D. Pope (1997: 131) even suggests that the real enemy was not necessarily or even usually the 'other side': in the Seven Years War (1756–63) the Royal Navy lost 133,700 men from disease and desertion, but only 1,512 through battle.[17]

Provided you lived long enough, there was the possibility of prize money, divided up in strict proportion between the crew and the officers. But with each seaman securing just under £4 after the capture of Havana, and the admiral and general securing £244,000 between them, prize money was never going to make ordinary seamen rich (Gilmour 1993: 191).[18] The consequence was, for the capture of a typical thirty-two-gun frigate in 1801, the equivalent of thirty-five years' pay for the captain, four years' pay for the lieutenants, and eighteen months' pay for the seamen.

If the delayed pay did not keep the sailors subordinate, the discipline might. The level of disciplinary violence seemed to increase throughout the eighteenth century, particularly during war (Rodger 1986). In theory, no captain could order more than twelve lashes without a formal court martial, but in practice, according to Admiral Duncan (reputably one of the strictest disciplinarians of the time), 'every captain has taken upon him to establish rules for himself' (Gilmour 1993: 417). The consequence, according to Poulsen, was that French sailors referred to British prisoners of war as 'Tigers', not because they were ferocious but because their backs were striped from innumerable lashings (corporal punishment in the French forces was abolished early on in the French Revolution) (Poulsen 1984: 132).

Before war was declared between the British and the French, in 1793, the navy had around 16,000 men. By 1797 this had multiplied over sevenfold to 114,000. Not only did this huge increase require extra pressing. It required taking men who ordinarily might not have been considered fit. Fit, not in the sense of being physically capable of withstanding the harsh conditions at sea, but fit in the sense of being appropriate. In effect, the rapid influx of new blood brought with it men who were more literate and more politically aware than had previously been the case. As Troubridge remarked, the 'trouble' was caused by 'lawyers'—that is, 'fellows who can read and write'. It was these kinds of people who, according to Troubridge, instituted mutiny, for 'Whenever I see a fellow look as if he was thinking I say that's mutiny' (quoted in Gilmour 1993: 417).

Admiral Collingwood was in agreement on this point, for:

What they call Billy Pit's men, the county volunteers, your ruined politicians, who having drunk ale enough to drown a nation, talked nonsense enough to mad it; your Constitution and Corresponding Society men, find politics and faction too rare a diet to fat on, took the county bounty and embarked with their budget of politics and the education of a Sunday School into the ships, where they disseminated their nonsense and their mischief. (quoted in Lavery 1989: 128)

In particular, the new pressing brought disaffected Irishmen into the fleet, often in a perverse attempt to stem the likelihood of revolt in Ireland, so that both local magistrates in Ireland and Lord Carhampton, Commander-in-Chief in Ireland, regularly 'exiled' Irish suspects to the Royal Navy. Gilmour estimates that 10 per cent of the fleet was Irish by the time of the mutinies and on some ships fully half the crew were Irish (Gilmour 1993: 417), and Manwaring and Dobrée (1937: 106) suggest a figure of between one-eighth and one-twelfth. Whatever the numbers involved, Irish rebels from the 1798 rebellion were not prosecuted and sentenced until June—*after* the naval mutinies—though many had entered the Royal Navy anonymously to avoid such a prosecution a little earlier (Durey 1998: 25).

There was also an increase in letters of complaint from sailors that coincided with political movements in Britain, Europe, and the world. By 1796 Tom Paine's *The Rights of Man* (1791–2) was well on its way to selling 200,000 copies in a population of England and Scotland that was little more than ten million (Neale 1985: 55). Jean-Jacques Rousseau's *The Social Contract* (1762) had also begun to make an influence on the language of complaint. A letter from HMS *Shannon* described 'the ill treatment which we have and do receve from the tiriant of a Captain from time to time, which is more than the spirits and harts of true English Man can cleaverly bear, for we are born free but now we are slaves . . .' (quoted in Manwaring and Dobrée 1937: 19). Not only did this comment reflect Rousseau's words; it also reverberated with the events in the Caribbean where Toussaint L'Ouverture was involved in the slave revolt against the French (C.L.R. James 1980).

Closer to home, in 1791 the Society of United Irishmen was formed to remove the English from Ireland and by 1797 the Society had forged links with both Protestant and Catholic organizations and with the French to secure their aims. At the same time the 'London Corresponding Society' was formed to try and secure the vote for all males and by 1795 it could organize a meeting of almost 200,000 people in London (equivalent to 20 per cent of the capital's population) to press their demands (Neale 1985: 60–1). In short, the political climate was often influenced by, if not saturated in, the radical pretensions of the day.

The Spithead Mutiny

Evidence of the impending storm was not difficult to see beyond the rash of individual ship mutinies in the previous years. Earl Spencer, the First Lord of the

Admiralty, had been made aware of problems in 1795 when Admiral Patton presented him with a report based on letters from the *Weazle* and the *Naussau*. This suggested a general mutiny was likely unless conditions were improved, but Spencer did nothing (Manwaring and Dobrée 1937: 17). Several petitions were sent to the Admiralty in late 1796, but these were not even shown to Spencer. However, on 11 December Captain Pakenham warned him in a letter that, since the pay of soldiers had been raised some two years earlier, naval lieutenants had just been awarded an increase, and naval captains were in the process of putting forward a claim, it was inevitable that the seamen would do the same (Manwaring and Dobrée 1937: 21). Spencer's reply thanked Pakenham for his note, for 'he should have been very sorry not to have been possessed on a subject of so much importance'. However, a pay rise was, in his words, an 'utter impossibility', an 'absolute impracticability' (quoted in Manwaring and Dobrée 1937: 22). As Manwaring and Dobrée (1937: 26) suggest, 'Spencer behaved with an astounding lack of wisdom, sometimes approaching idiocy'.

The organization of petitions against pay and conditions was necessarily clandestine, since it could be—and usually was—interpreted as mutinous action for which the death penalty was a likely consequence. Even before the Spithead mutiny, men aboard the *Charlotte* (Admiral Howe's old flagship) appear to have been coordinating the protests, sending drafts of petitions to other ships for comments and completion before each ship sent its own—unsigned of course—to the Admiralty (Guttridge 1992: 45).

One such draft went to the *Minotaur* in February 1797 asking:

MESSMATE,

If your ship's company approve of the enclosed petition you are requested to get a fair copy, and let us know on what day it will be convenient for you to send it . . . let it be directed to Lord Howe, without any signature at the bottom, only the ship's name and day of the month. Therefore wishing it success,

We are yours, etc., etc.,

THE CHARLOTTES.   (quoted in Guttridge 1992: 45)

A reply from HMS *London*, dated 26 February 1797, noted not just that the House of Commons should be the destination for the petition, not the Admiralty, but that the petitioners should 'proceed in caution, peace and good behaviour. Let no disorder or tumult influence your proceedings' (quoted in Manwaring and Dobrée 1937: 30).

The ageing Admiral Howe, hero of Cape St Vincent and long regarded as sympathetic to the seamen, also chose, initially at least, to ignore the eleven petitions that were dated February. He assumed they were 'fabricated by some malicious individual' with the intention of instigating 'a general discontent of the fleet' (quoted in Guttridge 1992: 47) and then took them to Spencer at the Admiralty. Since Howe was now retired at 71 years of age, he was replaced by Admiral Bridport. Spencer insisted to a meeting of the Admiralty on 22 March that nothing should be done that might generate 'unpleasant consequences'. By that he did not mean a mutiny by the fleet but a stream of abuse from the tax-paying public directed against him if pay rises were agreed (though Pitt admitted that 'the amount of the expense is comparatively of no consequence'—probably because he had just introduced income tax for the first time in British history and was expecting to raise £10 million (quoted in Manwaring and Dubrée 1937: 54)).[19] The same day Sir Peter Parker, Port Admiral at Portsmouth, received a twelfth petition signed by two 'Delegates' from each of the sixteen warships in the Channel Fleet, and wrote promptly to the Admiralty telling it that a refusal of duty was planned.[20] However, the Admiralty's information was that nothing untoward was planned by the seaman and Admiral Bridport went on leave until 10 April, unaware even of the existence of the original eleven petitions. Those seamen left behind were gravely disappointed that Howe had done nothing and concluded that: 'We flattered ourselves with the hopes that his Lordship would have been an advocate for us, as we have repeatedly, under his command, made the British flag triumph over that of our enemies' (quoted in Manwaring and Dobrée 1937: 35).

Captain Patton, Transport Officer at Portsmouth, became aware of the problem on 13 April and used the new 'telegraph' system (semaphore) to relay his message, 'Mutiny brewing at Spithead', to the Admiralty via the chain of telegraph situations on the hills (Temple Patterson 1968: 6). Two days later, on 15 April, boats carrying 'Delegates' rowed from ship to ship to discuss the matter and the *Defence*—which, until that time, had remained uncommitted—agreed to come into the conspiracy and received the following note from the *Royal Sovereign*:

FRIENDS,

I am happy to hear of your honourables courage towards redress. We are carrying on the business with the greatest expedition. We flatter ourselves with the hopes that we shall obtain our wishes, for they had better go to war with the whole Globe, than with their own subjects. We mean the day the petitions go to London to take charge of the ships until we have a proper answer from government. The signal will first be made by the *Queen Charlotte*. The first signal is the Union Jack at the main with two guns fired: this is for taking charge (and sending the officers and women out of every ship). The second signal is a red flag at the mizzen topmast head, and two guns: this is to send a speaker from every ship.   (quoted in Manwaring and Dobrée 1937: 37)

Somehow, the Port-Admiral, Sir Peter Parker, got to hear of the plan and immediately rowed out to tell Bridport, who reported it to Spencer. The latter sent the original eleven petitions to Bridport and ordered him to sea forthwith. Bridport responded on 15 April with some bitterness on being left out of the information loop, enclosing two new petitions, including one from his own crew, which he promised would be answered.

I had very much to lament that some answer had not been given to the various letters transmitted to Earl Howe and the Admiralty, which would, in my humble opinion, have prevented the disappointment and ill-humour which at present prevails in the ships under my orders. I therefore conclude that their Lordships will not direct the squadron to proceed to sea before some answer is given to these petitions, as I am afraid it could not be put into execution, without the appearance of serious consequence.   (quoted in Manwaring and Dobrée 1937: 39)

Spencer was unimpressed and ordered the fleet to prepare to sail and the squadron, under the Second in Command, Admiral Gardiner, to leave immediately for St Helen's anchorage (three miles south of Spithead) (see Fig. 3.1). Even though Bridport recognized the folly of the demand under the circumstances, he ordered Gardiner's squadron to weigh anchor, but the crew of Gardiner's flagship, the *Royal Sovereign*, refused. Immediately the crew of the *Charlotte*, no longer able to stick to their planned timetable, gave three loud cheers to mark the beginning of the mutiny. The mutineers then told the rest of the fleet to send two Delegates from each ship to the *Charlotte* that evening to form a 'General Assembly of the Squadron', nominally under the leadership of Valentine Joyce, a 26-year-old quartermaster's mate from the *Royal George*. Joyce was allegedly a United Irishman, who may previously have owned a tobacconist's shop in Belfast and been imprisoned for sedition. This is, however, unlikely, since he had been born in Jersey and his family had lived in Portsmouth for many years, where his father had served in the army invalid corps (Neale 1985: 166–7).[21] The Delegates included a quartermaster's mate, thirteen able-bodied seamen, several petty officers, two quartermasters, a gunner's mate, five 'mature' midshipmen (not youths), but no ordinary seamen. Most were English, with a minority of Scots, a handful of Irish, and one American (Manwaring and Dobrée 1937: app. 1). They were, in the words of Manwaring and Dobrée (1937: 44), 'no rabble of discontented scum, knowing nothing of the sea, but men whom their companions had learned to trust, the flower of all that was not quarterdeck [officers].' Even the officers interviewed after the event admitted that the Delegates were the 'best men aboard', 'the good and leading men', and 'the best behaved and reliable' (quoted in Temple Patterson 1968: 7).[22] As Bridport reported to the Admiralty that day: 'I see no method of checking the progress of this business but by complying in some measure with the prayer of the petitions' (quoted in Temple Patterson 1968: 7).

The thirty-two Delegates, two from each of the sixteen ships-of-the-line, took over the Admiral's cabin on the *Charlotte* and gave the Admiralty two days to reply to their requests:

1 that their pay should be increased;
2 that the weight of their provisions be raised to sixteen ounces to the pound, and of better quality; and that 'our measures may be the same as those used in the commercial trade of this country';
3 that while in a British port they should be given 'a sufficient quantity of vegetables, and no flour should be served';
4 that the sick men on board should be better attended and given 'such necessaries as are allowed for them and these be not on any account embezzled';

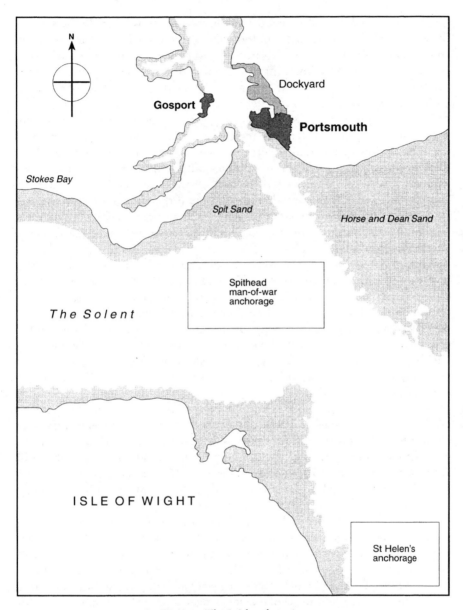

Fig. 3.1. The Spithead mutiny

5 that they should be given leave when possible in harbour, but they recognized that 'there shall be a boundary limited' and any seaman going beyond
it should be punished;
6 that a man wounded in action shall have his pay continued until he is cured
and discharged (D. Pope 1998: 123–4).

There was an additional demand from particular ships: that the complaints about certain officers should be addressed. In short this was the equivalent of an industrial strike not a revolution, for, as they told the reforming MP Charles Fox, 'we are not actuated by any spirit of sedition or disaffection whatsoever; on the contrary it is indigence and extreme penury alone that is the cause of our complaint.' (Manwaring and Dobrée 1937: 45).[23]

The Delegates maintained that all orders from officers were to be obeyed; indeed, the Delegates insisted that 'the greatest attention be paid to the orders of the officers. Any person failing in respect due to them, or neglecting their duty, shall be severely punished (but) no ship shall lift an anchor to proceed from this port until the desire of the Fleet is satisfied' (Manwaring and Dobrée 1937: 45). Furthermore, all officers would be sent ashore if their demands were not met promptly. Every sailor—and every marine—was also required by the Delegates to take an oath to support the mutiny 'that the cause we have undertaken be persevered in till accomplished'.

Bridport asked each captain to muster his crew and ascertain the grievances that were then transmitted to the Admiralty. Initially the Admiralty insisted that their requests would be 'taken into serious and immediate consideration' once they had sailed, but the mutineers were not persuaded. They did, however, maintain normal life, including at least one flogging of a miscreant, though other offenders were ceremoniously 'ducked' in the water, a punishment unknown to the navy at the time. When the Delegates travelled from ship to ship—and the rest of the crews were forbidden this privilege—they were treated as if they were officers and piped on board.

On 18 April Earl Spencer arrived in Portsmouth and offered the seamen between 2 and 4 shillings a month extra—very roughly a 15 per cent increase. But he offered nothing with regard to their claim for better quality and greater quantity of food, nothing to help the sick on board, nothing on the possibility of increased shore leave, no possibility of the wounded continuing to receive their pay whilst hospitalized, and nothing regarding the complaints about individual officers (Temple Patterson 1968: 8).

The following day the Delegates rejected the Board's offer, demanding a shilling a day extra for able-bodied seamen not between two and four shillings extra a month, an increase in the Greenwich pensions, the same pay for marines on land as at sea, a sixteen-ounce pound, and better food, adding that—'with the single exception of the French fleet being sighted—until the grievances before stated are redressed, and an act of indemnity passed, we are determined not to lift an anchor; and this is the total and final answer' (quoted in Poulsen 1984: 134). Of special concern were the actions of particular officers and some were so hated that entire crews were willing to provide their signatures to letters to the press.[24] Flogging was not the issue, but the abuse of discipline was considered a despicable crime. Then each ship was told to put ashore any officers deemed to be tyrannical and unjust—and 100 were. Yet the mutiny maintained order, such that the Prince of Württemberg was taken on a tour of the fleet by Spencer on the same day and the mutinous sailors duly cheered the royal procession around the ships (Manwaring and Dobrée 1937: 61). Even the *London Chronicle* was impressed by their discipline, noting that 'the seamen conducted themselves throughout the whole business with a sobriety, steadiness, unanimity and determination, that would do honour to a better cause' (Manwaring and Dobrée 1937: 62).

The Admiralty responded first by ordering Bridport to arrest the ringleaders and put to sea immediately. But after Bridport had informed it that the entire fleet was solidly behind the mutiny, the Admiralty decided to provide the demanded pay rise—but nothing else. Bridport told the mutineers that they would all be forgiven if they returned to duty (omitting to tell them Spencer's last requirement, which demanded an immediate cessation of the mutiny). At first the offer seemed to be acceptable, then Admiral Gardner took it upon himself to address the Delegates in person—before Joyce returned from a meeting on land. Gardner informed them, quoting from Spencer's new note, that 'if the men from the several ships assembled in the *Queen Charlotte* do not immediately accede to the terms offered they may rely on it that they will be brought to condign punishment and suffer the utmost vengeance of the law'. That was a clear threat to hang them all. At this point Joyce entered the meeting and insisted that only a direct pardon from the King would save them. 'Remember the *Culloden*!', he is alleged to have shouted, and few on board could have forgotten that ship's mutiny, which had allegedly been terminated when the Captain promised to pardon all concerned—but later hanged five mutineers.[25] It was little wonder, then, that the reminder dissuaded the mutineers from agreeing. Whereupon Gardner called them 'a damned mutinous blackguard set that deserves hanging . . . skulking cowards . . . I'll hang you and every fifth sailor in the fleet!' (quoted in Manwaring and Dobrée 1937: 62).

Predictably negotiations collapsed, Bridport's flag on board the *Royal George* was replaced with a red flag, and the guns prepared for firing. Spencer, in response, sent 10,000 troops to Portsmouth and ordered all the shore batteries to prepare for action. Meanwhile a small mutiny at Plymouth had resulted in bloodshed and several ships, including the *Leviathan*, joined the Spithead mutiny.

The mutineers now not only rejected the new deal but demanded a formal royal pardon. They also confirmed that they sought no more new demands (except higher pay than that offered): 'in order to convince the nation at large that we know when to cease to ask, as we know when to begin, and we ask nothing but what is moderate and may be granted without detriment to the nation or injury to the service.' However, they insisted that Parliament pass an Act augmenting their pay and addressing the other demands before any return to duties would be considered. Spencer belatedly accepted the situation and returned to London to secure the King's pardon and Parliament's acceptance. By 22 April the royal pardon had been secured, and on the following day the news, and another promise to redress the particular grievances against specific officers, was read out to the crews at Spithead. The Delegates agreed in principle but demanded the arrival of the original draft and the King's seal itself before accepting formally. However, the bulk of the fleet weighed anchor and moved down to St Helen's to wait for these, leaving four ships at Spithead, which refused to move until complaints against their own officers were addressed (Temple Patterson 1968: 10).

Further problems resulted after a letter from the Admiralty to all officers, dated 1 May, warned them to use 'the most vigorous means' against the first sense of any renewed mutiny and 'to bring the ringleaders to punishment' (Temple Patterson 1968: 10). Rumours of this paper soon circulated the fleet and the crew of the *Duke* burst into their captain's cabin and, when it transpired that Captain Holloway had destroyed the letter, seized and threatened to hang him, or subject him to 'a degrading punishment' if no copy was received forthwith. Simultaneously, when Spencer was asked in the House of Lords whether he had any communication on the recent events in the navy, he answered that he had none to make nor did he expect to have one (Temple Patterson 1968: 11). Reports of this exchange soon reached Spithead and confirmed to the suspicious mutineers that the government was stalling for time.[26]

On 3 May, two weeks after the agreement in principle, Parliament eventually passed a seaman's bill worth £370,000 in pay (a 3 per cent increase on the war budget). On the same day, Bridport was commanded to set sail for France to intercept the French fleet from Brest, but the wind was unfavourable so no order was given. The *original* royal pardon had still not been delivered and the information now leaking from London suggested that the sailor's demands would not be met. For instance, the demand for fresh meat not flour when in port 'cannot at this time be complied with', and the vegetables requested were out of the question. Indeed, 'instead of asking for more, they ought to be most thankful for that with which, at great expense to the country, they are now supplied'. Nor would anything be done about unpopular officers, since 'all animosities have ceased' (Temple Patterson 1968: 10–11).

Believing that he had done enough, Spencer wrote to Bridport on 6 May that he was 'truly happy to find that at length tranquillity and order seem to be perfectly established in your squadron' (Temple Patterson 1968: 10–11). Once again, he was wrong. The following day the wind changed and Bridport ordered a squadron of ships out of St Helen's to assess the news about the movement of the French fleet. All four ships involved refused and the men once again took up control of the ships, threatening to fire on the *Defence* when it initially refused to join what was actually a second mutiny. The General Assembly then sent Delegates back to the ships still at Spithead to discuss the issue with the crews, but Admiral Colpoys refused to allow them on board his ship, the *London*. When Colpoys's crew refused to obey him, his first lieutenant, Peter Bover, shot one of them and a minor battle ensued, leaving five dead (three sailors, one officer, and one midshipman), several wounded (including a Delegate), and Lt Bover on the verge of being lynched by the incensed crew. Joyce, however, interceded on Bover's behalf and he was saved (Temple Patterson 1968: 12).

The mutineers demanded that the three dead seamen should be buried after a procession through Portsmouth, but the military authorities refused and prepared the garrison defences to fire upon the 'invaders'. Fortunately, Portsmouth's mayor, Sir John Carter, intervened and a compromise route was agreed. Yet the incident hardened the resolve of the mutineers, who moved all the ships still at Spithead down to St Helens, and between the 7 and 9 May ordered 100 officers to be put ashore and demanded another royal pardon. Not all the officers were forced ashore, and, in particular, Admiral Colpoys, Captain Griffith, and Lieutenant Bover were imprisoned on board the *London*, awaiting what was popularly regarded as a 'sailor's court martial'. They were all subsequently found not guilty and released. The mutiny was not completely solid though, for the crew of the *Eurydice*, having been forced to banish their popular captain, rescinded their expulsion the following day, invited him back, and quit the mutiny.

Eventually—and with the threat of the Nore mutiny now hanging over them—the authorities gave in and on 10 May the final Act of Parliament was given royal assent. Even the Admiralty saw sense and replaced Spencer with Howe, who visited the *Royal George*, the *Queen Charlotte*, and the *Duke* on 11 May and more of the ships on the 12th. Most of the mutineers were satisfied, though the crews of the *Mars* and the *Duke* made one final attempt to increase their demands on prize money but to no avail. Yet still the crews were hesitant; the wording of the pardon was changed from 'promise our most gracious pardon' to 'extend our most gracious pardon'. On 13 May Howe was too tired to be rowed around the remaining ships and instead Delegates came to meet him on the *Royal William*. Many of these demanded the dismissal of yet more officers (one admiral, four captains, and fifty-four others). Howe finally managed to end the rebellion not by agreeing to this but by insisting that the demands be written as 'prayers' to the King begging for new officers, not demands for the removal of old ones. Howe had suggested courts martial for all the officers concerned to assess their competence, but the mutineers were adamant that they all be removed forthwith, and he eventually accepted their point. 'However ineligible the concession,' Howe wrote later, 'it was become indispensably necessary' (quoted in Manwaring and Dobrée 1937: 115). Just at this moment the rest of the Plymouth mutineers arrived in eight more ships, all flying red flags, who promptly demanded, and received approval for, the ejection of sixty-five unpopular officers (Guttridge 1992: 60).

On 15 May, after a month of mutiny, the Delegates landed in Portsmouth and were led through the town by a band playing 'God save the King' and 'Rule Britannia'. The Delegates were toasted in Portsmouth, dined with Howe, and led their crews on a celebratory march around Portsmouth, during which time four Delegates from the Nore mutiny spoke with Joyce. Within two days the Spithead mutineers had returned to normal duties at sea (Guttridge 1992: 60).

The Nore Mutiny

Three days earlier, on 12 May, as the Spithead mutiny was drawing to a successful close, men aboard the *Sandwich*, a depot ship, at the Nore off Sheerness (see

Fig. 3.2), also mutinied. The ship, which was built for 750, and had once served as Admiral Rodney's flagship in the West Indies, then housed 1,500.[27] Even the ship's doctor, John Snipe, had begged Captain Mosse to reduce the numbers to prevent further physical and moral decay. Captain Mosse duly forwarded the letter to the Admiralty with a covering note suggesting that Snipe's statement was, 'I am sorry to say, a true picture of our situation'.

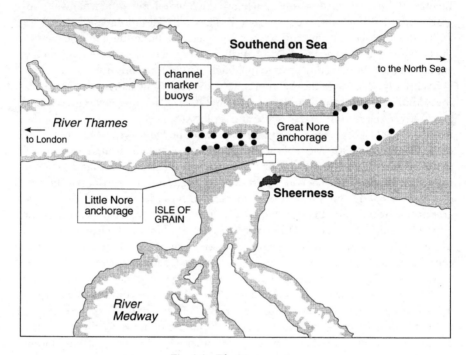

Fig. 3.2. The Nore mutiny

On the morning of 12 May Buckner, the Admiral at the Nore, and Captain Mosse were on board the *Inflexible* to participate in the court martial of a Captain Savage, who had lost his ship. The crew of the *Sandwich* took advantage of their absence and declared a mutiny, forcing Lieutenant Justice to leave and asking the other ships at anchor to join them, which they duly did. The crews then sent their most detested officers ashore, and demanded similar changes to those won by the Spithead mutineers. This mutiny was ostensibly led by Richard Parker, an ex-schoolteacher, born in Exeter, who had (re)joined the navy as a carpenter's mate, to escape debtor's prison in Scotland, as part of the quota for the county of Perth. Indeed, many on board the *Sandwich* were 'quotamen' whose level of education was often higher than that of the average seamen. On the previous two occasions that Parker had been in the service (he had served as a midshipman in the Royal Navy and in the merchant navy) he had once refused to pick up his hammock and been disrated (demoted) for disobedience. However, since

another Royal Navy captain had subsequently asked him to serve as a petty officer, his actions could not have been regarded as heinous (Manwaring and Dobrée
1937: 126). On the *Sandwich* Parker was 'captain of the maintop', the army
equivalent of an NCO.[28]

The Nore squadron was less significant than that at Spithead: it had fewer
ships in general and fewer warships (three line-of-battle, the depot ship the
Sandwich, and eight frigates), but it included Captain Bligh's *Director*, which
had put into Nore for repairs. Bligh, who was, of course, a survivor of the mutiny
on the *Bounty* in 1789, had on board the *Director* 100 seamen from the *Defiance*,
a seventy-four-gun man-of-war that, in September 1795, had been involved in a
mutiny over money and shore leave. Captain Bligh had been involved in regain-
ing control of the ship and the subsequent execution of five men, with two men
receiving 100 lashes each and four others receiving 300 lashes (Neale 1985:
132–64).[29]

But, despite the sprinkling of 'old mutineers', the make-up of the squadron was
regarded as less cohesive than the Spithead group, since it was regarded as a place
for escort ships to await their convoys or for ships to await repair, rather than the
home anchorage of a particular fleet. Nevertheless, all the ships at the Nore,
except the *San Fiorenzo*, which had just arrived from Spithead, joined the
mutiny, though even the *San Fiorenzo* cheered the mutineers aboard the sixty-
four-gun *Inflexible* after the latter fired one shot into the rigging of the recalcitrant ship.

Four Delegates from the Nore mutiny had been on board the *Royal George* to
hear Lord Howe relate the conditions for the ending of the mutiny on 15 May.
When they returned, the Nore Delegates decided to copy the Spithead policy of
excluding unpopular officers (including, once again, Captain Bligh from the
Director). They also drew up a code of conduct based on the Spithead code,
which again insisted that no 'private liquor' was to be allowed and strict discipline maintained and it seems to have been just as vigorously enforced: three men
were flogged for drunkenness; another was imprisoned for twenty-four hours for
'kicking a brother', and the boatswain of the *Prosperine* was tied up, a rope was
placed around his neck, and he was rowed round the fleet, much as a prisoner
about to be 'flogged around the fleet' would have been—but this time there was
no flogging, just degradation (Manwaring and Dobrée 1937: 134–5).

Rather more democratic than the Delegates of the Spithead mutiny, the Nore
Delegates constructed a system for each ship to elect its own governing group of
twelve, with one person elected as 'captain'. Above this was another elected
body, the 'general Committee of Internal Regulations' with a secretary and clerk,
which was to meet each morning aboard the mutineers' flagship, the *Director*.
Manwaring and Dobrée (1937: 135) suggest that, despite the organization behind
the mutiny, 'no demands were voiced, no manifesto issued or petition presented.
It seemed to be a mutiny in the air with no objective'. Yet at this time the Spithead
mutiny had still not ended, and the Nore mutineers had declared their solidarity
with the Spithead mutiny; the mutineers would, therefore, presumably have

mirrored the Plymouth mutineers and assumed that their demands were the same as those at Spithead. After all, it would not have been possible to discriminate between sailors' pay and conditions on the basis of whether they had taken part in the Spithead mutiny or not as the case may be. Certainly the mutineers at the Nore referred to their 'present cause' in the oaths that they were all required to take—as indeed had the Spithead mutineers. Nor was there anything seditious about the Nore at this point.[30]

On 19 May two of the four Delegates sent to Spithead, including Hollister, returned carrying copies of Howe's papers detailing the agreement. However acceptable the agreement may have been, there was one clear gap: without a specific royal pardon, exempting the Nore mutineers, they could all be hanged. Moreover, now that the Nore mutineers knew what their Spithead comrades had accepted, the former were in a position to formulate more specific demands where they saw fit. Admiral Buckner then met the Delegates on the *Sandwich* on 20 May and they handed him a document listing eight grievances that they required to be resolved before they would end the mutiny:

Article 1st.—*That every indulgence granted to the fleet at Portsmouth be granted to his Majesty's subjects serving in the fleet at the Nore, and on places adjacent.* [By definition, this was no different from the Spithead agreement.]

Article 2nd.—*That every man, upon a ship's coming into harbour shall have liberty (a certain number at a certain time, so as not to injure the ship's duty) to go and see their friends and families; a convenient time to be allowed each man.* [This had been on the list of the Spithead mutineers' demands but had not been granted.]

Article 3rd.—*That all ships before they go to sea, shall be paid all arrears of wages down to six months, according to the old rules.* [This, as they stated, was an 'old rule' and therefore not novel.]

Article 4th.—*That no officer that has been turned out of any of his Majesty's ships shall be employed in the same ship again, without the consent of the ship's company.* [This had been part of the Spithead mutineer's personal agreement with Howe.]

Article 5th.—*That when any of his Majesty's ships shall be paid, that may have been some time in commission, if there are any pressed men on board that may not be in the regular course of payment, they shall receive two months advance to furnish them with necessaries.* [This was to prevent the 'credit shops' and pursers charging extortionate sums and even Admiral Buckner agreed with this.]

Article 6th.—*That an indemnification be made to any men who run, and may now be in his Majesty's naval service, and that they shall not be liable to be taken up as deserters.* [Given the chaos generated by the various mutinies—and the fact that the punishment for 'desertion' was death, plus the problem of verifying whether deserting from a mutinous ship was 'desertion' or actually a manifestation of 'loyalty' to the Admiralty—this was a difficult issue for the authorities but could have been covered by the general pardon.]

Article 7th.—*That a more equal distribution be made of prize money to the crews of his Majesty's ships and vessels of war.* [This was a problem for the Admirals and officers but hardly a Jacobin claim for equality since no specific division was mentioned, and within ten years it was indeed granted.][31]

Article 8th.—*That the Articles of War, as now enforced, require various alteration, several of which to be expunged therefrom, and if more moderate ones were held forth to sea-*

men in general, it would be the means of taking off that terror and prejudice against His Majesty's service, on that account too infrequently imbibed by seamen, from entering voluntarily into the service. [Again, there is nothing specific in this that the Admiralty could not have negotiated around. Anyway, the removal of unpopular officers was itself already accepted and primarily rooted in their use and abuse of the same Articles of War.] The document ended:

The committee of the Delegates of the whole fleet, assembled in council on board his Majesty's ship Sandwich, have unanimously agreed that they will not deliver up their charge until the appearance of some of the lords commissioners of the Admiralty to ratify the same.

Given on board his Majesty's ship Sandwich, by the Delegates of the fleet, May 20ᵗʰ, 1797.

RICHARD PARKER
President. (Manwaring and Dobrée 1937:145–6)

The Lords of the Admiralty replied that they were 'extremely surprised' and that only Article 1 was acceptable. In turn this reply must have seemed equally surprising to the Delegates, since the demands were either identical to those at Spithead, or supported by their own admiral, or so indeterminate as to be easily negotiated away or satisfactorily watered down. But by 22 May the government's answer became much clearer when two militia regiments were marched to Sheerness—the nearest land to the Nore anchorage. However, far from being intimidated by this display of force, the mutineers, now sporting red ribbons in the hats of both men and women on board the ships, rowed over to Sheerness and, to quote Lord Collingwood, began 'shaking hands with their relations and friends amongst the militia' (quoted in Manwaring and Dobrée 1937:153). The failure of this threat of force from the government was made worse when the Lord Chancellor, Lord Loughborough, informed Spencer that the mutineers' suspicion about the royal pardon was unfortunately valid: it did not apply to any event that had occurred after its promulgation, thus a new pardon must be obtained. As if to rub Spencer's nose in it, Lord Howe then wrote to the Duke of Portland insisting: 'The extravagances of the seamen are not attended to, I think, in the manner they ought to be . . . I can only impute it to the incompetency of the persons who have the immediate superintendence in the department' (quoted in Manwaring and Dobrée 1937: 157).

Once again Spencer refused to meet the mutineers (who still held the majority of officers on board), but he reluctantly travelled to Sheerness with the new pardon, arriving on the 28th. At the same time he sent Captain Bligh, recently removed from his ship, the *Director*, to ask Admiral Duncan at Yarmouth whether the North Sea Fleet could be used against the mutineers. But all was not well with the North Sea Fleet either.[32] Thus, even though Duncan intimated to the Admiralty that he was sure the North Sea Fleet would carry out normal duties, he was privately far less convinced that it would assist in putting down the mutiny at the Nore. In fact, Duncan was near breaking point: 'I am fatigued to death and cannot hold it long . . . Sorry I am to repeat there is no dependence on any of us, I fear' (quoted in Manwaring and Dobrée 1937: 178). Yet when, on 27 May, Duncan ordered his fleet to sea to intercept the Dutch fleet believed to be leaving Texel, only the *Belliqueux* failed to move. That night Duncan captured four Delegates from the Nore who were intent on securing support from the North Sea Fleet, but even without their prompting the *Lion*, the *Standard*, and the *Nassau* then joined the *Belliqueux* and raised the red flag. By the next day the *Glutton*, the *Ardent*, the *Leopard*, the *Isis*, and the *Agamemnon* had joined the mutiny, leaving only four ships loyal to Duncan, including the *Trent*, which Duncan had threatened to fire into when it appeared to be deserting. It remained 'loyal', a pragmatic response to imminent destruction, which, bizarrely, Manwaring and Dobrée (1937: 179) call 'a striking tribute to his [Duncan's] personality'. Duncan's personal magnetism was clearly limited, because on 29 May the mutinous North Sea Fleet, now at anchor off Yarmouth, decided to send the *Agamemnon*, the *Ardent*, the *Isis*, and the *Leopard* to the Nore to support their comrades. Meanwhile the Yarmouth mutiny proceeded to develop regulations on exactly the same principles as the Spithead and Nore mutinies: strict discipline, respect for officers, but no movement until their demands were addressed—unless the enemy appeared (quoted in Manwaring and Dobrée 1937: 182).

By 31 May the entire fleet at Yarmouth had decided to join the Nore mutiny. At Sheerness Spencer had heard from Buckner that the mutiny was beginning to crumble and that seven ships, including the *San Fiorenzo*, were already flying the Admiral's flag and not the red flag. The mutineers, hearing of Spencer's arrival, rowed over to the Commissioner's house, where he was staying, demanding to see him. When he refused, they demanded—through Buckner acting as an intermediary—ratification that the Spithead conditions applied to them (including the royal pardon)—and that the Admiralty would at least 'consider' their additional demands (Guttridge 1992: 64). This was hardly revolutionary and was surely the best basis for negotiating a return to normality with little loss of face on either side. But Spencer rejected their demands outright and it was he, not the mutineers, that now insisted on a new demand and it was this decision, more than any other, that doomed the mutineers. Not only was he unwilling to accept any of their demands, but they must humbly approach him to secure the royal pardon from his hands. Spencer gave them until noon on 29 May to accept.

29 May was Restoration Day, the commemoration of the restoration of the monarchy, and the mutineers duly fired a royal salute, and flew the Royal Standard at the same time as the red flag; for them the dispute lay with the Admiralty not with the monarchy or government as such. Nevertheless a meeting rejected Spencer's demand for an unconditional surrender, and Parker was refused access to Spencer (Manwaring and Dobrée 1937: 161).

Spencer, meanwhile, was impressed by the actions of General Sir Charles Grey, who had organized an effective—if unofficial—blockade of the mutineers and replaced one of the two militia regiments at Sheerness with two more reliable ones. That unofficial blockade became official on 30 May, when Admiral Buckner warned the Commissioner and Agent Victualler at Chatham not to provide the mutineers with any further stores, while General Grey prevented the mutineers from landing. That night the *Clyde*, never a fervent member of the mutiny, slipped her moorings, and the following morning the *San Fiorenzo* did likewise, the latter being fired on by the remaining mutineers, though no one was injured. But the loss of these two frigates could hardly have mattered, for sailing in the opposite direction—indeed passing the deserting *San Fiorenzo*—came three ships-of-the-line from Duncan's North Sea Fleet, all flying the red flag.

On 31 May the enhanced mutiny still remained effectively blockaded and the Delegates decided to threaten to blockade London in retaliation (and not the other way around, as suggested by Tracy),[33] giving the Admiralty two days to consider 'The Final Determination of the North Sea Fleet'. Despite claims that this demonstrated the desperate political intentions of the mutineers, Graham, the magistrate co-opted by the government to investigate the mutinies, found only that 'the want of beer and fresh beef prompted them to revenge, and that and nothing else induced them to interrupt the trade of the river. It was done on the spur of the occasion, and with a view of obtaining a supply of fresh provisions' (quoted in Manwaring and Dobrée 1937: 187). It was, therefore, hardly what Guttridge (1992: 68) calls 'lunatic', an 'obsessive' dream to bring 'the admiralty to its knees'. But by this point the government appeared less interested in attending to the complaints of the mutineers and more on ensuring the unconditional surrender that Spencer had demanded on 28 May. On 1 June Pitt introduced a bill to Parliament 'the better prevention and punishment of attempts to seduce persons serving in the naval or military service from their duty and allegiance, and incite them to mutiny or disobedience'. During debate, on 3 June, the wording was amended to include the words 'maliciously and advisedly inciting them', after all, as Pitt insisted: 'The whole affair was of that colour and description which proved it not to be of native growth, and left no hesitation on the mind of any thinking man to determine whence it was imported' (quoted in Manwaring and Dobrée 1937: 191).

Thus, despite all the evidence to the contrary, the government had decided to consider the action as a rebellion inspired by the French Revolution, and not an industrial strike generated by the drop in relative conditions of the sailors and the disciplinary actions of some of their more zealous officers. A second bill enabled the Admiralty to determine whether any ship was in a state of rebellion and declared that after such a declaration any person remaining on board would be declared a felon and a pirate and any person helping or encouraging them would suffer the same penalty: death. A third bill outlawed the administration of unlawful oaths.[34] The rules of the game were now radically redrawn to the extent that whatever the mutineers did it could, and probably would, be interpreted by the authorities as the acts of pirates. Still the mutineers declared their loyalty to the Crown, insisting—as they released Captain Knight of the *Montague* and his wife to return to shore—that 'every Delegate has sworn himself that he has no communication with any Jacobins or people of that description' (quoted in Manwaring and Dobrée 1937: 197).

The mutineers even celebrated the King's birthday on 5 June—though it was the King who had insisted on the new legislation and it was the King who wrote to Pitt that 'the preventing of their getting fresh water will soon oblige them to submit'.[35] The same day, in a desperate attempt to placate the authorities, the mutineers relaxed their blockade on London, preventing only ships carrying provisions from continuing their journey. The blockade by the mutineers was effectively over after less than a week, but the official blockade of the mutineers by the authorities continued.

By now the mutiny had continued for almost a month and, as usual on any large naval vessel at the time, many of the sailors were ill. Probably assuming that the unconditional and unilateral termination of the blockade would assuage the Admiralty, and clearly believing the Admiralty to be composed of humane people in the main, around fifty sick mutineers then sought medical help from a hospital ship, but all were turned away on the orders of Buckner. The situation then appeared critical and on 6 June the mutineers asked Lord Northesk, Captain of the *Monmouth*, a known liberal and respected officer (who was later to serve as third in command at Trafalgar), to meet the Delegates (now numbering around sixty) on board the *Sandwich*. Once there he was asked to take a petition to the King proclaiming the loyalty of the mutineers, denying the newspaper claims that they were 'rebels' in a 'floating republic', or 'outlaws' that would 'force them to repose in another country'. They also gave 'fifty-four hours from 8 o'clock June 7 for a reply addressing their demands . . .' (quoted in Manwaring and Dobrée 1937: 204–5).

Unknown to the mutineers, at precisely the same time that they were trying to persuade Captain Knight of their loyalty, the Admiralty declared all the men to be rebels. The mutineers were now effectively finished, unless the government caved in, for any surrender would undoubtedly lead to executions. Their only real hope of survival lay in escaping to a foreign country: Ireland, France, Holland, and the West Indies were the favoured spots, though France and Holland were then ruled out because the mutineers still declared themselves patriots. William Gregory, a carpenter on the *Sandwich* who had been elected as President of the Committee of Internal Regulations, even suggested America. But the authorities were already alert to the possible loss of an entire fleet—and all the expense and embarrassment that would incur—and they promptly ordered the sinking of all the remaining markers and buoys indicating the safe channels through the sandbanks that had been progressively removed since 4 June. This left an unmarked channel about 200 metres wide towards London and an unmarked channel about 900 metres wide out to sea. But, without pilots or local knowledge, the mutineers were effectively trapped between the sandbanks leading out to sea and the forts guarding the entrance to London at Sheerness and on the Thames.[36] Since few sailors could swim, a grounding on the sandbanks usually resulted in death.

On 8 June Captain Knight returned bearing papers declaring that all those involved were rebels but that the ringleaders alone would be denied a pardon. At this juncture the mutineers seemed split on a response; some wanted to risk the sandbanks and sail away, possibly to Holland, but others appeared willing to sacrifice the lives of the Delegates, as long as their own could be saved. On the morning of 9 June Parker raised the signal to sail, but no ship moved and the Delegates agreed to meet in the afternoon to consider their next action. While they were away, the officers and 'loyal' crew members of the fifty-gun *Leopard* took control of the ship, cut it loose, and began drifting away from the rest of the fleet, and despite being under fire from several ships managed to reach land, where eighteen mutineers were immediately arrested.[37] The sixty-four gun *Repulse*—like the *Leopard*, one of Duncan's ships from Yarmouth—then followed suit but became stuck on a sandbar. At first Parker demanded that the mutineers fire upon the grounded ship, but he changed his mind and forbade any firing, at least until the *Repulse* had fired upon them, which it duly did. In the resulting exchange of cannon fire one of the lieutenants of the *Repulse* lost a leg, but otherwise no injuries were reported. At midnight the *Ardent* also slipped its cables and disappeared. The situation was clearly desperate for the mutineers and Parker wrote one more time to Captain Knight. He asked him to meet the King and to say that the mutineers would accept his pardon and return to duties providing only that all wages owed to them were paid, that the current ships' companies were kept together, and that no officers were to be returned to the ships without the consent of the crews.

But neither the King nor the Admiralty nor the government was interested in anything but what Nepean, the Secretary to the Admiralty, called 'unconditional surrender'. Even now many of the crews remained defiant, though fighting broke out on several boats between those wishing to surrender and those wishing to continue the mutiny. By 12 June twenty-two of the original thirty ships still remained at the Nore, though five ships deserted soon afterwards. Typical of the decision-making confusion was that which occurred on the *Swan*. The Delegates from other ships gathered the crew of the *Swan* on deck and asked them what they wanted to do; the half that voted to surrender were put into the boats to make their way to the *Isis*, which was already sailing away from the Nore. But when the 'loyal' crew of the *Swan* climbed on board the *Isis*, a battle between the officers and the mutinous crew was raging, and, after three sailors had been killed, the officers were imprisoned. Yet the following day the *Isis* was returned to the control of the officers by the crew and promptly left the mutiny (Manwaring and Dobrée 1937: 225–6).

As the mutiny disintegrated, one boat full of mutineers escaped from a naval ship and a £500 reward was offered to anyone capturing Richard Parker. On 12 June the crew of the *Sandwich* had voted to release their officers, but decided to reverse their vote the following day. That day, 13 June, a month after the beginning of the mutiny, Parker himself released the officers, chaired a meeting of the crew, and oversaw the vote to terminate the mutiny. Thereupon he handed the keys of the magazine back and was subsequently arrested and handed over to the authorities at Sheerness when the boat landed on 14 June and he was then imprisoned in Maidstone jail.

Back at the Nore, only the *Inflexible*, *Montague*, and *Belliqueux* remained—the crews, unlike all the others, being unwilling to sacrifice their Delegates' necks to save their own. The solution was quick in coming because three boatloads of sailors left the *Inflexible* and landed at Faversham, where they 'borrowed' a small boat and sailed to Calais, from where the 'borrowed' boat was returned courtesy of two boys.[38] Similarly, seamen from the *Montague* escaped to Holland. On 16 June these three ships finally surrendered; the mutiny was over.

In the following weeks Parker was one of 412 men court-martialled for the Nore mutiny. His court martial was ordered on 19 June under Admiral Sir Thomas Pasley, who received a note from Nepean suggesting that he could '. . . prove almost anything you like against him, for he has been guilty of everything that's bad'. Parker never really expected the trial to be anything other than a stitch-up, though Manwaring and Dobrée (1937: 235) claim it was 'as anyone who has ever sat on a court martial knows . . . scrupulously fair'.

Throughout the trial Parker denied acting in a disloyal or seditious manner and, while admitting his actions were contrary to the regulations, he insisted that his moderate leadership had prevented greater harm. When the court found him guilty and sentenced him to death Parker remained calm and responded:

I have heard your sentence—I shall submit to it without a struggle—I feel thus because of the rectitude of my intentions. Whatever offences may have been committed, I hope my life will be the only sacrifice. I trust it will be thought a sufficient atonement. Pardon, I beseech you, the other men; they will return with alacrity to their duty.   (quoted in Manwaring and Dobrée 1937: 236)

Parker's courage and magnanimity were inversely mirrored by the fear and depravity that gripped his accusers. Pasley, Spencer, and the King were all keen to have his body hung in chains 'on the most conspicuous land in sight of the ships of the Nore'. But their collective desire to indulge their taste for rotting flesh proved impossible to satisfy only because there was no precedent for this (Guttridge 1992: 72).

Parker's 'Dying Declaration', written two days before his execution, complained that they (the Delegates) had been beaten because they had prevented the crews from inflicting violence. He may well have been right, because Spencer knew they would not resort to violence and only the threat of violence—or the absence of any defence against the French—seemed to worry him. The mutineers, then, were victims of their own misplaced faith in the common sense and humanity of the establishment. As he wrote: 'never make yourself the busy body of the lower classes, for they are cowardly, selfish and ungrateful' (quoted in Gilmour 1993: 422).

But he also refused to apologize for his actions: 'I stand subject to human passion the noblest of which is a tender sensibility at every species of human woe. Thus influenced, how could I stand by and behold some of the best of my fellow creatures cruelly treated by some of the worst . . . I die a martyr in the cause of humanity' (quoted in Manwaring and Dobrée 1937: 265).

Leaving a small inheritance to his wife (who had vainly pleaded with the King for her husband's life), Parker was executed on 30 June on the *Sandwich* anchored just off the Isle of Grain, where scaffolding had been erected to allow the civilians sight of his death. Just after nine in the morning he mounted the scaffold on the forecastle, acknowledged the justice of his sentence, and again asked that his 'death may be deemed a sufficient atonement, and save the lives of others'. He then leaped off the scaffold and swung from the yardarm for an hour before being cut down and buried by his wife in the church of St Mary Matfellon, Whitechapel (Manwaring and Dobrée 1937: 238–9).[39]

Parker's dying wish was denied: fifity-nine of the 412 men court-martialled were sentenced to death, though only twenty-nine had their executions carried out, leaving twenty-nine others to be imprisoned and nine flogged—one sailor from the *Monmouth* receiving 380 lashes.[40] As Parker had predicted, the rest of the mutineers who were pardoned returned to active service 'with alacrity', and on 11 October, just four months after being labelled rebels, seven of the mutinous ships engaged the French fleet at the battle of Camperdown under Duncan.[41]

Analysis

The Philosophical Arts: Identity

Establishing the identities of the two parties involved is a useful way of evaluating the utility of the philosophical arts, because so much rests not on who the parties considered themselves to be, but how successful they were in representing that identity to the outside world. For example, both sets of mutineers regarded themselves as loyal sailors with legitimate grievances and on both occasions the Admiralty portrayed itself as a just employer but necessarily firm in the circumstances of war. However, while the Admiralty had to accept the 'honest tars' of the Spithead mutiny, it was able to corral public and government opinion into believing that the Nore mutineers were both seditious and inspired by the French republicans. And against this foreign bacillus the Admiralty could operate in a much more extreme way because, allegedly, the fate of the nation lay in the balance.

Gilmour is sure that the influx of political malcontents, imbued with the ideas of Paine and the French Revolution, were important in instigating the mutinies, and there certainly were mutinous letters delivered anonymously to the Admiralty. Guttridge also insists that political discontent was rife amongst the sailors, though this 'was not the only, nor necessarily even the main, issue at the heart of the mutiny. And Aaron Graham, a magistrate sent by John King, Under secretary of State to the Home Department, to uncover evidence of Jacobinism and sedition, found no evidence of it; indeed, no seditious pamphlets, which were apparently swamping the ships, were ever discovered. As Graham's report concluded: 'I am persuaded from the conversations I have had with so many of the sailors that if any man on earth had dared openly to avow his intention of using them as instruments to distress the country his life would have paid forfeit. Nothing like want of loyalty to the King or attachment to the government can be traced in the business' (quoted in Manwaring and Dobrée 1937: 110).

But, whatever the case, as far as the mutineers were concerned, it had little impact upon the success of the Spithead mutiny and the defeat of the Nore. This was not how the authorities chose to portray it. Indeed, the cartoonists of the day described the mutineers in precisely these terms, as puppets of 'foreign' revolutionaries. As Lavery (1989: 142) states: 'Some commentators, at the time and later, have seen it [the Nore mutiny] as a much more political affair than Spithead, more influenced by the radicals and revolutionaries ashore. There is no real evidence for this'. That said, the government and the Admiralty were acutely aware of, and frightened by, anything connected with Irish or French republican politics, so much so that the mere mention of the words 'tree of liberty' could attract punishment for the speaker and this did not simply mean a sharp dressing down: in 1805 a captain's clerk was given 150 lashes and two years' imprisonment for expressing republican views (Lavery 1989: 141).

Thus the ability of the Admiralty to interpret the identity of the mutineers in markedly different ways, the first as an unfortunate strike and the second as a seditious rebellion, played a significant role in allowing the first to succeed and the second to fail. That Parker and the Nore mutiny failed was partly to do with their misunderstanding of the power of those in authority to (mis)interpret the mutineers' intentions to suit their own strategic vision: a subordinate and cowed navy. In short, the Nore mutineers mistook their truth for the accepted truth; they radically failed to imagine how their actions could be portrayed as the despicable actions of despots seeking a republican dystopia rather than as the unfortunate actions of loyal subjects seeking legitimate redress.

The Fine Arts: Strategic Vision

On the face of it, however, it was certainly not self-evident to Parker why the Nore mutiny should have gone so disastrously wrong, especially so soon after the Spithead mutiny had been so successful. Nor it is clear whether Joyce provided qualitatively better leadership. Obviously much of the problem lies in our lack of information surrounding the actions of these two individuals. Despite this, Gilmour and Temple Patterson claim that the Nore mutiny failed because the leadership was much poorer. According to them, Joyce and the Delegates had remained in control at Spithead, had assured the government that they would sail if the French fleet appeared, had allowed normal trade to continue into Portsmouth, and had maintained discipline on board with minimal violence. And for Manwaring and Dobrée the successful mutineers are to be congratulated for their carefully 'thought out demands', their avoidance of arrogant displays, their concern for the country's trade, and their refusal to put 'anybody forward as being at their head'. Yet Parker and the Delegates behind Nore had done these things: they had certainly affirmed that their intentions were not to overthrow the Crown and that they too would fight the French should they appear; they had also allowed trade to continue with the exception of one week's blockade; they had allowed trade to continue even after it was clear that the authorities were not willing to lift their blockade of the mutineers; and they had maintained discipline. So the strategic vision of the two leaders of the mutinies appears little different—at least to their respective Delegates.

Nor is there any suggestion that the Nore mutineers were not in 'error' until the Spithead mutiny was resolved, after which time their 'muddle-headed affair' was 'wild and foolish'. On the contrary, even the Lord Chancellor admitted that the resolution of the Spithead mutiny implied nothing for the Nore, because the royal pardon did not cover the latter. Moreover, when there was a clear possibility of resolving the mutiny, on 28 May, it was Spencer who prevented a conclusion not Parker. We can only surmise that the Admiralty, government, and King wanted blood, not a negotiated settlement, and that the catastrophe at Nore was less the fault of the mutineers' errors than the strategic vision—the preferred result— always sought by the authorities. Bloodletting, for an already humiliated group of state representatives, was not a failure but a success.

Certainly Parker had additional objectives but these were for more leave, fairer distribution of prize money, and an amnesty for returning deserters—these were hardly 'insane' demands, nor were they the 'half-baked radical pretensions' that Steve Pope (1998: 74) decries. On the contrary, in 1802 King George issued a pardon for all deserters provided they returned to their ships (Tracy 1998b: 252–3). Dundas's reform of the Navy Pay Office Regulations in 1802 removed further complaints and in 1803—and again in 1805—the division of prize money was restructured to make it more equitable (Tracy 1998b: 345–51, 353). Yet for Guttridge (1992: 73), the Admiralty had learnt a 'twofold lesson from those events, namely, that legitimate grievances of the lower deck were best promptly redressed and that impossible demands were best resisted without compromise'. This receives support from Gilmour (1993: 420), who suggests that the Nore failed because its 'objectives were not clear', but, since Gilmour previously insists that the 'new' demands 'were not unreasonable', we have to be rather cautious here too.

What is also worth considering is the extent to which these various writers explain the success of Spithead and the failure of the Nore in terms of requisite reward. By this I mean that they assume that the strategic vision of the Nore was necessarily immoderate, excessive, political, incompetent, evil, and so on because it failed. Had it succeeded, then all of these descriptions would have been inadequate and the similarities between the two mutinies would no doubt have been revealed in much greater depth. In effect, the explanation for the result is drawn ex-post facto from the result: a success deserves to succeed and a failure deserves to fail. Within this rationale lies a liberal philosophy that also condemns the Nore not just because it failed but because it is read as an extremist response to a situation where good (i.e. British) common sense, pragmatism, and moderation could have prevented bloodshed. Ironically, the latter claim is probably accurate, except that most of these qualities lay on the side of the mutineers and it was the extremist, uncompromising, and ideologically driven strategy of the authorities that resulted in bloodshed (Manwaring and Dobrée 1937: 252). In fact, Gilmour (1993: 420) is probably closer to an explanation than many with his argument that the Nore mutineers failed because the timing was wrong. That is, they restoked the fires that the government had just extinguished and 'had the Nore been the first mutiny most of them [the new demands] would have been granted'. Not only was it not the first mutiny, but the first had been resolved by Howe, and Spencer retained control over the second and was clearly 'intent on their [the mutineers'] capitulation'.

The Martial Arts: Organizational Tactics

If Parker's failure was at least in part a failure of imagination, were the organizational tactics deployed by the Nore mutineers also responsible for their appalling demise? In other words, if the *what* was exposed by its imaginative naïvety, was the *how* also weak? Certainly the Nore is condemned for its excesses, but the condemnation is rooted in a very partial analysis: 'Officers had been expelled from their ships' (as they had from the Spithead); 'all the ships refused duty except for the essential routine' (precisely as had the Spithead crews); the *San Fiorenzo* had been fired on when it had refused to support the mutiny (the *Royal William* at Spithead had been threatened with this but had complied before the mutineers' cannons were fired); and there existed a 'blatant atmosphere of violence', though several had been injured in the Plymouth mutiny and the Spithead mutiny had seen five dead, including one officer and a midshipman (Manwaring and Dobrée 1937: 138–9). In fact, the Spithead mutineers had illegally imprisoned Admiral Colpoys, Captain Griffith, and Lieutenant Bover and tried them for murder in a 'kangaroo court'. In contrast, at the Nore only one officer was injured throughout the mutiny. It is difficult to see, then, in what way 'the mass uprising at the Thames Estuary base of the Nore was an altogether nastier business', as Steve Pope (1998: 74) maintains. Similarly, Manwaring and Dobrée wax lyrical about the 'magnificent' organization at Spithead and the attempts by the Spithead mutineers to secure redress through constitutional means until all options were foreclosed—but this was exactly as occurred at the Nore.

Partly, again, this was a problem of communication, because the Nore mutineers simply failed to ensure that their version of events was heard. But were the actual tactics different as a consequence of the timing of the mutinies? If we look at Spithead first, Joyce and the mutineers constructed a carefully trodden path that sought to use the legitimate monopoly of violence claimed by the state against it. Nothing was done to deny or cast doubt upon the legitimate authority of the naval authorities—beyond refusing to sail—thus hampering the Admiralty's deployment of force on the grounds of the illegitimate and illegal acts of the crew. But at the Nore the only trump card in the hands of the mutineers—their control over London trade—was now used against them, for rather than the action actually threatening the authorities, it provided them with just the evidence they needed to paint the mutineers as Francophile republicans not loyal suffering sailors.

The Admiralty had learned from Spithead and was in a much stronger position because its network of alliances was now stronger than that of the mutineers. Where Howe at Spithead did not blockade the mutineers and could not physically contain them, Spencer at the Nore could and did both. Howe's network included a frightened government, a public sympathetic to the mutineers because many of them would have come from the area, and very little else. Spencer had a government hardened by its previous defeat, a public that had little sympathy for the largely non-local mutineers, the local sandbanks, and the political will to see the act through. In effect, Howe deployed a neutralizing approach designed to limit the likely damage, but Spencer developed a dominating approach intent on destroying the mutineers rather than limiting the damage they might cause.

Moreover, with Spencer back in the driving seat, or rather at the tiller, the unravelling of events took on a different colour. Where Howe may have resolved the dispute by concession, Spencer resolved it through force. Where Joyce's principle stand was to keep as far within the law as possible, and to ensure that the Admiralty's far greater potential coercive resources were hamstrung by that same conditional requirement for legitimate action, Parker's attempt to do likewise failed because the law had changed. And, with the legal impediment to retribution cast aside, the Nore mutineers could no longer use the prerequisite legitimacy of the state's action as a mechanism to prevent it from deploying its resources. In short, the resource-inversion principle of Spithead no longer worked in the changed legal conditions. At that point the Nore mutineers' only remaining option was violent assault or desertion, but, because they still assumed the Spithead approach was viable, they were themselves hoist by their own petard. Indeed, it may well be *because* Howe had facilitated the mutineers' victory that Spencer was intent on preventing a rerun of history. In effect, Spencer seems to have taken 'on board' the familiar element of negotiating theory that insists that unconditional concessions merely encourage more demands, and decided instead to make it very clear to the mutineers that only unconditional surrender could be countenanced. Thus at Spithead it was the mutineers who exploited the tactic of resource inversion by tying the Admiralty into its own net of legitimate action but at the Nore it was the Admiralty who encouraged the mutineers to use what little power they had to show the country what 'brigands' they really were. It was Spencer who literally gave them enough rope to hang themselves.

The Performing Arts: Persuasive Communication

Finally, is there any sense in which the performative actions of the parties involved contributed to their failure or success? Both Gilmour (1993: 420) and

Tracy (1998a: 217) claim that the Nore failed partly because 'No attempt was made to preserve a blur of anonymity over an ostensibly collective leadership'. The point is supported by Poulsen (1984: 136), for whom Parker's overt leadership 'lost the valuable anonymity that had been so useful at Spithead'. Given that both authors name the leaders of both mutinies (Joyce and Parker) and that Joyce was personally dined by Lord Howe after the mutiny, this cannot be significant; indeed, it is difficult to see what anonymity there was. Furthermore, it would have been relatively easy for most of the Delegates to be identified by someone in the crew—indeed, this was how the eventual courts martial of the Nore mutineers came to decide who was worthy of execution. And, since both Joyce and Parker were previously known to the authorities and both allegedly had criminal records, there is little that separates them in this area. Gilmour insists, though, that there is an issue about the actions of Parker. Parker took upon himself the title of President and 'adopted the trappings of power and undermined the anonymity that had prevailed at Spithead' according to Gilmour (1993: 420). In effect, Gilmour asserts that Parker was too vain and pretentious, becoming the focus of animosity from both the Admiralty and his erstwhile followers.

For Guttridge (1992: 64), Parker's 'hold' over the mutineers was achieved 'through oratory at once pretentious and incoherent . . . he betrayed a recklessness that bordered on insanity'. Unfortunately, Guttridge provides not a shred of evidence of any speech, nor does Parker's behaviour appear to differ greatly from Joyce's. W. E. Edwards, writing in 1925 (p. 665), considered the mutiny to have been 'a violent and criminal movement led by a dissolute and insubordinate sailor', but again provides no evidence .

Manwaring and Dobrée contort themselves with their explanations for the Nore. For them, Parker was a critical figure and the source of many errors. He was a 'smouldering, swarthy figure . . . a gaol-stained nobody . . . a man of vivacity and intelligence, of much more education than most of them, who knew the ways of the Navy and had been an officer . . . it is no doubt true that he was not among the first movers of the mutiny; if he had been, it could hardly have flared up so soon, and perhaps it is true that he accepted his elevation with reluctance.' Yet this same cool-headed ex-teacher and reluctant leader is simultaneously 'excitable, neurotic even'. At one point he is described as the 'self-appointed president', then he is 'made President' by others. We can surmise from this that Parker's performances are held to be responsible for the defeat of the Nore mutineers by several commentators, though none of their accounts seems to hold as much water as Parker's ship did. Indeed, where we do have evidence of Parker's performative abilities from his court martial, he appears as a leader of some character and rhetorical ability, pleading for his followers' lives and resigned to sacrificing his own if this is the necessary price.

But the significant performances are probably not on the ships but on the land, not by Joyce or Parker but by Howe and Spencer. For it is Howe's bravura performance under immense pressure that defuses a potential disaster for the authorities and it is Spencer's resolute refusal to negotiate under any circumstances, and his maintenance of support from the King and government, that effectively seal the Nore mutineers' fate.

Conclusion

We can summarize the issue by establishing first that, although the precise significance of leadership is difficult to establish, for the data are thin and the interpretations too varied to facilitate any kind of consensus on this issue, it does seem that the victors in both mutinies—Joyce and the mutineers in the first and Spencer and the Admiralty in the second—succeeded by inverting the resources of their opponents: they turned strengths into weaknesses. However, it is not clear—at least to me—that this was an intentional principle upon which the events turned. Parker may have been a poor leader and Joyce a good one, but Parker may simply have been unlucky in using a strategy whose utility had been enervated in its first embodiment.

The Spithead mutineers managed to retain the identity of honest but exploited loyal sailors, bravely standing up for their legitimate rights against a deaf, incompetent, but largely honest Admiralty. At the Nore, the mutineers' attempt to construct an image identical to that of their Spithead comrades was undermined by the Admiralty, whose control over the media and isolation of the mutineers persuaded the public that the Nore mutineers were, at worst rebels and revolutionaries, and at best ignorant people led astray by political incendiaries. Thus the red flag at Spithead represented just a refusal to work; the red flag at the Nore symbolized revolution. Admiral Howe wanted to solve the Spithead mutiny by seeing the royal flag fluttering from the yardarm of the flagship; Spencer wanted to solve the Nore mutiny by seeing disloyal rebels fluttering from the yardarm of the flagship; they both achieved what they wanted.

Notes

1. The 1651 Navigation Act prohibited the import of goods that were not carried in British ships in a successful attempt to undermine Dutch domination over the North Sea.
2. A 'fleet' comprised at least ten ships-of-the-line; a 'squadron' had less than ten ships but included some ships-of-the-line; a 'flotilla' had no ships-of-the-line (S. Pope 1998: 27).
3. Sheerness lies at the western end of the Isle of Sheppey and there is some speculation that the island may have been the site for a much earlier tale of heroic tragedy—*Beowulf*, the earliest surviving piece of intact literature in 'English'. See Simon Hall (1998).
4. Admiral Duncan was equally eloquent in his attempt to erase history: 'Fain would the historian pass over, in the strictest silence, an event, the recital of which brands with shame that character, which, till then, stood foremost in the ranks of honour ... Fain would we ourselves banish the recollection of it from our minds, and consign to everlasting oblivion an act, which, by comparison, raises rebellion into a venial offence' (quoted in Tracy 1998a: 221).

5. Until 1790 women convicted of 'coining' (cutting the edges off solver coins) had their bodies publicly burnt after hanging, while male traitors had their heads chopped off. Capital punishment for murder was abolished in Britain in 1965, but it remained on the statute book for treason and piracy under civil law and for five offences under military law, including mutiny, assisting the enemy, and obstructing operations.

6. Discipline on board ship had always been harsh. In Henry VIII's navy, c.1530, murder was punishable in a particularly grotesque fashion: 'If any man kill an other within the shippe, he that dotheth the dede shall be bownd quicke to the dead man, and so be cast into the see' (Booke of Orders for the Warre both by Sea and Land, written by Thomas Audley att the Command of the Kinge Henry the VIII,' quoted in Bald 1991: 30). Drawing a weapon to strike your captain was not regarded so heinous a crime and only warranted losing the arm that drew the weapon. Arson in a royal dockyard remained punishable by death well into the twentieth century.

7. The Articles of War formed the regulations that covered mutiny: number 19 concerned 'Mutinous assembly' and 'Mutinous language', article 20 concerned 'Concealment of mutinous design', article 22 related to 'striking, or attempting to strike, a superior officer', and article 34 covered, simply, 'Mutiny' (Lavery 1989: 141).

8. The Incitement to Mutiny Act, passed in 1797 as a direct result of the Spithead and Nore mutinies, was removed from the statute book only in November 1998.

9. In the same year the crew of the Janus mutinied, as did the notorious Bounty in 1789, the Culloden in 1793, the Windsor Castle in 1794, and the Defiance in 1795. One of the men involved in the suppression of the mutiny on the Defiance was Captain Bligh and the only men hanged for participating in the mutiny on the Bounty were hanged aboard the Brunswick, anchored at Spithead in 1792 (Neale 1985: 66).

10. But perhaps the most notorious individual act of mutiny occurred in February 1797 aboard the Hermione, when Captain Pigot had threatened to flog the last man down from the rigging, causing three sailors to fall from the mizzen mast and die instantly. Pigot, contrary to all traditions of death outside battle conditions, had all three thrown overboard immediately without a religious service. The next day a dozen sailors were flogged and that night Pigot and around ten other officers were murdered. The 150 mutineers then sailed for Venezuela and disappeared, though thirty-three were subsequently caught and twenty-four of these hanged (Neale 1985: 2–4).

11. The term 'press' was a corruption of the payment or 'prest' (from old French prest)— a loan or advance—that was made to pressed men.

12. S. Pope (1998: 50–2) suggests the following wages for seamen in 1793: landsman (least experienced) £10.60 per annum; ordinary seaman (worked the sails and rigging) £11.30 per annum; able-bodied seaman (took the helm, mended sails, understood guns) £14.00 per annum; petty officer (responsible for commanding sections of the ship) £20–£27 per annum.

13. Resistance to impressment was common and the local magistrates often supported the local population against over-zealous impressment gangs. The law, then, was not axiomatically on the side of the press gang; if it did not carry the correct warrant, or if it was not led by the appropriate officer, then the local population could—and frequently did—resist the gang, often with extreme violence. For example, between 1790 and 1800 there were twenty riots in London alone when press gangs were resisted, and on one occasion a mob of 500 destroyed two naval recruiting offices after a press gang had murdered the master of the merchant ship. Occasionally prisoners of war were recruited and common criminals were often an easy target, though

the navy preferred to avoid these where possible and to take those convicted of minor offences—such as debtors—rather than those accused of drunkenness or violence. Since pressing of landmen (i.e. men without naval experience) could actually prove counterproductive to the efficiency of a ship—to say nothing of it being illegal—pressing at sea was usually preferred by the navy, and this usually involved the stopping of merchant ships inward bound—and it also often resulted in widespread resistance and violence, with death a not uncommon feature (Manwaring and Dobrée 1937: 24).

14. Hawkins suggested it first in 1593. (D. Pope 1997: 144–5).

15. Poulsen talks of sailors using the salt beef and pork to carve tobacco boxes and using cheese to replace lost buttons on their coats, so we can assume that quality may not have reached ISO9000 standards (unless it was for boxes and buttons) (Poulsen 1984: 131).

16. Faith (1998: 6) suggests that many of the conditions are still evident in some of the world's fleets—namely, a prohibition on the crew leaving the ship when in harbour, the absence of edible food and drinkable water, and wages delayed by up to eighteen months.

17. D. Pope (1997: 264) concludes that, as bad as conditions at sea were, they were far better than those afflicting the British army wherever it served in similar places abroad.

18. D. Pope (1997: 234) suggests that the usual division was into eighths: one for the admiral, two for the captain, one between all the lieutenants, and so on down to the ordinary and able-bodied seamen, who shared two-eighths between them.

19. In the event income tax raised only £6 million, but it was sufficient because the tax was (temporarily) removed under Addington, Pitt's replacement (*Guardian*, 9 Jan. 1999).

20. The last petition had ended, 'We, your petitioners, thereby humbly implore that you will take these matters into consideration and with your accustomed goodness and liberality comply with the prayers of your petitioners, and we are in duty bound ever to pray, &c.' (quoted in Poulsen 1984: 134).

21. The United Irishman was an organization led by Wolfe Tone, which initially sought the peaceful removal of religious discrimination and parliamentary reform until forced into subversion.

22. Admiral Duncan thought otherwise for, in his opinion, 'the core of the mutiny was formed of land lubbers, or half and half sailors, who, in a gale, are almost impediments to the honest and spirited exertions of good and practical seamen' (Temple Patterson 1968: 7). Admiral Colpoys, on the *London*, also regarded them as a rabble and tried to resist the *Charlotte's* men when they approached, but Bridport told him not to get involved.

23. Nevertheless, when the *Royal William*, the Port Admiral's ship, refused to join the mutiny, it was threatened with cannonfire unless the crew changed its mind; it did. On the other hand, when two smaller ships attempted to join the mutiny on 20 April, they were refused permission by the Delegates and told to fulfil their normal duties.

24. For example, all 200 crew aboard the *Nymphe* claimed that they were 'kept more like convicts than free-born Britons . . . Flogging is carried on to extremes, one man received three dozen for what was termed silent contempt—after being beat by a Boatswain's mate, the man smiled . . .' (Manwaring and Dobrée 1937: 66).

25. The *Culloden*, a notoriously old and leaky ship that had fought at the Glorious First of June just five months before, had been involved in a mutiny under Captain Troubridge when the crew refused to take it out to sea from the St Helens anchorage on 9 November 1794 on the grounds that it was unseaworthy. Since more ships were lost through accidents than through enemy action between 1792 and 1815, the *Culloden*'s crew were probably acting extremely rationally (S. Pope 1998: 28, 29). The *Culloden*'s crew then agreed to 'surrender' on two conditions: a new ship (or the repair of the *Culloden*), and 'your Lordships word and honour not to punish any man concerned in the present business . . .'. But the Admiralty was not interested and on 9 December sent Troubridge and Captain Pakenham to resolve the matter. According to the *Culloden*'s crew, Pakenham gave them his word that no one would be punished; according to Pakenham this was not true. True or not, one mutineer was sentenced to 800 lashes (he was later pardoned), and five were hanged (Neale 1985: 68–118).

26. Spencer's inactivity could hardly have come at a worse time, for simultaneously a letter arrived at the Admiralty reporting that the crew of the *Marie Antoinette*, a Royal Navy schooner in the West Indies, had murdered both their officers and escaped (D. Pope 1998: 122–3).

27. Poulsen, (1984: 136) puts the numbers at 400 and 1,600 respectively; Guttridge, (1992: 62) has 367 and 1,100.

28. A Non-Commissioned Officer—that is, a corporal or sergeant

29. One of the leaders of the mutiny that was not punished, because he was never recognized by the authorities, was Matthew Hollister, a gunner's yoeman, in control of the storeroom wherein lay the powder room. Hollister was one of the four Delegates who met Joyce at the end of the Spithead mutiny (Neale 1985: 168–9).

30. As a popular song went:

> Then at the Nore the lions boldly roused,
> Their brethren's cause at Spithead they espoused,
> Each swore alike to the King he would be true,
> But one and all the tyrants would subdue,
> Their gallant hearts the chains of bondage broke,
> Not to revolt, but to evade the yoke.

> (quoted in Manwaring and Dobrée 1937: 136.)

31. After 1808 the admiral's share was reduced to a third of the captain's quarter and the petty officers and ratings shared half the value between them (S. Pope 1998: 85).

32. The *Adamant*, one of Duncan's line-of-battle-ships, refused to obey orders on 13 May, and a sloop, the *Albatross*, had also proved troublesome on 16 May. On 27 May the crew of the *Montague* refused to weigh anchor until they had been paid 6 months of the 13 months' back pay they were owed—unless the enemy fleet was in sight.

33. Tracy (1998a: 217) wrongly implies that the government blockaded the mutineers *after* the mutineers blockaded London.

34. After the mutiny, the authorities were astonished at the significance allotted to their oaths by the mutineers and subsequently insisted that all sailors take an oath of allegiance to the monarch.

35. The King, George III, was known as 'Farmer George' because of his interest in agriculture; he was also known as 'Mad George', suffering from increasing bouts of insanity.

36. In contrast, the channels at Spithead were between *c*.1,700 metres and 3,500 metres wide—so wide that blockade was virtually impossible.

37. Seven of the twenty-nine mutineers executed at the Nore were from the *Leopard*.

38. Although forty-one people from the *Inflexible* were subsequently court-martialled, not one was punished—suggesting that all the 'ringleaders' had indeed flown to France.

39. Spencer was allegedly so distraught at the execution that he gave Parker's widow between £1,200 and £1,400. This would have been the equivalent of 100 times Parker's expected total salary had he lived and remained in the Royal Navy, but she lived on charity and died in poverty in 1840 in London. It would be unusual in the extreme for a man who wanted to see Parker's body swinging in chains to have been so guilt stricken as to pay such a huge sum to his widow. We can surmise that the magnanimous 'Spencer tradition' is as full of holes as Parker's ship was when the mutiny broke out.

40. This was not the end of rebellion. Two months later three marines were executed in Plymouth for sedition and there were fifteen other single-ship mutinies that year. Mutinies also broke out in St Vincent's fleet off Cadiz. On the *St George* a mutiny broke out in protest at the death sentence passed on two sailors convicted of buggery, but the mutiny was put down and four of the protesters were then hanged at the same time as the original two condemned men. That day was a Sunday and several officers protested about executions on the Sabbath—excluding Nelson, who congratulated St Vincent for 'had it been Christmas Day instead of Sunday I would have executed them'. Later that year the crew of the *Marlborough* mutinied and St Vincent ordered the crew to haul their own mutinous leaders up to the yardarm. By the end of 1798, fifty sailors had been hanged; according to Guttridge (1992: 75), 'it was the only sane response'. On 14 March 1800 a sailor called Jackson led a mutiny on the frigate *Danae* and sailed the ship to Brest, where he, along with the other mutineers, was arrested by the French authorities. One of the mutineers, John McDonald, alias Samuel Higgins, was subsequently executed. Jackson survived—as indeed he had done the Nore mutiny, where he had been Parker's secretary. In December 1802 three sailors were hanged on board the *Gibraltar*, an eighty-four-gunner, which they had unsuccessfully tried to take over (Tracy 1998*b*: 105–6, 285–6). Mutinies also broke out again in the Channel Fleet. In 1805, the year of Trafalgar, there were twelve courts martial and eleven men sentenced to death aboard one ship. Fifteen more mutinies occurred in 1813 (Lavery 1989: 141–3).

41. When the victorious fleet returned to the Nore on 30 October, to be reviewed by the same King that had actively sought the destruction of his own sailors, he was said to be distraught when the bad weather prevented the royal yacht from sailing out to them. He was not distraught on his own part; on the contrary, he remarked: 'think of the disappointment of those brave fellows, whom I long to thank for defending me, protecting my people, and preserving my country' (Manwaring and Dobrée 1937: 240). We can be less sure that the sailors felt the same disappointment.

4

Nursing the Media: Social Leadership in the Crimean and English Hospitals

> To understand God's thoughts we must study statistics, for these are the measures of his purpose.
>
> (Florence Nightingale (quoted in Darwin 1979: 363))

This chapter has a slightly different intent from the previous two. The last example was rooted in two leaders facing similar circumstances, with one notably more successful than the other. That success and failure were rooted not in two radically different sets of demands or even strategies on the part of the mutineers but rather in the way the arts of leadership were deployed successfully, first by Joyce and the Spithead mutineers, and then by Spencer and the Admiralty. Again this is not to reinvoke either the situational or the contingency approach to leadership, which suggest that the circumstances determine which leader or which style works best. Rather it is to insist that what leaders do—or do not do—can play a critical role in constructing those very circumstances that they believe themselves to be in: leadership is an active constructor of circumstances not a passive sufferer of them.

In this chapter we will consider a case where the same individual, Florence Nightingale, faces different circumstances: in the first she is apparently successful but in the second she is considerably less so. In the first case Nightingale succeeded in persuading the army, or rather the government, that the army's care of the sick and wounded was grossly inadequate and positively counterproductive to the war effort. Her leadership, supported by the public outcry against the incompetence of the military and army medical leadership, facilitated the wholesale reconstruction of the military hospital service. Thus in the Crimea the resources of her opponents—the British Army's leaders and medical profession—were used directly against them, for the more they took control over events the less viable appeared their medical system. How else could a single woman and a 'motley collection' of 'nurses' have achieved so much against the might of the British military establishment?

However, Nightingale's policy of operating *within* and not *against* the parameters of the establishment was markedly less successful once the war was over, when public attention was focused elsewhere (the *defence* of the army against the Indian mutineers). And when her research began to focus attention beyond the army and directly at the government itself and the general medical profession, the establishment closed ranks against her.

Nightingale's first major biographer, E. T. Cook, regarded her as a 'passionate statistician' and there is little doubt that she put an inordinate amount of faith in the persuasive effects of 'facts'. The consequence was that, rather than take up an overt leadership role in personally mobilizing public opinion against the military establishment on her return from the Crimea, she preferred to rely on her rendering of the 'facts' to the political establishment. But this time the establishment used Nightingale's resources against her: her expertise in facts was almost rendered irrelevant, because the 'facts' were (and are) often easier to deny or deflect than public opinion. Yet the more the army and the politicians filibustered the more she threw incontrovertible facts at them—and the more confident they became that she would fail. And, although she did make a considerable impact on the development of civil nursing, her ardent ambition to stop more of the soldiers she called her 'children' dying from quite unnecessary causes was marginal.

Nightingale was a leader whose success depended to a large extent on persuasive communication, but she was not a great or even an effective public speaker. She was, however, one of, if not the, most prolific letter-writers of all time: at least 15,000 of her letters are still in existence in various collections and there may be another 5,000 that have disappeared, often destroyed at her insistence (Vicinus and Nergaard 1990: 1). She knew how to mobilize political support at home and her campaign to reorganize the military service in Scutari benefited from the wide-scale and novel press coverage of the blundering military authorities. But her limitations were also grounded in the limits of communication: mortality statistics were no match for military stasis, and moral fortitude paled into insignificance before media fickleness.

Nightingale's legacy is as controversial as her career. Long regarded as the founder of British nursing, her birthday (12 May) has been celebrated as International Nurses Day by the International Congress of Nurses for many years. But in 1999 delegates at the annual conference of the British health union, Unison, suggested she should be dropped as the nurses' icon, given her authoritarian disposition, her submissive attitude to doctors, her antipathy to feminism, her questionable success in the Crimea, and her cosseted and traditional upbringing. She was, according to Marie Idle, 'a woman who not so much kept her nurses under her thumb, but under the boot' (quoted in Brindle 1999). Kelly (1999) suggests that Nightingale was actually anything but conventional, for 'she was a lesbian, and a feminist, a lifelong rebel and a vociferous campaigner for better public health' (as well as being addicted to chloroform). In fact, critical attacks upon the Nightingale legacy have been in existence from the Crimean War period itself, though they were most clearly detailed in Lytton Strachey's *Eminent Victorians*, first published in 1918. This implied that the Victorian establishment supported the creation of the mythical 'Lady of the Lamp' in order to divert attention away from their own imperialist follies. Yet much of the legend was decidedly anti-establishment. Whatever her success rate in the Crimea—Small (1998) has suggested that her administration killed more soldiers than it saved—and Nightingale accepted this even if some of her hagiographers did not), my concern here is to understand the complexities of leadership rather than the specific utility of nursing techniques.

Florence Nightingale, Early Life

Florence Nightingale took her first name from the city in which she was born in 1820 and her second name from her father's uncle. Her father, William E. Shore, had assumed the name Nightingale at the age of 21 on acquiring an inheritance from this uncle and was subsequently known as W.E.N. He had already inherited the lead mine on the property as a minor, was now a man of considerable wealth, and when he went up to Cambridge he had an income of around £8,000 a year (almost half a million pounds a year in contemporary terms). Her mother, Frances (Fanny) Smith, came from a large family and her father had been an MP for forty-six years and a leading abolitionist. In 1818 W.E.N. and Fanny married and moved to Italy. As a rich, cultured and liberal gentleman W.E.N. had no need for work and much preferred his library to anywhere else. The following year Florence's elder sister Frances Parthenope (Parthe) was born in Naples (the Greek name for the city was Parthenope) and in 1821 the Nightingales returned to England to live in a new house, Lea Hurst, on W.E.N.'s Derbyshire estate in Lea. The house was considered too cold and too small, but was used as a summer house for the family. In 1825 the Nightingales moved to Embley Park, Wellow, Hampshire, which became the main residence from then on. As befits a wealthy upper-middle-class English family at the time, the Nightingales spent the summer at Lea Hurst, the winter at Embley Park, and during the spring and autumn 'season' they lived in London.

Florence became obsessed early on that she was a 'monster', unlike ordinary people, and claimed that much of her childhood—and later life—was spent in 'a dream' where she would withdraw into her own imagination and act out heroic deeds. By 11 she was already a passionate and prolific letter-writer. According to Florence's own autobiography, or her *Curriculum Vitae* as she called it: 'I never learnt to write till I was 11 or 12, owing to a weakness in my hands . . . the first idea I can recollect when I was a child was a desire to nurse the sick. My daydreams were all of hospitals and I visited them whenever I could. I never communicated it to anyone, it would have been laughed at; but I thought God had called me to serve Him in that way' (quoted in McDonald 1998: 1).

In 1832 W.E.N. decided to educate the girls (now aged 13 and 12) himself, particularly in Latin, Greek, Italian, French, German, history, philosophy, and mathematics. A governess was employed to teach music and drawing and, after W.E.N. had failed to gain the seat as Member of Parliament for Andover in 1835, he withdrew from political life to concentrate upon his library, his riding, and his daughters. Florence then became W.E.N.'s constant companion in the library, while Parthe remained at Fanny's side in the drawing room.

Life had become one long social circus with innumerable events for the extended family, but Florence was already desperate from something more substantial: 'I craved for some regular occupation, for something worth doing instead of frittering time away on useless trifles' (quoted in Woodham-Smith 1982: 13). W.E.N. had other ideas and decided to take the girls to Europe to broaden their experiences before they were 'presented' to society, but Florence was shaken and then strengthened by the first of several religious experiences she had. As she wrote (then aged 17) 'On February 7th, 1837, God spoke to me and called me to His service' (quoted in Woodham-Smith 1982: 17). She heard the voice as outside her, not inside her head, but she was unsure as to what exactly she was supposed to do. However, she now became more confident, knowing she had been called for something special.

In September 1837 the Nightingales travelled to Paris while Embley Park was rebuilt and Florence met Mary Clarke (Clarkey), something of an intellectual and a Bohemian whose rebellious lifestyle proved attractive to Florence.[1] W.E.N. and Florence became interested in the cause of Italian independence and, in September, visited Geneva, then the home of many Italian patriot refugees, avoiding the Austrian authorities who controlled much of Italy at the time. The contrast between the hedonistic city of Florence and the commitment of the refugees in Geneva, who had given up everything to fight for freedom, seemed to have forced Florence to reconsider her priorities.

In March 1839 the Nightingales returned to England, and Florence, having tasted the high life in Europe, worried about the role chosen for her by God. Since he had not spoken to her for two years, she assumed it was a result of her lifestyle in Europe and wrote a note to herself that she must learn from this that 'the desire to shine in society' is a sin to be avoided not a pleasure to be sought (Woodham-Smith 1982: 31). Such a lesson was to have a profound consequence on Florence's attempts to reorganize the military health service after the Crimean War.

Like many women of the romantic era of Byron, especially middle-class women, Florence was considered to have 'delicate' health and was assumed prone to exaggeration and overt emotional instability. But her most painful problem was what, precisely, God had called her for? In a bitter note of reflection she wrote to herself: 'All I do is done to win admiration' (Woodham-Smith 1982: 41).

Florence (then aged 22) met Richard Monckton Milnes, a 33-year-old heir to an estate in Yorkshire and a philanthropist, poet, and politician. Monckton Milnes announced himself in love with Florence, but, though she liked him, she had more significant things in mind for her future than marriage. The 'Hungry Forties' had left much of the country in the desperate throws of poverty and disease and Florence began to perceive that her future role was helping such people. At last, in the spring of 1844, Florence's long search for a goal was resolved: she would work in hospitals helping the sick. As she recalled in 1857, 'since I was 24 there never was any vagueness in my plans or ideas as to what God's work was for me' (quoted in Woodham-Smith 1982: 48).

However, work of any kind was anathema to Florence's social class, and work in a hospital was just about as low as one could get without being out on the street. For the rest of the year she strove in vain to find a way of escaping from home and entering upon her vocation, but she was constantly ill and often confined to bed, where she wrote at length to whoever would read her letters. Her grandmother, Mrs Shore, was ill over the summer of 1845 and, for the first time, Florence was left alone to nurse someone. But her experience of freedom was tinged with the realization that she knew nothing about nursing. As she noted: 'I saw a poor woman die before my eyes this summer because there was nothing but fools to sit up with her, who poisoned her as much as if they had given her arsenic' (quoted in Woodham-Smith 1982: 55).

From then on, the tender care that Florence had assumed was enough to nurse people took second place to the expertise and training that were required. Her only problem was how to acquire it. She hatched a plan to work with Dr Fowler, a family friend who was head physician at Salisbury Infirmary. Her mother, Fanny, accused Florence of having an affair with the 'low vulgar surgeon' and her sister Parthe had what the family regarded as 'hysterics'. As far as the other Nightingales were concerned, the only people who entered hospital as patients were those unable to secure private care at home—and the consequence was hospitals that mirrored the deprived and depraved environments from which the patients came. Nurses were popularly regarded as no better, and it was unclear whether the patients or the nurses were more prone to drunkenness.[2] At this time the only respectable way for middle-class women to earn a living—and it was far more preferable not to have to earn a living—was by being a governess, and there were 21,000 of these by 1850 (Trollope 1994: 61). Thus, Florence had spent eight years since 1845 trying to understand the nature of her calling from God and she was to spend the next eight years trying to find a way of realizing her mission. As she wrote in her diary on 5 December 1845: 'God has something for me to do for him—or he would have let me die some time ago' (Trollope 1994: 61).

Her immediate reaction to her family's distress was to sink ever deeper into depression: 'This morning I feel as if my soul would pass away in tears, in utter loneliness . . . I cannot live—forgive me oh Lord, and let me die, this day let me die' (quoted in Woodham-Smith 1982: 60). More positively she began her self-education on hospitals and sanitation, reading very early in the morning before the rest of the family awoke. She read whatever she could lay her hands on in terms of the official Blue Books, and the series of official inquiries into the health of the poor in the late 1830s and early 1840s. This habit of very early rising persisted right through her active life, because, as she later recalled: 'Women never have a half-hour in all their lives (except before or after anybody is up in the house) that they can call their own, without fear of offending or hurting someone. Why do people sit up so late, or, more rarely, get up so early? Not because the day is not long enough, but because they have no time in the day to themselves' (quoted in Johnson 1996). Or, as she more pointedly stated in a letter to Hilary Bonham Carter: ' "Ladies' " work has always to be fitted in where a man is' (quoted in Vicinus and Nergaard 1990: 19). The more she read, the more she realized that this was her future life, and she endeavoured to cut herself off from others in an attempt to ensure that the temptations of high society would never again take hold of her.

In 1847 Richard Mockton Milnes asked Florence to marry him, but she could neither accept, because of her intended vocation, nor refuse, because she clearly felt something for him. The strain of her existence proved too much for her and she collapsed, sure that death was upon her. She was wrong by another sixty-three years, but it prompted Selina (Sigma) and Charles Bracebridge, a well-travelled and well-heeled childless couple who were already family friends to rescue Florence and take her to Rome. There she returned to the life of the English gentry abroad, with a long succession of parties and functions. In Rome Florence met Elizabeth (Liz) and Sidney Herbert, another rich and cultured couple whose activities in politics were matched by their philanthropic pursuits.

On her return home, Richard Mockton Milnes, after two years of waiting, was finally rejected, despite the fact that she admitted that she adored him and dreamt of him at night. But she was terrified of her life ending in a closed circle of entertaining and enjoyment when God had demanded so much from her, for 'Marriage had never tempted me. I hated the idea of being tied for ever to a life of society, and only such a marriage could I have . . . I was tempted after several years' resistance, it was such an easy escape out of my difficulties . . . An accident prevented it. I will believe that it was God who saved me from casting myself down from the Temple' (quoted in McDonald 1998: 2).[3]

She came to be an inveterate hater of family life, at least as she had known it: 'The family uses people *not* for what they are intended to be, but for what it wants them for . . . if it wants someone to sit in the drawing room, that someone is supplied by the family, though that member may be destined for science, or for education, or for active superintendence by God' (quoted in Trollope 1994: 26).[4] But Florence was in a distinct minority, especially when it came to the value of education for women, because the common assumption at the time was that an inverse correlation existed between an education and a viable existence. Education, it was assumed, merely distracted women and made them less likely to fulfil their allotted role in life—the raising of a family.[5]

Once again the Bracebridges rescued her from domestic suffocation and took her down the Nile and to Greece. In July, when they reached Berlin, Florence visited several hospitals and charitable institutions and from 31 July to 13 August 1850 visited Kaiserwerth on the Rhine, a religiously run institution that embodied a hospital, school, and women's jail. She left 'feeling so brave as if nothing could ever vex me again' (quoted in Woodham-Smith 1982: 82). But it did, for as soon as she returned home and explained where she had been, Fanny and Parthe, as usual, had what Florence regarded as hysterics; W.E.N., just as typically, disappeared to his library. Parthe even persuaded Florence to give up helping at a local school and Florence was, once more, enslaved to her family. There was nothing but misery in front of her. As she wrote: 'In my thirty-first year I see nothing desirable but death' (quoted in Woodham-Smith 1982: 86). Gradually it dawned upon Florence that she, not God, would have to make the first move and that move could not be incremental but must be revolutionary, for 'there are knots which are Gordian and can only be cut' (quoted in Woodham-Smith 1982: 88).

The following year, with Parthe remaining ill, the family decided to visit Carlsbad, and Florence was permitted to visit Kaiserwerth again—as long as it remained a secret within the family. Between 6 July and 7 October Florence was a student there and the Spartan regime and religious framework were heaven on earth for Florence: 'This is life. Now I know what it is to live and to love life, and really I should be sorry now to leave life . . . I wish for no other earth, no other world than this.' When Florence rejoined her mother and sister they treated her as if she had 'just come out of prison' (quoted in Woodham-Smith 1982: 92).

She planned to enter Catholic hospitals run by nuns in Dublin and Paris, but her mother would hear none of it and the plan was abandoned. Aunt Mai stepped in and demanded that Fanny set a time—four years—when Florence would be free to do as she pleased, and reluctantly, very reluctantly, Fanny agreed. Moreover, when a doctor declared that Florence was making Parthe ill, the last reason to stay had been broken. In fact Florence's plan to visit hospitals in Dublin and Paris were thwarted by a family illness. But in February 1853 she travelled to Paris for a month, where she visited hospitals and watched operations. She also developed a questionnaire on hospital and nursing administration that she circulated to hospitals throughout Europe and, with W.E.N.'s £500 annual allowance (around £30,000 in contemporary terms), she began to carve out a niche of her own.

In March 1853 she heard God speak again and she decided to serve the poor. The Institution for the Care of Sick Gentlewomen in Distressed Circumstances, a charitable institution, was in financial and administrative trouble and Liz Herbert suggested that Florence should take up the post of Superintendent. Florence agreed and was appointed by the board of governors—to the disgust of Fanny and Parthe, who both took to their beds—especially after a rumour spread that Florence was 'going into service' (quoted in Vicinus and Nergaard 1990: 63).

Florence was to receive no salary for her work and personally paid for a Matron to assist her. On 12 August she set up 'An Establishment for Gentlewomen During Illness', 1 Harley Street, London. She immediately set about reorganizing the administration of the hospital: hot water was piped to each floor, and lifts were installed to carry the patients' food between floors. The board demanded that she took in only Church of England women and Florence immediately tended her resignation unless she could take in whomever she wanted, irrespective of their religion. The committee reluctantly agreed to this. She had absolutely no time for what she called 'do-gooders' and was interested only in practical benefits; as she noted, 'from committees, charity, schism, from the Church of England, from philanthropy and all deceits of the devil, Good Lord deliver us' (quoted in Woodham-Smith 1982: 118). But, a letter to her father revealed that her success came only when she began to play politics, rather than suffer from it:

When I entered 'into service' here, I determined that, happen what would, I NEVER would intrigue among the committee. Now I perceive that I do all my business by intrigue . . . Last general committee I executed a series of resolutions . . . and presented them as coming from the medical men . . . these I proposed and carried in committee, without telling them they came from *me*, and not from the medical men; and then, and not till then, I showed them to the medical men, without telling *them* that they were already passed in committee . . . The medical men have had two meetings on them and approved them all *nem. con.*, and thought they were their own!   (quoted in Woodham-Smith 1982: 119–20)

By the end of 1853, for the first time in many years, Florence appeared to believe that she had at last found her calling and made a success of it. But by the beginning of 1854, with the administration working like clockwork, she began to fret at the limited scope of her new enterprise, her 'little mole hill', as she called it. The mountain that faced her was the entire hospital system and Florence began to accumulate data on the conditions afflicting hospital nursing in particular. With pay and conditions reflecting the low status of the nurse, Florence was well aware that changing the nurse was the key to changing nursing and hospitals. Cholera broke out in the summer of 1854, around Drury Lane and westward towards Middlesex, and Florence, amidst great personal danger, volunteered to manage nurses in cholera wards; it was just a foretaste of what was to come.

The Social, Economic, and Political Background

The mid-Victorian years in Britain that Florence Nightingale lived through marked a period of intense political activity in Europe, a merry-go-round of minor political change at home, and the steady strengthening of the British Empire, which kept British focus anywhere but on Paris, Vienna, Berlin, or Moscow. True, the political make-up of British governments in the mid-nineteenth century was anything but stable: there were six general elections between 1847 and 1868 and all returned coalition or minority governments that lasted only as long as the horse-trading lasted. But this was nothing compared to the revolutions that wracked so many European countries and were so chillingly announced by Marx, somewhat prematurely it has to be said, as the death knell of capitalism.

Underlying the fragility and instability of the British governments was the great surge of middle-class expectations, eroding the landed aristocracy's prior domination and gradually establishing the liberalization of the economy and the state. It was under this political framework that John Stuart Mill's *Principles of Political Economy* (1848), Smiles's *Self-Help* (1859), Darwin's *On the Origin of Species* (1859), and Spencer's equivalent sociological papers all surfaced and all generated a resonant message to the British population: independence, individualism, self-help, and self-respect. Also critical was the related liberalization of the 'taxes on knowledge'—the stamp duties on newspapers and customs duties on paper. During the 1850s and 1860s, with the removal of tax and duties, and technical developments such as linotype composition (1844) and the rotary press (1846), the newspaper industry exploded in a frenzy of print, to the extent that by 1863 over 1,000 newspapers existed, the vast majority recent arrivals. Moreover, these could now produce 30,000 copies of a newspaper in just one hour (Matthew 1986: 466–8; Young and Jesser 1997: 21). It was this media development that first whetted and then fed the public's feeding frenzy for sensational news—and there was little more sensational than the blundering of the British army in the Crimean War and the 'lady of the lamp', as Nightingale rapidly became known.

But as well as inducing the rapacious principles of economic self-interest, the Victorian period also heralded the age of public service. Primarily, but not wholly, voluntary in motive, public service and philanthropy endeavoured to establish a network of organizational forms that rescued and supported those deei ied worthy of effort. Hence the Royal Society for the Prevention of Cruelty to Animals was founded, the exploitation of children at work was limited, and vast public works erected schools, hospitals, sewerage systems, and the like. Yet it was not really until after 1850 that urban conditions changed markedly for the better.

The rise of living standards gradually altered the gender balance at work to the extent that, with the exception of northern factories, social status increased as the distance between, and visibility of, the work and income link increased. The highest status devolved upon those aristocrats who appeared not to work at all, the lowest upon those who were so poor that the entire family had to work. Thus, for those from the wealthy middle class with links to the political and landed élite, such as the Nightingale family, the prospect of a daughter working was social anathema; to work in a hospital where only the poverty stricken and destitute ended up was social suicide. Domestic work, for such families, was what servants did and between 1851 and 1871 the number of domestic servants increased by 60 per cent, twice the growth of the population (Briggs 1994: 264).

The role of middle- and upper-class wives and daughters was wholly nonutilitarian where possible and administrative where necessary. They should

not only wear fine clothes and practise 'accomplishments' such as music, drawing and decorative needlework but should patently have the leisure to enjoy them. The result was the rise of the 'perfect lady', the Victorian ideal of the completely leisured, completely ornamental, completely helpless and dependant middle-class wife or daughter, with no function besides inspiring admiration and bearing children.   (Perkin 1972: 159)

Florence Nightingale ridiculed such perfection in her novel *Cassandra*, written in 1852, for 'suppose we were to see a number of men in the morning sitting round a table in the drawing-room, looking at prints, doing worsted work, and reading little books, how we should laugh!' (quoted in Golby 1986: 246).

If the governments' domestic policies were oriented around freeing the economy and creating an infrastructure to support the population of the richest nation on earth (and a group of 'perfect women'), the foreign policy was generally aimed at protecting and extending the trade that supplied the wherewithal for this prosperity to continue. Only when other nations appeared to infringe upon what the Victorians seemed to regard as their God-given right to rule the waves, and the trade routes within them, did they become concerned. One of those routes was the Mediterranean and one of those concerns was Russia.

The Ottoman Empire had been in decline for many years when the Russian Tsar embarked on a policy of expansion to take advantage of the frailty of the 'sick man of Europe' and gain access to the Mediterranean via the Black Sea. On the pretext of protecting orthodox Christians, Russia entered Bulgaria (nominally still part of the Ottoman Empire) in July 1853 and Turkey promptly declared war on Russia and pushed the invaders back. In November 1853 a Russian fleet, using explosive shells for the first time, attacked and sank the Turkish fleet at Sinope, leaving only 358 of the 4,490 Turkish sailors accounted for after the action. The victory turned a political problem into a military nightmare, for the British and French now regarded the Russian threat of greater expansion into the Mediterranean as both dangerously real and unacceptable. Unfortunately for the British government the population was, at best, disinterested in the issue, at least until *The Times* published news of the 'massacre' and demanded a vigorous defence of oppressed religious minorities (Goldie 1997: 15–16). The Austrians, erstwhile allies of Russia, demanded an immediate Russian withdrawal, which was complied with, but the Anglo-French alliance was intent on deterring any further attack and, after declaring war on Russia in March 1854, decided to attack Russia at its Crimean base of Sebastopol. As ever, the war was to be over by Christmas and, as ever, it was not.

The Military Background

By 1815 Wellington's army had achieved lasting success against Napoleon's *Grande Armée*, primarily through training, discipline, and skill rather than patriotic fervour or morale. However, with the exception of Ireland, the forty years of relative peace that followed had left the British army without a specific role, bereft of political support and subject to the fetish for cost-cutting that saw its annual budget decline from £43 million in 1815 to around £10 million by the time of the Crimean crisis. Parallel reductions in troop numbers occurred, from 234,000 in 1815 to around 100,000 by 1850.[6]

As in the Royal Navy, recruitment and desertion were constant problems in the British army, even though the only criteria for entry were minimal height (which varied with demand) and minimal health. But the social chasm between the aristocratic officer corps, devoted to their regiments (rather than the army, through the purchase of commissions—unlike the French meritocratic system), and the ordinary soldiers, devoted to drink and survival, persisted throughout the first half of the nineteenth century. There were reformists who attempted change, usually through individual and paternalistic schemes to cut the consumption of alcohol, provide reading rooms, and end Wellington's tradition of treating soldiers as 'scum'. There was even some reduction in the maximum number of lashes permitted for the various offences (declining from 1,500 in 1795, to 500 in 1829, to 50 in 1846) before it was abolished altogether in 1881 (D. Edwards 1978).

But these reforms, and the reformists behind them, were far outnumbered by the inertia protected by the traditionalists, typified by the Horse Guards and supported by the other five elements of military administration (the War Office, Colonial Office, Home Office, Treasury, and Ordnance). This Kafkesque nightmare of self-interested bureaucracy ensured that almost all attempts at reform, such as those attempted in 1836 by Lord Howick, failed.[7] A report by Marshall and Tulloch had also attempted to improve the diet and barrack accommodation in the 1830s, but their influence was minimal, as was that of the Colonial Secretary, Grey, whose attempts to reduce the recruitment problem by encouraging short-term careers (ten-year enlistment rather than twenty-years) was vigorously and successfully watered down by Wellington before his death in 1852.

There was little public concern for the plight of the ordinary soldier (except for removing corporal punishment) and thus little chance of ensuring the necessary degree of public outrage that had, for example, managed to minimize the exploitation of child labour through factory legislation (McGregor 1984).[8] The results were conditions that in some ways were worse than those in prison. Space per soldier was typically about half that allowed to civil prisoners until late into the nineteenth century, washing was done in tubs used for overnight urine, half of their daily pay was withdrawn to pay for food, and married soldiers lived with their wives and children (where they were permitted) in the same room as single soldiers (Burroughs 1994: 160–73). The high command were also uninterested in the treatment of the wounded—a pattern of behaviour that makes Nelson's activities even more unusual (see Chapter 7). The Medical Officer of the Scots Greys, Dr Brush, told the Hospitals' Commission in the Crimea that no general officer ever visited his hospital nor enquired about the troops, and Dr Marlow of the 28th Regiment was equally scathing (Woodham-Smith 1982: 158).

It was not just a lack of concern but also part of a culture of masculinity in which wounds were badges of courage and pain a test of character. After all, Lord Raglan, the Commander-in-Chief in Crimea, had watched his own arm amputated without anaesthetic after Waterloo—calling upon the doctor who threw it away to bring it back, since it had a ring on the finger given to him by his wife. But he had not been on active service for the forty years since then, and at 66 years old was hardly a good choice for command. Nor was Lord Lucan, the cavalry commander, who had retired sixteen years earlier and rejoined the army at Varna (see Fig. 4.1), much to the amusement of his troops, who had difficulty comprehending the outdated commands he used. Lucan's brother-in-law, Lord Cardigan, commander of the Light Brigade, was equally inadequate: he had never seen active service at all and forbade his troops from wearing cloaks at night because he regarded them as 'effeminate' (Mulvihill 1997: 26).

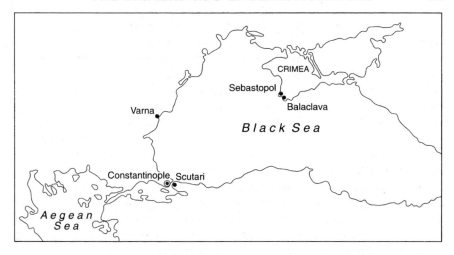

Fig. 4.1. The Crimea

The overall result of the developments in the forty years since Waterloo was that the army facing the prospect of a war against Russia was both depleted in strength and disoriented in strategy. It could and did just about fulfil the requirements for national and colonial defence but it did not envisage how to fight against a European enemy of immense size at a considerable distance from home. The very essence of the British army was organized around a battalion (usually around 600–800 men); thus coordinated action by brigades (around 5,000+) or divisions (15,000+), let alone whole armies, was entirely outside the experience of any serving officer. Nevertheless, in the summer of 1854, 26,000 British troops embarked for an attack upon Sebastopol in the Crimean Peninsular.

The Crimean War: From Calamita to Calamity

'The finest army that ever left these shores' was the description given by *The Times* to the British army embarking for the Crimea at Portsmouth, but even by the standards of journalism this was being economical with the truth (quoted in Goldie 1997: 15). In 1852 it had just forty cannon in total and could probably muster about the same firepower as one of Nelson's frigates. In fact, the army's state was a constant source of irritation to *The Times*, particularly when the French seemed so much better organized, not just militarily but even to the extent of each regiment having their own *vivandière*, a woman recruited to provide food, drink, and medical help to the soldiers. In Varna, where the Anglo-French armies first gathered, diarrhoea, dysentery, and cholera broke out, and before any allied soldier saw a Russian 10,000 of them were dead (Mulvihill 1997: 34).

However, despite the problems, *The Times* demanded an immediate attack upon Sebastopol and Raglan reluctantly accepted his mission and sailed for

Sebastopol in September 1854. So depleted was the land transport that the (by-now) 30,000 British troops that embarked for the Crimea at Varna, in what is now Bulgaria, had only thirty-one wagons with them and much of the equipment was left behind to pack in as many troops as possible. Anglo-French–Turkish armies of 64,000 troops managed an unopposed landing on the Crimean coast, but poor preparation, organization, and leadership deterred them from taking Sebastopol immediately. The British landed at Calamita Bay on 13 September, left what little stores they had landed with on the coast, and marched inland to fight the Battle of Alma exactly a week later. As Dr Alexander, 1st class Staff Surgeon to the Light Division, noted on their landing: 'My God they have landed this army without any kind of hospital transport, litters or carts or anything' (quoted in Gold 1997: 41). Private Cameron of the 93rd Highlanders would have agreed, for 'My comrade and I got grass or anything we could gather for a bed and lay down, having a stone for a pillow, and then the rain came pouring on us. So we lay on our backs holding up our blankets with our hands, so as the rain would run down both sides, and so keep our firelocks and ammunition dry' (Gold 1997: 40). The results were appalling: between June and August 1854 20 per cent of the entire expeditionary force were hospitalized with cholera and related diseases—and no shot had yet been fired (Vicinus and Nergaard 1990: 78). At least thirty-eight officers—who may have bought their commissions only recently to see some 'action'—had already seen enough and tendered their resignation to deal with 'urgent private affairs' back home. Luckily Lord Cardigan had remembered to bring his own private yacht to live on—so he did not have to suffer the consequences of failing to bring any tents.

Despite effective use of the new rifles by the British against the Russians at the Battle of Alma, it was not a crushing victory—though the headline in *The Times* on 2 October 1854 read 'The Fall of Sebastopol'. The confusion of war was also reported by Russell in *The Times*, for 'The French General is dying. The English General . . . in order to take Sebastopol was marching round it! The Russian General, anxious to save Sebastopol, was marching away from it! Neither had the least notion what the other was doing' (quoted in Gold 1997: 49).

As the siege of the city began, the Russians attempted to relieve the city through attacks at Balaclava and Inkerman, both of which failed, with the latter attack resulting in 12,000 Russian casualties to the allies' 3,000. The ensuing winter caught the British completely unprepared and resulted in dreadful losses and a public outcry against the army's incompetence. The French, supported by a small force of Sardinians, then took centre stage and repulsed one final attempt by the Russians at the Battle of the Tchernaya on 16 August 1855, where once again the allies' losses (2,000) were quadrupled by the Russians' (8,000).

The Crimean War, in many ways, was the first industrialized conflict and it was marked by a series of technological innovations. The old musket with its spherical lead ball shot was replaced on the Anglo-French side by the rifle (with 'rifled' spiral grooves along the inside of the barrel to impart spin) and its associated Minié bullet (with a cylindrical head and hollow base), which, in theory, increased the killing range of the infantry from 100 to 300 or even 500 yards. The war also witnessed rapid developments in steamship technology that enabled the allies to resupply their armies faster than the Russians—without a railway network to the area—could resupply theirs; by around 1870 the comparative advantage of sea supply over land supply had been reversed, and with it much of British military tradition.[9] In many ways the most important development adopted at the time was the electric telegraph system and Samuel Morse's code, available across the English Channel in 1851. For the first time governments could maintain contact with—or override—their commanders in the field (as Napoleon III did repeatedly), and newspaper reporters could ensure their reports reached home only two days after the events—rather than the weeks it had taken in Nelson's day. However, the line between Balaclava and London was not complete until April 1855—that is after the horrendous winter that Nightingale and the British Army struggled through. Until that time battle reports still took weeks; for example, the Battle of Balaclava, which took place on 25 October 1854, was not reported in *The Times* until 14 November. On the other hand, because the British Parliament was in recess from 14 August to 12 December, the news was consistently dominated by the war and not by the usual political machinations (Kerr 1997a: 70).

Naturally, while the military sought to make use of any technical invention they could, they were less than impressed by innovations that appeared to undermine their control.[10] Henry Crabbe Robinson covered Wellington's campaign for *The Times*, but William Howard Russell, also of *The Times*, is often regarded as the first professional war correspondent, followed by Thomas Chenery from the same paper, Nicholas Woods of the *Morning Herald*, and J. A. Crowe of the *Illustrated London News* (which also sent six artists and boasted a circulation of 100,000 during the conflict) (Mulvihill 1997: 23). Like Wellington before him, Lord Raglan had little time for reporters, noting to his superiors that 'the enemy had no need of a secret service, all they had to do was read *The Times*' (quoted in Young and Jesser 1997: 23). In fact, Raglan delayed the post in both directions to ensure that his report of affairs reached London first and he was forewarned of impending trouble before anyone else. As Fred Dallas remarked about the strange postal system in operation:

You will scarcely believe that the mail has been in since Saturday morning, this being Monday night, and except Lord. R's own bag, not a single officer has yet received his letters! The mail has been wandering about and no one knows why. The postmaster tells us that every obstacle also has been put in the way of the mails going away from here and it is shrewdly suspected that Lord Raglan is at the bottom of it as he does not like our accounts getting to England, as soon as his.   (quoted in Pye 1997b: 111)

And, even if the military mail and newspaper correspondents could be controlled, there were still the 'TGs' or 'Travelling Gentlemen'—tourists who wandered over the battlefields at will (one of whom was given a medal for good conduct by mistake).[11] Nightingale was well aware of the power of the media and suggested after the Crimean War that one of the reasons for the failure of reforms in the army was 'the degree to which, in England, the newspapers influence people's opinion or rather talk' (quoted in Goldie 1997: 292). Unfortunately, she failed to alter her own strategy to suit such a philosophy and continued to be indignant that her portrayal of the 'facts' proved less efficacious than the media's construction of the 'news'. But, as governments came to recognize the power of the media, the freedom secured by Russell and colleagues in the Crimean War quickly evaporated.[12] After the Crimea, factual reporting was not allowed to hinder the war effort nor cast doubt upon military commanders. From then on, in the words of Senator Hiram Johnson in a speech to the US Senate in 1917: 'The first casualty when war comes is truth.'

But immediately after the Battle of Alma the consequences of the army's maladministration became clear, not just to the military victims but also to their families back in Britain. In the absence of any kind of anaesthetic, and without any candles or lamps, surgeons performed amputations by the hundreds but had no bandages to cover the bleeding stumps that remained. In his despatches from the front and the hospitals in the second week in October, 1854, Howard Russell, war correspondent of *The Times*, railed against the ineptitude of the authorities:

It is with feelings of surprise and anger that the public will learn that no sufficient preparations have been made for the care of the wounded. Not only are there not sufficient surgeons . . . not only are there no dressèrs and nurses . . . there is not even linen to make bandages . . . Not only are the men kept in some cases for a week, without the hand of a medical man coming near their wounds, not only are they left to expire in agony, unheeded and shaken off . . . (but) the men must die through the medical staff of the British Army having forgotten that old rags are necessary for the dressing of wounds.   (quoted in Woodham-Smith 1982: 134)[13]

Two weeks later, at the Charge of the Light Brigade on 25 October 1854, 110 soldiers died in one of the most (in)famous military actions of the war, the direct result of misunderstood orders in which Lord Cardigan and his 632 cavalrymen charged the 'wrong' guns. But far worse was to come, for within three months around 290 soldiers were dying every week in one of the most infamous military inactions of the war. Colin Campbell, an officer of the 46th Foot noted: 'The actual loss to the army of the Light Cavalry was not so important as has been imagined, as many horses would have died of starvation if they had not been killed then; and as for the men, we bury three times the number every week and think nothing of it' (quoted in Kerr 1997a: 71).

These men, along with cholera victims numbering 1,000 a week, were sent back from the Crimea to the Turkish town of Scutari (now Üsküdar), where a disused artillery barracks was turned—without any supplies or furniture of any kind—into an overflow Barrack Hospital when the General Hospital became full. Russell left little to the imagination as he detailed the conditions that British soldiers were experiencing in Scutari:

The dead laid out as they died, were laying side by side with the living and the latter presented a spectacle beyond all imagination. The commonest accessories of a hospital were wanting, there was not the least attention paid to decency or cleanliness—the stench was appalling . . . the sick appeared to be tended by the sick and the dying by the dying. (quoted in Young and Jesser 1997: 23)

To rub salt into the symbolic wounds that Russell opened up, he noted the superiority of the French army in surgeons, organization, supplies, and nurses. This was enough to stir even the most disinterested reader and the search for an instant scapegoat landed, paradoxically, at the doors of the one of the few politicians who had an interest in the sick: Sidney Herbert, Secretary *at* War (the Secretary *for* War was a different appointment and the division of responsibility was partly to blame for the ensuing chaos).

Responsibility for the health of the army was divided between the Principal Chief Medical Officer in the Crimea, Dr Hall, the Commissariat, under the Commissary-General, Mr Filder, a Peninsular veteran, who had three clerks, and the Purveyor's Department, under the Purveyor in Chief, Mr Ward, a 70-year-old veteran of the Peninsular War who had two clerks and three messenger boys. These three, Dr Hall, Mr Ward, and Mr Filder, had no authority to suggest changes in the system to Lord Raglan, the Commander-in-Chief, and, as Woodham-Smith (1982: 153) notes, 'A commissary officer did not rank as a gentleman, while the purveyor was despised even by the commissary'.

The division of responsibility between the Commissariat and the Purveyor was confused but basically split between the external focus of the Commissariat, who was responsible for purchasing and delivering the supplies needed by the army (principally food and fuel), and the internally focused Purveyor, who was responsible for cooking and distributing the food. The Purveyor had no control over the condition or quality of the supplies, while the Commissariat had no responsibility once the goods had been accepted by the Purveyor. The potential confusion was compounded by the problem of the sick and wounded, who could not eat normal rations. 'Medical comforts'—that is, food for invalids—remained the responsibility of the Purveyor. So confused did this system become that, when Filder testified before the Roebuck Committee the following year, he was unable to explain where the division of responsibility lay. But, though the medical authorities might look down upon the Purveyor with disdain, they could not afford to cross him: a doctor could prescribe a special diet for a patient—taking the responsibility for provisions from the Commissariat to the Purveyor—but if, for any reason, the Purveyor failed to provide the provisions, the doctor was powerless to do anything about it. Moreover, the Purveyor could supply only materials for which he was authorized through a system of warrants; anything not authorized through a warrant became the personal responsibility of the doctor requiring it and there was a pending lawsuit regarding exactly this kind of unauthorized expenditure (Woodham-Smith 1982: 154).

The system for ensuring strict administrative control over expenditure and the consumption of supplies demanded that everything had to be authorized by the signatures of two doctors, one of whom had to be the Senior Medical Officer. The duty surgeon was required to complete up to six different records of the material consumed by each patient every day, and a daily report on the state of the hospital was demanded by the Inspector-General. The consequence of this bureaucratic blitz was that Dr Menzies, Senior Medical Officer at the Barrack Hospital, spent his entire day filling in forms and seldom entered the wards at all (Woodham-Smith 1982: 156).

When Scutari Hospital was overwhelmed with casualties and cholera victims, Menzies was forced to open the Turkish Barracks as a second hospital, but it had been left empty and dilapidated. As a result, when he asked the Purveyor to organize the necessary equipment for the new hospital, the latter, naturally, filled in the appropriate forms and forwarded them to the Commissariat, who, naturally, returned the forms with the appropriate inscription 'None in store'. In fact, the system worked perfectly and all involved had done exactly as required, as became clear when the Roebuck Committee questioned Dr Menzies about the failure to provide clean shirts for the patients. Since, Dr Menzies claimed, he had requisitioned the shirts from the Purveyor in the manner required, the fact that no shirts arrived was not his concern. And, since the Purveyor argued, he had completed the appropriate warrant and passed these on to the Commissariat, his responsibility for the problem was also nil. Of course, the Commissariat had a cast-iron alibi: he had returned the forms with 'None in store' written on them in the required manner so everyone was happy—except the patients who still had no shirts nor any chance of ever getting any.

But there was more to this than simply mind-numbing stupidity. The British soldier, according to the traditionalist view, did not expect anything better and should not receive anything better. Since the average soldier was regarded as a drunken animal—'the scum of the earth',—as Wellington insisted—and would respond to discipline only if maintained in such a position, such luxuries as special food, clothing, and attention would be deleterious for the morale of the entire army. Ward, the Purveyor, told the Hospitals Commission that he was amazed at the luxury he had been asked to provide for the sick and wounded, since his own experience in the Peninsular War with Wellington was that they had not even bothered with beds in hospitals, let alone special comforts.

The Times, under the editorship of John Thadeus Delane, demanded that 'the daughters of England' should help the wounded in their hour of need. The Duke of Newcastle, Secretary of State for War, tried to find someone capable of directing and controlling a body of nurses for the Crimea but despaired at the likelihood (Trollope 1994: 82). Herbert was informed by the military authorities, in particular Dr Hall, Inspector General of Hospitals, that The Times was grossly exaggerating and that everything was well in the Crimea, but Herbert nevertheless told Lord Stratford de Redcliffe, British Ambassador to Turkey in Constantinople (now Istanbul), to purchase whatever was required to facilitate the care of the sick and wounded. He also wrote to Florence, on 15 October, asking her to take a party of nurses out to Turkey to help, noting that:

It would be impossible to carry about a large staff of female nurses with the Army in the field. But at Scutari, having now a fixed hospital, no military reason exists against their introduction . . . I receive numbers of offers from ladies to go out, but they are ladies who have no conception of what an hospital is, nor of the nature of its duties; and they would, when the time came, either recoil from their work or be entirely useless, and consequently what is worse—entirely in the way. Nor would these ladies probably ever understand the necessity, especially in a military hospital, of strict obedience to rule . . . There is but one person in England that I know of who would be capable of organizing and superintending such a scheme . . . Would you listen to the request to go and superintend the whole thing? You would, of course, have plenary authority over all the nurses, and I think I could secure you the fullest assistance and co-operation from the medical staff and you would also have an unlimited power in drawing on the Government for whatever you thought requisite for the success of your mission . . . If this succeeds, an enormous amount of good will be done now, and to persons deserving everything at our hands; and a prejudice will have been broken through, and a precedent established . . . If you were inclined to undertake this great work, would Mr and Mrs Nightingale give their consent?   (quoted in Goldie 1997: 23–6)

In fact, Florence had already made arrangements to do just this anyway, having acquired the approval of the Home Secretary, Lord Palmerston, and the Foreign Secretary, Lord Clarendon. She also cleared her trip with Dr Smith, Director of the Army Medical Service, who denied that anything was needed by the army but provided her with a letter of introduction to Dr Menzies, Chief Medical Officer at Scutari. Indeed, the general opinion of the army medics was that female nurses were an 'unwise indulgence unfavourable to medical discipline and to the recovery of the patients' (quoted in Woodham-Smith 1982: 159). Still, with Florence's powerful political backers it was unwise to parade their hostility.

When Florence first broached the idea to her family, Mrs Nightingale and Parthe were adamant that Florence should not go, but when the government asked for their permission their attitudes changed instantly and they gave every assistance to their newly famous daughter and sister. Her appointment, as 'Superintendent of the Female Nursing Establishment of the English General Hospitals in Turkey', was unanimously approved by the Cabinet and her authority was 'everything relating to the distribution of nurses, the hours of their attendance, their allotment to particular duties . . . subject of course to the sanction and approval of the chief medical officer'. This left much room for the subsequent disputes with the army authorities: was she restricted to Turkey or did the appointment include the Crimea as well? And what was the division of responsibilities between the medical officers and the superintendent of nurses?[14]

Expecting a flood of patriotic and experienced nurses to volunteer for the jobs, the London House of the Herberts became the selection headquarters but few came forward. Indeed, even the ones recruited seemed to be concerned more with the monetary rewards than any notion of valour or sacrifice.[15] Mary Stanley, on the selection committee, wrote to Liz Herbert afterwards that: 'All London was scoured for them . . . We felt ashamed to have in the house such women as came.

One alone expressed a wish to go for a good motive. Money was the only inducement' (quoted in Woodham-Smith 1982: 142).[16]

So, despite the inducement of double the average nurse's wage, on 21 October
1854 Florence set off for Turkey with just thirty-eight nurses—two short in the
quantity required but many more short in the quality hoped for. Fourteen of the
thirty-eight were already professional nurses and the remaining twenty-four
were members of various religious institutions: five catholic nuns from the con-
vent in Bermondsey, five catholic nuns from the orphanage in Norwood, eight
Anglican sisters known as the Sellonites, and six High Church sisters from St
John's House. Florence was less than enthusiastic about the utility of some of the
nuns: 'fit more for heaven than hospital, they flit about like angels without hands
among the patients and soothe their souls while they leave their bodies dirty and
neglected' (quoted in Woodham-Smith 1982: 145).

She was even less enamoured of various 'ladies' who arrived at Scutari to help
but could not bring themselves to touch the sick or wounded. All the nurses
signed a contract submitting themselves to the absolute control of Florence and
she warned them that 'misconduct' with the troops would lead to instant dismissal. After a trying voyage the party arrived at Constantinople and transferred
to the hospitals at Scutari through the barrack gateway—over which Florence
later insisted should have been inscribed: 'Abandon Hope All Ye Who Enter
Here.'

Scutari: 'Abandon Hope All Ye Who Enter Here'

Scutari, it turned out, was not a town close to Constantinople but
Constantinople's principal cemetery and barracks. There were few shops, except
drinking dens and brothels, and the place was frequently cut off from
Constantinople by the storms that swept the Bosphorus. On 5 November,
Nightingale entered the Barrack Hospital and found what she feared most: no
furniture, no medicines, no supplies, and hundreds of sick and wounded. She
quickly discovered that many of the supplies had been abandoned at the
embarkation point in Varna and that the individual packs of the wounded and
sick soldiers were often left in the Crimea. The consequence was that they arrived
without changes of clothes or eating utensils, but, since these were not within the
authorized warrants of the Purveyor, he refused to supply them; indeed, he
would have been held personally responsible for such an unauthorized expenditure. The precise state of the hospital was the source of contention from the very
first day. Dr Menzies wrote to Dr Hall on 8 December 1854 suggesting that
Nightingale was 'surprised at the regularity and comfort which appeared in every
one of our wards'. Indeed, after the war the Reverend Mother Bridgeman also
insisted that the hospital had been in a good condition when Nightingale arrived.
However, the Reverend Osborne, a friend of Herbert's, suggested the opposite
was true and completely agreed with Nightingale's own report (Goldie 1997:
33–4).

The forty women in the party were housed in six rooms (the equivalent space given over to a single major elsewhere in the hospital) and one of which still contained the body of a dead Russian.[17] Florence and Mrs Bracebridge slept in the water-closet room and the rest slept in the kitchen and the other four rooms. Altogether there were two beds, a few chairs but no tables and no food. Lord Stratford, the British Ambassador, who had lived in a palace in Constantinople for almost sixteen years and insisted on taking twenty-five servants and seventy tons of plate whenever he travelled away, had been authorized to purchase whatever was necessary to equip the hospitals but he had demurred. In fact, he visited the hospitals only once, when Florence dragged him in. Thus when Dr Menzies, alarmed at the slur on his character implied by the attacks in *The Times*, insisted that nothing was needed in Scutari, Lord Stratford informed Sidney Herbert that Menzies's view was correct. He even suggested that the public funds raised by *The Times* to help the wounded in Crimea be diverted to building a church in Constantinople. Yet the hospital did not even have an operating table. Not that the nurses made any difference, since the doctors refused to have anything to do with them and they remained unable to practise what they had come for, even though the hospital was hopelessly understaffed.

Florence decided that her best policy was to work within and not against the system and, since no arrangements had been agreed for the use of nurses, she insisted that the nurses remain in their rooms until official requests were made by the authorities for help. Indeed, she had little option, because she had no authority over the hospitals, only over the nurses. Ironically, then, she was persuaded by the army to adopt a policy of resource-inversion: she would wait until their maladministration got so bad that their own monopolization of control and consequential chaos would, with media help, force them to ask her for help. She divided the nurses up, with twenty-eight for the Barrack Hospital and ten for the General Hospital and waited—but not for long. On 8 November, four days after arriving at Scutari:

we had 1,715 sick and wounded in the Hospital (among whom 120 cholera patients), and 650 severely wounded in the other building called the General Hospital . . . when a message came to me to prepare for 510 wounded . . . we had but an hour's notice . . . we now have four miles of beds, and not eighteen inches apart . . . In all our corridor I think we have not an average of three limbs per man.   (quoted in Trollope 1994: 83)

Eventually, Florence managed to work her way into the hospital system through her control over the kitchen in the General Hospital. Food for the 2,500 patients here had been cooked in one of the thirteen giant coppers and consisted of a piece of meat tied up in a cloth and heated (since the water seldom boiled) until the 'cook'—an orderly and not a trained chef—decided to serve what was regarded by most as an inedible concoction. On the second night Florence cooked arrowroot soup and, with medical permission, distributed it to the troops. From then on, and at her own expense, the nurses' kitchen provided all the invalid food for the Barrack Hospital, but all of it was requisitioned and double signed by the medical authorities. As she wrote to Herbert in February 1855, looking back at her first few weeks, 'it is obvious that what I have done could not have been done, had I not worked with the medical Authorities and not in rivalry to them' (quoted in Goldie 1997: 88).

The British troops encamped at Balaclava had already been exposed to cholera, typhoid, dysentery, and scurvy, and now they had the Russians too. Raglan had chosen Balaclava as the base from which to attack Sebastopol because the harbour appeared so good, but it harboured more than just water in it and within days cholera spread through the troops. Worse was to follow, because the troops had very few supplies with them and no method of moving supplies should any arrive. When winter arrived and the Russians attacked on 25 October, the sick and wounded were taken off and transported to Scutari in their hundreds, where they began arriving on 9 November. Conditions were, if anything, worse in hospital than in the Crimea. With over 1,000 cases of acute diarrhoea, twenty chamber pots, and blocked waste pipes, the General Hospital soon became awash with excrement and alive with diseases: erysipelas, gangrene, cholera, dysentery, diarrhoea, typhoid, and scurvy turned the whole place into a death trap for anyone entering it. The cellar under the hospital, which was home to hundreds of women and children attached to the soldiers, was originally the channel for the effluent from above. However, as Lady Alicia Blackwood discovered (one of the few 'ladies' that Florence tolerated because she endeavoured to help rather than look on), the drainpipe had a dead baby wedged in it to limit the outflow (Trollope 1994: 84). Augustus Stafford, an MP on a private visit to Scutari, tried to persuade someone to unblock the waste pipes but nobody could be prevailed upon to take responsibility for it, since it appeared beyond anyone's official remit. He even offered to pay for the work himself, but could not find anyone to organize the work.[18]

By 14 November, just when it appeared that the situation could not possibly worsen, it did. A hurricane blew away many of the tents at Balaclava, including the hospital tents, and sank all the vessels in the harbour, including the *Prince*, which had just arrived with the stores that had been ordered. Five days later the *Avon* began taking the wounded on board in preparation for the trip to Scutari, but the ship remained where it was in Balaclava for three more weeks with the wounded on deck covered only by coats or a single blanket.[19] The strain was so great that the administration collapsed, with neither the Purveyor nor the Commissariat able to complete their beloved forms; the whole vast apparatus of forms and responsibilities, bedpans and amputations, was grinding to a halt. Even the washing of the wounded—considered a 'minor detail' by the Purveyor—was difficult, and Nightingale estimated that each casualty could look forward to a wash once every eighty days. It was, she noted, 'a sad joke that a large reward has been offered for anyone who is personally responsible, barring the Commandant' (quoted in Vicinus and Nergaard 1990: 88). *The Times* report of 23 December 1854 summed up the situation:

the noblest army ever sent from these shores has been sacrificed to the grossest mismanagement. Incompetence, lethargy, aristocratic hauteur, official indifference, favour, routine, perverseness and stupidity reign, revel and riot in the camp before Sebastopol, and in
the harbour of Balaclava, in the hospitals of Scutari and how much nearer home we do not
venture to say.   (quoted in Pye 1997b: 111)

At this point Florence offered to purchase whatever was needed with the money
she had brought with her (£30,000—about £1.8 million in contemporary terms,
raised from readers of The Times and the government) from local suppliers and,
with everything pre-ordered on official forms, signed by the requisite medical
officer, she, Mr Stafford, Mr Macdonald of The Times, and the Reverend
Osborne (a voluntary chaplain) ventured into Constantinople daily. With the
purchase of brushes the floors and giant urinal tubs were washed for the first
time; then some soldiers' wives were employed to wash the patients' clothes. By
December she had purchased the winter clothes that the army had forgotten to
issue to its troops, as well as eating utensils, operating tables, towels, bandages,
soap, and everything else necessary for a military hospital in a major war.[20]

When, in early December, Lord Raglan intimated that a further 500 casualties
were on their way, the hospitals were already overflowing and the only remaining option was to open the fourth wing of the Barracks, which had been badly
damaged by fire. Once again the Ambassador refused to provide the funds and
once again Florence used her own money and some from The Times fund to
employ 200 Turkish workers to repair the damage and prepare the wards. As she
wrote to Herbert, the Ambassador 'refuses blankets at 19 shillings, which the
French buy up at 20 shillings. The Ambassador refuses to obtain buildings which
the French instantly lay hold of' (quoted in Goldie 1997: 96).[21]

A handful of the nurses had proved themselves valuable to Miss Nightingale,
but the majority had not. Particularly galling was what she regarded as their lack
of discipline, such as attempting to provide nursing to suffering troops without
the express permission of the medical authorities and when direct physical contact with certain parts of the patients' bodies was (rightly, as far as Nightingale
was concerned) the job of the (male) orderlies and not the nurses. Or, worse, publicly denouncing the medical authorities, as Sister Elizabeth Wheeler, one of the
Sellonite Sisters, had done through The Times in December 1854. In the ensuing
inquiry in London Wheeler was asked to resign, but the damage had been done.
Nightingale had wanted to show the authorities what disciplined nurses could
achieve; instead they were demonstrating precisely the reasons why the army did
not want them around.

She was even more upset when it was announced in the same month that a further party of forty-six—including nine 'ladies', fifteen nuns, and twenty-two
nurses—led by Mary Stanley, her old colleague—was on its way to Scutari.
Given the difficulties Nightingale already faced, the prospect of yet more undis-
ciplined nurses, and, worse, the prospect of a group of fiercely independent Irish
nuns under Mother Bridgeman and a group of 'assistant ecclesiastics', filled her
with horror. Always a devout Christian, Florence had no time for what she

regarded as those who came to preach rather than to nurse, and even less time for the religious conflicts that would bedevil her future relations with the army authorities. She reacted furiously to Stanley Herbert, reminding him of his prior confirmation that no other group would be sent and offering her resignation. When the party arrived on 15 December 1854, Nightingale refused to accept them and demanded that they return—which they could not, since the party had already spent the £1,500 they came with—equivalent of £90,000—on the outward journey. The party was eventually put up by the Ambassador, where Mary Stanley insisted that the nurses clean for, and attend to, the 'ladies'.

As December turned into January the situation in the hospitals grew worse, with over 200 extra casualties a day arriving. With the Stanley party turning into a political fiasco, Nightingale eventually agreed that some of the existing nuns could be removed to make way for some of the Stanley party, but the compromise pleased no one. The outgoing nuns from Norwood left in tears and under protest, while the incoming nuns, under Mother Bridgeman (or the Reverend Brickbat, as Nightingale called her), refused to recognize the authority of Nightingale in nursing matters, or Father Cuffe, the existing Catholic priest, in spiritual matters. With the Protestant sisters fighting amongst themselves as well as the Catholic nuns, and all fighting each other and Miss Nightingale, it was little wonder that Florence was relieved when, at Lord Raglan's request, eleven Sellonite sisters went to the Balaclava General Hospital under Elizabeth Davis. Simultaneously, Mary Stanley, Mother Bridgeman, and ten nuns removed themselves to the hospital at Koulali (just to the north of Scutari)—which went on to have the highest mortality rate of any hospital in the war. However, the threat to the overall experiment in nursing for the army remained high.

In January 1855, the haemorrhaging of the British Army reached its peak and still no stores arrived. On the contrary, a shipload of cabbages was dumped in Balaclava harbour because nobody had ordered them. Similarly, the 20,000 lb. of lime juice that arrived in the middle of December remained untouched until February because no one had ordered it—yet, of 1,200 men that arrived at Scutari on 2 January, 85 per cent had acute scurvy. Even while men lay on the hospital floor without blankets, there were enough in store for each patient to have three, but, since the warrants did not allow for replacement blankets to be issued to soldiers who had lost them, they could not be used.

There were now more men in hospital in Scutari (12,000) than camped before Sebastopol (11,000), and Nightingale's workload and significance increased daily, yet she continued to write fortnightly to Sidney Herbert about the situation. In January she wrote two letters outlining plans for the complete reorganization—and centralization—of the hospitals at Scutari. But, despite all her efforts in cleaning up the hospitals, in January a cholera epidemic broke out killing not just hundreds of troops but four surgeons, three nurses, and the Purveyor himself. Nightingale frequently worked for twenty-four hours continuously and dressed wounds on her knees for eight hours at a time. Though anything but a soft-hearted romantic, she made it a rule that no man she was responsible for ever died on his own and in the winter of 1854–5 she personally witnessed around 2,000 deaths. A nurse accompanying her on her nightly rounds described the scene: 'It seemed an endless walk and one not easily forgotten. As we slowly passed along the silence was profound; very seldom did a moan or a cry from those deeply suffering fall on deaf ears.' The troops were equally enamoured of her presence: 'She was full of life and fun when she talked to us, especially if a man was a bit down hearted,' wrote one. 'What a comfort it was to see her pass even. She would speak to one and nod and smile to as many more; but she could not do it all you know. We lay there by hundreds; but we could kiss her shadow as it fell and lay our heads on the pillow again content,' wrote another (quoted in Woodham-Smith 1982: 206–7).[22]

Scutari had become the graveyard of the British army, not because of the fatal wounds inflicted by the Russians in battle but because of the insanitary conditions that prevailed. Indeed, Nightingale's primary preoccupation was not medicine but sanitary science.[23] More soldiers died of diseases that rampaged through the hospitals than those who remained untreated out of the hospitals. In January and February 1855 there were, on average, 2,349 men in hospital and during the same time there were 2,315 deaths. It was probably worse for the Turkish troops, who no longer had any hospitals since the British and French had moved in.

In January, John Arthur Roebuck, Radical MP for Sheffield, proposed a Select Committee to inquire into 'the condition of the army before Sebastopol'. It amounted to a vote of (no) confidence in Aberdeen's government, and, when the proposal was passed, Lord Aberdeen resigned—as indeed did Sidney Herbert—and Lord Palmerston became the Prime Minister. Since the latter was an old friend of the Nightingales, the change in Prime Minister did not augur badly for Florence, and, when another of her patrons, Lord Panmure, combined the two offices of the Secretary at War and the Secretary for War in one office, the future looked a little brighter. Panmure, with a little help from Florence and pressure from another of her friends, Lord Shaftesbury, ordered a Sanitary Commission to investigate the hospitals at Scutari and in the Crimea, and a Commission of Inquiry into the Supplies for the British Army in the Crimea (the McNeill and Tulloch Commission).

When Nightingale gave evidence to the Sanitary Commission, the extent of her knowledge of hospitals became apparent, for she said she had visited every hospital in London, Dublin, Edinburgh, and Paris, and many in the rest of Britain, Germany, and France. The Sanitary Commission discovered that the Barrack Hospital had been built over a completely inadequate drainage system, such that the entire building sat in what was little more than a giant cess pit. Worse, the water supply flowed through the carcass of a dead horse, while the open privies next to the water supply contained no less than 556 handcarts of rubbish, with twenty-six dead animals, including two dead horses (Woodham-Smith 1982: 205).

The mortality rate in Scutari in February 1855 was 43 per cent. By April it had declined to 11 per cent and by May to 5 per cent (I. B. Cohen 1984: 131). By the time the emergency had passed, in the spring of 1855, Florence was exhausted and the squabbles of the past returned, but nothing was to prepare her for her next engagement with the opposition in the form of the Chief of Medical Staff on the British Expeditionary Army: Dr John Hall.

Nightingale versus Hall

Hall joined the Army Medical Service in 1815, but had qualified as a doctor only thirty years later. He had a reputation as a martinet and had been associated with the death of a soldier given 150 lashes in Hounslow Barracks. He held no truck with chloroform and appears to have terrorized his subordinates through a complex system of confidential reports. He was not a willing member of the Crimea expedition but had failed to achieve a posting home from India. On arriving at Scutari in October 1854 he had pronounced the hospital fit for use and thereafter he stuck to his opinion, as did his subordinates.

In the teeth of both his and others' opposition, Nightingale opened a small reading room in Scutari and when she discovered how many soldiers were illiterate asked if she might—at her own expense—employ a schoolteacher. This idea was rejected vigorously by Lord William Paulet, then the Military Commandant, on the grounds that it would spoil 'the brutes' (quoted in Goldie 1997: 127). She even became an unofficial banker to the troops, who gave her money to send to their families at home—not trusting the military authorities to do the same. At one time she was handling £1,000 a month—almost £60,000 in contemporary terms. She wrote to Queen Victoria asking for her support to secure a proper scheme for remitting money home, though Lord Panmure pointed out that 'The soldier is not a remitting animal; all who are inclined to do so, do remit continually, but there are many so selfish and brutish, whose appetite is their God, and everything is offered up to satisfy its sensual longings.' However, remittance systems were established and £71,000 (around £4.2 million now) was sent home in the first six months of 1855 (Woodham-Smith 1982: 240).

When Paulet was replaced by General Storks, the official attitude to drunkenness also changed dramatically and it became a court-martial offence to be found drunk. Games and recreation rooms were opened and four teachers were employed. At last Scutari appeared to have been organized properly and Nightingale decided to go to Balaclava, where Dr Hall's own General Hospital and the tented Castle Hospital remained problems for her, both because of their higher mortality rates and because the nurses insisted on remaining independent of Nightingale's authority. This was especially the case with regards to the 'Free Gifts'—that is, parcels of gifts sent out by virtually every town in Britain to the troops—which included the new 'balaclavas' and 'cardigans'. The problem was that, although Nightingale ensured a rigidly egalitarian and openly administered distribution of these, she did not believe that the Balaclava hospitals did the same and was particularly concerned with the antics of Elizabeth Davis. When Nightingale arrived on 5 May 1855, exactly six months after arriving at Scutari, she was cold-shouldered by the authorities and within a few days was taken ill with 'Crimean Fever', possibly typhus. While recovering she was advised to return to Scutari and she was put on board the *Jura* by Dr Hadley, the Senior Medical Officer at the Castle Hospital and a close friend of Dr Hall. In fact the boat was not stopping at Scutari at all but heading directly back to England, and only the quick work of Mr Bracebridge prevented Nightingale from a premature exit from the area. She returned to Scutari on a private yacht and by July had recovered.

Meanwhile, Lord Raglan had died and been replaced by another veteran of the Peninsular War, the even less sympathetic General Simpson, who (rightly) said on hearing of his appointment: 'They must indeed be hard up when they appointed an old man like me' (quoted in Cherfas 1997a: 137). Yet, the end of the war was now in sight, with Sebastopol falling to the allies on 8 September 1855. Nevertheless, British troops had played only a minor part in the final assault and General Simpson was condemned for failing to secure an honourable part in the action for his troops. Nightingale then resolved to act in the best interests of the nursing experiment when it came to dealing with the rebel nuns. However, as she travelled to Balaclava to resolve the problems, *The Times* printed a lecture given by Mr Bracebridge in Coventry in which he attacked the army, the doctors, the purveyors, indeed, everyone except Miss Nightingale, who, he claimed, had resolved all the problems in the matter of a few days. Naturally, those whom Nightingale had intended to placate closed ranks against her, assuming she was the moving spirit behind the report. Hall was furious and so was Nightingale, for the report undermined all she had attempted to do over the last year. Hall told his officials to ignore her and made an official complaint when Nightingale's new invalid kitchen at the Castle Hospital failed to provide officers with toast for twenty-four hours. Despite the setbacks she had at last come to believe that she had achieved what she had set out to do. As she wrote in the official report: 'It is obvious that the experiment of sending nurses to the East has been eminently successful, and that the supplying (of) trained instruments to the hands of the Medical Officers has saved much valuable life and remedied many deficiencies' (quoted in Goldie 1997: 147).

Her satisfaction did not last long. When a new wave of cholera broke out in Scutari in November, she despaired. 'The victory is lost already', she wrote to Aunt Mai (quoted in Woodham-Smith 1982: 243). Even the French system, long regarded as superior to the British, cracked under the strain of another typhus and cholera outbreak, and within the first three months of 1856 53,000 French soldiers were admitted to hospital and 10,000 were never discharged alive (Cherfas 1997b: 175).

In December FitzGerald, the Chief Purveyor to the Crimea, and a long-time ally of Hall, compiled a 'Confidential Report on Nightingale', which accused her and her nurses of most crimes known to the army, in contrast to the nuns of Mother Bridgeman, who were regaled as the true heroines of the Crimea. It even accused Nightingale of seeking to maintain Miss Wear as Superintendent of the

General Hospital in the Crimea against the explicit wishes of Dr Hall, who knew of Miss Wear's failures. Yet this was a direct inversion of the truth, for it was Hall who had protected Miss Wear when Nightingale had tried to remove her in May 1855. She wrote to Colonel Lefroy on 28 January 1856 trying to make clear that the problem was not Hall's lack of concern for specific issues but the complete absence of any kind of system:

Again, I repeat, I say these things to you not to complain of Dr Hall, who is an able and efficient officer in many ways—and who, I think, has been justly provoked in many ways. Dr Hall is indefatigable in *detailed* work, and wants only a governing system to work under. But he is wholly incapable of originating one. And we have no system for *General* Hospitals, in time of war.   (quoted in Goldie 1997: 206)

In January 1856 the McNeill and Tulloch Commission into the Supply of the British Army confirmed what Nightingale had said all along: many of the deaths in the winter of 1854–5 (when, of course, she was directly involved) had been unnecessary and a direct or indirect consequence of blunders made by individuals and by an inept system. Yet almost every officer named in the report as in some way responsible for the disaster had promptly been promoted in February. Even Dr Hall received a KCB, or Knight of the Crimean Burial grounds, as Nightingale called it. Still, the report caused a storm of protest from the officers named and Panmure agreed to a Board of General Officers at Chelsea to evaluate it. Nightingale's response, evident in a letter to her mother, was caustic and revealing: 'When the people of England rise, as they did against the Corn-laws, about these late Promotions, I shall believe in them. But now, what can we expect other than more Sir John Halls, more Sir Richard Aireys, more Lord Cardigans? We are just where we were . . . Put not thy faith in people' (quoted in Goldie 1997: 208).

In February Mr FitzGerald refused to honour her bank drafts and refused to accept she had any authority in the Crimea, but Hall, sensing FitzGerald's report had gone too far, distanced himself from his former ally while maintaining his disregard of her request to bring nurses to the Crimean hospitals. Since her original authority had mentioned Turkey but not the Crimea, she obviously had no authority there. By the beginning of March she was exhausted, both physically because of her work and spiritually not only because she saw her work unravelling but also because the very people who had caused the problems were everywhere in ascendance again.

Yet back home the populace had taken Florence to their hearts; she was their new Joan of Arc, their 'Lady of the Lamp' (a term first used by the *London Illustrated News* in February 1855). Her 'shadow on the pillow' had acquired a cult status, as returning soldiers spoke of her endeavours on their behalf in contrast to the ineptitude and disinterest of the army. Just as Nelsonian memorabilia had flooded the country after the Nile and Trafalgar, so Nightingale cups, lamps, pictures, postcards, and songs flooded the country. At Sidney Herbert's instigation, a public meeting was held to consider how best to honour her work, and it decided to establish a 'Nightingale Fund' to promote the training of nurses. Even the army was asked to contribute a day's pay (one shilling for privates), and, though Hall refused, the equivalent of 216,000 soldiers provided a day's pay. By June 1856 the fund had attracted £45,000 (well over £2.5 million in contemporary terms) primarily from wealthy middle-class individuals (Baly 1997: 13–17).

Initially, Nightingale had little time to organize training through the fund and it was never intended that the fund should set up a permanent Nightingale Nursing School, since it was assumed that the need for nurse training was so obviously required that, once the fund had provided the seed-corn, it would be a self-sustaining system supported by public demand. Nightingale was overwhelmed and accepted control over the funding only because its destiny was, as yet, unclear in her mind. She claimed never to have read the newspapers that were sent out to her and thus it came as a surprise that she had become a celebrity back home (Woodham-Smith 1982: 252). But she was not interested in any heroic roles; indeed she was mortified by the possibility, and though this may have been an attractive personal aspect of her modesty, it prevented her from using her popularity to push the establishment further in the direction she hoped they would move.

On 10 March she received a letter from the now Sir John Hall asking her to bring ten nurses to the Crimea. It is not clear why Hall suddenly agreed to this, but the decision may have been prompted by the actions of Colonel Lefroy. Lefroy had been sent on a secret mission on behalf of Lord Panmure and had visited the hospitals in Scutari and the Crimea and informed Lord Panmure that Nightingale's perspective was correct and that Sir John Hall and his colleagues were doing everything in their power to discredit her. Lord Panmure was then persuaded to issue a General Order through Sir William Codrington—that is, an officially published order from the highest military authority in the country, which effectively and publicly censured Hall. It was published on 16 March and stated that, 'It appears to me that the medical authorities of the Army do not correctly comprehend Miss Nightingale's position as it has been officially recognized by me . . . Miss Nightingale is recognized by Her Majesty's Government as the General Superintendent of the Female Nursing Establishment of the military hospitals of the army . . .' (quoted in Goldie 1997: 229). Woodham-Smith (1982: 250) argues that this was, at last, a 'triumph. It was more than she had ever asked. It was a complete defeat for the Hall party, the Stanley party, the Salisbury party.' Indeed, it was a complete vindication of her position, but it had come too late to make any serious difference, because a peace conference in Paris had already declared an armistice.

Fitzgerald and Hall still managed to make her life as difficult as possible; she was refused any army rations for ten days and had to feed her nurses from her own pocket. But Fitzgerald had taken the feud too far and other doctors began to turn against him. Beatson from the General Hospital in Balaclava suggested that Fitzgerald 'even presumes to question the validity or authority of a requisition because a word is spelt differently from the accepted mode—although I do not consider him a competent philologist to decide such a point' (quoted in Goldie 1997: 243–4).

Eventually Hall abandoned Fitzgerald, yet the former remained opposed to Nightingale. Having found the General Hospital in Balaclava in a state of infestation, Nightingale and the Bermondsey nuns had spent three days cleaning it—only to have Hall report that they had turned a previously 'admirable' hospital into a 'disgusting state' (quoted in Woodham-Smith 1982: 252). But she was now devoted not just to nursing in general but to ordinary soldiers in the British Army in particular, whose courage in the face of enemy terror and official disinterest was a revelation to her. As she wrote to Parthe in March 1856:

I have never been able to join in the popular cry about the recklessness, sensuality, and helplessness of the soldiers. On the contrary I should say . . . that I have never seen so teachable and helpful a class as the Army generally. Give them opportunity promptly and securely to send money home and they will use it. Give them schools and lectures and they will come to them. Give them books and names and amusements and they will leave off drinking. Give them suffering and they will bear it. Give them work and they will do it. (quoted in Goldie 1997: 221)

The war ended officially on 27 April with the ratification of the Treaty of Paris. No mention was made of the rights of religious minorities, the Danube became an international waterway, and the Black Sea was deemed neutral; and Sebastopol, that city over which so many had died, remained as it was before the war—in Russian hands. Of the 98,700 British troops who went to the Crimea, only 5,500 (6 per cent) had died from wounds, while 17,600 (18 per cent) had died from disease, and, as ever, most of the casualties fell upon particular elements of the army. Despite their allegedly better administration, the French lost 24 per cent to disease and suffered 100,000 deaths in all, while the Russians may have lost as many as 500,000—half their army (Baly 1997: 7–8; Kerr 1997*b*: 178).

Florence knew that, for her and the British soldier, peace had come not too late but too soon—before any significant long-term reforms had been won:

As I stood on the Heights of Balaclava, and saw our ships in the harbour so gaily dressed with flags while we fired a salute in honour of peace . . . I said to myself, 'More Aireys and more Filders, more Cardigans, more Halls. We are in for it then all now and no hope of reform.' Believe me when I say that everything in the Army (in point of routine versus system) is just where it was eighteen months ago . . . In six months all these sufferings will be forgotten.   (quoted in Goldie 1997: 246–7)

She was right but she did not help her own cause. As the army embarked for home, so did her nurses, and she managed to find many of them work back home. She also forbade them from writing or publishing anything about their experiences. On 5 May Lord Ellesmere spoke of her in the House of Lords:

The angel of mercy still lingers to the last on the scene of her labours; but her mission is all but accomplished. Those long arcades of Scutari in which dying men sat up to catch the sound of her footsteps or the flutter of her dress, and fell back content to have seen her shadow as it passed, are now comparatively deserted. She may probably be thinking how to escape, as best she may on her return, the demonstrations of a nation's appreciation of the deeds and motives of Florence Nightingale.   (quoted in Woodham-Smith 1982: 255)

The Coldstream Guards, the Grenadiers, and the Fusiliers all offered to meet her wherever she landed, the Government offered to bring her back in a warship, the mayors of Folkestone and Dover vied with each other to be the first town to welcome her home, but she would hear none of it. In her own mind she was coming home a widow not a heroine: 'Oh my poor men, I am a bad mother to come home and leave you in your Crimean graves—73 per cent in 8 regiments in 6 months from disease alone—who thinks of that now?' (quoted in Woodham-Smith 1982: 256). She was distraught and wrote to Parthenope about the Chelsea Inquiry:

To me it is a melancholy sign of England's decay that a report, such as Colonel Tulloch's and Sir John McNeill's . . . should have failed . . . if they can do nothing, who can? . . . As for me I have no plans. If I live to return, what I should like to do, after a short visit home, would be to go to some foreign Hospital where my name has never been heard of and . . . work there as a nurse for a year. . . My health is too broken for a position of responsibility and power. (quoted in Goldie 1997: 267–8)

There was no great homecoming: she left Constantinople on 28 July with Aunt Mai, travelling incognito as Mrs and Miss Smith, and, when she reached the station in her home village on 7 August, she walked home alone.

Woodham-Smith (1982: 256–7) considers Nightingale's actions in the Crimea changed the image of the British soldier for ever: 'never again was [he] to be ranked as a drunken brute, the scum of the earth. He was now a symbol of courage, loyalty and endurance, not a disgrace but a source of pride.' Vicinus and Nergaard (1990: 158) are of the same opinion: 'She was to have a profound influence upon government health policies in regard to public sanitation, the army in India and the Army Medical Corps.' Similarly she transformed the status of nurses: 'never again would the picture of the nurse be a tipsy, promiscuous harridan. Miss Nightingale had stamped the profession of nurse with her own image . . . (but) she ended the Crimean War obsessed by a sense of failure. In fact, in the midst of the muddle and the filth, the agony and the defeats, she had brought about a revolution.' But in many ways her return to England marked the end of her successes and the beginning of her failures.

Post-Crimean Crises

By August 1856 Nightingale had decided that the blood of her 'children' must not be seen to have fallen for nought: 'I stand at the altar of the murdered men, and, while I live, I fight their cause' (quoted in Johnson 1996: 1). She wrote to Lord Panmure and Stanley Herbert pleading with them to take action to reform the army's health administration while the memories of the war were still strong, but for the most part politicians were on vacation and preferred to forget about the inglorious 'victory'. But her letters were as much for advice as demands, for, as she wrote to Colonel Lefroy:

What shall I say to Lord Panmure, to the Queen, and to Sir B Hawes? . . . Would it not be better for me to ask humbly and directly for a Female Nursing Dep't in the Army Hospitals

... or should I state boldly the whole case at first? ... I should ... much like to consult with you, whose opinion is necessarily so far better than mine, as to what reforms are desirable and what are practicable?   (quoted in Vicinus and Nergaard 1990: 160–1)

She became ill again as she fretted at the inaction around her, but she felt unable to initiate anything herself. As a woman and a heroine, she considered that anything from her would be seen by the military establishment as tainted. Even when various people asked her for recommendations, she refused to help, sensing that a trap was being laid to destroy her credibility. So great was her paranoia that she never made another significant public appearance or issued a public statement in the remaining fifty-four years of her life. Thus the one person who could have mobilized the public behind radical reform refused to do so because she suspected she could not achieve what a man could and because she regarded publicity-seeking as immoral and counterproductive. 'The buz-fuz about my name has done infinite harm. If only I could find a mouthpiece. If I could leave one man behind me ... who would work the question of reform I should be satisfied, because he would do it better than I' (quoted in Woodham-Smith 1982: 262).[24]

In fact, the establishment expected her to reveal the incompetence and disasters she had witnessed, and, as 'the voice of the people of the present' (as Dr Pincoff, a civilian doctor at Scutari, called her), she was in a formidable position. But she rejected this strategy and operated along the lines that had seemed to her to work in Scutari and before this at her Harley Street institution. She would demonstrate rationally to the authorities that she was right and that would suffice—despite the fact that this policy had not brought about the movement she desired. As a woman she felt that attacking the military authorities could not succeed; only working with them offered any hope. For the military authorities this played straight into their hands, because Nightingale's belief that her greatest strength was her command of the facts could do little harm to a culture long practised in disinformation and no longer under the media spotlight; they had effectively inverted the utility of her resources.

Parthe, noting that her sister's fanmail arrived in 'hail storms', was astonished at her behaviour: 'her indifference to praise ... is quite extraordinary' (quoted in Woodham-Smith 1982: 262). In the event it was Parthe who wrote the acknowledgement letters, since Florence refused. And it was not until Queen Victoria summoned her for her views on the Crimean War that Florence suddenly returned to the quest with a vengeance. She compiled reams of statistics on death rates, sickness, and diet and visited the Queen privately several times, certain that Victoria had persuaded the government that a Royal Commission to examine the problems had been accepted by her but aware that Victoria had little power to instigate one. Lord Panmure, the Secretary of State for War, did have such powers, and, after a meeting in November 1856 between Victoria, Panmure, and Nightingale, he agreed to her proposal. He also accepted her suggestion that the replacement for the Director General of the Army Medical Department, Dr Andrew Smith, who was retiring, should not be Sir John Hall.

With Sidney Herbert as the chair, the Royal Commission into the Health of the Army looked set to sweep away all the problems that Nightingale had faced.[25] But when February arrived without notification of the start of the Commission, she fell ill again with frustration, unable to appreciate the government's desire to avoid any increase in public expenditure on the army, least of all its health service. Her illness was probably also partly in response to the Report of the Chelsea Board, which had heard the appeal of the officers named in the McNeill and Tulloch Report and had, as Nightingale expected, cleared every single officer of any blame. Indeed, it blamed the entire catastrophe of the Crimea on a missing consignment of pressed hay!

Despite Panmure's assurances that the Commission would start soon and that she should provide a confidential report of her own experiences, she was very pessimistic in March. 'Lord Panmure', she wrote, 'has broken all his promises, defeated the Army Reformers at every point, simply by the principle of passive resistance, the most difficult of all resistances to overcome, the easiest of all games to play. I think our cause is lost' (quoted in Woodham-Smith 1982: 278). So discouraged was she that she appeared to alter her own rules of working with the authorities by threatening to publish her own report by late May 'unless there has been a fair and tangible pledge by that time for reform' (quoted in Woodham-Smith 1982: 279).

The threat, supported by public disquiet at the whitewashing of the Chelsea Board's exoneration of the five senior officers, worked and Palmerston was forced to honour McNeill with a KCB and Tulloch with membership of the Privy Council. Nightingale was ecstatic: 'Victory!' she wrote 'They have been borne to triumph on the arms of the people.' On 5 May 1857 the Royal Warrant was issued and the following week it began to hear evidence. It looked, at last, as though Nightingale's approach had borne fruit: she had led the way to change. Her own submission to the Commission emerged as the 1,000-page report: 'Notes on Matters Affecting the Health, Efficiency and Hospital Administration of the British Army'. It was never published, for it put the blame squarely on the shoulders of those responsible, the army, the military health authorities, and the government.

Those who had become the Reformers of the British Army—Nightingale, Herbert, and Dr Sutherland (who called himself 'one of her wives')—now christened themselves the 'band of brothers'. They worked under Florence, their 'Commander-in-Chief', from the Burlington Hotel—'the little war office'—where they shared meals at their 'mess' and planned their 'campaigns' against the traditionalists. The collection of material for the commission went extremely well, though Nightingale refused to appear in person and submitted evidence only in written form—specifically, reams of tables, figures, and comparative statistics proving to the Commission that the hospitals had killed more men than the war and linking the health of the army to its efficiency as a fighting system. Plans for diets, for hospital design, construction, and administration, education, and many other elements of army life were detailed, but her main target was not the individuals responsible for the Crimean débâcle but the system that allowed it to occur. Indeed, it was her evidence of the state of the peacetime army that jolted the reader more than any more revelations about the Crimean War. She argued that the peacetime army had a mortality rate twice that of the civilian population and this was despite that fact that the army recruited only the fittest young men.[26] Eventually, the report of the Commission was published in November 1857, but, as she reminded herself on numerous occasions, 'Reports are not self-executive.' In other words, writing the report was only the first in a long series of battles to achieve victory in the war against the army traditionalists.

Nightingale's principled approach mirrored that which had proved so successful in the Crimea. But the opposition was no longer the same: rather than using the resources of the army and the political establishment to undermine their own claims to efficiency, she was trying to meet them head on—and failing signally. While the press in the Crimea had monopolized popular interest with their descriptions of events, battles, and catastrophes, the news value of 1,000 pages of statistics was, at best, marginal, and at worst never able to compete directly with the establishment.

On 7 August, Herbert wrote to Panmure warning him about the contents of the report and suggesting that the government would do well to start the reform procedures before the report came out. To that effect he suggested following Nightingale's recommendations, namely that four sub-commissions be started, looking at: sanitary order in the barracks; the inauguration of a Statistical Department for the army (she had recently become a Fellow of the Royal Statistical Society); the beginnings of an Army Medical School; and the reconstruction of the Army Medical Department. But the strain was too much for Nightingale and she collapsed again on August 11, assuming, once more, that she was about to die. She was not, but she used her illness to protect herself and her work, for each time her mother or sister arrived Florence fell ill until the doctor informed her family that for her own survival she must be left alone.

Despite her illness Florence toiled away all day on getting the sub-commissions ready for work, but Panmure, while recognizing the depth of public support behind the Reformers, was also aware of the power of the Traditionalists to obstruct any change and to bring his government down. Recognizing the danger, Nightingale at last developed a campaign to mobilize the public through the press and she persuaded Herbert, Lord Stanley, Edwin Chadwick, and Henry Reeve, the editor of the *Edinburgh Review*, to write and publish favourable material. Nightingale herself published an unsigned pamphlet entitled *Mortality in the British Army*, which she sent to every individual of authority she could think of, adding notes such as: 'This is confidential . . . please do not leave it about,' thus ensuring maximum publicity. In the publication she developed what she called a 'Polar Area' diagram or 'coxcomb' (pie chart) to illustrate the statistics of mortality and illness and not only popularized the material but, in Audain's view (1998: 1) 'revolutionized the idea that social phenomena could be objectively measured and subjected to mathematical analysis'. Fig. 4.2 is a representation of

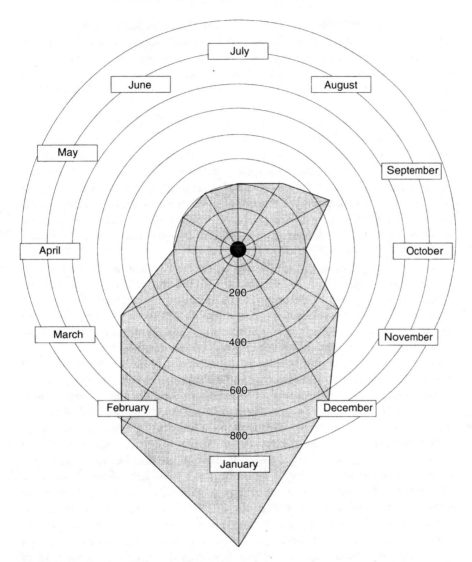

Fig. 4.2. Polar area or coxcomb of mortality in the army in the East, April 1854–May 1856

Note: Annual rate per 1,000; inner black circle represents mortality rate of Manchester.
Source: Reconstructed from the original (Nightingale 1858).

an original from the report (in Goldie 1997: 94). Yet, despite her belief in the utility of 'facts' to persuade others to act, she had previously accepted that 'facts'
were not always reliable. As she wrote to Lefroy in April 1856: 'C.J. Fox said,
"No, don't read me history. For that I *know* is false." I have learnt to say, "No
don't show me Returns. For those I know (are not false, but) give a false impression" ' (quoted in Goldie 1997: 94).[27]

By December 1857 she had got her way and Panmure had agreed to the four sub-commissions. But in February 1858 Palmerston's government fell, and with it Panmure and, by way of retirement, Dr Andrew Smith, Director General of Medical Department of the British Army. Next in line was her old Crimean enemy, Sir John Hall, but Nightingale ensured that Alexander, not Hall, replaced Smith.

Everything—at long last—seemed to be moving in her direction and she published her *Subsidiary Notes as to the Introduction of Female Nursing in Military Hospitals in War and Peace* in 1858. This was to be the basis of the great reform in nursing that she so desperately sought, but it was never enacted. She had belatedly recognized the power of the press and the critical significance of mobilizing popular support to undermine the establishment; but it was too late, for the favourable tide soon ebbed. The problems began with the Indian Mutiny, or what had recently become known as the War of Independence, which broke out in early 1857 (L. James 1997: 233–98).

Nightingale wanted to go to India and repeat her Crimean work, but Herbert insisted that she stayed put and continued with the work she had started. Then Herbert himself fell ill in November 1858 with the beginnings of his fatal kidney problems, but Nightingale was unsympathetic. Their work was too important for either of them to worry about their personal health; after all she would die soon anyway, so why should his minor problems impede them?

But their work was simply eclipsed by events in India, as the majority of infantry regiments in Bengal mutinied and the press had a field day reporting the hideous massacres of British troops and civilians, and the equally horrendous reprisals by British troops. Even so almost 9,000 of the 11,000 British deaths were the results of disease and illness rather than the attacks of the mutineers. But the reconstruction of events by the press ensured that 'Christian martyrdom' and heroism against the 'animalistic' native population became the norm. The xenophobic approach was no doubt aided by the speed with which the mutiny was successfully put down, allaying any remaining public concern over the viability and utility of the army (Burroughs 1994: 185–6). Thus one of the greatest resources of the army—its military power—was no longer available to Nightingale for her own purposes, because that window of opportunity had been shut by the mutiny and it successful termination by the British. To many readers of *The Times* on 8 July 1857 this was just as well, because, in the words of one retired officer, 'without India, Britain would subside into a third rate state' (quoted in L. James 1997: 278). Three days later 20,000 letters, many of them private, arrived from India and many quickly found their way into the national and provincial press. Thackeray insisted that few consumers of these dire revelations knew much about India, but this was less relevant than the pre-existing tradition of reporting the area in the most lurid terms. By the summer of 1857 the mutiny was the consistent headline story in all major British newspapers and in true Dickensian fashion the grisly developments were relayed in weekly instalments. Dickens himself added fuel to the fire: 'I wish I were commander-in-chief in

India,' he wrote on 4 October; 'I should do my utmost to exterminate the Race upon whom the stain of the late cruelties rested' (quoted in L. James 1997: 283).

Few stood against the rabid tide of hate for the mutineers and the patriotic flood of support for the suddenly heroic army. The *Manchester Guardian* demanded vengeance, Christina Rossetti and Tennyson wrote poems, the *London Illustrated News* had a field day with its pictures of hangings and mutineers being tied to cannons and blown apart. Edward Hopley and Joseph Noel . Paton painted scenes from imaginary events and even the Church was swept up in the fever: the Bishop of Carlisle demanded 'severe punishments', while Dr Cumming lashed out at those guilty of 'whining sentimentalism'. The rape of British women in particular stimulated a frenzy of repulsion at home—even though there was no substantiated evidence that mass rape had occurred. So soon after the blunders of the Crimea, it was probably inevitable that the military would be under investigation again, but this time there was a different scapegoat: the soon-to-be-removed East India Company. Thus the probability that the mutiny had been against the British in general and the British army in particular was conveniently displaced by the 'fact' that the conflict had really been between the company and its Indian troops (L. James 1997: 286–95). But the damage had been done to Nightingale's campaign, because now the victorious British army had put the world back the way it was supposed to be. After all, as the *Edinburgh Review* proclaimed, was it not 'the glorious destiny of England to govern, to civilize, to educate and to improve the innumerable tribes and races whom Providence had placed beneath her sceptre' (quoted in L. James 1997: 294). Moreover, the Indian Mutiny had demonstrated beyond debate—at least to most of the British decision-makers—that assuming such people could be civilized quickly with kindness was erroneous, for only the stern hand of discipline had saved a worse catastrophe. The same logic applied to the British army's own soldiers—kindness did them no good.

When a commission was set up to investigate the health of the army in India in May 1859, Herbert was invited to chair it and, within a month, to become the Secretary of State for War in the new Palmerston government. Florence, on discovering that there were no existing records on the health of the troops in India, set to work drafting a 'Circular of Enquiry'. This was sent to so many respondents in India that the returns filled an entire room and resulted in a 1,000-page report and her *Observations by Miss Nightingale* published in 1862. The Reformers believed that most of the cards were stacked neatly in their favour, but they made the mistake of taking the cards at face value, when the game was much more like poker than 'happy families'. With consummate ease the officials of the War Office turned Nightingale's obsession with working through the system against her and they began a long campaign of what Clausewitz would have recognized as 'friction'. Minutes of the meetings went missing or were delayed by every possible means. Minutes concerning the diet of the War Office cat seemed to take priority over those of its soldiers, and after seventeen months' discussions there was still no agreement on whether the cat should live on rats she caught or whether the War Office should provide milk for her—in which case, how much and at what cost? Even when Herbert himself took over at the War Office, the delays continued: the Army Medical School was given a list of appointments to its staff, but their salaries were not paid; building land for the School was bought, but no buildings appeared. When the Reformers forced the day by recruiting students and setting an opening date in 1860, the first ten students found empty buildings. And, since Gladstone had taken over as Chancellor of the Exchequer, the funding for any public work, least of all military work, became the last priority on the Treasury's list.

Still Nightingale soldiered on, issuing *Notes on Hospitals* in 1859, in which she described the administrative chaos of the civilian hospitals as very close in kind to that pervading those in the military; it was not individuals who were at fault, it was the system; or, rather, the lack of system. The results of the existing confusion drove her to establish what to our eyes may seem a bizarre first principle: 'It may seem a strange principle to enunciate as the very first requirement in a Hospital that it should do the sick no harm' (quoted in Johnson 1996: 1).[28] The problem lay in the fabric of the buildings and the ignorance of the professionals: poor ventilation, poor hygiene, and poor nursing generated 'hospital diseases' that killed more than did the diseases the patients entered with.[29] Hospitals did not even use the same classification of diseases, so that no comparison could be made between them. With her own single classification scheme, plus its attendant model statistical form, all this was soon to be put right.

She also published *Notes on Nursing*, and, having decided that a Training School for Nurses could not operate independently of the existing hospitals, persuaded St Thomas's Infirmary to host it, against strong internal and external opposition. Most of this came from those who considered training an unnecessary and rather 'forward' issue. The consequence was that the first batch of Nightingale nurses—who were intended to act as trainers for other nurses—was chosen on the basis of criteria so strict that only fifteen were taken on in 1860, the first year. They were provided with uniforms, food, and lodging plus £10 per annum for their year-long training period. They were also required to complete a diary, to attend lectures, and to submit to a monthly report by Mrs Wardroper, the Matron of St Thomas's, where their moral as well as technical record was perused in considerable detail.[30]

Despite, or perhaps because of, this, the school was, in Woodham-Smith's view (who follows Cook's 1913 analysis) a success, and a Training School for Midwives was opened at King's College Hospital the following year. However, the Midwifery School collapsed within two years, as did Herbert's health. In fact, the early record of the Nursing School was not especially promising: four were dismissed, one died, and only four nurses survived to their second year. After ten years only 196 had entered the school, some just as observers, and sixty-four of these had been dismissed (five for insobriety) (Baly 1997: 42, 214).

By the spring of 1860 Herbert had been told that, unless he gave up the War Office, he would die. Nightingale, having herself 'proved' that death could be postponed through hard work, demanded that he continue his work with her. By January 1861 his plan for War Office reorganization lay ready for execution, but he was too ill to do much with it, much to Nightingale's fury, for he had 'not one cardinal symptom of confirmed disease'. In June he collapsed but again she railed at him for his ruination of their work when he still had 'many years of usefulness' (quoted in Woodham-Smith 1982: 366). Herbert died on 2 August 1861 and Nightingale collapsed and questioned her own faith—though not her guilt, for how could God 'involve the misfortune, moral and physical, of five hundred thousand men' when all he had to do was 'set aside a few trifling physical laws to save him' (quoted in Woodham-Smith 1982: 369).

Thirty years later, little of the temporary gains that Nightingale and Herbert had secured still existed, as the scandals of fever-ridden barracks in Dublin demonstrated, and it was this embarrassment not their labour that led to the barrack building programme in the 1890s (Spiers 1994: 190). As Woodham-Smith (1982: 372) concludes about Herbert's term of office, it 'was a period of great and promising beginnings fated to come to almost nothing'. But they had at least established that, in principle, the health of the soldier was as important as his sickness. They had also initiated the beginnings of the statistical branch of the Army Medical Department, an Army Medical School, a Sanitary Code, a new military hospital at Woolwich, and recreational rooms for soldiers in barracks. But Nightingale saw many of these and other improvements unravel almost as soon as Herbert was dead. As she wrote to Harriet Martineau on 14 September 1861: 'Alas! Seven years ago this month I have fought the good fight with the War Office. AND LOST IT. Every day his decisions . . . his judgements are over-thrown . . . We have lost the battle. Now all is over . . . except desperate guerrilla warfare. I am worn out and cannot go on long' (quoted in Woodham-Smith 1982: 377–9).

In 1865 the temporary Barrack and Hospital Commission, which she had set up with Herbert, became the standing Barrack and Hospital Commission; Nightingale was sent many of the papers to that committee, and commented on them, but she did not attend the meetings (Woodham-Smith 1982: 402). Nightingale's most vigorous campaign was reserved for the Contagious Diseases Act that primarily concerned prostitution and venereal diseases. The number of prostitutes in mid-Victorian England seems to vary with the author, but any-where between 30,000 and 380,000 were involved in what the contemporary establishment regarded as 'the great social evil'. With syphilis on the increase, the Medical Department recommended the licensing and inspection of prostitutes as the only practical response, but to Nightingale this, once again, treated the disease but not the cause. It was a health problem not a medical problem in her mind, hence the resolution related to the living conditions of the soldiers. Indeed, since the main cause of death, as far as Nightingale was concerned, was the environment not the medical condition of the body, she wanted nurses to be students of sanitation not disciples of disease. As she was fond of saying: 'There are no specific diseases' (Briggs 1994: 267). She was, therefore, very interested in the statistical work of Quetelet, who asserted that behaviour could be explained by—and therefore changed through—the conditions within which humans found themselves. If the conditions were healthy, then the people would be healthy. Consequently, if the conditions were improved, the reliance by soldiers on prostitutes would decrease and with it venereal disease. But, despite her copious reams of statistics that 'proved' the prostitute licensing system, already used by the French army, did not work, and her suggestion that prostitutes who survived five years with the army should not be 'policed' but given 'good service pensions', her campaign failed. In 1864 the Contagious Diseases Act became law and she responded, characteristically, saying that the War Office 'deserved the Victoria Cross for their cool intrepidity in the face of the facts'.

From about this time Nightingale became even more of a recluse. She had previously refused to see anyone except individually and with a prior appointment—even if she had invited the said person as a guest to her house.[31] Now she declined to see her remaining friends too and allowed a masseur to massage her rheumatic back only on condition that no noise and no word resulted. Even when she invited Clarkey to stay, she wrote to her (in the same house), regretting that she would not be able to find time to meet her. The Queen of Holland tried to make an appointment but was refused; the only people she saw were those directly involved in her work, for 'I cannot live to work unless I give up all that makes life pleasant' (quoted in Woodham-Smith 1982: 430). Only an occasional niece or nephew and the Oxford academic Jowett, with whom she had a long friendship almost wholly by letter, seem to have escaped the anti-intruder system.[32]

By 1869 her last hopes of political influence disappeared with the accession of Gladstone, whose own Christian morality led him to regard a standing army as an immoral institution that was progressively unnecessary amongst civilized nations and thus unworthy of either attention or resources.

In 1871 there had been moves to allow women to train as doctors, much to Nightingale's distress, for, in her eyes, the problem lay in the absence of nurses and midwives not in the absence of doctors. Since she had never found her gender a hindrance to her own career, she could not understand why others did, nor why they sought equal rights to vote when voting was, to her at least, an irrelevancy. And, with pauperism, the workhouse, and the starving on the streets of Britain, 'does Mr Mill really believe that the giving of any woman a vote will lead to the removal of even the least of these evils?' (quoted in Woodham-Smith 1982: 487–8).

Looking after her increasingly wayward mother drove Nightingale to despair and one after another all her friends and elder relations died. Considering herself a failure, she was mystified by her survival: what was God's purpose in keeping her alive? Thus 'by 1879 she had reached a depth of despair; progress in India was at a standstill; out of the effort and sacrifice of twenty years nothing had been achieved . . . No commission had been set up on irrigation, sanitary works recommended more than fifteen years ago had not even been begun. Reform in India had failed' (Woodham-Smith 1982: 546).

It had also failed in the army.[33] A Commission of Inquiry in 1882, another in 1890, and the subsequent Boer War eventually led to the formation of the Queen Alexandra Imperial Nursing Corps and the reorganization of the Army Medical Department into the Royal Army Medical Corps. But, as Baly suggests: 'Miss Nightingale and the Fund were never successful in establishing a military nursing service on the lines laid down in the *Subsidiary Notes*.' And one of the main reasons was that Nightingale continued to insist that nurses should report to their superintendent in medical matters but the army refused to have anyone within its ranks that was not subordinate to military command. As she herself noted in a letter to Mrs Herbert in November 1855: 'The real grievance against us is that we are independent of promotion and therefore of the displeasure of our chiefs—that we have prospects to injure—and that, although subordinate to the Medical Chiefs in office, we are superior to them in influence and in the chance of being heard at home. It is an anomalous position' (quoted in Goldie 1997: 179). Paradoxically, then, despite Nightingale's insistence on working within the system (which included political lobbying), she failed to recognize that the system would not work with her, and it did not reform along her suggested lines until the First World War (Baly 1997: 117).

By now her influence on the government was at its lowest ebb and she turned back to the workings of the Nightingale Training School, which had had some successes and was established in New Zealand, Canada, and Australia, but was in urgent need of reorganization at home—so urgent that she made her *first* visit there in 1882. She was especially keen that her twin concern for the technical *and* the moral side of nursing must be continued and she managed to retain an interest in almost all the new recruits, forever searching for the combination of middle-class education—but not 'lady nurses'—and working-class effort (Baly 1997: 12).

She also reactivated her concern for the state of military hospitals when Mrs Hawthorn, the wife of a colonel in the Royal Engineers and cousin of General Gordon, alerted her to continuing abuse of military patients by their orderlies. A Committee of Inquiry accepted that orderlies were habitually drunk, ate the patients' food, and did little for the sick, but, despite the anodyne suggestion that 'improvements were necessary', nothing happened. Moreover, when the military campaign in Egypt began in 1882, Nightingale reported that it was just like the Crimea again: not enough supplies, those that existed were in the wrong place, too little medical equipment, the wrong uniforms for the climate, poor cooking arrangements, and a much larger proportion of casualties through sickness than through military action. For all the reorganization that had occurred since the Crimea, the emphasis had been on making economies not making efficiencies. Once more Nightingale rolled into action for the second Committee of Inquiry. Once more the Queen gave her backing to the suggested reforms and once more the army reported that all the recommendations had been carried out, but they were not.

From then on her entire life was spent in her bedroom in South Street, but she still managed minor successes: in 1896 she intervened on behalf of troops in Hong

Kong, whose barracks had been the source of bubonic plague. She still remained a difficult patient and, despite being almost blind, insisted that, after being tucked up in bed at night by her nurse, she would get out of bed and tuck the nurse in (Baly 1997: 12).

In 1899 800 women nurses of the Army Nursing Service Reserve were sent out to South Africa to find, once again, that Nightingale's efforts with the army had achieved little. The description of Number 11 Field Hospital by Sister X replicates that of Florence in Scutari: ' no linen of any sort . . . no pillows except flat straw bolsters . . . rows of white and yellow boned, hollow eyed men were lying or siting up in their beds' (quoted in Trollope 1994: 98).

By the end of the Boer War (in which 66 per cent of the British army's deaths were due to disease rather than combat) the situation had, at last, begun to change; the Army Nursing Service was reorganized and the establishment's approval for women nurses in military hospitals was established through the Queen Alexandra's Imperial Military Nursing Service in 1902. By then Nightingale was not always aware of her surroundings, as blindness became total and her memory began to fail, but it was not until 1906—when she was 86—that the India Office stopped sending her official papers on sanitation. In 1907 she was awarded the Order of Merit by King Edward VII, but it is unclear whether she knew what was being awarded. By 1910, the jubilee of the foundation of the Nightingale Training School, there were over 1,000 such training schools in the USA alone, but Nightingale was probably unaware of it by then; she no longer spoke and died in her sleep on 13 August (Woodham-Smith 1982: 593). She refused to be buried in Westminster Abbey and was buried in East Wellow.

Analysis

The Philosophical Arts: Identity

Nightingale's personal identity was clearly related to a determined stand against the mores of the society into which she was born; it was, in effect, a mirror-image of the traditional Victorian model for middle-class women. But she also assumed that she could achieve protection for 'her' soldiers by simply holding a mirror up to their appalling conditions. What she failed to recognize was that identities— including her own—were as much a product of myth and mystery as of truth. For all her efforts, the identification of the British soldier as anything other than Wellington's 'scum of the earth' was inordinately difficult to challenge, let alone change. This was particularly so in the context of war and mutiny, when the first victim was always going to be truth.

Ironically, she served her soldiers best when she was directly involved in saving them, for this left others to present and represent their identities back home in the media. And when the 'other' was either the incompetent army authorities or the 'barbarian' Russians, then the poor bloody infantry could rely on a sympathetic reading back home. But when Nightingale herself returned home, her own refusal to exploit her new identity as national heroine and the eruption of the Indian Mutiny destabilized the fragile movement for change within the army and allowed the traditionalists to maintain the status quo. In effect, Nightingale eventually lost the battle of identity to the army establishment because she assumed the first phase of victory was merely a reflection of reality. It was not; it was a construction of reality.

At the height of her unwanted fame an entirely new icon industry erupted, cast in her image, rather like that which trailed behind Princess Diana. And, as with Diana, the 'good causes' that Nightingale coveted were temporarily carried forward on a surge of public support, and the identities of the common soldier and the hospital nurse were temporarily lifted out of the gutter, within which they had lain for years. But the Angel of Mercy had long since abandoned any interest in personal vanity and she was unable to disentangle the personal adoration from the political power that was derived from it. Probably the only person who could have kept the soldier and the nurse from slipping back into the gutter that she had temporarily saved them from was Nightingale, but she interpreted her situation as one where private guilt prevailed over the social advancement of the causes that were so close to her own identity and her heart. In sum, the crisis of her own identity inhibited her from identifying the crisis that, with judicious exploitation, could have given her 'children' the protection they so desperately needed. Once she had returned home and once the crowd had drifted away from the theatre that was the Crimean War, her reliance on rational facts and statistics was never going to engage the public and seldom dented the establishment's armour.

The Fine Arts: Strategic Vision

In contrast, Nightingale's strategic vision in the Crimea was relatively clear and potentially achievable—it was, in short, a concrete utopia. That vision was the elimination of unnecessary deaths amongst the army—unnecessary being those caused by poor medical facilities and military inaction rather than those caused by direct hostile action. The army, in contrast, was completely focused on defeating the Russians—but it had neither the resources nor the skills to achieve this and this strategic failure made Nightingale's vision even more important as a consequence.

When she returned to England, the strategic vision did not alter—she merely wanted to extend the goal into the future to prevent any more soldiers dying from military incompetence and she wanted to extend the medical—or rather health—principles into civilian life. But the army's strategic objective had radically altered. In the Crimea it had sought (and in reality had failed) to defeat the Russians; in England the army was involved in self-protection and damage-limitation exercises. For that role it was remarkably well equipped and positioned and wheeled out all its prodigious network of supporters to forestall any attempt at radical reform.

In sum, and rather like the case of the naval mutinies, it was not the strategic vision of the 'rebels' that changed, it was the strategic vision of the authorities;

they had learned the lessons of strategy formulation more quickly and more comprehensively than their challengers.

Nightingale also failed at home because her visions were often abstract utopias. For example, her plans to modernize India's water and sewage systems were probably very astute as examples of what *could* and *should* be done if the British government could muster the political will and the economic resources for it, but this was *never* a remote possibility. And much the same can be said of her visions to modernize the army medical services and restructure the civilian health services. She may have been right in what was necessary to achieve these, but the connection between vision and will was never strong, least of all when no crisis appeared to bring the nation's health service—such as it existed—to its knees. Nor was she likely to succeed in India when the last thing the British public were interested in doing was funding improvements to a country few Britons believed worthy of improving. Nightingale was certainly imaginative in *what* could and should be done—but *how* these things could be achieved was often beyond her.

The Martial Arts: Organization Tactics

Nightingale's concern that the organizational system, not the individuals, was the problem was very probably correct, but the focus of the newspapers—and often therefore the establishment—was upon the identity of the scapegoats required for ritual humiliation. In the Crimea public sympathy for the soldier was whipped up into a frenzy by the papers but, despite Nightingale's concerns, was allowed to misdirect the focus onto the effect not the cause of the problem. The cause of the problem was the institutionalized inertia and the inability of the government to change the military establishment; the effect of this was to allow incompetent individuals free rein and little responsibility. Worse, it allowed people to prosper at the expense of the soldier. Either by default or by shrewd tactical awareness, Nightingale refused to engage in a war of attrition with the army that she believed she could not win. As a consequence she waited for the army to ask for her help and, in its blind adherence to tradition, it did not ask her until it became a national scandal, thanks to the media reporting of the medical chaos. Thus the army's resources were mobilized against themselves, for the more they kept Nightingale at arm's length the worse the situation and the embarrassment became.

But back home the opposite occurred, for Nightingale missed the opportunity to mobilize the public outrage into a mass movement for change. This was partly because she thought the public incapable of such action and partly because the army then recovered and neutralized her barrage of facts and reports by their astute use of delaying tactics. Partly it was also the result of the deflection of public hostility onto the backs of the East India Company and the Indian mutineers. From then on Nightingale responded with a campaign of attrition that was never going to work; she simply did not have the resources for it.

Nightingale's refusal to take an overt role in maintaining and channelling public outrage against the military establishment was deeply rooted in her belief that working within—not against—the system was the only way to succeed. Thus, rather than focus the public's mind—which she regarded as 'untrustworthy'—on the systemic problems, she chose to focus the government's mind instead. The result was to relapse into the same institutional quagmire that had generated the problem in the first place. Public outrage *may* have coerced the government into taking on the military establishment, but reams of facts, however rational and compelling, were no match for ranks of privilege.

The public outrage was directly stimulated and massaged by the newspapers not by any political party or individual (like Nightingale) with mass public support. The result was that the interests of the newspapers, not the interests of the soldiers, took priority, and, when the Crimean crisis no longer filled the pages of the papers, it no longer filled the consciences of the readers either. Quite the contrary. Although the Crimea remained of concern right up to the time when the Treaty of Paris was ratified in April 1856, and although Nightingale was hailed as a heroine on her return in August 1856, her immediate convalescence allowed the public concern to evaporate. When public outrage returned in May the following year, it was directed not at the military establishment—which after all had apparently succeeded at Sebastopol—but at the Indian mutineers, whose attacks upon British troops and civilians now generated support for the very same establishment. In effect, the window of opportunity that had existed during and directly after the termination of the war was dissipated through the absence of an organized political opposition, the consequential over-reliance upon the press, whose fickleness was legendary, and a coincidental development in India. The shift of spatial attention from the Crimea to India and the withering of temporal interest in Crimean military failure in the face of a mutiny against the same army swung public outrage against Nightingale's concerns. Within a year of her return, her facts on the military had become overshadowed by the fate of the mutiny. Nightingale's *Subsidiary Notes* were intended to operate within the body of the army, but to the army the words were those not of a welcome nightingale but of an unwelcome cuckoo.

The Performing Arts: Persuasive Communication

Finally, did Nightingale's actions in the performing arts make a significant difference to the relative success in the Crimea and relative failure in Britain? In terms of the conventional role of actor or actress, we can be certain that Nightingale does not rank amongst the greatest—or even the known—thespians: she simply avoided all public speaking. But, as a writer of letters and a constructor of research reports, there have probably been few that have been as prodigiously productive. Yet the issue is really how effective she was in using her performing arts to muster support for her case—and the answer is not very.

As an icon, as an Angel of Mercy, her performance was probably critical, for it allowed the press to mobilize public opinion on her behalf, but it was nevertheless markedly under-exploited by Nightingale, because she was always so guilt-ridden. Nightingale's performances were seldom properly related to the rapidly shifting context and she tended to rely upon cold 'facts' to persuade people, when many of her own greatest performances were deeply rooted in a recognition that facts do not speak for themselves.

Conclusion

Baly suggests that the debate about the role of Nightingale in the establishment of nursing persists to this day, 'ranging from those who attribute all the ills nursing has suffered, such as poor pay, harsh discipline and long hours, to her legacy, to those who say that if only she were alive today with her vision, all would be well' (Baly 1997: p. vii). Certainly E. J. M. Hill,[34] insists that 'No other person in the history of nursing has demonstrated the genius for administration or the educated imagination that created a profession where none existed previously.' The Nightingale Fund continues to this day, although its leading role in nurse training diminished sharply after her death in 1910. Civilian nursing did change as a consequence of Nightingale's intervention, but it was neither a radical nor a rapid change and was more the result of political compromises between the hospitals' desire for cheap labour, doctors' demands for subordinate help, and the training bodies' attempts to instigate a body of trained nurses (Baly 1997: 4).

There is little doubt that, but for Nightingale, the losses of the British Army would have been far higher and the slow move towards modernization of military and civilian health systems delayed yet further, but the deaths in Scutari hospital multiplied despite her presence because the system was so inadequate. In short, Nightingale's formidable organizational skills eventually outmanoeuvred the incredible organizational incompetence of the army in the Crimea, but by then it was too late to save most of the soldiers destined to die. And back on home turf the army had closed ranks and Nightingale's strategy then appeared amateurish against the professional networks of the military élite. In the Crimea she had used the army's power against itself, so that its monopoly of incompetence garnered increasing public support through the press for change. But at home the army used her power against herself, happy in the knowledge that her fixation with facts and proper procedures would never seriously threaten a militarily successful army staunchly defending the British Empire from the 'barbarians' all around them. Nightingale was a remarkable person and her efforts in the Crimea were extraordinary, but they were not enough to make a radical or permanent change to the status quo.

Notes

1. The following year they travelled back to her birthplace, Florence, the intellectual and cultural capital of Europe at the time, and Florence spent much of her time attending high-society balls and visiting the galleries and the opera. After each performance she

wrote down a score so that she could compare it with previous and future performances.

2. Baly (1997: p. viii) suggests that drunkenness amongst nurses was much exaggerated by Nightingale. Anyway, since the only forms of analgesic were alcohol and laudanum (opium)—aspirin became available only in 1899—the ubiquitous nature of alcohol was hardly shocking and one of the chief 'cures' seems to have been whisky—up to two pints a day according to Trollope (1994: 82).

3. Nightingale was convinced that marriage would see the end of all her hopes to fulfil God's work, for, as she wrote in *Cassandra*:

> Behind *his* destiny woman must annihilate herself, must be only his complement. A woman dedicates herself to the vocation of her husband; she fills up and performs the subordinate parts in it. But if she has any destiny, any vocation of her own, she must renounce it, in nine cases out of ten . . . A man gains everything by marriage; he gains a 'helpmate', but a woman does not . . . The true marriage—that noble union, by which a man and a woman become together the one perfect being—probably does not exist at present on earth.   (Quoted in Golby 1986: 249–51)

4. She was also an inveterate hater of traditions that restricted women in their activities:

> Why cannot a woman follow abstractions like a man? Has she less imagination, less intellect, less self-devotion, less religion than a man? I think not. And yet she has never produced one single great work of Art, or Science, or Literature . . . And why? . . . Is it not because *the habit* of never interesting herself much, in any conversation, printed or spoken, which is not personal, of making herself and her own feelings the subject of speculation . . . of making all she says autobiographical . . . (this) renders her powerless to rise to any abstract good, or general view. It cuts her wings, it palsies her muscles, and shortens her breath for higher things.   (quoted in Vicinus and Nergaard 1990: 31)

5. One such example occurred at a dinner party when Florence was sitting between Sir Henry de la Beche, an early initiatory of the geological map of Britain, and Warrenton Smyth, an Egyptologist. After she had shown herself to be their equal in their own subjects, Sir Henry commented to Warrenton Smyth after the meal on her attractiveness: 'A capital young woman—if only she hadn't floored me with her Latin and Greek!' (quoted in Trollope 1994: 28).

6. Of these, 23,000 troops were stationed in India, 32,000 in Europe, and 45,000 in Britain. A posting overseas was, for many soldiers, a death warrant—not because of any violence or conflict but because of disease. While the mortality rate for home-based soldiers ranged between 15 per thousand to 18 per thousand between 1815 and 1853, the rate for soldiers in the Gold Coast regiments was 668 per thousand, for regiments in Jamaica 130 per thousand, and for regiments in South Africa 15 per thousand. As might be expected, the mortality rate for officers was half that of ordinary soldiers (Burroughs 1994: 165).

7. Howick did manage to secure good conduct badges, libraries, games facilities, and regimental savings banks, but these were of limited utility when the entire corpus of regulations and institutions dehumanized most soldiers.

8. On the contrary, while reformists operated along Rousseau's philosophy, or what we might now consider McGregor's Theory Y model of human nature—where people are considered naturally responsible but made irresponsible by the institutions within which they work—the traditionalists within the army were driven more by the Hobbesian Theory X. In this case the soldiers were assumed to be naturally ignorant

and brutish and therefore only harsh discipline could inhibit their behaviour from reverting to its animalistic worst (see Grint 1998*a*: 123–4).

9.   The Crimea heralded several remarkable developments in unrelated areas: Isambard Kingdom Brunel developed a prefabricated hospital that saw service at Renkioi, near Scutari; Alexis Soyer designed a portable stove, the basic design of which formed the framework for a similar unit in the Gulf War of 1991; even Charles Dickens entered the fray, with a clothes drying machine, fifteen of which were sent to the Crimea in 1855 (Pye 1997*a*: 92–3).

10.   The Duke of Wellington had complained during the Napoleonic Wars about the role of newspapers; as he wrote to the War Office: 'I beg draw your Lordship's attention to the frequent paragraphs in the English newspapers describing the position and numbers, the objects, the means of attaining them possessed by the Armies in Spain and Portugal . . . This intelligence must have reached the enemy at the same time as it did me, at a moment at which it was most important that he should not receive it' (quoted in Young and Jesser 1997: 22).

11.   These were not restricted to the allied side: at the Battle of Alma a group of thirty Russian women had set up a picnic to watch the events of the day (Pye 1997*b*: 123). The fears of the military about the role of the media were highly prescient: MacGahan's reporting in the *Daily Mail* of Turkish atrocities in the Bulgarian uprising of 1876 are conventionally regarded as having turned the tide of public opinion in Britain, and James Creelman's despatches did the same for American opinion during the Japanese attack upon Manchuria in 1894.

12.   Russell had his official accreditation withdrawn by both sides in the American Civil War after he reported what he saw rather than what he was supposed to see. Even stalwarts like Baden Powell, hero of the siege of Mafeking during the Anglo-Boer War, had to be protected by the editor of *The Times*, after his policy of starving the black population to save the white population was reported by their correspondent Hamilton (Young and Jesser 1997: 29).

13.   For Russell, the 'thin red streak' of the Highlanders repulsing the Russian cavalry earlier in the day was subsumed beneath the Light Brigade's 'courage too great almost for credence—demi-gods could not have done what we failed to do'. But the words of French General Bosquet persisted longer in the memory: 'C'est magnifique, mais ce n'est pas la guerre. C'est de la folie' (quoted in Kerr 1997*a*: 67, 69). Tennyson's 'The Charge of the Light Brigade appeared in the *Examiner* just seven weeks later. When William Simpson subsequently drew the battle, Lord Cardigan, now safely back on his yacht, objected to the first two versions and only Simpson's third effort received the commander's approval, despite the fact that he had made only one significant change, for 'the real truth was that in the last sketch I had taken greater care than in the first two to make his Lordship conspicuous in the front of the brigade' (quoted in Kerr 1997*a*: 71).

14.   Copies of her instructions and authority were sent to Lord Raglan, Dr Hall, Mr Ward, and Mr Filder. Herbert also arranged for a 'Committee of Enquiry into the State of the Hospitals and the Condition of the Sick and Wounded'. This was to comprise Maxwell, a barrister, and two doctors: Cumming and Spence. It would have no powers of action but was merely a fact-finding mission and Florence was to provide official reports to them, and unofficial reports to Herbert.

15.   This is in sharp contrast to the call at the beginning of the Boer War for nurses, where the recruiting offices were overwhelmed (Trollope 1994: 95).

16. In fact, one of the most influential women in the Crimea, Mary Seacole, who ran a popular canteen called 'Mary Seacole's British Hotel' near Balaclava, was turned down by Nightingales' recruiters, probably because she was black. Seacole eventually paid her own way to the Crimea and went on to win the admiration of several high-ranking officers, who subsequently organized a music festival after the war when she became penniless. Mary was born in Jamaica in 1805 to a black mother and a Scottish soldier.

17. In a letter to William Bowman, the surgeon, she insisted that she was the equivalent in rank to a Brigadier-General, 'because 40 British females, whom I have with me, are more difficult to manage than 4,000 men' (quoted in Vicinus and Nergaard 1990: 84).

18. The situation on the Russian side was no better. As Pytor Alabin recalled after the Battle of Inkerman:

> The sick and wounded were packed tight like herrings in a barrel. They were in their dirty clothes and linen, covered in blood, stained beyond measure; the men were unshaved, unwashed, many had not had their dressings changed more than once since the battle on Inkerman; lying on plank beds with their uniform for a pillow and cloth trousers for bedding—for those who still had them—many had no bedding at all; the only coverlet for many of the wounded and sick was their immutable greatcoat'. (quoted in Pye 1997a: 79)

19. When Lord Raglan got to hear of the situation, he demanded that the Chief Medical Officer, Dr Hall, sack the Principal Medical Officer, Dr Lawson, which he reluctantly did, but he soon retrieved the man's career by getting him appointed Senior Medical Officer at the Barrack Hospital.

20. She even recruited Lady Stratford, the ambassador's wife, to help, asking her to provide twelve heavy wagons to move heavy material up to the hospital. The twelve heavy wagons turned up as seven glass and gilt coaches and five other smaller carriages, complete with a bill, which Florence was obliged to pay. She was not amused, for Lady Stratford, 'in consequence of want of practical habits of business, with the kindest and most benevolent intentions, was nothing but good and bustling and a time waster and an impediment' (quoted in Woodham-Smith 1982: 176).

21. Not that her nurses proved to be the objects of efficiency she had hoped for. One admitted that, when she arrived, she was 'prepared to submit to everything . . . But there are some things, Ma'am, one can't submit to. There is the caps Ma'am, that suits one face and some that suits another. And if I'd known, Ma'am, about the caps, great as was my desire to come out to nurse at Scutari, I wouldn't have come Ma'am' (quoted in Goldie 1997: 36).

22. Throughout this whole period she wrote all her own correspondence, all the requisition forms, and all the numerous letters the troops and nurses asked her to write on their behalves, and she also wrote to the mothers and wives of the dead.

23. Unlike her Russian counterpart Pirogov, who personally performed over 4,000 operations, though Pirogov also thought that administration was critical and that two of his major problems were 'the insatiable rapacity of the hospital administration' and the 'stupidity of the official medical personnel' (quoted in Pye 1997a: 87).

24. Quoted in Woodham-Smith (1982: 262). In the winter of 1858 Nightingale sent a copy of her 'Notes on Matters Affecting the Health, Efficiency and Hospital Administration of the British Army' to Harriet Martineau, then a writer on the *Daily News*. While happy to allow her to use the material for articles concerning the army, Nightingale was adamant that her name could not be associated with the feminist

articles that Martineau became famous for. As Nightingale said: 'I am brutally indifferent to the wrongs or the rights of my sex,' though she was keen on equal property rights, for 'till a married woman can have possession of her own property there can be no justice' (quoted in Baly 1997: 187).

25. At first Panmure sat on the process and hoped that, by sending Nightingale plans of the new military hospital then being built at Netley, on the Solent, he would assuage her wrath. But she simply took the plans apart, brick by brick, and demanded a radical rethink—and an early start to the Royal Commission. Still Panmure resisted, and Netley was completed despite her criticism (it was demolished in 1966).

26. As she noted, 'Yet with all this, the army from which the injured lives (unfit civilians) are subtracted dies at twice the rate of mortality as the general population. 1500 good soldiers are as certainly killed by these neglects yearly as if they were drawn up on Salisbury Plain and shot . . . Our soldiers enlist to death in the barracks' (quoted in Woodham-Smith 1982: 297).

27. Ironically, even her own Polar Area diagram contained errors—see Small's (1998) reconstruction.

28. In fact, it had been known for many years that hospitals were a source of infection and that the mortality rate amongst nurses was far higher than most other occupations (Baly 1997: p. viii).

29. Indeed, Nightingale tended to be a supporter of the miasmatic theory of illness: diseases generated spontaneously from filth and were not really the result of 'germs'. Even when she became more sympathetic towards germ theory, she still insisted that cleanliness was critical to health.

30. Each month every nurse was supposed to be evaluated on her

   Personal Character, Moral Character and Acquirements of Nurse. Personal Character included: Punctuality, Quietness, Trustworthiness, Personal Neatness and Cleanliness, and Ward Management. Moral Character involved: Sobriety, Honesty and Truthfulness. Acquirements of Nurse included: Dressing, Applying Leeches, Enemas, Management of Trusses, Rubbing, Helpless Patients, Bandaging, Making Beds, Waiting for Instructions, Sick Cooking, Keeping Ward Fresh, Cleanliness of Utensils, Management of Convalescents, Observation of the Sick, General Remarks. (Baly 1997: 229–30)

31. Such eccentricities were manifest in her novel *Cassandra*, where the context was not a strange old person, but a woman struggling to be independent in a man's world. There women 'are taught from their infancy upwards that it is a wrong, ill-tempered, and a misunderstanding of "woman's mission" if they do not allow themselves *willingly* to be interrupted at all hours' (quoted in Golby 1986: 247).

32. Jowett once referred to her as 'Florence the First, Empress of Scavengers, Queen of Nurses, Reverend Mother Superior of the British Army, Governess of the Governor of India'. She replied that she was closer to the 'Maid of all (dirty) work' (quoted in Vicinus and Nergaard 1990: 300).

33. In 1880, when Britain was engaged in a war against Arabi Pasha in Egypt, the War Office looked to the nurses at the military hospitals in Netley and Woolwich (the latter named the 'Herbert'). Nightingale's response to an enquiry from Colonel Lindsay reveals her assumption that neither place had been successful—despite the Nightingale Fund's claims: 'Does he call nurses "trained" at Netley? Training there had been an utter failure and at the Herbert it has not been tried' (quoted in Baly 1997: 115). Nightingale's pessimistic review was echoed over a century later by Summers,

who noted that doctors at the turn of the century were still complaining that 'the whole system of female nursing in the army appears to have been clumsily grafted on to the old system of nursing by orderlies . . . The graft has not taken root' (Summers 1988, quoted in Baly 1997: 216).

34. Chair of the Department of Nursing Education, University of Kansas Medical Centre, in 1998.

5

Scarlet and Black: Military Leadership at Isandhlwana and Rorke's Drift

We saw countless things dead. Dead was the horse, dead too the mule, dead was the dog, dead was the monkey, dead were the wagons, dead were the tents, dead were the boxes, dead was everything, even to the very metals.

(Muziwento, a Zulu boy who visited the camp area just after the battle of Isandhlwana (quoted in Knight 1998: 122))

Fifty years after Florence Nightingale had made her reputation in an army hospital in the Crimean War, the hospital at Rorke's Drift, as reconstructed in the film *Zulu*, was the site of another epic story of individual heroism and leadership. Facing enormous odds, about 100 fit British soldiers, mainly of the 24th Foot,[1] resisted around 4,000 Zulus in a daylong battle. Proportionately more Victoria Crosses (one for every twelve defenders) were won here than in any other battle—using metal taken from the Russian guns captured in the Crimea. Moreover, this success came hot on the heels of a major military catastrophe at Isandhlwana, where 75 per cent of a much larger British force (around 1,800) had been killed by a Zulu army that Wood (1984: 143) estimates at around 20,000. The failure and success of the two armies within a twenty-four-hour period provide a fourth valuable comparison of leadership, and the differences could hardly be clearer. Writing a school textbook in 1925, less than fifty years after the event, Edwards was clear on the reason for the 'Annihilation of a British force at Isandhlwana'. It was quite simply 'owing to the carelessness of Lord Chelmsford, who despised the enemy and neglected to laager his wagons and to throw out scouts'. In contrast, the 'Heroic defence of Rorke's Drift' was primarily achieved through the leadership of Lieutenants Chard and Bromhead, who thus kept the Zulus out of Natal. Subsequently, and no doubt having learned by his mistakes, 'Lord Chelmsford routed the Zulus at Ulundi' (W. E. Edwards 1925: 106). Morgan is also convinced that the problem was leadership: 'Incompetent generalship (a feature of British military operations in South Africa) led to the death of 800 British troops at Isandhlwana (the rest were colonial African troops), one of the very few occasions in colonial wars in which spears triumphed over guns' (Morgan 1986: 508). This was, of course, only a temporary setback, and the Zulus were virtually liquidated at Ulundi (1879). Finally, Murray extends the responsibility for failure to include both the general and his subordinate officers who all 'underestimated their opponents' (Murray 1995a: 245).

The leader of the expedition against the Zulus in 1879, Lord Chelmsford, had divided his forces, and the Zulus moved around his advance troops unseen. On 22 January they smashed into the British camp at Isandhlwana; there, because of serious tactical errors by British officers on the spot, and the imbecility of the supply system that required written receipts from the defenders for ammunition as it was being used, the Zulus killed almost everyone. As far as success is concerned, Murray (1995a: 245) continues the expanding net of responsibility to include technology: 'Later that day and night, victorious Zulus struck the small outpost of Rorke's Drift, defended by barely 100 soldiers—including the sick. In an epic defence, the British fought off waves of Zulus; the killing power of rifles devastated the attackers.' Similarly, Troup (1975: 150–1) suggests that t.ie Isandhlwana defeat occurred when 'their ammunition was done . . . At Ulundi, the guns won.'

In what follows I first outline the background to the Anglo-Zulu conflict before detailing the two battles that we are primarily concerned with and then assess the reasons for the contrary results. It will become clear that many issues are important, not least the role of luck or fortune, but ultimately leadership is the axis around which success and failure rotate. And once again the principle of resource-inversion provides a persuasive explanation for why some leaders succeeded where others failed.

Background to the Anglo-Zulu War and the Invasion of Zululand

The Dutch had been the first Europeans to show any significant interest in the Cape area of South Africa, though the Portuguese adventurer Vasco de Gama first sighted what became known as the Natal area on Christmas Day 1497, naming it *Terra Natalis* in honour of Christ's birth. Henceforth, Europeans called the area south of the Thukela River, Natal. In 1652 the Dutch East India Company set up a trading post at the Cape, but it was not particularly profitable, though the Dutch government was as keen to tax the colonist-farmers as the colonist-farmers were to evade government control by moving north. The British took control of the Cape in 1795 following a war, gave it back shortly thereafter, but in 1806 the British government decided to buy it from the Dutch as an insurance policy against French encroachment into India. Hostility between the Boer farmers and the British authorities continued to smoulder away until the British abolished slavery in 1833 and the Boers decided to take their slaves north in the Great Trek. By all accounts the British government was glad to see the back of the recalcitrant Boers, but the anti-slavery lobby managed to persuade the British Parliament to pass the Cape of Good Hope Punishment Act in 1837, which extended British sovereignty to the 25th parallel—to include the (e)migrating Boers. With little prospect of enforcing the Act, with a government insisting on reducing costs wherever possible, and with contradictory demands from religious groups in Britain and Boer groups in the countryside, there was little chance of any kind of satisfactory policy. Into this turmoil came the Zulus.

The Zulus had migrated in the fourteenth century as part of the Nguni, a pastoral people, going south to the south-east African coast, which had been occupied since at least the sixth century. The Nguni, though generally peaceful, did engage in war, but were renowned for their *ubuntu* or humanity. But by the beginning of the nineteenth century, as pressure on land increased from the local population and the expansionist policies of the Boers, the Nguni were dominated by one of their own tribes, the Zulus, first under Dingiswayo and then under Shaka. Dingiswayo and Shaka reconstructed the Zulu nation into a military society and it struck terror into all its neighbours as the Zulu regiments, or *impis*, spread. The black Diaspora or *Difaqane* that resulted from the violently expansionist Zulu movements dispersed as much as 20 per cent of the entire African population (Keegan 1993*a*: 3).

Zululand was always identified by the people who aligned themselves to the Zulu king, rather than by any physical boundaries, and that political alignment was often fluid, as rival chiefs fought and conspired to gain and retain control. Indeed, Shaka was really the first to construct the semblance of a Zulu *nation* and this was primarily achieved through the Zulu army. However, the Zulu army was not a professional group differentiated from the civilian base like the British army. *Amabutho*, or regiments of warriors, were formed on an age basis once the warriors reached 18 years of age, and warriors were prohibited from marriage until Shaka gave his assent. Sometimes, but not always, this involved the *impis* 'washing their spears' in (human) blood, but, despite the Victorian British predilection for assuming 'savages' were inevitably linked to sex and violence, permission to marry was not dependent on killing or war. Thus the regional and ethnic divisions that had previously divided the area were dissipated by the age-related identities formed through the Zulu army and marked by differentiated regimental shield and costume designs. In fact, the individual regiments or *ibutho* were just as likely to be called up to engage in some civilian work as any military requirement and seldom were all the regiments called up at the same time. Once the warriors had married, they were allowed to wear a top-knot or head-ring (*isococo*), which marked out their mature status and ensured that their responsibility reverted back from the Zulu king to their local chief and their own families. Hence, for as long as possible, Zulu kings prevented their young warriors from marrying—sometimes until they were in their late thirties (Knight 1995).

Shaka also allegedly replaced the wooden throwing spear—which proved relatively ineffective—with the metal-tipped stabbing assegai. Knight suggests that such weapons preceded Shaka but that he brought the weapon into better use and allied its greater lethality to a stronger and larger shield and also to a far more disciplined military battle strategy and system of fighting tactics. This demanded close-order discipline from his troops as they repeated their tactic of *Impondo zankomo*, 'the beast's horns', in which the enemy would be crushed between two encircling horns as the centre or 'chest' held the enemy's attention. A fourth group, the 'loins', would be held back in reserve. Whether this tactic was invented by Shaka is uncertain, but it was certainly effective against weakly armed or disorganized opponents and the British army was well aware of it (Knight 1995). Whatever else the whites thought about the Zulu nation, it was generally regarded as having the only marginally credible black army and it was the army alone that provided the Zulu king with power.

Eventually, in 1828, Shaka was murdered by his own family and replaced by Dingane, Shaka's half-brother, who attempted to strengthen the foundations Shaka had built, though Zulu influence to the south of the Thukela river was always marginal. Shaka's apocryphal alleged parting cry was to reinforce this problem: 'Sons of my father, you will not rule this land when I am dead, for it will be ruled by the white people who come from the sea' (Knight 1998: 7). Those whites who had first moved north from Capetown into Zululand settled during Shaka's reign in what was then called Port Natal, and were treated by Shaka as any other group—that is, as a client kingdom under his protection upon land temporarily ceded and protected by him in return for future service. But the whites, like many of the local population, believed their allegiance to the Zulu nation had died with Shaka and by the mid-1830s the thirty odd whites at Port Natal and their 2,000 retainers sought greater and greater independence, with bloodshed a not uncommon consequence (Knight 1998: 18–19).

In 1837, during the Boers' Great Trek, Dingane had been approached by the Boers to buy some land from him. He had initially agreed but became suspicious of Boer intentions when the Boer leader, Retief, refused to hand over some captured cattle and his followers began to settle in the area before any agreement had been reached. At a celebration to mark the agreement, all seventy Boers and their thirty servants were murdered. Dingane then proceeded to kill the 531 Boers and servants living around Port Natal. A series of clashes between the Zulus, the Port Natal traders, and the Boers followed, ending in the Battle of Thukela on 17 April 1838. There, a small detachment of eighteen Europeans and their auxiliaries' army of about 500 were effectively destroyed by a much larger Zulu army, though the number of Zulu dead may have been as high as 2,000. This battle marked the end of any possibility of peace between the white settlers and the Zulus and it also signalled the undoubted military ability and bravery of the Zulu army (Knight 1998: 30–4).

The following year, Dingane sent around 10,000 Zulu troops to destroy the remaining Boer camps, and between 13 and 14 August they attacked the settlers, who had 'laagered' their wagons into a defensive circle that the Zulus failed to overcome. A larger Boer force, composed of almost 500 men, then drove deep into Zulu territory and, on 16 December 1838, laagered their wagons near the Ncome river, where they were attacked by between 12,000 and 16,000 Zulus. But the Zulus were unable to manoeuvre properly because of the confined territory within which the Boers were laagered, and their attacks withered under the storm of rifle fire and a ship's cannon that had been brought along. The river allegedly turned red with Zulu blood. The Boers claimed to have killed 3,000 Zulus while suffering only three wounded themselves, and the Battle of Blood River, as it became known, secured Natal from Dingane. Subsequently, one of the Zulu leaders, Mpande, split from Dingane, taking 17,000 followers with him. Dingane's 'loyalists' were then defeated by his erstwhile colleague and Dingane himself was murdered, leaving Mpande as the new Zulu king. The Boers then declared Natal to be independent of Britain and proceeded to claim almost half of the Zulu kingdom as their own (Knight 1998: 45–50). While British politicians were favourably inclined towards this development, the delay in affirming independence coincided with Boer expulsion of 'surplus Africans', and the British government was spurred into retributive action in 1843, reclaiming Natal and forcing the Boers to trek yet further north to the Transvaal, re-establishing the original Zulu border (Glover 1997).

Mpande rebuilt the divided Zulu kingdom, and in 1832 the most important of his wives, Ngqumbazi, bore a son, named Cetshwayo ('the slandered one'), whom Mpande presented to the Boers as his heir. The Boers promptly clipped his ear, as if he was a cow. However, Mpande later changed his mind and tried to ensure that Mbuyazi, a son by a different wife, would secure the throne. The subsequent struggle for power, between Cetshwayo's followers, the uSuthu, and Mbuyazi's followers, the iziGqoza, ended with the Battle of Ndondakusuka on 2 December 1856, which left more than 5,000 iziGqoza warriors, and at least twice and perhaps three times that number of non-combatants, dead (Knight 1995: 40). Cetshwayo remained as the (still disputed) heir to Mpande, who died peacefully in 1872. The following year Cetshwayo, eager to dissuade any further potential rivals, called upon the British administration in Natal, which he (like Mpande before him) had long cultivated, to attend his crowning as King of the Zulus, though he remained embarrassed by the tinsel crown placed on his head by Theophilus Shepstone, then Natal's Secretary for Native Affairs (Knight 1998: 51–66).

Cetshwayo's coronation in 1873 marked a new burst of interest in the region by the British government, which until then had continued its general policy of disinterest in southern African affairs (the first diamond had been discovered by whites only six years earlier in 1867). British concern occurred only in so far as the sea route to India and the Far East was threatened, and, while the British navy remained unchallenged at sea, the British army could hardly have expected to be defeated by what it referred to as 'a pack of naked barbarians' (Glover 1997: p. x). When the Suez Canal was opened in 1869, offering an alternative route to the East, government interest in southern Africa dipped yet further and it seemed unlikely, notwithstanding the new diamond finds, that such an inhospitable place would provide anything like the opportunities opening up in the USA and Australia. However, if British southern Africa was to 'pay its way' with its natural resources, then a transport infrastructure and a rationalized administration were necessary. Thus the Colonial Secretary, Lord Carnarvon, attempted to persuade the Cape Colony, the Orange Free State, and the Transvaal to form a confederated South Africa (along Canadian lines) and, despite Boer hostility, ordered the said confederation in 1877, using British troops to occupy Pretoria. The annexation of the Transvaal immediately threatened the Zulus—long hostile to the Boers—and, when Shepstone authorized the ceding of disputed land along Blood River by the Zulus to the Boers, it left Cetshwayo astonished by the betrayal of his former British allies (Knight 1998: 68–70).

The Colonial authorities, especially Sir Henry Bartle Frere, despatched as the new British High Commissioner to South Africa, were unmoved by Zulu protests and certain that peace in the region could not be maintained unless the Zulu army—then allegedly numbering some 40,000, but probably closer to 25,000—was disbanded or destroyed (Knight 1995: 35). Cetshwayo had threatened bloodshed in a letter to the Lieutenant-Governor, Sir Henry Bulwer, and it did seem unlikely that he would be able to restrain his army indefinitely, but it is by no means certain that the Zulus were willing to put their entire community at risk for the sake of a strip of land. The British authorities were far less circumspect, as Laband and Knight (1997: 1) suggest: 'The Anglo-Zulu War of 1879 was engineered by Sir Bartle Frere.'

In mid-September two Zulu regiments, or impis, began massing on the Natal border and in October news came that the rest of the Zulu army was massing at the Zulu capital Ulundi. Chelmsford called on the Boers in the Transvaal to assist in repelling any likely invasion, but only forty turned up, along with the advice to laager his wagons, which Glover (1997: 62) asserts was 'sound but impractical. Laagering was a difficult and peculiarly Boer skill'. Since Chelmsford seems to have mastered the difficulties of laagering several times after Isandhlwana, we must assume that either he improved rapidly or Glover is wrong.

Frere was clearly looking to provoke Cetshwayo in order to destroy the Zulu army, and, when the sons of a local Zulu chieftain crossed the border in pursuit of two of his escaping wives, Frere's plans took a giant leap forward in combating what, according to the Natal Witness, was self-evidently a 'Zulu Outrage'. On 5 October Frere spoke at length about his 'mission' at a banquet at Pietermaritzburg:

his long experience of native races led him to conclude that there was every reason to hope that they were capable of being raised from the state of barbarism in which they are at present; especially when we remember how ten centuries had raised us from a similar state to the state of civilization we now enjoy. We cannot expect the kaffirs to advance at a rate much greater than that (at) which we ourselves proceeded.   (quoted in Laband and Knight 1997: 9)

Frere, obviously keen to start the thousand-year civilizing mission of the British Reich as soon as possible, invited Cetshwayo to a meeting in December 1878. Ostensibly this was to discuss the results of the boundary commission sitting at Rorke's Drift, a Swedish mission station on the Natal side of the Mzinyathi river that separated Natal from Zululand, named after Jim Rorke, an Irish trader who had built the station in the 1840s. The commission, chaired by Sir Henry Bulwer, was intended by Bulwer to resolve the problem peacefully, but it merely exacerbated it, suggesting that the land was Zulu but the Boers could live there. But this was the least of Zulu problems, for Frere also demanded that the two Zulu 'invaders' be surrendered and gave the Zulu king twenty days effectively to demobilize his army permanently by abolishing the *amabutho* system and to abolish the tradition of the king's approval as a precondition for marriage. With no response from Cetshwayo (and Frere never expected one, for his demands meant the effective end of the Zulu state), the High Commissioner handed the resolution of the problem over to Chelmsford on 11 January 1879, the expiry date for his ultimatum (Glover 1997: 43–56; Knight 1998: 72–3).

Chelmsford, Lieutenant-General Commanding in South Africa, whose paternal great-uncle had fought with Nelson at Copenhagen, had been commissioned into the Rifle Brigade in 1844 as a 17-year-old. He had fought in the Crimea and Abyssinia and had been involved in suppressing the Indian Mutiny. He had acquitted himself well in the so-called Nine Kaffir Wars in the Transkei in 1877–8. However, his victories over the Xhosa had taught him that the local population fought using guerrilla tactics and rarely undertook formal battles. It was commonly assumed by the British army that the Zulus would do the same—even though they were aware of the Zulu preference for 'the beast's horns'—and guerrilla tactics would certainly have limited the advantages of British military technology. But Zulu military strategy had always been to use mass, rapid, and violent assault against its enemies, and it was not until Isandhlwana that such an assumption underwent a radical revision.

In a pamphlet widely distributed within the British army, 'The Zulu Army' was described by Chelmsford as being between 40,000 and 50,000 in number, composed of regiments based on age; and, according to Morris (1994: 262), the 'white regiments (with white shields) were over 40 years old, married and veterans of conflict. The black regiments (with black shields) were under 40 and unmarried'. In fact, each regiment was distinguished from every other by the particular colour and pattern of their shields and headdress to the point where the warriors would often identify more with their regiments than their families or tribes by adopting their regimental name in place of their familial name (Knight 1995: 14).

Chelmsford also recognized from the beginning that suppressing the Zulu army was altogether more difficult than anything else he had attempted. He originally had just 2,000 troops against their army, and the land was virtually impassable to a conventional army, laden with wagons and artillery, though a Zulu army could move at will across any part of the 200-mile border between Zululand, Natal, and the Transvaal. As he commented on taking command: 'the distribution and number of Imperial and Colonial troops gave no hope of my being able to prevent an invasion should Cetshwayo give orders for it to be made' (quoted in Glover 1997: 60). In fact, Cetshwayo's army was probably no greater than 29,000 at its height, and at no time could he muster more than 25,000 for a single campaign (Knight 1998: 77). However, the speed at which the Zulus could deploy their forces across the ground meant that the British eventually began to plan their campaigns on the assumption that they were facing cavalry not infantry—but it took the defeat at Isandhlwana to confirm to the British just how successful Cetshwayo's army could be (Knight 1995: 13). Indeed, the Zulus never really altered their battle tactics to take advantage of the firearms in their possession and preferred to use guns as adjuncts to their throwing spears, firing one round from close range before rushing the British positions with their stabbing spears. In contrast, the Xhosa used firearms to ambush the British in small groups and the BaSotho adopted firearms to develop mounted infantry (Knight 1995: 214), the muskets that most Zulus who had firearms carried were very inaccurate above 100 yards and Zulu ignorance of the sighting system ensured that even under 100 yards most of the British targets were relatively safe.

In December 1878 the government partially acceded to Chelmsford's request for more troops by sending two battalions of infantry and two companies of engineers. But, as Chelmsford prepared for an invasion in January 1879, he still had only around 5,000 British troops, 1,000 European colonial volunteers, and 7,000 ill-trained and poorly armed Natal Africans in the Natal Native Contingent (NNC). The British authorities were reluctant to arm, uniform, and train the NNC properly in case they rebelled, so the policy had been to arm only one in ten recruits with a rifle (of obsolete pattern), and to distinguish the other 90 per cent from the Zulus only by the red headband that the NNC troops were obliged to wear. In addition, Chelmsford had accumulated transport (10,000 oxen and 1,000 wagons and carts) to carry supplies only for what was thought to be a six-week campaign. It was nowhere near enough for his original invasion plan using five columns, but it was just about sufficient for three.

Chelmsford's tactics for dealing with such a large enemy force were simple. As long as the Zulus could be kept at a distance, the Martini rifle, though only single loading, was more than capable of destroying large numbers of Zulus, however disciplined, brave and determined they may be, and doing it at distances up to 720 metres. Until Isandhlwana, the British army had operated on the general basis of linear formations: long extended lines of riflemen so that the killing power of their weapons could be maximized. Such tactics had been deployed by most modern armies since the sixteenth century, when the arrival of muskets began to make pikes obsolete, and with them the familiar box or square formation. However, Isandhlwana soon persuaded Chelmsford to return to the defensive square to prevent flanking attacks from poorly armed but more numerous and very mobile Zulus (Spiers 1994: 202).

In terms of strategy, the military tradition of concentrating strength against the enemy was difficult to apply. The country did not lend itself to a swift and condensed attack by the British, laden down with their supplies along narrow and poorly built roads, but it did lend itself to the Zulus counter-attacking in precisely this way. For Chelmsford, the danger was of him slowly chasing a small element of the Zulu army while the rest moved behind him to invade Natal and the Transvaal. Indeed, Glover (1997: 64) argues that no single route into Zululand could have withstood a concentrated modern army across it without considerable engineering work, which Chelmsford could not manage in the time available to him. His solution was to split the army into three self-sufficient columns, using the only three passable routes across rivers and on tracks direct to Ulundi. This would, in theory, prevent Cetshwayo from leaving Zululand and force him to a showdown that the British should win through force of arms, before destroying Ulundi. Glover (1997: 650) suggests 'the experience of two of the three columns showed that he was right but in the third his theory was not proof against the blunders of his subordinates'.

As the British massed on the borders, Cetshwayo assembled his chieftains, but it rapidly became clear that the British had little intention of seeking a peaceful solution to the problems. By 6 January 1879—five days before the ultimatum expired—British troops had already crossed the border and begun stealing cattle, and by 12 January Chelmsford's column had attacked the home of a local chieftain living along the border. Once Zululand had been invaded, Cetshwayo ordered his army to undertake the ritual purification rites that were traditional before any battle and then called forward pairs of regiments, roughly similar in age, and encouraged them to challenge each other for honour and valour in the forthcoming conflict. Among those called were the uMbonambi regiment. Then, as with the British, since it was not the tradition for the king to lead the battle itself, he entrusted the army to Ntshingwayo kaMahole and Mavumengwana kaNdlela, his two most respected generals, though each regiment or impi had its own commander.[2] He ordered them to negotiate where possible, to march slowly, attack only in daylight, never to attack a fortified position, and not to enter Natal. On 17 January the largest-ever Zulu army moved off. Cetshwayo had originally told them that the fighting would last just one day—partly because he was confident in victory (as long as they obeyed his instructions) and partly because the Zulu army could not mount a long campaign because they had no system for maintaining an army in the field (Knight 1995: 173).

Opposing the Zulus were Colonel Wood, who took command of the northern column, brevet (acting) Lieutenant-Colonel Glyn, who commanded the centre (with Chelmsford accompanying him), and Colonel Pearson, who commanded the southern column. Chelmsford established his headquarters at Helpmakaar, twelve miles south-west of Rorke's Drift, where he left a small detachment to guard the crossing point and moved east. He was immediately faced with the problem of getting his 220 wagons (5 metres long, 4 tons in weight, each pulled by sixteen or eighteen oxen) across the waterlogged path that was the road. On 20 January, nine days into the campaign, the column had moved only nine miles from Rorke's Drift and set up a supply camp at the base of Isandhlwana Hill, which rises ninety metres above the plain. On 21 January, with no prospect of the column advancing in the poor weather, and needing to return some of the wagons for more supplies from Helpmakaar (since he had taken only two weeks worth of supplies), Chelmsford ordered Major Dartnell to undertake a reconnaissance south-west. The following day, messages from Dartnell suggested that a large force of about 700 Zulus had been sighted and he asked for permission to attack. Chelmsford at first rejected the request, since he knew the main Zulu army was approaching and wanted a fixed battle by the camp. But a subsequent report suggested that 2,000 Zulus faced Dartnell, and Chelmsford, assuming this was part of the main army, eventually took off with Glyn in support of Dartnell. He was accompanied by half the remaining force and intended to inflict an early and devastating defeat on the Zulus, hoping this would discourage any further Zulu action. He left brevet Lieutenant-Colonel Henry Pulleine in command of the camp and ordered Lieutenant Smith-Dorrien to ride back to Rorke's Drift to order Colonel Durnford to bring his troops, then guarding the drift, up to Isandhlwana to replace those he was taking to Dartnell.

Brevet Colonel Durnford had been the chief military engineer in Natal for many years but had been held responsible for a botched attempt to arrest a Zulu chieftain in 1873, in which several of Durnford's men had been killed and he had been injured. Since then Durnford had been regarded by Chelmsford as a hot-head, desperate to rebut charges of incompetence, and Chelmsford had recently warned him that, 'unless you carry out the instructions I give you, it will be my unpleasant duty to remove you from your command . . . I trust you understand this plain speaking . . .' (quoted in Morris 1994: 322). Since Durnford was senior by three years to Lieutenant-Colonel Pulleine, Glover and Morris assert that it was clear that Durnford would be in overall command of the camp, though Pulleine would retain control of his own troops. Unfortunately for all of them, the Zulu army was not where Chelmsford expected it to be; instead it was five miles north of Isandhlwana, hidden by the Nqutu Plateau (Glover 1997: 75; Morris 1994: 356).

Isandhlwana, 22 January 1879

Lieutenant-Colonel Pulleine, educated at Marlborough and Sandhurst, had joined the army, like Chelmsford, at 17. He had been in South Africa for five years already but had seen no active service—indeed, it was this lacuna that had per-suaded him to petition Chelmsford to join him, which he had done on 17 January between Isandhlwana and Rorke's Drift. Pulleine's main task was to ensure that the wagons were returned via Rorke's Drift whilst Chelmsford and Glyn were out seeking the Zulus. The camp at Isandhlwana contained room for 4,500 troops living in lines of tents, which were staked in front of the 220 wagons and carts. Behind the wagons lay Isandhlwana Hill, which lay north–south down to the track back to Rorke's Drift. The map in Fig. 5.1 provides a rough guide to the land and the events of the day.

Colonel Glyn, in laying out the camp, had assumed that the line of tents would fit within the north–south boundary of the Isandhlwana, which was impassable from the west, and which therefore left only the east as the major battle line, with the exception of the extreme northern and southern perimeters. Indeed, Morris (1994: 329) considers it 'the best campsite for miles about', enabling either a solid square in front of the site or a line against the hill itself. However, the tents

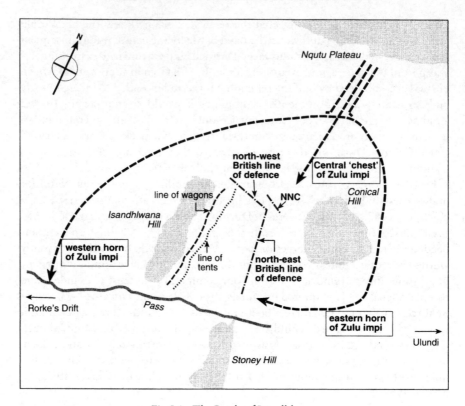

Fig 5.1. The Battle of Isandhlwana

extended south beyond the protective wall of the hill, and, moreover, the southern and northern aspects of the hill could easily be climbed by the lightly armed
Zulus. Protecting the camp were around 900 British infantry soldiers of the 24th
(2nd Warwickshire) Regiment, two artillery guns, 118 colonial cavalry, and
around 420 others from the NNC, who between then could muster around sixty
rifles. The possibility of laagering the wagons had been mooted, but Chelmsford
had discounted it because he wanted the wagons to return through Rorke's Drift
for provisions on the morning of the 22nd and because 'There never was a position where a small force could have made a better defensive stand' (quoted in
Glover 1997: 73).

Moreover, laagering wagons could not be done by oxen but required the
efforts of around fifty men to shift the wagons with their fixed rear axles.
Entrenchment was a possibility—indeed, entrenchment of permanent camps
was part of Chelmsford's own standing orders—but the ground was considered
too stony and Chelmsford had obviously taken a calculated risk that his lookouts
would provide sufficient warning of any impending attack for the troops to line
up and provide concentrated defensive fire (Morris 1994: 331). Because

Chelmsford had also taken half of the column with him to support Dartnell, he ordered Pulleine not to send fifty wagons back until an escort could be provided and to keep lookouts posted, which Pulleine did, sending all his cavalry to maintain lookouts to the north and south. Since his back (the west) was protected by Isandhlwana Hill, he saw no need to cover it.

At 06.00 on 22 January some Zulus were spotted on a ridge overlooking the camp and Pulleine ordered the 24th Regiment to stand to. Then just after 08.00 firing was heard to the east of the camp and a scout reported a large band of Zulus in the north-east. Pulleine ordered the entire garrison—about to eat breakfast—to arms. He left the north-western and north-eastern patrols out, but pulled the southern patrol back into camp, and sent a message to Chelmsford that the Zulus—though he did not say how many—were advancing on the camp. It took two hours for the message from Pulleine to get to Chelmsford, and it would have taken three more hours to get any troops back to him—and, of course, it was in the opposite direction to the one Chelmsford wanted to go. So, since Chelmsford did not think Pulleine was in any real danger, he ordered Pulleine to move forward to him, rather than attempting to move back to Pulleine.

At 08.10 many of Pulleine's troops were lined up in two lines right across the north-western and north-eastern front of the camp. Such a deployment might have been sufficient against a slow-moving enemy of moderate numbers, since the greater firepower of the British would have been able to hold such an attack at bay—providing the ammunition supply was adequate and the line remained firm. None of these conditions prevailed. About the same time a messenger arrived announcing that the main Zulu army had split into its familiar three prongs with two disappearing back into the hills while the third continued moving away towards the north-west.

At 10.30 that morning Durnford's own Native Natal Horse, and their 300 rifles, accompanied by two rocket sections, arrived at Isandhlwana from Rorke's Drift. But, when a force of 500 Zulus was spotted moving east away from the camp, towards Chelmsford's forces, instead of taking command of the camp from Pulleine, Durnford proposed riding after them, taking all his men plus a third of the remaining British infantry that Pulleine had left to guard the camp. At first Pulleine refused, then accepted the request, only to be persuaded by his own Lieutenant Melville that it would be foolhardy. Reluctantly Durnford accepted the refusal but demanded that the men be sent to help him should he get into difficulties. By 11.30 Durnford had left and by 12.15 he had run into an impi of Zulus, about 4,000 strong, near Conical Hill. Pulleine now had one portion of his defence with Durnford moving east at about a mile distance, one portion about a mile north-west, and another two miles north-east. The north-eastern group, led by Captain Shepstone, then ran into the main Zulu army, numbering about 20,000 and began falling back southwards to the camp.

The Zulus had not intended to attack until the following day, the 23rd, but, on being discovered, the leading regiments decided they had little option except to attack immediately (Laband and Knight 1997: 60). Their local commanders were markedly less enthusiastic about such an immediate assault but could not prevent the Zulu warriors from attacking spontaneously. The lack of discipline led to unnecessarily high casualties because the attackers could not coordinate their movements but approached the British in piecemeal fashion, allowing the defenders to concentrate their fire on whichever group was nearest. Precisely the same problem bedevilled the attack on Rorke's Drift and Khambula Hill, and, though the Zulu commanders were aware of it, they remained unable to prevent it, such was the enthusiasm for battle and the competition between the Zulu regiments for the honour of being the first to breach the British lines (Knight 1995: 188–9).

At about the same time that the first Zulu assault began gathering strength and Shepstone raced back to tell Pulleine of the imminent attack, Chelmsford's demand that Pulleine should strike camp and join him came in. Pulleine obviously ignored this command but then seems to have made a fatal error. Chelmsford had assumed that the camp was safe—even against a large Zulu army—providing the troops were concentrated in firing positions close to the wagon line (there was, after all, half a million rounds of ammunition available). However, Pulleine ordered the opposite to occur, for his already scattered troops were not ordered to retreat and regroup at the camp. Instead he sent some of the remaining troops out to reinforce Shepstone in the north-east and Durnford in the east at Conical Hill. The hubris of the British was about to demonstrate that even hugely superior technology could not transcend the resource-inversion the British brought upon themselves.

The group of NNC troops posted at the point where the north-western and north-eastern lines of imperial troops met were poorly trained and lightly armed—they had thirty rifles between 300 of them and only five rounds of ammunition for each weapon. Just behind the NNC, and firing over their heads, were the two 7-lb guns. The consequence of Pulleine's decision to move *out* to reinforce the extended line, rather than call the outlying troops *back* to a concentrated position, was that, even when the outlying troops' initial retreat was stopped by the reinforcements, the new extended lines of defence left large areas of undefended gaps. At full deployment there were only 600 men covering one mile of space—roughly three yards each—with the outlying troops hundreds of yards, and in some cases well over 1,000 yards, from the ammunition.

Just after 12.15 Durnford, now well past Conical Hill, turned to see the huge Zulu army approaching the camp behind him and threatening to cut him off from it. Durnford, facing the eastern horn of the Zulu attack, made an ordered retreat, retiring, then dismounting to fire at the attackers, and then remounting to retire a little further to repeat the process. While this was going on, the rocket section had been cut off, surrounded, and almost wiped out before Durnford's troops managed to rescue the remnants. Eventually Durnford's group made a stand in a river bed against the encroaching Zulu impi.

To the north-west, the British line under Younghusband, Mostyn, and Cavaye had stopped the Zulus at a distance of 200–300 yards and the north-eastern line had also managed to halt the onslaught, and at this point it looked as though the impetus of the attack was spent. But many of the troops had expended their 40–100 rounds of ammunition and, after fighting for between thirty and sixty minutes, they were running low. Ammunition in the camp was plentiful, but it was controlled by two quartermasters, who serviced the two different battalions. Pullen controlled ammunition for the 1st battalion, and was stationed at the extreme south of the camp, between 1,000 and 1,800 yards from the 1st battalion's companies mainly in the northern line. Bloomfield controlled the ammunition for the 2nd battalion and was stationed in the centre of the camp, 1,100 yards from his companies. The runners from the northern companies of the 1st battalion naturally approached Pullen's wagon first, but he sent them on to Bloomfield, 500 yards further south or, if they were native troops, told them to find their own wagon. Lieutenant Smith-Dorrien was himself admonished by Bloomfield for taking the 'wrong' ammunition. Simultaneously, Durnford sent runners back to the camp for ammunition but returned empty handed when Bloomfield refused them any. Captain Essex, one of the five surviving officers, suggests that when he returned to camp during the retreat he had little difficulty replenishing his troops with ammunition and that one of the quartermasters—presumably his own— was shot dead trying to help him load up a wagon with ammunition. However, as he returned to the front, the first gaps in the line were already appearing as individual NNC troopers ran back to the camp (Laband and Knight 1997: 59).

Much is also made of the infamous ammunition boxes, whose lids were screwed down, making access difficult without the mysteriously missing screwdrivers (Morris 1994: 372). Wood (1984: 144) agrees, also suggesting that the ammunition wagons were too far from the fighting. Glover (1997: 80) merely talks about 'minor disputes as quartermasters tried to get their own ammunition' and he repeats the problem of the ammunition boxes. Whatever the cause of the ammunition problem, Durnford rode back to the camp to confer with Pulleine and they seem to have agreed to order a retreat to a smaller defensive position. But, as the British troops rose to begin retreating, their firing slowed everywhere. Ntshingwayo, either recognizing the opportunity or worried by the apparent failure of the attack, ordered Ndlaka, one of his subordinate commanders, to rally the uKhandempemvu regiment, which had halted in the face of furious British rifle fire. And since it was normal for regimental commanders to lead from the front—unlike the senior commander, who usually directed from an observation post in the rear—Ndlaka quickly responded. He reminded the uKhandempemvu of their boast to outperform their rival regiment, the iNgobamakhosi, and the uKhandempemvu rose *en masse*, followed very quickly by iNgobamakhosi (Knight 1995: 216–17; 1998: 118–19).

The British were now effectively retreating at a rapid walk, stopping only to fire, but the NNC troops in the centre of the line—with the least ammunition, the lowest proportion of guns, the weakest officers, and the poorest training—broke lines and ran back, along with most of their British officers, followed by the two artillery pieces. This left a 300-yard gap at the apex of the line and the Zulus rushed through it, attacking the adjacent British troops in the rear (Morris 1994: 371–5). Glover (1997: 79), following the account of Captain Essex, suggests not only that most of the NNC were stationed behind the imperial troops' line but that those that were firing were 'seen to be blazing away at an absurd rate'. Since only around 10 per cent of them had rifles, and even these had only five rounds each, it is hard to explain how this could possibly have happened nor what they were allegedly shooting at. Nor, indeed, would there have been any gap in the line if they were behind the regular troops. In fact, Glover makes no mention of the NNC's retreat, followed by the artillery pieces, and explains the disastrous rout by concentrating on Durnford's actions.

The extended north-eastern line that Pulleine had made to rescue Durnford now also became a tragic weakness. Durnford had almost run out of ammunition and retreated, leaving the line without cover on the southern flank, and, as Lieutenant Pope ordered his southernmost company in the line to wheel around and fall back to the camp, the eastern horn of the Zulu swept behind it. This horn struck the camp from the south-east, while the western horn moved behind Isandhlwana Hill to cut the track back to Rorke's Drift. The British line then disintegrated, as the troops ran back into the camp, fragmenting the remaining troops of the 24th Foot into small groups and undermining any chance of defeating the Zulus. With defeat imminent Pulleine ordered Melville to escape with the colours, escorted by Lieutenant Coghill, but both men were shot escaping. Durnford made a last stand with about seventy surviving men until their ammunition also disappeared. Back at the camp the surviving sixty men under Captain Younghusband backed up the southern face of the Isandhlwana until their ammunition also gave out and then made a final bayonet charge to their deaths.

At 17.00 it was all over. Of the 605 men and officers of the 24th, three had survived. Of the total strength of 1,774 as the battle had commenced, 1,329 were dead (Glover 1997: 69–82). About 400 men fled south back towards Rorke's Drift, but most were killed by the western horn of the Zulu Impi, which had moved behind the Isandhlwana. Only five officers and around fifty-five soldiers of the British Imperial Army survived (Knight 1998: 122; Morris 1994: 382). Over 1,000 of the Zulus were dead in and around the camp and 1,000 more were soon to die of their wounds. In addition, almost all the 3,000 cattle plus innumerable horses, mules, and dogs had been killed. In short, approaching 6,000 carcasses lay strewn all around. The Zulus took no prisoners and they stripped the camp bare, taking over 1,000 Martini rifles and 500,000 rounds of 0.45 ammunition— clearly, a shortage of ammunition in the camp had never been a problem for the British.

Cetshwayo was not in jubilant mood after Isandhlwana, despite the 'victory'. He asked the returning army 'When will the rest come before me?' and when he was told of the Zulu losses he exclaimed that 'an assegai has been thrust into the belly of the nation . . . There are not enough tears to mourn for the dead' (quoted in Morris 1994: 386). Moreover, despite his order that no Zulu was to cross the border, a reserve regiment, the oNdini, which had not been involved in the attack and was led by Cetshwayo's brother Dabulamanzi, moved swiftly on to Rorke's Drift to destroy the British supply depot there. Dabulamanzi already had a reputation for rashness and the attack upon Rorke's Drift merely confirmed Cetshwayo's opinion of him. Cetshwayo, restricting his Zulu army to a defensive war, now waited as his troops returned to bury their dead and bring in their crops, but, although his army was severely shocked by the losses it had sustained, the British were in a considerably worse state of shock. Had Cetshwayo decided then to invade Natal, there would have been little to stop him, but he did not, and that temporal suspension allowed the British to recover and to reinforce the army that eventually destroyed him.

Chelmsford had become aware that action of some sort had occurred at Isandhlwana, because at 12.30 he had heard cannon fire and could see the flash of the guns, but since it did not continue he assumed the attack had been beaten off easily. The second and third messages about the attack may not have reached Chelmsford *verbatim*, for he did little about them, assuming they all referred to the same initial (and limited) action. However, he decided to return to the camp personally at 15.30 and met Commandant Lonsdale, who had returned sick to the camp during the height of the battle—and promptly rode straight out again. Chelmsford was himself now in great danger, caught between his advance party and the main Zulu army, but he ordered Glyn to move back with the infantry and guns in an attempt to retake the camp. Then his scouts warned him that smoke could be seen near the Oskaberg mountain, near the crossing point of the Buffalo River, Rorke's Drift.

Rorke's Drift, 22 January 1879

In overall command of Rorke's Drift, including the thirty-six men in the hospital, was acting Major Spalding, temporarily promoted and one of Lord Chelmsford's staff officers. The Drift was a crossing point on the Buffalo river and Spalding decided to ride back to Helpmakaar to demand an additional company to guard the crossing point. Spalding left Lieutenant Chard in temporary command, even though there were several other officers who appeared to outrank Chard. Captain Stephenson was in command of a unit of the NNC but his commission was a 'colonial' rather than a 'regular' one and, like his NNC troops, Stephenson was regarded as inferior to Chard's regular or imperial troops. These comprised eighty-four men of B Company, 2nd battalion of the Twenty-Fourth (2nd Warwickshire) Foot—who were virtually all Welsh. B Company was commanded by Lieutenant Bromhead, who was senior in age and service to Chard, but Chard had entered service as a first Lieutenant straight from Woolwich whereas Bromhead had entered as a 2nd Lieutenant and thus remained junior to Chard. Lieutenant Chard, a 32-year-old Royal Engineer with eleven years' service, was at the time without any hint of the leadership skills that were to be ladled upon him by an adoring British press. He had been eighteenth out of nineteen in his passing-out exams at the Royal Military Academy at Woolwich, which churned out 'competent technicians rather than leaders of men in battle' (Glover 1997: 2).

When firing had been heard at around lunchtime on the 22nd, the officers at Rorke's Drift had assumed only that a skirmish was underway. Shortly after Spalding had ridden off, two messengers arrived from Isandhlwana with tales of the tragedy there and the news that one part of the Zulu wing was now heading straight for the drift. Since Chard could not really hope to outrun the Zulus back to Helpmakaar with all the sick and wounded on wagons, his only real alternative was to make a stand, though neither Chard nor Bromhead seems to have been certain until retired Sergeant Dalton persuaded them to stay. Chard then sketched out the defensive perimeter, while Bromhead and Dalton began to organize the work itself. The hospital building—which was only a large house in reality—and the perimeter area were then fortified using two-foot-high biscuit tins, weighing approximately 100 lbs., and mealie bags weighing well over 100 lbs. Six men barricaded themselves into the main rooms of the hospital with the sick and wounded, since it was decided that there was no time to evacuate them. With a four-foot-high mealie bag and biscuit-tin wall (with the northern line on top of a two-foot ledge) enclosing the two ends of the site (see Fig. 5.2), Dalton opened up a quarter of the fifty ammunition boxes and the order to fix bayonets was given; it was 16.30.

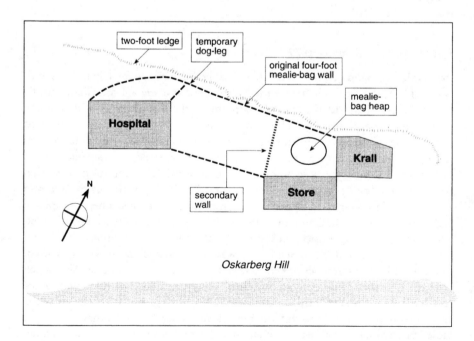

Fig. 5.2. The Battle of Rorke's Drift

Survivors of Isandhlwana then began drifting in, including 100 cavalry under Lieutenant Vause, who had been escorting Durnford's baggage up to Isandhlwana before they turned back, but they did not stay long, retreating to Helpmakaar despite originally claiming that they would stay and fight. Shortly afterwards, Captain Stephenson and his NNC cavalry deserted, leaving a defensive position designed for 350 men to be held by just 140, thirty of whom were in hospital and with only the eighty-one of B company to be relied upon. Chard immediately set about bisecting the existing compound with a new wall made from the biscuit tins and mealie bags;[3] at the same time the first attack from a 4,000-strong Zulu impi was unleashed from the western end at the hospital building.

For an hour and a half the Zulus engaged in desperate hand-to-hand fighting all the way around the perimeter wall. As this developed, Zulus with rifles tried, usually unsuccessfully, to pick off defenders along the northern wall from the 500-foot Oskarberg Hill behind them, but most of their shots went high. The chaplain, acting as ammunition carrier, delivered the cartridges from the opened cases in front of the storehouse. At 18.00 the pressure was intense and all attempts at 'volley fire'—the 200-year-old infantry tactic in which alternate ranks of three lines of rifles shot whilst the other two reloaded to ensure continuous firing[4]— had long since been abandoned. The loopholes dug in the outside walls of the hospital with a pickaxe provided only a limited field of fire and the Zulus were now up to the walls themselves and about to break in, having already set the thatched roof on fire. Nine of the original patients and four of the defending soldiers (all of whom were awarded Victoria Crosses) escaped to the relative safety of the reduced compound. By 22.30 the defenders held only the secondary enclosure around the mealie-bag heap, which Chard rebuilt into a citadel with room for both the wounded and around twenty soldiers, should the Zulus break into the new enclosure. They had now been fighting for six continuous hours without let up, but at almost no time had the Zulus coordinated their attacks upon all points thus allowing the defenders to concentrate fire wherever necessary. Since the defenders were without food or water, Chard then led an assault team out into the yard to recover the water cart. It was not until 02.00, after almost ten hours' fighting, that the frontal assaults stopped, and not until 04.00 that the firing died down. The burning hospital provided light for the defenders to ensure that no Zulu broke into the secondary enclosure and lived. With fifteen of the original troops dead and ten severely wounded, there was little chance that the defenders would be able to survive the expected renewal of fighting when the light returned. They had already fired 20,000 bullets.

But when dawn broke the impi had gone, leaving 370 bodies in the immediate vicinity of the building and a further 100 in the river, left there by the Zulus themselves. At 07.00 one of the native troops reappeared and simultaneously the Zulu impi appeared to the west of the Oskarberg. The Zulus had not eaten for three days and were also exhausted; they soon melted away towards Isandhlwana, passing within 100 yards of Chelmsford's equally exhausted party moving in the opposite direction. Neither side attempted to obstruct the other's progress.

The Aftermath

When news of the events reached Natal, panic set in amongst the European population, and Pietermaritzburg and Durban were barricaded in advance of the expected attack. It never came, because the Zulu impis had never intended to enter Natal and simply went back to Zululand. However, Rorke's Drift was widely reported as having 'saved Natal'; it was, to quote one of the earliest 'eyewitness' reports, the time 'when a mighty wave of victorious barbarity . . . was checked by our little band' (quoted in Laband and Knight 1997: 62).

Chelmsford did not attempt to clear his name, because he felt he had nothing to clear: the responsibility for the disaster at Isandhlwana was Durnford's and he was dead; the camp could have been defended with the available force, but it was not. The court of enquiry made no decision as to the responsibility for the disaster. Durnford's relatives insisted that Chelmsford had chosen the wrong site, had failed to laager the camp, had irresponsibly ridden after a decoy group of Zulus, and had not specifically told Durnford to take command from Pulleine. In Morris's words (1994: 439): 'the indictment sounded impressive, but the points were not telling.'

The campsite was adequate and it did provide sufficient time to see any attack and sufficient cover to defend against one—providing the troops were properly organized. It was not intended to be a permanent site nor was Chelmsford *irresponsibly* seeking out the Zulus—that was his intention all the time so that he could bring superior weapons to bear on a larger force. Moreover, even though there was some confusion about the messages from Pulleine, it would not have been possible for Chelmsford to return in time—nor did he assume it would be necessary.

Back in England, despite the shock that ran through the country, Disraeli, the Prime Minister, was more concerned with the Afghan War, and the possibility of renewed conflict with Russia, rather than with the Zulu war, but the latter was a major political embarrassment. By March the reinforcements requested by Chelmsford were on their way and the country was searching for a scapegoat for the South African catastrophe. Frere was censured for sending Cetshwayo an ultimatum without the Cabinet's approval, while on 9 February Chelmsford wrote to the Secretary of the State for War asking that an officer of the rank of Major-General should be sent out 'without delay' because of the 'strain of prolonged anxiety, physical and mental' (quoted in Morris 1994: 447). This was widely interpreted as a request to resign, though he denied it, replying that it was just a request to send an able second-in-command to take over some of his onerous responsibilities.

In fact Chelmsford had already planned the second invasion of Zululand, this time with a large contingent of colonial troops from Natal who would not be able to defeat the Zulus but would be able to weaken them sufficiently for the imperial troops to finish the Zulus off for ever. Wood, commanding the original northern column, had already seen one of his supply convoys destroyed and eighty men killed at Myer's Drift on 12 March after the wagons had been inadequately laagered and the local convoy's commanding officer had failed to post advance lookouts.

Meanwhile Colonel Pearson, leader of the original southern column, was short of supplies and cut off at Eshowe, though not in any immediate danger from the Zulus. On 23 March a Zulu envoy approached Pearson, on behalf of Cetshwayo, to ask why the British were invading and to offer the troops safe conduct back to Natal; it was refused.

Chelmsford asked Wood to draw off some of the Zulus planning to attack the relief column nearing Eshowe, and Wood decided to attack at Hlobane, a mountain range on 28 March. Two small forward columns were caught on the plateau by an army of around 22,000 Zulus and ninety-four British troops were killed and eight wounded. Wood now had about 400 men within a laagered camp—with ammunition boxes opened—and on 29 March the Zulus bore down on his camp. Just after 12.00 hours, employing the now standard tactic of inducing one Zulu wing to attack before the other was deployed properly, the right wing of the impi was tempted to attack first after being provoked by a small cavalry attack by the British Frontier Light Horse. Eleven thousand Zulus then attacked but were beaten back by four artillery pieces and sustained rifle fire. By 14.00 the chest and left wing of the Zulu army were in position and they attacked for three hours before retreating. The Zulus lost 2,000 dead and innumerable wounded, while the British lost twenty-nine dead and fifty-five wounded (Morris 1994: 467–97).

By the beginning of April, Pearson's men had been under seige for ten weeks, and by the time Chelmsford's relief party was closing in they were beginning to die of disease. Chelmsford's column, led by him personally, arrived on 2 April. He had clearly learned much from Isandhlwana: ammunition boxes were carried on every wagon, every box had the screws taken out, and every wagon had a spare screwdriver—just in case. Every evening of the final approach the wagons had been laagered and a defensive trench dug. When the battle occurred, at Gingindhlovu, near the Inyezane river, the Zulus led by Somopo had already missed several opportunities to attack the column as it crossed one of the rivers— as Cetshwayo had ordered—and made headlong charges against the square. Chelmsford used additional rockets, artillery, and, significantly, four hand-cranked Gatling guns firing 300 rounds per minute. These were first used by the British in 1874 against the Ashantis and fired 1-inch bullets. Despite the military insistence that the Gatling gun was a piece of artillery, and must therefore be mounted on a fixed carriage—making it virtually impossible to traverse— Chelmsford was adamant that it 'should not be attached to the artillery, but should be considered as essentially an infantry weapon' (quoted in Ellis 1993: 63). The 10,000 strong Zulu army broke into three sections to attack three of the four faces of the defensive square formed by the British and at 1,000 yards the Gatling guns began scything through them. Only one Zulu broke through the square, a 12-year-old boy who was subsequently adopted by the Navy crew manning one of the Gatling guns; he later joined the British navy. Around 700 Zulu bodies lay before the square, several hundred more were killed later in the retreat, and 400 guns, taken from the troops at Isandhlwana, were recovered. On average, the infantry (about 3,400 men) had only fired seven cartridges each. The British losses were thirteen dead and forty-eight wounded (Morris 1994: 463–5).

Chelmsford returned to Durban on 9 April to continue planning the second invasion, safe in the knowledge that the flanking columns were no longer at risk, and that it was not at all likely that the Zulus would invade Natal. With the reinforcements from Britain, Chelmsford now had 16,000 imperial troops and 7,000 colonial troops to take on the remaining 20,000 surviving Zulus. So was Chelmsford's ability as a leader rectified by Gingindhlovu? Well the British Cabinet did not think so and sent Sir Garnet Wolseley to be his superordinate officer in June, just as Chelmsford had embarked on a second attempt to destroy the Zulu army at Ulundi. Wolseley was keen to reach Chelmsford before Chelmsford reached Ulundi, because, according to Wolseley, though 'a gentleman and a very nice fellow . . . the Lord forbid that he [Chelmsford] should ever command troops in the field' (quoted in Morris 1994: 550).

On 1 June the 22-year-old Crown Prince of France, Napoleon Eugène Louis Jean Joseph, son of Napoleon III, who was accompanying Chelmsford as a rather unwelcome 'spectator', was killed by Zulus. He had been engaged on a 'sketching trip' on 'safe ground' but, explicitly against Chelmsford's orders, had an escort of only seven soldiers and a guide, to establish a new campsite. When the search for his body commenced the next morning, 1,000 troops were involved. Chelmsford, who had only reluctantly accepted the prince into the force, was in yet deeper trouble. Ironically, the death caused far more of a sensation in Britain than had Isandhlwana, though it was a problem more for Queen Victoria than for the government of the day. Forty thousand people attended the prince's funeral at Chislehurst (Morris 1994: 536).

Cetshwayo had good reason to fear the worst, particularly after the British retribution for Isandhlwana had proved so vigorous that a dispute over territorial control looked more and more like a policy of extermination. Morris (1994: 558–9) certainly suggests that the ultimatum given Cetshwayo was impossible to comply with because he did not have complete control over the situation and at least three attempts to negotiate with the British were rejected. Nor did Chelmsford feel free to act as he thought fit, for the newspaper journalists followed and reported his every move. As he complained on 10 June 1879, it was 'more than probable with such a large number of newspaper correspondents in camp, that many false impressions may be circulated and sent home regarding our present operations either intentionally or ignorantly' (quoted in Laband and Knight 1997: p. v).

As late as 14 June Cetshwayo sent a messenger to bargain with Chelmsford, but the messenger missed Chelmsford's column and was threatened with death when he tried to approach another British camp. Cetshwayo then sent gifts of cattle to Chelmsford and promised that two field guns captured at Isandhlwana would be returned. Chelmsford, however, wanted an entire Zulu regiment to surrender, something that even Cetshwayo could not order. Indeed, the regiment did not even allow the cattle to be surrendered.

On 29 June, with Wolseley hot on his heels to grab the glory, Chelmsford decided to save his reputation and attack. He gave a Zulu messenger, who had returned the French prince's sword, a final demand for 1,000 Martini rifles taken at Isandhlwana (and conspicuously not used to the Zulus' advantage afterwards) instead of the surrender of an entire Zulu regiment and gave Cetshwayo until 3 July to comply.

Chelmsford, now cleared of blame for the prince's death, was camped barely forty miles from Ulundi with 10,000 troops. By 2 July, just four miles from Ulundi, Chelmsford received a telegram from Wolseley demanding that Chelmsford reunite his two columns and desist from attacking until Wolseley could take personal command of the (soon-to-be-victorious) British forces. But by this time Cetshwayo had left Ulundi, taking with him the Dutch trader who was the only one able to understand English at Ulundi. On 4 July, Chelmsford gathered 5,300 troops, complete with field artillery and Gatling guns, and formed a large empty square; opposing them were 20,000 Zulus. Brigadier General Wood had earlier suggested entrenching the square, but Chelmsford would have none of it: 'They'll only be satisfied if we beat them fairly in the open—we must show them we can beat them in a fair fight' (quoted in Morris 1994: 569).

'They', in this case, referred not just to the Zulus but to the British government and public back home; whether assegais versus artillery, rifles, and Gatling guns is 'fair' is another matter. No Zulu came within thirty yards of the square and within thirty minutes the battle was all but over. Thirty-five thousand cartridges were fired by the British, who had lost eleven dead and eighty-eight wounded; the Zulu dead littered the floor and were estimated at 1,000.

The very next day, on 5 July—just before Wolseley's arrival—Chelmsford requested permission to return to England, which he did on 27 July. Cetshwayo was exiled to Capetown and Zululand was split into thirteen kingdoms. All Zulu men were free to marry when and whom they wanted, but no military system was permitted. In all, around 8,000 Zulus had been killed and 16,000 wounded. On the British side, 1,083 men had been killed, and 243 wounded; over 1,000 colonial troops had died. The war had cost the British over £5 million. By September the last British troops had left Zululand. The House of Shaka had fallen.

Analysis

The Philosophical Arts: Identity

We began this chapter by comparing the allegedly poor leadership of Chelmsford and the ostensibly heroic leadership of Chard as significantly—if not wholly—responsible for the defeat at Isandhlwana and the victory at Rorke's Drift respectively. It should be clear that, however 'heroic' Chard was, (a) there were literally thousands of heroes on both sides of the Anglo-Zulu wars and (b) Chelmsford was by no means the sole cause of the initial British catastrophe.

Of course, a major cause of the British catastrophe was the Zulus and we should look to the role of identity amongst them for important clues to their initial success and subsequent failure. In the first place it was the competitive identities rooted in honour between the various regiments that explained why so many were so willing to risk their own lives. But it was also this that inhibited coordinated attacks and allowed the British to concentrate their fire upon one group at a time. Relatedly, it was the British disparagement of the NNC troops that ensured they were so badly resourced and led and consequently the first to break at Isandhlwana.

At a political level, the identities of the two warring parties were also to prove critical, for, while the Zulus saw themselves as simply defending their homes and families, the British, or at least the British establishment, saw the Zulus as dangerous barbarians who had to be destroyed if British control over South Africa was to be secured. And, while the Zulus saw the British as merely concerned with maintaining order and controlling the Boers, they were manifestly wrong, for it was the British who were the 'real' imperialists not the Zulus. That misunderstanding of the *who* question proved catastrophic for Cetshwayo.

The Fine Arts: Strategic Vision

The strategic vision of the Zulus and British was clear *on* both sides but not clear *to* both sides. By that I mean that the British were intent on destroying the Zulu army and nation but the Zulus were not aware of this until too late. Cetshwayo intended to defend his kingdom, with force if necessary, but not to go beyond the boundaries of Zululand in the hope that this would deter the British from seeking his destruction. He was wrong, and his inability to see the real objective of the British Army prevented him from adopting more appropriate organizational tactics. In sum, Cetshwayo could not imagine that his erstwhile ally against their common enemy—the Boers—would seek the annihilation of his kingdom. Here is another important lesson for leadership: leaders have to divest themselves of their own assumptions about the opposition and step into their shoes; not so much sleep with the enemy but walk in their shoes to try and establish what they want—and to what extent they will go to achieve it. As we shall see when we consider Hitler, his opponents constantly underestimated his willingness to contemplate any action to achieve his objective.

The Martial Arts: Organizational Tactics

Wood suggests that two factors explain the difference between Rorke's Drift and Isandhlwana. First, the British could not maintain the necessary 'killing gap' between themselves and the Zulus at Isandhlwana; in other words, the rate of fire was insufficient to prevent the Zulus closing with, and overwhelming, the British (Wood 1984: 143–4). Secondly, the ammunition supply was too far from the front line and the ammunition boxes remained impervious to attempts to open them without screwdrivers. 'All for the want of a horseshoe nail!' is how he sums up the problem. Wood goes on to suggest that, important though the firepower and the discipline of the British troops were, they were insufficient in themselves to explain the victory at Rorke's Drift and the defeat at Isandhlwana; after all, both battles had the same two features. The difference, according to Wood, was the fortifications and the adequate ammunition: 'And those fortifications would never have been built had it not been for provident and active leadership by leaders who converted a highly vulnerable supply base into a defensible base for firepower . . . It took leadership of a high order not only to make preparation for defence but to ensure that the defence held out until the enemy reached his breaking point . . . through sheer force of will' (Wood 1984: 145–6).

But the Zulus lost the war primarily because their martial rather than their fine arts were inadequate. In other words because their organizational tactics were inadequate. This is not to suggest that the Zulu warriors were individually inadequate in their courage or skill but that their leaders failed to utilize their resources adequately. For example, although their army was sufficient to *dominate* their neighbours for many years, and although such a policy had secured the throne for Mpande against Dingane and later Cetshwayo over Mbuyazi, the Zulus' actual battle tactics (as opposed to Cetshwayo's more sophisticated theoretical tactics) never altered, even when the balance of resources began tilting sharply against them. At Rorke's Drift the Zulu field commander, Dabulamanzi, had ignored Cetshwayo's advice not to attack defended positions and Dabulamanzi had failed to coordinate the attacks on the compound. In short, they had not exploited their resources properly: they had attempted a battle of attrition that might have worked if the internal competition between regiments and the poor communications had not inhibited a single and sustained assault on all four walls. The competition between Zulus for martial glory and their undoubted bravery should have been resources in their favour, but instead the Zulus were deployed in ways that facilitated the survival of their British enemies.

Since the most significant resources available to the Zulus were the size, speed, and bravery of their army, a resource-inversion principle would suggest that the British should have encouraged their enemy to attack strongly held defensive positions where the greater killing power available to the latter could have been most effective. For the Zulus, initially without access to many firearms, the British technical superiority should have been used against them by encouraging a level of overconfidence bordering on conceit for the Zulus. However, it is more likely that Cetshwayo's tactic of attacking the British as they crossed the rivers was the one most consciously intended—in this case as a tactic of neutralization, where the British technical superiority could not be properly deployed in the restricted arena. The Battle of Isandhlwana was a good example of resource-inversion operating to the Zulus' advantage—though it is unlikely that this was ever a conscious tactic. The Battle of Rorke's Drift was an example of resource inversion operating in favour of the British—though again it is doubtful that the British intended and could even have hoped that the battle would turn out as it did. The Zulus had lost primarily because their leader, Dabulamanzi, had ignored Cetshwayo's advice not to attack defended positions and because Dabulamanzi had failed to coordinate the attacks on the compound. In short, they had not exploited their resources properly. The British defenders survived because their leaders, Chard, Bromhead, and Dalton, organized appropriately to prevent the Zulus closing and using their superior numbers to overcome their inferior technology.

The Performing Arts: Persuasive Communications

It is important to remember that the first battles were fought before the telegraph system had reached South Africa, so that, for example, twenty days elapsed after the fighting in Africa before Charles Norris-Newman's report on Isandhlwana was read in Britain (Laband and Knight 1997: p. vi). Its effect upon the British population can only be guessed, but the government immediately authorized the reserves and reinforcements that Chelmsford had long demanded. Furthermore every national newspaper of any repute sent a correspondent along with these reinforcements to report on 'the adventures' of the thin red line.[5] Chelmsford's prior and subsequent military campaigns suggest that he was, by and large, a successful military leader. Certainly, as his initial report on Isandhlwana suggests, apart from noting the bravery of Durnford's 'mounted Basutos', he was unable to explain the disaster.

As Table 5.1 suggests, at Gingindhlovu and Ulundi Chelmsford achieved the lowest casualty rate amongst his own troops whilst executing his orders to oversee the elimination of the Zulu army and the House of Shaka. He may well have inflicted unnecessary death and destruction upon the Zulu nation, but these were never articulated as reasons to question his leadership skills. He had entrusted the camp at Isandhlwana first to Pulleine, an officer with limited experience of battle—but with a thorough knowledge of conventional tactics—and then to Durnford—an experienced field officer who had already shown himself to be a

TABLE 5.1. *Comparative losses of the Anglo-Zulu war*

Battle	Zulu dead		British dead	
	Nos.	%	Nos.	%
Isandhlwana, 22 Jan.	2,000	10	1,329	75
Rorke's Drift, 22 Jan.	470	12	15	11
Hlobane, 29 Mar.	2,000	18	29	7
Gingindhlovu, 2 Apr.	700	7	13	0.4
Ulundi, 4 July	1,000	5	11	0.2
Waterloo, 1815			15,000	22
Somme, 1 July 1916			21,060	13.5

Note: absolute numbers of dead and as per cent of original numbers

loose cannon. But between them they should have managed to organize the defence of Isandhlwana rather better than they did.

Chard, on the other hand, had provided the proper—that is, traditional— defensive system, which had enabled the men at Rorke's Drift to survive the Zulu onslaught. Chard had also provided several demonstrations of personal bravery, but on any account heroism was one thing that was seldom lacking on any of the battlefields of Zululand. Certainly the defenders of Rorke's Drift were brave— but then the defenders of Isandhlwana suffered a much greater chance of death or injury than those at Rorke's Drift: there were 1,329 (75 per cent) total British casualties at Isandhlwana and only fifteen (11 per cent) at Rorke's Drift. Moreover, of the soldiers fit for action before the latter battle only six were seriously wounded and only one soldier died in the battle itself—and that as a consequence of leaving his post and running headlong into the Zulus; all the other casualties and deaths were from those already in the hospital (Glover 1997: 133). It was far more likely, then, that a defender at Rorke's Drift would survive without a scratch than that a defender at Isandhlwana would survive at all. And, since the proportion of the enemy killed was virtually identical, one can only assume that the bravery of the defenders at Isandhlwana was at least as great, and probably much greater, than those at Rorke's Drift.

Rorke's Drift was the scene for the highest ever number of Victoria Crosses, but no Victoria Crosses were issued for action at Isandhlwana. Was this because the defenders of Isandhlwana were not brave? I doubt it. Was it because the first was a victory and the second a defeat? I do not think so. The answer is much more mundane than this, but it is also profound: posthumous awards had yet to be created. The implication of this is that what counts as bravery is something that is constituted by discourses that turn 'acts' into examples of 'bravery' by dint of formal recognition. In other words, unless an act is observed and recommended by someone in authority as an act consistent with formal definitions of bravery, it cannot be considered brave. In effect, bravery is recognized as such only when it is performed according to the requirements of the recognition system. For example, there are probably thousands of acts of consummate bravery by Zulu warriors whose chances of death were far higher than those facing the British side—but you will be hard pressed to find them recounted or recognized in most texts on the battles.

A glance at the proportion of deaths in the battles also highlights the problem of assuming that Isandhlwana was a failure in terms of inflicting casualties upon the Zulu attackers. Far from it: the proportion of Zulu dead was higher than at either Gingindhlovu or Ulundi, the two battles that allegedly destroyed the Zulu army. The significance of this implies that the British 'victory' at Rorke's Drift occurred on the back of a destruction of about 12 per cent of the enemy force— only marginally higher than the Zulu casualty rate at the British 'defeat' at Isandhlwana. The implication, assuming that the latter figures are correct, is that the victory must have been rooted in something other than enemy casualties.

Of course, the proportion of casualties on the British side was significantly higher than any other battle in the campaign, in both absolute and relative terms, and, given the inequality between assegai and rifle, the shock of the defeat was that much greater. But it cannot be the case that absolute casualties are the most important issue, because the subsequent battle of Waterloo generated far higher absolute casualties for the British—yet was a victory. Indeed, since the death of the French crown prince was allegedly regarded in Britain as a greater tragedy than the death of over 1,300 imperial and colonial troops, we must assume that even the relative numbers killed were not the issue that drove headline writers back in Britain. Glover (1997: p. x) is clear that Rorke's Drift achieved its significance only because the British government wanted it that way and because the British public needed it that way. In other words, the defeat at Isandhlwana—and the disproportionately high casualty rate—were both a major political embarrassment and a necessary precondition for the public to accept Rorke's Drift as something other than the typical small-scale battle between hostile, but poorly armed, natives and the imperial troops of Britain. Isandhlwana had turned the British world upside down, but Rorke's Drift had turned it back the 'right' way again. This is important, because the method by which news was communicated ensured that the 'official' line usually prevailed.

Conclusion

In the long run the war effectively terminated the careers of many involved: Cetshwayo—now that he was beaten—became an icon for those Victorian British seeking the 'noble savage' and he was paraded through the streets of London in 1882 to polite applause wherever he went. And leading those seekers was Gladstone, eager to displace Disraeli's imperialist expansionism, which had led to the deaths of '10,000 Zulus . . . slain for no other offence than their attempts to defend against your artillery, with their naked bodies, their hearths and homes, their wives and families' (quoted in Knight 1995: 43.) After all this, Frere was recalled, the Confederation policy abandoned, and the Zulus left to their ignominious fate.

Overall, the resource-inversion tactics provide a significant explanation for the fortunes of the various parties, though it is not the case that either side consciously adopted the principle. Clearly, maintaining a 'killing gap' made sense to the British, just as eliminating the gap made sense to the Zulus, but this exploitation of one's own strengths is different from exploiting the strengths (rather than the weaknesses) of the other side by a policy of inversion. It was taking advantage of the Zulu propensity to mount competitive headlong assaults against the British that ultimately enabled the British to destroy the Zulu kingdom. But also critical was the demonizing of the Zulu identity by the British and the misunderstanding of the British strategy by the Zulus. It was not simply the rifle that won the war; it was leadership and the lack of leadership that proved critical.

Notes

1. Renamed the South Welsh Borderers in 1881.
2. Morris (1994: 360–2) suggests there was no formal head of the army.
3. According to Wood (1984: 136), it was Bromhead, not Chard, who built the wall.
4. This was originally developed by Maurice of Nassau in the 1590s (Parker 1995: 154) and refined by the British from the days of Marlborough (Chandler 1994: 85; Guy 1994: 104–6).
5. Quoted in Laband and Knight (1997: pp. xii–xiii). For instance, when Archibald Forbes, working for the *Daily News*, carried the first report of the Battle of Ulundi from the battlefield to the nearest—and new—telegraph station in August 1879, the report of his 'ride' was subsequently emboldened by the *Illustrated London News* into one where Forbes, 'bold, unwearied, dauntless, solitary horseman . . . volunteered to carry Chelmsford's despatch . . . in fourteen hours, entirely alone, over a rugged and mountainous country without any proper roads, and with no small risk of being cut off by the straggling bands of the enemy . . . he twice lost his way. He performed this valuable public service with such intrepid courage . . . that we trust he will receive from her majesty the Queen a suitable honorary distinction . . .'. The correspondent of the *Natal Mercury* was rather less generous, for 'the account of his [Forbes's] ride . . . has very amused those who know the man, and the road he had ridden over and the feat he had performed. Mr Forbes was not asked to carry despatches . . . there was nothing extraordinary about the matter, for unless he had been irresponsible for his actions he could not have missed the track left through the country by 600 Ox wagons, 2,000 cavalry and 10,000 footmen, and travelling at a time when it was perfectly safe to ride' (quoted in Laband and Knight 1997: 57).

Part Two

Situating Extreme Leaders

6

Henry Ford: The Blind Business Visionary

Strange, mused the Director, as they turned away, strange to think that even in Our Ford's day most games were played without more apparatus than a ball or two and a few sticks and perhaps a bit of netting. Imagine the folly of allowing people to play elaborate games which do nothing whatever to increase consumption. It's madness.

(Aldous Huxley, *Brave New World* (1955), 35)

Henry Ford was, in the eyes of many, the leading figure of modern capitalism: he gave us Fordism—not just a way of manufacturing but a new form of industrial organization.[1] Indeed, according to Henry himself, he 'invented the modern age'. Thus Ford must rank as one of the great inventor-leaders of all times.[2] Henry Ford, it seems, did this primarily through the invention of the assembly line at Highland Park that Charlie Chaplin later parodied in *Hard Times*—even though assembly production long pre-dated Ford and was in operation in a Venetian arsenal by the late fifteenth century (George 1972). Moreover, it was Charles Sorenson and P. E. Martin who introduced it to the Ford plant (Batchelor 1994: 44). Ford apparently invented mass production—*the* twentieth century industrial systems—even though Colt revolvers and Singer sewing machines had been mass produced long before the Model T hit town. He also invented the overhead conveyor belt—though the Chicago slaughtering yards had been handling carcasses this way long before Ford visited them. He invented the standardized product—the model T that came in one colour [black] and one model (Doray 1988: 70)—yet the Model T actually had nine different body styles and was originally green, then always black, and then one of five colours. He invented interchangeable parts—but again Colt and Singer beat him to it outside car production, and inside it was Henry Leland's Cadillac Motor Company that introduced it (Gartman 1979: 197). He invented flow technology, yet Edwards suggests that Rhode Island textile merchants had already introduced flow technology at the beginning of the nineteenth century, and, anyway, it was Walter P. Flanders not Ford himself who first introduced the idea to the Ford Motor Company (R. Edwards 1979: 113; Batchelor 1994: 44). And even if he didn't invent the moving assembly line, he certainly employed it to good effect, securing huge productivity gains from it, according to Hounsell—even though the greatest advances were achieved either before the moving assembly line had been introduced or were derived from technical and organizational changes that had little to do with the moving assembly line (Hounsell 1984; Williams *et al.* 1993). Yet, ironically, although Ford's mass-production, 'just-in-case' system of huge-stocks-of-everything is forever contrasted to the Japanese 'just-in-time' production systems, it was Ford who, with Chrysler and General Motors, pioneered the development of just-in-time's predecessor and progenitor: 'the hand-to-mouth' system. Ford invented the mass market itself with his famous Model T—a motor car that even the people who built them could afford—yet the definition of 'mass market' remained unclear and could have been applied to several products before.

He provided the unheard of wages of $5 a day in 1914 that enabled his employees to buy Model Ts 'and set in place the foundations of a consumer economy where well paid workers created demand' (Morgan and Cruz 1997: 3), though few Ford workers either earned $5 a day or stayed long enough to earn the required sum for a Model T. Indeed, Ford's wages were seldom high by the standard of the day in the USA. He enabled vast numbers of Americans to own cars because his prices were so low, but he persisted in assuming that price was critical long after many of his former customers had drifted away to the cars of General Motors and Chrysler, where the competitive edge was in novelty and product enhancements not simply price. He set a precedent with his groundbreaking union deal in 1941, which set the pattern for post-war industrial relations—even though Ford detested the unions, and his official and unofficial police force machine-gunned labour activists and assaulted them.

He was a pacifist who spent a vast personal fortune leasing a 'peace ship' to sail to Europe and stop the First World War—but he simultaneously made an even bigger fortune with his production of munitions, boats, tanks, planes, and jeeps in both wars. He said history was bunk and then spent a lot of time, money, and effort ensuring that his version of the past prevailed over contrary reports, and he left America with Greenfield Village, the first historical theme park based around reconstructed eighteenth- and nineteenth-century buildings. He pontificated endlessly on the importance of family life to America—and gradually destroyed his own.

He also invented the modern corporation—yet the Ford Motor Company was almost wholly driven by the needs of production. Finance, marketing, cost accounting, managerial structure, and all the other accoutrements of modern corporations were of little or no interest to Henry Ford (though they were to General Motors), and the company came close to collapse on several occasions as a consequence of his engineer's tunnel vision. Ford also pioneered 'in-sourcing' to secure control over every possible element of car production, even to the point of buying a huge Amazonian rubber plantation, though he also resorted to outsourcing when it suited him and, eighty years later, once again the Ford Company pioneered the outsourcing of car assembly in the Ford Amazon plant in 1999 (*Financial Times*, 4 Aug. 1999).

Henry Ford also regarded himself as a leader of the American people—as indeed were all business people in his eyes. But his belief that he understood the people better than their political leaders is best represented by his claim during prohibition that, 'in the matter of liquor . . . the people are now, as they have ever been, against it' (Ford 1991: 124). He could not have been more wrong.

Nevertheless, he was not just *a* successful business leader; he was *the* successful business leader—the icon of the early twentieth century. He was not just one of *the* greatest mass producers; he was a mass of contradictions, though, on the whole, a successful mass. He was, to put it concisely, a leader whose organizational success rested not on engineered organizational clarity but on invented organizational paradox.

He achieved this not by mobilizing his workforce through great speeches—because, like Nelson, he was a poor public speaker. His morality was not a great driver either, and, though he did have a particular philosophy of life, it did not enthral his followers—employees or customers. He was not regarded as charismatic and many of his actions achieved machiavellian notoriety. He could not threaten his followers with extreme coercion, as Hitler could, though some of the actions of the Ford Motor Company towards its own employees, especially union activists, fell little short of wielding the sword. And Henry's son, Edsel, certainly seems to have lived under the Fordist sword of Damocles for virtually all his life. Nor could Ford invoke the divine right with which monarchs buttressed their thrones—though again, Ford sometimes appeared to act *as if* this were the case. He was a risk-taker, as indeed are all leaders, but not in the Nelson school of absolute personal risk; indeed, Ford was adamant that risk-taking *à la* financial investment in stocks and shares was not just bad business but immoral.

Ford was notoriously bad at many things and often isolated. He could, however, *seduce* colleagues, employees, and customers alike. He could seduce colleagues away from traditional investments to invest in his apparently crazy schemes that had so often failed in the past by displaying before them his vision of undreamed-of wealth. He could seduce his employees to leave their traditional path of work limitation and collective representation to sweat their lives out as individual slaves to the machine in his factories by dangling what was often regarded as a carrot of astonishingly high wages. However, getting them *into* work was one thing; getting them to *do* some work when they were there was altogether a different problem, and the difference illuminates the gap between the theory and the practice of organizational power, the indeterminacy gap. Ford could seduce his customers away from their traditional horse-drawn buggies and from alternative cars, from alternative investments and purchases, and from their own cultural inertia by promising them a product that would revolutionize their lives, but he could not guarantee a sale, let alone a return customer. Because Ford assumed he had the *absolute* solution to the problem of family transport, he took little interest in the *relative* utility of the car. As far as Ford was concerned, once everyone had a Model T, demand would eventually dry up. But, as Veblen had predicted, and as General Motors embodied, once everyone had a Model T, those who could afford it wanted something different. Veblen called this 'conspicuous consumption', the overt demonstration of superior material wealth over those recently able to acquire the latest consumer good, but Ford was conspicuously consumed by a different driver: not infinite consumer demand but insatiable producer control.

Again, the discontinuity between *what* Ford thought should happen—his strategic vision of a world full of perfect Model Ts—and *how* it was to be achieved—his organizational tactics—undermined his dream. Ford assumed he had found *the* solution to the *how* problem when he began displacing people with technology wherever he could. Thus the unreliable human was turned into the reliable machine, and, where complete displacement was not possible, the indeterminacy of the human was coerced, cajoled, and, if necessary, dominated by the machinery of production. Yet Ford failed in this vision and was constantly forced to provide supplementary mechanisms for controlling people. Since large numbers of them left, rather than put up with his designs and demands, his technology could reach only those people who stayed. But the quality and quantity of their work were never as reliable as Ford assumed and he was forced to employ large numbers of quality inspectors, of shortage-chasers, of company spies and company informers, simply to compensate for the weakness of the technology. It could not, after all, dominate or determine production.

F. W. Taylor had held much simpler views on the utility of seduction as a mobilizer of effort: only money mobilized because only money seduced. The cash nexus was therefore not just the *critical* link between employer and employee, between the strategic vision and the organizational tactics, between the *what* and the *how*; it was the *only* link. Furthermore, Taylor was adamant that brain and hand should be separated so that the managers could scientifically establish the one best way of executing a task and workers would be forced to adhere regidly to this. Ford remained dogmatically glued to the Model T, but his workers had to remain flexible to cope with the endless changes in production practices as Ford strove continuously to improve efficiency. Ford's seduction strategy was also far more complicated than the *homo economicus* that Taylorism and Scientific Management implied. For Ford, at least early on, the seduction of wages still required its opposite for effective motivation—morality; workers had to be shown how to behave and what to do with their new-found wealth. In sum, Ford sought to dominate his workers, just as he dominated his managers and his family. Domination, or, if necessary, a battle of attrition until he achieved domination, was just about the only organizational tactic that Ford used.

By the end of Ford's life the irony of the situation was to become all too clear. The replacement of the paternalistic cash nexus with the amoral (and sometimes immoral) stripped-down cash nexus stimulated not simply a greed for more money, and through this a subordination to Ford, but a desire for protection from the depredations of Fordist amoral market capitalism through the very thing Ford feared most: a labour union. Ironically, then, not only did Ford's anti-collective strategy invoke the kind of collective behaviour it was designed to avoid, but all Ford's failures and successes were premised upon the opposite foundation stone: it was through collective effort alone that anything—success or failure—resulted. Ford succeeded because he built a successful organization, and then he almost lost everything by dispersing that same organization. If Ford could not dominate his colleagues, he sacked them, as he did with the team that designed and built the Model T: Harold Wills, the original draughtsman, was forced out in 1919—to build his own car; the Dodge brothers withdrew their investment to build their own vehicles; James Couzens, a coal-yard clerk that drove Ford's production line along, resigned to become Mayor of Detroit and later entered the senate; John R. Lee, who had helped build the Sociological Department, left at the same time (1919) to help Harold Wills; William Knudsen, the Danish engineer, having failed to overcome Ford's more favoured Dane, Charles Sorensen, left to help design the Chevrolet for General Motors that undermined the Model T. As Ford noted when Knudsen had gone, 'I let him go not because he wasn't good, but because he was too good—for me' (quoted in Lacey 1986: 274). In effect, Ford removed all those people who had a talent equal to his or the temerity to argue with him; the consequence was that no one could stop Ford's slide after the Model T had peaked. He dominated all those he could and sacked all those he could not—and they included the people who could have stopped him making many of the mistakes he made.

The paradox of Henry Ford was no more clearly evident than in the way Ford's initial success was rooted in the elimination of indeterminacy. In the new world of the Model T nothing was to be left to chance or variation; control over processes, people, and product was to be complete—the vagaries of nature and humanity were to be subordinated to the precision of the machine. But it was precisely this precision, this replicability, this conformance to standards imposed by Ford that saw his lead over competitors erased. The customers of the 1930s did not want the determinacy and invariability of a Ford whose alleged embodiment of the perfect vision rendered it beyond improvement. Instead they wanted change, variation, new models, fashionable accessories, and individualized cars. Ford may have initiated modernism but he wanted to control his progeny; instead it nearly destroyed him. But Ford was also phenomenally successful—how did he achieve this?

The Bland Watchmaker

Henry Ford was born on 30 July 1863 in a wood clearing in Dearborn, Michigan, thirty-one years after his Irish relations arrived in the USA, and twenty years after his own parents, poor Protestant farmers from southern Ireland, had fled the potato famine. While Henry's parents were originally poor, Henry, the eldest son, was by his own account brought up in comfortable conditions on the 120-acre farm (Ford 1991: 17). He went to the local one-room, one-class school at 7 and, although not a notable student, excelled—according to his own account—at mechanical repair and construction, though this is disputed by his sister Margaret. In 1876, when Henry was 12, his mother died shortly after giving birth to her eighth child. Henry seems to have been devastated by the event; for him the home had become 'a watch without a mainspring' (quoted in Lacey 1986: 11).

Not long after this tragedy Henry saw his first motorized vehicle, a steam-powered wagon whose owner had converted the now commonplace agricultural steam engine to drive the wheels of a wagon. For Ford this was his moment of destiny and set him further on a path of conflict with his father, William Ford, who, in Henry's account, wanted to keep his son on the land and had a distinct disdain for mechanical devices of any kind. Again, Henry's sister Margaret disputes all this and Lacey suggests that Henry's fixation with his mother made it impossible for him to admit that his father had ever encouraged him (Lacey 1986: 15). By the age of 16, Henry had left home and moved to Detroit. In his own version of events he simply left home against the wishes of his father, but there is substantial evidence to suggest that, on the contrary, his father helped him get his first job in Flower Brothers machine shop.

When Henry arrived in Detroit in 1879, the city had around 80,000 inhabitants but was hardly a thriving industrial conurbation; yet within thirty years it ranked third to Chicago and New York, with its thriving iron, lead, and salt mines, fishing and forestry. The first metal stoves were built there in 1864 and the first refrigerated beef was shipped from Detroit in 1869. Detroit rapidly became the machine capital of America and by 1903 it produced almost half of all US car production. After a short apprenticeship at Flowers, Henry joined the Detroit Dry Dock Company and maintained himself by undertaking evening and weekend work as a watch-repairer. Despite Henry's assertions about his disdain for his father and the land, he returned every autumn to help his father with the harvest, and, at the age of 19, having completed his mechanical apprenticeship, he left Detroit and returned home to work the land with his father. In the event, his first job was repairing, maintaining, and using a neighbour's small steam engine, which he trailed around the local farms to undertake cutting, threshing, and sawing jobs. This led to a job working as a local representative for Westinghouse, the manufacturers of the steam engine, and Henry seems to have regarded this period of his life with great affection, nostalgically returning to the country for harvest celebrations long after he had actually left the land behind.

On 1 January 1885, Ford met his future wife, Clara Jane Bryant, at a local dance—though, in her words, 'he made absolutely no impression on me'. He also, allegedly, kept the original programme as a momento. In fact, as Lacey suggests, the programme was a fake, reconstructed many years after the event, demonstrating yet again what the *Chicago Tribune* called Ford's 'congenital reshaping of history' (*Chicago Tribune*, 25 May 1916) and throwing a different light on his most famous quote: 'History is more or less bunk' (though Ford was really concerned with the way traditions, once established, prevented people from realizing new dreams). As his words continued, history is 'tradition. We don't want tradition. We want to live in the present, and the only history that is worth a tinker's damn is the history we make today' (quoted in Batchelor 1994: 1).

Henry and Clara were married in 1888 and initially lived in the small 80-acre farm his father had given him. Henry soon found work repairing machinery around the area and in Detroit, and it was there that he first came across the 'silent Otto', an internal combustion engine that Ford immediately realized could be redesigned to drive a vehicle in a way not dissimilar to the steam-engined contraption he had seen as a boy.[3] However, the new device was driven by electricity, about which Ford knew virtually nothing, and he took a job in Detroit with the Edison Illuminating Company as a mechanic-engineer in a power station. Once the station was up and running, it more or less looked after itself—an idea that Ford may have applied later to his own workshops. Ford and three other engineers spent a considerable amount of time building small engines and considering how to build a horseless carriage—which they did in a shed near Ford's lodgings. As one of his colleagues, Frederick Strauss, recalled: 'Saturday nights we had quite a crowd. Henry had some sort of magnet. He could draw people to him; that was a funny thing about him' (quoted in Batchelor 1994: 18). This was not the first motor car by any means, since European vehicles had existed since about 1885, but there were, until 1893, no such contraptions in the USA.

In 1893 Edsel Ford, Henry and Clara's only child, was born, and within a year Ford had received a double promotion to chief engineer and taken up teaching mechanics at the local YMCA, where he met Oliver Barthel and Barthel's employer, Charles B. King, who were also building a car. In fact, theirs was finished marginally earlier than Ford's, and the first car ran on the Detroit streets in March 1896. However, King's car was a slow-moving, heavy, and luxurious affair. In contrast, and right from the beginning, Ford employed a design for his *Quadricycle* where the reduction in weight meant reduced cost and increased speed, which, by happenstance, also established the basic principles for a mass-produced car. In June 1896, having had to demolish the shed to get the vehicle out, Ford took his first car on to the streets.

Three years later, in 1899, the Detroit Automobile Company (the first car company in the city) was formed with $150,000 of capital. This huge sum was supplied by Ford's old acquaintances: William Maybury, Detroit's mayor, who had hosted Henry and Clara's wedding; William Murphy, a multi-millionaire; the McMillan brothers, who controlled the Michigan Telephone Company and most of its transport network; the Detroit Dry Dock that Henry had worked for; and a whole host of other city dignitaries and magnates. In January 1900 the first vehicle, a delivery van, drove out of the factory with Henry and a reporter from the *Detroit News Tribune* on board. Despite the rapturous reception in the press, the company was bankrupt in less than a year after Henry had realized that he could not control the entire company and simply withdrew.

But Murphy still thought Ford could make a success of cars and sponsored Henry's new development, a racing car featuring a spark plug covered in porcelain, courtesy of a local dentist, that was to feature in the Grosse Pointe race between the new world record holder, Alexander Winton, and Henry Ford. Ford won when Alexander's quicker engine blew up.

It was also around this time that Ford became interested in reincarnation, perhaps because it rationalized all the events and experiences of life—even if they were not employed until the next one. This idea, derived from a book entitled *A Short View of Great Questions*, provided Ford with the kind of simple explanation for complex events that he always sought. As Lacey (1986: 58) argues, 'His great gift, the secret that was to make him successful, was the ability to make complex things simple.' Hence, when Ford was asked to explain the pacifism that he clung to during the early part of the First World War, he would insist that his birth, on 30 July 1863, shortly after Gettysburg, must have been premised upon the death of a soldier. Reincarnated or not, Ford had stumbled across an organizational principle that would take his name around the world: simplification. It is by no means certain that Ford was aware of the significance of this, because his return to business conspicuously failed to embody the principle. In November 1901, on the back of his famous Grosse Pointe victory, Ford's second car company, the Henry Ford Company, with $60,000 of capital, opened for business. Despite the failure of his first venture, Ford immediately began designing not a simple commercial vehicle but a second complex racing car. However, Murphy had prepared for another such scenario and this time brought a trouble-shooter, Leland, who demanded Ford returned to the original design work. Ford refused and was fired, leaving the Henry Ford Company with the commercial designs for a Ford car that would become the first Cadillac of the renamed Cadillac Automobile Company, and subsequently, in 1909, the General Motors Corporation. Ford had now formed and left two of the 502 car companies in the USA that existed between 1900 and 1908; he was still in the majority, because 302 of these did not last beyond the first decade of the twentieth century (Lacey 1986: 62).

The Ford Motor Company

Henry's new venture was with Tom Cooper, a famous cycling champion, and C. Harold Wills, a draughtsman. Between the three of them they designed two new racing cars, and chose the '999', the opposite of Ford's previous lightweight machines, to participate in the Grosse Pointe race of 1902—which he duly won in another new American record time. However, it was with Alex Y Malcolmson, a Detroit coal merchant, that Henry developed his next commercial project, Ford & Malcolmson Ltd, in 1902, and the intent from the start, this time, was to build a passenger car. Malcolmson employed James Couzens, with a reputation as a ruthless accountant, to keep Ford in order and the new Model A began its life under the renamed Ford Motor Company. As was usual for the time, the manufacturing of the car was left to outsourced subcontractors, with the factory concentrating on final assembly, but the company was so undercapitalized that Ford was forced to maintain his concentration on the job in hand, rather than wandering off to develop new models as he was wont to do. And at 39 years of age Ford was not really in a position to renege on his commitments.

A large number of small investors backed Ford, including Charles H. Bennett, and, with each car costing around $554 to produce, leaving $150 profit, Ford Motor Company began—after a shaky start—to make a profit. Initially it made twenty-five cars a day with 300 employees (Zoia 1996). By March 1904 658 model As had been sold. The same year Ford announced three new models (B, C, and F), with the Model B as a luxury vehicle, but he still could not match the 'Merry Oldsmobile', which was $150 cheaper, as a mass-market product.[4] Luckily for Ford, the Olds factory burned down in 1905, leaving them without a production plant and without the finance to re-source it. As a consequence, Olds developed what became known as 'hand-to-mouth' inventories: they outsourced whatever they could, because they had virtually no production plant left, and they minimized stock levels, because they could not afford to accumulate any surplus inventories. Since the early car manufacturers tended to use many of the same parts, and because many of the parts' manufacturers were also concentrated around Detroit, what we now refer to as 'just-in-time' systems developed spontaneously (Schwartz and Fish 1998: 52). Although Malcolmson insisted on moving further upmarket with the Model K, Ford and Couzens saw the real challenge and opportunity at the other end of the market. But to make this work they needed to reduce costs dramatically, preferably by overturning the outsourcing policies and getting as much of the vehicle as possible built within the Ford plant itself. To this end, the Ford Manufacturing Company was initiated in 1905 excluding Malcolmson, who promptly began a new business of his own in competition with Ford. Ford was now the majority shareholder of his own company and, as he was driven home that night, allegedly said to his driver, one of the mechanics, Fred Rockelman, 'Fred, this is a great day. We're going to expand this company, and you'll see that it will grow by leaps and bounds. The proper system, as I have it in mind, is to get the car to the multitude . . . The car will have a universal effect. We won't have any more strikes or wars' (quoted in Lacey 1986: 84, 132).

In 1906 Ford announced they would produce 10,000 Model Ns at a price of $450. This was truly the equivalent of the computer developments that occurred in the 1990s: a colossal reduction in cost in conjunction with an incredible increase in power. However, mass production was not machine production and the effort simply required larger numbers of workers; even then, prices could not be held to those advertised and the first Model N was priced at $600. The Model N, and its enhancements, the Models R and S, generated spectacular growth and $1 million profits for Ford, and all other models were dropped as the company concentrated its production. But the car that Ford had in mind was the Model T.

The Model T

In the winter of 1906–7 Ford began to design a completely new car—his twentieth in five years—based on the use of vanadium steel, which had made the Model

N stronger, lighter, and more reliable (Womack *et al.* 1990: 26). This car, Ford predicted, would be different:

I want to build a motor car for the great multitude. It will be large enough for the family, but small enough for the individual to run and care for. It will be constructed of the best materials, by the best men to be hired, after the simplest designs that modern engineering can devise. But it will be so low in price that no man making a good salary will be unable to own one.   (quoted in Batchelor 1994: 20)

Ford had insisted that no 'scientist' was necessary to enhance the company's knowledge of special alloys. Instead, the most talented of the shopfloor workers were employed, with a short training period, to oversee Ford's metal develop-ment, and it was with vanadium that Ford began to construct the plans for the Model T—an all new car. When the car was nearing assembly, Ford sent out the particulars to his sales agents, many of whom assumed it was another of Ford's practical jokes (for which he had become famous). But, within three months of announcing the car publicly, in October 1908, Ford was forced (temporarily) to close the order book, the demand was so great, and, with 500 workers producing 100 cars a day, at a price of $850 each, Ford was moving into large-scale produc-tion. And, for all his relish for continuous improvement and his engineer's inabil-ity to leave things as they were, Ford decided that the only person who was going to be free to play around with the product was himself:

It is strange to think how, just as soon as an article becomes successful, somebody starts to think that it would be more successful if only it were different. There is a tendency to keep monkeying with styles and to spoil a good thing by changing it . . . Therefore in 1909 I announced one morning, without any previous warning, that in the future we were going to build only one model, that the model was going to be 'Model T', and that the chassis would be exactly the same for all cars.   (quoted in Sargant Florence 1961: 109)

The rapid increases in production that resulted from the change of direction and focus were the consequence of two particular features: work slides between workers who slid their completed work down to the next operative, and radical advances in the division of labour. This effectively eliminated the need for work-ers to walk between sections and simultaneously facilitated supervision, because there was now no reason for any employee to be anywhere except at his or her direct point of production (Gartman 1979: 198–9). The only 'slack time' now operating was the time it took to move parts where slides were inappropriate—and the moving assembly lines soon began eating into this. Horace Arnold sug-gested that what Ford had done through the assembly line was make control easier, since it was now much clearer who was slacking and who was not. As he says, before the assembly line the 'boss could never nail, with certainty, the man who was shirking, because of the many workpiles and general confusion due to the shop floor transportation' (quoted in Lewchuck 1987: 62). It looked as though Ford had solved the problem of friction, the puzzle of indeterminacy, by making his organization more transparent to his controlling gaze. Self-taught shop-floor workers, not university-educated engineers, had enabled him to see better and now he could dominate his workforce physically rather than continue a constant battle of attrition with them.[5]

Costing $825, the Model T was not the mass vehicle Ford had dreamt of, yet. But, at the equivalent of a teacher's annual salary, it sold 10,000 in the first year. The success was based upon innovation, rather than cost: it had a powerful engine, semi-automatic transmission, and a magneto that replaced the previous heavy batteries. There were no doors, speedometer, or internal fuel gauge[6] and the car's suspension was designed for potted lanes not surfaced roads—but then there were very few of the latter anyway. By the end of 1918 approximately half the world's cars were Model Ts and by the end of production, in 1928, Ford had produced fifteen million (Lacey 1986: 97).

In 1909, just as the Model T was hitting record sales, the company was hit by a suit claiming patent infringement on behalf of the Association of Licensed Automobile Manufacturers (ALAM), a consortium of car-makers who had all accepted the claim of George Selden to have patented the internal combustion engine. Although a New York judge decided against Ford, Henry refused to accept defeat—or the heavy financial claims made against the company—and eventually won at the appeal court in 1911. From this point on, Henry Ford became an American folk hero, fêted in the press as the man who stood up to the ALAM trust, which, it was alleged, was clearly intent on milking all and sundry. Far from suffering from his identity as a farm-boy made good, Ford became represented as an archetypal honest mechanic, a self-sufficient and independent family man who stood for the 'traditional' values of America and who wanted to help the lives of his fellow Americans. As the business magazine *Management Today* makes clear: 'As is proper for an American folk-hero, Ford had humble beginnings' (*Management Today*, Dec. 1996, 86). Humble or not, they were certainly perceived as being in sharp contrast to the besuited business executives of the new corporate élite in ALAM, who were evidently trying to exploit the average American. Thus, at a point where Ford could have been put out of business by a very powerful lobby group, he unwittingly managed to invert their strength because their very power became symbolized as a self-interested attack by the rich on the poor.

The Model T inaugurated the mass-production line as a method of assembly when the Highland Park factory was opened in 1909. Mass production was not a novel idea in the USA but Ford insisted that his version was the only true mass-production system, for it operated around the assembly line itself and combined dedicated machinery, the automated flow of materials, and large production runs. The consequences were twofold: first, prices dropped dramatically and, secondly, the difficulty of retaining workers to operate 'on the line' forced Ford to pay high wages. Ultimately, the high wages generated the precise conditions for mass consumption and the era of industrial modernism was ignited.

Although the new factory was designed with the new reinforced concrete that allowed much larger areas of space and huge swathes of windows, the first production of Model Ts in 1910 used the old assembly system in which sections of the car were built in one spot before the whole chassis was moved on to the next dock. There were no moving assembly lines as yet, even though the principles of assembly-line production were well known to Ford, from the Singer and Colt factories and from the slaughtering yards in Chicago, which used overhead conveyor belts for disassembling the animal carcasses. But demand was so high that the docking-station method could not cope—as the car production figures suggested: in 1909/10, Ford manufactured 18,664 Model Ts. The following year this had almost doubled to 34,528, and by 1911/12 it had doubled again to 78,440 (*Management Today*, December 1996: 86).

Interchangeability was a critical element of Ford's approach, because he could not afford the time to remachine each part that needed fitting and he was a zealot at 'working-to-gauge' (Womack *et al*. 1990: 27). The idea of interchangeability had originally emerged in the late eighteenth century in France with General Jean-Baptiste de Gribeauval's concerns for gun production. But its development had been taken furthest first by the partnership of the American government's Ordnance Department and Samuel Colt armoury in the 1850s and then by the Singer Sewing Machine Company in the 1880s. Ford also adopted some of Frederick Taylor's methods of Scientific Management, though Ford was more concerned to displace labour by technology wherever possible rather than to enhance its efficiency. Ford also had little time for the scientifically derived work efforts that Taylor claimed he could establish.[7] If there was a scientific level of effort then it might prevent the kind of continuous improvements that Ford knew he could extract from his workers simply through the ubiquitous 'speed up' for which the word Ford became synonymous. Moreover, Ford's homespun engineering skills and policy of promoting from the shop floor always militated against Taylor's insistence on separating conception from execution: thinking from doing; management from labour. Ford had nothing but disdain for 'book learning' and often looked to his shop-floor workers to provide suggested improvements to the production process. If any employee refused to remain flexible and insisted on doing a task in his, or occasionally her, way, Ford had no compunction about instant dismissal. Paradoxically, then, despite Ford's image as a man who refused to change with the times, he introduced a continuously changing process and product—the only condition was that it was Henry Ford himself who set the parameters for all these changes. Thus the last Model T produced in 1927 was almost totally different from the first Model T of 1908—but it was still a Model T. The only changes were those personally approved by Henry Ford and these could not be seen to undermine the original power train and chassis, and, as the car developed, it simply got heavier, slower, and noisier, and shook its passengers more.

Ford also wanted to replace the outsourcing of parts with in-house production, since, on average, Ford reckoned he could produce the same part for half the price—the diametrically opposite view of what became taken (even by Ford) as 'common sense' in the 1990s: outsourcing. Thus, while 68 per cent of the value of each early Model T was bought in, by 1915 this figure had been reduced to 52 per cent (Williams *et al.* 1992: 521). It should also be remembered that Ford's reliance upon outsourcing left him dependent on others—something that he never felt comfortable with.

What Ford was developing was the perfect machine, not the perfect labourer beloved of Taylor. This fixation with perfection—that was apparently all his own doing—was never so graphically displayed as when, in 1912, Ford returned from a trip to Europe to be faced with a 'new' red, low-slung Model T, built in his absence by his own design team. Ford ripped the car apart with his own hands. It was an act of hand disassembly that presaged a radical assault upon the organization of hand assembly: the assembly line was coming.

The Moving Assembly Line

The first moving assembly line was introduced on 1 April 1913 at Highland Park, where the magneto assemblies were produced; it cost $3,500 in 1913 prices (Winter 1996*b*). On that day the workers arrived to find their traditional benches gone and a new, waist-high rail system instead, upon which the magnetos travelled. Through a series of experimental changes, assembly time fell from twenty minutes under the hand-assembly system down to thirteen and then five minutes. The changes also did away with the need for skilled workers. By the summer of 1913, as the experiments expanded throughout the plant, the final chassis assembly came under scrutiny and, according to Arnold and Faurote, who observed the new system shortly after it had been introduced, the 12.5 hours labour time per chassis was halved to just under 6 hours. When further improvements were made, it went down to 1.5 hours (Arnold and Faurote 1915). However, as Williams *et al.* (1993: 70–1) suggest, the figures are dubious, since indirect labour costs were eliminated from the calculations and neither the innovations in machine-shop technologies nor the introduction of gravity slides were eliminated from the figures allegedly derived from the moving assembly line. Wherever the savings came from, with such reductions there were concomitant labour reductions, and, with 100 of the 600 employees on the assembly floor operating as full-time component carriers, Ford was keen to wield the redundancy axe as quickly as possible (Gartman 1979: 20). The secret, according to Ford, was that

The man who places a part does not fasten it. The man who puts in a bolt does not put on the nut; the man who puts on the nut does not tighten it. . . . No workman has anything to do with moving or lifting anything . . . let the conveyor do the walking. Save ten steps a day for each of 12,000 employees, and you will have saved fifty miles of wasted motion and mis-spent energy.   (quoted in Lacey 1986: 109)

One consequence was that labour costs were cut in half by late 1914 (Wilson 1996: 30). But it was not just 'mis-spent' energy that Ford was interested in, it was also 'un-spent' energy, and much of the efficiency was secured through speed-ups. As Ford admitted: 'We regulated the speed of the men by the speed of the conveyor' (quoted in Gartman 1979: 202). The suggestion that his employees were reduced to robots through the machinery is very dubious, since they could always refuse to operate at such speeds, but without any collective organization to support such displays of resistance the workers were individually isolated and very vulnerable to Ford's disciplinary system. Nevertheless, workers covered for each other to facilitate the development of extra breaks and spent such a long time in the toilets, having an extra cigarette break, that Ford was forced to employ extra supervisors to watch out for such 'toilet loafers' (Batchelor 1994: 53).

Thus Ford persisted in trying to dominate the production process by replacing people with technology wherever possible. Moreover, the technology appeared less subjective than a human controlled system, and therefore ostensibly less open to dispute and negotiation. As Ford suggested: 'Real leadership is unobtrusive and our aim is always to arrange the material and machinery to simplify the operations so that practically no orders are necessary' (Ford 1926: 99). What such an approach to control also ensured was that any quality problems remained the problem of the quality inspector, not the individual machinist. Ironically, then, despite Ford's attempt to place the control over quantity and quality outside human hands, the production system was very dependent upon human quality inspectors. In 1916 over 600 inspectors were employed and, although some of these were deployed to inspect materials coming in that were obviously beyond the direct machine control so beloved of Ford, the majority of inspectors were deployed internally, checking on both the product and the process quality (Wilson 1996: 28). Still Ford pushed for a further displacement and he began to reverse his prior Taylorist trend to divide work unto the maximum degree, and began reintegrating the tasks under technological control: 'Now we are heading back to the old days except that where one man did the whole of a job, now a machine as far as possible does all of the job' (quoted in Wilson 1996: 29). In short, the fewer people involved the better.

Ford's displacement of skilled workers by machines also opened up a sizeable source of labour for employment—and thereby increased the utility of dismissal as a disciplinary weapon. When it took between five and ten minutes to train almost any operator on almost any job, and when the task cycle time had been reduced from 514 minutes in 1908 to 2.3 minutes in 1913, the interchangeable part was accompanied by the interchangeable worker in the interchangeable organization (Womack et al. 1990: 28, 229). Ford had created a carrot and stick controlling system, where the good wages dragged workers in and the very real fear of losing these same wages acted, often almost literally, to enthral them. Fig. 6.1 shows that the numbers of cars produced per worker doubled from just under nine in 1909 (the numbers are per ten workers) to just under eighteen in 1916. At the same time, labour hours per car dropped from 357 in 1909 to 134 by 1916. But what is also important is that the moving assembly line, introduced in 1913, did not, in and of itself, make the largest single difference to the productivity increases. However, 'the Chain drive (continuous assembly) proved to be a very great improvement, hurrying the slower men, holding the fast men back from pushing work on to those in advance, and acting as an all-round adjuster and

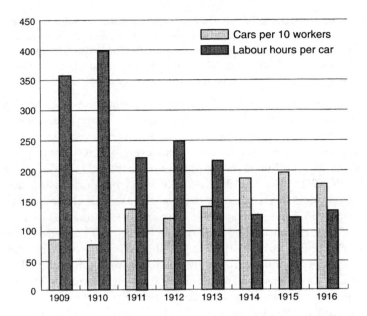

Fig. 6.1. Model T production in hours and workers
Source: Reconstructed from Williams, Haslam, and Williams (1992).

equalizer' (quoted in R. Edwards 1979: 118). For Edwards, following Arnold, the technology not only dominated the pace and method of work but displaced the supervisors; henceforth disputes at work were mediated by technology; in the end, 'it succeeds in maintaining speed without obtrusive foremanship' (quoted in R. Edwards 1979: 119). And, with a supervisor/worker ratio of just 1 : 58, it was apparently clear that the technology now embodied the primary disciplinary mechanism. Ford's penchant for dominating tactics appeared to have fused perfectly with the machine.

This fetish for the elimination of waste of any kind also marked Ford's decentralization policy. Moving completed cars around the USA put a $75 charge on each one, as Ford could squeeze only three vehicles on each freight car. However, by packing them as knock-down kits, he could get twenty vehicles into a freight car. By 1915 he had established twenty-four branch assembly sites across the USA, and by 1911 he already had plants in Windsor, Ontario, and in Trafford Park, Manchester (Williams *et al.* 1992: 521).

In 1913, when Ford was producing 200,000 units, Peugeot, the largest French manufacturer, managed a mere 5,000, while the largest British firm, Wolseley, barely reached 3,000. Ford's Model T was often regarded by the British, long locked into performance cars for the élite, as 'cheap and nasty'. Certainly, some of the skilled craft-workers recruited to Trafford Park were unimpressed with Ford's attempt to deskill them: in 1913 a twenty-two-week lock-out at the body shop occurred. As one British engineer remarked:

In America, I understand, the labour available is much more amenable to systematized working. In England there is difficulty in getting a man to do exactly what he is told, because he is apt to think a great deal more for himself than do his fellows in America. Therefore the system in this country has to be more elastic and less precise than many American systems are said to be.   (quoted in Batchelor 1994: 73)

Indeed, the predominance of the USA as a car producer became ever clearer in the inter-war period: in 1924 there was one car for every seven US residents, in the UK the ratio was ten times greater at one car for every seventy-eight residents, and in Germany greater still, at one car for every 470 residents. Most West European countries, including the UK, did not reach the 1924 US level of car ownership until the 1960s (Bowden 1991: 246). But even when the British decided that the car market might stretch beyond the upper and middle classes, and the first Model T competitor, the Morris Oxford, arrived in 1913, the Model T was still 25 per cent cheaper, even after its rapid rebuild from the kit imported to Trafford Park (Church 1994: 6; Morales 1994: 60). William Morris visited the USA twice in 1914 to study production methods but was hardly in a rush to copy their techniques: he first introduced a hand-powered assembly line in 1919 but did not invest in a powered line until 1934 (Batchelor 1994: 75).

With the Ford system now mechanized, production levels doubled again, but this time the workforce, rather than doubling to keep pace with demand, actually fell from 14,336 to 12,880. Yet, although Ford seems to have been intent on continuous improvements in design, he was also an adherent of continuous avoidance of administration, to the point where it began to unhinge the production system. In the event, Couzens ensured that the administration was taken out of Ford's personal hands, while continuous improvements in design were restricted so that they did not impede production. Additionally, a network of 450 agents was established across the country to sell the cars.

The $5 Day

Away from his cars, Ford relaxed by bird watching and he made some effort on behalf of the Weekes–McLean Bill to protect migratory birds, which subsequently became law in 1913. Ford also dabbled in the ideas of John Burroughs, Ralph Waldo Emerson, and Henry David Thoreau. From Emerson in particular, Ford accepted that spontaneous action was preferable to reason, 'for too much rationalization can be a dangerous thing' (quoted in Lacey 1986: 114). This may seem paradoxical for a man so rigidly glued to rationalizing the assembly line, but Emerson was no hater of machines and Ford's actions were also those of a free spirit, and account for at least some of his early industrial failures.

Free spirit he may have been, but 'generous employer' was not the kind of epithet attached to Henry Ford in 1913. The 'going rate' for employees at the time was around $2.50 for a ten-hour day, and Ford, like virtually every other employer, only paid the going rate and laid off workers as soon as demand slowed or production was interrupted. In October 1913 the pay was increased to range from $2.34 to $4 in an effort to stem the massive labour turnover, that reached 380 per cent by Christmas 1913. At the time 70 per cent of the turnover comprised 'five-day men'—that is, workers who stayed for only one wage packet and simply failed to come back to work and were presumed to have left after five days of absence. Only 4 per cent of the workforce qualified for the annual bonus payable to all those with three or more years' service and by early 1914 Ford's absenteeism was still running at 10 per cent, despite the fact that the company was then making 96 per cent of all American-made cars sold at less than $600.

But Ford was not just a visionary with tunnel vision and a tactician with only one tactic; he was also a performer in his own right and knew how to rationalize a problem into an innovation. With what had now become typical for Ford, a press statement in January 1914 announced the solution to the 'five-day men'. 'The Ford Motor Co., the greatest and most successful automobile manufacturing company in the world, will, on Jan. 12, inaugurate the greatest revolution in the manner of rewards for its workers ever known to the industrial world' (quoted in Batchelor 1994: 23). The haemorrhaging of 'five-day men' was reduced by 90 per cent by increasing the pay to $5 a day. It included a large profit-sharing element, and was payable only after six months' continuous service. It was also linked to an eight-hour day (from nine), which simultaneously enabled the shift pattern to change from two nine-hour shifts to a continuous cycle of three eight-hour shifts. By this time Ford was well aware of the significance of media coverage, and the unwelcome advances of the syndicalist trade union, the Industrial Workers of the World (IWW). On the morning of the wage changes the press was suitably impressed: 'A Magnificent Act of Generosity' ran the headline of the *New York Evening Post*. 'God bless Henry Ford' cried the *Algonic Courier*. And a 'lordly gift' opined the *Toledo Blade* (quoted in Batchelor 1994: 24).

In fact, Ford hoped the money could also be used to 'Americanize' the workforce, 70 per cent of which were then composed of twenty-two different nationalities. John R. Lee, head of Ford's Sociological Department, explained the approach: 'It was foreseen that $5 a day in the hands of some men would work a tremendous handicap along the path of rectitude and right living and would make of them a menace to society in general and so it was established at (the) start that no man was to receive the money who could not use it advisedly and conservatively' (quoted in Batchelor 1994: 49). Those who were not regarded as 'heads of families'—that is, women workers, unmarried men under 22 years of age, workers with less than six months' service, married men having 'family troubles', or anyone 'living unworthily'—were refused the increase. Living 'unworthily' included living off credit—a moral sin for the puritanical Ford, but a 'sin' that was also to cost Ford dear when, bucking the trend, he held out for many years against offering cars for sale on credit terms. Two years later there were still 30 per cent earning less than the magic $5 (Serrin 1974: 130). When Ford discovered in 1919 that eighty-two of his female employees had husbands who also worked, he sacked them. After all, he reminded the readers of *Ladies Home Journal* in 1923: 'I consider women only a temporary factor in industry . . . Their real job in life is to get married, have a home and raise a family. I pay our women well so they can dress attractively and get married' (quoted in Batchelor 1994: 50).

The new shift patterns required an extra 4,000–5,000 employees, and within a few days 15,000 increasingly desperate individuals milled around outside, eventually attacking the Ford workers and being dispersed by the Highland Park Police's water cannon. The *Wall Street Journal* was sanctimonious in its condemnation of Ford for trying to introduce 'spiritual principles into a field where they do not belong'. This, the paper suggested, had inevitably led to chaos and social disorder, and, worse, it was obvious that Ford could not sustain the wages. In fact, Ford could easily sustain them, for at Christmas he had restructured the assembly lines to make them continuous, thereby cutting the total vehicle assembly time down from 400 hours in early 1910 to 130 hours in 1916. Most of these hours were reduced by displacing external by internal labour. The implication of this is that the majority of the saved labour time and reduction in material costs occurred *before* the moving assembly inaugurated by the magneto line in 1913. For example, the overhead conveyor was in operation by 1912 (Williams *et al.* 1992: 522–5). Hence, although the moving assembly line came to acquire an iconic status, the symbol of the new dawn, it was in the more mundane elimination of waste and workshop materials handling that most of the advances in productivity were achieved—where, for instance, simply putting machines in the sequence for part completion and moving them closer together reduced the distance travelled by engine black casting from 4,000 feet to 334 feet (Williams *et al.* 1992: 527). In short, it was organization not technology that was mainly responsible for Ford's leap in productivity.

Waste in terms of overstocking was also eliminated throughout 1915 by running with stocks for only three days, production for much of the time—though the factory was designed to run with twenty-five days' of stock in hand (Williams *et al.* 1992: 543). One consequence was that, whenever a bottleneck occurred, 'shortage chasers' were mustered to solve the problem—something that would not have been necessary had the technology operated to plan (Wilson 1996: 29). At this stage the development was more the consequence of a radically expanding demand, which simply pulled material through the plant almost faster than Ford's employees could make the cars. Earnest Kanzler had an even more radical method of lean management up his sleeve, which he deployed five years later as the post-war slump hit Detroit: he outsourced the problem to Ford's dealers (see below). However, the 'hand-to-mouth' system that had now reappeared at Ford was again seen as a problem not a solution, particularly when the massive turnover of staff so disrupted the assembly line that massive overproduction mountains and underproduction bottlenecks were becoming regular occurrences. Furthermore, in an era where control and predictability were the measures of organizational success, the contingent unpredictability and innate instability of the hand-to-mouth approach persuaded Ford that something better was needed. Indeed, since Ford was convinced that the Model T was already perfected and since the market appeared like a sponge, devouring anything and everything that Ford could make, the fear that stockpiles of parts would soon be obsolete and thus uneconomic was consigned to the dustbin.

More than this, Ford had learned from Emerson that, in essence, you got what you paid for—and only if you paid good wages would you get commensurate workers. Ford liked to portray the $5 a day as an act of consummate economy; it was, he said, 'one of the finest cost-cutting moves we ever made' (quoted in Lacey 1986: 122). But Lacey suggests that underlying this bravado was a real desire to pay what Emerson called 'full compensation'. Moreover, Ford was intent on ensuring that the employees recognized the difference between the $2.34 'basic-wage' element of the pay packet and the $2.66 'profit-related pay'. Ford's newly created Sociological Department tried to ensure the latter was wisely spent by having each of its fifty inspectors questioning workers, spouses, and neighbours as to the final destination of the $2.66. Ford hoped that the money would not be spent in any of the 500 brothels that spread through the area, easily outnumbering the churches. As Lacey concludes, courtesy of the Ford Sociological Department, and in a fine parody of *Brave New World*, 'Cleanliness was next to Fordliness' (Lacey 1986: 124). And though Fordliness was typically patriarchal, the disabled were not discriminated against. By 1919 almost one-fifth of the entire workforce was disabled in some way, including one worker with no hands and four who were totally blind; there were also between four and 600 ex-convicts on the payroll. On the other hand, many rejected his iron discipline, and, when 900 members of the orthodox Greek and Russian churches took time off work to celebrate Christmas in January, they were unceremoniously sacked.

Ford's promotion of the disabled was partly connected to his assumption that everyone should earn a living rather than rely on charity. But it was also linked to his assumption that most of his workers were happy to work in a system that he himself admitted was soul- and body-destroying for those individuals blessed with talent.

Repetitive labour—the doing of one thing over and over again and always in the same way—is a terrifying prospect to a certain turn of mind. It is terrifying to me. I could not possibly do the same thing day in and day out, but to other minds, perhaps I might say to the majority of minds, repetitive operations hold no terrors. In fact, to some types of mind, *thought* is absolutely appalling . . . The average worker, I am sorry to say, wants a job in which he does not have to put forth much physical exertion—above all, he wants a job in which he does not have to think.   (quoted in Batchelor 1994: 52; emphasis added)

Ford's tactics were, then, clearly grounded in an evaluation of his internal 'opposition'—that is, his employees—as congenitally weak. Therefore his domination of them was not simply in his own interests and not even just in the interests of the company; it was actually in the interests of the employees themselves. Ford had managed to create a series of strategic visions in his head in which everything he did was in the interests of everyone—whether other people realized it or not.

This ruthless and arrogant approach to business was often hidden beneath a veneer of innovation and generosity, so that Ford managed to take the moral high ground at the same time as he dug a pit for his opponents. For instance, in 1914 he introduced what must have been the first 'cashback' scheme in history, giving $50 to every Model T purchaser, an act that cost the company $11 million. But the effect of this was to reduce the sum available to the other shareholders, and at the time the Dodge Brothers were both major shareholders (owning 41.5 per cent between them) and they were intent on using their Ford profits to develop the first Dodge car, in direct competition with Ford's Model T. Thus Ford effectively neutralized the power of the Dodge brothers by rendering their shareholding of marginal value. By 1916, after Henry had threatened to withhold another $58 million in profit, the Dodge Brothers had had enough and sued Ford, complaining that his action—of continually reducing prices even when demand was increasing—was contrary to the basic laws of the market and therefore clearly designed to undermine their own profit taking. The 1908 Model T price of $825, for instance, had been reduced to $345 by 1916 and all the time demand increased. Ford's response was that he was not in business simply to make money but also to provide the largest possible number of ordinary people with a means of transport and with a job. Such a marketing approach operated to expand the US car market quite dramatically—in sharp contrast to most European manufacturers, especially the British, where a radically unequal distribution of income, coupled with high taxation, and high initial and running costs, prevented all but the top quarter of the population ever being in a position to buy a car (Bourden 1991: 255).[8] But Ford's ability to reduce the price of the Model T was not based on the savings derived from the reorganization of the production system and the reduction in direct labour costs associated with this. On the contrary, as Fig. 6.2 demonstrates, internal labour never generated more than around a quarter of the costs of the materials involved in Model T production between 1909 and 1916. In effect, the price reductions were achieved only through a permanent clampdown on the costs of materials and bought-in components: it was insourcing that built the foundations of Ford's early success. What withholding the profits and the expansion of sales also did was lay the foundation for the River Rouge site.

Originally, Ford had talked of the River Rouge plant not only in terms of its enormous size (2,000 acres) but also within his vision of a vertically integrated plant where Ford owned everything—that is, the mines for the ore and coal, the plantations for the rubber, the ships, and everything else in between, including the blast furnaces. But the plant was also his private possession, a personally owned Henry Ford tractor plant rather than a collectively owned Ford Motor Company plant. The Rouge plant, the largest industrial complex in the world at the time, opened in 1918, mass producing warships. As promised, Ford bought rubber plantations in Brazil—Fordlandia—by the Amazon on a site four times the size of Rhode Island, coal and iron mines in northern Michigan, as well as forests and fleets (Davis 1998: 32). The Dodge brothers were very concerned that such a huge investment could not possibly support just a tractor plant. They were right. At the end of 1918 Henry Ford resigned from the presidency of Ford Motor Company, giving Edsel the chance to take over; meanwhile Henry, now in com-

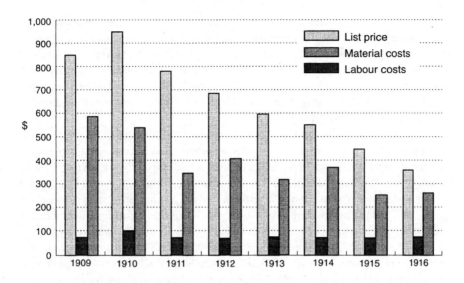

Fig. 6.2. Model T: price, labour, and material costs, 1909–1916
Source: Reconstructed from Williams *et al*. (1993: 76).

plete control of the new company, was going to build a car to rival the Model T
that he would sell for half the price. The intention of this drastic action by Ford
was to reduce the value of the original Ford Motor Company stock and force the
Dodge brothers and the other five major shareholders to sell their shares back to
Ford. In the event it cost Ford $105 million, but even this colossal sum was prob-
ably an undervaluation of around 400 per cent (Lacey 1986: 176). By 1920, then,
Ford had achieved his goal; he and his son Edsel were now in total control and
they had undermined the power of the Dodge brothers and the other shareholders in a costly battle of attrition. The rival car and the rival company mysteriously
disappeared and, while Edsel was nominally in charge of 'business', Henry
retained control of engineering.

The First World War: Peace Ship versus Warship

Hard-nosed as he was, Ford remained true to his early pacifism as the First World
War spread through Europe, and in 1915 insisted that he would give up his entire
fortune (then estimated at over $30 million) if it would bring peace to the world.
He even offered prizes and investments for peaceful endeavours of various kinds.
In 1915 he charted the *Oscar II* as a Peace Ship, and held a press conference to
announce how it would end the war—except that he had no idea how it would
end the war. And, with his usual ineffective display of public speaking, he merely
managed to embarrass himself. In the words of the *Detroit Free Press*, there is
'not the slightest evidence that Mr Ford had a definite plan as to what he is going

to do when he gets to Europe' (quoted in Lacey 1986: 139). In sum, Ford's legendary organizational skills were once more revealed as inadequate to the task—
as indeed they would have been for any single individual. The difference between
Ford and most other individuals was that he did not recognize a barrier even
when it appeared right in front of him. The *New York Herald Tribune* was even
more scathing in its sarcastic headline: 'Great War Ends Christmas Day: Ford to
Stop It' (quoted in Batchelor 1994: 25).

The voyage was a disaster in terms of its intentions, but Ford at least won some
of the journalists over, for whom he was 'an inarticulate Christ', and 'a mechanical genius with the heart of a child'. Indeed, when asked by an adviser why he
had risked so much, Ford replied: 'I do not want the things money can buy. I want
to live a life, to make the world a little better for having lived in it' (quoted in
Lacey 1986: 144). In the event, Henry became ill on the trip and returned to the
USA, where he was greeted more as a foolish Don Quixote who had at least made
an effort to stop the war (he spent almost $500,000 on the escapade) than as a
complete idiot. 'No matter if he failed,' said the *New York American*, 'he at least
TRIED' (quoted in Batchelor 1994: 26). Ironically, then, Ford's inabilities as a performer on the world stage had once again worked in his favour, for, just as he had
beaten the ALAM trust with his naïvety, so he emerged from the shambles of the
Peace Ship as an honourable leader in dishonourable times.

Ford's performative ability was much better suited to persuading people to
part with their money for guns rather than their guns for money. By 1917, even
though Ford remained committed to peace, the German announcement of unre-
stricted submarine warfare against all shipping suspected of carrying material to
the allied side led Ford to do an about turn. Instead of executing his original
threat to burn down Highland Park rather than use it for war, he asserted that the
entire plant would be turned over for war production—but without taking one
cent of 'blood money' for it. In the event, helmets, armour plate, aeroplane
engines, and tanks were all churned out from Highland Park. The 'Eagle' anti-
submarine boat was also produced in the new River Rouge plant, which turned
out to be a blessing for Ford, since it encouraged the government to foot the bill
($3.5 million) for Ford's new development—though only one boat was commis-
sioned before the war was over.

Ford's role in war work, especially during the First World War, was as controversial as his political views and character. Despite his pacifist views, Ford made
a considerable sum from building munitions and military equipment, but managed to display this 'blood money' as a patriotic gesture. Indeed, in 1922 *The
Truth about Henry Ford*, a book written by Sarah Bushnell, allegedly with the
cooperation of Mrs Ford, suggested that Ford had donated all of the $29 million
profit made from war work to the US Treasury. In fact, Ford had not paid any
sum to the Treasury, but the political embarrassment caused by the concerns
about 'blood money' failed to stimulate any such payment afterwards, even
though the legend of Ford's generosity persisted until the Second World War
(Lacey 1986: 162–4).

In 1916, at President Wilson's personal request, Henry Ford stood for the Senate representing Michigan and his election campaign was geared to his inability to speak publicly—he simply refused to make a single speech in the entire campaign and then exploited rather than suffered from this tactic. As Ford (1991: 120) later said in his own defence: 'It is not the men who are doing the talking who are solving our problems, but the men who are at work.' He still managed a creditable performance, even after his son, Edsel Ford, had refused to enlist and had subsequently been made exempt on the grounds of already supervising war work and being an only son. Henry Ford lost the election but only by the slimmest of margins in the November 1918 election.

Undeterred by this defeat, and spurred on by the recent excitement of political influence, in the same month Henry Ford bought the local newspaper, the *Dearborn Independent*, intending to make it both an organ for broadcasting his own views and a national paper of repute. He hired several conventional reporters, including William Cameron, and, through Cameron, Ford began to outline his homespun wisdom in 'Mr Ford's Own Page'. As already mentioned, Ford was never a great public speaker and was at his worst during a case for libel against the *Chicago Tribune* in 1919, which had accused Ford of being an anarchist and ignorant to boot. To test the latter, the lawyers for the *Chicago Tribune* asked him, 'Have there been any revolutions in this country?' To which Ford replied, 'Yes . . . in 1812.' Asked if there were any others, Ford denied it. He was then asked, 'Do you know that this country was born in revolution?' He answered, 'Yes, in 1776.' 'Did you forget that revolution?' asked the *Chicago Tribune*. 'I guess so,' came Ford's reply. The court found in favour of Ford—he was not an anarchist—but awarded him only six cents in damages. The highbrow newspapers had a field day in their indictment of Ford's ignorance. But, like the British population in Nelson's day, the rest of the population seemed to feel that not only was Ford actually made human by this weakness, but it was right and proper that the power of the land should not be restricted to the clever. Arthur Brisbane, a journalist with a syndicated column in rural newspapers, asked his readers to 'cut this [newspaper column] out and mail it with your name signed: Dear Ford: I am glad to have you for a fellow citizen and I wish we had more of your brand of anarchism, if that is what it is.' The appeal was immensely popular and Ford's reputation for simple honesty and trustworthiness was enhanced yet further (Batchelor 1994: 27). Once again, Ford's weaknesses had been turned into strengths, for the more 'ordinary' Ford appeared to be, the more his customers supported him. After all, the Model T was not a luxury car for the élite, it was an 'ordinary' car for the 'ordinary' people. In effect, Ford's personal character mirrored the characteristics of his car and Ford's personal identity became conflated with the cultural icon of American identity: the rags-to-riches story of a poor citizen who made it from farm to fame on the basis of his own hard work and endeavour.

It was not always clear whether Ford was as simple as his critics made out but whenever his apparent simplicity won over their sophistication the public cheered him. Thus five leading art dealers assembled what they considered to be the greatest 100 paintings available in the world and then created three books full of copies of the originals—in an attempt to persuade Henry to buy them. But they were devastated when Ford asked why he would want the originals at such exorbitant prices when, as a gift, they had already provided such marvellous books of copies. After all, Ford's financial success was based on exactly this principle: replication.

Depressions and Downsizings

With the end of the First World War, plus the addition of an electrical self-starter to solve the problem of the crank starting, Ford's now ubiquitous Model T was poised to break the million mark, as one car in three bought in the USA was now a Model T. But the depression of 1921 caught Ford dangerously close to a cash-flow crisis. Ford, typically, slashed car prices—by over 30 per cent on some versions of the Model T. At these prices Ford was losing $20 a car and he instigated some radical cost-cutting measures. The administration staff was cut by over 50 per cent; 60 per cent of the telephones were removed and those most unnecessary luxuries of all, pencil sharpeners, were thrown away. More importantly, Ernest Kanzler, who was married to Edsel's wife's sister, was brought in to run the Fordson tractor plant, and, having recognized the futility of carrying so much stock, he (re)instigated the hand-to-mouth system. By 1924 it had developed to the point where stock was often used on the same day that it arrived. Kanzler was then brought to Highland Park and the River Rouge plant to replicate the savings. Ford later explained the results:

Let us say one of our ore boats docks at Fordson at 8 A.M. on Monday . . . Ten minutes after the boat is docked its cargo will be moving toward the High Line and become part of a charge for the blast furnace. By noon Tuesday, the ore has been reduced to iron, mixed with other iron in the foundry cupolas, and cast. Thereupon follow fifty-eight operations which are performed in fifty-five minutes. By three o'clock in the afternoon the motor has been finished and tested . . . If the motor . . . goes into the assembly line for the Detroit district, then the completed car will be delivered before Tuesday afternoon.   (quoted in Schwartz and Fish 1998: 56)

Not that Ford was alone in this approach. All three major US producers operated hand-to-mouth systems in the 1920s and General Motors boasted, for example, that the time between painting a wheel and fixing it to the car was reduced from eighteen days to four hours (Schwartz and Fish 1998: 57).

A second cost-cutting tactic was literally to outsource the problem. With around $88 million in cars and stock, Ford clearly had a lot to save and he simply shipped each of his 6,000 dealers more cars and more spares than they had ordered. Since, until this time, a Ford franchise was the equivalent of a gold mine, the excess stock was 'outsourced' on a huge scale to the dealers and their total subordination to his company left them with little or no room to manœuvre.

Moreover, by cutting and delaying payments for materials, Ford soon removed his financial crisis, and, after a couple of months idle, Highland Park reopened with just nine workers per car, rather than the fifteen it had used before the shut-down at Christmas 1920. In all, 20,000 of Ford's 70,000 employees were not rehired, including the entire Sociological Department. From then on, the attempt by Ford to institute a new moral philosophy of work—by paying high wages but monitoring how it was spent through visits to employees' homes—disappeared. Ford was now not just another employer; on the contrary, as Bill Klann, a pro-duction assistant, recalled, 'Ford was one of the worst shops for driving men' (quoted in Lacey 1986: 351).

One of his main targets now became the $60 million of stock lying around Highland Park and the River Rouge plant and, as he recalled,

We found out how to use less money in our business by speeding up the turnover ... (and) reducing the cycle of manufacture from twenty-two to fourteen days. That is, raw mater-ial could be bought, manufactured and the finished product put in to the hands of the dis-tributor in (roughly) thirty-three per cent less time than before. We had been carrying an inventory of around $60,000,000 to insure uninterrupted production. Cutting down the time one-third released $20,000,000.   (quoted in Schwartz and Fish 1998: 54)

But again, each organizational 'solution' generated—or, rather more accurately, 'dispersed'—another organizational problem. The shift to hand-to-mouth inventories also left Ford very vulnerable to outside suppliers, to the extent that Ford began employing trackers to monitor the shipment of raw materials and parts to Ford from all over the country. 'Men are stationed at junctions and other points throughout the country to see that (railway) cars are not delayed ... if a car is overdue more than one hour, the fact is known at headquarters' (quoted in Wilson 1996: 29).

By 1923 Model T sales had topped 2 million and well over half the cars built in the world were Fords. Each year technical advances were incorporated into the car and by 1925 you could even have a Model T in one of five colours.[9] But in the same year market share dropped to 45 per cent (from 57 per cent) and Ford responded this time with another performance of innovative note: he extended 'the leisure hours of the workforce'—in other words, he cut the working week by a day to reduce production. An annual 'cull' of workers was now common prac-tice in Ford's: each summer a percentage would be fired and each autumn a smaller percentage would be rehired—often at lower rates than they had origi-nally received. By 1926 market share had dropped to 34 per cent—primarily at the hands of General Motors' Chevrolet, then run by Alfred Sloan and ably abet-ted by several of the men Ford had 'let go' in the 1920 'downsizing'. While the Chevrolet was designed for the surfaced roads, rather than the mud tracks that had first borne the Model T, and while General Motors offered customers credit purchases and annual design changes, Ford offered none of these. Nor did he think the Model underpowered or noisy, nor did it need a gear box, nor hydraulic brakes, nor a redesigned body; since, like its designer, it was already virtually perfect, it did not need any changes. Nobody else thought like this, but then nobody else was in sole command of Ford Motor Company. The obvious reason for the failing sales, according to Henry Ford, was the inadequacy and incompetence of the sales force. The solution was to expand the dealerships so that competition between Ford dealers was encouraged. But Ford dealers, now weary of selling fertilizer from the Rouge plant and ensuring that every purchaser took out a subscription to the *Dearborn Independent*, began leaving in droves. Kanzler attempted the impossible—suggesting that Henry Ford was wrong—in a six-page letter to the old man (Ford was now 63), worked out with Edsel's blessing. But, while Edsel was away in 1926, Henry proved he was right by sacking Kanzler. After all, he argued, 'The Ford car is a tried and proved product that requires no tinkering. It has met all the conditions of transportation the world over . . . The Ford car will continue to be made in the same way. We have no intention of offering a new car at the coming automobile shows' (quoted in Batchelor 1994: 57).

But even Henry could not turn back the tide, and, on 26 May 1927, Henry Ford, with Edsel at his side, drove what was to be the last of 15 million Model Ts off the Highland Park assembly line. Sixty thousand Ford workers in Detroit were left without work for six months until the new Model A was unveiled in December 1927. The delay was a consequence of Henry's inability to recognize the change of the times and to reorganize in time for the change. His anarchic management structure—such as it existed—and lack of experience in developing new models threw the company into chaos. Resolving that chaos cost a fortune, perhaps as much as $250 million in terms of lost sales as well as setting up costs for the new Model A (Batchelor 1994: 63). Yet even this stagnation did not fundamentally impair Ford's fortunes, because the market was so enormous that demand made the technological investment viable—in a way that was seldom the case in the smaller European markets. Thus, for example, in 1937 the US manufacturers still produced over ten times more cars (four million) than the UK manufacturers did (390,000). Equally significant, 85 per cent of the US market was dominated by the big three (Ford, General Motors, and Chrysler), while in Britain, Morris, Ford, and Austin controlled only 61 per cent of the domestic market (Bowden 1991: 261).

At 65 Henry Ford, still with an annual income measured in multiples of million dollars, and with Edsel Ford still President of the company, should perhaps have been looking forward to retirement, but a control freak like Henry could never let go of the reins. And, even though father and son were always physically in touch with each other, they seldom seemed to be able to touch each other emotionally. Henry simply demanded and Edsel simply acquiesced. For Henry, such acquiescence was a sign of weakness that could be cured only by him and only by a long-term strategy of humiliation. On one occasion while Henry was away, Edsel had organized the building of a new office block to house the expanding needs of the administration. When Henry returned and asked Edsel what the building was for, Edsel started by saying that they needed more room, and that the first development was for the accountants on the fourth floor. Within twenty-four hours Henry Ford had stripped the existing Accounts offices of every stick of furniture and sacked every single member of the department, telling Edsel that if he needed any more room the fourth floor was now vacant. Edsel subsequently found jobs for all the sacked staff but the acquiescence to his father merely provoked Henry to further displays of ritual humiliation in a vain attempt to get Edsel to stand up for himself (Lacey 1986: 264). In fact, so problematic did accountants find working for Ford that the financial system became something of a mystery—to the extent that one department was found to have been so understaffed that it began *weighing* corporate invoices in bundles rather than paying them individually (Lacey 1986: 430). The organizational slimming that Henry was so fascinated by had become organizational anorexia. This was hardly the sign of an organizational genius and more the manifestation of an organizational ignoramus.

Yet, while the organization hovered on the edge of catastrophe, the product appeared infallible. Within one week of the new Model A being released to the dealers, 25 per cent of the entire American population had visited a showroom. It was state-of-the-art technology and yet remained, at a price of $495, over $100 cheaper than the rival Chevrolet. The Model A was built at the Rouge plant, which at the time was the first integrated car plant where virtually every component was produced in house on the twenty-seven miles of conveyor belts, using raw materials from Ford's mines and plantations. But the research, testing, and production facilities were so poor in comparison to those available to General Motors that each early Model A cost Ford $300 in after-sales repairs. It took Ford six months to switch from Model T to Model A; it took General Motors six weeks to change its Chevrolet model in 1929; Ford was a great engineer and an even better entrepreneur, but he was not a great manager of organizational change.

The Model A took 34 per cent of new sales in 1929, ahead of Chevrolet, but this was the last time in Henry's lifetime that Ford could look back at the competition. And while the move to total integration and conveyor-fed production at the Rouge plant generated an immediate increase in productivity, it was a one-off improvement that the mechanical nature of the plant both institutionalized and set in concrete. Where Highland Park had been a place of constant change and constant improvement, the fully mobilized Rouge was, ironically, the immobilizer of change and constant improvement (Williams *et al.* 1992: 545). By comparison, the Chrysler plant building the 1935 Plymouth achieved a degree of versatility in production that makes contemporary claims to just-in-time production and flexibility look distinctly tardy and Ford's concern for uniformity positively medieval:

The entire output of the plant is made only to order from the dealers. Orders coming in are sent daily to the control room. Here thirty-five copies are made and sent to the points from which all necessary variable parts of the car are despatched to join the embryo chassis on its way to completion. Timing is so perfect that the specific car ordered by the specific customer comes together as rapidly and smoothly as though the 1,800 cars produced daily at the Plymouth plant were identical instead of varied ... The whole thing takes only seven days from the time the order is received.   (*Fortune*, Aug. 1935, 114, 117, quoted in Schwartz and Fish 1998: 62)

There were some radical technical advances associated with the Rouge plant at the time, but they were few and far between. For instance, the V8-engined version of the Model A, called a Model B, which Ford developed in 1932, provided such acceleration that many gangsters and criminals of the day, including John Dillinger and Bonnie and Clyde, used them as getaway cars. When Bonnie and Clyde were killed in 1934, their Model B was riddled with 107 bullets but the local Ford dealer drove it away from the scene without any trouble (Lacey 1986: 311–12).

As the Depression deepened in America, and as Detroit's unemployment queues lengthened, Ford reduced the cost of his cars and increased wages to $7 a day for unskilled workers, because 'the average man won't really do a day's work unless he is caught and cannot get out of it' (quoted in Lacey 1986: 305). But Ford simultaneously laid off expensive skilled workers and outsourced their work to some of the most exploitive sweatshops of Detroit. By 1932 the wage rate had dropped back to $4 a day and the number of Ford employees was halved from 101,069 to 56,277. Car production in Ford and the rest of the USA had also collapsed, as Fig. 6.3 shows.

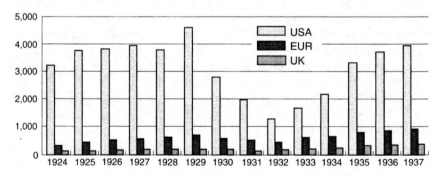

Fig. 6.3. Output of motor cars, 1924–1937
Source: Reconstructed from Bowden (1991: 244).

For those black Americans who lived in Inkster, a shanty town that housed the now unemployed foundry workers from the Rouge plant, Ford had a better idea. He paid them just $1 a day to work, funnelling the other $3 into a fund to revive the community of Inkster itself, because, in Ford's mind, black Americans were incapable of organizing themselves properly. As his 1917 *Ford Guide* reminded them: 'Black people came from Africa where they lived like other animals in the jungle. White men brought them to America and made them civilized' (quoted in Batchelor 1994: 51). Not so the Jewish population, for Henry Ford's anti-Semitism had long held Jews responsible for organizing a grand financial conspiracy against virtually everybody, but particularly the farmers, whose increasing productivity always seemed to generate lower not higher prices. This combination, Ford insisted, could be explained only by recourse to a conspiracy of Jews, not by the operations of the free market. Ford's anti-Semitism came in full public view as his *Dearborn Independent* lambasted the Jews in every copy of the paper for two years, as the 'invisible government', as he called the 'world Jewish conspiracy', sought to control the international economies. Lacey (1986: 208) calls Ford the 'Great Simplifier' and this surely is an apt title, reflecting Ford's bias to explain complex events by the simplest possible explanation. However, when Ford began considering a personal race to the White House in 1922, he had the anti-Semitic articles stopped: 'Jewish hostility might not matter too much so far as car sales were concerned, but it could cost a lot of votes in urban areas' (Lacey 1986: 210). When, in 1924, Ford decided not to pursue his political ambitions, the anti-Semitic articles returned with a ferocious attack on Aaron Sapiro, a Jewish lawyer who had organized the Californian farmers into a cooperative system. Sapiro sued Ford and after five years Ford was forced to apologize to Sapiro and to the Jewish people in general; he closed the *Dearborn Independent*. He did not, however, close his anti-Semitic mind, and Ford became the only American to be quoted by Hitler in a positive light as 'in a nation of one hundred and twenty millions . . . (the) single great man' (quoted in Lacey 1986: 218). Years later, in 1938, when Ford was 75, he accepted the Grand Cross of the German Eagle, the highest award possible for a foreigner—and he accepted it along with another recipient, an erstwhile competitor of his, James Mooney, the Director of Overseas Operations for General Motors (GM).[10] Both companies had subsidiaries operating in Germany during the war, though both denied they had any control over them. Yet Ford made it clear in September 1939—at least in private—that there was no war in Europe: 'The whole thing has just been made up by the Jew bankers' (quoted in Lacey 1986: 387). Ironically, Ford's last heart attack occurred shortly after he had watched newsreel film of a concentration camp (Lacey 1986: 218–19).[11]

Labour Problems

Ironically, it was also Ford, alone again, amongst the employers of Detroit, who responded positively to a call in 1926 to promote more liberal policies towards black Americans. By this time around 10,000 blacks worked for Ford, over 10 per cent of the total. Ford even promoted black supervisors over white workers, much to the consternation of most white workers, and in the Rouge foundry all workers and all supervisors, up to the plant superintendent, were black (Lacey 1986: 222–3).

Yet some of these same black Americans were soon to be involved in Ford's most violent labour dispute: the Ford Hunger March. Under the organizing umbrella of the Communist Party, 3,000 people, some of whom seem to have been unemployed ex-Ford workers, marched to the Rouge plant on 7 March

1932, in a protest about speed-ups, favouritism in hiring and firing, better hours and conditions, and the right to join trade unions. Walter Cunningham, a worker who resigned in 1932 and published his memoirs under the title *J8*, was probably typical of the protesters. J8 was his work number and Cunningham complained that, as far as Ford's was concerned, a number was all he represented, since he had been shorn of all the rest of his individual identity (Batchelor 1994: 53).

The marchers, without official permission, planned to march from Detroit to the Rouge site through Dearborn, and, while the Detroit police allowed them through, the Dearborn police, then little more than Ford's private police force, with the help of the Ford Service personnel, ordered the marchers to disperse and fired tear gas into the crowd. In the chaos that followed, the crowd rushed the plant fence, were drenched with water cannon by the Fire Department, and were then machine-gunned by the police. Four demonstrators were killed and twenty injured. The press was united in its condemnation of the killings and 15,000 mourners—many of them Ford employees—followed the red-flagged coffins through Detroit. But this did not stop many of these same employees finding themselves sacked by the end of the month as Ford's complex espionage system matched the photographs of the mourners to the faces of employees (Lacey 1986: 343–6).

Discontent continued to smoulder at Ford's, but the American Federation of Labor (AFL), dominated by craft unions, remained unable—or unwilling—to organize proper union representation for the mass of unskilled and semi-skilled workers at the company—much to Henry's relief. The following year, though, Roosevelt's National Recovery Act (1933) encouraged the AFL to try again and strike threats began to emerge in Detroit's other car manufacturers. At the bequest of President Roosevelt, the Congress of Industrial Organizations (CIO)—a more militant union confederation—met him in 1934 to find a way out of the threatened labour action and within a year the AFL had, in the eyes of car workers, negotiated away their rights. The 1935 (Wagner) National Labor Relations Act, which reinforced the National Recovery Act, provided greater legal support for unions and by 1936 the United Auto Workers (UAW) was formed to represent the interests of car workers. It affiliated to the CIO and within a year the UAW had organized General Motors and Chrysler, leaving Ford as the only non-union major car manufacturer.

Securing the right to hand out UAW pamphlets on 26 May 1937, exactly ten years after the last Model T was produced, four local activists, including Walter P. Reuter—who had worked for Ford at one time but had been sacked in 1932 (possibly for campaigning for the Socialist candidate in his Ford car)—were attacked by thugs in the Ford Service Department. It became known as 'the Battle of the Overpass'. Reuter, who went on to become the leader of the UAW (and helped organize the March on Washington for Jobs and Freedom in 1963 (see Chapter 9), was beaten up and dumped over the edge of the overpass. One of his colleagues had his back broken and another spent ten days in hospital. Despite this, a survey in *Fortune* magazine within weeks of the 'battle' put Ford as the person most likely to have 'been on the whole helpful to labor' (Batchelor 1994: 31). Once more, Ford's identity as a national icon seems to have protected him from the criticism that might have ruined other individuals.

Partly, this protection came through Ford's personal distancing from responsibility for industrial problems, for all company dealings with the unions were organized by Harry Bennett. So adamant was Ford that the unions would play no part in his plants that he would have nothing whatsoever to do with them and forbade Edsel for mentioning the issue. Bennett, an ex-sailor and boxer, had originally worked for Ford as an artist after the First World War, and came to run what Lacey (1986: 359) calls an 'empire of darkness'. Ford's management structure—since it was part of the administration—was entirely informal: there were few titles and many were unaware of who was responsible to whom or what job certain people did. Bennett's job was to act as Henry Ford's unquestioning henchman in charge of Ford's Service Department from the early 1920s. Bennett was a notorious man: he shot hats off visitors too impolite to remove them from their heads in his office, he kept lions and tigers as pets, and he mixed with the Detroit underworld, especially the likes of Chester LaMare, who ran the mafia-controlled bootlegging operation during prohibition. Bennett also had the personal support of the FBI's director, J. Edgar Hoover. Bennett allegedly organized 'outside squads' of thugs to terrorize labour activists at each Ford plant and one such squad of twenty-eight men was 'mistakenly' arrested by a sheriff outside the Kansas Ford plant in 1937. The men were carrying twelve shotguns, fourteen revolvers, and sixty other weapons, but were released without charge. Despite this kind of activity, as Lacey (1986: 372) acknowledges, Henry Ford's overall public support hardly wavered through this period. He was still the archetypal all-American boy made good.

Yet the UAW was not to be denied forever and it brought several charges against Ford for breaches of labour legislation and over the Battle of the Overpass. Bennett managed to persuade Homer Martin, the moderate leader of the UAW, to call off the lawsuits in exchange for unspecified advances, and the consequence was a split in the UAW between the radicals led by Reuter, now leading the UAW-CIO, and the moderates led by Martin, now in the UAW-AFL. Bennett bribed Martin and supported his organization while letting the 'outside squad' loose on the UAW-CIO. But the court case against Ford was resurrected and supported by the Supreme Court in February 1941. Two months later, on 1 April 1941, the Rouge workers stopped work in a one-hour sit down that forced the company to rehire a number of shop stewards that Bennett had just fired. Within seven weeks the ballot to determine which union would represent the workers was—to Bennett's and Ford's horror—won overwhelmingly by Reuter's UAW-CIO (Serrin 1974: 130). Worse than that, Ford's own proposal for a union-free shop won less than 3 per cent of the vote. It was, as Sorensen, a senior Ford executive, said, 'perhaps the greatest disappointment he had in all his business experience . . . he never was the same after that' (quoted in Lacey 1986: 377).

The negotiated settlement to the dispute rocked the rest of the automotive world through its apparent generosity to labour. Ford plants were to be UAW-CIO closed shops, back-pay was to be provided, all Service Department officers were to make themselves known, wages were to be increased, and, most unbelievable of all, Ford's was to operate an automatic check-off system deducting union fees directly from employees' wage packets. Henry Ford was adamant that the deal was unacceptable—though he seems to have been shocked when he discovered that Ford wages were lower than those of either Chrysler or General Motors. However, Edsel Ford favoured it and Henry's wife, Clara, appalled at the violence of Bennett and the effect it had had upon Edsel, threatened to leave Henry unless he accepted it (Serrin 1974: 130–1). In fact, Ford also had several lucrative war-work deals signed up with the government—but these were dependent upon a change in labour relations, and without these deals there was little future for Ford. Henry Ford also reckoned that, if he gave the union a little, they would keep coming back for more, but, strangely enough, if he gave them everything they wanted they would fall out amongst themselves. What Ford also reckoned was that, by offering the 'check-off' system, Ford would become the union's bankers and retain some control over them (Serrin 1974: 131–2). Thus the unions came to Ford's and were successfully installed because Henry could not continue without them. Had he been more successful with car sales, he would not have been so dependent upon the government's war contracts, but his almost congenital inability to listen to the advice of others denied him this avoidance route.

Family Problems

One of these government war contracts was an order for 6,000 Rolls Royce Merlin engines for the Spitfire, then suffering terrible attrition at the hands of the Luftwaffe during the Battle of Britain. Edsel immediately agreed, but Henry refused point black when he was required to work directly with the British. In the event, Ford became the third largest American defence contractor in the Second World War—the 'arsenal of democracy'—building all kinds of vehicles, including jeeps, the Sherman tank, engines, gliders, and—in 1942—B-24 bombers at the rate of 'one an hour', according to Henry Ford, from the new Willow Run plant. In fact, the first six months' production generated only fifty-six B-24s, as the mass production line failed to produce any kind of mass. Also failing was Henry Ford, now with two heart attacks to his credit and his memory going. Edsel was also failing, possibly suffering from stomach or liver cancer and undulant fever; he died on 26 May 1943, exactly sixteen years after the last Model T was built, and at the age of 49, of what Eleanor Clay Ford, his wife, called 'a broken heart' (quoted in Lacey 1986: 398). For Eleanor, Henry Ford and Harry Bennett had killed her husband, and only after she had confronted Henry with this did he begin to question his relationship with Edsel. Nevertheless, Henry wanted to appoint Harry Bennett as the new President of the company, but eventually decided to appoint himself, now just a month short of his eightieth birthday, and he began sponsoring the rise of Bennett's sidekicks. So great was the consterna-tion in Washington that a major defence supplier was being run by what Lacey calls 'a senile old man and the collection of hoodlums and semi-criminal fixers surrounding Harry Bennett' that J. K. Galbraith, then deputy director in the Office of Price Administration, suggested taking the B-24 out of Ford hands alto-gether to protect production (Lacey 1986: 404). By August 1943, thanks to Clara Ford, Eleanor Clayton Ford, Earnest Kanzler, and Frank Knox, then the US Secretary of the Navy, Henry Ford II, at 25 years of age, Edsel's eldest son, returned to Detroit from his training in the navy. His grandfather, Henry, was disgusted, for Henry Ford II was guilty of numerous errors: marrying, converting to Catholicism, answering back, disliking Harry Bennett, and so on. Henry Ford even went so far as attempting to redraw his will to ensure that Henry II was kept out of power for ten years after Henry's death—or permanently if possible. With Henry Ford now distinctly feeble, Henry Ford II began the slow process of under-mining Harry Bennett's network of support by firing most of them one by one. By September 1945, with help from Clara and Eleanor, the strategy had worked, and, at the age of 82, Henry Ford finally admitted that he could not continue in office and handed over the presidency to his grandson. His grandson's first exec-utive action was to sack Harry Bennett—followed by more than 1,000 others. Virtually his second was to hire a group of ex-Air Force 'Whizz Kids', among them Robert McNamara, who had touted themselves as a group of consultants able to solve any industrial problem, at a price. Ford certainly had some organ-izational problems: in 1945 the company was losing $9 million a month (1945 prices) (Winter 1996a).

After his grandson's takeover, Henry Ford became more withdrawn and taci-turn. He spent more time than ever in Greenfield Village, especially in the school-house that was a replica of his own first school. Far from being 'bunk', history was now all that Ford could look forward to. He became more and more inter-ested in reincarnation, and assumed his niece was the reincarnation of his mother, teaching her to drive in the car that 'her son' had made famous. On 7 April 1947, the River Rouge flooded, swamping the power plant, and Henry Ford tried to visit the plant for the first time in months to see the damage, but the flood water kept him back and he never saw his creation again. That night, at the age of 83, Henry Ford died. It is alleged that 100,000 people filed past his coffin and the whole of Detroit came to a standstill for one minute as his funeral service started. He died with $26.5 million in a personal account and left around $700 million in financial reserves. Just over fifty years later, on 11 September 1998, it was announced that William Clay Ford, the 41-year-old great-grandson of Henry Ford and nephew of Henry Ford II (the last family CEO, who eventually left in 1980), was to lead Ford into the next century. By this time the company was val-ued at £44 billion, it had an annual turnover of £72.7 billion, it was the second largest producer of cars (7.5 million, just behind General Motors at 7.5 million), and it had 364,000 employees. In January 1999 the company bought Volvo for £3.9 billion to add to its stakes in Jaguar and Mazda and take it back to the top of global car manufacturers. Exactly a century after Henry Ford initiated his first car company (the Detroit Automobile Company), Ford had returned to the number one position with 14 per cent of the world market (*Guardian*, 29 Jan. 1999).

Analysis

The Philosophical Arts: Identity

Whatever else Ford was, he was identified by most Americans at the time as the all-American boy. In this identity—much of it constructed from a past every bit as mythical as his museum—Ford played the boy from a poor rural Irish background who pulled himself up by his bootstraps and made himself one of the richest men in America. Indeed, it was this 'native' rooting that ensured Ford's performances in front of the media were read as a reflection of his honesty rather than his naïvety.

Ford's financial success has a related cultural reverberation: the Model T was configured as *the* American icon: it was a car that espoused equality for all—at least all who could find enough well-paid work to buy one—and it was a product that raised Americans above every other nation in a way that no other product could. In short, just as Ford himself symbolized the new American of the twentieth century, so the Model T symbolized the new America.

Ford also symbolized a global change: the movement towards mass production in which American technology and American know-how would lead the world. Thus the triple images that Ford became identified with involved him as an iconic leader of the American people, the Model T as an icon of the American masses, and mass production as an icon of American industrial leadership.

The Fine Arts: Strategic Vision

Ford had a simple and single overwhelming vision: to produce a car that would revolutionize the transport of the ordinary American citizen. Everything was subordinated to this vision and it figured so prominently in Ford's life that it became impossible to disentangle his private vision from the one that he charged his company with achieving.

His personal vision was as closely aligned to this corporate strategic vision as possible so that he was able to make demands on his followers that could be represented as responsibilities to the social needs of the collective not the private needs of the leader. The downside of this indivisible vision was, of course, that Ford drove his family as though its members were his employees.

Ford's desire to promote what he perceived to be American values—that is, competitive individualism—was not considered by the mass of the population to be problematic—even if many of those who worked with or for Ford had very different interpretations of his vision. In short, he created an organization that was perfectly adapted to his vision of business success, but, as Henry grew increasingly myopic in his refusal to see anything outside his own tunnel vision, the organization became clouded by organizational cataracts. However, the overriding desire to achieve one's vision often turns a strength into a weakness; a commitment becomes all consuming, destroying rather than achieving the vision. Unlike many leaders, Ford was not stopped before the vision began to degenerate nor did Ford generate an open organization where followers were encouraged to compensate for his own errors or were free to criticize him when necessary.

The Martial Arts: Organizational Tactics

Ford has traditionally been associated with organizational brilliance and innovation. In fact, many of the organizational innovations were not his but he still managed to retain the credit for them. None the less Ford did manage to align the skills of his employees and colleagues to the organizational tactics—at least in the beginning. His leadership was clearly founded on his organizing skills, but these worked best when he left subordinates to get on with their jobs—as made manifestly clear in the early years of the Model T. But Ford rarely allowed this to continue, and, for all his obsession with controlling the organization, it usually proved beyond even Henry's grasp. The friction generated within his factories undoubtedly enabled his competitors to flourish and eventually overtake Ford; indeed, many of his competitors were ex-Ford employees whom Ford personally had fired for recalcitrance.

Ford preferred to minimize the risks less by inversing or neutralizing the competition wherever possible than by dominating or removing them. Yet his constant price reductions, facilitated by his cost control and insourcing rather than innovative productive methods, always unbalanced his competitors—and even his shareholders and partners. As a consequence, a series of costly attritional battles developed between Ford and the Dodge brothers, between Ford and his dealers, between Ford and his son, and between Ford and anybody else who got in his way. That he survived these battles was more a consequence of the initial strength of the product and the weakness of the competition rather than a confirmation of the value of his tactics. Ford could have been more successful and retained more supporters had he chosen alternative tactics—but Ford was a control freak not a sophisticated tactician. Under such a leader, when Ford got things right he proved unassailable, as his Model T made manifestly clear. But the Model T was a joint product from a talented team; when Ford got rid of this team and still erred, there was no one to tell him he was going wrong.

Tactical errors are as responsible as tactical successes for the outcome of contests. Ford had many opponents—the unions, his competitors, his managers, his employees, his family, and the government to name a few. Since Ford's initial product was so popular, he never developed into a great tactician, because he could usually dominate his opponents. Most of the time Ford could play one off against another to ensure his success, and their general inability to rise above internal feuds and stand against Ford collectively allowed him to dominate them until very late in his life.

The Performing Arts: Persuasive Communication

Ford misread the mood of the American public and consumers on several occasions but they remained loyal to Ford the individual, if not Ford the product. His relatively ordinary background enabled many to identify themselves with him and this, in turn, ensured that his greatest weaknesses in communication and in adapting to the changing times and fashions were construed by the general public as manifestations of his honest intent not his poor performance.

But underneath this 'honest Henry' veneer was a calculating leader who invested heavily in observing his own employees, who developed rules for moral behaviour that penetrated the entire lives of his employees and who remained wedded to the idea that the only person capable of taking the leading role in the great Fordist production was himself. Hence some of his persuasive methods verged on paranoia and operated through fear and coercion, not through positive inducement.

On the other hand, Henry Ford had, like Nelson, a knack for stealing headlines and turning problems into solutions. For example, the $5 day was forced upon him but he paraded it as the volitional policy of a generous boss. And he apparently turned his manufacturing plants into the 'free' 'Arsenals of Democracy' yet used government funds to develop his own manufacturing ability and made a small fortune out of his war work. Ford may not have agreed that leadership is a performance rather than a set of rules, but his performances suggest otherwise.

Conclusion

Noble suggests that Ford was unique, neither a professional engineer nor a scientist but more a 'mechanically minded inventor'. 'He never fully shared the corporate liberal vision, preferring to prevent unionism at all costs, enforcing a strict puritanical code of behaviour for his workforce to enhance its productivity, and raising the wage level to ensure its co-operation, loyalty, and ability to buy his cars' (Noble 1977: 283). There is little doubt about Ford's eccentricities: he funded the Henry Ford Hospital in Detroit, treating it like a human garage, and refused to stay in bed after a hernia operation. He held that illness and crime were correlated, and that meat and protein should never be mixed in the stomach; thus he ate meat at lunchtime and potatoes in the evening. He pioneered the use of Soya beans as a food source and industrial material in the USA, even using it for the boot lid of a 1937 model, and he organized experiments to assess the viability of extracting automotive fuel from plants. He also built Greenfield Village, a 'living-history' project, which he sought to ensure represented the 'real' history of the USA as he—a self-confessed adherent of reincarnation—had known it, several times over. And, since Henry liked watchmakers and did not like banks, he had three watchmakers' shops built in the village—but no banks (Batchelor 1994: 12). He even made dancing lessons for senior managers mandatory. Not content with earthly manœuvrings, Ford instituted the first US airmail service, built the first all metal multi-engined plane, and developed the first radio system for guiding commercial aircraft. Many of these later developments occurred next to Greenfield Village, so Ford could link the farm-boy nostalgia of his past with the engineered future in the Henry Ford Museum, opened in 1928, in what rapidly became America's first theme park. The prime exhibit was Henry Ford—the all-American boy.

Notes

1. See Allen (1992), Williams *et al.* (1992) and Grint (1998*a*) for discussions on the meaning of 'Fordism'.
2. 'Forbes 400', *Forbes*, 13 Oct. 1997, 230.
3. Internal combustion cars were already in existence in France, Germany, and the USA.
4. The 'Merry Oldsmobile' was then selling at 4,000 units per annum (Batchelor 1994: 39).
5. In fact, the self-taught machinist was much more typical than a professional engineer throughout the car industry (Flink 1988). The related fixation with the division of labour reached its zenith some years later, in 1916, when an ex-Ford employee applied for a job in a Swiss automobile factory on the basis of being a 'skilled erector of automobiles'. When asked what he did, the man replied 'I screwed on nut No. 58' (quoted in Gartman 1979: 203).
6. I once drove a Fiat without an internal fuel gauge and when I asked how I could tell when the fuel was low I was told the system was foolproof and very reliable: when the car ran out of fuel, it would stop.
7. Taylor gave a four-hour lecture to Ford management in 1909.
8. Bowden calculates that the average annual tax per 1,000 cc was £1.67 in the UK, £1.10 in France, 90p in Germany, and a mere 20p in the USA. By 1999 the three top Fortune 500 companies by revenue were all car-makers: GM, DaimlerChrysler, and Ford (Microsoft was 284th). The UK, virtually alone among major economies, has no indigenous car-makers of any scale, and, as BMW has found to its cost, British manufacturing quality and productivity remains poor. Rover has not made a net profit since 1975 and retains only 6.4 per cent of the domestic market. With the exception of specialist motor engineering (such as Formula One and Indy Car production, which is dominated by Britain), British car manufacture is all but moribund. See Whisler (1999).
9. The original Model Ts had been green, but the discovery that black paint dried more quickly than green led to the (in)famous remark about customers having 'any colour you liked—as long as it was black'.
10. In 1935 GM's subsidiary Opel won a contract to build Blitz trucks at Berlater and it was these trucks that transported German infantry into Poland and Russia. Even after the invasion of Czechoslovakia, Alfred Sloan, GM Chair, insisted that the Nazi contract should be supported. Bradford Snell, the historian of GM, commenting on the role of Switzerland and GM in the Nazi war effort, has suggested that 'The Nazis

could have invaded Poland and Russia without Switzerland. They could not have done so without GM' (quoted in *Guardian*, 1 Dec. 1998).

11. In September 1945 a US Army report accused Ford of operating as 'an arsenal of Nazism, at least for military vehicles' (quoted in *Guardian*, 1 Dec. 1998).

7

Horatio Nelson: Determining the
Indeterminate Military Hero

You can't step twice into the same river.
(Heraclitus)

At some point between 1793 and 1815 Britain was at war with France, the United States, Spain, the Netherlands, or several other European powers. Both temporally and spatially it was an era of conflict that was excessive even by the standards of the previous century. The British navy often, but not always, dominated the seas and it did so primarily through violence—real or intended. The period saw the beginnings in Britain of income tax (to pay for the wars), the Ordnance Survey (to plan the country's defence), and the national census (to map and organize the population). Traditionally, Britain is seen as a nation ill at ease with a standing army and more reliant upon a permanent navy to protect its trade routes and homeland from external enemies.[1] Yet by 1809, if we include the regular army, the militia, the volunteers, and the navy, over 786,000 men—around one-sixth of the entire adult male population—were under arms. Many of these were anything but volunteers in the true sense of the word: the navy 'impressed' its seamen, the army 'crimped' its soldiers, and, in Scotland, the 'tenant-at-will' system provided many crofters with little option but to join the ranks of one of the many Scottish regiments (Esdaile 1995: 144–5). Yet, as we saw in Chapter 3, the dislike of the 'press' did not surface as a complaint of the mutineers at Spithead or the Nore. There were undoubtedly some genuine volunteers for the wars against the historical foe, the French, but, as Esdaile notes (1995: 145), 'patriotism did not figure high'. Even Wellington accepted as much, for 'English soldiers are fellows who have enlisted for drink. That is the plain fact—they have enlisted for drink' (quoted in Esdaile 1995: 146). The navy was hardly more popular: eighty-one (12 per cent) of the 703 seamen on board *Victory* at Trafalgar were foreign and Esdaile (1995: 146) suggests that perhaps only 15 per cent of the naval crews in 1812 were genuine volunteers. Under these circumstances, the avoidance of error through training and skill, and the construction of order derived through discipline rather than patriotic enthusiasm, were the essential prerequisites of Nelson's and British military success.

Nelson was not the formulator of British government or naval strategic visions, but he was responsible for carrying some of it out, and he had his own strategic vision to execute, which ran in parallel to the official one and sometimes overrode it. That vision included seeing off the French invasion and strengthening British naval dominance, but more important to Nelson were two private visions. One was almost always on his mind and one developed only when he was already 35 years old and coincided with the onset of the French wars—but it was a marital not a martial vision. The first personal objective that drove Nelson in a personal crusade against the French was the desire to become the greatest British naval hero that had ever lived. To achieve this he had to marry his personal crusade to his military mission—the destruction of the French navy—and the seamless link between the two parallel visions enabled Nelson to do whatever he thought necessary to achieve it; he was, indeed, the archetypal machiavellian. The second personal vision was to spend the time not engaged in a death or glory rampage around the oceans with Emma Hamilton, with whom he became besotted. Only one thing mattered more to Nelson than Emma, and that was glory, and there was only one way to achieve a permanent place in the annals of British history—and that was to die achieving his military mission.

Nelson was undoubtedly fixated by his strategic visions and there are few if any examples of leaders of repute who have achieved success by being anything but fanatical in their pursuits. However, many leaders are fanatics without achieving the iconic status that Nelson secured, and I shall suggest that much of Nelson's success was based, among other things, on organizational tactics that few other Admirals could match. Much of Nelson's success, as with so many other leaders, can also be firmly placed in the errors of his competitors or enemies. Some of these errors he was able to induce by deploying the neutralizing and inversion tactics discussed before, while others were the products of Machiavelli's *fortuna*, or luck. Either way, Nelson's success was not preordained and his actions could have led to personal, naval, and national disaster on several occasions. But, as Napoleon was fond of saying, 'The greatest general is he who makes the fewest mistakes.' Nelson got away with his mistakes, his enemies often did not. In a rule-bound environment, the opportunist cannot operate without breaking the regulations—and this is precisely what Nelson did: he took advantage of the opportunities proffered up by fortune, where others held back; he embodied the dictum *carpe diem* (seize the day). This ability was facilitated by his apparent lack of fear. Mirroring samurai traditions, Nelson apparently accepted that death was likely but accepted it rather than worried about it; indeed, ironically, his quest for immortality was feasible only if he died engaged in its pursuit.

Nelson's exploitation of organizational tactics should not, however, be reduced to an assumption that successful leaders are simply those that lead from the front at the right time and in the right place. In many ways Nelson was a model leader, but the modelling he was involved in was proactive and sophisticated. It did not assert that being in the right place and time to be first over the parapet was enough. Rather, making sure everyone *knew* that you were first over the parapet was just as critical and making sure that you would not be the only one going over was the only way to enhance the likelihood of collective success. Even this cannot guarantee success: the interpretation of intention, action, capacity, and so on is an essential feature here and it is not sufficient to list the differences between military forces as explanations of the success of one side over the other. In other words, we should remain sceptical about the 'inevitable' victory of the British over the Combined Franco-Spanish Fleet at Trafalgar because of the alleged superiority of British gunnery or leadership or seamanship and so on. Indeed, we should remain sceptical over the significance of Trafalgar—if by this it is suggested that an objective analysis can evaluate its importance without having to worry about the role of interpretation and persuasion before, during, and after the battle itself. But, if the unfolding of events is indeterminate this is exactly why opportunism is so important to leaders; it is the exploitation of the window of opportunity that so often signifies the difference—often wafer thin— between success and failure, victory and defeat.

Without doubt Nelson has emerged as an extraordinary military leader, perhaps Britain's—and almost certainly England's—greatest hero, but the question is why? In myth Nelson stopped the French invasion through Trafalgar—but the French army had already left the embarkation ports two months before Trafalgar. In myth Nelson destroyed the French navy and set it back 200 years— but within nine years the French navy was larger than the British. Clearly, the invented myth has more resonance than the reality. Does this national exemplar gain his place then because of self-evidently unique personal characteristics, there from birth, and, if not, how did he come to be perched on top of a column in Trafalgar Square rather than anyone else? To lead by example requires leading by paradox. By this I mean that the example demonstrated cannot be repeated either in space or in time, or, to quote Heraclitus again: 'You can't step twice into the same river.' In other words, the temporal sequence cannot be repeated because the water is not the same water. I shall suggest that this paradox at the heart of Nelson's leadership is not that he was a humane exemplar amidst a mass of the most exemplary form of institutionalized bullying, but that the archetype he constructed rested upon its opposite. In other words, that his personal action involved breaking rules, regulations, and norms at times of his own choosing because this brought him the spatial control, the military success, and the personal glory he so desperately sought. But, although he chastized those who failed to follow in his footsteps, his very success depended upon them failing: either because this enhanced his reputation by comparison or, equally important, because his success demanded mass compliance to his requirements. Had his fellow officers or opponents undertaken what he had shown was possible, his own symbolic stature would have shrunk; had his sailors manifested the same disregard for regulations that he had, the British navy could not have been as successful as it was. Thus, although Nelson is often regarded as *the* exemplary leader, the English martial icon bar none, we shall see that this modelling was neither a direct reflection of his action nor was it a pattern of action that could have been copied by his followers without undermining his own success.

In effect, a great part of Nelson's leadership skill was in recognizing and aligning the particular skills and competences of his own followers with organizational tactics that made the most of such skills and competences. The contrary
holds for his competitors and opponents. But there is more to Nelson's leadership
than this, and for much of the time we need to remember the power of his performing arts, for in many ways he was foremost in promoting his own career, his
own version of events, his own successes, and his own heroic death. Thus the
hero of Trafalgar who allegedly saved Britain from an imminent French invasion
probably did less for the country's direct security than Admiral Cornwallis, who
was both Nelson's superior officer and responsible for maintaining the blockade
of the Franco-Spanish fleet. But Cornwallis was involved in a mundane activity
that held little interest for the media or the general population and he made little
attempt to ingratiate himself to a generally unknowing and uninterested country.
In contrast, Nelson was a professional in every sense of the word, a spin doctor,
a miracle-worker, a 'man of the world', and a man beyond this world. In short,
Nelson could be said to have invented—and most certainly embodied—the cult
of the heroic leader.

The Social and Political Background

The American War of Independence, which ended in 1783, was the first and only
major defeat in war for Britain. Despite this—or more likely because of this—
Britain was the only major European power not to experience some form of revolution or crisis amongst the ruling élite. However, although the war against
France between 1793 and 1815 (excluding the intervening periods of truce) cost
roughly six times the national income at the time, the cost was less significant
than the political threat to the élite: the all-successful French *Grande Armée* was
led by men without inherited rank or property. 'The diadem of Bonaparte',
bewailed the *Edinburgh Review* in 1809, 'has dimmed the lustre of all ancient
crowns of Europe; and her nobles have been outshone and out-generalled, and
out-negotiated, by men raised by their own exertions from the common level of
the populace' (quoted in Colley 1992: 150). For a time, the legitimacy of the
British élite was questioned by radicals such as Thomas Paine, John Wade, and
William Cobbett, and, with no more than 400 aristocratic families dominating
the land, and a demonstrable failure of leadership at the top over the loss of the
American colonies, their position in the face of a meritocratic, egalitarian, and
successful French alternative looked difficult at best. But by the end of the first
decade of the century, not only had the French Revolution begun to devour its
own progeny, thereby undermining radical sympathies in Britain, but the visible
threat of a French invasion force made any fears of an imminent revolution in
Britain—already much exaggerated—rapidly disappear. Of course, under the
pressure of an external enemy many internal divisions are dissolved and it must
have seemed bizarre to note that many of the British élite still spoke French—the
language of polite society throughout Europe—which Nelson learned after sev-

eral attempts. The British élite also dressed in delicate French fashions, even when the country was at war with France. However, such fashions went into sharp decline as the crisis of the élite continued and one consequence was the search for a more British version of patrician culture, itself instilled by the now very popular public schools, where patriotic duty was wedded to militaristic virtue (Colley 1992: 170–2). This new cult of heroism rapidly became the hallmark of the élite, and wounds suffered in the service of one's country ranked as high as wealth accumulated for services to the county; at last the élite had found itself a niche. Moreover, with that niche came a change of dress—from effete French fashion to military uniform—and a change of intent—death at the moment of victory (as achieved by General Wolfe in 1770, and subsequently by Nelson in 1805, and by General Sir John Moore in 1809). There could be no better ending for adherents of the cult of heroism.[2]

For Nelson, the cult of heroism was to prove even stronger than to most of the British élite—which he attempted to mimic but was never accepted by, for:

> Those most susceptible to the ideal were often not so much the great landowners, or peers of the realm equipped with gilt-edged genealogies, but relative newcomers to the élite who had less to lose and more to prove . . . Nelson only practised to a remarkable degree what the cult of heroic individualism fostered very broadly among the class he aspired to . . . And it was this calculated exhibitionism, this theatre that embarrassed and appalled many of his more genuine patrician contemporaries. For it seemed to caricature to a vulgar degree the very style and strategy that they themselves were increasingly adopting. (Colley 1992: 182–3)

Thus military uniforms oozed ostentatious licence and 'served to distinguish members of the British élite from the rest of the population, while at the same time underlining their wearers' patriotic function' (Colley 1992: 186). Nelson subsequently became the archetype for the professional middle-class officer, willing to sacrifice his life for his country. Ironically, it was his exaggeration of this element of the performing arts, this overt display of fashionable clothing, that so endeared him to the mass and so alienated him from the élite.

At the same time as dress codes changed, so too did moral codes, for the fashion of the male élite maintaining mistresses, which had been common in the late eighteenth century, died out as the French aristocracy died out. From then on, sobriety accompanied the uniform—and one of the other reasons why Nelson was so loathed by the élite was because his private life not only broke the new moral code that the élite set itself; it actually reminded the public of what the élite had previously been like. Paradoxically, in Nelson's case, the linkage between the 'jolly tar' with his 'girl in every port' may have exonerated him from such a 'crime' amongst the common sailor and populace. That is, while it was now scandalous for politicians or aristocrats or generals to acquire mistresses, Nelson avoided the public disquiet (though not the élite disquiet) because he was regarded as doing what all sailors did—he was 'one of the boys' not 'one of the toffs'.

The Naval Background

The Royal dockyards were the largest single employer in Britain at the time of Trafalgar, Portsmouth was the largest single industrial complex, and its main products, ships-of-the-line or men-of-war, were the largest and most complex single artefacts produced, sometimes carrying 1,000 people and far more armaments than an army. So great was the armament on board a typical man-of-war that, for comparison, Nelson's fleet at Trafalgar carried six times more fire power than Napoleon's Waterloo army, at one-fifth of the cost and at five times the speed (Keegan 1993*b*: 47). The Royal Navy itself was managed by the Admiralty, which was answerable to the First Lord of the Admiralty, a political appointment within the Cabinet.[3] At the beginning of 1793, when Britain joined the first European coalition against France, there were only twenty-five ships-of-the-line in service. By October 1793 there were eighty-four (Lavery 1989: 180). By 1801 the number of French ships-of-the-line had also been reduced through war and loss, from sixty-five to forty-one, while the British navy, at the same time, had 108. With the war inducing a shortage of timber, however, the British were forced to use substitutes for their usual Baltic timber, thereby reducing the average life of a ship from around forty to a mere eight years as dry rot wrought havoc.[4] The result of the conflict over resources was that by 1814—nine years after it had allegedly been destroyed for ever by Nelson, the French navy, with limitless supplies of timber and under the direct orders of Napoleon, outnumbered the British fleet 104 to 99 (Esdaile 1995: 151–2).[5]

A ship was distinguished by its rating, class, and guns, and there was some overlap between the systems, but basically the largest warships, or ships-of-the-line, or line-of-battle ships, were first-raters, with three decks and 100 guns or more. From here rates increased (from second to sixth) as decks decreased (from three to one) and as guns decreased (from 99 to 0). By and large, ships with less than 64 guns tended not to be deployed as line-of-battle ships by 1793 and all rated ships were captained by a full or 'post' captain. Since ship size tended to be limited by the size of timbers, not only were larger ships more expensive to build and run; they were also far more difficult to build.[6] HMS *Victory* was built in 1758 (Nelson's birth date); it was a first-rater, with 104 guns, and the largest ship ever built at that date for the Royal Navy, needing 850 sailors to sail it and originally costing £63,176. It lasted about forty years as a fighting ship.[7]

But, while ships were very similar, except in size, captains were very different. Precisely what a captain ought to do once at sea was very much left up to the individuals themselves, as Dudley Pope (1997: 33) comments:

Apart from a routine for the necessary paperwork, there was no drill laid down for the handling of the guns, no sail drill and no set uniform for anyone except officers and certain warrant officers. As soon as a captain took command of a ship he gave a copy of his own standing orders to the first lieutenant . . . the officers . . . promptly threw away the copies they had made of the previous captain's standing orders and copied out the new ones, which were usually quite different.

However, there were strict regulations drawn up for the conduct of battle itself and it was these that Nelson so often ignored in the war at sea.

The training of potential officers to fill these ships was never very systematic in the British navy. There was a Naval College at Portsmouth, but only a very small minority of officers went through this route, the rest, which included Nelson, being trained as a midshipman aboard a ship. Fifty per cent of the officer corps originated, as did Nelson, from the professional middle classes, far more than entered the officer corps of the army, which remained the repository of men from the very top of the social hierarchy (Hibbert 1995: 7). In effect, the navy's recruitment net was wider than the army's, though those who staffed the most senior positions in both services were almost exclusively of aristocratic heritage. Part of Nelson's popularity may well have been his 'middling' origins, which allowed him to mix with Admirals and able-bodied seamen alike—though he was never comfortable with, nor made to feel comfortable by, Britain's aristocracy.

Midshipman was the probationary rank for officers undergoing training; most but not all were young men or boys. Most youths would have entered at around 12 years of age as 'captain's servant' or able seamen. Some servants were on the muster for pay but not on the ship, and several captains were disciplined for 'false muster'—either making money from the abuse or ensuring their sons or relatives' sons could accumulate seniority without the problem of actually sailing (D. Pope 1997: 65). 'Powder monkeys', responsible for carrying powder between the magazine and the guns and for the general servicing of a gun crew, joined from the age of 6. A first-rate vessel[8] might carry as many as twenty-four midshipmen, most of them between 15 and 22 years of age, though some maintained this junior status until well on in life.[9] Promotion to officer status from the lowest entry point (common seaman) was possible, but Lavery (1989: 92) calculates that only 3 per cent of entrants as common seaman were likely to achieve a commission. Normally, after six years of good experience and service, and at an age of at least 19, the examination for commission as a lieutenant was taken, which could include all kinds of questions on seamanship and naval tactics. From then on, those who passed the examination had to await a vacancy—and if the country was at peace this could take some time. Officers were not specialized but had to know all aspects of the navy, from sailing and navigation to gunnery. Promotion beyond lieutenant was primarily a combination of patronage, seniority, and demand.[10] Patronage—or 'interest' as it was referred to—was a very powerful support system in the navy at the time and nepotism was its twin. After 1797, however, Admiral John Jervis introduced a limited number of promotions for those who exhibited exceptional talent—and for those without significant political support inside or outside the navy the only real hope for promotion lay in displaying such talent in battle (S. Pope 1998: 93). Lavery argues that, although Nelson had acquired a helping hand early on from his uncle, his later promotions tended to rely much more upon this form of distinction, but, as we shall see, Nelson was given rather more than an initial helping hand (Lavery 1989: 95–7). Above lieutenant, the career ladder moved from Commander—in control of a small vessel such as a sloop—through Captain in control of a rated ship—to Commodore (in temporary control of a squadron of ships), to any of the nine, and later ten, grades of Admiral (Rear Admiral, Vice Admiral, Admiral of the [in seniority] Red, White, and Blue squadron; Admiral of the Fleet).[11] Since promotion was, in theory, solely by seniority, there was a mechanism for bypassing admirals considered too old or incompetent to command; such men became Admirals of the Yellow squadron—that is, they were virtually retired, allowing a junior admiral to take command. This was probably just as well because in 1799 there were forty Admirals (excluding Admiral of the Fleet), forty-two Vice Admirals and forty-nine Rear Admirals. All British commissioned officers (almost 3,000 in 1799) were entitled to half pay when their duties were not required—i.e. during peacetime—and, since there was no retirement nor retirement pension scheme, officers had to rely upon the acquisition of prize money or invalidity pension (Tracy 1998b: 336). [12]

In contrast, promotion in what remained of the French navy, after the departure of most of the officer corps in the early post-revolutionary years, could be very rapid. The old officer corps had been removed in 1791 and a decree in 1793 further thinned out the already meagre remnants. By 1794 the French navy was led by Admiral Villaret-Joyeuse, who only two years previously had been a lieutenant. Villeneuve, no longer sporting his aristocratic 'de', was promoted Vice Admiral in the same year (Keegan 1993b: 34). Equally damaging, the 1793 decree abolished the corps of gunners, on the grounds that it was an 'aristocracy of the sea'. As Lavery (1989: 281) comments: 'Revolutionary fervour was enough to make good soldiers, but sailors need technical skills which could not be learned without long years of experience.' French naval schools were instituted in 1800 to begin the process of training the new officer corps, but they could not be expected to have turned the navy round within five years. As for the French seamen, there were only 60,000 at the beginning of the wars—half the number available to Britain.

Competent officers manned the Spanish fleet but their crews were even weaker than the French. In 1787 the Spanish navy needed 89,350 sailors to crew it, but it had only 53,147 registered mariners and, of these, only 5,800 had ever sailed beyond the shallows of the Spanish coastline. Spain, therefore, used conscripted 'landmen' to fill the gaps, as well as having a much larger proportion of marines than the British ships had.[13] The excessive reliance upon untrained and inexperienced 'sailors' by the French and Spanish navies was to have devastating consequences in their battles with the British and the relative advantage of the British was well known to their enemies. For example, just prior to the battle of the Glorious First of June in 1794, a captured French officer on board the seventy-four-gunner *Defence*—having attested that the French crews were better than the British—remarked to William Dillon that the five minutes it had taken to tack would normally taken fifteen in an equivalent French ship (Dillon 1999: 15). Robert Eastwick (1999: 110), captured by the French frigate *La Forte* in 1799, was astonished at the apparent lack of discipline amongst the French sailors—though he admitted that they 'went through their duty with alacrity'.

Naval Warfare

The fallout from the French Revolution inaugurated nine significant sea battles in which the Royal Navy engaged. The British did not suffer any major defeats, but four of the engagements were indecisive and three of the five victories had been against allies of the French (the Spanish, Dutch, and Danish) rather than the French fleet itself. Only the 'Glorious First of June' and the 'Nile' had witnessed a decisive British defeat of a French fleet. However, the Danes, Dutch, and Spanish never recovered—leaving the British free of a North European threat for the first time in a century—and, though the French recovered, they never challenged the British again. All the battles except the Glorious First of June were fought close to land, with the battles of Copenhagen and the Nile actually fought against fleets in harbour (Keegan 1993b: 42–3; Lavery 1989: 280).

Between 1793 and 1815 166 British warships were captured or destroyed by enemy action, including five ships-of-the-line. But the figures for Britain's enemies were much higher (1,201 ships, including 159 ships-of-the-line). As Lavery (1989: 317) argues, the 'habit of victory' was secured not through greater numbers but by greater fire power, superior tactics, superior crews, and superior confidence, an assumption of invincibility that few French or Spanish ships seemed to be able to break. When Napoleon was aboard the *Bellerophon* on his way to exile in St Helena, he remarked, 'I can see no sufficient reason why your ships should beat the French with so much ease. The finest men-of-war in your service are French; a French ship is heavier in every respect than yours, she carries more guns, those guns are of a larger calibre, and has a great many more men.' He also said, 'What I admire most in your ship, is the extreme silence and orderly conduct of your men . . . How much might be done with a hundred thousand such soldiers (marines) as these' (quoted in Lavery 1989: 321). Ironically, Napoleon had put his finger on the critical difference without being aware of it.

In fact, both the French and Spanish navies operated a national register of seamen who could be conscripted at any time; the Spanish even resorted to drafting in soldiers to man their ships. Yet the quality of human resources was critical, as Lyon (1996: 9) asserts: 'From Quiberon Bay to the Nile and from Lissa to the *Shannon/Chesapeake* action it was the best trained officers and crews that won, even against considerable numerical and material odds.' Villeneuve, for example, reckoned that the Spanish quota system filled the Spanish fleet under his command at Trafalgar with 'herdsmen and beggars' (quoted in Keegan 1993b: 38).

Naval warfare during the period was seldom a war to the finish between major fleets. Just finding the enemy fleet at sea was difficult enough—which explains why most sea battles were fought just offshore—and, with only wind power to assist their movement (which often provided the escaping fleet with sufficient headway to avoid battle altogether), battles of attrition were few and far between. It was information on fleet movements that could win or lose a battle, but so often that information was bewildering in its diversity—as illustrated by Nelson comparing his notes on the intended direction of the French fleet at

Toulon in 1804: 'Bull (the Civil Commissioner in Malta) is sure they are going to Egypt; the Turks are sure they are going to Greece; Mr Elliot (the British Minister at Naples) to Sicily; and the King of Sardinia to his only spot . . . I trust, and with confidence, they are going to Spithead' (quoted in Keegan 1993b: 23). In fact, Nelson guessed wrong on this occasion and on several other occasions: in Egypt in 1798, and in January, March, and again in June of 1805.

Once the enemy had been found, the chances of engaging them still depended upon whether they could be caught—and very often a battle could commence only if both sides decided to stand and fight.[14] It also required weather that would permit gunfire: a storm and rolling seas made firing the guns with any accuracy virtually impossible. Even when battle was commenced, the chances of catastrophic casualties and outright defeats were slim. For all the ferocious cannon that a ship could fire into another, few ships sank from gunshot alone and it was not really until the new age of iron ships and explosive shells that fleet engagements could involve the loss of an entire naval force. Hence, when Nelson appeared to achieve the unachievable—by virtually obliterating (or in his words, 'annihilating') enemy fleets—his leadership became elevated above others. When his greatest victory coincided with the apparent failure of invasion (though in fact Napoleon had already cancelled the invasion before Trafalgar), Nelson was boosted from naval hero to national icon. And, when he died in securing this victory, in replication of the Christian sacrifice, his status moved from national icon to what C. White (1995) calls 'immortal' hero. After all, this had always been Nelson's intention; to be, 'living or dead, the greatest man in his profession that England ever saw' (quoted in Keegan 1993b: 28).

Given the shape of warships, it was likely that most guns would align with the sides and thus a ship could not advance upon another and fire at it at the same time. The consequence was the development of the broadside and the line of battle. Ships of enemy fleets would line up one behind the other and sail past each other firing a succession of broadsides as the opposing ships were brought to bear. By 1690 rigid battle instructions were prepared and those who disobeyed them, like Admiral Mathews off Toulon in 1744, could find themselves court-martialled. The so-called permanent-instructions, thirty-three of them in total, sought to ensure adherence to the pattern. A tradition, rather than part of the permanent instructions, was that the British fleet always fought from the 'weather gage'—that is, with the wind behind it. This provided it with a greater degree of control over timing and it facilitated its aggressive tactics. However, it also meant that an approaching British fleet, under a strong wind, was likely to have its lower gun deck on or under the water line and this often required a strong degree of self-discipline as the ships bore down on the enemy. It was also the case that British strategy was quite different from that of the French. The French dominated the land and their navy served as an adjunct to the army; thus its overall strategy was to facilitate army movements and not necessarily to dominate the seas. The British army, however, was considerably weaker than its French opponent, while the country's strength lay in its colonial empire and trade domination. For this to be maintained, the British navy had always taken precedence over the army—hence its title as the 'senior service'—and its role was not to move troops but to control the seas. In effect, the French navy's role was to await instructions until needed by the army; the British navy's role was to maintain supremacy and prevent the French navy from supporting the French army. And since the French army appeared invincible there was little need for the French navy to set about protecting the country from invasion by the British. In fact, then, the French fleet operated under the opposite assumptions to its British counterpart—as a permanent threat of invasion as opposed to a permanent safeguard against invasion. The French fleet 'tended to concentrate on specific tasks, whereas the British one was designed for the more general control of the seas. British ships would seek battle when there was any prospect of victory, but the French tended to avoid it unless it was absolutely necessary—their role was to carry out a specific mission, and a sea battle would cause delays, or even the abandonment of the objective' (Lavery 1989: 282).

The possibility of alternative tactics, including 'breaking of the line' by attacking at a right angle to the enemy line and the consequent mêlée (individual contests between ships within the larger battle), was originally discussed on paper by a French Jesuit, Paul Hoste, in his book *L'Art des armes navales*, written in 1697 and published in English in 1750 and again in 1762. A similar argument was put by a Scottish merchant, John Clerk (Clerk of Elgin), in his 1782 work *Essay on Naval Tactics*. This was believed by many to be the inspiration behind Rodney's successful attack in the Battle of the Saintes in the same year, though he had simply turned the line of battle at right angles to the enemy, slicing through their line with his own rather than cutting the line so as to secure a temporary and local numerical superiority and then engaging the enemy ships—in effect temporarily to neutralize a section of the enemy's fleet. In 1788 le Vicomte de Grenier suggested the triple lines of attack adopted later by Nelson. And in 1790, Lord Howe, Commander of the Channel Fleet, and an avid reader of Clerk, issued some supplementary instructions, which encouraged the greater use of individual initiative and the breaking of the line by individual ships as an accepted alternative to the line of battle.[15] Of course, such a tactic exposed the weaker bow section of a boat to an enemy for as long as it took to engage it at close quarter, passing either to fore or aft and using its own broadside to rake the enemy in turn. This tactic could work only if the enemy gunners were unable to cripple each ship as it approached. The utility of the tactic can be best appreciated at Trafalgar, not with Nelson leading the northern column on the *Victory* but with Collingwood leading the southern column on the *Royal Sovereign*. After receiving comparatively little damage or casualties from its approach run, the *Royal Sovereign* parted the French line between the Spanish flagship, the *Santa Ana*, and the French ship *Fougueux*. Firing double-shotted broadsides[16] into the stern of the *Santa Anna* and the bow of the *Fougueux*, the *Royal Sovereign* allegedly inflicted over 400 casualties in one go (Lyon 1996: 121). But the associated danger to the attackers involved in the tactic can also be appreciated by considering the casualty list of British sailors, which, though radically shorter than that of either the French or the Spanish, nevertheless reflected the vulnerability of the first ships in each column. Of Nelson's fleet, the second and third highest casualties occurred on the *Victory* (159) and the *Royal Sovereign* (141) respectively; only the *Colossus* received more (200): as a double-decker seventy-four-gun ship, it had been engaged with three enemy ships simultaneously.

Breaking of the line was not always effective: Bryon had failed in a similar attack against the French in the late 1770s.[17] Individual breaking of the line obviously diminished the control of the admiral over the fleet and thus such tactics required both better seamanship from individual captains and crews and also greater faith in the same by the admiral.

Gun performance also seems to have played a crucial role in naval battles—it was not simply a matter of accumulating larger and more guns than your opponent; it was how well the guns were used that mattered. The significance of gunners can be established by comparing the number of instructions set down by the Admiralty for them: thirty-three. In contrast, bosuns had only eleven and lieutenants only twenty-six. A gunner had to pass an examination before three already qualified gunners and a 'mathematical master' (D. Pope 1997: 86). Most guns at this time were smooth-bore muzzleloaders, classified by the weight of ball—which was generally restricted by the weight of ball a gunner could carry and the weight implications the gun had for the stability of the ship. The largest conventional guns were 42-pounders used on old British first-raters, but these were already obsolete well before Trafalgar. In fact, the French navy's largest guns—their 36-pounders—were a similar size to the British 42-pounders and their excessive weight may have been one of the reasons for the slower rate of fire of the French ships (Lyon 1996: 79).[18]

The *Victory* carried thirty 32-lb. guns. Capable of penetrating two feet of oak at one mile, they weighed 55 cwt. and were 9'6" long. A 24-pounder could penetrate 2'6" of oak at point-blank range.[19] The larger guns were used on the lowest gun deck to facilitate stability, although from 1779 the top deck often carried heavy carronades, whose short wide barrel prevented much accuracy over distance, but firing a 68-lb. shot could devastate enemy ships at close range. *Victory* carried two such guns. In fact, accuracy was so poor that sights were not generally used until the American successes in 1812 against the British (Lyon 1996: 11).

Gun practice occurred on most British warships every day, but live shot was seldom fired because it was always in short supply. Typically, ships carried around sixty rounds of solid shot per gun, plus five rounds of grape shot and three rounds of double-headed hammer shot for use against rigging and masts (Lavery 1989: 87, 172–8). By tradition, British gunners fired on the downward roll of the ship, bouncing cannonballs off the water into the ship's hull, while French gunners fired on the upward roll, aiming for the masts and rigging. This was no doubt facilitated by the different aspects taken up by the opposing ships: a British ship attacking with the wind behind it would, as mentioned above, have its guns pointing slightly down while the French would be pointing slightly up. This may also be one of the reasons for the generally heavier French and Spanish casualties in sea battles. But the critical issue was the rate of fire, in which British sailors had achieved a renowned superiority by the time of Trafalgar, both through better training and because of the use of flintlock ignition mechanisms, rather than the hand-held linstock devices still used by most French and Spanish ships. The flint-lock or gunlock normally ensured instantaneous discharge, but a linstock could burn for several seconds before discharging, making the task of aiming the gun and gauging the roll of the ship very difficult. A further advantage acquired by the British was the use of flexible tools for cleaning and dampening the cannon. This enabled the guns to be cleaned and reloaded with the gun ports lowered, thus speeding up the routine and protecting the crew from enemy rifle fire (Dillon 1999: 22).

The effects of guns upon crews could be harrowing: a single cannonball decap-itated Nelson's secretary before his very eyes at Trafalgar, while a 'double-headed shot' (two cannonballs fired from the same gun simultaneously) killed eight marines standing in line. On average, 5 per cent of the crew of each ship would die on every long voyage and 3 per cent would die in battle (S. Pope 1998: 72). The greatest risks occurred in the West Indies. In the first six months of 1796 the *Hannibal* lost 200 men to yellow fever, almost four times more than any ship involved in the Battle of Trafalgar and twice the total losses to disease of Nelson's Mediterranean fleet of eleven ships and 6,500 men over the two-year period lead-ing up to Trafalgar.[20] Disease, not the French or the Spanish, was the real enemy for most British sailors at the time of Nelson—but there is little that counts as heroic in falling to yellow fever and Nelson was adamant that he would die a hero's death (D. Pope 1997: 139, 142).[21] To become a hero, Nelson needed to mobilize his followers and supporters through discipline and rewards—and keep some of them alive.

Methods of Mobilization

Although much has been made of the lashings in the British navy, and keel-haul-ing, the actual use of the lash appears to have varied considerably (D. Pope 1997: 213).[22] A young midshipman with Collingwood on the *Mediator* suggests that floggings occurred only about twice a year, though 'starting'—hitting a sailor with a short length of rope called a 'starter'—was very common. Lashings were also very common amongst newly pressed sailors, for whom even swearing was punishable by the lash, though, as William Richardson (1999: 7) noted at the time, 'not severely, few getting more than seven or eight lashes'. Captains, in the-ory, could not order more than twelve lashes at any one time without instigating a court martial, but many captains appeared to take little notice of such regula-tions.[23] In 1795 one captain had awarded two deserters seventy-two lashes each, and the Admiralty, on reading his report, made no comment upon it (D. Pope 1997: 221). Precisely what damage could be done through lashing is difficult to tell; as Dudley Pope comments, 'Three dozen lashes could kill one man; another would survive 200.' Some men were 'lashed around the fleet', with the number of lashes (up to 600) divided between the number of ships on station. And, though not all the lashes would be inflicted at one go, the prospect of a lashing must have made some impact on even the most hardened rating. At the age of 15, Nelson joined the *Seahorse*, a twenty-gun frigate captained by George Farmer, a renowned martinet who, on average, flogged two of his men every week (Pocock 1994: 18). Nelson himself, though not known as a 'flogger', was quite prepared to flog and hang those he considered guilty of crimes, and he was directly involved in the mass execution of Neapolitan rebels in 1799. But, while there were many great 'floggers' in the navy, none appears to have survived his employment as a great 'leader'. So was the seduction of sailors through anticipated financial gain a clear differentiator? After all, prize money was alleged to be quite considerable and Nelson himself was often in dispute with his superior officers over the share allotted to him.

Prize money (until 1808) was distributed according to a fixed scale. Three-eighths went to the captain (unless he was under an admiral, in which case the admiral took one of the captain's eighths). A further eighth was for the captain of the marines, while another went to the lieutenants, ensigns, quartermasters, and other non-commissioned officers. One-eighth went to the midshipman, sergeant of marines, and petty officers, and the last quarter was divided equally between the remainder of the crew (Lavery 1989: 116). As a consequence, the capture of an average-sized prize might net the captain thirty-five years' pay, the lieutenants four years' pay, and each sailor about eighteen months' pay. Clearly vast fortunes could be won—or lost—through the successful capture of enemy merchant ships, and the seductive allure of such riches would undoubtedly have attracted many people and encouraged them to risk their lives rather more frequently than otherwise might have been the case. However, in Nelson's case, the pursuit of prize money was never his major concern and more a means to an end than an end in itself. Therefore, those who served with Nelson may have been *less* rather than *more* likely to have exerted themselves on his behalf. The capture of enemy warships was more important to Nelson but much less financially profitable. Though the acquisition of promotions and honours could only be achieved through such 'prizes', ordinary sailors and marines were seldom in a position to benefit from such gestures (Lavery 1989: 116). Enemy warships accumulated 'head money' or 'gun money' rather than prize money, such that the capture of an enemy seventy-four-gun ship would result in £10 per gun divided amongst the crew, usually resulting in around £1 per sailor. But this was nothing compared to taking a merchant ship, and, given the greater dangers attached to attacking an enemy warship, the seduction of honour probably played a small part in most sailors' incentives.[24]

We should also remember that the average sailor, pressed or not, was not necessarily appalled by the prospect of fighting at close range; after all, that is what they were there for. Steve Pope (1998: 79) goes even further to suggest that: 'Victory was assumed and it might mean some small reward in prize money, but fighting was something sailors did for pleasure anyway, and many reacted to the prospect of killing or maiming Britain's enemies like the bloodthirsty xenophobes they were.' So how did Horatio Nelson come to lead this mob?

Nelson's Early Years

Horace[25] Nelson, one of eight children, was born in 1758 to Edmund Nelson, a Cambridge-educated rector at Burnham Thorpe, Norfolk, and Catherine (née Suckling), who was distantly related to Robert Walpole and who died when he was 9. Horace was sent to board at the Royal Grammar School at Norwich, then to a local private school, where Greek and Latin were taught by a Welsh parson, John Price Jones, with a reputation for flogging boys. Horace Nelson's main claim to fame through these years was his growing reputation for bravery. He stole Jones's pears 'because every other boy was afraid'; late home one day, he was scolded by his grandmother and asked why fear had not driven him home? 'Fear', he is alleged to have replied, 'I never saw fear. What is it? It never came near me' (Hibbert 1995: 6). It was the tradition for boys from the lower professional classes, such as Horace, to join either the Royal Navy or the Church. Horace only ever wanted to go to sea and already had a relation in the service— his uncle, Captain Maurice Suckling, then commanding the *Dreadnought*. Suckling had defeated a superior French squadron in 1757, on 21 October to be precise, a date that became an annual celebration in the Nelson family long before Trafalgar (Schom 1992: 244; Pocock 1994: 3). In 1770 the Spanish invaded the Falkland Islands, so the bulk of the navy was taken out of 'reserve' and Captain Suckling was sent to command one of the ships to relieve the islands. In the event, the war never happened, but it encouraged Horace to ask his uncle for a position on his ship. To which Maurice—adopting the more familiar Horatio as a more suitable name for a potential naval officer—replied: 'What has poor Horatio done, who is so weak, that he should be sent to rough it out at sea. But let him come, and the first time we go into action a cannon ball may knock off his head and provide for him at once' (quoted in Grabsky 1993: 76).

So on 1 January 1771 Nelson entered the navy at the age of 12 as a midshipman, joining his uncle's ship *Raisonnable*. Nelson's spelling and grammar remained poor throughout his life as a consequence of his leaving school early. His uncle was almost immediately transferred to the command of the *Triumph*, a guardship on the Thames. Hence Horatio was put on board a merchant ship bound for the West Indies to gain more experience of the sea. On his return, in 1773, he joined the *Carcass* on an expedition to the North Pole and was disciplined for leaving the ship to hunt a polar bear—which almost attacked him after his gun had misfired (Hibbert 1995: 14). Within the first two years of his service Nelson had already established a valuable lesson. It was not what you did that mattered, but how that act was interpreted by the audience: hunting the polar bear was the act not of an indisciplined youth but of a youth without fear. He had achieved success with his first naval 'performance'.

He then joined the *Seahorse*, a twenty-gun frigate captained by George Farmer, and sailed to India, where, in 1775, he contracted malaria at the age of 15. He was so ill that he was transferred to the *Dolphin*, and, under the influence of his fever, experienced a 'vision' off the coast of West Africa—a 'radiant orb', which he assumed to be a manifestation of royal patriotism. 'Well then,' he allegedly said to himself, 'I will be a hero and, confiding in Providence, I will brave every danger.' As Hibbert (1995: 16) notes: 'Thereafter he was rarely to doubt that he was a man of destiny.' This is important because until this time there is little that marks Nelson out from any other midshipman, and this 'transformation' clearly instilled him with the confidence to take his undoubted natural courage further. He had already acquired performing arts; now Nelson acquired a strategic vision that was never to leave him and provided the bedrock of all his actions: he was going to be a hero. But, while a belief in some form of fate may prove to be a clue to Nelson's qualities, it was not sufficient to invent a career ladder. For this he needed more than luck. What helped was his uncle, Captain Suckling. In 1775, when the American War of Independence broke out, his uncle, unusually for a guardship captain, was promoted Comptroller of the Navy and a senior member of the Navy Board, thus massively increasing Nelson's patronage or 'interest'. This transformed Nelson's meritocratic—and therefore heroic— struggle through the ranks into a narrative of sponsored success that mirrored rather than outshone that of almost every other admiral at the time (Pocock 1994: 21).[26]

Two years later, in 1777, at 18 years of age, Nelson presented himself to the Admiralty to determine his suitability for promotion. Captain Suckling was on the Board but asserted that he did not tell the other members of his relationship— though, since the normal minimum age for promotion was 19, one wonders just how ignorant the other two members of the Board were. Nelson, speaking with a 'strong Norfolk dialect', passed the exam and later, as Lieutenant Nelson on the frigate *Lowestoft*, leaped aboard an American merchantman in rough weather to claim it as prize for his captain after the first lieutenant had refused. Later a schooner was captured and renamed the *Little Lucy*, and Nelson was given command, whereupon he quickly captured an American schooner, the *Abigail*. In a few short months, Nelson had 'seized the day' to enhance his own reputation at the expense of a weaker—or less foolhardy—first lieutenant and begun his solo career as a leader at a very young age. Such early experiences of leadership are often regarded as vital to the later development of leaders and Nelson's potential rapidly increased with the declaration of war by France against Britain. In March 1778 Rear Admiral Peter Parker—as Pocock (1994: 26) notes, 'with an eye to future favours' (with the Comptroller of the Navy)—appointed Suckling's nephew as third lieutenant aboard his own ship. Captain Suckling died three months later, but by the time the news had arrived (in October) Parker was so impressed with Nelson that he promoted him to Commander of the brig *Badger*, patrolling the eastern seaboard of Central America, and he became Nelson's new patron.

Captain Nelson

Within a year, in June 1779, Nelson was again promoted, this time to Captain of the frigate *Hinchinbroke*. During this time he shared accommodation, when in Jamaica, with Captain William Cornwallis, whose housekeeper was a Jamaican woman, Cuba Cornwallis, a slave freed by Cornwallis. It is not clear whether this was the West Indian 'gypsy' Nelson recalled on the eve of Trafalgar who, when foretelling his glorious future, got to 1805 and proclaimed: 'I can see no further!' (Hibbert 1995: 356). 'Ah Katty, Katty, that Gypsy!', he is reputed to have exclaimed to his sister a little while earlier (Pocock 1994: 315). Whoever the fortune-teller was, her prophecy was powerful enough for Nelson to remember it for the rest of his life and it may well have helped him to face great danger with equanimity. After all, if you can be persuaded that your life is assured for the next twenty-six years, what fear can you have?[27]

At the age of 21, with Spain at war with Britain, Nelson on 3 February 1880 ordered what may have been the first of many floggings, this time of two men, 'for neglect of duty and insolence' (Pocock 1994: 36). But his progression from harmless boy to coercive man made little impact upon Captain Polson of the King's American Regiment, charged with leading an expedition against the Mosquito Coast of Spanish Nicaragua. As Polson recalled: 'A light-haired boy came to me in a little frigate, of whom I at first made little account' (quoted in Hibbert 1995: 23). Nelson was required only to land the expedition, but, once more seizing the opportunity, he volunteered to help with navigation, worked closely with Edward Despard,[28] and led a frontal assault upon the Spanish battery at Bartola. Nelson later wrote his 'Sketch of my Life', in a vein of self-congratulations that was to mark almost all his writing and turned his act into a performance:

Major Polson, who commanded the soldiers, will tell you of my exertions: how I quitted my ship and carried troops on boats one hundred miles up a river . . . it will then be told how I boarded an outpost of the enemy, situated on an island in the river; that I made batteries, and afterwards fought them, and was a principal cause of our success . . . I shall recover and my dream of glory be fulfilled. Nelson will yet be an Admiral.   (quoted in Hibbert 1995: 29)

Nelson was, therefore, disconcerted to be sent to the North American Station during the War of Independence. It was noted as the station for making prize money, but Nelson was adamant that he would rather be in the West Indies—'the station for honour' (Hibbert 1995: 34). Honour was, however, coming his way, for he soon met Prince William Henry, third son of the King, and struck up an acquaintance that Nelson assumed could do nothing but good for his career. Prince William was less sure, for 'Captain Nelson appeared to be the merest boy of a captain I ever beheld . . . My doubts were, however, removed when Lord Hood introduced me to him. There was something irresistibly pleasing in his address and conversation' (quoted in Pocock 1994: 58).[29]

When the American War of Independence ended in 1783, Prince William made an official visit to Havana, using the *Albermarle* as his royal yacht, and Nelson was now firmly ensconced as one of the navy's favourites. He wrote to Captain Locker (Nelson's captain on the *Lowestoft*) saying that Admiral Parker 'treats me as if I was his son and will, I am convinced, give me anything I can ask of him: nor is my situation with Prince William any less flattering' (quoted in Pocock 1994: 59). As a naval and royal favourite, Nelson could—apparently—do no wrong and he considered standing for parliament, but was unsure which party to stand for and had no reputation either as an administrator or as an orator. Eventually he decided on the Tory party but he was unable to find a constituency and forgot the issue. In March he became captain of the twenty-eight-gun frigate *Boreas* and sailed to the West Indies, where he called a midshipman to his cabin on hearing that his father was a Whig: 'There are three things, young gentleman, which you are constantly to bear in mind: first you must always implicitly obey orders, without attempting to form any opinion of your own respecting their propriety; second, you must consider every man as your enemy who speaks ill of your King; and, thirdly, you must hate a Frenchman as you do the devil!' (Hibbert 1995: 43). Note here the significance of the first, and therefore presumably the most important thing to bear in mind: 'always implicitly obey orders'. As a boy Nelson had frequently done the opposite; as a midshipman himself he had again disregarded his captain's orders. Now, however, his own success depended on others doing as he told them, not as he had done.

His increasing emphasis on adherence to the letter of the law grew in conjunction with his concern at what he saw as lax discipline in the navy. For example, on sailing to Antigua he protested in person and letters about the Commissioner of the island flying an inappropriate flag. Then he increased his already rising unpopularity in the area by enforcing the Navigation Acts (taxation) against merchant ships heading to North America. The Acts were known to be unenforceable, so a blind eye had been turned to them by the authorities, but Nelson required the rules to be enforced and had several writs taken out against him by shipowners. Nelson's pique seems to have been motivated by the 'treasonable' behaviour of the colonists rather than by the inviolability of the taxation laws, for 'the residents of these islands', he complained, 'are Americans by connexion and by interests and are inimical to Great Britain. They are as great rebels as ever were in America' (quoted in Pocock 1994: 72). Yet he himself subsequently broke the law on importing goods without taxation when he smuggled a cargo of tamarind into the country because 'the duty . . . is so enormous that no person can afford the expense' (Hibbert 1995: 63).

But, despite his unpopularity with most of the white islanders (he had no concerns for the black islanders), he did impress at least one, a Mrs Frances Nisbet, a widow with a 5-year-old boy Josiah, daughter of a judge on the island of Nevis in the West Indies.[30] She had been the wife of a doctor who had died from some tropical illness, and, though she herself was without fortune, Nelson looked optimistically at her prospects, for her uncle owned several estates on the island.

Prince William added further honour by attending their subsequent wedding in 1787. His fellow officers were not impressed. One said of the bride that she had 'a remarkable absence of intellectual endowment'. Another, Captain Thomas Pringle, complained that 'The Navy, Sir, has now lost one of its greatest ornaments . . . It is a national loss that such an officer should marry. Had it not been for that circumstance, I foresaw Nelson would become the greatest man in the Service' (Hibbert 1995: 60).[31] Irrespective of his marriage, for a man desperate for glory the next five years were remarkably frustrating, for, without the means to achieve it—a war—like most captains, he spent the next five years unemployed on half-pay.

The Early Construction of the Myth

Within a year of marriage, Nelson was reduced to writing to his erstwhile friend Prince William, asking for an appointment for his wife in the Royal Household, but he received no reply. Then 1789 brought the French Revolution; this was anathema to a royalist like Nelson, but, paradoxically, it brought about precisely the inversion of the status quo he needed to restart his career at sea—providing war with the old enemy was declared. He again badgered the navy for a commission, but, unbeknown to Nelson, his friendship with Prince William annoyed the King—who disliked his son intensely.[32] For a man with such support, coupled with his own virulent pursuit of bureaucratic requirements, the future looked bleak indeed. As Lord Hood said to him: 'the King was impressed with an unfavourable opinion of Captain Nelson' (Hibbert 1995: 71). Nelson was devastated—an ardent, indeed, *the* ardent royalist, rejected by the very person whom he had sworn to defend with his life. Yet, he declared, 'Neither at sea nor on shore, through the caprice of a minister can my attachment to my King be shaken. That will never end but with my life' (quoted in Pocock 1994: 92).

Four years into his forced early retirement Nelson was increasingly desperate, as, probably, were the other 446 post captains without a command (D. Pope 1997: 20). He wrote to the Admiralty again: 'If your Lordships should be pleased to appoint me to a *cockle-boat* I should be grateful.' But he received no response. However, the execution of the French king suddenly made war look likely and the following January (1793) he was required to attend the Admiralty; as he wrote: '*Post Nubila Phaebus* [After clouds comes sunshine].' Nelson, now aged 34, was about to restart his quest for glory, this time in command of the *Agamemnon*, a sixty-four-gun ship.

On 1 February 1793 France declared war on Britain and in the September Nelson sailed to Naples and met Emma Hamilton, the second wife of Sir William Hamilton. Emma Hamilton, born Emily Lyon in 1765, daughter of a Cheshire blacksmith who had died two months after her birth, was brought up by her grandmother and went into domestic service at 12. She then worked in an exclusive 'club' called the 'Temple of Health' in London, where fertility could be restored in the 'Celestial Bed'. At 16 she had a child by an unnamed naval officer and became mistress first of Sir Harry Fetherstonhaugh and then of Charles Greville. A striking beauty in her early years, many portraits were made, but she had very little education. Greville decided to marry someone of his own social class and, with one eye on the fortune of his uncle, Sir William Hamilton, Greville 'presented' her, now aged 26, to him. Hamilton, a 60-year-old widower, agreed to take her on in Naples and, despite the British public displeasure at the relationship—Emma made close friends with the Queen of Naples—they were eventually married in 1791 (Pocock 1994: 174–5).

In May 1793 Nelson sailed into Cadiz, impressed with the Spanish ships—but not with their sailors: 'in vain may the Dons make fine ships; they cannot make men' (quoted in Pocock 1994: 105). Since the Spanish navy was virtually bankrupt, this was hardly surprising (S. Pope 1998: 25). When the Spanish fleet—temporarily allied to Britain—joined the British squadron under Hood, their combined movements were all too brief and the Spanish admiral signalled to Hood that he would have to return because he had been at sea for sixty continuous days—an excuse Nelson found incredible (Pocock 1994: 106). More importantly, it persuaded Nelson that the Spanish were no match for the British and that he need not fear an engagement with them—irrespective of the relative numbers involved on both sides. Escaño, head of the Spanish General Staff in 1795, was of a similar opinion, for 'all the ships, with few exceptions, are in a bad state of repair and without the means to change the situation. Even the weakest of enemies could destroy them with ease . . . If we have to enter into battle this squadron will bring this nation into mourning, digging the grave of the person who has the misfortune to command it' (quoted in C. White 1998: 30). So dire was the situation that, when the *Santissima Trinidad* sailed in 1797, it had only sixty experienced sailors on board, out of a total complement of 900 (C. White 1998: 31).

On 22 October of the same year Nelson began forming the same opinion of the French. The French grain harvest of that year had failed—dragging the economy deeper into debt—and the French navy was persuaded to seek supplies from wherever it could. So poor was morale that Rear Admiral Villaret-Joyeuse, in command of the Brest fleet, threatened to guillotine any captain failing to carry out his orders. But Nelson, having chased five smaller French ships in the *Agamemnon*, was still unable to capture or destroy the French ships, instead himself suffering some minor damage and seven casualties (one dead). But the report of the action to Hood revealed that his skills in the performing arts could compensate when his martial arts failed him, for he claimed that he had severely damaged the largest French frigate, the *Melpomène*. Simultaneously, however, he sent a different report to his elder brother Maurice (who had originally been a clerk in the excise office but had moved to the administrative Navy Office in London), with an eye to establishing a more positive informal perspective. In that report he explained how he had been outgunned three to one by the French ships yet had *still* managed to fight successfully (Pocock 1994: 112). The Nelson legend construction machine was beginning to move. Yet Nelson was hardly the only brave English captain: in November 1794 Sir Sydney Smith sailed right into Brest harbour, counted the French fleet at anchor, and sailed out again without suffering any damage, so poor was the condition of the French navy and port defences (Tracy 1998a: 111).[33]

As was made clear above, one of the few ways that members of the élite and the armed forces could demonstrate their social value was through the cult of heroism, and nothing manifested this better than the acquirement and display of wounds. Nelson's first wound occurred in 1794 when he lost most of the sight of his right eye as a French shell exploded in sandbagged ramparts in Corsica. His summary was perfectly aligned to the professional dismissal of injury: 'the blemish is nothing . . . so my beauty is saved' (Hibbert 1995: 96).[34] More significantly for Nelson, General Stuart, Commanding Officer of the land forces, failed to mention him in his report, despite 'three actions against ships, two against Bastia in my ship; four boat actions, and two villages taken and twelve sail of vessels burnt'. Once again, Nelson wrote to his brother to ensure that an unofficial résumé of his actions would circulate throughout the Admiralty: 'I am now pointed out as having been this war one hundred and twelve times engaged against the French, and always successful to a certain degree. No Officer in Europe can say as much . . . Mine is all honour' (quoted in Hibbert 1995: 97).[35]

The Myth Develops

By now Nelson was beginning to regain some of the favouritism that had supported his early career. In 1796 Admiral Sir John Jervis replaced Hotham, who had replaced Hyde Parker, who, in turn, had replaced Hood, all in quick succession.[36] Nelson got on well with Jervis—so well, in fact, that a less favoured captain was tempted to remark to Nelson that 'You did just as you pleased in Lord Hood's time, the same in Admiral Hotham's and now again with Sir John Jervis. It makes no difference to you who is Commander-in-Chief' (quoted in Pocock 1994: 126–7). Jervis offered to secure Nelson (now aged 38) a promotion to vice admiral but instead a promotion only to commodore was confirmed by the Admiralty, along with command of the *Captain*. With French advances in Italy, Spain switched sides from Britain to France, and, much to Nelson's disgust, the British decided to retreat from the Mediterranean under the pressure of the combined enemy fleet.

In December 1796 Nelson's performing arts were given their severest test when he left the *Captain* and joined the frigate *La Minerve* on a reconnaissance patrol back into the Mediterranean, where, accompanied by *Blanche*, another frigate, he attacked and captured a Spanish frigate, the *Santa Sabina*. Nelson then wrote his official report of the victory. But, as he did so, further Spanish ships sailed towards him and he was forced to cast off the prize—and its British prize crew—and escape. Rather than scrub the original report of his capture of the *Santa Sabina*, Nelson wrote a second report and sent them both to the London *Gazette*, where they were both published—though C. White (1998: 23) suggests the victorious version received more attention than the inglorious one.

With rumours of a mutiny at home beginning to spread, the British fleet in the Mediterranean in retreat, and Ireland near rebellion, Jervis was overheard suggesting that 'A victory is very essential to England at this moment', and, on 14 February 1797, his suggestion was realized (quoted in Pocock 1994: 129).[37] With fifteen ships under his command, facing twenty-three Spanish (the British claimed there were twenty-seven), Jervis's ships opened fire at 11.30. Noting the division between the sections of the Spanish fleet (brought about by an attempt to tack under pressure that tested the skill of the Spanish crews to the utmost), he opted to intercept at the gap and defeat one section before the other section could return, in a neutralizing tactic that was also a prelude to Nelson's neutralizing tactics at Trafalgar. However, when Jervis gave the order to tack in succession and engage the enemy—with each ship reaching the position of the leading ship before it turned—Nelson realized that tacking in succession would give the Spanish time to close the gap. In defiance of explicit orders, and once more seizing the moment, he tacked immediately, taking the *Captain* out of line and heading for four 100-gun triple-deckers and the *Santissima Trinidad*, a four-decker 140-gun ship, then the largest warship in the world, intending to force the gap apart. Such was the time lapse in these forms of warfare that Nelson did not engage the enemy until about 13.30 and did not reach the *San Nicholas* until about 16.00. Pocock suggests that this apparently suicidal mission was nothing of the sort, since Nelson probably calculated that, even with 500-plus guns ranged against him, his rate of fire from the *Captain*'s seventy-four guns—possibly ten times greater than the Spanish rate—would probably discharge more shot at the Spanish than they could at him (Pocock 1994: 130). In short, he could win the battle of attrition, especially given the state of the Spanish ships and their crews. Whatever the calculation, the *Captain*'s masts and rigging were rapidly shot away and Nelson then ordered the *Captain* to ram the *San Nicolas*, which, in consequence, ran into the *San José*. White (1998: 65) claims that Nelson personally led the boarding party, even demanding that Miller, who had intended to lead it, step aside, and allegedly shouting, 'No Miller, I must have that honour.' But it seems more likely that Lieutenants Berry and Pearson led the boarding party against the *San Nicholas* and Nelson joined them later—though even this was considered an inappropriate course of action for a commodore, and, with seven British dead and ten wounded, the risks were clearly high (Tracy 1998a: 180–1). He then personally led—or rather was second in line in—a boarding party against the *San José*, allegedly shouting: 'Westminster Abbey or Glorious Victory!' C. White (1998: 66) suggests that this was extremely unlikely and that it was probably an invention of Emma Hamilton's, placed into the text of James Harrison's 1806 biography by her. Whatever the content of his orders were, luckily for Nelson and the rest of the boarding party, the crew of the *San José* surrendered immediately and there were no British casualties.[38]

The manœuvre was widely regarded as extremely hazardous, some captains suggesting that he had risked the entire fleet by weakening the collective position, others suggesting that the tactic was correct but that he should have taken the rest of the rearguard squadron with him (Bethune 1999: 82). When Captain Calder, the Fleet Commander, correctly suggested that Nelson had acted in defiance of the Admiral's instructions, Jervis allegedly responded: 'It certainly was so, and if ever you commit such a breach of your orders, I will forgive you also' (quoted in Pocock 1994: 132). What Jervis should have added was 'as long as you are as successful'. However, since Nelson appears to have been the source of this account, we should remain wary of assuming its accuracy.

Precisely how influential Nelson had been was subject to some dispute by Admiral Parker on the *St George*, who insisted that it was his ship, in addition to one or two others, that had battered the *San José* into submission *before* Nelson's ship had arrived. Moreover, Parker claimed that, because the *San José* struck her colours[39] before Nelson's ship had arrived, Parker decided to move on to the *San Nicholas* and leave the already surrendered ship to be formally possessed by Nelson. Nelson merely acknowledged the letter but refused to entertain Parker's claims (Tracy 1998a: 191–2). Even Nelson's friend, Captain Collingwood, suggested that, when he arrived alongside the *Captain*, 'I happily came to his relief, for he was dreadfully mauled' (quoted in C. White 1998: 63). And, as C. White (1998: 68) suggests, without detracting from Nelson's personal heroism, both Spanish ships had been pounded by four British ships for two hours before any boarding occurred. However, the point is that, whichever captain had the better martial arts, Nelson's better performing arts won the day and secured the rewards.

As news of the Battle of Cape St Vincent spread back to Britain, Nelson asked Sir Gilbert Elliot to try and ensure he received a knighthood and an Order of the Bath (the right to wear a glittering star) and not a baronetcy (since he could not afford to maintain a hereditary title at this time). Instead he received nothing at first and blamed Calder. Nelson, never one to let history rest, then wrote his own account of the battle and got two other (junior) officers (Berry and Miller) to sign it as their own (they demand to be recognized in his account); it was subsequently published by a third captain (Locker) in the newspapers (Hibbert 1995: 112). As Nelson mentioned to Locker: 'if you approve of it you're perfectly at liberty to insert it in the newspapers, inserting the name of "Commodore" instead of "I"' (quoted in C. White 1998: 77). The performative massaging of history worked: he was promoted Rear Admiral of the Blue and received a knighthood and an Order of the Bath.[40]

Death and honour may have been inseparable for Nelson but neither was of interest to his wife and she pleaded with him to disengage from enemy action from now on. His response was typically dismissive: 'Life with disgrace is dreadful. A glorious death is to be envied' (quoted in Hibbert 1995:). Just how inglorious death could be was shown very soon afterwards when Jervis, now named St Vincent, sentenced two men to death for a homosexual act—'an unnatural crime', as it was termed.[41] Jervis subsequently sentenced four others to death for leading a mutiny against the original sentence and intended to proceed with the hanging of these men immediately, as it happened on a Sunday, despite some concern by the other officers about an execution on the Sabbath. Nelson was not one of those so concerned, even though he regarded himself as an ardent Christian: 'I very much approve of it being so speedily carried into execution, even though it is *Sunday*' (quoted in Pocock 1994: 137). Thus a man who wilfully broke an explicit order from his commanding officer, and put the lives of all his men at unnecessary risk, for the sake of his own pursuit of glory condemned others for what many of the crew, at least in Jervis's ship, thought was beyond the need of discipline. Nelson was keen to parade his own insubordination, since it had contributed to a victory, but he was even more keen to parade that of others—if necessary, by a rope from the yardarm—whose 'insubordination' contributed little and threatened even less.

That Nelson was inordinately brave is without doubt: in July 1797 he had yet another premonition of death whilst planning an amphibious operation to land 4,000 troops at Santa Cruz in Tenerife. As he suggested to Admiral Jervis: 'My plan could not fail of success, would immortalize the undertakers, ruin Spain and has every prospect of raising our country to a higher pitch of wealth than she ever yet attained' (quoted in C. White 1998: 99). Quite how it would achieve these objectives is unclear, but the planning went wrong even before the operation had started, for the army refused to release any troops and Nelson had to make do with just 900 seamen and marines. The raid was a disaster on the first attempt through the surrounding hills. The second attempt on the next day was a frontal assault on the town led by Nelson himself, after a deserter had suggested that the defenders were 'frightened to death' and a collective Council of War had supported the idea. In the event Nelson was shot in the right arm by a musket ball before he had even reached land, crying out: 'I'm a dead man.' He was taken back to his own ship, which he climbed up one handed without help and then ordered the surgeon to remove his right arm. He was given opium to deaden the pain and within thirty minutes was back in command. But when the excitement of the action was over he sank into depression as he realized he could not continue to command with one arm and one eye.

Furthermore, his contempt for the Spanish had only contributed to the scale of the defeat at Tenerife: 153 British were dead or missing, over 100 were wounded, and the captured British sailors were forced to march through the town as they were escorted back to their ships. For once the Spanish had managed to invert the British superiority. Nelson's hair turned white, he lost many of his upper front teeth, and from then on he was rarely seen smiling in public and often took opium at night to relieve the pain. As Lady Spencer, wife of the First Lord of the Admiralty, described him: 'A most uncouth creature I thought him . . . He looked so sickly it was painful to see him and his general appearance was that of an idiot; so much so that, when he spoke and his wonderful mind broke forth, it was a sort of surprise that riveted my whole attention' (quoted in Hibbert 1995: 132).

Yet, contrary to his fears, he was awarded a hero's welcome back in Portsmouth as the dashing hero of the victory at St Vincent and the 'gallant' defeat at Tenerife, which was blamed on the politicians (Pocock 1994: 146;

C. White 1998: 141). This seems to have come about because the distance between Britain and Tenerife ensured that the version of events read by the public allowed a heroic gloss to be poured over what might have been regarded as an outright failure. As the *Naval Chronicle* put it: 'The unfortunate failure of this expedition, occasioned by a variety of unforeseen circumstances, is well known; but it redounds highly to the credit of every officer and man concerned, that the failure resulted not from any defect in the plan of attack, or from any error or incapacity of execution' (quoted in Tracy 1998a: 197). In effect, the 'surf', the 'rocky coast', and the 'extraordinary great force' opposing them were to blame. The first two were self-evidently errors of planning not 'unforeseen circumstances'; as to the 'extraordinary' force, which official figures suggested amounted to 8,000 regular soldiers, there were, in reality, 1,699, half of whom were irregular militia men armed with sickles not rifles (C. White 1998: p. ix). But performances are not rooted in such 'truths' and it suited all the powerful lobbies concerned to accept Nelson's account of the 'glorious' defeat rather than to look a little more closely at the tactical disaster.

His monetary problems were also resolved by the prize money, his rear admiral's pay, and a disability pension. He was now 38 years old and had fought in four major fleet battles, six attacks against land batteries, ten attacks upon individual ships, and three captures of towns. As far as he was concerned his best years were behind him, but Napoleon was in front.

The Battle of the Nile, August 1798

Napoleon had assembled a huge invasion force to wrest Egypt from its formal ruler, the Turkish sultan, and its informal rulers, the Mamelukes—a group of slave soldiers. Once Egypt was taken the greater prizes lay further east, especially India, though several French historians[42] remain sceptical that Napoleon ever really had a clear political or even military strategy. Britain had already been forced out of the Mediterranean when Spain had joined France in the war against Britain, and, in early May, Napoleon sailed with forty-two warships of varying sizes (including thirteen ships-of-the-line) and around 273 troop transporting merchant ships. Nelson, now on his own flagship the *Vanguard*, had orders to search for Napoleon's armada with thirteen ships-of-the-line and two smaller vessels.[43] Nobody knew where Napoleon was headed, but Nelson's task was to find him and prevent him from going wherever he was intending to go. Ironically, in what was one of Nelson's greatest victories, he failed to achieve the task set him.

Nelson eventually found the empty transport ships off Alexandria on 1 August, though the French Admiral Brueys's main battle fleet had anchored at Aboukir Bay. There, in theory, the anchorage was relatively safe, with the larger ships anchored at the southernmost point—the point most vulnerable to attack—since the northern end was shallow, and the northernmost ship had anchored close to shore to prevent any enemy ship sailing between the line of

French ships and the land. Since it was also late, Brueys assumed Nelson would not attack until the following morning and so continued to unload his ships. Indeed, Napoleon had insisted that a large proportion of the crews help the army scavenge for food and water, leaving Brueys distinctly vulnerable. In fact, in a subsequent report by a French officer, it was suggested that the French had wanted to engage the British under sail but had less than the minimum 200 sailors on each ship to manage this. Moreover, many of those on land simply ignored the order to return to their ships hoisted at 14.00 on sighting the enemy fleet. But Nelson's exploitation of the moment came to fruition at Aboukir, for, rather than waiting until morning, at 15.00 he ordered the British fleet to attack. And, rather than sailing down the seaward side of the line of French ships, three of the British ships managed to squeeze down the landward side. Nelson had not so much 'seized the day' as seized the French fleet.

The French fleet should have been safe. There had been several examples of an anchored fleet close to the land prevailing over a larger attacking fleet in the American War of Independence. And, at the Battle of St Kitts in 1782, a British fleet under Hood had managed to stave off a French attack when anchored in Frigate Bay, though Hood had been forced to move his line of ships closer to the shore when a French ship had tried to get to the landward side of the line. Nelson, as usual, discussed tactics with his captains before the battle, so that, as Sir Edmund Berry put it, 'every one of the Captains of his squadron was most thoroughly acquainted; and upon surveying the situation of the enemy, they could ascertain with precision what were the ideas and intentions of the Commander, without the aid of any further instructions' (quoted in Grabksy 1993: 83). Yet, as Nelson approached the bay he had *asked* Captain Hood 'What he thought about attacking that night', rather than either telling him what would happen or simply following any alleged prepared plan (see Tracy 1998a: 266). Finally, Nelson said to his officers—for at least the second time—'Before this time tomorrow I shall have gained a peerage or Westminster Abbey.' Nelson had intended that a couple of British ships would anchor alongside each of the most northerly French ships (see Fig. 7.1) and, if possible, slip between them and 'double up' along both sides, thereby neutralizing the southern end of the French line and engaging in a battle of attrition that he could win. However, as the British fleet drew near, he saw the possibility of outflanking the French ships on the coastal side rather than risking going through the line and getting caught upon the inevitable cables that would be strung out between the French ships to prevent the British entering the line. Nelson then called to Captain Hood in the *Zealous* to lead the British fleet into the battle formation with Nelson on the *Vanguard* in the centre of the column— as was typical for the day. Hood was then asked to see whether he could take his ship around the top of the French line. In fact, Hood's ship was overtaken by Captain Foley's *Goliath*, the only captain with a map of the waters, and it was he, apparently without direct orders from Nelson, who rounded the French line at its most northerly point at about 18.30 just as darkness approached. The *Goliath* then swung back south on the landward side, followed by the *Theseus* and the

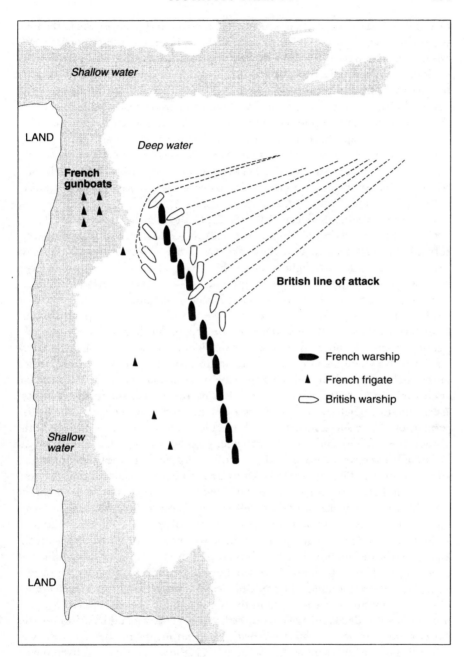

Fig. 7.1. The Battle of the Nile

Orion. The first five French ships receiving broadsides from both sides of the twin British line, which now extended down to the eighth French ship (Pocock 1994: 164). Even the second-smallest British ship, the *Leander,* a fifty-gun double-decker, conventionally thought too weak to use in a battle, became directly involved as it slipped between two French ships—whose cables should have prevented such an action. The *Leander* anchored and fired broadsides at the bow of the *Franklin* on the port side and the stern of the *Peuple Souverain* with impunity, because such ships carried no forward- or rearward-facing guns of any significance (Lyon 1996: 81–2). In fact, the order to send out cables between the ships to prevent the British getting between them, and to allow the French ships to swing a little to bring their broadsides to bear, was given at 17.00 but seems to have been ignored (Tracy 1998a: 271).

Late in the evening, between 21.00 and 22.00, the French flagship, the 120-gun *L'Orient,* blew up. Admiral Brueys, hit three times, and with both legs shot away, refused to surrender or to leave the deck, even as fire broke out around him, saying: 'A French Admiral ought to die on his own quarterdeck' (quoted in Lyon 1996: 84). Immediately afterwards Captain Casa Bianca was mortally wounded, but his son—who was later immortalized in Heman's poem 'The boy stood on the burning deck'—refused to leave him.[44] Meanwhile Captain Dupetit-Thouars continued to resist the British attacks despite having both legs and one arm shot off in short succession; he died directing the fight from a brantub placed on deck for him. Elsewhere, in a desperate attempt to avoid the fire of *L'Orient,* which spread debris up to half a kilometre away, it seems that many French ships cut their cables and drifted out of line, allowing the British yet further access.[45] Certainly the French subsequently argued that, but for the explosion, the British would not have been so successful.[46] Rather less valorous were the actions of the ships at the southern end of the French line. Two ships-of-the-line (one with Rear Admiral Villeneuve on board) and two frigates fled the scene the following morning at around 11.00 and escaped. Afterwards Villeneuve claimed that Admiral Brueys had had no plans for the southern end to support the northern end of the fleet, because he had assumed that Nelson would attack the south, and, anyway, the southern ships could not have reached their distressed comrades in time to help. Lyon (1996: 86) suggests that Villeneuve should not be saddled with the blame for the defeat; however, it is the case that five French ships-of-the-line and three frigates played virtually no part in the battle, either escaping directly or running themselves aground in the panic to escape. Thirteen of the seventeen French ships were captured or destroyed in the battle and the French suffered between 1,700 and 5,000 dead and 1,500 wounded, while 3,000 were taken prisoner—the latter being released, because the British had no means to feed them. It was, according to a British sailor, 'An awful sight . . . the whole bay was covered with dead bodies, mangled, wounded and scorched, not a bit of clothes on them but their trousers' (quoted in Lyon 1996: 88).

The British, in contrast, suffered around 218 dead and 617 wounded. Most of the British casualties were onboard those ships that had attacked the seaward side of the French line and Lyon (1996: 88) suggests that this was because the French were not expecting an attack from the landward side and had therefore not prepared the guns on that side properly. Certainly, the only three ships that were fit enough to continue the action until the French fire had ceased altogether were the three ships that had anchored on the landward side of the French fleet: the *Zealous*, *Goliath*, and *Theseus*. Nelson himself was wounded in the head by shot fragment and had spent much of the battle below deck preparing—yet again—for his own death, while Captain Berry took over. But when the surgeon told Nelson that it was merely a flesh wound, Nelson returned to the deck and omitted all reference to his wound in his official dispatch, thereby increasing his merit when it became known—as it surely would—that he had been wounded.

When Nelson had approached Aboukir Bay, he was thirty-ninth of forty-two rear admirals in the seniority list but a well-known naval figure (D. Pope 1997: 31). When it was over, Nelson was a national hero; he had, at last, achieved the glory and fame he relished—as well as undreamed-of wealth—and he had achieved it by defeating what had appeared to be the undefeatable Napoleon.[47] Admittedly Napoleon, who had long disembarked his troops, set about occupying Egypt, defeating the Mamelukes by the Pyramids. But his army was now marooned and it was eventually defeated by a British amphibious landing in 1801—the first British army victory over Napoleon. As Lyon (1996: 91) concludes: 'No other battle between fleets of approximately the same size in the age of fighting sail was quite so strikingly complete, not even Trafalgar . . . most of all it was the achievement not just of Nelson, but of his "band of brothers" as well.'

How had Nelson achieved this? First it should be clear that in the battle itself Nelson's personal part had not been significantly greater than that of any other captain. Indeed, the actions of Foley and Hood and their respective crews were probably greater in terms of personal bravery. Nelson had demanded that the fleet attack as soon as it had sighted the enemy, giving the French little time for preparation, but, as mentioned above, the French should have been safe. But they were not. *If* Captain Trullet of the *Guerrier* had anchored his ship properly, then Captain Foley's *Goliath* would have been unable to round it and begin the 'doubling-up' on the French line that saw each French ship in turn attacked by two British ships simultaneously. Moreover, because the French assumed the *Guerrier had* anchored properly, the port guns of their ships were unprepared. *If* the cables between the French ships had been properly laid, no British ship would have been able to break through the French line anyway, leaving the British with little option but to engage in a traditional line of battle with precious little chance of overpowering their stronger opponents. Finally, even accepting all this, *if* Villeneuve and the unengaged French ships at the southern end of the line had weighed anchor and come to the rescue of their northern colleagues, all might not have been lost. As it was, all was lost, through a combination of fatal initial mistakes by the French and daring by the British. Nelson had gambled that his aggressive audacity would eliminate French static defence and he was right—but it was a gamble, it was not preordained. He had given the French no time to prepare and had eliminated their spatial safety by sailing down both sides. But it is important to remember that Nelson's audacity and tactical skill did not, by themselves, bring the victory; it was the mistakes by the French that allowed Nelson and his 'band of brothers' to exploit the opportunity. That opportunity was constructed not from British 'luck', but from French error. In effect, Nelson had inverted the apparent strength of the French by exploiting the side that should not have been exploitable; he could not have *known* this would happen, but in reality it was the only tactic that might have secured such a victory.

Nelson returned to Naples after the battle, and on the way malaria and sea-sickness persuaded him, for at least the third time, that he was about to die. But Lady Hamilton was not about to let that happen. She had grown 'monstrously fat', according to Sir Gilbert Elliot, but she still paraded around Naples with a headband emblazoned with the words 'Nelson and Victory' on it, and arranged a party with 1,740 guests for him. She fainted on seeing him, while Miss Knight, daughter of Admiral Knight, spoke of Nelson as 'little and not remarkable in his person either way'. But later she was struck by his 'great animation of counte-nance and activity in his appearance'. Lord Keith, however, was more concerned about the activity of his host rather than his subordinate and was heard to remark that 'Lady Hamilton has had command of the Fleet long enough!' (quoted in Hibbert 1995: 149, 152). The British newspapers, having ridiculed Nelson for failing to find Napoleon's fleet in the first place, now regarded him as the saviour of Britain. A new dance—the breaking of the line—became fashionable, and huge crowds gathered in London and across the country to celebrate Nelson's name and the victory (Pocock 1994: 182). The Sultan of Turkey sent Nelson a *chelengk*, a mechanical diamond ornament, with a clockwork star, which he ostentatiously attached to his hat. The Russian Tsar, in turn, sent him a dia-mond-encrusted box and the East India Company gave him £10,000. The British government made him a baron with a £2,000 p.a. pension, but Nelson was pri-vately furious because he had expected to be made a viscount. This was probably not simply an oversight, because his public and private antics after the battle con-siderably embarrassed the naval and political establishment, hence he was appointed as second-in-command to Parker for the subsequent Baltic operation, rather than put in command himself (Tracy 1998*b*: 149).

As far as the French were concerned, the Battle of the Nile was more significant than Trafalgar, because the latter battle occurred *after* the invasion of Britain had been called off while the former made the invasion unlikely in the extreme since the British navy appeared as invincible as the French army. The French navy may still have been able to facilitate an invasion of Britain, but only if it could out-smart or outrun the British; it would not be able to defeat the British at sea. Thus, as Lyon (1996: 69) notes: 'Trafalgar was merely an epilogue, a battle in which the French and their allies were doomed from the start, and furthermore they knew it.' However, although Napoleon abandoned his army in Egypt, he did not return in disgrace, as the British press suggested; rather, he was greeted as the only undefeated general in France, entering Paris in 'Egyptian dress' (Rapport 1998: 16). Indeed, by November 1799 he had been appointed First Consul, after the *coup* against the deeply unpopular Directory. Nelson may have emerged as the hero of the Nile, even if we have seen how much of the victory should have been laid at the feet of his followers and the errors of the French. But the threat to Britain was not in Egypt; it was in France.

The Neapolitan Episode, 1799

With the French making inroads into what is now Italy, Nelson was responsible for the evacuation of the Neapolitan royal family to Palermo when Naples was invaded. The whole episode began badly for Nelson, for it was he who had encouraged the Neapolitan king to take Rome back from the French invader, but the Neapolitan troops were no match for the French. At Palermo, Nelson suffered from his usual nausea, chest pains, indigestion, and breathlessness, now considered to be symptoms not of the heart condition he feared but of Da Costa's syndrome, or 'Soldier's Heart'—a stress-related condition. He also became infatuated with Emma and started the relationship that became the scandal of London, although this inhibited him not one jot. After all, as he constantly asserted to all who would listen, his love for her was perfect love and therefore beyond the reproaches of mere mortals.[48]

With the Neapolitan army failing to retake Naples, he had little sympathy for the defeated leaders and sent word to the Duke of Clarence that the two generals should be arrested for cowardice and treachery: 'If found guilty . . . shall be shot or hanged. I ever preach that rewards and punishments are the foundations of all good government' (quoted in Pocock 1994: 195).[49] The Neapolitan army and 'The Christian Army of the Holy Faith'—an irregular force led by Cardinal Ruffo—had besieged the French with their republican supporters in Naples for weeks, and in June a truce had been agreed. The French, and whichever of the rebels wanted to leave, would be allowed to do so when transport could be arranged. But Nelson, urged on by the Neapolitan royal family, decided otherwise, and threatened to bombard the city from the sea until it surrendered unconditionally. Cardinal Ruffo met Nelson and it was agreed that the British would not attack but allow the rebels and the French to evacuate. However, once the rebels had left the castles and boarded the small boats to flee, Nelson ordered them all to remain in the harbour under armed guard. Nelson then personally chaired the court martial of Commodore Carraciolo, who had commanded the Neapolitan fleet and deserted the royalist side when the royal family had itself deserted Naples. Refusing to allow a stay of execution, or accept Carraciolo's plea to be shot rather than hanged from the yardarm like a mutineer,[50] Nelson had him taken aboard a Neapolitan frigate, hanged, and his corpse tossed into the sea. All this took place while Nelson entertained the Hamiltons to dinner on board his own flagship, the *Fourdroyant* (Pocock 1994: 203). Some days later Carraciolo's corpse, weighted down with leg irons, resurfaced, and, 'standing' half out of the water, drifted slowly past Nelson's ship until it was taken in tow and buried ashore.

In the months that followed, from a giant gibbet in the Piazza del Mercato, hundreds of men and women who had been involved in the rebellion—many of them former friends of the Hamiltons—were executed before huge crowds by two executioners, 'one clutching their legs, another—often a dwarf—clowning on their shoulders to the cheers and laughter of the drunken mob' (Pocock 1994: 204). As Midshipman Parsons noted, shocked by the display, 'grieve to say that wonderful, talented and graceful beauty, Emma Lady Hamilton, did not sympathise in the manner expected from her generous and noble nature' (quoted in Pocock 1994: 204). We should also note that Nelson not only supported the executions—which would not have occurred at all had he not broken the agreement to evacuate the French—but vigorously rejected all attempts to spare any individual (Pocock 1994: 204; Hibbert 1995:192). As far as Nelson was concerned, a king could obviously desert his own people with equanimity, but his people could under no circumstances desert their own king. Wisely, in the circumstances, the Neapolitan King decided not to set foot on his own land for the time being. The King did, however, demonstrate his enormous generosity to Nelson for saving his throne by giving him the title 'Duke of Bronte'.[51]

Élite Disdain and Popular Acclaim

The new duke clearly relished his ennoblement and promptly decided that Admiralty orders took second place to his own love life. Lord Keith had left Nelson in charge of the blockade of Malta and ordered him to watch for an attempt by the French to rescue their beleaguered army in Egypt, but Nelson left Malta and went to Palermo instead—on account of his health theoretically, but Lady Hamilton was of course still there. Subsequently, Lord Keith twice ordered Nelson to send ships to Minorca before he finally agreed to do so, ensuring a rebuke from the Admiralty in due course—which characteristically he dismissed: 'My conduct is measured by the Admiralty by the narrow rule of law when I think it should have been done by common sense' (quoted in Pocock 1994: 206).

Yet common sense was something that many thought Nelson left behind whenever Lady Hamilton was in the room. His affair with her was now common knowledge and the subject of considerable ridicule in the navy. He seemed completely besotted with her. Lady Elgin described her as 'very handsome at dinner, quite in an undress . . . she is indeed a Whapper! and I think her manner very vulgar. It is really humiliating to see Lord Nelson. He seems quite dying and yet as if he had no other thought than her' (Hibbert 1995: 199).

When the Hamiltons decided to leave Palermo and return to England, so did Nelson—chastened, no doubt, by a brusque note from Lord Spencer at the Admiralty requesting him to do so. Horatia, Lady Hamilton's daughter by Nelson, was conceived on the voyage, but the scandal mattered little to the mass of the British population, who greeted him wherever he went. The British King virtually ignored him, however, and Nelson's relationship with his wife grew increasingly tenuous. In November, whilst attending a play at the Theatre Royal in Drury Lane, his wife Fanny stood up, screamed, and fainted. Nelson was palpably embarrassed and was never seen in public with her again.

The ostracism of Nelson and Lady Hamilton by the élite social circles now began in earnest. Just after the new year (1801) had started, Nelson left his wife for the last time and was promoted to vice admiral. He became the subject of many bawdy caricatures in the press as news emerged of the break-up of his marriage, and the relationship with Lady Hamilton became the gossip of the country when Horatia, daughter of Lady Hamilton and Nelson, was born. Horatia was brought up by a Mrs Gibson elsewhere and never acknowledged Lady Hamilton as her mother. Nelson planned her christening as the daughter of Johem and Morata Etnorb,[52] but Lady Hamilton dissuaded him for fear of the publicity and scandal. Few had a good word for either of them. An Austrian visitor, Franz Cullenbach, commented that '[she] never stopped talking . . . [he] seemed as clumsy and dim on land as he is adroit and notable at sea', while a German visitor said that 'he was one of the most insignificant figures I ever saw in my life . . . a more miserable collection of bones and wizened frame I have yet to come across'. According to Melesina St George: 'She is bold, forward, coarse, assuming and vain . . . [He] is a little man without dignity' (Hibbert 1995: 216, 218). The Queen refused to meet her and the King generally ignored them both. Friends and enemies alike ridiculed them both: Sir William Hotham argued that Nelson's vanity had led him to 'unpardonable excesses and blinded him to the advantages of being respected in society'. Lady Elizabeth Foster remarked that the 'foolish little fellow Nelson has sat to every painter in London. His head is turned by Lady Hamilton, who sometimes writes him four letters a day' (quoted in Hibbert 1995: 231). Even Lord Minto, one of Nelson's greatest friends, talked of how at the dinner table she crammed 'Nelson with trowelfuls of flattery, which he goes on taking as quietly as a child does pap . . . she leads him about like a keeper with a bear' (quoted in Schom. 1992: 251). As ever, though, the ordinary population viewed Nelson quite differently. He was fêted wherever he went; he had broken all the social conventions of polite society, but this was not polite society and it seemed that the more Nelson outraged the establishment the more the mass took him to their hearts.[53] The local papers and cartoonists had a field day ridiculing the three of them: Nelson and Lord and Lady Hamilton, and it persuaded Nelson and Lady Hamilton to invent pseudonyms for each other, but it did not prevent them from writing to each other. Nelson got Lady Hamilton to write to him as an ordinary sailor called 'Thompson', and he wrote to her, sometimes four times a day, once saying that he loved her so much that he 'can be trusted with fifty virgins naked in a dark room' (quoted in Hibbert 1995: 245). It was a situation he was unlikely to face as he sailed north to fight the Danes.

The Battles of Copenhagen and Boulogne, 1801

When Russia, Prussia, Sweden, and Denmark formed an alliance to resist British attempts to restrict Baltic trade with the French, the British immediately decided to dissuade them all by force of arms. Nelson sailed to the Kattegat to blockade the Baltic under Admiral Parker and possibly attack the Danes at Copenhagen. Parker was always concerned about the dangers of battle, because the Danes had moored their ships in such a way that the Nile tactics could not be repeated, so he asked Nelson to discuss the options as they approached Copenhagen, raising the possibility of avoiding conflict altogether.[54] As Nelson returned to his ship, the *St George*, he wrote to Troubridge, a long-time colleague: 'Little did I think it was to converse on *not* fighting' (quoted in Pocock 1994: 233; emphasis added). And, in an oft-rehearsed phrase, he wrote to Parker: 'I am of the opinion the boldest measures are the safest' (quoted in Pocock 1994: 233).

Parker realized the fleet was outgunned by the Copenhagen batteries and, deciding discretion was the better part of valour, withdrew half the fleet, leaving Nelson to attack with the other half. On the other side, the Danish version suggests that the British ten ships-of-the-line easily outgunned their seven block-ships (Tracy 1998b: 157). Whatever the relative numbers, on 2 April the attack started, with Nelson clearly assuming the battle of attrition would inevitably go his way. But immediately Nelson's ships were in trouble: within two hours two ships were flying distress signals and one was aground. Knowing that Nelson would not retreat, Parker allegedly ordered the recall signal, noting that this would provide Nelson with the face-saving excuse to retreat if he needed one and that otherwise he would ignore it. The signal was relayed to Nelson, who demanded that the lookout stop looking at Parker's ship and watch the Danes for the surrender signal. He then put the telescope to his blind eye, saying: 'I have a right to be blind sometimes. I really do not see the signal' (quoted in Hibbert: 1995: 261). Ever after the story was one of Nelson valorously disobeying orders for the benefit of the nation, but Parker subsequently insisted that it was never his idea to hoist such an order and it took an hour to persuade him that it should be raised. By then it may well have been intended as a face-saver for Nelson, not as a demand for compliance; indeed, Tracy (1998b: 150) suggests that a retreat at this time would have been suicidal. Thus are heroes invented. Or, in the rather more florid words of the *Naval Chronicle*, 'Thus will a severe but just lesson be taught to all our puny rivals, of the folly and imbecility of any attempt to dispute with Britain the Sovereignty of the Ocean' (quoted in Tracy 1998b: 151).

Eventually, after around 1,000 casualties on both sides, Nelson sent a signal to the Danes suggesting a ceasefire—'to save the brave Danes', who were 'no longer resisting'. The Danes—obviously unaware that they were beaten—sent a response asking the purpose behind the flag of truce, to which Nelson reaffirmed his opinion that the Danes had lost. At last the Danes accepted a ceasefire and Nelson went ashore to meet the Danish Crown Prince the next morning. In his own version of events, Nelson said that he was received 'with Cheers and *viva*

Nelson . . . my reception was too flattering, landing at Portsmouth or Yarmouth could not have exceeded the blessings of the people'. Yet, according to a Danish observer, he was received with 'neither cheers nor murmurs' (quoted in Hibbert: 1995: 265; see also Pocock 1994: 239 and Tracy 1998*b*: 188 n. 19). After receiving a day-long bombardment and 1,000 casualties, only a man in Nelson's mould could interpret the silence of the Danes as cheers. He went even further, writing later to Lady Hamilton: 'I received as a warrior all the praises which could gratify the ambitions of the vainest man and the thanks of the nation . . . for my humanity in saving the town from destruction. Nelson is a warrior, but will not be a butcher' (quoted in Pocock 1994: 240). A fourteen-week armistice was agreed, but, to Nelson's astonishment, there was little public acclaim for the battle; after all, the Danes had not been enemies for a thousand years and posed no threat, so few could understand why force was necessary. This was particularly so when it turned out that the Tsar had been assassinated a week before the battle when Parker had considered avoiding the conflict, which, in the event, was an unnecessary waste of human life. For Nelson this was not important and he succeeded Parker as Commander-in-Chief and was created Viscount Nelson—but he remained outraged that no medal was given for the battle. For once, his performative powers seemed to fail him.

On his return home he went to the naval hospital to seek out the health of those sailors wounded at the battle and spent time with each one, but he did not seek out his wife.[55] She wrote twice to him, congratulating him on the victory and asking him to return to her, but he ignored the first letter and returned the second, writing on the envelope: 'opened by mistake by Lord Nelson but not read' (quoted in Hibbert 1995: 274).

Whatever his concerns over what he saw as the fickle nature of the British population, the Admiralty sought to assuage their fears of an imminent French invasion—which Nelson never really thought possible—by appointing him to the command of the Channel Fleet. But simply guarding the Channel was too tame for Nelson and he decided that raiding the invasion flotilla being assembled at Boulogne was a better way to spend his time. Thus, on 1 and 15 August he organized attacks upon Boulogne, but the raids were failures: forty-four of the British attackers were killed and 128 wounded (Lyon 1996: 104). Once again Nelson underestimated his enemies and the difficulties of attack. He was even crossed by a blackmailer, who threatened to reveal his mismanagement of the attack, to which he replied: 'Very likely I am unfit for my present command . . . but you will, I trust, be punished for threatening my character.' As a result of the débâcle, posters were put up in the country suggesting that life with Nelson meant an early death for any sailor (Grabsky 1993: 85), and jokes about his failure to lead the attack personally swept through the fleet (Pocock 1994: 252.)

Nelson was also unable to get permission to go to London to see Lady Hamilton and assumed a conspiracy was afoot because of the Admiralty's disquiet about his relationship with her. In September he bought Merton Place in Surrey, a modest country house, in which, according to Lord Minto—one of the few visitors—'not only the rooms, but the whole house, staircase and all, are covered with nothing but pictures of her and him'. Nelson wrote to Emma of his plans for Merton, where 'We will eat plain, but will have good wine, good fires and a hearty welcome for all our friends, but none of the great shall enter our peaceful abode. I hate them all' (quoted in Pocock 1994: 259).

In October, his moderate ability at public speaking became clear when he gave his maiden speech in the House of Lords to little acclaim; Nelson apparently had what Dudley Pope (1997: 211) calls a 'high-pitched Norfolk drawl'. His second speech was regarded with open disdain by his opponents: 'How can Ministers allow such a fool to speak in their defence?' wrote William Huskisson, former Undersecretary of War to Lord Dundas, the War Minister (quoted in Pocock 1994: 267). Nevertheless, Lady Hamilton assured him that his oratorical skills made a political future a certainty. His colleagues, including Captain Hardy, persuaded him otherwise.[56]

The new year (1802) brought a double blow. In March peace between France and Britain was declared and the following month Nelson's father, Edmund, died. Nelson had always respected his father, but Edmund's gentle rebuke of Horatio for his actions with Lady Hamilton undermined Horatio's claims to be innocent of immorality. Nelson refused to go to the funeral, not as a mark of his dispute with his father, but to avoid meeting his wife.

Always more interested in his own death, Nelson asked Benjamin West, who had painted *The Death of General Wolfe* in 1770 (Nelson's boyhood hero), why there were no similar pictures. 'Because there are no more subjects,' replied West, 'but I fear your intrepidity may yet furnish me with another such scene, and if it should, I should certainly avail myself of it.' 'Then I hope to die in the next battle,' replied Nelson (quoted in Hibbert 1995: 384). He was to get his wish.

Despite the Boulogne fiasco, Nelson had by now become what Pocock (1994: 276) calls: 'a national hero in his lifetime'—a unique phenomenon. He was instantly recognizable, even by those who had never seen him before; the shops were littered with mementoes, serious and lewd, and the papers were still full of ribald coverage of the *ménage à trois*. In July and August the threesome toured the south and west of England. Oxford made him a freeman of the city and both he and Sir William Hamilton received an honorary doctorate of civil law from the university (LLD). The *Morning Herald* suggested Sir William's degree should have been not LLD but ASS. The *Morning Post* suggested that Nelson's should have been a degree in divinity, since he knew so much about 'cannon laws'. After Oxford the party drove off to Blenheim Palace at Woodstock,[57] but the Duke, a critic of their antics, refused to see them, suggesting he send a servant with some cold food out to the park—if they cared to eat outside. Nelson stormed off suggesting that he had expected no better from 'the great' (Hibbert 1995: 303). But, while Nelson was now a virtual pariah amongst the upper classes, he was little short of a messiah to the lower classes. Travelling through Gloucester and Wales, Nelson was fêted everywhere by the local population and numerous pubs were renamed 'Lord Nelson'.[58] After Nelson had made a speech at Monmouth, the

local bookshop-owner asked if he could print copies of the speech, to which
Nelson replied, 'I am an old man [he was 43] and may not live long. It is my wish
that posterity should know my sentiments. Therefore do it' (quoted in Hibbert
1995: 308). The company finished their tour in the Midlands, and in a
Birmingham theatre received standing ovations as they entered; the social élite
may have ostracized Nelson, but for the mass of the population he could do little
wrong.

Ironically, the death of Sir William Hamilton in April 1803 did not free Nelson
and Lady Hamilton to enjoy each other's company without concern. Nelson had
hoped that she would move permanently to Merton, but, insisting on continuing
the pretence of a platonic relationship with Nelson, she moved to a separate
address in London. Their chances of a permanent union were then rudely shattered when, on 14 May, Britain declared war on France again. Nelson was
appointed Commander-in-Chief of the Mediterranean fleet; he joined his new
flagship the *Victory* and began to blockade the French Mediterranean fleet at
Toulon.

War, Invasion, and Indecision

The *Victory*, built in 1758 (Nelson's birth date), was a first-rater of 104 guns. At
the time it was the largest ship ever built for the Royal Navy and needed 850 men
to sail and fight. At Trafalgar their average age was 22; fifty were over 40, one was
only 10, and four were 12. William Robinson (1999: 166–7), who sailed on the
Revenge at Trafalgar, also suggests that the crew included one woman, Jeanette
of French Flanders, who was disguised as a man and served with her husband
until he was killed in the battle, whereupon her identity was discovered.[59] The
crew also included eighty-one foreigners:[60] these included twenty-two
Americans, three Germans, seven Dutch, two Swiss, six Swedes, four Italians,
three French, nine West Indians, and one Russian. Some of these—for instance,
the French sailors—would probably have been Royalist sympathizers, but most
of the others would have been sailors unable to secure work because of the blockade imposed by the British navy on many foreign ports or would have been (illegally) pressed (D. Pope 1997: 108). When fully victualled, the *Victory* had enough
food and water (or small beer) for four months and enough ammunition for three
years (Keegan 1993*b*: 46). It needed all of this: for the next twenty-nine months
the campaign to prevent a French invasion wore on, with Trafalgar as the culmination of the long campaign involving a thirty-ship blockade of the main French
and Spanish fleets from Gibraltar in the south to Brest in the north. For the
British, the campaign primarily involved riding out storms and calm weather a
little way off each of the ports—a boring, unpleasant, and unheroic job but one
that was essential. But it was not a campaign that easily lent itself to glory and, as
Schom suggests, it had no appeal to Nelson.

The man responsible for commanding and maintaining the Channel Fleet throughout this
arduous two-and-half-year period and, in the final analysis, the one responsible both for

successfully preventing the French invasion of Britain and for deciding on the necessity of creating and dispatching to Spanish waters the nucleus of the fleet that Nelson was to command at Trafalgar—Admiral Sir William Cornwallis—was, however, never thanked by a grateful nation for his singular services. Unlike Nelson, Cornwallis was not known to the man in the street and was never stopped and cheered by patriotic Londoners, nor was he a boastful man. Indeed, he was the antithesis of Nelson, a quiet, retiring gentleman who assiduously avoided public acclaim as much as Nelson relished it. Unlike Nelson, too, he was neither a self-publicist nor even an adequate chronicler and left much less material for historians to study than did almost any other admiral of the time (Schom 1992: 2–3).

While Cornwallis commanded the Channel Fleet, Nelson commanded the Mediterranean Fleet off Toulon.[61] The threat of invasion stimulated a shift from cold to hot pressing and from 27 July all men between 17 and 55 were required to drill and train to defend the nation. Army recruitment expanded rapidly in Britain between 1803 and 1805—when 'anxiety had given way to panic' (Schom 1992: 54)—from around 75,000 to 100,000, but many of these conscripts (45,000 in all) bought themselves out with a substitute, while 8,000 men already serving deserted. Meanwhile the navy budget was raised by 50 per cent to facilitate the building of eighty-three more ships.

The French, meanwhile, under Napoleon's keen but ignorant naval eye, set about building an invasion fleet. Napoleon seems to have had little time for naval warfare, but, when his imperial ambitions were thwarted only by British naval power, he undertook what Keegan (1993b: 12), recalling Alexander the Great, called 'defeating the enemy fleet from the land'. William Pitt, on the other hand, began the arduous and complex process of constructing a network of allies to strangle French ambitions and the first fruits of this appeared on 29 June 1804 when an Anglo-Russian pact was proposed.

While disdainful of the French navy, the British should have been a little more chary of their preparations, for Napoleon had ordered over 1,000 new ships for the invasion, followed by a second order for a further 1,000 ships within months of the first order; these were to carry over 150,000 troops to England. Napoleon, with no naval experience, supervised the design of the fleet himself and maintained that flat-bottomed vessels were perfectly adequate for the invasion, but the ships proved unseaworthy. Despite all the frantic ship-building and the port-construction programme, the invasion could not occur until the entire French fleet was reunited—and Nelson's role was to ensure that the French Mediterranean Fleet stayed in the Mediterranean—or, preferably, made a run for the Straits of Gibraltar, which would enable his fleet to destroy them.

In May Napoleon wrote to Vice Admiral Laurent Truguet (to sack him), because, 'in spite of my very real intention that the vessels in . . . Brest weigh anchor every day (so) that the crews get the essential practice they need in their work . . . in order to harass the enemy . . . not a single vessel has put to sea since the beginning of the year, which has resulted in the enemy blocking an impressively large squadron with just a handful of ships' (quoted in Schom 1992: 171). What Napoleon could not understand was soon explained to him, for, although

Brest harboured more and better ships than the British just outside the harbour, their new Vice Admiral, Honoré Ganteaume, reported that, despite the fact that the French sailors had undertaken gunnery practice in the calm of the harbour, 'if it came to sailing in bad weather we would all be embarrassed (for they) all lack the will, strength and courage to succeed' (quoted in Schom 1992: 172). Ironically, Ganteaume, unlike Villeneuve, was happy to leave harbour and fight the British, but Napoleon had actually forbidden him to go and fight the blockade because he wanted all the Brest ships in perfect order when the time for the invasion came. As he instructed Ganteaume, 'A Naval victory under these circumstances serves no purpose. You have but one objective, that of fulfilling your mission. Sail without fighting' (quoted in Schom 1992: 203).

On 2 June Admiral Latouche-Tréville was ordered to sea from Toulon to draw the British fleet south, then to turn and head for Cherbourg and embark the invasion fleet for Britain by the end of September at the latest. But the Admiral died before he could sail, leaving Napoleon desperately short of seasoned naval commanders. In contrast, even the undermanned British ships were capable of maintaining their stations under the worst possible conditions for months on end, thanks, in part, according to Schom, to 'a plentiful supply of extremely diligent naval officers *at every level*' (Schom 1992: 173; emphasis in original). Napoleon chose Vice Admiral Villeneuve as Latouche-Tréville's replacement. Villeneuve was to leave Toulon and participate in one of the four simultaneous attacks upon British territories in the Americas, Africa, Asia, and Ireland. He was then to unite the fleets, return to France, break the Channel blockade, and facilitate the invasions of England and Ireland.

Cornwallis, on learning of some of the plans, and discovering that British sailors captured by the French were being held as prisoners in 'neutral' Spanish jails, ordered a squadron to intercept some Spanish ships and prevent their treasure from falling into Napoleon's hands. In the event, a fight broke out on 6 October and one of the Spanish ships blew up, taking 240 Spaniards and untold treasure to the bottom of the Atlantic.

By November, reports of poor morale from the French army waiting to invade were common, and it was no longer certain that an invasion would even occur, because the French fleets were unable to break out and unite. The weather, however, intervened to help France, for terrible gales damaged five of the watching British ships and they returned to Plymouth for repairs. By the end of 1804 the navy had lost fifteen warships, primarily to storms, and the entire blockade had been washed away. But there was better news on the diplomatic front for Britain, because on 3 December an Anglo-Swedish agreement was signed, providing—for all its allies—£1,250,000 for every 100,000 continental troops deployed against France (Schom 1992: 148–59).

This painstakingly slow construction of a political and military alliance against France was rapidly and radically undermined on 12 December, 1804, when Spain, smarting from the attack on its ships and encouraged by Napoleon, declared war on Britain. This dramatically changed Nelson's assumption that a

French invasion could not succeed. With the French, Spanish, and Dutch fleets now available to support a flotilla, an invasion became plausible.

The year 1805 started auspiciously for the French. On 1 January the French fleet at Rochefort escaped the blockade and disappeared. On 4 January the Franco-Spanish Pact was signed, putting the Spanish fleet of about thirty ships-of-the-line at the disposal of the French, and requiring Spain to provide funding and troops for the invasion of Britain(Schom 1992: 190). But the Spanish, especially after epidemics in the southern ports, were as short of troops as the French were of experienced sailors. By comparison, the British were extremely experienced; for example, the majority of British officers at Trafalgar had already experienced action, including eleven of *Victory*'s seventeen lieutenants.

Villeneuve, one of the few French veterans, but also a veteran of Nelson's attack at Aboukir Bay, which had, in Schom's opinion, left the French admiral with 'an intense fear of that English admiral for the rest of his life', reached Toulon, where he was ordered to leave at the earliest opportunity to sail to South America (Schom 1992: 194). He delayed leaving until 18 January 1805 and within three days was back, after a battering from a storm. Within the first three weeks of 1805 all the French fleets and squadrons had evaded the British blockade to make the first significant escape since May 1803, when hostilities had resumed, but this success was marred by Villeneuve's failure and the onset of a deep sense of personal foreboding. On 22 January Villeneuve wrote to Napoleon, asking to be relieved of command:

I should like to point out to you that *about all one can expect from a career in the French Navy today is shame and confusion . . .* It is my most ardent wish that the Emperor decide not to commit any of his squadrons to the hazards of these events, for if he does *the French flag will be seriously compromised.* In reality *it is utterly impossible for us to defeat the enemy when both sides are equal, indeed, they will beat us even when they are a third weaker than we are . . .* I should view it with the greatest pleasure if the Emperor would replace me in this command.   (quoted in Schom 1992: 198; emphasis in original)

Napoleon refused to accept Villeneuve's resignation—there was no alternative available—but he referred to Villeneuve as a man of 'double vision' after he imagined twice as many enemies as there were (Schom 1992: 240). Napoleon then wrote to General Lauriston, army commander of the troops that Villeneuve was supposed to embark, suggesting that 'I really believe your Admiral does not know how to command' (quoted in Schom 1992: 199). Napoleon's own naval inexperience became manifest soon after: on 26 January he issued his fourth invasion plan, rescinded two weeks later by his fifth plan, in which the Spanish navy was given a significant role for the first time. But this all hinged on Villeneuve, who had again tried but failed to escape from Toulon in February. On 2 March the fifth invasion plan came into operation, with Ganteaume, Missiessy, and Villeneuve all ordered to rendezvous at Martinique, where, under Ganteaume's command, all forty-plus ships would return to breach the blockade and arrive at Boulogne between 10 June and 10 July. At last, almost a month later, on 30

March, Villeneuve escaped from Toulon and sailed to the West Indies, but Napoleon had already revoked the invasion plan and was now working on plan number six, omitting a move to the West Indies and replacing this with a simultaneous invasion of Ireland and England. Just to ensure that everyone—or rather no one—knew what to do, Napoleon cancelled plan number six and, on 13 April, the seventh invasion plan was launched—the West Indies diversionary trip was back on. Paradoxically, Villeneuve was now in command of the Combined Fleet—despite his previous attempt to resign—but Ganteaume now failed to leave Brest as required, and, to make the issue far more complicated than it already was, the Anglo-Russian Treaty was signed, opening up France's eastern flank to yet another incursion and forcing Napoleon to reconsider the invasion of Britain altogether.

The risk to Napoleon's career was matched in the same month by the risk to Nelson's. On 18 April Nelson learned that Villeneuve's fleet had passed through the Straits of Gibraltar and was not headed, as he suspected, to Egypt. Nelson, as commander of the Mediterranean fleet, had no warrant to leave his station, but he proposed to leave immediately and chase Villeneuve wherever he went. As he wrote to Simon Taylor, an old friend, 'I flew to the West Indies without any orders, but I think the Ministry cannot be displeased' (quoted in Schom 1992: 217). This decision, which Schom calls 'the greatest risk of his career', effectively left the Mediterranean without any British fleet and exposed the routes to Egypt and India (Schom 1992: 212). There was no significant enemy fleet left in the Mediterranean by this time, but Nelson had no way of knowing whether Villeneuve's escape to the Atlantic was anything more than a ruse to lure him away, after which they could return—as indeed they tried to in October. But, as so often before, luck was with Nelson and on 12 May Nelson put into Lagos Bay, Portugal, for stores to take his fleet to Villeneuve's destination: the West Indies.[62]

Within a month Nelson had arrived only to learn that, through poor information from General Brereton, commanding officer of the army on St Lucia, he had just missed Villeneuve's fleet. As Nelson wrote: 'I am as miserable as you can conceive. But for General Brereton's damned information, Nelson would have been, living or dead, the greatest man in his profession that England ever saw. Now, alas! I am nothing' (quoted in Schom 1992: 222). In fact, despite Napoleon's orders to remain in the West Indies and rendezvous with Ganteaume's fleet, Villeneuve returned to France immediately he discovered Nelson had arrived in the area, omitting to land the 12,000 troops he had been sent to land in the first place. Nelson duly informed Cornwallis that the combined enemy fleets had left and were heading back. If this Combined Fleet managed to break the blockades at Brest, Rochefort, Cadiz, and El Ferrol, the British would face a combined total of fifty-eight French and Spanish ships-of-the-line. On 20 July Nelson himself returned to Gibraltar (he had been at sea for almost two continuous years) and sailed for England for rest and recuperation.

Meanwhile, on 22 July Vice Admiral Calder's squadron intercepted Villeneuve's returning Combined Fleet off Cape Finesterre in an indecisive battle that saw the Spanish ships in the thick of the action. Calder, with fifteen ships, attacked the Combined Fleet of twenty-six, but his inability to press home the attack rendered the effort—in the eyes of the Admiralty—unworthy of the name of a battle, and thereafter it became known as 'Calder's Action of 22 July' (Keegan 1993*b*: 28). Napoleon later blamed the Spanish for poor fighting qualities, when, in the event, it had been Spanish bravery that had led them to receive the greatest damage from the British fleet. Napoleon even claimed a great victory over the British, when, at best, the battle had achieved nothing for either side. Admiral Calder was subsequently severely reprimanded by a court martial for his refusal to continue the battle, but he did at least dissuade Villeneuve from heading further north to the Channel; instead he sailed to Vigo Bay.

By 2 August the invasion flotilla had 1,339 armed and 954 unarmed vessels, and, in two practice embarkations on 3 August, Napoleon claimed that the entire army (163,645 men and 9,059 horses) was on board in ninety minutes (Lyon 1996: 110). However exaggerated, boarding was the easy bit; getting the ships out of the harbour took at least two tides and required calm seas with no enemy. It was, therefore, still imperative that the British were drawn away from the Channel, but the realistic possibilities of a successful invasion were small. As Lyon comments: 'Napoleon's plan looked good on paper, but relied too much on precise timing, failed to take account of the weather and the practicalities of operating and co-ordinating sailing fleets over long distances, and above all discounted the skill, knowledge and sense of priorities of the enemy.' Nevertheless, Napoleon ordered Villeneuve to sail first to Ferrol and then on to Boulogne for the invasion. Villeneuve, responding in a letter to Decrès on 6 August, was typically pessimistic: 'I believe that all my men will remain at their posts, but no one will be fighting whole-heartedly. I foresaw all this before leaving Toulon' (quoted in Schom 1992: 219). As ordered, on 10 August Villeneuve set sail from Ferrol—not north to Boulogne and the invasion but south to Cadiz. 'What a Navy! What an Admiral! All those sacrifices for nought!' exclaimed Napoleon when he heard what Villeneuve had done, for now there could be no invasion. 'Where', Napoleon continued, 'did my Admirals learn that they can make war without taking risks?' (quoted in Keegan 1993*b*: 30). By 13 August Villeneuve knew he was already beaten: 'Our naval tactics are antiquated. We know nothing but how to place ourselves in line, and that is just what the enemy wants' (quoted in Keegan 1993*b*: 30). On the same day Napoleon, realizing that Nelson was in England, again ordered Villeneuve north to Boulogne, thus to break the blockade immediately: 'Never will a fleet have run such risks, and never will my soldiers and sailors have spilt their blood for a greater or more noble purpose . . . Nelson and Collingwood are off the battlefield . . . what a splendid opportunity we should be missing . . . What a perfect occasion, *if only I had a real man there*' (Napoleon, quoted in Schom (1992: 24), emphasis in original). Villeneuve, however, while categorical that his fleet was doomed, could not accept that he was the problem: 'Because of the lack of experience by my officers and sailors, because of my captains' lack of wartime experience, and as a result of everything put together, this fleet is incapable of sailing and is doomed to failure ... *I cannot conceal my belief that we have no chance of winning* ... My Lord put an end to this situation' (quoted in Schom 1992: 243; emphasis in original). Napoleon may not have been listening, but Villeneuve made sure Napoleon would be unable to launch the invasion, because on 21 August, the day before Napoleon's final review of the invasion flotilla at Boulogne, and the last day that Napoleon hoped to see his fleet, Villeneuve, sailing in the opposite direction, reached Cadiz. 'Indeed, Sire,' as General Lauriston, commander of the invasion troops wrote to Napoleon, 'the fear of Nelson has got the upper hand of him ... This squadron needs a *man* and above all an admiral who commands confidence and attachment ... The captains have no heart left to do well; attention is no longer paid to signals ... discipline is utterly relaxed' (quoted in Keegan 1993*b*: 31). By 24 August, with his failing economy,[63] without Villeneuve, and with the Russian and Austrian armies massing on his eastern flank, Napoleon was left with little choice about what to do (Schom 1992: 271). Two days later, on 26 August, the *Grande Armée* marched away to fight in continental Europe, and the French navy's role was changed from protecting the invasion flotilla to preventing the British forces joining with the Russian forces via the Mediterranean. As Keegan (1993*b*: 30) rightly notes, 'a Russo-Austrian coalition threatened his power as the survival of Britain's seaborne empire never could'. If the threat of an invasion was over, the threat of a full-scale continental war had increased to a near certainty.

Nelson's Penultimate Return

Nelson had reached England on 19 August for twenty-five days' leave after twenty-seven months at sea. He thought himself a failure, having missed Villeneuve twice, and expected to be sacked from the Mediterranean post. But he need not have worried, for the country, if anything, was in the grip of even greater war hysteria than it had been in 1803 and 1804. The population appeared desperate for a visible heroic saviour, even if Nelson had achieved little in his role as Commander of the Channel Fleet while the invisible Cornwallis had achieved considerably more as Nelson's superior. Everyone *knew* the French were coming, the only questions were when and where? Hence, in the words of *The Times*, 'as soon as Lord Nelson's flag was descried at Spithead, the ramparts, and every place which could command a view of the entrance of the harbour, were crowded with spectators. As he approached the shore, he was saluted with loud and reiterated huzzas, as enthusiastic and sincere as if he had returned crowned with a great naval victory' (quoted in Schom 1992: 255). But his leave was dramatically cut short when, on 2 September, Captain Blackwood informed Nelson that the Combined Fleet had been spotted in Cadiz harbour. Nelson was immediately returned to Commander-in-Chief of the Mediterranean Fleet, with responsibilities including Cadiz. Nelson seems to have been a little uncertain as to the future, for, as he confided to Alexander Davison: 'half a Victory would half content me ... But I will do my best ... I have much to lose, but little to gain; I go because it's right and I will serve my country faithfully' (quoted in Schom 192: 263). He then went to an upholsterer in Brewer Street to have his coffin—which he had now carried round for six years—prepared and engraved, 'for I think it highly probable that I may want it on my return' (Schom 1992: 264). On 12 September, his last day at Merton, Nelson and Emma exchanged wedding rings and were blessed by a priest. By 14 September he had re-embarked upon *Victory* at Portsmouth as hundreds of people saw him off from the beach. At dinner that night he informed the chaplain that he wanted to be buried in St Paul's Cathedral not Westminster Abbey and told the story of a West Indian fortune-teller who, when she got to 1805, proclaimed: 'I can see no further!' (quoted in Hibbert 1995: 356).

Napoleon, meanwhile, had at last lost patience with his admiral, and on 17 September ordered Rosily to replace Villeneuve, but Rosily was delayed in Spain after an accident. In fact, Napoleon had all but abandoned the navy at Cadiz: the French section had lost 10 per cent to desertion or illness and there was no money to buy food or repair the ships after their trip to the West Indies. Ten days after Napoleon's order, Nelson joined the British fleet off Cadiz—much to the relief of many of the officers, who were, until then, serving under Collingwood, regarded as a taciturn martinet. His second-in-command, Calder, was still unaware that the 'victory' he believed he had won in August was already regarded as a lost opportunity by the Admiralty (Pocock 1994: 317–18). Nelson lost no time in explaining his battle plan to his 'band of brothers' the captains, and within three days of his arrival all of them had dined with him on board *Victory*. As he wrote later, in his usual immodest style, 'When I came to explain to them the *Nelson touch* the effect upon them was like an electric shock . . . some shed tears . . . all approved. It was new, it was singular, it was simple. It must succeed, if ever they will allow us to get at them!' It was, of course, not new, but it was simple—rather than sail parallel to each other, Nelson intended to split the enemy line with three attacking columns and then encourage every British ship to engage the enemy in single combat.

Villeneuve remained very nervous of the British fleet, but when Villeneuve became aware that six of Nelson's twenty-nine ships-of-the-line were due to leave for revictualling duty, the odds against the British improved with their twenty-three ships against the Combined Fleet of thirty-six. The odds in favour of Villeneuve grew yet stronger on 29 September when Nelson was ordered by the Admiralty to have Calder return to London to face a court martial for his (in)action in his previous engagement with Villeneuve. He was to leave his own ship, the ninety-gun *Prince of Wales*, and return in a smaller ship; however, Calder insisted on returning in his own ship and, though Nelson needed it for the forthcoming battle, he acceded to Calder's request. Once again Nelson had refused to obey an Admiralty order and once again this put the British fleet at unnecessary risk.

Nelson spent October desperately hoping to entice the Combined Fleet out of Cadiz. Captain Blackwood's five frigates maintained a daily vigil outside the harbour, relaying signals back to Nelson via the revolutionary alphabetic flag system devised by Sir Home Popham, which replaced the ideograms previously used to transmit entire words or ideas (Schom 1992: 285). Most of the remainder of the fleet kept fifty miles over the horizon to avoid scaring Villeneuve into remaining in port—though he knew of Nelson's arrival almost as soon as it occurred. By 8 October, as Villeneuve prepared to execute Napoleon's orders to sail immediately, he held a council of war with the fourteen most senior officers of the Combined Fleet, but the meeting disintegrated in confusion and enmity. As he noted afterwards to Decrès:

Everyone acknowledged that the ships of our two allied countries are for the most part badly armed and manned (and) that several vessels and their new crews have never been to sea . . . All our observations led us to recognize unanimously that the enemy fleet . . . is much stronger than ours, which, nevertheless, will be forced to fight it at the most unfavourable moment, just as we were leaving port . . . everyone agreed as to the necessity of waiting in port until a more favourable occasion presented itself.   (quoted in Schom 1992: 303)

The Spanish admiral Escano reported that they were 'lacking nothing—but good crews, which we could never remedy' (quoted in Keegan 1993b: 53). In effect, the entire fleet decided to stay put and refused to obey Napoleon; they had neither the confidence nor the carelessness to risk a battle.

The following day Nelson put the finishing touches to his tactics in a letter to his captains. They would attack in three columns at a line perpendicular to the enemy fleet. The third prong was to act as a mobile reserve. Since the Combined Fleet was larger than his, the intention was to dissect the enemy line into three sections, the foremost of which would be left alone and would, anyway, take some time to turn around and help its colleagues: it would, in effect, be temporarily neutralized. As he said, 'I look with confidence to a Victory before the Van of the Enemy could succour their rear, and then that the British fleet would, most of them, be ready to receive their twenty sail of the line or to pursue them should they endeavour to make off' (quoted in Keegan 1993b: 51–2). The problem, of course, was that this method of attack meant the two ships leading the double main prong would be under raking fire for perhaps half an hour before they reached the enemy line.

Raking fire—firing at the bow or stern of a ship—attacked the weakest parts of the vessel, inflicted the most damage, and received the least in return: hence its effectiveness. But to get to the position of raking an opponent, a ship usually had to suffer raking fire in its approach. Keegan argues that 'breaking the line' proved to be the solution to indecisive engagements, 'but it would have to await a revolution in signalling and, consequent on that, the dissolution of a naval way of thinking against anything but the most formal linear organization' (Keegan 1993b: 44).[64] Yet, as we have already seen, Commodore Dubordieu's breaking tactics against the British at Lissa in 1811 failed, partly because the strategy worked only when it was aligned with your own side's strengths and your opposition's weaknesses. In the Lissa attack the strategic plan of the French was misaligned with their own skills. The British had already experimented with breaking tactics before Nelson refined it and the significance of signalling seems much overplayed. The signals that Nelson deployed during the battle were apparently just three: 'engage the enemy more closely', which he had already given the captains of his ships before the battle; 'England expects . . .', which had no tactical significance whatsoever and seems to have been designed specifically for public consumption back home; and his signal that he intended to stop the enemy from reaching Cadiz—an obvious point given the direction of his ship. Indeed, the whole point of the mêlée tactics was that it left individual captains free to use their initiative to destroy the enemy and unreliant on orders from him.

Villeneuve faced the opposite tactical problems, and his concern for the lack of experience of his fleet compared to the British was well founded. As his chief of staff, Prigny, argued, 'the British had scarcely weighed anchor for eight years', whereas, in Schom's view, 'it was the first time several thousand of its [Combined Fleet's] "sailors" had ever ventured beyond a beach' (Schom 1992: 303, 310). Yet despite this—as we shall see—Villeneuve erred in his tactical approach, confusing his fleet by changing his mind about the intended destination and thus scrambling the already precarious order into disorder.

Nelson's view on the problem of so little sailing experience was clear, for 'ships and seamen rot in harbour' (quoted in D. Pope 1997: 134). But, despite the collapsing morale in the Combined Fleet, on 10 October, just two days after he had informed Napoleon that it would not sail, Villeneuve ordered the fleet to sail, then promptly cancelled the order on the grounds that the weather was closing in. Eight days later the weather was of considerably less significance, because Villeneuve had been informed that Vice Admiral Rosily was travelling to replace him. Villeneuve thus ordered the fleet to sail immediately, informing his captains that he would 'tolerate no shameful behaviour which could in turn discourage our crews and bring about our defeat . . . courage and the love of glory was to guide them. Should it come to a battle, any commanding officer not under fire will not be considered to be at his post, and a signal from me pointing this out will be taken as a stain upon his honour' (quoted in Schom 1992: 310). This was, of course, almost identical to Nelson's own order of the day.

The following day Nelson ordered what turned out to be his last floggings: two sailors were given thirty-six lashes each for drunkenness and at 08.00 the following day, 21 October, he received the signal he had been waiting for: the Combined Fleet had been spotted leaving Cadiz at 06.00 heading for the Straits of Gibraltar.

The Battle of Trafalgar

In December 1804 Villeneuve had already guessed what Nelson's tactics were to be—contrary to Nelson's assumption that he would 'surprise and confound the enemy'. Villeneuve repeated his prediction to his captains on the morning of the battle: 'The enemy will not limit their tactics to forming the usual battle line parallel to ours . . . they will endeavour to surround our rear-guard, and cross through in order better to envelop and defeat us, carrying away those of our vessels they will have isolated' (quoted in Schom 1992: 307).

As Villeneuve's fleet, now numbering thirty-three ships-of-the-line, approached Gibraltar on the morning of 24 October, attempting to flee into the Mediterranean, Nelson's fleet of twenty-seven ships closed in. Villeneuve ordered his line to form three columns in preparation to fend off the Royal Navy, then, forty minutes later, deciding that he could not make the Straits of Gibraltar, he ordered the fleet back into a single column to make for Cadiz; the process took ninety minutes for the four-mile-long column to head back. At 08.30 Nelson was informed that the Combined Fleet was heading straight for him, now with Rear Admiral Dumanoir's rear squadron taking the vanguard position. As Schom argues, if Villeneuve had chosen to flee, he might have escaped Nelson but he would not have escaped Napoleon.

At 11.25, with his usual eye on the history book, Nelson hoisted his famous signal, saying to Blackwood: 'I'll now amuse the fleet with a signal' (quoted in Lyon 1996: 119). 'England confides that every man will do his duty.' But 'confides' was not in the signal book and therefore required spelling out by letter. The word 'expects' was substituted for speed. Collingwood (the second in command) was annoyed at the banal message, as were Lieutenant Ellis's men: ' "Do our duty! Of course we'll do our duty! Let us come alongside of 'em, and we'll soon show whether we'll do our duty." Still, the men cheered vociferously—more I believe from love and admiration of their Admiral and leader than from a full appreciation of this well-known signal' (quoted in Grabsky 1993: 101).

Nelson's officers were concerned at another aspect of his legendary example— his uniform with all its decorations, which would draw the attention of the enemy's sharpshooters. But Nelson refused to change, saying that 'he did not fear to show them to the enemy'. Yet Nelson was far from alone in this: Villeneuve also wore his dress uniform, complete with a chest full of medals. So did Captain Cooke of the *Bellepheron*, refusing to remove his epaulettes as the ships closed, despite the insistence of his junior officers, saying: 'It is too late to take them off. I see my situation but I will die like a man' (quoted in Keegan 1993b: 76). Captain Cooke, like Nelson, did indeed die that day.

In fact, the situation did not go to plan. Nelson's three-pronged attack was cut to two after six ships from Gibraltar under Admiral Louis failed to show up in support; and the Combined Fleet was not in a single battle line but in an untidy string of ships, which prevented any simple cutting manœuvre. Moreover, Nelson could not pick out Villeneuve's flagship to attack, and, rather than the British line cutting the Combined Fleet in two and surrounding the rearguard, in the event the first British ships were isolated, surrounded by the Franco-Spanish fleet and subject to murderous bombardment. Since, in terms of fire power, the Combined Fleet still formed a formidable enemy, with six more ships-of-the-line (33 against 27), an extra 420 guns (2,568 against 2,148), and an extra 13,000 men (30,000 against 17,000), the dangers of a terrible defeat should have been clear to all (Schom 1992: 315).

Normally, as at the Battle of the Nile, the flagship would not have led the column into attack, but Nelson and Collingwood clearly assumed that their ships, being the largest, would be best able to take the raking fire for longer. More importantly, they would be able to demonstrate leadership by example. In fact, Pocock suggests that the light winds made it impossible for the two British approach lines to manœuvre into line abreast before reaching the enemy, allowing the enemy ships to concentrate their fire on the two leading vessels. Yet there is no other claim that this dispersed approach was Nelson's real plan, and, since both Nelson and Collingwood ordered several ships to change places in the line approaching the enemy, and Nelson explicitly rejected Hardy's suggestion that the *Téméraire* exchange places with *Victory,* such a line-abreast approach cannot have been intended (Pocock 1994: 325). The approximate deployment of ships is reproduced in Fig. 7.2. As Nelson's column approached the Combined Fleet, Captain Blackwood again asked Nelson to consider directing the battle from his frigate (*Euryalus*), which he refused, and Blackwood then asked Nelson what he would consider as a victory, suggesting that 'if fourteen ships were captured, it would be a glorious result'. Nelson relied: 'I shall not, Blackwood, be satisfied with anything short of twenty' (quoted in Lyon 1996: 118–19).

Villeneuve commented after the battle to Blackwood, then his captor, that, as soon as the British deployed for an attack, led by the first and second in command, he called his officers together to point out to them what was happening and told them, 'Nothing but victory can attend such gallant conduct' (quoted in Lyon 1996: 119). You do not need a Ph.D. to know what kind of motivational error this was.

At 11.40 Nelson decided to head for the vanguard because he still could not see Villeneuve's flagship, which was the *Bucentaure,* a relatively small eighty-gun ship. Five minutes later all the Combined Fleet ships, except the *Bucentaure,* hoisted their colours, then the *Bucentaure* did the same, and Nelson reverted to his original plan and headed for Villeneuve at the centre of the enemy 'line'. At 11.50 the first shot fell close to *Victory* and Captain Blackwood left, shaking Nelson's hand and saying: 'I trust on my return to the *Victory* I shall find your Lordship well and in possession of twenty prizes.' To which Nelson replied: 'God bless you Blackwood. With a heart very sad, I shall never speak to you again' (Hibbert 1995: 369). In the fifteen minutes between the *Victory* coming under fire and itself breaking the line, four broadsides were fired against it, according to Keegan (1993*b*: 68), suggesting a firing rate of at best merely one broadside every 3½ minutes. In this brief period *Victory* suffered one-third of its entire battle casualties (thirty wounded and twenty dead). By 12.04 *Victory* had broken through the line and engaged the enemy, becoming entangled with the French ship *Redoubtable,* whose sailors had been trained in small arms fire by their Captain Lucas, and Nelson was unable to fire a broadside into it. A minute later the first broadside from the *Bucentaure* hit *Victory* and at roughly the same time *Redoubtable* fired a broadside from the other side. All of *Victory*'s masts were hit and the double wheel torn away, leaving forty seamen to manhandle the tiller on

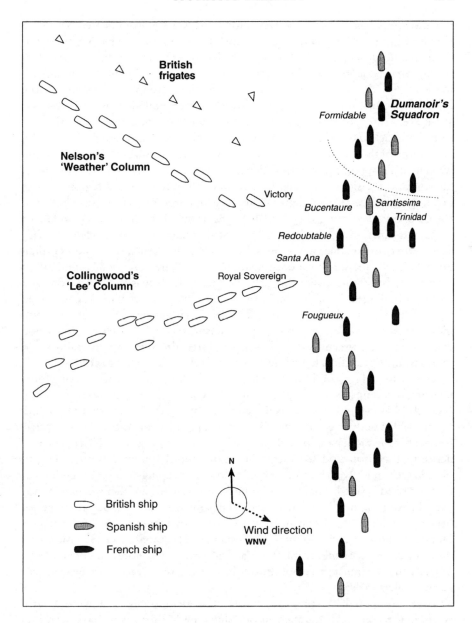

Fig. 7.2. The Battle of Trafalgar

the lower gun deck. 'This is too warm work to last long,' commented Nelson to Hardy, Captain of the *Victory*. Meanwhile the French ships *Neptune* and *Redoubtable* closed in on the *Victory*, which had yet to fire a broadside. At 13.00 the first broadside from *Victory* hit the *Bucentaure*, the fifty guns, double and treble loaded with shot for short-range destruction, dismounted twenty of the *Bucentaure* guns, and half of her crew were killed or wounded instantly (Pocock 1994: 326). At 13.10 Hardy swung *Victory*, into the *Redoubtable* and the two ships were locked together. Royal Marine Second Lieutenant Rotely, on *Victory*, later wrote of this period in the battle: 'We were engaged on both sides; every gun was going off . . . recoiling with violence, reports louder than thunder, the decks heaving and the sides straining. I fancied myself in the infernal regions, where everyman appeared a devil. Lips might move, but orders and hearing were out of the question; everything was done by signs' (quoted in Grabsky 1993: 96). At 13.25, just ninety-five minutes after the first shot had been fired, Nelson was hit, as were forty others, mainly marines, by fire from the French sharpshooters high up in the masts and rigging aboard *Redoubtable*.[65] 'They have done for me at last Hardy. My backbone is shot through,' he cried out. He was extremely accurate: a musket ball, fired from the top of the *Redoubtable*'s mizzen mast, had passed through his left shoulder, cut through his left lung, severed a branch of the pulmonary artery and shattered his spine.[66] Nelson was carried below to the orlop deck, where the surgeon was operating on forty already wounded sailors and marines amidst candlelight and decks painted red to camouflage the blood.

Later, when Hardy told him he had achieved a 'brilliant victory', taking fourteen or fifteen ships, Nelson replied: 'That is well, but I had bargained for twenty' (Pocock 1994: 330). Then, as his life ebbed away, he demanded that Hardy did not throw his body over the side (the common practice for British fleets in battle but not for the French or Spanish) and asked Hardy to kiss him. There is no evidence that Nelson said 'Kismet', the Arabic word for fate. With feeling in Nelson's lower body gone, and the cold gradually creeping through his abdomen, Dr Scott tried easing his pain by rubbing his chest, while another seaman fanned him. 'I wish I had not left the deck for I shall soon be gone . . . Doctor, I have not been a *great* sinner . . . Remember that I leave Lady Hamilton and my daughter Horatia as a legacy to my country . . . Never forget Horatia . . . Thank God I have done my duty . . . Drink, drink, fan, fan, rub, rub . . .' (quoted in Pocock 1994: 331). At 16.30, almost three hours after being shot, the surgeon, Dr Beatty, pronounced Nelson dead.

The effect upon the *Victory*'s crew was self-evident to those that were aboard. According to one, 'All the men in our ship [the *Victory*] who have seen him [Nelson] are such soft toads they have done nothing but blast their eyes and cry ever since he was killed' (quoted in Schom 1992: 356). And a boatswain's mate, responsible for piping the hands to quarters after the action, could not get a sound out of his pipe because of his tears (Pocock 1994: 333).

Meanwhile the battle had been raging above Nelson's head, with the *Téméraire* attacking the *Redoubtable*. The French Captain, Lucas, surrendered, as well he might, for 522 of the *Redoubtable*'s crew of 643 had been killed or wounded. The *Victory's* casualties, in contrast, were fifty-seven dead and 102 wounded, leaving almost 700 unscathed. The *Bucentaure,* with 450 casualties and surrounded by five British ships, surrendered, and the grossly unequal casualties between the two sides made manifest the significance of the difference in gunnery. The *Leviathan,* which had engaged the Spanish ship the *San Agustín,* had only twenty-six casualties, while the Spanish ship had 380 casualties. After a two-hour battle the *Santa Ana,* with 340 casualties, surrendered to the *Royal Sovereign* with 141 casualties. The French *Swift-sure* with 260 casualties and the Spanish *Bahama* with 141 casualties surrendered to the most badly mauled British ship, the *Colossus* with 200 casualties.

Rear Admiral Dumanoir's ten ships of the van ignored both the noise of the battle, and the signals from Villeneuve to engage the enemy, by sailing away from the battle for a full two hours after its commencement (Keegan 1993*b*: 79). Pocock (1994: 329) suggests that the light wind prevented the return of the van, but, since the ships made no attempt to turn and when they did four simply escaped, this cannot be a valid excuse. This fatal error allowed both Nelson's and Collingwood's columns to engage the Combined Fleet on roughly equal numerical terms in a battle of attrition that the British were always likely to win. As Schom (1992: 349) reports, if Dumanoir's squadron had indeed done as they were expected—or as they were later ordered—the entire battle could have been altered. Three hours later half of Dumanoir's squadron arrived but it was too late to alter the course of events. One of the two early returnees, the *Intrépide*, engaged with and surrendered to the *Orion* after suffering 320 casualties to the *Orion's* twenty-four. Four ships of Dumanoir's squadron, including his own, sailed right through the battle, refusing to engage the British and headed away, to be captured a week later.

The aggression of the British fleet had not been restricted to the *Victory* or the *Royal Sovereign,* the two flagships. *Belleisle, Mars, Achilles,* and *Colossus* engaged six, five, four, and three enemy ships simultaneously, yet the Combined Fleet also had its equivalents: the *Intrépide* surrendered only after losing all its masts, suffering 242 dead, and being surrounded by six British ships. The *Fougueux* listed 546 casualties (three-quarters of the crew). The French ship *Achille,* attacked by the British *Prince,* blew up leaving 499 dead, while there were no deaths aboard the *Prince* (the only British ship without casualties). Keegan (1993*b*: 84) concludes: 'had there been more commanders of the stamp of Infernet, Lucas or Cajigal . . . in the Combined Fleet, Nelson's Trafalgar enterprise might have perished through its very recklessness. He had counted . . . on compensating for inferior numbers by the unorthodoxy of his approaching manœuvre . . . (and) the inaccuracy of the enemy's gunnery'. In the event, Villeneuve knew Nelson's tactics but was still unable to make him pay for it. Once again, it had been the tactical errors of the opposition that had allowed the British to exploit the situation.

Few of the British ships had been damaged below the water line and few of the men below deck had been injured: only two of *Victory's* casualties came from the lower gun deck and most had been on the top decks. In contrast, Lucas on the *Redoubtable* (which lost five-sixths of its crew) said afterwards that he knew of nothing that had not been hit and that most of his casualties had occurred in the deep Orlop deck (Keegan 1993*b*: 85.) The heaviest casualties were clearly amongst the Combined Fleet, but the officer corps of both sides lost disproportionately. On the British side, Nelson and the two captains, Cooke and Duff, died with 22 per cent casualties amongst the deck officers, while the Combined Fleet had twelve of its thirty-three captains killed or wounded. Casualties amongst British sailors were approximately 9 per cent overall. Schom (1992: 358) suggests fourteen French and Spanish ships eventually fled the battlefield, leaving nineteen of the original thirty-three against Nelson's twenty-seven (Schom 1992: 358). In fact only eighteen ships are listed as prizes. Lyon argues that fifteen French and Spanish ships deserted—four with Dumanoir sailing south, which were later caught, and eleven with Gravina heading north-east towards Cadiz (Lyon 1996: 133). Whatever the actual number, the results of the desertion—with several ships never firing a single shot—left the balance of forces redistributed in Britain's favour. To simplify the situation, if we take an average French or Spanish ship to have 78 guns and 909 crew (with the British equivalent at 80 guns and 629 crew) the loss of fifteen ships left the Combined Fleet with a total of 1,404 guns (down from 2,568) facing the British total of 2,148. Moreover, the average casualty rate demonstrates the critical significance of rate of fire. Assuming all the Combined Fleet fought at Trafalgar, each ship took about 210 casualties—marginally under a quarter of the entire force, compared to the average British casualty rate of 10 per cent. Overall, 17 per cent (8,500) of all those who took part in the battle (50,000) were killed or injured, compared to a casualty rate of 29 per cent at Waterloo. And, while Wellington's 'defensive' strategy saw him escape with hardly a scratch from sixteen battles, Nelson's 'offensive' strategy saw him gradually destroyed piece by piece and killed at his only major battle on the high seas (Keegan 1993*b*: 89–90). Even allowing for the fact that many—though by no means all—of the deserting ships carried casualties, each French or Spanish combatant at Trafalgar was between three and six times more likely to end up a casualty than the average British combatant—depending on how many Combined Fleet ships are counted as having been engaged in the battle. The difference in casualty rate cannot be accounted for by the difference in the number of guns, but might be explained by two aspects of the tactics deployed. First, the different tactics used by the opposing crews, with the British aiming at the hull to kill the enemy while the French and Spanish aimed at the rigging and masts to disable their enemy. And secondly, and probably more importantly, the familiar one of rates of fire. With the British crews training daily and the French and Spanish crews training hardly at all, it would seem that the rate of fire of the British guns was anywhere between twice and six times faster than their enemy. The time taken to fire broadsides varied not just with training but also with the conditions, because the guns had to be run in and back out again for each firing. Collingwood's ship, *Royal Sovereign*, fired three broadsides in ninety seconds, while the *Victory* managed the same in two minutes (D. Pope 1997: 199), while the French and Spanish continued to use the slow burning matchlock fuse achieving a firing rate of merely one broadside every 3½ minutes at best (Keegan 1993*b*: 60, 68; D. Pope 1997: 206).

It was not bravery then that distinguished one side from the other in the battle itself; after all, most of the casualties were French and Spanish, so there could not have been a lack of valour on the part of those that stayed. It may have been the lack of bravery that was significant on the part of the deserting ships, and had these remained to fight the results might have been quite different. Rather, it was a consequence of the ability of the British to dominate their enemies in the battle of attrition won through the greater rapidity of the British guns, aligned to the better sailing experience and abilities of the British sailors.

Eighteen enemy ships had been destroyed or captured, but, since Collingwood rescinded Nelson's last order to anchor after the battle, only four prizes ever reached Gibraltar (four were scuttled, two escaped, and the rest sank in the storm) where Dumanoir's four captured ships made the prize look more respectable. No British ship had been taken or sunk. In total there were 6,953 (4,408 dead) French and Spanish casualties and 20,000 prisoners of war. On the British side there were 1,690 casualties (449 dead). Nelson was put into a tub of brandy to preserve his body and then transferred to a lead-lined coffin in Gibraltar a week later. He was 47 and, despite his lifelong hypochondria, his autopsy reveals no major damage to any organ except that caused by the musket ball.

The country was transfixed by the combination of the victory and the loss; although it was not the case, it appeared that Nelson had given his own life to save the nation—it was a replica of the Christian tradition of self-sacrifice. 'Every newspaper and periodical printed ballads, orations and hymns in Nelson's praise.' 'I never saw so little public joy,' acknowledged Lord Malmesbury, and, instead of victory jubilations, mourning lamps appeared in windows across the country. The *Annual Register* noted: 'There was not an individual in the country who did not feel that it [victory] was purchased at too dear a rate' (quoted in Schom 1992: 361). *Victory* reached Portsmouth on 4 December 1805 and the body, now in his own coffin made from the mast of the *L'Orient*, lay in state from 5 to 7 January. His funeral was attended by thousands lining the streets to St Paul's Cathedral, where the seats allotted to the public were filled six hours before the service took place. Ten thousand sailors marched in the procession, which meant that the head reached St Paul's Cathedral before the rear had left Whitehall 1½ miles away. Forty-eight sailors from the *Victory* were to fold its white ensign and place it upon the coffin, but they tore one section off the flag and ripped strips off as mementoes. The Prince of Wales was the chief mourner at the state funeral, though this was much against the King's wishes. Lord St Vincent refused to attend: 'Lord Nelson's sole merit was animal courage, his private character most disgraceful in every sense of the word . . . and [Lady Hamilton] was a diabolical bitch' (Hibbert 1995: 388).

The establishment may still have excluded Nelson from their midst, but the rest of the population did not: fifty streets and several towns were named after him and Trafalgar Square, with its 145-foot Nelson's Column, was completed in 1843. £90,000, plus an annual annuity of £5,000 and the title 'Earl Nelson of Trafalgar and Merton', was granted to Nelson's heirs (his brother William in the first instance). Nelson's sisters were given £10,000 each, and his widow an annual pension of £2,000. The Prince of Wales asked that Nelson's last wish—that the country look after Lady Hamilton—be met. It was not; neither she nor any other woman was allowed to attend his funeral, and all hope for Lady Hamilton faded when William Pitt died a fortnight after the funeral. She continued to spend wildly, was imprisoned for debt, and eventually fled—ironically—to Calais with Horatia, where Emma died a virtual alcoholic in 1815, aged 50. Horatia, who knew the identity of her father but not her mother, married a curate in 1822, had a large family, and died in 1881. Nelson's wife, Frances, died within a year of her son, Josiah, in Exmouth in 1831, aged 73 (Pocock 1994: 341). Villeneuve was captured, imprisoned, and returned to France in 1806, only to 'commit suicide' on 22 April at Rennes. His was one of the most unlikely 'suicides' in history: he had six stab wounds to the chest. On 7 December 1805 Napoleon (who had heard the real story on 16 November) announced that the Battle of Trafalgar had been a great victory for the Combined Fleet, with nineteen British ships sunk and 10,471 British casualties (Schom 1992: 362). Almost 200 years later, on 27 June 1999, Louis Napoleon Bonaparte-Wyse, a descendant of the Emperor's brother, shook hands with Anna Tribe, great-great-great-granddaughter of Nelson and Emma Hamilton, in a ceremony in Alexandria to celebrate the findings of a French excavation of the site of the battle of Aboukir Bay.

Analysis

The Philosophical Arts: Identity

Just as Henry Ford became identified as an icon of America in the early twentieth century, so Nelson became the iconic military hero of Britain, in particular the greatest leader of the senior service. This was anything but an accident, for, as we shall see, this was always Nelson's personal vision.

It is also important to remember that Nelson's identity was formed at around the same time that the identity of the British nation—as opposed to the component parts of it—was formed. That formation, at the time of war against the French and in the face of widespread fear of invasion, added considerably to his popularity.

Nelson's identity carried a visibility that few other individuals at the time could hope to match because he was instantly recognizable, even to those who had never seen him before. Thus his small stature, his self-evident war wounds, his love of ostentatious uniforms, and his thirst for public adulation and recognition all turned him into the equivalent of a contemporary pop star.

The Fine Arts: Strategic Vision

Nelson had one overriding vision and it was extremely clear: he wanted to become Britain's greatest-ever naval hero. Almost everything that he did was channelled into achieving this and he managed to align this personal ambition to the strategic vision of the Admiralty in a seamless conjunction. That enabled him to take inordinate risks not just with his own life but with the lives of many of his followers, for he could represent his exorbitant demands for their sacrifice as offerings for their nation rather than as stepping stones for their admiral. In effect, Nelson's ability to embody the nation's strategic vision made it difficult for his followers to resist him.

Nelson's appeal to the general population also lay in the complexity and heterogeneity of his character: he was simultaneously a national hero and a man smitten with the same weaknesses that ordinary mortals suffered from; his background was middle-class English, but his moderate social class did not prevent him from mixing with the lowest sailor or the highest of the land.

As long as the two agendas (organizational and personal) were sufficiently entwined, subordinate agendas that manifest weaknesses or flaws were not necessarily critical, especially if they could be represented as flaws that could be rationalized as demonstrating a link to 'ordinary' people. One might argue here that Nelson was the turn of the (nineteenth)-century equivalent of Clinton. However, the overriding desire to achieve one's vision often turns a strength into a weakness; a commitment becomes all-consuming, destroying rather than achieving the vision. There are (at least) two ways to avoid this shift from strong focus to tunnel vision:

1. know when to stop or be stopped before it happens—the latter happened to Nelson;
2. generate an open organization where followers are encouraged to compensate for the leader's own errors and are free to criticize that leader whenever necessary.

The Martial Arts: Organizational tactics

It is organizational tactics that are frequently regarded as the origins of Nelson's greatness. Yet 'breaking the line' was not an original idea; nor were his mêlée tactics revolutionary, nor his action at Aboukir Bay, since this was exactly what the French Admiral de Grasse had tried to do to Rear Admiral Hood at Frigate Bay, St Kitts, in 1782 (Lyon 1996: 55–62).

Moreover, at Trafalgar Villeneuve knew what Nelson planned—even if the French admiral failed to do anything with this knowledge. This surely was a crucial element of Nelson's success: it was not that he was an especially original tactician, but he took others' ideas and refined them and he simply made fewer mistakes than his enemies. Thus his greatest successes, the Nile and Trafalgar, were won by a fatal combination of his tactical audacity and his opponent's tactical ineptitude.

The Nile was a victory rooted in inverting the French apparent strength against the landward side. Trafalgar was a victory secured by neutralizing a large proportion of the Combined Fleet by breaking the line.

The Performing Arts: Persuasive Communication

Perhaps Nelson's greatest leadership skills were not in battle, nor in securing the unflinching support of most of his followers, but rather in persuading others, especially the British media and the Admiralty, that whatever he did was a manifestation of his unique abilities. This is particularly important when defeats and mistakes occur, because it is relatively easy to secure praise for clear-cut victories but much harder to represent defeats advantageously. Hence, Nelson's greatest mistakes, at Tenerife, at Boulogne, and missing several enemy fleets, were forgiven because they were conveyed—often by him—as gallant errors of judgement. Even his infamous (in)action during the mass executions of the Neapolitan rebels failed to dim his public adoration, probably because a population at war is seldom so xenophobic.

His performances also exemplified the cult of the hero in its earliest and critical days after the French Revolution when a frightened nation looked for an icon to rely on. Nelson fitted the requirements perfectly: he led from the front, put himself at greater risk than virtually anyone else, and expected all his followers to do likewise—though we have already seen that he may well have expected to live at least until 1805.

But the kind of example he demonstrated could not be mirrored by others without threatening the very platform of his own success. That is, while Nelson broke rules and regulations whenever he felt it appropriate, had his followers done the same his strategy would surely have failed. His demand that others follow his example would have meant individual captains *not* following his battle orders but doing whatever they thought appropriate; it would have meant individual sailors *not* accepting the Admiralty's regulations whenever they thought it less sensible than their own endeavours; it would have meant other whole fleets leaving their stations to chase the enemy irrespective of the risks this raised for others. Thus, Nelson's exemplary leadership could not have been followed; by following his example, Nelson wanted every other captain to do exactly as he told them, not exactly as he did. Of course he wanted them all to demonstrate bravery and to use their initiative within limits, but those limits were set down by an iconoclastic leader; he could and did disobey his superiors, but he did not allow any of his subordinates the kind of leeway that the Admiralty allowed him. Other captains and admirals who transgressed Admiralty rules could expect far less tolerance than Nelson received.

More importantly for us here, Nelson's success as a leader was not the simple reflection of an outstanding individual with a remarkable sway over his followers. His success had to be massaged by himself and others from early on; he did not rise through the ranks simply on merit but through a useful relation in his uncle and by acquiring a string of influential friends. He was not the bravest individual in the navy at the time, because there is no way of assessing this claim and there must have been hundreds of equally brave individuals on all sides of the various conflicts. But there were few as adept at seeking publicity in an age where the cult of heroism had taken a feverish hold over the minds of that very same élite that had such difficulty accepting Nelson. And there were even fewer leaders who generated a network of popular and professional supporters who were strong enough to transcend this ostracism by the social élite and to downplay his flagrant breaking of Admiralty orders.

Finally, we should note that Nelson at Trafalgar made little use of flags to signal his requirements—except to say, 'engage the enemy more closely' (Lavery 1989: 256–9). Indeed, in 1803 he made clear that signalling during a battle left too much to chance. After all, 'He was fully assured that the admirals and captains of the fleet I have the honour to command will, knowing my precise object, that of a close and decisive battle, supply any deficiency of my not making any signals, which may, if extended beyond these objects, either be misunderstood, or if waited for very probably from various causes be impossible for the commander-in-chief to make' (quoted in C. White 1998: 70). In sum, the communications that Nelson made were not signals for the present but signals to the future: he was literally writing his own history.

Conclusion

Napoleon may have been more imaginative in his renditions of the battles than the British press were, but what are we to make of Nelson's leadership? Schom considers Nelson's character, and thus presumably his leadership skill and style, to have been based on loyalty: 'perhaps the most important principle or precept of his life he appears never to have articulated. That one had to be honourable, do one's duty, give one's life if necessary to protect Britain, be loyal to fellow officers . . . above all . . . that every responsible person had to think for himself' (Schom 1992: 248). But there is a clear tension here between the absolute loyalty owed to one's country and peers and the duty to think independently. Independence of thought and action is surely one of Nelson's characteristics, but this was often articulated and executed at the expense of loyalty to his superior officers and to the Admiralty. He frequently disobeyed direct orders *because* of his independence of thought and action. For Grabsky, 'He was vain, ambitious, disfigured by battle, adulterous, and almost wrecked by a life at sea. He disobeyed orders, made up his own rules and was pensioned off for five years. Nevertheless, every 21 October, on British naval bases and warships throughout the world, glasses are raised to 'the immortal memory' of Horatio Nelson (Grabsky 1993: 75).

Notes

1. The discomfort with a standing army is often related to the era of the republican Commonwealth under Cromwell, when, for a time, military rule displaced not just the monarchy but parliament too.

2. As General Patton argued over a century later.

3. The dockyards were run by the Navy Board and all the victualling was organized by the third arm, the Victualling Board, a semi-independent bureaucracy. Guns, ammunition, and land fortifications were the remit of the Ordnance Board.

4. At this time a 'ship' was anything with more than three masts; anything with less than three masts was a 'boat' (S. Pope 1998: 35). The shortage of 'compass' timber (naturally curved) meant that when ships were broken up such wood was transferred to the new ship—along with the wood rot spores that had probably rendered the original ship unusable (D. Pope 1997: 53).

5. A British government report in 1783 into the state of the domestic timber available for shipbuilding suggested that, while 234,000 loads (one load was 50 cubic feet) were available in the previous survey of 1618, by 1783 only 50,000 were available (D. Pope 1997: 35). A conventional seventy-four-gun double-decker ship took about 2,000 oak trees to construct—the equivalent of fifty acres of forest. Some ships were built in the royal dockyards but many more were built in private yards, such as Buckler's Hard near Southampton. The design of most European ships differed little at this time, unlike the considerable differences that were visible at the time of the Spanish Armada in 1588. French ships did tend to be marginally faster than British ships, and British ships tended to be marginally stronger than French ships, but the frequent capture and reflagging of enemy ships—and the difficulty of telling which ship was which during battle in the absence of flags—suggests that similarity was the norm (Lavery 1989: 40). Throughout the 1790s British ship-designers struggled to keep up with the French and Spanish designers. In the early part of the decade it became clear that the quicker French ships had a longer length in relation to their beam, and British designers immediately began to copy the 'solution'. However, by the end of the decade captured Spanish ships, which were also quicker than their British counterparts, had revealed the opposite design features, so British designers reverted back to their original in the hope of keeping up (D. Pope 1997: 56).

6. The *Santisima Trinidad*, a four-decker 136-gun Spanish ship captured at Trafalgar, was the largest ship in the world at the time of its launching in 1769 at Havana. It was designed by Matthew Mullan, an Irish designer, using the longer timbers that grew near Havana.

7. That shipbuilding was an art not a science can be assessed by the thirty-eight tons of corrective ballast that were needed to keep *Victory* sailing properly (S. Pope 1998: 29).

8. The 'rate' originally referred to the pay 'rate' of the captain (Lyon 1996: 20).

9. Billy Culmer, who entered the service in 1755, was promoted only in 1790, at the age of 57 (Lavery 1989: 90).

10. G. H. Fortye remained a lieutenant for fifty-five years (D. Pope 1997: 78).

11. The Red, White, and Blue divisions were instigated by the Commonwealth Navy of the 1650s, with the Admiral of the Red division being the most senior.

12. Widows of officers were granted the full pay of their husband for one year; orphans were allowed one-third of the same their mother was entitled to (Tracy 1998*b*: 340). G. V. Jackson held the record for the longest non-active service. He joined the navy in 1801, gained command of a ship in 1818, was put on half-pay in 1828, then aged 31, and remained there until 1876, by which time seniority had pushed him to becoming an Admiral, having last served in any capacity forty-eight years previously (Pope 1997: 80).

13. 30% of the Spanish crews were marines rather than the 20% that was common in Royal Navy ships (Lavery 1989: 284–5).

14. In 1813, for example, the battle between the British frigate *Shannon* and the American frigate *Chesapeake* began only after both captains had issued challenges to each other (S. Pope 1998: 80).

15. Nelson called Lord Howe 'the greatest sea officer the world has ever produced'.

16. 'Double shotted' means using two cannonballs or two canisters of grapeshot per cannon.

17. Dubordieu, an avid admirer of Nelsonian tactics, had deployed precisely the same two lines with his combined Franco-Venetian squadron of seven ships in an attack upon a smaller squadron of four British ships commanded by Captain Hoste (previously one of Nelson's favourite midshipmen) in the Battle of Lissa in 1811. Dubordieu even signalled 'Remember Nelson!' to his ships as they attacked. In the event, the better discipline, training, and support of the smaller British squadron saw off its attackers, with British casualties at around 190 dead and wounded, while the Franco-Venetian squadron lost two ships and had about 470 casualties.

18. A 24-lb. gun had a point-blank range—that is, the range at which a horizontally fired gun delivers its shot without dropping—of 200 yards; with a nine degree elevation its range was over 2,200 yards, though most battles tended to be fought at very close range, perhaps between zero and 100 yards (D. Pope 1997: 44). However, since ships were seldom stable, and the gun's traversing could be achieved only by a crude combination of different pressures on the gun tackle and handspikes to lever it, while a wedge, or quoin, was used for elevation, accuracy was seldom guaranteed except at very short range.

19. In 1782, when an artillery officer suggested that the navy might use redhot shot, Lord Howe was horrified. 'I think it, Sir, quite horrid enough, without having recourse to anything more (than) . . . cold shot' (quoted in Tracy 1998*b*: 11).

20. But the *rates* of casualties were often considerably higher amongst the army than the navy, especially when sent to Africa or the West Indies. For instance, of the 8,700 soldiers sent to defend Jamaica against a French invasion in 1795, 6,000 had died from unspecified fevers within the year. Indeed, a death rate of between 30 and 40% was the norm rather than the exception in the West Indies at the turn of the century, primarily of yellow fever.

21. Even dying for one's country is often less ennobling in the popular imagination than dying whilst on a pleasure cruise. Compare, for example, the 1,517 deaths from the *Titanic* with the 4,500 deaths that resulted from German bombing of the British *Lancastria* in June 1940 off St Nazaire. One became forever linked to tragedy and heroism, while the other was forgotten—as Churchill intended, since he banned information about the event (Stuart Hall 1998).

22. Keel-hauling involved attaching ropes to a miscreant and pulling him—there are no records of it ever happening to a woman, though there were often women passing as men on board—under the keel for the length of the ship. It was deemed illegal from the eighteenth century in Britain but used in the Dutch navy as late as 1813. In 1802 a report was filed of two sisters who had served in the Royal Navy as men (Tracy 1998b: 270).

23. Not all captains resorted to the lash. Captain Bond, of the sloop *Netley*, which carried an experimental sliding keel in 1798, punished minor offences by making the offender wear a scarlet cap with black tassels; more serious miscreants were made to wear a wooden collar (Nagle 1999: 105).

24. Head money for capturing slaves—£5 per head—was eventually removed from the statute book in November 1998. As late as 1799 the Royal Navy was still involved in freeing British slaves. For example, in May of that year six Britons were freed after fourteen years' slavery in Algiers (Tracy 1998*b*: 8). Later head money was increased to around £4 per sailor (D. Pope 1997: 232).
25. The name Horatio was gradually acquired through childhood.
26. He was, for example, directed, via Suckling, to join the *Worcester*, a sixty-four-gunner at Portsmouth where the *Worcester*'s captain, Mark Robinson, held a dinner party for the Mayor to meet the now 16-year-old probationary Lieutenant Nelson, the nephew of the Comptroller of the Navy, who was also about to stand for Parliament in Portsmouth (Pocock 1994: 21).
27. There is an issue about the significance of fatalism in leadership because many leaders were convinced that their future was preordained by God. Thus, for example, Patton, Florence Nightingale, Joan of Arc, Nelson, and Martin Luther King were all 'certain' of their calling.
28. Edward Despard later attempted to lead a rebellion against the King, and, though Nelson spoke on his behalf, Despard was executed in 1802 for his troubles.
29. He was not always so irresistible. In 1781, as Captain of the *Albemarle*, a 28 gun captured French frigate, Nelson tried to press his, as yet, unrecruited crew on board from four English merchant ships. He fired twenty-seven cannon shot at them before they agreed to heave to. Paradoxically, after two years at sea under Nelson the pressed *Albemarle's* crew subsequently decided to 'Turn Over' (stay with the Captain) *en masse* after the crew was paid off in 1783. Yet earlier Nelson had preferred to enforce compliance rather than risk desertion when anchored in the East River for he had the ship moved further from land to prevent desertion—since few sailors could swim. Indeed, the Admiralty did not encourage its sailors to swim for just this reason. In the event, two men still deserted, one of whom was the corporal of the Marines charged with preventing desertion! (Pocock 1994: 58–9). (In 1998 the British Navy warned of a crisis in its ranks—20 per cent of new recruits could not swim (*The Guardian*, 16 September 1998)).
30. Nelson fully supported the rights of whites to own slaves, so we can assume he was not a great favourite of the black islanders. Indeed, he (and King George III) positively detested the abolitionist Wilberforce. As Nelson admitted, he was 'bred in the good old school, and taught to appreciate the value of our West Indian possessions, and neither in the field nor the Senate shall their [slave owners,] just rights be infringed, while I have an arm to fight in their defence, or a tongue to launch my voice against the damnable doctrine of Wilberforce and his hypocritical allies' (quoted in Thomas 1997: 545–6).
31. Even his successful efforts to intervene on behalf of a deserter from the *Rattler*, who was condemned to death (winning him not only a reprieve but a pardon), led to a letter of rebuff from the Admiralty for exceeding his powers. Having upset just about everyone, Nelson was probably glad to return to the Nore in September 1787, where the *Boreas* became the receiving ship for 1,000 pressed men. But the discontent of the press spread to his crew, such that he ordered eight of them to be flogged. Unremarkably, the crew of the *Boreas* declined to 'Turn Over' with Nelson in November 1787, when they were paid off (Hibbert 1995: 62). Almost as soon as the crew had been discharged, one of them, James Carse, allegedly murdered a prostitute. In the case that was heard against Carse in December 1787, Nelson spoke for

him, arguing that he had served his captain well and could only have committed the offence because of insanity brought on by sunstroke received during his service in the West Indies. Carse was declared guilty but insane and he was imprisoned for life (Pocock 1994: 82).

32. The Prince of Wales, then weighing sixteen stone, and refered to by Charles Lamb as the 'prince of Whales', was, according to Schom (1992: 25), 'a notorious reprobate', even before reaching his majority with personal debts of £600,000 (four per cent of the country's annual budget).

33. Two years later, when Villaret-Joyeuse was ordered to prepare the Brest fleet to land a French army in Ireland, he refused, insisting that supplies and morale were too poor to guarantee success; he was dismissed and replaced by Admiral Morard de Galles— who also failed (Tracy 1998a: 155–6).

34. Subsequently, there have been suggestions that the problem from the sand was probably temporary and that the permanent damage was caused by continuous exposure to sea and sun. Certainly by 1800 Nelson's colleagues had begun to note that his good eye also had a film forming over it (Pocock 1994: 118, 208).

35. After Corsica Nelson sailed to Leghorn, Italy, for repairs and apparently had an affair with Adelaide Correglia, an opera singer known as Nelson's 'Dolly' to his fellow officers (Pocock 1994: p. ix). By the March of 1795 Nelson was chafing at the bit, which prevented him from establishing his name. He was refused permission by Admiral Martin to continue chasing the French fleet off Toulon and wrote to his wife: 'my disposition cannot bear tame and slow measures. I wish to be an Admiral and in command of the English Fleet'(quoted in Hibbert 1995: 100). Captain Freemantle was invited to dine with Nelson and Dolly, and Nelson began to reveal an emotional aspect to his character that became increasingly apparent as his affair with Emma Hamilton strengthened: 'Dined with Nelson,' wrote Freemantle; 'Dolly aboard . . . he makes himself ridiculous with that woman' (quoted in Pocock 1994: 125).

36. The Spanish fleet went through a similar upheaval, changing Admiral of the Fleet three times in six weeks in 1796, but, unlike Parker, Admiral Ramos had no experience of senior command.

37. By May the mutinies at Spithead and Nore (see Chapter 2) had become common knowledge, and, though sympathetic to some of the grievances of sailors, Nelson had no time for mutineers. He had defused a mutiny on the *Blanche* in January and said of the Nore mutiny: 'At present we are all quiet in our fleet and, if the Government hang some of the Nore delegates, we shall remain so'(Hibbert 1995: 102).

38. There was, however, a new British recipe: 'Nelson's New Art of Cookery'. 'Take a Spanish . . . ship and after well battering and blasting them for an hour, keep throwing in your force balls and be sure to let these be well seasoned . . . as soon as you perceive your Spaniards to be well stewed and blended together, you must throw your own ship on the two-decker . . . skip into her quarter gallery window, sword in hand. The moment you appear . . . the Spaniards will throw down their arms and fly' (quoted in Grabsky 1993: 81).

39. Striking the colours—removing the flag—was an accepted signal of surrender in naval warfare at the time. But in 1801 the Speedy, a brig carrying only ninety crew and fourteen 4-lb. guns, captured the Spanish frigate *El Gamo* with 319 crew and thirty-two twelve and twenty-four pounders, after a British sailor cut the Spanish flag down. The Spanish crew believed their captain had surrendered and promptly lay down their arms (Cochrane 1999: 133–6).

40. The reception of the Spanish naval officers could hardly have been more different: the commander, Don Joseph Cordova, was deprived of his rank, discharged from the navy, and prohibited from ever appearing at court or in any major port. Four captains received similar punishments and several others were publicly reprimanded and humiliated (Tracy 1998a: 200–1).

41. Strictly speaking, the penalty for homosexual activity was death, but at the time the usual punishment for 'going to another man's hammock' was 100 or 200 lashes (Pocock 1994: 137).

42. For example, Leprévost.

43. Vice Admiral Sir John Orde was so incensed when Earl St Vincent chose Nelson instead of himself to lead the attack against the French that he resigned and challenged the Earl to a duel. Sir John was subsequently arrested and bound over to keep the peace just hours before the duel was due to be fought. The Earl, it seems, had little intention of obliging Sir John (Tracy 1998b: 66–7).

44. When L'Orient disintegrated (the noise was heard fifteen miles away in Alexandria), a large chunk of the mast hit the Swiftsure, setting fire to it. The fire was successfully doused and Swiftsure's captain, Hallowell, later used the wood to make a coffin for Nelson, which Nelson kept in his day cabin from then on. He was eventually buried in it.

45. A naval excavation of the site between 1997 and 1999 established the distance from the spread of debris on the seabed. One 3-ton cannon was found 150 metres from the ship. There were two explosions, one of the ship's powder and one of the powder carried for the invasion. Seven cut anchor cables were found close by—demonstrating the fear that the explosion generated and the desperate attempts to move away. Some of the remains of the 1,700–2,000 French sailors were also found (Beeston 1999).

46. See the French accounts in Tracy (1998a: 271–6).

47. Between 1 October 1798 and 1 October 1799 Nelson received over £27,000 in gifts from various grateful dignitaries. At the time an average sailor might have earned about £17 (Lavery 1989: 130; Tracy 1998a: 262).

48. He wrote to her while at sea of his dreams: 'in one of my dreams . . . I was . . . sitting between a Princess, whom I detest, and another. They both tried to seduce me and the first wanted to take those liberties with me which no woman in this world but yourself ever did . . .' (quoted in Pocock 1994: 193).

49. Cowardice in the Royal Navy was something that allegedly only seems to have affected the officers. As S. Pope (1998: 92) puts it: 'An exposed target on the quarterdeck, and almost the only man aboard with the leisure to contemplate danger or the authority to avoid it, the captain was uniquely vulnerable to bouts of discretion.' Yet Dillon (1999: 24–5) provides two examples from just one action where ordinary sailors deserted their place during battle.

50. It was British practice to execute officers by shooting but to hang seamen from the yardarm.

51. Bronte was a 30,000-acre rock-strewn estate with one farmhouse on the slopes of Mount Etna, Sicily. Patrick Brunty, Irish father of the Brontë sisters, changed his name in honour of Nelson.

52. These were allegedly quasi-anagrams of Nelson and Lady Hamilton.

53. For all the attention he meted out to her, Nelson's insecurity became most manifest over the relations between Lady Hamilton and his erstwhile friend, the Prince of Wales. Nelson was petrified that she would be seduced by him. Nelson wrote to her:

'Does Sir William (Hamilton) [for she remained living with her husband throughout the affair] want you to be a whore to the rascal? I see clearly you are on SALE'
(quoted in Hibbert 1995: 239). And later: 'He [Prince of Wales] will put his foot near
you . . . telling you soft things . . . Don't let him touch you . . . God strike him blind if
he looks at you—that is high treason and you may get me hanged by revealing it . . .
I know his aim is to have you for a mistress . . . I am in tears. I cannot bear it . . . no-
one, not even Emma, could resist the serpent's flattering tongue' (quoted in Schom:
1992: 252).

54. Nelson suggested that Parker would not talk to him at first, but Nelson asked one of
his sailors to catch a turbot, a favourite food of Parker's, and had the fish sent straight
to the Admiral's boat. Thereupon Parker thanked Nelson and asked his advice on the
forthcoming battle (see Tracy 1998b: 160–1).

55. Occasionally, as during the Battle of the Glorious First of June, 1794, a hospital ship
accompanied the battle fleet (Dillon 1999: 13).

56. Nelson had once risked his entire ship's crew for Hardy in 1797 when escaping from
chasing Spanish ships. A sailor had fallen overboard and Hardy had organized the long-
boat to search for him, and, as the enemy ships closed in, Nelson refused to leave the
search party. The Spanish, fearing an ambush, failed to close in (Bethune 1999: 65–6).

57. This is the same palace that Richard Branson dropped off Frank Zappa, as discussed
in Chapter 2.

58. At Tenby a man said that: 'The whole town was at their heels. The lady is grown
immensely fat and equally coarse, while her "companion in arms" has taken the other
extreme—thin, shrunk, and to my impression, in bad health . . . Poor Sir William,
wretched but not abashed, followed at a short distance, bearing in his arms a puppy
and other emblems of their combined folly' (quoted in Hibbert 1995: 306).

59. Ships often carried the wives of some of the officers on board, and occasionally
sailors' wives too. In the Battle of the Glorious First of June, 1794, for example, the
Naval Chronicle noted that 'During the action the sailors' wives, who were on board
some of the English ships, fought with the most determine valour, at the guns;
encouraging and assisting their husbands' (quoted in Tracy 1998a: 93).

60. Dudley Pope (1997: 109) has seventy-one.

61. In fact, it was rare for any admiral to command more than twenty vessels at any one
time, so widely dispersed were the 266 rated ships of the Royal Navy. Between
January 1803 and January 1804 only five seventy-four-gun ships were added to the
Royal Navy and one of these had been captured by the French, so that by May 1804 it
only had 405 vessels in all, excluding the very light harbour boats. By January 1805
there were only eighty-three ships-of-the-line, several having been lost in the attacks
upon the French ports (Schom 1992: 41).

62. Despite the intense hostility of the British for the French, the former—including
Nelson—were as keen as the latter to put down any slave rebellions or insurrections
in the West Indies. Thus a secret agreement between the two countries in 1802
allowed the French to transport French troops unhindered to the French West Indies
to quash 'Toussaint and his ferocious followers' (Tracy 1998b: 264).

63. The new Banque de France owed 92 million francs and the franc had lost 58% of its
value compared to the Spanish currency.

64. Though he does suggest otherwise elsewhere (1993b: 8).

65. In contrast, Nelson had forbidden sharpshooters from operating from the fighting
castles for fear of setting fire to the sails and rigging.

66. Nelson had witnessed an almost identical injury to a sailor on the *Victory* several months before and was well acquainted with the symptoms he was then suffering (Beatty 1999: 178). In 1815, after peace was declared, a Colonel Drinkwater Bethune, who had known Nelson, reported that he had met a man in Paris who knew of the sharpshooter that shot Nelson, and he had shot the officer with the 'decorations' because he suspected he was indeed the Admiral (Hibbert 1994: 371). That sharpshooter survived the battle and returned to France—though the British marines claimed that, at the time that Nelson was shot, only two sharpshooters remained in the rigging of the *Redoubtable* and both were killed by the marines and some midshipmen with rifles (Beatty 1999: 183).

8

Adolf Hitler:
The Political Emotionasaurus Rex

He who fights with monsters might take care lest he thereby become a monster. And if you gaze for long into an abyss, the abyss gazes also into you.

(Friedrich Nietzsche, *Jenseits von Gut und Böse*, iv. 146 (quoted in Darwin 1979: 363))

It may seem ironic that Adolf Hitler—the most evil leader of all leaders—also embodied the four arts of leadership and took them to levels seldom seen before or since. A painter by 'trade', Hitler painted a vision—or rather a dystopia—of a German empire that sucked a large proportion of the globe into the maelstrom of war. And through his performing arts, notably his speeches, he persuaded a large proportion of the German population to embody the new German identity and engage in acts of barbarism that have rightly gone down as the greatest crimes against humanity ever recorded. He also seemed to have been a gifted organizational tactician, whether neutralizing the internal opposition, taking over large areas of Europe by 'peaceful' diplomacy, overwhelming the Franco-British forces in May 1940, or reaching the gates of Moscow in December 1941. But he did not achieve this alone, nor does it explain why it all went wrong for him, and right for the Allies, from 1943.

Hitler was reluctant to engage in war with the British, not because he was particularly concerned with British military prowess—he was not—but because he regarded the British as second only to the Germans in their 'Aryan' purity.[1] But identity is imagined, for to be 'English'—as Hitler usually referred to the British—implies having a whole raft of things in common with every other English person. Yet the diversity of people living in Britain then and now needed to be transcended through what Anderson (1991) refers to as a collective leap of the imagination. In effect, because the English—or any other population— hardly know each other, they have to imagine the similarities that apparently bind them together. But, to follow Jenkins (1996: 28), to say that something is imagined does not mean that it is imaginary. Identity is constructed not discovered; it is a product of the imagination rather than a product of history, let alone science. It is *imposed* upon a population rather than *emerging* from one and it does not reflect what is a deep essence *within* a people but is essentially steeped *upon* a people. It is not an event but a process: 'Social identities exist and are acquired, claimed and allocated within power relations. Identity is something over which struggles take place and with which strategies are advanced: it is means and end in politics . . . Social identity is a practical accomplishment, a process' (Jenkins 1996: 25). We should, therefore, consider the construction of identities as accomplishments of the artist not discoveries of the scientist, and this is why leadership has such an important role to play both in the development of social identities and in the deployment of these identities as a mechanism for mobilizing a population in pursuit of a strategic vision. In this mobilization there are few leaders so successful as Hitler—and few identities so strongly constructed on such a fragile foundation as that which enwrapped the German population so strongly during Hitler's Third Reich. Of course, there was much more to Hitler's leadership than the construction of an identity, but this was the bedrock upon which the Nazi scaffold—metaphorically and literally—was built.

Identifying Germans and Non-Germans, Humans and Hon-Humans

In 1841 Thomas Carlyle published *On Heroes, Hero Worship, and the Heroic in History*. In it, Carlyle discussed how a natural élite was alone capable of ruling, and that the truly great leaders were individuals whose astonishing personal abilities were matched by empathy for the times they lived in. When a great leader recognized, and operated in and through, the great movements in history, they could act as agents of momentous change. For Hitler such a leader was represented by Wagner's mythical Siegfried and Herman the Cherusker, or Arminius as he is known, the Germanic leader who defeated the Romans in AD 9, heralded as the precursor of the German nation and celebrated in his 'heroic' monument in the Teutoburger Wald (Kershaw 1998: 77).[2] Despite Carlyle's virulent anti-Semitism, he was not a particularly favourite author of Hitler's, though the model for Carlyle's 'great' leader was also Hitler's: Frederick the Great. Goebbels (Hitler's propaganda chief) read sections of Carlyle's biography to Hitler in the last month of the war in a vain attempt to boost the Führer's collapsing morale (Steinweis 1995: 33). Was Hitler one of these leaders around whom the tide of history turns? Certainly there have been more biographies of Hitler than of any other man, and it is upon Hitler's head that much of the blame for the Second World War and the mass extermination of Jews, gypsies, gays (and anyone else that fell foul of the Nazi regime) lies. Thus, if there ever was a 'great' leader—though the term 'great' is a misnomer here if it implies anything positive—to fit Carlyle's 'great-leaders-of-history' approach to leadership, Hitler is one such leader (see Fest 1974).

But the consequence of this kind of approach to leadership leads to a search for the demonic powers that literally 'enthralled' the German population, and to the eventual conclusion that such powers are, like Weber's notion of charisma, unique to a mere handful of individuals across time and space (Weber 1978). A variant of this is to insist that Hitler was not alone, but that a small 'criminal clique' helped him (see Bartov 1994: 43). Both variants mean that the sins of the

Nazis died on 30 April 1945 with the death of the Führer and the collapse of the Nazi state. After all, how can anyone be guilty of a sin if he or she is coerced by magic or by fear for his or her own survival?

The contrary structural argument would imply that Hitler was little more than the pawn of history, a rivulet playing the role ordained by the plate tectonics of, for example, (capitalist) economics and (bourgeois) politics. In this extreme counter-case the critical events of the world are inevitable, and, once again, the actions of individuals are 'irresponsible' because individuals have no choice. Even if we dismiss the more extreme versions of this approach, we can still visualize a totalitarian society in which the sinews of control are so great and their reach so long that no form of resistance is possible or plausible because the population is 'atomized' or simply disorganized by the apparatus of the Nazi state (see Bracher 1973). Thus, Hitler's power rested upon a state construction of unparalleled sophistication. In this approach whether Hitler was a charismatic leader is irrelevant; what matters is that resistance was useless: only decisive military action by a state or states of even greater power could have removed him and the Nazi state.

The irony at the heart of Hitler's leadership is that neither of these explanations—and the structural account (capitalist puppet) was as popular with the former East German scholars as the voluntarist account (demonic individual) was with the former West German scholars—is viable. Mass voluntarism, not just systemic coercion, freedom of choice not just the limits of choice, lie deeply buried within the Nazi system (Kershaw 1991: 6). Yet it was the system that ensured Hitler's success. Rees (1997: 10) puts it with cold clarity:

There was massive voluntary collaboration with the Nazi regime; in which many Germans were happy and content under Nazi rule in the 1930s; in which members of the Nazi élite lied when, after the war, they claimed they were 'acting under orders'; in which thousands eagerly profited from the downfall of the Jews; in which a majority of Germans in 1932 knowingly voted for parties committed to overthrowing German democracy.

In Geyer's (1987: 62) terms, 'the Nazi state did not require that everyone become a Nazi as long as the National Socialist leadership could convince Germans of the benefits of racist rule'. Ideological politics were thus the promise of participation in the domination of others for one's own and the common German benefit. As late as 1951 half of the citizens of the (West) German Federal Republic still regarded the period between 1933 and 1939 as the best in German history (Herbert 1987: 97). It would appear, therefore, that, far from Nazi propaganda constructing a German identity—and an identity for all those deemed enemies of the state by the Nazis—that misled a substantial proportion of the population into either supporting them or at least not standing up to them, the Nazi propagandist, in Huxley's (1936: 39) words, 'canalize[d] an existing stream [for] in a land where there is no water he digs in vain'. This does not mean that coercion was an insignificant element of Nazi control. Clearly, nothing could be further from the truth. However, the point I wish to make is that it was not *just* coercion that maintained Nazi control; collaboration, and collaboration above and beyond that required for self-preservation, was an axial principle upon which the Nazi behemoth rolled over European civilization and all but eliminated European Jews. And in this latter bestiality lies a vital explanation for the behemoth, for it was fundamentally and vigorously rooted in the identification of 'the other' and, therefore, in the identity of the German population. This 'race' of Aryans was, in Hitler's strategic vision, destined to dominate the world by destroying the enemy of 'civilization': the Jews. In short, Hitler's construction of the German master race, risen like a phoenix from the shame and ashes of 1918, was a construction, an invention—not a discovery—of an identity whose survival depended upon the elimination of another constructed, and not discovered identity: international Jewry.

Jews in Germany long pre-date the anti-Semitism that Carlyle stoked, but that very anti-Semitism was also long-lived: Jews, for instance, were not allowed to own land in what was to become Germany until the second half of the nineteenth century. Yet, at less than 1 per cent of the population and, in general, a very assimilated minority (only around 20 per cent still wore clothes associated with Jews), Germany was no more anti-Semitic than any other European country. Indeed, Jews from Hungary and Russia had fled to Germany to avoid the pogroms of the 1880s, and they had even fled Poland after the First World War to avoid increased anti-Semitism (Hobsbawm 1994: 120; Hodgson 1995: 205; Rees 1997: 21). German Jews may have been relatively assimilated, but they were not represented in all occupations: Jews made up about 16 per cent of all German lawyers, but almost no judges were Jews. About 17 per cent of all bankers were Jews and around 10 per cent of all doctors; but there were very few Jewish academics or hospital consultants. In fact, there were very few Jews: in 1934 they numbered 503,000 or around 0.76 per cent of the population (Carr 1987: 70; Rees 1997: 17).

Germany was, for many people, the last place to expect someone of Hitler's ilk to emerge: it was the cultural and intellectual centre of Europe and, as the largest single nation in continental Europe, it also had one of the most sophisticated labour and socialist movements. Indeed, the German identity was one superimposed by Bismarck in 1871 upon a manifestly disparate and pluralist society. Conservatives might have expected a future of immense stability, given the economic power of German industry. Liberals might have expected the steady expansion of the fledgling democracy and the profusion of further German philosophers, writers, and composers. Radicals might have expected the political left to take power by revolution or evolution. Whatever the future held at the beginning of the twentieth century, it was not one as primary instigator and loser of two world wars, nor one in which Germany would organize mass murder on a scale never before seen. All three perspectives were terribly wrong: economic stability was the one thing that was notably missing from Germany in the first half of the century—primarily as a direct result of the financing of the First World War; a large proportion of the cultural élite emigrated for good; and the great movement of the left watched in disbelief as the mass of Germans raced to defend the colours in the First World War and defended the colour of the race in the Second. How did Hitler and the Nazi party manage to construct such a popular and repellent strategic vision from the relatively positive soil of Weimar Germany?

'The Stab in the Back' by 'the November Criminals', 1918

The German military had long believed that the working class was untrustworthy and, until 1910, had expanded the German navy at the expense of the army, because the latter was forced to recruit from the 'unreliable' masses. So certain was the army command that the workers would rebel if an aggressive war was started by Germany (as they intended in July 1914), that they made contingency plans to arrest the entire leadership of the main working-class political party, the Social Democratic Party (SPD). They also planned to draft the leaderless masses immediately into the army, where extreme coercion would ensure compliance. However, Bethmann Hollweg, the then Chancellor, removed this necessity by persuading the SPD that the aggressive intentions of Russia would require a pre-emptive war in *defence* of the Fatherland. But this was almost the only thing that went to plan, since in the ensuing war the German attempt to knock France out through the Schlieffen Plan soon broke down, giving the Russians time to mobilize. This also left Germany with a war on two fronts, which the plan had been designed to avoid.

The war left almost ten million dead, a quarter of these German. It also left a huge financial debt. Desperate to avoid increasing direct taxation at the beginning of the war, the German government pushed up indirect taxation and issued war bonds that could be repaid only through reparations secured from the defeated enemy. When the opposite happened, the war bonds became worthless—though German complaints about *Allied* reparations remained shrill. Equally vocal was the political right's concern for the consequences of victory on the workers, for they would surely demand a greater level of political participation and reward. Alfred Hugenberg, a director of Krupp, had the preferred solution: 'We would be well advised, in order to avoid internal difficulties, to distract the attention of the people and to give fantasies concerning the extension of German territory room to play' (quoted in Berghahn 1987: 52). As Berghahn (1987: 55) suggests, the rapidly congealing strategy of the political right in 1918 was to combine 'annexations abroad and dictatorship at home'.

Notwithstanding the stalemate on the Western front, the first part of the plan had already borne fruit with the annexation of Poland, Finland, the Ukraine, the Baltic provinces, and Bielorussia, following the Brest-Litovsk Treaty with the new Soviet Union in March 1918. This is important, because it sets the contexts for Hitler's constant complaints about the diabolical unfairness of the later Versailles Treaty. The victorious German state at Brest-Litovsk removed huge swathes of land from Russian control without hesitation or compunction. When a similar 'surgery' was practised upon the defeated German state in 1919 at the Treaty of Versailles, Hitler was not alone in proclaiming the Germans to be the novel victims of an unspeakable sin. Such 'surgery' was common practice amongst the victors in war; after all, that was how Alsace-Lorraine had come under German jurisdiction after the Franco-Prussian war of 1870.

The second part of the German plan drew nearer in 1917 as the SPD's hold over the German masses back home fragmented to the left with the Independent Social Democratic Party, led by Hugo Hasse, and, further left still, to the Spartacus League, led by Rosa Luxemburg and Karl Liebknecht, which subsequently formed the core of the German Communist Party (KPD). But by mid-September 1918 the Allied armies had made significant inroads against all German positions and all Germany's allies (Turkey, Austria, and Bulgaria) were in the throws of peace negotiations. Ludendorff, adviser to Hindenberg and virtual co-controller of Germany during the second half of the war—having scuppered the previous attempts to end the conflict on the grounds that victory was assured—now accepted that victory was impossible and called for an armistice. The result was that all the sacrifices now became wasted and the citizens and soldiers of Germany turned upon their own leaders (Craig 1981: 397). By the middle of October 1918 industrial disputes took on an ever more radical political coloration, with demands that the Emperor should be deposed. Admiral Speer, head of the German navy, then ordered it to attack the British fleet in a suicidal mission 'to restore the honour of the fatherland', but the sailors mutinied in response. On 4 November one of the socialist leaders persuaded the mutineers to return to state authority—on three conditions: that their Sailors' Council was recognized as a legitimate body; that there would be no attack upon the British; and that their leaders were released from prison. But the rebellion spread and on 5 November the sailors at Wilhelhmshaven, Germany's largest naval base, mutinied. By 7 November no military garrison in the north remained loyal to the state. That same day Kurt Eisner led a revolutionary *coup* in Munich, and declared Bavaria an independent socialist republic. The events signalled the collapse of state control and the government resigned, as did the Kaiser, who fled to Holland with the crown prince. The new Social Democratic government, now responsible for a republic, came into being on 9 November 1918, two days before the armistice, under the Reich Chancellor Friedrich Ebert, a moderate social democrat. At a stroke, the defeat of Germany was spirited out from under the feet of the generals and right-wing politicians responsible for it and reborn in the laps of the social-democratic republicans. Ludendorff, a primary candidate for (mis)leading Germany into this abyss, stated as much on 1 October 1918 to the German High Command. In what can only be regarded as a breathtaking inversion of the truth he told them he had 'asked His Majesty to bring those people into the government who are largely responsible for things having turned out as they have. We shall, therefore, see these gentlemen enter the ministries, and they must now make the peace which has to be made. They must now eat the soup which they have served us!' (quoted in Berghahn 1987: 59). Two days later, on 11 November, an armistice was agreed. German troops surrendered, but, without exception, the boundaries they were defending at the time were greater than those at the beginning of the war in 1914. The German army, bloodied but undefeated, was persuaded by right-wing politicians and the military that they had been 'stabbed in the back' by left-wing politicians—the 'November Criminals'—at home. As Herbert Richter remembered: 'We did wonder because we didn't feel beaten at all. The front-line troops didn't feel themselves beaten, and we were wondering why the armistice was happening so quickly, and why we had to vacate all our positions in such a hurry, because we were still standing on enemy territory and we thought all this was strange' (quoted in Rees 1997: 16).

In fact the government was also under intense pressure from a rash of industrial disputes led by the Workers' Councils, and by political revolts led by the Spartacists. Fearing the development of another full-blown communist revolution along Russian lines they—they being the Social Democratic government—opted for an immediate peace. This, they assumed, would give them both the time and the resources to put down the revolutionary developments at home that threatened all their interests, even if it meant accepting a disadvantageous peace that endangered some of their interests. The point that it was the conservative government and military leadership that had prevailed throughout the war, which had self-evidently failed to achieve victory at enormous cost, and that the German army was retreating rapidly—though by no means defeated—by November 1918, did not prevent right-wingers (including Hitler) from concluding that it was the political left that had caused the dishonourable defeat of Germany. After all, had not the Supreme Army Commander, Ludendorff, promised them victory right until the end? Clearly, ran the political right's interpretation of events, betrayal had turned certain victory into catastrophic defeat; it was not the political right that had led to this ignominy, it was the political left. And some elements of the political left were led by Jews; *ergo*, ran the twisted logic of the right, the Jews betrayed the Germans. Thus was the first foundation stone for the rise of Hitler *constructed*. The identity of the scapegoat was transformed within a few days from incompetent generals to evil Jews.

Ebert, nominally in charge of a society that was rapidly disintegrating into chaos, then received a phone call from Ludendorff's replacement, Groener, offering the loyalty of the German army in return for the suppression of political revolutionaries and industrial strikes, and the Ebert–Groener Pact was born. In fact, the Workers' Councils, which had formed a Congress of Councils in December 1918, were not revolutionaries, though they had called for the reconstruction of the German army, but Groener demanded that Ebert denounce the Congress or face the withdrawal of the army's support. Ebert vacillated but, despite his Social Democratic colours, his disposition was taken to imply support for the army and for the political right over the left. It was enough for further demonstrations by the left in early January and a poorly organized and ineffective *coup* attempt by the Spartacists in Berlin on 5 January. The army, by now in complete confusion, responded with the construction of irregular units of the so-called Free Corps

(*Freikorps*),[3] and on 10 January Ebert gave their nominal leader, General Lüttwitz, a free hand to root out the Sparticists in Berlin.[4] Over the next few months the Free Corps brutally put down left-wing demonstrations and insurrections right across Germany, the most significant being in Munich, where Eisner's assassination in February sparked a self-declared but short-lived Soviet Republic in April 1919 led by revolutionaries, a majority of whom were Jewish. Hitler was present during this but appears to have taken no part.

Not only had the right now constructed a powerful myth explaining, or more accurately inventing, the identity of those who had lost Germany the war—democrats, the left, and the Jews—but the Social Democratic government had prevailed over the brutal execution of its previous comrades. The result was to unite the right, split the left, and leave Corporal Hitler with a golden opportunity that he would not fail to exploit.

The Weimar Republic and the Versailles Treaty

The National Assembly, chosen in January 1919, which met in Weimar to construct a new constitution, was led by Ebert's Majority Socialist Party, which had achieved 38 per cent of the votes. The democratic philosophy behind the new constitution was never as deeply rooted as its constructors hoped. Many right-wing members of the Assembly appear to have supported the developments just to appease the Allies, and, when the Allies imposed what the right-wingers regarded as harsh terms, their support for democracy disappeared as quickly as it had arrived. But several aspects of the constitution worked in favour of political extremes; and, in particular, the use of proportional representation provided a safety net for minority interests that under a first-past-the-post system would probably have withered rapidly. The constitution also facilitated the use of referenda, which Hitler later used to great effect to buttress his support in 1933 (when he took Germany out of the League of Nations), in 1936 (when he ordered the reoccupation of the Rhineland), and in 1938 (at the unification with Austria—the *Anschluss*). The National Assembly also adopted an emergency-measures clause, Article 48, which heralded disaster for democracy, though it was probably aimed at supporting it against communism. Article 48 stated: 'Should public order and safety be seriously disturbed or threatened, the President may take the necessary measures to restore public order and safety; in case of need, he may use armed force . . . and he may, for the time being, declare the fundamental rights of the citizen to be wholly or partly in abeyance' (quoted in Craig 1981: 417). Finally, for our purposes, Article 54 guaranteed the positions of judges, a guarantee that, almost without exception, worked in favour of the right and against the left. For example, leaders of right-wing *coups*, such as Hitler, received a maximum of five years' jail; leaders of left-wing *coups*, such as Eugene Leviné and Max Hölz, received either death sentences or long prison sentences. Similarly, between 1919 and 1921 the thirteen murders of right-wingers by the left resulted in eight death sentences and a total of 176 years' imprisonment. In contrast, the

314 murders of left-wingers by the right led to just one life sentence and a total of thirty-one years' imprisonment (Berghahn 1987: 76).

When the text of the Versailles Treaty reached the German government on 7 May 1919, the entire cabinet was aghast and attempted to negotiate changes to several elements, but to no avail. The Allies rejected the amendments on 16 June and gave them five days to accept the treaty or face the consequences of refusal. Among other things, the treaty demanded: the reduction of the German army to 100,000 troops, without armour, aircraft, or offensive weapons; the navy was to have no warship greater than 10,000 tons and no submarines; the General Staff and the élite training schools were to be disbanded; and the Emperor and military leaders were to stand trial for violating the rules of war. Until these terms were completed, the Rhineland, which was to be permanently demilitarized, would be occupied by Allied troops.

Whether the conditions were as harsh as the critics maintained is an issue of some debate. The German intention in 1914, according to the 'September Programme' of war aims, was 'the safeguarding of the German Empire for the foreseeable future in the East and the West. Hence France must be so weakened that it cannot rise again as a great power. Russia must be pushed back from the German frontier as far as possible, and its rule over the non-Russian peoples must be broken.' The details included acquiring the French coast from Dunkirk to Boulogne, Belgium was to become a 'vassal state', Holland would be independent in theory but in practice a 'subject state', and Germany would dominate Europe economically, politically, and militarily; in effect, the first superpower would be born (Kagan 1997: 208). This was considerably harsher than anything the Germans were to suffer, and the treaty forced on the new Soviet government at Brest-Litovsk was itself tougher than Versailles. As Kagan (1997: 293) concludes: 'Viewed from a relevant comparative perspective, the peace imposed on Germany at Versailles was not unduly harsh.' But as I have already suggested, the persuasive utility of such a 'truth' is limited, especially when a more enticing alternative is in the process of construction. The 'myth' of November was now safely aligned with the 'myth' of Versailles and both were already gnawing away at German self-esteem and democracy. The parties that signed the agreement, the Social Democrats and the Catholic Centre Party, would not be forgiven for they had ceded 25,000 square miles of territory and six million people. In addition, they lost 65 per cent of Germany's iron ore, 72 per cent of its zinc, and, through the lost colonies, a further million square miles, and twelve million people (Kagan 1997: 289–90).

The German military reacted with disgust, and a series of minor mutinies culminated in the Kapp Putsch, when disaffected troops marched on Berlin in March 1919 and declared a new government. The military command, in the person of General von Seeckt, refused to intervene in support of the government, but a strike by Berlin workers, and the ineptitude of the military rebels, led to a speedy collapse within four days. However, the failed putsch provoked the left to mobilize, and a 'Red Army' of 50,000 workers occupied the Ruhr, only to be routed by the army under von Seeckt, who now decided that the loyalty of the army could not be questioned—as long as the opponents were left-wingers (Craig 1981: 415–33). 'The threat to liberal society and all its values', suggest Hobsbawm, 'seemed to come exclusively from the Right; the threat to the social order from the Left' (1994: 123).

The defeats of the left were made complete with the election for the Reichstag in June 1920, which saw the vote for the Social Democrats slide from 11.5 million to just over six million, though the Independent Socialists increased their representation and the Communists secured their first representatives. However, despite being the single largest party, the SPD declined to form a Reich government and, with the exception of a brief period between 1928 and 1930, it never did again until Hitler was dead.

Adolf Hitler: The Early Years

Adolf Hitler was born in Braunau, on the Austrian side of the border with Bavaria, on 20 April 1889 (he did not acquire German citizenship until 1932). Alois Hitler, his alcoholic father—who had been brought up Alois Schicklgruber (his mother's maiden name)—was a 52-year-old customs officer when Adolf was born, while his mother, Klara Pölzl, was the 29-year-old second cousin of Alois, and his third wife. Alois died in 1903 when Adolf was 14, and, though Klara doted on her son, his general arrogance and laziness ensured that he failed to take his school leaving certificate when he was 16. He then spent two years in Linz, posing as an artist, but failed to gain entrance to the Vienna Academy of the Arts. In 1907 his mother died of cancer, following an anaesthetic provided by a Jewish doctor, and it has been suggested that this provoked a deeply rooted, but unconscious, connection between Jews and the death of the only thing dear to him. However, recently uncovered evidence shows that the family doctor, Ernest Bloch, a Jew, had tried to help Adolf in 1895 when the young Hitler was suffering from nightmares, possibly brought on by beatings from Alois. Bloch had suggested Adolf be sent to a psychoanalyst in Vienna (possibly Freud), and, although Alois forbade it, Bloch appears to have been the only Jew that Hitler personally saved from death, instructing Martin Bormann to grant Bloch safe passage to Switzerland in 1938 (Hellen 1997: 3).

Hitler, again refused entry to the Vienna Academy of the Arts, became a vagrant in the city, eking out a living from his meagre inheritance by selling postcard sketches. He may also have come under the influence of Vienna's violently anti-Semitic mayor, Karl Leuger (Kershaw 1991: 20). Hitler later wrote in *Mein Kampf*: 'I began to see Jews, and the more I saw the more sharply they became distinguished in my eyes from the rest of humanity . . . Was there any form of filth or profligacy, particularly in cultural life, without at least one Jew involved in it?' (quoted in Rees 1997: 22).

Bullock, one of Hitler's greatest biographers, considers Hitler a paradoxical creature: 'Everyone who knew him was struck by the combination of ambition, energy and indolence' (Bullock 1962: 35). Within a year he had entered a charitable Home for Men, but by 1913 had drifted to Munich, in Germany, to avoid military service in Austria. In Munich he was arrested for evading military service but excused on the grounds of physical weakness. Yet, when the war came in 1914, he eagerly joined the Bavarian army as a regimental runner, where, although he did not rise above the rank of corporal (he was considered lacking in leadership skills), his undoubted bravery and devotion to duty earned him two decorations, one of which was an Iron Cross. In many ways the time in the trenches was the crucible for Hitler's character formation and he often looked back to this period of *Kampfgemeinschaft*—a community of warriors, born in the struggle at the front. It was only there that the internal divisions of German society were transcended by the collective will to survive and to win, and it was to this fondly remembered historical memory that Hitler always intended to return, dragging Germany, riven by social, political, and economic differences, with him.

He was in a Pomeranian hospital, recovering from the effects of a mustard-gas attack in 1918, when the armistice was signed, and, after he had recovered from the shock of defeat, he was employed by the army to observe extremist groups. On 12 September 1919 Corporal Hitler, then 30 years old, entered the Sterneckerbräu beer hall in Munich, at the behest of his commanding officer, to observe the activities of the new right-wing German Workers' Party (DAP) (one of seventy such organizations). The German army was not fearful of such groups; on the contrary, it intended to develop covert links with those it thought most useful and planned to arm them when necessary (Williamson 1996: 14). After engaging in an argument, Hitler was asked to join the party by the founder, Anton Drexler, who was impressed by his rhetorical skills (which he had first honed in the army education unit to which he was attached) and force of character. Hitler claimed to have been one of the very first members of the party (number seven to be precise) and thus to have set up the founding structure, though in fact he was number 555, as Drexler pointed out in 1940. Since Hitler was renowned for his memory, we must assume this to have been one of the many historical reconstructions he was to be involved in (Rees 1997: 25).

The National Socialist Workers' Party

The first German Workers' Party programme was developed in February 1920. Apart from its violent anti-Semitism and anti-Marxism, it had little to differentiate it from any other of the myriad right-wing extremist groups. Hitler's own *Weltanschauung* (world view) stressed racial superiority, national community, and leadership. His strategic vision for Germany, which he developed between his days in Vienna and his early post-war period in Munich, changed remarkably little over the next twenty-five years—though he combined this immutable end with very mutable means to secure it. Its initial supporters were mainly the Bavarian petty-bourgeoisie (Pine 1997: 23).

By 1922 his world was wholly Manichean in origin; everything was either good or evil, right or wrong, and associated with this fanatically held view was a penchant for the radical over the moderate, which mirrored the ceaseless drift towards rabid extremism. Weber's discussion of charisma suggests that the retention of power by a charismatic requires the perpetual demonstration of success: dynamism not stability had to be the watchword for Hitler's survival (Weber 1978: 1111–57). Thus, if there was an extreme option, Hitler would prefer to take it, because only through extreme measures could his most feared and despised enemy, 'Jewish Bolshevism' manifest in the Soviet Union, be subdued. In his mind it was Jewish Bolshevism that had led to German defeat in the First World War and it was, at least by the middle of May 1923, Hitler's personal quest to ensure that Jewish Bolshevism be eradicated in the coming Second World War. Put simply, Hitler believed that humans naturally formed groups, which were naturally hierarchical, and that an eternal struggle between and within groups was a biological imperative. The 'natural' hierarchy that he invoked led from the very bottom, composed of Jews, to the next rung up, the slavs, to the top, where 'Aryan' or 'Nordic' races prevailed—dominated by German 'Aryans'. Within the German 'Aryan' society a naturally operating law of the jungle would project the Nazis to the top, overlaid by the SS[5] who, in turn, were dominated by him.

The SS originated in 1922–3 as the 'Adolf Hitler Shock Troops'—a personal bodyguard to protect him both from left-wing assailants, and from the Nazis' own SA (*Sturmabteilung* (Storm Troops)), whom Hitler had recognized as an internal threat to his power from their inception. The SA themselves developed as bodyguards for all Nazi speakers and under Röhm developed into a semi-autonomous private army. Indeed, Röhm assumed that one day the SA would replace the German army—hence the strained relations between the organizations even after the Nazi takeover of power.

As far as Hitler was concerned, he had not chosen this 'mission', it had been chosen for him, and, in the characteristic form of a charismatic, he felt he had no option but to accept his 'calling'. Kershaw's conclusion is apt: none of the myriad other ultra right-wing parties, and none of the other Nazis, had Hitler's combination of 'demagogical brilliance, his mobilizing capability, and the unity and all-encompassing "explanatory force" of his ideological vision' (1991: 31).

Yet we must be careful not to be sucked into the maelstrom of personality cults here. Hitler seems to have been an effective speaker, but this does not mean everyone was enamoured of him. Hans Frank, the Nazis' legal expert, certainly was, because the first time he heard Hitler speak he was 'positively spell-bound'. So was the Hitler Youth leader, Baldur von Schirach, who was quickly convinced that Hitler was 'the coming saviour for Germany' (quoted in Kershaw 1991: 33–4). It was not far from this position to the cultivation of the 'Führer Myth': not only was Hitler the saviour of the nation; he could do no wrong and consequently any wrongdoing by the Nazis must have taken place without his knowledge. Herbert Richter, a German diplomat, thought otherwise: 'I immediately disliked him . . . I found him rather comical, with his funny little moustache. I was not at all impressed by him . . . He had a kind of scratchy voice . . . And he shouted so much' (quoted in Rees 1997: 35). Nor does being an 'effective speaker' mean utilizing the kinds of sophisticated linguistic constructions adopted by Martin Luther King (see Chapter 9). Kershaw, for instance, regards his speeches as full of banal platitudes and simplistic explanations, but he reminds us that the words themselves should not be decontextualized (1991: 50–1). On the theatrical stages where Hitler often spoke, with thousands of uniformed party members all holding flaming torches and all carrying huge Swastikas unfurled against a darkening sky, it would have been relative easy for any 'effective' speaker of Hitler's skill, pandering to the worst excesses of the majority, to have whipped the crowd into a frenzy. In the words of one of Hitler's contemporaries: 'All propaganda, according to Hitler, has to limit its intellectual level to the understanding of the most stupid among his audience. Banal "Black against White!" rather than intricate thoughts. . . . The theme must be explosive . . . No wisdom from the council table. Stir up anger and passion and stoke the fire until the crowd go berserk' (quoted in Kershaw 1991: 51).

Hitler, therefore, was uninterested in 'theory'; indeed, he was contemptuous of 'educated intellectuals' and was much more concerned with leadership than with theory: 'For leading means: being able to move masses' (quoted in Kershaw 1991: 51). And that 'movement', the dynamic release of energy, was a clear competitive edge over other parties. What seems to have mattered was not the intellectual ideas underlying Nazism—such as there were any—but the construction of a radical potency, a visceral will to power. Rationality is the last thing we should consider in explaining the attraction of the Nazi party, for 'it was the dynamics of the party, its parades, the ceremonial blessing of banners, the marching columns of the SA, the uniforms, the bands etc., which captured the imagination of the masses' (Broszat, quoted in Welch 1995: 5). Through such measures the Nazis developed their identity as 'the community of the people' (*Volksgemeinschaft*)—the classless and 'partyless' society based on the 1920 party programme *Gemeinnutz geht vor Eigennutz* (common good before the good of the individual) (see Welch 1995: 16). This was markedly different from the conventional conservative political party, yet simultaneously it looked backwards in much the same way that many of its rivals did. This Janus-like ability to appear radically novel and conservatively traditional also differentiated the Nazis from their left-wing enemies. While the Social Democrats looked primarily sideways, in support of the much-decried Weimar Republic, the Communists looked only forward to the new utopia, with little if any regard for the cultural heritage of its supporters.

For Hitler the past, imagined or real, was a treasure trove to be plundered at will in pursuit of the new Germany, and this new identity was best developed by contrasting it to all kinds of mythical forms that threatened to besmirch the new 'Aryans'.[6] In short, solidarity and difference were foremost in his mind: solidarity with his fellow German 'Aryan' warriors (though he was a dark-haired, brown-eyed, Austrian of moderate stature and not the tall, blond, blue-eyed Viking he was besotted with). In his mind: 'All great cultures of the past perished only because the originally created race died out from blood poisoning' (quoted in Kershaw 1991: 28). A direct line ran from this to educational policies that spelled out to children the 'science' of race and eugenics, and from there to the Spartan practice of infanticide. As Hitler claimed in a 1929 rally at Nuremberg: 'If every year Germany had one million children and eliminated 700,000–800,000 of the weakest, the end result would probably be an increase in national strength' (quoted in Welch 1995: 68).

By February 1921, the German Workers' Party was renamed the National Socialist German Workers' Party (Nazi) to appeal to socialist and nationalist supporters. The 'socialist' element was Hitler's interpretation of the trench camaraderie in which class and statuses had been stripped away to leave just 'Germans'. It was 'nationalist' because it opposed all those that opposed the rise of Germany. This conflation of concerns is important, because it enabled Hitler and the Nazis to recruit from a much more heterogeneous—and therefore larger—audience than any 'purist' right-wing party could have done; in effect, it mobilized from below rather than from above (Hobsbawm 1994: 117).

In fact, Nazi support from the urban working class was slim—workers' support for the KPD, and especially the SPD, remained relatively robust—and its main avenues of expansion in the early period were amongst the rural Protestant populations of northern and north-eastern Germany. Its critical feature, according to Berghahn (1987: 11), was its negative philosophy: 'anti-Republican, anti-socialist, anti-Communist, anti-Versailles, anti-Semitic and anti-capitalist (at least anti-large industrial capitalist).'

By August 1921 Hitler was already the Nazis' greatest orator, and violence between the SA and opponents of the Nazis became a frequent occurrence. One such attack occurred in September in the *Löwenbräu* cellar and Hitler was arrested for violent breach of the peace. In January 1922 Hitler was found guilty and sentenced to three months' imprisonment, the minimum possible. The judge, Georg Neithardt, then successfully recommended to a superior court that the sentence be further reduced to one month's prison plus probation.

By November 1923 a crisis in Bavaria over the refusal of the local government to control the Nazi press, and a threat by the Bavarian nationalists to leave the German republic, persuaded Hitler to attempt a putsch in Munich. Hitler led a group of armed SA and *Freikorps* soldiers against von Kahr's nationalists who were holding a meeting in the *Bürgerbräukeller*. The meeting broke up and the following day Hitler led a group of 3,000, including Ludendorff, Himmler, and Göring, to relieve Röhm, who had taken over the War Ministry building with another *Freikorps* unit. When their way was blocked by armed police, one of the police was shot dead, and in the resultant violence fourteen marchers, two of the rebels in the War Ministry building and three policemen, were killed. The Nazi flag, carried at the head of the march, was spattered with blood and became the symbol of the Nazis' first significant action. The *Blutfahne* (Blood Banner) was subsequently used to consecrate the flags of the SA and the SS. The Nazis now had their first martyrs and their first 'holy' relic. One of the martyrs was Ulrich

Graf, who had stepped in front of Hitler to protect him from the police bullets (Williamson 1996: 18).

Hitler stood trial charged with high treason in February 1924 and it looked like the end of the line for the Nazis. It was not. Hitler became a national celebrity after he denied the legitimacy of the court to try him. As he pontificated to the judges:

It is not you who pronounce judgement upon us, it is the eternal court of history which will make its pronouncement upon the charge which is brought against us . . . You may pronounce us guilty a thousand times, but the goddess who presides over the eternal court of history will, with a smile, tear in pieces the charge of the Public Prosecutor and the verdict of this court. For she acquits us. (quoted in Rees 1997: 29–30)

Hitler need not have worried—and probably did not—for one of the judges was his old friend Neithardt. He had already acquired other friends in high places in Bavarian élite circles, within the police and in the military, though outside Bavaria the Nazi party was all but banned for their part in the putsch.

The five-year sentence for high treason was, as he expected, soon commuted to ten months and he wrote *Mein Kampf* (My Struggle) while in prison. But he had also learned something of greater significance: his route *to* power—as opposed to his use *of* power—had to be constitutional. That is to say, to achieve his strategic vision he had to change his organizational tactics so that his opponents could be neutralized, because he could not be certain of dominating them and could not risk a battle of attrition at this stage.

He was released from prison in December 1924, and by February 1925 the Nazi party—which had fallen apart in his absence—was allowed to reform in Bavaria. But the SA, under his arch-rival Röhm, had grown from 3,000 when he entered prison to 30,000 when he left. Hitler quickly removed Röhm from control and formed the SS to ensure his own safety. At this stage the SS was restricted to an élite unit of ten individuals in each district (except in Berlin) whose oath of loyalty was not to the Nazi party but to Hitler personally. The SS were also given custody of the *Blutfahne*—much to the distress of the SA, who responded by demanding a limit on the growth of the SS to no more than 10 per cent of the size of the SA (Williamson 1996: 18–19).

But by then the hyperinflation (which had seen the Mark–dollar parity rise from 4:1 in 1914 to 4.2 trillion:1 in 1923, and which led the Allies to accuse the Germans of deliberately undermining their own economy to devalue the cost of reparations) was long over, and the party receded back to the political margins. However, the isolation provided Hitler with the time to develop a control over the party seldom held by any leader of any party. The decision-making apparatus of the party was simple: Hitler made all the final decisions—he dominated the party. The process for taking an issue to Hitler to be decided was also simple: whoever won the battle of ideas secured the right to take the idea to Hitler for approval or not as the case may be. Darwinian struggle—as Hitler understood it—rooted in the power of might, not rational argument rooted in the power of right, was the essence of the Nazi party, and it was later to become the essence of the Nazi state. As Hitler argued in 1928: 'In this struggle the stronger, the more able, win while the less able, the weak, lose. Struggle is the father of all things . . . It is not by the principles of humanity that man lives or is able to preserve himself above the animal world, but solely by means of the most brutal struggle' (quoted in Rees 1997: 36). Or, as he asserted in the midst of the war in September 1941:

God does not act differently. He suddenly hurls the masses of humanity onto the earth and leaves it to each one to work out his own salvation. Men dispossess one another, and one perceives that, at the end of it all, it is always the stronger who triumphs. Is not that the most reasonable order of things? If it were otherwise, nothing good would ever have existed.   (quoted in Rees 1997: 36)

This is important, because Hitler's own domination of the party rested upon a permanent mobilization for struggle; without struggle—with peace—the Nazis would probably have suffocated on their own inefficiencies. And, as the struggle began visibly to fail, as it did from 1942, the level of Nazi terror over its own population increased to buttress the declining faith in the Führer. Civilian executions, for instance, increased from 339 in 1940 to 1,120 in 1941 and then accelerated in 1942 to 3,393, to 5,684 in 1943, and to 5,764 in 1944 (Berghahn 1987: 169–70). In other words, there could be no 'normalization' period when the traditional German élite took back power from the Nazis, because that élite had itself become mobilized into, not outside of, the system (Kershaw 1994: 204, 207).

Not that the intentions of the Nazis were markedly different from many officers in the *Reichswehr* (Imperial Forces—at this time, the army). In 1926 Colonel Stülpnagel, with the approval of Seeckt (head of the *Reichswehr*), sent an assessment of German foreign policy to the Foreign Office. It asserted the following objectives:

1. liberation of Rhineland and Saar;
2. abolition of the (Polish) corridor and return of Polish Upper Silesia;
3. *Anschluss* (union) of German Austria;
4. abolition of the demilitarized zone;
5. a solution to the 'French problem', by war or peace, to preface European 're-establishment';
6. an inevitable war with the Anglo-American powers (Berghahn 1987: 96).

This more or less directly mirrored Hitler's own concerns and ensured that many officers accepted, if not supported, his intentions. But still the electoral game seemed a long way from a successful conclusion. The general election in May 1928 saw the Nazis secure just 2.6 per cent of the popular vote and it looked as though the battle for survival had sidelined the Nazis for good. However, an agricultural crisis, quickly followed by the 1929 Wall Street Crash and the Depression, changed the contours of German politics back in the Nazis' favour. Dependent as it was on exports, the German economy crumbled under the American-led depression and, in March 1930, with unemployment at three million, Heinrich Brüning of the Catholic Centre Party became Chancellor and inaugurated a strictly deflationary programme that was rejected by the Reichstag (Böhme 1978: 111–12). Brüning responded by enacting Article 48 of the Weimar Constitution, which enabled him to rule by presidential decree (with President Hindenberg's support) and—unnecessarily, given this—Brüning called for new elections in September (Kershaw 1991: 38).

By this time unemployment had reached five million and the election saw the expected rise in support for extremists. The Nazis (who had now swallowed up virtually all the other extreme right groups) secured 18.3 per cent of the vote and the Communist Party also rose in popularity, from 10.6 per cent to 13.1 per cent. Since both extremes were openly anti-democratic we can assume that by this time almost one-third of the German electorate were using their existing democratic vote to vote democracy out of existence. Brüning was well aware of this but tried to use the threat of an extremist *coup*, and the consequent collapse of the German economy, to force Germany's creditors to stop the demand for reparations. Simultaneously he rejected the offer of Social Democratic support in return for a weakening of his anti-inflationary measures, which had, for example, cut the real value of state employees' salaries by 80 per cent. This was against a background where the index of industrial production fell from 100 in 1929 to 58 in 1932, and the value of exports and imports was cut by half (Berghahn 1987: 116, 118). Brüning also rejected the idea of securing Nazi support, since Hitler had now demanded nothing less than the Chancellorship as the price.

But for Brüning's action the Nazis might never have resurfaced as a real threat, but the new election further undermined democratic support for the republic and facilitated the rise of the Nazis and the Communists. With no hope of any majority government, Brüning continued to govern with Hindenberg's blessing until May 1932. But the rash of elections, both for the Reichstag and for the Presidency, ensured that the German population was also permanently mobilized for political gain at the same time as the political system became increasingly centralized around the Chancellor and the President.

Paramilitarism, particularly conducted by and through young men, was the visible icon of this political polarization, with armed and unarmed groups of the left and the right patrolling 'their' territory and 'invading' that of their enemies. The result, as Berghahn suggests, was that an array of radically polarized and militant groups swarmed around the streets without ever appearing to be able to *affect*, let alone *effect*, political policies. The mass of rather young extremists fought for political control of the streets, but real political control lay in the hands of the extremely few and rather old in Berlin (Berghahn 1987: 120–1). Nevertheless, while many groups on the right offered a programme that, in the light of day, was not markedly dissimilar from that of the Nazis, it was the latter who generated the most heat. Their programme was awash with symbols, with flags, with torchlight processions, with energy, and with determination. This was not the politics of doorstep discussion, rather it was the politics of door destruction: the Nazis were nothing if not masters of street theatre. Propaganda in the form of endlessly repeated simplistic solutions to complex problems was the key to power, and emotion not reason was the force that turned the key.

By June 1932 the situation had hardly stabilized and the Lausanne Conference at last recognized the inability of the German economy to continue with reparations and terminated them, but the conference failed to agree to German demands for equality in armaments. When the German delegation walked out in protest, pressure was put on the most reluctant ally, the French, to agree to German demands, which it eventually did in December 1932. As a result, even before Hitler came to power, the rearmament game was already agreed. So indeed was the framework for German expansion, because the German government (still non-Nazi at this time) had agreed to push for the break-up of Poland and the return of all lands ceded at the end of the First World War (Kaplan 1997: 326–8). All Hitler had to do was pick up where his predecessors left off. And, since the French were too weak to act alone against Germany, the Americans were uninterested in European problems, and the British still persisted in their belief that the First World War had been an unnecessary result of an arms race and an unstable alliance system, their collective weakness was not difficult to recognize. In short, while the Allies migrated towards disarmament, the Germans, and not just the Nazis, were heading in the opposite direction. But Hitler could, as yet, not openly flout international agreements and hence demanded that Britain and France disarm immediately to the level of German armament. Since, as he knew, they would not agree to this, he then had an excuse for walking out of the talks (Kaplan 1997: 338). There were many on the Allied side who warned that he could not be trusted, but they were not in power. And, since few bothered to read *Mein Kampf*—and it was not translated into English until 1939—the Germans slid into war at the same time and speed as the British slid in the opposite direction towards peace and appeasement (Kaplan 1997: 426).

The Rise to Power

In May 1932 Hindenberg secured the votes of the Catholic Centre Party and many Social Democrats to defeat Hitler and Thälmann (the Communist candidate) for the Presidency, but the defeat of the political extremists did not undermine extremist violence—which was leaving hundreds dead. In the ensuing Reichstag elections on 31 July 1932, the Nazis secured 37.4 per cent of the vote and 230 seats, making them the largest single party and marking the democratic highpoint of Nazi popularity. Until recently most research has suggested that the vast majority of Nazi voters were the disaffected petty bourgeoisie: the shopkeepers, small business owners, farmers, and so on. However, it now appears that, although the vote of the working classes for the Social Democrats and the Communists remained high, a small minority began to drift towards Nazi support (Crew 1994*a*: 18). However, as Fig. 8.1 suggests, the overwhelming support for the Nazis probably came at the direct expense of the conservative parties, not at the expense of the left or centre.

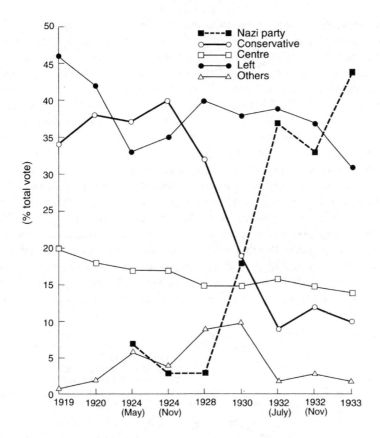

Fig. 8.1. Reichstag elections, 1919–1933
Note: Conservative = DDP, DNVP, DVP, WP; Centre = Z/BVP; Left = SPD, KPD, USPD. (SPD: Social Democratic Party; USPD: Independent Socialists Party; KPD: Communist Party; DDP: Democratic Party; DNVP: Nationalist Party; DVP: People's Party; Z/BVP: Centre Party/Bavarian People's Party; WP: Economy Party.)
Source: Reconstructed from Smith (1979: 22).

The reason seems relatively clear: by 1932 the Nazis had achieved 37 per cent of the vote on the back of the Depression and the consequent mass unemployment. It is important to note here that by 1932 the anti-democratic parties—the Communists and the Nazis—had a majority of the vote, as Fig. 8.2 suggests. And, though we should treat all data with caution (especially the unemployment figures, since they were collected on different premises throughout this period), there is a clear correlation between the trend in unemployment and the trend in anti-democratic voting. In fact, a closer inspection of the data suggests that the most critical link is *not* between Communist voting and unemployment but between Nazi voting and unemployment. Again, we must be wary of the data, but they suggest that only after 1928 did the Nazis pick up support from the effects of unemployment. Even this does not necessarily mean that the worse the crisis became the more likely the unemployed were to vote Nazi, since it may have been the results of the despondent democratic right shifting further right, as Fig. 8.3 suggests. Moreover, the Catholic centre parties retained most of their votes, as did the SPD and KPD. What seems to have happened is that the Nazis captured first the Protestant rural and small-town voter, and subsequently other members of the Protestant middle class (Berghahn 1987: 114). This is rather ironic, since the Nazi propaganda was initially aimed at the urban workers and the agricultural policy was developed only in response to increased support from rural labourers. In almost every large town or city (above 100,000 inhabitants) the Nazis fared consistently more poorly than in the rural areas, villages, and small towns. Since the SPD and the KPD were already active in the cities—and had built up significant organizational loyalties—the Nazis prospered only where no party had previously trodden. But they also secured many votes from the civil service and from the upper middle class. Even some working-class areas were drawn to the Nazis, particularly Protestant workers in parts of Saxony—and it should be remembered that, however limited working-class support was, around 55 per

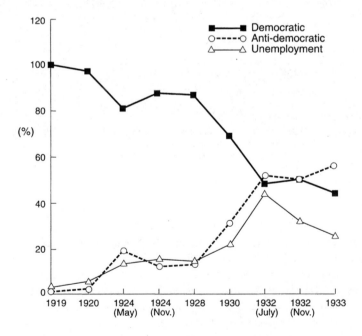

Fig. 8.2. Democracy, votes, and unemployment, Germany, 1919–1933
Note: Democratic = DDP, DNVP, DVP, SPD, USPD, WP, Z/BVP; Anti-democratic = KPD, Nazi.
Sources: Smith (1979); Harman (1982); Furtado (1993); Hodgson (1995).

cent of the SA had working-class origins. By July 1932 around 25 per cent of Nazi voters were working class. Thus, although Nazi support was relatively broad, it remained over-represented amongst Protestants, rural-dwellers, small towns, the older voters, and the lower middle class. In fact, the more the population represented the archetypal factory proletariat, the less likely they were to vote Nazi (Geary 1998). As Beghahn concludes: the 'Germans' did not vote for Hitler; a minority of Germans did, but a majority of Germans voted against democracy. In short, it was not just the Nazis that were the problem; it was those who were theoretically against the Nazis but who failed to act against the Nazis that were also the problem.

Fig. 8.3 suggests that, when we split the anti-democratic votes up between the Communist Party and the Nazi party, it was the Nazis that benefited most from unemployment. Again, this does not mean that *all* the unemployed voted Nazi. On the contrary, many of the unemployed were from the most urban areas and

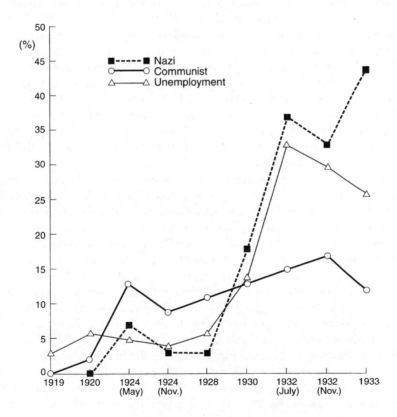

Fig. 8.3. Anti-democratic votes and unemployment, Germany, 1919–1933

Sources: Kendal (1975: 354); Smith (1979); Harman (1982); Berghahn (1987); Furtado (1993); Hodgson (1995); Rees (1997: 61).

voted Communist, while only around 13 per cent voted Nazi. But it may have been that the *threat* of unemployment persuaded the (still) employed middle classes to shift from the traditional right to the Nazis. But whatever the links, and whatever the precise numbers, there was little doubt that by this time Germany had become 'a republic without republicans' (Berghahn 1987: 74). The German military sealed the republic's fate by withdrawing support from Brüning in May 1932. Their preferred option, von Papen, was elected in his place and he immediately lifted the ban on the SA and illegally suppressed the regional Prussian government on 20 July 1932, at this time still operating under a coalition of Social Democrats and the Catholic Centre Party. With the SPD failing to do more than merely protest at von Papen's action, Hitler saw his opportunity and, after the election, saw President Hindenburg on 13 August, when he demanded the right to be Chancellor in place of von Papen. Hindenburg refused, wary of Hitler's extremist intentions. However, by the second election of 1932 Nazi support was waning and the economy starting to recover. As Goebbels wrote in his diary: 'We must come to power in the foreseeable future. Otherwise, we'll win ourselves to death in elections' (quoted in Kershaw 1991: 54).

Von Papen, however, could not provide the kind of right-wing support the élite was looking for and he too was removed in November 1932, to be replaced by Von Schleicher on 2 December. The elections brought yet worse news for the right, because, while the Communists managed to continue their steady growth from 14.6 to 16.8 per cent, the Nazi's vote dropped from 37.4 to 33.1 per cent, despite intensifying the propaganda campaign.[7] The party was in turmoil as its financial base crumbled, and Strasser, leader of the northern Nazis, resigned from the party after Hitler had prevented him from assuming the Reich Vice-Chancellorship offered by Von Schleicher.

Just after the November 1932 election, a petition signed by Schacht, the former head of the national bank, amongst others, appealed to Hindenburg to make Hitler the Chancellor, and Hindenburg, though distrustful of the Nazis, was even more wary of the Communists and confident he could 'box Hitler in' now the latter's popularity was dwindling. In December 1932 the cabinet received a report from the army suggesting that, in the event of civil unrest between the Nazis and the Communists, it would be unable to maintain law and order. The result was a series of secret meetings between von Papen and Hitler, at which von Papen agreed to back Hitler's demand for the Chancellorship, as long as von Papen was made Vice-Chancellor and only two other Nazis entered the cabinet (Göring as Minister without Portfolio and Frick as Minister of the Interior). It was an error that even Ludendorff could see, complaining as he did to President Hindenburg that 'this accursed man will cast our Reich into the abyss and bring our nation to inconceivable misery. Future generations will damn you in your grave for what you have done' (quoted in Kershaw 1998: 377). On 30 January 1933, in a perfectly legal manœuvre, Hitler became Chancellor.

We should be wary of assuming that the depression or mass unemployment inevitably led to a Nazi takeover; neither had led to fascism in the USA and it did not automatically result in Germany either. Indeed, there were several opportunities overlooked or missed. Brüning's action was significant in reviving the Nazis and the Nazi party itself was extremely unstable with a very high turnover of membership. In fact, as Fig. 8.4 suggests, until very late in the day it was virtually non-existent as a political force.

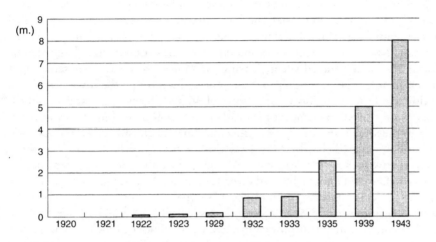

Fig. 8.4. Nazi party membership, 1920–1943

The Communist Party (with an equally volatile membership), then towing the line from Moscow, insisted on treating the Social Democrats as 'Social Fascists', seeing no difference between them and assuming, incredulously with hindsight, that Hitler's inevitable failure would leave room for them to take over. The Social Democrats were equally culpable, preferring the sanctity—and irrelevance—of opposition to the necessarily grubby compromises of power. And the business and social élite thought they could use Hitler to curtail the political left and the trade unions, only to step back into power when they judged it appropriate. They were all manifestly wrong. The establishment had allied itself with the extreme right to gain protection for German civilization from the left; instead it inaugurated the end of German civilization, undermined by the right.

There was nothing inevitable about Hitler's rise to power; by a combination of propaganda and terror he had manipulated his supporters and enemies into a position where his limited political support made him appear susceptible to outside pressure. In short, he inverted the power of his opponents because it appeared that their predominant strength made them, not him, the arbiter of Germany's fate.

His identity as the saviour of the nation was still largely disputed, but his identification of the political left and the Jews as *the* German problem—and the Nazis strategic vision as *the* solution—provided him with the platform to construct a political system and a German identity that would act as a polarizing magnet, dragging half the German population towards him at the same time as the other half were flung into the political and social wilderness.

The Consolidation of Power, 1933–4

The political left was stunned by Hitler's acquisition of legitimate power. A typical episode occurred in Breslau the following day: a protest meeting was called by the Communist Party, but it was broken up by the police, who shot one of the Communists dead. The local Communist Party was subsequently banned. The Social Democrats stayed silent, fearing the same treatment. That same night 50,000 people took part in a pro-Nazi procession through the town centre and within a month an auxiliary police force of SA and SS ensured that the political opposition stayed quiet. By April, Breslau trade-union headquarters was occupied by the SA. The multi-pronged, incremental, and quasi-legal attack upon the opposition ensured that by May 1933 there was no official opposition. More importantly, because the violent assaults upon the opposition appeared uncoordinated, they could not be blamed directly upon the Nazi leadership but had the requisite effect of ensuring their opponents remained cowed, and of keeping the left's leaders isolated from the left supporters (Bessel 1987a: 4–7). Hence, through a subtle concoction of neutralization and attrition, Hitler slipped into power.

Initially the Nazis were far less successful with their attempts to dominate the Jews. Although such assaults had continued in a disorganized way, it soon became clear to Hitler—and more particularly to Hindenberg—that such violence was becoming counterproductive (especially in the light of continuing mass unemployment). Hitler attempted to control the violence by channelling it into a one-day boycott of Jewish businesses, called for 1 April 1933. It was not a great success and further planned boycotts were abandoned, though the SA continued to upset the Nazi leadership by their very visible and violent action. In September 1933 the 120 members of the *Stabswache* (Headquarters Guard) of the SS were retitled the *Leibstandarte* SS Adolf Hitler (SS Bodyguard Regiment Adolf Hitler). They became the forerunner of the *Waffen* (weapons, or armed) SS, and the first armed group that was independent of the Nazi party and bound by their oath of unconditional loyalty to Hitler (Williamson 1996: 22, 32).[8] By this time the SS itself had grown from 2,000 members in 1932 to 30,000 in 1933. But they were still swamped by the SA, now 400,000 strong.

Overwhelmingly young (80 per cent were under 30), with a high proportion of the unemployed and a rapid turnover of membership, the SA were deeply rooted in the macho violence of young men allegedly protecting the 'nation': an unstable unity of tradition and novelty. Similarly, when the Nazis became more firmly established, their development of youth culture, in and beyond the Hitler Youth for boys and the League of German Girls, provided a focus for youth opposition to family control— but always in subordination to the state (Peuket 1987b).[9] Likewise, the National Socialist Organization of Women supported travel and training for women who had previously been confined to village life; thus Nazism appeared to 'liberate' people at the same time as it constrained them (Wilke 1987).[10]

The development of such 'party cultures' was typical rather than unusual in Germany, for until their abolition both the KPD and the SPD had developed strong and extensive 'proletarian cultures' manifest in sports clubs, educational organizations, party newspapers, and political programmes, and the Nazis were careful to mirror and replace these (Berghahn 1987: 85–6). Great emphasis was placed on reaffirming the new German identity at every opportunity and aligning it to Hitler's strategic vision, to the extent that by 1934 the number of radio sets available had increased to six million. By 1939 over 70 per cent of households had a *Volkssempfänger*—a state-subsidized 'People's Receiver'—which could not receive foreign broadcasts, and state broadcasts were replayed through loud speakers in public places, factories, offices, schools, and restaurants. And, while Churchill barely broadcast at all to the British public during the war, Hitler made fifty speeches on radio in 1933 alone. However, it soon became apparent that Hitler's speeches in a recording studio lacked the passion of his public performances and from 1934 he never spoke on radio again directly from a studio; all his performances were live from some public arena or other (Welch 1995: 33–4).

Hitler was also careful to continue the German foreign policy that had been established for many years—and this is one of the reasons that the Allies assumed he was little more than just another Chancellor. But, after a short period of grace, he set about changing Germany with radical intent. Both Hitler and his establishment supporters wanted an end to democracy and an end to communism but Hitler worried about a likely communist *coup* if he pushed immediately for a ban. Instead, he opted for new elections in March, as a method of securing plebiscitary support more than anything else (which indeed it was). He also banned newspapers and demonstrations critical of the government, releasing his supporters onto the streets to terrorize the opposition. The plebiscites were not a means of *demonstrating* support for Hitler; they were a mechanism for *mobilizing* that support. They were, in effect, tools for the construction and confirmation of the new German identity rather than simply means for measuring that identity. Hence it was not coincidental that he held them just after his most significant political successes, especially in foreign affairs (Kershaw 1991: 104–5). And, although many of his supporters were not rabid anti-Semites, he did articulate some of their concerns sufficiently well for them to trust him. In particular, he spoke of a 'people's community', a *Volksgemeinschaft*, a future society that rejected the anti-capitalism of the left but also supplanted the élitism of the traditional right with a new volatile mix of concerns about the community of 'little businessmen', of farmers, of families, of those who achieved success by merit not birth. In pursuit of this mythical identity the Nazis constantly reiterated such phrases as 'One People! One Reich! One Führer!' And the radio, newsreel, and newspapers blitzed the population with calls to help the community in a variety of ways. This involved restricting their diet to a 'one-pot' (*Eintopf*) meal once a week, or collecting food and money for the 'Winter Help' (*Winterhilfe*) programme for the poor and needy, or by attending the subsidized People's Theatre or People's Cinema, or even by saving for the ultimate leveller: the People's Car (*Volkswagen*). Even trade unions, the institutionalized vehicle for the representation of workers' sectional interests, became transformed by the drive for a people's community. Thus by January 1934 the Law for the Ordering of National Labour cemented the Labour Front (DAF) as the sole representative of the workers. 'Within it [DAF] workers will stand side by side with employers, no longer separated into groups which serve to maintain special economic or social distinctions or interests . . . the high aim of the Labour Front is to educate all Germans who are at work to support the National Socialist State and to indoctrinate them in the National Socialist mentality' (quoted in Welch 1995: 55).

The indoctrination buttressed the national community by emphasizing the value of hard and unsavoury jobs (*Adel der schweren Arbeit*), by developing the 'Beauty of Labour' (*Schönheit der Arbeit*) to improve working conditions, and through the 'Strength through Joy' (*Kraft durch Freude*) movement to organize the leisure activities of the workers. Although such policies and programmes may not have persuaded many workers that the new utopia was coming, there is some evidence that they did generate a degree of national solidarity and that the Volkswagen and holiday schemes in particular were immensely popular (Welch 1995: 57–8). And behind the Nazis' industrial policies stood well-known German businesses, such as Volkswagen, Daimler Benz, IG Farben, Siemens, Krupp, Degussa, Allianz, Bertelsmann, and Deutsche Bank, that were unwilling to resist, and apparently happy to profit from, Nazi policies of anti-Semitism and slave labour. Not until 14 December 1999 did sixty-five of the biggest businesses in Germany admit moral responsibility for complicity in Hitler's regime and agree a £3.2 billion fund to compensate their collective victims (Hooper 1999: 15).[11] Of course, the actual policies of the Nazis also supported the élites by smashing the political left and the trade unions and they, in turn, were supposed to have supported the Nazi future, in which class and other divisions between ('Aryan') Germans would disappear in the face of external enemies and internal 'traitors'. Hitler was aided in his quest to remove the internal 'traitors' by the demented actions of van der Lubbe, a Dutch communist who allegedly set fire to the Reichstag on 27 February, giving Hitler the pretext for what he already intended (it was widely believed that the SS set fire to it). Using Article 48 of the Weimar Constitution and the Reichstag Fire Decree, anything deemed to be critical of the new state was banned, and basic rights of association, freedom of assembly, and the press were abolished. Within two months 25,000 political opponents were rounded up and sent to the newly created 'concentration camps', or 'protective custody' as it was called, run by the newly formed units of the SS *Totenkopf*, and by 1939 ten times this number had met the same fate (Berghahn 1987: 131). Generally, though, most prisoners were released after a year or so, providing they agreed not to talk about their experiences or re-engage in political activity deemed to be against the state, and by 1937 only around 7,500 inmates remained (Kershaw 1991: 75).

In March 1933 the Nazis took 44 per cent of the vote, which was a relatively poor showing given Goebbel's exploitation of the national radio and the terror the Nazis had imposed on the opposition (fifty-one anti-Nazis were killed). This control was further enhanced by the Enabling Act, which virtually gave Hitler *carte blanche* over the future of Germany. It was also the main reason for calling the election in the first place, since it freed the Chancellor from dependence on the President and legalized a dictatorial regime intent on silencing all opposition. For a short while the Nazis were forced to continue a coalition with the German National People's Party, but the parliamentary façade did not last long. In practice, the Communist Party was finished, although it was never banned, because all the deputies and about half its membership (150,000) were imprisoned or murdered.

One might have expected the *Reichswehr* not to intervene; after all, Hitler promised to restore their honour and their power, and—unless the threat came from the left—they prided themselves on being an apolitical and professional military service (Fest 1997: 18–22, 38). But the 250,000 members of the *Reichsbanner*, the paramilitary force of the SPD, held no such view. Indeed, they had trained for precisely such an eventuality when the extreme right overthrew democracy. Yet they too stood back waiting for the call to the barricades from Otto Wels, their leader, but they waited in vain. The SPD leadership simply did not know what to do, because Hitler had achieved power legitimately and all the plans of the left were premised upon him seizing power illegitimately. A mass demonstration was called in the Lustgarten in Berlin on 30 January, but it lacked the spectacle of the Nazis' victory parades, and the pessimism of the speakers did little to mobilize their defences; Wels merely assured them that 'harsh rulers don't last long' (quoted in Fest 1997: 34). By February 1933 the first resignations from the SPD had already begun (Fest 1997: 22, 29). The KPD's equivalent paramilitary force, the *Rotfrontkämpferbund*, even switched sides to support the Nazis following the Comintern line against the 'true' enemy of the workers: the 'Social Fascist', otherwise known as the SPD. On 1 May the trade unions, whose general strike in Munich in 1923 had helped destroy Hitler's putsch, also stood aside, swore allegiance to Hitler, and were persuaded to march with their new masters in a new National Workers' Holiday parade. The very next day they were abolished. Hitler was himself surprised at the 'miserable collapse' of his opponents and he was evidently expecting some form of backlash, but the left had immobilized itself in defence of legitimate political activity and that immobility soon turned to mortality. Perhaps Hitler might have echoed the words of Rosa Luxemburg's, the murdered victim of the last right-wing pogrom in 1918: 'Where is the German proletariat?' It was frozen by its own tactical failure, which had been derived from a strategic vision that imagined Hitler could achieve power only illegitimately. Two months later the SPD was banned, followed by the liberal parties, the DDP and the DVP, and, in June, the Catholic and Centre parties, the Z/BVP, followed suit. They had all been neutralized.

The Vatican even reached a Concordat with Hitler that stated that no Catholic clergy would involve themselves in political activity.[12] The Protestant Church split, with the majority reaching a similar position to the Catholic Church, while a minority, under Pastor Martin Niemöller, vigorously denounced the regime. By the middle of July 1933 the Nazi party was the only legal party left and within six months even the local administrations had lost their power.

The takeover of power was constitutional but it was far from peaceful: at every level of political and civilian administration the existing authorities were forcefully evicted and replaced by Nazis within a month, and by October 1933 26,000 people had been arrested. Far worse, the SA—now numbering three million—erected torture chambers around the country and between 1933 and 1945 225,000 people were charged with political offences and 27,000 German citizens were executed for treason against the state, as were twenty thousand German soldiers (Berghahn 1987: 170). After 1939 no trial was legally necessary and on 26 April 1942 the last meeting of the Reichstag agreed that formal laws could not bind Hitler, as the new supreme head of justice. But the fact remains that Hitler's acquisition of the legal trappings of state was itself legal; he did not need to loose the SA onto the opposition to attain power—they let him take it. This did not mean that Hitler intended to provoke his supporters to yet further violence. On the contrary, the continuation of terror tactics on the streets of Germany, especially by the SA, was beginning to test the patience of both the business establishment and the army leadership—which had been treated with kid gloves so far. Röhm, the leader of the SA, had already openly talked of a second revolution to merge the army and the SA, and chafed at the way Hitler seemed to prefer the support of the existing élites in the *Reichswehr* to the new radicals of the SA that had carried him to power. Thus, when Röhm declared that 'the SA will be the arbiters of Germany's fate', Hitler determined to remove him (quoted in Winston 1997: 25). Himmler, then the leader of the SS, concocted a story about Röhm planning a *coup*, and on 30 June 1934 Röhm and between 85 and 1,000 (depending on the source) of the SA leadership were murdered in the 'night of the long knives' at Hitler's command by the SS and Gestapo (*Geheime Staatspolizei*—Secret State Police). Included in the casualty list were von Bredow and von Schleicher, two army generals, and one consequence was that the SA was now clearly subordinate to the SS in general, and Hitler in particular. A second consequence was that not only did Hitler now appear to have saved the nation from the untrammelled violence of the SA, but the *Reichswehr* had proved itself unwilling to intervene against him, even when he murdered their own leaders. The *Reichswehr* stayed clear of the event because they were only too pleased to see the SA subordinated to them, but they failed to see that their own action also put them subordinate to the SS.

Hitler carefully nurtured his relationship with the *Reichswehr* by paying the SS through the police budget and by ensuring that the *Waffen* SS never expanded beyond 10 per cent of the size of the army. And, while the physical requirements for membership of the SS were higher than those for the army, and their age was slightly higher, the educational requirements were lower. Indeed, many of the *Waffen* SS recruits were rural-dwellers, though most of the army's recruits were from the urban areas (Williamson 1996: 36). Initially Hitler was unsure about the military value of the *Waffen* SS, but after their role in the assault on France, and more particularly their successes in Russia, he agreed to an expansion of their divisional strength from the three existing units: *Leibstandarte Adolf Hitler*, *Das Reich*, and *Totenkopf* (Goldin 1998: 29–30).

What the army also failed to recognize was the difference in their respective approaches to violence: the *Reichswehr* prided itself on exclusive control over institutional violence for the protection of the state; the Nazis in general, and the SS in particular, wanted the protection of the *Reichswehr* to institutionalize the violent expansion of the state. Once again, Hitler had managed to invent a situation that would facilitate the identification of the Nazis and himself with order and stability not terror and instability.

Shortly afterwards Hitler pulled off yet another *coup*, this time wearing the uniform of the SA and identifying himself as one of them, not one different from them. Speaking before 97,000 SA men at Luitpold Stadium, he insisted that personal loyalty to him was the only way to ensure their domination. In fact a system of personal oaths to Hitler was then established, not by Hitler but by Field Marshal Blomberg in an attempt to ingratiate himself and the army to Hitler. This unconstitutional move (because the Oath Act of 1 December 1933 required oaths to be sworn to the office of leader not the individual incumbent of the office), was the act that many German soldiers, sailors, airmen, and even civil servants (who were required to give the 'Heil Hitler' salute from 1933) believed bound them irrevocably to the fate of Hitler. By 1939, with his opponents silent, exiled, or dead, he was able to relax, secure in the knowledge that, at last, a majority of those Germans left would have been either active or passive supporters or else of no significance (Fest 1997: 51–5; Kershaw 1991: 70–89).

How had Hitler managed this astonishing success? Of particular importance was that Hitler had learned from the past and the left had not. Thus, what neither the unions nor the political left had trained for was precisely what Hitler had planned: a legitimate and (relatively) peaceful transfer of power. Of course, thereafter, violence became an everyday occurrence, but Hitler had broken no law in acquiring power, so how could the left justify breaking the law to seize power from him? In Fest's profound oxymoron, the ' "legal revolution" dumbfounded not only Hitler's opponents but his allies as well' (Fest 1997: 11). The army could now revert to course with their claims of political impartiality and so could the civil service. As for the rest of the population, notwithstanding a substantial minority of anti-Nazis, the last fourteen years of the Weimar Republic seemed to have brought little of comfort to the middle classes ruined by the hyperinflation, or to the unemployed stilted by the Depression, or to the nationalists, still smarting for the shame and ignominy of the Versailles Agreement. It must indeed have seemed that democracy, after the defeats in Spain and Italy, was being confined to the dustbin of history: the future was national unity under

Nazism. The conservative right, of course, particularly von Papen, assumed they would be able to control Hitler, but they were as arrogantly wrong as the left. But the past also belonged to the Nazis, because their propaganda reiterated the yearning for a return to the stable and authoritarian unity of the past. Before Weimar, had not Germany prospered under Bismarck's stern conservative gaze? Only the Nazis merged past and future together in a heady mix of romantic myth and utopian alternative. That neither the past nor the future was anything like the invented or constructed model proclaimed by Hitler and Goebbels was less relevant than the yearning by a significant proportion of the German population for such a concoction (Fest 1997: 19).

Political Darwinism and Political Tropism: Working towards the Führer

With Hindenburg's death on 2 August 1934, Hitler now combined the Presidency and the Chancellorship in one office under the new nomenclature, the Führer. Yet the concentration of power led not to a ruthlessly efficient government machine but to the growth of jungle warfare, as 'turf disputes' between different individuals and rival departments were actively encouraged by Hitler (Bartov 1994: 44). Otto Dietrich, Hitler's press chief, captured the result well; 'in the twelve years of his rule in Germany, Hitler produced the biggest confusion in government that had ever existed in a civilized state' (quoted in Rees 1997: 57). However, the internal confusion was also a manifestation of the radically dynamic element of the state: there was confusion, but it was a confusion born of the energy with which the various individuals and groups competed in a Darwinian struggle of survival to fulfil their own, and the Führer's, dreams.

Undertaking no more than a couple of hours' work a day, Hitler contrived to let the war of the fittest resolve all subordinate problems, and, as long as the resultant victor produced a policy that was in alignment with his general intention, that policy would prevail. Kershaw (1991: 8) confirms this in the words of Werner Willikens, State Secretary in the Ministry of Food, in a speech on 21 February 1934: 'it was the duty of everybody to try to work towards the Führer along the lines he would wish.' This point is crucial, for

the destructive and self-destructive nature of Nazism cannot be reduced to Hitler's own personal drive to destruction . . . It was 'immanent' to the system of Nazism . . . Without a readiness widespread among many who were by no means convinced or avid Nazis to 'work'—directly or indirectly—"towards the Führer", the peculiar form of personalized power exercised by Hitler would have been devoid of social and political foundations.' (Kershaw 1991: 194)

In other words, as long as subordinates operated in a relatively 'tropic' manner— that is, in response to the assumed direction of the source of light and power (Hitler)—their freedom to develop policy was considerable. This was reinforced by Hitler's antipathy towards administration: he preferred watching American western films to developing the minutiae for organizing civil life. Rees describes how this led to the development of the euthanasia programme in 1939, not because Hitler had always planned it, but because the father of a disabled child wrote to Philipp Bouhler at the Office of the Chancellery of the Führer asking for his son to be 'put down' (Rees 1997: 80–5). Knowing Hitler's attitude to racial purity, manifest in the existing laws introduced in 1934[13] and legitimizing compulsory sterilization of between 200,000 and 350,000 [14] gypsies, alcoholics, and the mentally ill, Bouhler suggested a system for medical examination and 'termination' for the mentally disabled, and this became state policy (Noakes 1987). None the less, in response to a sermon by Bishop Galen on 3 August 1941, which revealed that German citizens were being murdered by the state, public protest, especially in Westphalia and particularly in Münster, effectively—if temporarily—halted the euthanasia programme on 24 August (Welch 1995: 71). But by the end of the war only 5,000 German gypsies remained alive, and 500,000 from elsewhere in Europe had been murdered, as had 71,000 Germans with mental disabilities of various kinds. These were initially killed by the 'T4' group using gas— the system subsequently adopted to eliminate the Jews when the T4 group was transferred from Germany to Poland (Berghahn 1987: 168; Hodgson 1995: 206, 208).

By 1935 the Nuremberg Laws prevented Jews from holding citizenship of Germany, and from marrying 'Aryans', but by 1937 only 120,000 of Germany's original 503,000 Jews had left the country. By 1938, though, with the economy expanding rapidly, the large German industrial concerns pushed Hitler to 'Aryanize' the rest of the economy, and by the end of the year Hitler had banned all Jewish firms from receiving state contracts and all Jewish professionals from working with 'Aryan' clients. Eventually, all Jews were forced to sell their businesses to 'Aryan' competitors. By 1939 a further 78,000 had left, but the annexation of Austria increased the number of Jews by a further 190,000 and the occupation of Poland brought still more under German tutelage (Carr 1987).

Educational policy, which had remained vigorously nationalistic even during the Weimar period (Craig 1981: 423–4), became even more subservient to the interests of the Nazis. In Hitler's words: 'No boy or girl must leave school without having been led to an ultimate realization of the necessity and essence of blood purity' (quoted in Pine 1997: 23). Almost immediately Jewish children were excluded from school and Nazi philosophy quickly seeped into the lessons. For example, a 1941 textbook stated:

Everyday, the state spends RM 6 [Reich Marks] on one cripple; RM 4.25 on one mentally-ill person; RM 5.50 on one deaf and dumb person; RM 5.60 on one feeble-minded person; RM 3.50 on one alcoholic; RM 4.80 on one pupil in care; RM 2.05 on one pupil at a special school; and RM 0.45 on one pupil at a normal school.

1. What total cost do one cripple and one feeble-minded person create, if one takes a life-span of forty-five years each?
2. Calculate the expenditure of the state for one pupil in a special school, and one pupil in an ordinary school, over eight years and state the amount of higher cost engendered by the special school pupil.   (quoted in Pine 1997: 27)

One might not expect such overt propaganda to make headway against the usual recalcitrant youth, but it seems to have had some effect. As one German remembers:

> No one in our class ever read *Mein Kampf*... On the whole we didn't know much about Nazi ideology. Even anti-Semitism was brought in rather marginally at school ... Nevertheless, we were politically programmed: to obey orders, to cultivate the soldierly 'virtue' of standing to attention and saying 'Yes, Sir', and to stop thinking when the magic word 'Fatherland' was uttered and Germany's honour and greatness were mentioned. (quoted in Peukert 1987*b*: 27)

Such an approach was doubtless helped by the popularity of the Nazis with the teaching profession: by 1937 the National Socialist Teachers' League (NSLB) represented over 95 per cent of all teachers (Welch 1995: 61). Since membership was virtually compulsory anyway, this was hardly a surprising proportion—but it was still possible to resign from teaching. With the Hitler Youth such a strong organization, we might suggest that at least some of these teachers were more concerned about being 'turned in' by their pupils for disloyalty as much as any predilection for Nazism, but this is the point: the absence of overt resistance allowed the regime to flourish and to take ever-more radical and diabolical steps. Yet this should not divert our attention from the main point: the vast majority of teachers 'volunteered' their support by remaining in post. At the level of government officials and ministers a similar phenomenon occurred. In effect, it was not a case of Hitler directly coercing individuals to develop and enact policies but the opposite: Hitler's subordinates, of their own volition, volunteered policies that they thought he would approve of. This was not simply a consequence of Hitler's lack of interest; he positively encouraged—that is, constructed—rampant competition by developing overlapping functions and thus remained the only person with any clear idea of the overall state of the government (Geyer 1987). Kershaw (1991: 113) suggests: 'Hitler was thus paradoxically the indispensable linchpin of the governmental apparatus, but at the same time largely detached from and scarcely involved in its deliberations.' For example, once he had become Chancellor he had five private offices:

- Office of the Reich Chancellery, under Hans-Heinrich Lammers;
- Office of the Chancellery of the Führer, under Philipp Bouhler;
- Office of the Presidential Chancellery, under Otto Meissner;
- Office of the Hitler's Personal Adjutant, under Wilhelm Brückner;
- Office of the Führer's Deputy, under Martin Bormann.

A parallel development occurred in the activities of the Gestapo. The common assumption may be one close to Orwell's *1984*, in so far as the ever-present eyes and ears of the state authorities cowered all opposition underground. 'Never before,' suggested Jacques Delarue's *History of the Gestapo*, 'in no other land and at no other time, had an organization attained such a comprehensive penetration (of society), possessed such power and reached such a degree of "completeness" in its ability to arouse terror and horror, as well as in its actual effectiveness' (quoted in Mallmann and Paul 1994: 169–70). In Mallmann and Paul's (1994: 169–70) terms, the Gestapo appeared to be: 'omniscient, omnipotent and omnipresent'. But, as *1984* suggests, it is the denouncement of 'traitors' and 'enemies of the state' by ordinary people, by neighbours and children, that makes the system work. That 'system' was supported by the 'Malicious Practices Act' of 1933, which made offensive or subversive remarks about the state a criminal offence. But, as Gellately makes clear, there were simply not enough Gestapo officials to spy on and terrorize the civilian population—their work had to be undertaken through the voluntary denunciations of 'ordinary' Germans (Gellately 1991). Since the Gestapo records in all but three towns were destroyed at the end of the war, we have little to go on in evaluating this, but, if we assume that *Würzburg* is representative, then 80 per cent of the 18,000 files collected on people between 1933 and 1945 are unsolicited denunciations by non-members of the Nazi party. The 'myth' of Gestapo domination was, of course, perpetrated by the regime to enhance its control and, in and through this, it did indeed assume greater power: if no one can be trusted, the construction of organized opposition becomes extraordinarily difficult—even if there is a collective hatred for the regime. In fact, there does not seem to have been this collective hatred. Rather, as Hitler was well aware, terror was not sufficient to rule; the people needed an idol to identify with, and he was that idol (Kershaw 1994: 202). It is under these circumstances that we should understand Franz Vogt, a former Social Democratic Party deputy, who suggested in 1936 that 'one must assume that, in each factory, there is at least one informer for every twelve of fifteen workers' (quoted in Mallmann and Paul 1994: 168). Suspicion alone would have been sufficient to deter many people from resistance.

Such an assumption also protected the political left from admitting what was the uncomfortable truth: the Nazi regime persisted through consent at least as much as through coercion. Given that a typical region like the Western Ruhr and Lower Rhine contained four million people but only 281 Gestapo agents, this would have meant not one agent for about every fourteen people but one for every 14,000 people. Naturally, there would have been many more unpaid informers, but this is the point: the fabric of the Gestapo rested on the façade of professionalism and—to those who believed themselves under observation—an unknown and unknowable number of voluntary denouncers. In Düsseldorf, for instance, only 15 per cent of all proceedings resulted from observations of Gestapo employees or paid informers. In Würzburg almost two-thirds of cases concerned with 'race pollution' came from private denunciations and only one case came directly from Gestapo agents. Indeed, the number of 'crimes' increased so rapidly that the Gestapo began having problems coping with the paperwork. Heydrich (Himmler's assistant) even threatened to send false denouncers to the concentration camps to curb the enthusiasm of the civilian population for denouncing their neighbours.[15]

By 1935 virtually all significant internal opposition to Hitler had been silenced. As a report from the then exiled Social Democratic Party revealed, the great strength of the Nazis was that they had disorganized the opposition. The same went for the cabinet: with fewer and fewer meetings, and Hitler refusing to intervene between disputing parties (on the grounds that the stronger would win eventually), by 1939 there was virtually no one left to dispute, caution, or advise Hitler.

Political and Military Adventurism with a 'race of carnivorous sheep'

In return for his support in achieving power, Hitler made Schacht the Minister of Economics in 1934, and it was through his deficit financing of rearmament that the long decline into mass unemployment was reversed. Hitler had little knowledge or interest in economics, he simply gave Schacht his requirements and assumed that they would be complied with, and chief amongst these requirements was the provision of funds to rearm the *Reichswehr*. For many Germans, especially soldiers, the reconstruction of the armed forces was an essential stepping stone to reversing the shame of Versailles, but for Hitler it was a bridge to the Russian steppes. In *Mein Kampf* he talked of the need for *lebensraum* (living space) for the German population. In essence this argument again centred on his interpretation of Darwin. Since resources were allotted to populations on the basis of their might not their right, it was the right of the German population to take over whatever land they needed. Most of this lay in the East—as he made abundantly clear in his *Second Book*, sometimes referred to as his *Secret Book*, because, although written in 1928, it was not published in his lifetime. 'We must stop the endless German movement to the south and west, and turn our gaze towards the land in the east . . . If we speak of soil in Europe today, we can primarily have in mind only *Russia* and her vassal border-states.'

There were, of course, considerable tracts of land to the west, in France, which would have to be defeated first before the Russian expansion began. And in Britain, but Hitler believed that the British—or the English, as he referred to them—were almost on a par with the Germans in terms of their racial purity and superiority. Hitler had wanted a non-aggression pact with Britain from 1933, with the German empire facing east and dominating the European continental land mass while the British faced west, controlling the seas and a colonial empire. Initially, Hitler seems to have considered 'the east' only in terms of Austria and Czechoslovakia, but later his attention would be turned towards the Slavic peoples of the Soviet Union. Not only did Hitler regard them as infinitely inferior to the 'Aryan' nations; they were also communist to boot and allegedly led by Jews. The solution to both problems was simple: if the Soviet Union was destroyed, so would be communism and the Jews, and the victory would provide all the land that Germany needed.

In the beginning this seemed to work: in 1935 an agreement signed by Eden and Ribbentrop, on the British government's assumptions about the pacifism of its electorate, allowed the German navy to reach 35 per cent of the British surface fleet and to equal the submarine fleet (Rees 1997: 87–96). Since the British had signed the agreement without French knowledge, the latter naturally experi-enced the episode as yet another blow to allied unity. However, Schacht was well aware that deficit finance to support public works and defence spending, in the long run, would generate high levels of inflation and unfulfilled consumer demand; in the medium term the Nazi economy would simply disintegrate. For Hitler the medium term was unimportant, what mattered was strengthening the German military *now*, because, by 1938, with the Nazi sympathizer Edward VIII gone from the British throne, an Anglo-German pact looked doubtful. Moreover, with unemployment down from six million when he had taken office to under one million, his economic reforms appeared little short of a miracle and his popular standing in Germany appeared extremely high. In fact, real wages rose little during this period and support for the Nazis from the industrial work-ers, as measured by the Nazi German Labour Front (DAF), increased little, though the cultural and sporting facilities provided through DAFs derivative, the 'Strength through Joy' movement (KdF), was rather better received.[16] However, other social groups, especially state employees, the middle classes, professionals, and the self-employed (though not the farmers), did much better. With the index of industrial production increasing from 66 in 1933 to 132 in 1939, assisted by cheap credit, industrialists also became firm supporters of Hitler, especially those involved in his major economic concern: rearmament and the mobilization of the economy and society for war (Berghahn 1987: 140–5). Thus the identity of het-erogeneous groups became channelled through the Nazis—one did not need to be a Nazi to find reasons to support them. However, the closer the relationship between such groups and the Nazis became, the more their identities became irre-deemably locked together. For example, both Auto-Union and Krupp became directly implicated in the Nazi war machine, because keeping mobilization secret from the Allies was a little difficult. But with the help of industry—such as Auto-Union's production of 'lorries', which were, in fact, military vehicles, and Krupp's development of 'agricultural tractors', which were actually tanks—it generally worked well.

In 1936 Hitler's four-year plan involved mobilizing for the very war that the rearmament programme needed to pay for itself. Without apparently plotting to radicalize his relatively conservative cabinet, Hitler (always a political oppor-tunist) removed his Minister of Defence, Blomberg (known to his subordinates as the 'rubber lion'), after his newly married wife was discovered to have posed for pornographic photographs. Hitler also sacked his army commander, Fritsch, after Göring framed him on charges of homosexuality. Without these two the next layer of the military hierarchy was easily removed and sixty generals either resigned or were moved. In Hitler's words, he wanted his military leaders to be 'mastiffs who had to be held fast by the collar lest they hurl themselves on every-one . . . [instead] I'm the one who always has to urge these dogs on' (quoted in Rees 1997: 105). Hitler then abolished Blomberg's position as War Minister and his office, and, at Blomberg's suggestion, appointed himself commander-in-chief of the armed forces in the new office of the *Oberkommando der Wehrmacht*

(OKW) led by Wilhelm Keite. As usual, Hitler then set the OKW against the OKH (*Oberkommando des Heeres*), the high command of the army. Blomberg protested that Keitel was merely an office manager, to which Hitler replied: 'That's just the kind of man I need . . . a man with the brain of a movie usher' (quoted in Fest 1997: 62). Hitler had, at last, divested himself of the need for élite support—and, in particular, army support, led as it was by what he called 'cowards'; he was, in reality, what he had been creating for many years: the Führer.

Having secured his domestic position, Hitler was now ready to take on his international enemies. He openly admitted that Germany had an airforce and announced, contrary to the Versailles Treaty, that Germany would conscript an army of 550,000 soldiers—that is, one larger than the French. In October 1935 Mussolini invaded Abyssinia and asked Hitler for help transporting his troops. At first Hitler assumed that the British would simply block the Suez Canal and force Mussolini to back down; but when they did not, he had the green signal for an adventure of his own: the remilitarization of the Rhineland. On 7 March 1936 Hitler marched around 36,000 soldiers and police in—though General Gamelin, commander of the French army, estimated their numbers at over a quarter of a million. In fact the French and Belgian army had three times the numbers of the Germans, and the large Czech and Romanian armies had also offered to assist in any allied move against Germany, but none came and yet another opportunity to stop the behemoth wilted.

The demilitarized Rhineland had effectively prevented any kind of instant assault upon France, Belgium, or the Netherlands, whilst simultaneously keeping Germany open to French attack, and for Hitler 'the forty-eight hours after the march into the Rhineland were the most nerve wracking in my life. If the French had then marched into the Rhineland we would have had to withdraw with our tails between our legs, for the military resources at our disposal would have been wholly inadequate for even a moderate resistance' (quoted in Kagan 1997: 360–1). In the event, neither France nor Britain had any intention of taking military action against the German move and both simply hoped that it would mark the limit of German expansion. In short, they had misread the new German identity: it was not a harmless sheepdog masquerading as a wolf to protect its flock of sheep, it was a wolf masquerading as a sheepdog, and a wolf content to sacrifice its flock of sheep if necessary. In effect, German aggression had won the day, Hitler had invented the future.

The mood in Britain was certainly not bellicose, for, as a taxi-driver allegedly commented to Eden, 'I suppose Jerry can do what he likes with his own back garden, can't he?' (quoted in Kagan 1997: 359). Kagan is adamant that a vigorous response to Hitler at this time, while not resolving the problem of Germany, would have humiliated the Führer and mortally wounded his public standing, but, as a result of weak leadership on the part of the British and the French, Hitler's audacious move went unchecked. We should note at this point that the wolf's identity was still forming—and, had Hitler's bluff been called, his identity would have been shown to be markedly less confident than it appeared in public.

But the negotiable nature of that identity rapidly congealed as a direct result of the Anglo-French vacillation. He cowed both his external and internal enemies and he could now plan for his final assault upon all of them.[17]

Yet paradoxically, Hitler, now aware that his rearmament's programme was critically reducing the supply of raw materials to the economy, was forced to push Germany towards autarky in preparation for war. In August 1936 General Fromm, head of the General Army Office, argued that at the end of this period, when rearmament was completed, the choices available to Germany would be reduced to two: either use the armaments in war to recoup the costs in booty and reparations from the defeated enemies or roll back the *Wehrmacht* (as the *Reichswehr* was now called) and allow civilian spending to displace it (Berghahn 1987: 154–5). Like most of the officer corps, Fromm was not against military expansion; the only difference between this group and Hitler was the officers' fears that Hitler would precipitate a crisis and drag them into war before they could be certain of success. For them it was just *when* not *if* Germany should embark upon a war of revenge and expansion. But for Hitler the situation was intimately configured through the relative will of the combatants. In his mind, and rightly at first, the will of the Allies to go to war over the reoccupation of the Rhineland, over Austria, and over Czechoslovakia was irredeemably weak. He underestimated their resolve in Poland—though it made no immediate difference. However, this prescient strength of will was also Hitler's major weakness, because, when he came up against the British and more particularly the Soviet Union, their will and ability to resist more than matched his will to succeed—and at this point the economic and military limits of the German war machine became ever more evident.

On 5 November 1937 Hitler called his chiefs of staff together and told them that he intended to secure 'living space' for the German people in the east. There was little need to explain why this was necessary—it was simply part of the Darwinian struggle of the fittest for survival. But note how such a rationale was seldom applied in retrospect to Germany's defeat in the First World War: the Allies had won only because of the traitorous acts of Jews and communists at home, not because the German nation had shown itself to be weaker than its neighbours.

The 'rightful' reassertion of German superiority would have to be achieved by 1943–5, because after that Germany's military efficiency would decline in line with its economy. The strategy, if not the tactics, had been declared in *Mein Kampf*, but by this time Hitler had realized that an alliance with Britain was no longer possible. The concern of Fritsch, Blomberg, and Neurath, his military leaders, that Germany was not ready to fight a war to acquire Austria and Czechoslovakia was dismissed by Hitler. After all, the British and French had not intervened in the occupation of the Rhineland and he did not think they would do so over these two adventures either.

Four months later, on 8 March 1938, after Hitler's increasing demands for integration of Austria into Germany, the Austrian Chancellor Schuschnigg announced a plebiscite for the Austrian population to decide the issue. But Hitler coerced him into dropping the scheme, after securing an agreement from Mussolini that Italy would not object (as it had done after a (failed) *coup* attempt by the Austrian Nazi party in 1934). Several days of indecision and panic on Hitler's part preceded the decision to enter Austria and it was Göring (always more concerned with German political and economic domination than the ideological extremes that drove Hitler) who ordered the army in. On 12 March Hitler, having driven past many broken-down German vehicles on the way, paraded through Vienna to an ecstatic reception. That ecstasy did not include the 76,000 people arrested, primarily Austrian Jews who were almost instantly attacked and humiliated by Austrian civilians and German soldiers alike. By the summer of 1938 one-third of Vienna's Jews had been expelled or left voluntarily. The French and British were alarmed, but, as Hitler had gambled, unwilling to intervene. Churchill was also alarmed and demanded collective action to prevent an even greater catastrophe brought on by Hitler's acquisition of the 'gateway' to Europe, but his interpretation of what would stop Hitler bore no fruit amongst the barren Anglo-French orchard.

Czechoslovakia was a little more difficult for Hitler. Three million ethnic Germans in Sudetenland had been enclosed when the state was formed after the First World War, and Hitler regarded it as a political insult to have ethnic Germans ruled by what he regarded as mere slavs. Hitler encouraged the Sudeten Germans to adopt the new greater German identity and to agitate for a return to German sovereignty, and he ordered their leader, Henlein, to demand conditions that the Czechs would not be able to accept and thus be provoked into war. The Czechs had defence agreements with the French and the Soviet Union, but the Soviets refused to intervene without the French and the French demanded British assistance. Once again military assessments of the forces exaggerated the strength of the Germans and grossly underestimated those available to help the Czechs. Even General Beck, Commander-in-Chief of the German army, resigned in protest at the imminent war that he (and every other general) assumed Germany could not win. Again, we should reinforce the point that the officers' concerns and Beck's resignation were not because they disagreed with Hitler's intentions, or that this would inevitably lead to war; rather, they feared that the kind of war Hitler would provoke would be one that they could not win. In fact, it is not self-evident that Hitler wanted a *world* war; what he wanted was a war to ensure German supremacy on continental Europe (westwards and then eastwards), possibly followed by an attack upon Afghanistan, Africa, and India. Once this was secure, a war against the Anglo-American powers was, in his mind, probably inevitable (Berghahn 1987: 155, 159).

The new French leader, Daladier, was of the same opinion as the German generals—Hitler could and must be stopped. He warned Chamberlain that Hitler could be stopped only by collective force, but the British Prime Minister was adamant that peace must be preserved at all costs—after all, he argued, Britain (as a direct consequence, amongst other things, of Chamberlain's own appeasement policy) was too weak to defeat Germany. In fact, even the German officers who had been plotting to overthrow Hitler if he declared war had pleaded with the British that only a show of force could stop him, but the British were uninterested in this, let alone in helping the plotters. After all, as Hugh Dalton had said, were not all German conservatives little more than 'a race of carnivorous sheep?' (quoted in Fest 1997: 78).

A week later Daladier received a report from General Gamelin that the French could not achieve victory against the Germans either and thus intervention was ruled out. Hence, as the war approached, the common assumption amongst many on all sides was that no one could win. Without consulting his Cabinet, Chamberlain flew to meet Hitler on 15 September in Berchtesgaden, returning with a face-saving (for the British and French) agreement that a plebiscite would be held, just in Sudentenland, to evaluate the wishes of the Sudentenlanders. The French accepted the position, as long as Britain supported France in guaranteeing the integrity of the rest of the Czech state, and the Czech government, under Beneš, was shamefully forced to accept the dismemberment of its own country on 21 September. Chamberlain then flew to Hitler in Bad Godesberg to present him with the text of the agreement, but Hitler had already recognized the weakness of the Allies and simply upped his demands to an immediate German occupation of the area. Chamberlain was still willing to negotiate to avoid conflict, but the Czech government mobilized for war and France insisted that it would support it—and expected likewise from the British—if the Czech government refused Hitler's ultimatum. Chamberlain was still convinced he could deal with Hitler, but he agreed to the French demand and both countries began to mobilize for war. Hitler ordered his troops to the borders with Czechoslovakia and the second motorized division was required to pass by the Chancellery building on Wilhelmstrasse in Berlin to mobilize the masses for war. But no rapturous crowds appeared to cheer them on and Hitler was, apparently, visibly shaken by his miscalculation of public support and the sudden appearance of the Allies' backbone (Fest 1997: 95). On 28 September, after Chamberlain had spoken to the House of Commons about his reluctant decision to mobilize, Hitler—suddenly alarmed that the Allies might defend Czechoslovakia after all—backed down and offered a formal guarantee to accept the sovereignty of the rest of the Czech republic.

Those German officers plotting a *coup* against him were aghast that their pretext for action had disappeared and it merely worsened when Chamberlain immediately organized an international conference to discuss the problem at Munich. This accepted everything Hitler had demanded at Bad Godesberg with the single exception that the occupation would take ten days and not one day. The Czechs were again forced to accept immediately and Chamberlain returned to London, with his 'piece of paper' that, he claimed, ensured 'peace in our time'. He was right, assuming that 'our time' meant the six months that intervened before Hitler's army marched into Prague on 15 March 1939, by which time the *Waffen* SS, the militarized wing of the SS, had become an independent part of the *Wehrmacht*.[18] Even then, after Hitler had finally gone beyond the restoration of

German land ceded by the Treaty of Versailles, Chamberlain remained adamant that Hitler's action was not a sufficient reason to go to war. For had not Hitler been forced to intervene to stop a civil war in Czechoslovakia? And—in a parody of logic that would have looked better in *Catch 22*—did not the subsequent disintegration of the Czechoslovakian state mean that there no longer existed a state with which Britain had a defence agreement?

It has been argued that the real value of Munich was in allowing time for the Allies to rearm in time for the inevitable war in 1939. There is even some evidence that Hitler was unhappy with the result, since he had hoped to start the war in 1938 (Veranov 1997: 83), and was reputed to have been worried that his attack upon Poland would be forestalled because 'at the last minute, some bastard will produce a mediation plan' (quoted in Fest 1997: 109). However, he now assumed that he could ignore the British and French, for 'I saw them at Munich. They are little worms' (quoted in Kagen 1997: 412).[19] But Kagan (1997: 408) notes that, even after Munich, Chamberlain continued to oppose further defence expenditure, and the rearmament programme that occurred under his leadership was instigated *before* he took power.

The Times—the most pro-appeasement paper of all—supported the transfer, but Churchill, supporting Attlee's criticisms, suggested instead that Britain

had sustained a total and unmitigated defeat . . . We really must not waste time after all this debate upon the differences between the positions at Berchtesgaden, at Godesberg and at Munich. They can very easily be epitomized if the House will permit me to vary the metaphor. £1 was demanded at pistol's point. When it was given, £2 were demanded at the pistol's point. Finally, the dictator consented to take £1 17s. 6d and the rest in promises of good will for the future . . . We are in the presence of a disaster of the first magnitude which has befallen Great Britain and France . . . The government had to choose between shame and war. They have chosen shame and they will get war.   (quoted in Kagan 1997: 406, 411)

By April 1939 Hitler was able to announce to the Reichstag—since he no longer bothered calling any cabinet meetings—an array of achievements, not for the Nazis but for Germany—because in his eyes, and many others', the identity of the former was indistinguishable from the latter and both were channelled through him:

I have overcome the chaos of Germany, restored order, massively raised production in all areas of our national economy . . . I have succeeded in completely bringing back into useful production the seven million unemployed who were so dear to all our own hearts . . . I have not only politically united the German people, but also militarily rearmed them, and I have further attempted to tear up page for page that Treaty, which contained its 448 articles, the most base violations ever accorded to nations and human beings. I have given back to the Reich the provinces stolen from us in 1919. I have led back into the homeland the millions of deeply unhappy Germans who had been torn away from us. I have recreated the thousand year historic unity of the German living space, and I have attempted to do all this without spilling blood and without inflicting on my people or on others the suffering of war. I have managed this from my own strength, as one who twenty-one years ago was an unknown worker and soldier of my people.   (quoted in Kershaw 1994: 202)

These were the words of a wolf in sheep's clothing, but, as we are about to see, even the sheep were carnivorous.

War against the Jews

Hitler's expansion east through Poland had already been prepared in the previous November, when von Rath, a German diplomat, was murdered by Herschel Grynszpan, a Polish Jew recently expelled by the Nazis. Goebbels persuaded Hitler to let the SA loose on the entire German Jewish population, since the Nazis held all Jews to be collectively responsible. The resulting pogrom on 9 November 1935, called Kristallnacht (Crystal Night) because of all the broken glass from Jewish shop windows, saw around 400 Jews murdered, 30,000 arrested and sent to concentration camps, and 6,000 businesses destroyed (Hodgson 1995: 204). The 'Jewish Question' then moved to the 'Jewish Desk' of Eichmann, who began to organize their removal to Poland.

The maelstrom that had swirled around in the dreams of the Nazis now became the nightmare for all their enemies within striking distance, and the possibilities of anyone controlling it were severely reduced, as Hitler's power increased in line with the state's curtailment. The cabinet no longer met, a substitute 'Ministerial Council for the Defence of the Reich' met only six times under Göring, its chair, and anyone seeking access to Hitler had to do so through Martin Bormann, Secretary of the Führer from 1943. Such audiences became ever rarer and thus the heads of various departments or branches of the state simply took on greater powers, often in competition with each other for resources and policy formulation and execution. The result, in Kershaw's (1991: 143) words, was that 'the "mafia" mob had taken over the state'.

German territorial ambitions on Poland were partly fuelled by the transfer of what had been East Prussia to the Polish state after the First World War, but the Anglo-French guarantee of Polish sovereignty in March 1939 posed a problem for Hitler. So far his tactics had worked, but now a war was likely. War with Poland was not the problem for Hitler because he had little regard for the Polish defence forces. But he did not want to become embroiled in that traditional German nightmare, a simultaneous war on two fronts: one with the Anglo-French and one with the Soviet Union. The British had made some efforts to interest Stalin in an alliance, but they had stalled amidst mutual suspicion. Hitler took that as a cue for action and the result was a non-aggression pact with the Soviet Union (with the return of Russian territories ceded during the previous war), the Molotov–Ribbentrop pact, signed in August 1939. With his back covered (and an attack upon the Soviet Union postponed but not cancelled), Hitler made one last effort to interest the British in an Anglo-German pact, but it came to nothing. He made no such overtures to France, since he believed the French needed to be militarily defeated before they would accept a subordinate position in the future German-dominated Europe. He then prepared for the final part of his immediate plan—an invasion of Poland—and on 1 September German troops invaded on the pretext of Polish aggression. On 3 September Britain and France declared war on Germany (Rees 1997: 98–123) and another attempt to topple Hitler from within the ranks of the military was set aside (Fest 1997: 110–12).

The German invasion of Poland was quick and brutal, for the Polish military forces were simply no match for the *Wehrmacht*. Hitler's intention in Poland was to divide the country up between the 'Warthegau' region and the 'General Government' region. Warthegau separated Germany from East Prussia and had been ceded to Poland after the First World War. Now Hitler demanded that it be what we now call 'ethnically cleansed', leaving it as a 'pure' German province, populated by ethnic Germans moved from the east as part of the agreement with Stalin when Soviet forces invaded the Baltic states. General Government was to be the (temporary) dumping ground for all those Poles regarded by the Nazis through their gigantic classification programme as 'impure' or unwanted, including Poles, Jews, communists, gypsies, the intelligentsia, the disabled, and so on. As Hitler made quite clear, he wanted 'nothing but labourers' from the future Poland (Berghahn 1987: 162). Greiser, head (*Gauleiter*) of the Warthegau region (and himself a Polish speaker of German descent), ruthlessly segregated Germans from Poles and issued a directive insisting that those now classified as Germans must cease all friendly contact with those classified as Poles on pain of being 'placed in protective custody' (quoted in Rees 1997: 142).

SS *Einsatzgruppen* (task forces), who were ostensibly under military law and followed the *Wehrmacht* into Poland, murdered whomsoever they liked as soon as they were over the border and little attempt was made by Hitler to limit or even organize the violence. As Greisner wrote to Himmler: 'during our last discussion concerning the Jews . . . he [Hitler] told me I could proceed with them according to my own discretion' (quoted in Rees 1997: 126). Forster, head of the West Prussian region, though also a Nazi, tended to assess the racial origin of the population in his region by mass, often asking those who wished to be regarded as German to sign a list. Despite Greiser's and Himmler's complaints to Hitler about Forster's acts, no action was taken by the Führer against him. It was simply not Hitler's method to intervene in disputes between subordinates: the law of the jungle would sort out who was 'right'.

That initial 'law of the jungle' involved the execution of anyone regarded as offering any form of leadership to the Poles and then the concentration of Jews in ghettos, especially in Cracow, Warsaw, and Lodz, where thousands were literally robbed and starved. By the winter of 1940 the starvation of the Lodz Jews[20] was temporarily ameliorated by Greiser's decision to make the population work for food. But there was, at this time, still no long-term plan for either the Jews or the Poles, though self-evidently Hitler had long regarded the Jews as beneath contempt; indeed, their identity as the epitome of all that was subhuman was a necessary foil to the superhuman identity of the 'Aryan' race. In January 1939 he had talked of annihilating the Jews if world war broke out. Indeed, in 1940, after the fall of France, there had been a plan to transport all Jews to Madagascar, after all their wealth had been confiscated to pay for it.

General Blaskowitz, commander of the Ober-Ost region in Poland, along with several other military commanders, complained to Hitler about the public slaughter of Poles and Jews, primarily because of the impact this had on the rest of the Polish population and indeed the German soldiers who perpetrated the actions: 'Every soldier feels repelled and revolted by these crimes which are being perpetrated by nationals of the Reich and representatives of State authority' (quoted in Rees 1997: 131). Hitler remained unmoved, speaking only of the 'child[ish] attitudes' of the army leadership who tried to wage war with Salvation Army methods. In fact, Hitler simply moved the areas out of the army's responsibility and, in May 1940, had Blaskowitz sent to France instead. However, we should recall Michael Geyer's conclusion: 'total and terroristic warfare . . . without regard for the population or—more generally—for the social costs of war did not just represent the horrific image of a war of annihilation conducted by the SS, but reflected the "normal" image of war of the *Reichswehr*' (quoted in Berghahn 1987: 164).

Many of the executioners were not German. In Lithuania and Latvia, invaded in June 1941, the Lithuanian police were involved in rounding up all known Jewish men, who were often forced to write letters to their families requesting food and money. They were then summarily executed, some in Kaunus by the infamous Lithuanian 'death dealer' with an iron bar, watched by civilians and German troops. Locals then used the letters to secure food and money from the dead Jews' families, who were unaware that their relatives had already been murdered.

By around autumn 1941, probably in response to German achievements—or lack of them—against the Soviet army in Operation Barbarossa, the executions had spread from Jewish men to Jewish women and children. But, as Alfonsas Navasinskas, a non-Jewish Lithuanian observer of the mass murders in Butrimonys on 9 September 1941 by *Einsatzkommando 3* (Lithuanian soldiers under German control) put it: 'Nobody spoke up for the Jews, nobody said a word. It was as if it were all quite normal' (quoted in Rees 1997: 186). Even those who undertook the executions, such as Petras Zelionka, seemed unmoved by the actions: 'They were only the Jews, no one was our countryman' (quoted in Rees 1997: 189–91). Himmler was also concerned about the mass shootings, not because he had suddenly developed a moral conscience but because he thought the act of shooting people at close range could damage the psychological health of the Germans involved.

By September 1941 German Jews were required to wear a yellow star and they too began to be transported east. As Hitler had prophesied on 25 October 1941: 'the Jew would disappear from Europe' (quoted in Rees 1997: 202). Up until September 1941 it still appeared that no systematic genocide was intended for all Jews, but at this point Hitler authorized the deportation of all German Jews to Poland. The 5,000 German Jews who arrived in Kaunus were shot immediately in November, but those arriving in Lodz and Minsk were spared. The confusion over their fate, and that of the so-called *Mischlinge*—those regarded by the Nazis as of 'mixed blood'—eventually forced Heydrich to call a conference in Wannsee for 9 December to resolve 'the problem'. However, this was cancelled on 8 December, the day after Japan had—to Hitler's surprise as well as that of the Americans—bombed Pearl Harbour. The European war had now turned into a global war and, just as Hitler had promised, the onset of a global war spelt the annihilation of the Jews. Goebbels's diary entry for 13 December, the day after a speech by Hitler to fifty Nazi leaders, spoke of his determination to 'settle things once and for all. World war has arrived, the destruction of Jewry has to be the necessary consequence' (quoted in Monteath 1998: 4). After this point there could be little doubt about their fate, and the plan for executing the 'final solution'—rather than discussion of 'the problem of the Jews'—was agreed at the reconvened Wannsee Conference in January 1942 (Kershaw 1991: 156).[21] By the winter of 1941–2, 500,000 Jews had already been shot and by 1942 extermination camps (as opposed to concentration camps) had been opened in Sorbibor, Treblinka, Majdanek, and Belzec, and an extermination extension built to the Auschwitz concentration camp at Birkenau. By March 1942 about three-quarters of all the six million victims of the Holocaust were still alive; a year later about three-quarters were dead, most of them murdered in Poland. The destruction of European Jews was, as Browning describes it, not a slow war of attrition but a *Blitzkrieg*, executed at a time when the *Wehrmacht*—under enormous pressure from the Red Army—could least afford the manpower necessary to undertake the task (Browning 1994: 302). In fact, the numbers involved in the mass murder were small and did not require the diversion of many scarce resources from the eastern front. Two groups were used: Latvians, Lithuanians, and Ukrainians were selected from the prisoner of war camps and trained up into private armies under the control of the SS; and recruits from various elements of the German police forces were fused into battalions of Order Police (*Ordnungspolizei*).[22]

Browning's research concerns Reserve Police Battalion 101 from Hamburg, stationed in Lublin in the General Government region of Poland. Two-fifths of the battalion were interrogated after the war, and, while the average age was 39, the vast majority had been recruited as unskilled workers from Hamburg. Only a quarter were members of the Nazi party, and, given that Hamburg had been a stronghold of the left before 1933, we can assume that many of these middle-aged reserve policemen were anything but the fanatical Hitler Youth that were then fighting the Red Army in the east and would soon be fighting the Western Allies in the West. A typical example of their actions occurred on 12 July 1942 in the village of Jozefow, when this motley group, having separated out the young men to transport to a work camp in Lublin, shot dead at close range 1,500 old men, women, and children. The conventional assumption about this kind of barbaric act is one where the individual perpetrators had no option but to carry out the orders of their superior officer, or find themselves in the firing line themselves. This was not regarded as a defence in law by the Allies after the war and it was, and always is, possible to refuse any order—on pain of punishment or death. However, what makes the Jozefow massacre of Jews so important is the testimonies of the subordinates, which suggest that coercion was *not* a prominent factor in them carrying out orders. Thus, for example, on the day before the killings, the officer in command, Major Trapp, had allowed a reserve lieutenant who felt, on hearing the orders, that he could not participate in the killing of women and children to escort the men to Lublin. The lieutenant was subsequently transferred to Hamburg and promoted to adjutant to the Police President. On the morning of the 12th, Major Trapp informed his battalion of their task and asked any individual unwilling to participate to step forward. About a dozen did, and these were subsequently given extra guard duties and so on, but no individual was disciplined, let alone court-martialled, sent to a concentration camp, or shot. The rest were then formed into companies: one to round up the Jews in the village, one to form firing squads in the nearby forest, and the third to accompany the Jews from the village to the forest. Trapp himself stayed in the village—much to the annoyance of his troops—and was heard by his driver weeping and exclaiming: 'If this Jewish business is ever avenged on earth, then have mercy on us Germans' (quoted in Browning 1994: 307).

Having completed the round-up, the men of the first company were then shown how to execute people at close range from behind, and, though the captain refused the request of several men to change duties, the sergeant was more accommodating and several men left to guard the route to the forest. The rest of first company was divided into squads of thirty-five men each—the same number that would arrive on the transport lorries from the village. As each lorry arrived, the squad marched parallel to the Jews and, when the latter were ordered to lie face down on the ground, each guard shot his victim. By lunchtime it became clear that the shootings would continue into the night unless they were speeded up and men of the second company were ordered to join their colleagues in the execution area, along with a large supply of vodka. Again the men were asked whether they wanted to drop out and one did. At least four of the second company asked to be relieved of their duty after they had begun to murder Jews, and a small but unrecorded number of the first company did likewise. By the evening all 1,500 Jews were dead and by the end of 1942 there were virtually no Jews left alive in the northern Lublin district. On interrogation most of those involved in the shootings claimed that they had had no choice, and when faced with the counter-evidence proclaimed that they had not heard the offers or that peer pressure and the guilt of appearing weak before their comrades were stronger than the guilt of murdering the weak. As one of the 'refusers' stated afterwards: 'I was not a career policeman and also did not want to become one . . . and I had my business back home' (quoted in Browning 1994: 313). In other words, one's professional career could be hindered by refusing, but not one's personal safety. Browning concludes that the search for explanations of the difference between those who obeyed and those who refused that day in Jozefow does not reveal fanatically rabid anti-Semitic Nazis, on the one hand, and staunch preservers of human morality, on the other. In fact, many Nazis found anti-Semitism to be rather low on their list of priorities, particularly compared to its position in their leader's mind. Rather, then, there is just: 'crushing conformity and blind, unthinking acceptance of the political norms of the time on the one hand, careerism on the other' (Browning 1994: 314).

Jozefow was just the tip of a bloody iceberg, and an iceberg upon which no German was ever apparently executed or sent to a concentration camp for refusing to murder a Jew or any other unarmed person. Goldhagen's summary of the evidence suggests that only fourteen Germans ever claimed self-preservation as an excuse for participating in such murders and none of these fourteen cases stands up to scrutiny (Goldhagen 1996: 379, 380). Nor is it the case that the killers *thought* they might be killed for refusing; in all the Police Battalions and *Einsatzgruppen* that we know about we also know that the participants knew their participation was voluntary; Himmler even wrote an order to this effect. Those that chose not to say 'no' in effect chose to say 'yes'.

Within a year 750,000 Jews in territories captured from the Soviet Union had been murdered, including 33,000 from Kiev who were shot by just two Germans, helped by Ukrainian 'packers', in the ravine at Babi Yar (Hodgson 1995: 212). But shooting Jews was too slow for Hitler and, after experiments with gassing victims in vans in 1941, the mass gassing in camps began early in 1942 using Zyklon B. The 'final solution' to the Jewish 'problem' led directly to death camps like Treblinka, where at least 800,000 people were gassed between July 1942 and August 1943. German control over this grisly process (even Himmler was physically sick after watching his first gassing) was significantly limited: only fifty Germans, aided by 150 Ukrainians and 1,000 Jews, were involved at Treblinka. At most, the ratio of controllers to controlled was 1 : 666, but the fate of the Jews was never absolutely self-evident. Treblinka 'station' had false 'timetables' to prevent panic, the victims were forced to strip naked for the deinfestation 'showers', and the entire 'processing' took just two hours from the train stopping to the bodies being dumped in mass graves (Rees 1997: 170). In Auschwitz the process could take as little as thirty minutes if the prisoners were regarded as too old, too young, or too weak. Those selected for slave labour, on average, lasted for about nine months, but despite the oppression there are many accounts of individual and collective resistance that give the lie to the common assumption that *all* the prisoners went quietly to their death—even if most apparently did. For example, a Soviet prisoner recalled how a Belgian woman carrying a child of about 3 was 'looked over' by the SS guard, who said to her:

'Come with me to the barracks and I will postpone your fate a few hours.' Instead of an answer the young woman pointed to the child in her arms. 'That's not what I have in mind' cried the guard, tearing the child out of the mother's arms. The child began to laugh, thinking that the officer wanted to play, and leaned forward, apparently intending to give the German a kiss. Without a moment's hesitation, the SS guard swung the child in a wide arc and smashed its head against the concrete wall. The child didn't even have time to cry out. In a rage the young mother snatched the pistol from the holster on the German's belt and managed to shoot him and several other SS officers before they finally overpowered her and tortured her to death in the anteroom of the gas chamber.   (quoted in Bishop 1999*a*: 14)

On a collective level there were revolts at Sobibor, Treblinka, and Auschwitz, but, and this is a crucial, since much of the evidence of individual and collective resistance died with the resisters or was destroyed by the SS, we know only what has been recorded, not what happened (see Langbein 1994).

There is little evidence that all the guards at the camps were psychopaths or otherwise mentally ill. On the contrary, the majority seemed to have been ordinary people who found themselves in bestial situations and either did nothing to prevent its continuation or found mechanisms for identifying their victims in the same way that Hitler identified them: as worthless or even deserving of their punishments.[23] Elsewhere many Germans subsequently argued that they knew nothing about such crimes, though it is probably safer to conclude that, at best, they chose not to know, not to ask, and not to think. Whatever happened, neither Hitler's coercion alone nor just the Nazi coercion alone could have exterminated six million people—the entire process hinged on a bloody complicity. In Kershaw's (1983: 227) apposite phrase: 'The road to Auschwitz was built by hate, but paved with indifference.' One did not have to positively identify with Hitler and the Nazis to ensure the system continued; one had only to say nothing or do nothing to stop it. The same applied to the military machine.

War in Europe

The invasion of France, which Hitler had announced to his generals on 27 September 1939, the day Warsaw fell, stimulated an immediate protest on their collective part. There were even discussions about a mass resignation, but they came to nothing; nor did another plot to kill Hitler (Fest 1997: 132, 136). The success of the German Blitzkrieg in France was not based, as it had been in Poland, on surprise and the superiority of numbers and weapons. The Allies were warned well in advance by sources within the German military about the date for the attack—though it was changed twenty-nine times (Fest 1997: 141). The French Somua tank, in particular, was better than anything the Germans could field, especially the Panzer 1s, which were really training tanks used to fill up the gaps in the German lines (Deighton 1995: 163–4). Indeed, as Fig. 8.5 suggests, except in aircraft, the German offensive was initiated on inferior not superior numbers. However, German tank tactics were superior to those of the French. While the French spread their tanks thinly over the ground in defensive formations, the Germans concentrated theirs in attacking groups. Moreover, the speed of tank warfare generated the possibility of very rapidly changing situations that required instant decision-making, and this had led the Germans to construct battle tactics in which senior leaders led from the front. In addition, and for the same reason, local tank commanders were given 'mission goals' but not 'mission methods' (Kirk 1997). The result was that, while French tanks were locked into long lines of communications and chains of command, German tanks operated along the principles of 'deep leadership': those on the ground were given the

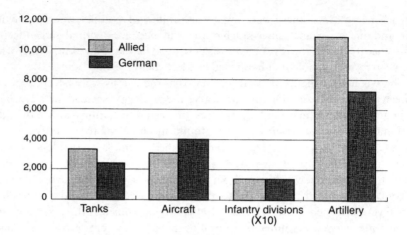

Fig. 8.5. Allied and German forces, May 1940
Note: Allies include troops from Britain, France, Belgium and the Netherlands.
Source: Veranov (1997: 104).

freedom to use their initiative. But the fundamental issue was not tactical but strategic, not military but political.

The military establishment—on all sides—operated on the basis of rationally evaluating the size and capacity of the armed forces available. France, Britain, Belgium, and Holland had roughly equal numbers of troops, more tanks, more artillery, but fewer aircraft than Germany, and the technical quality was generally similar. Therefore, the situation was *self-evidently* one where Germany should not attack. But Hitler's approach was not rooted in any allegedly 'objective' assessments of technical capacity; it was rooted in a political assessment of his enemies' will to resist and therefore concentrated on the relationships between the humans and the non-humans, not just the things in themselves. Not only did this radically unnerve his military advisers, but, when it worked, they could not explain it rationally and thus resorted to notions of superhuman 'genius'.

When Hitler managed to secure Austria and Czechoslovakia without military force, his skill as a politician was explicable by his shrewd gambles, but then politics was always about gambles and bluff, hence he was just a good poker player. Yet his military success proved more difficult to explain, because war was the preserve of military experts, and military expertise was, allegedly, a science, not the preserve of lucky amateurs. Only a 'genius', therefore, ran the argument, could have organized the audacious defeats of Norway, Belgium, Denmark, the Netherlands, and France, and, because 'genius' cannot be taught or learned, the military experts simply subordinated themselves to it.

The consequence of Hitler's military 'genius'—because it was not rooted in any strategic novelty or coherent military doctrine—was to displace rational planning with a pseudo-Darwinian free for all. Unlimited application of force, immediate exploitation of local advantage, and competitive conquest were the roots of *Blitzkrieg*, rather than a new and highly integrated approach to mobilized warfare. Hitler, at this stage, did not so much lay out detailed and rational plans for action as set the dogs of war loose upon his enemies. His enemies, expecting, and therefore preparing to resist, a rational war of manœuvre, found themselves savaged by the speed and ferocity of their assailants, who competed with each other to be first to the enemy capital (Geyer 1986: 584–7). Just as Hitler's domestic strategy was to let his subordinates fight between themselves to 'work towards him', so he did the same with the military. For the invasion of France, the planning of 'Case Yellow' had originally followed traditional German staff patterns, and when von Manstein suggested an altogether bolder attack, which exposed the attackers to incisive enemy counter-attacks, he was overruled by his superior von Brauchitsch, who had von Manstein posted. However, von Manstein, adopting Hitler's preference for competitive behaviour and radical ideas that 'worked towards him', approached Hitler directly. Within twenty-four hours von Brauchitsch had been ordered to adopt the new 'Sickle Stroke', which Hitler paraded as his own idea (Flitton 1998).

The approach worked: six weeks after the beginning of the attack, on 17 June, the Germans were in Paris, and the French surrendered four days later. According to the SD (German Security Services) an 'unprecedented social consensus' greeted Hitler's elimination of the final stain from the First World War (Fest 1997: 143). He had achieved everything he had planned for and was hailed by his previously pessimistic military advisers as a genius. But his assault upon Britain was 'from a military perspective, not feasible and from Hitler's perspective, pointless' (Geyer 1986: 577).

Operation Sea Lion, the invasion of Britain, was unlikely to have succeeded at its intended date of September 1940, and there is some evidence that it was never really a priority for Hitler (Berghahn 1987: 158). Nevertheless, an invasion in May 1940—after what should have been the capture of the British Expeditionary Forces at Dunkirk—would have had a much stronger chance (Roberts 1997: 296–302). But Hitler did not want to engage the British in war and assumed that, once France had fallen, Britain would negotiate a peace. Indeed, this *may* have been why a halt to the encirclement of Dunkirk was called on 24 May, though Veranov argues that he feared losing his tanks in the sand when they were still needed to defeat the French forces in the south. Hence he wanted the *Luftwaffe* to finish the job (Veranov 1997: 122–5). However, it seems more likely that the commander of the German Fourth Army ordered the halt to tighten up the line and, in the forty-eight hours of confusion that followed as Hitler tried to restore the advance, a third of a million Allied troops escaped. Certainly, Hitler's military advisers assured him that Britain was not the most important enemy, nor could the *Kriegsmarine* (navy) or *Luftwaffe* defeat the British on their own (Magenheimer 1998: 22). There were, in fact, several attempts to construct a truce with Britain in May and June 1940, but Churchill was adamant that there would be no surrender and no peace deal.[24] On 21 June, two days after the French surrender, Ribbentrop, the German Foreign Minister, insisted:

The Führer does not desire the destruction of the British Empire. He asks that England renounces some of her possessions and recognize the *fait accompli* (on the continent) . . . If England chooses war, it will again be total war, pitiless, decisive until the destruction of England and the Empire. If England chooses peace, the Führer will be happy to collaborate in the reconstruction of a Europe in which order and peace will be assured . . . (quoted in Berghahn 1987: 158)

That peace would also have benefited Germany. Between July and August 1940 seventeen *Wehrmacht* divisions were demobilized, not because the war was all but won, but because the German armaments industry could not keep pace with the demand. The soldiers were to enter the factories to build the guns they would use when they returned to the *Wehrmacht* (Magenheimer 1998: 66).[25] The mobilization of the German economy for war, ironically, was extraordinarily tardy. In 1944 almost a quarter of industrial production was still devoted to consumer goods and Hitler constantly resisted the deployment of women into the factories or the reduction of the 220,000 civil servants to free up scarce labour for war work. No central control over arms production occurred until 20 June 1944, two weeks after D-Day, though the greatest production actually occurred simultaneously—despite the Allied bomber offensives of the previous years.[26]

When Britain neither surrendered nor recognized the *fait accompli* in Europe, Hitler (having already ordered his staff to prepare detailed plans for attacks upon the Azores, the Canary Islands, Gibraltar, the defence of Finnish nickel mines, and the Italians in North Africa) turned east towards his most important enemy: the Soviet Union, the land of 'Jewish Bolshevism' and the enemy of all civilized people, as he insisted (Craig 1986: 494).

War in the Soviet Union

This war, as he constantly reminded his commanders, would be different from any other: it would be a war of annihilation. Four *Einsatzgruppen* were formed under Himmler and particular reference was made to the 'Commissar Order' (formulated by the *Wehrmacht* as well as the SS): Red Army political commissars 'as a rule, [were to be] immediately shot for instituting barbaric Asian methods of warfare' (quoted in Fest 1997: 172).

Once again, the senior commanders, this time Halder, Bock, and Brauchitsch, discussed resigning in protest, but once again they did not. Nevertheless, it was unclear what Hitler's objectives really were: did he want to defeat the Soviet Union, or eliminate the Jews, or replace Communism? These were not identical aims and were clearly likely to Contradict each other. Nor is it clear to what extent the Soviet Union was already planning to attack Germany when the Germans invaded (see Magenheimer 1998: 41–51).

Operations in Greece and Yugoslavia delayed the German assault upon

Moscow long enough to ensure that, despite the remarkable successes of the German forces in July and August 1941, the winter of 1941–2 stopped them short of their target. But even without the delays the dispute about the strategy would have remained. In fact, so confident was Hitler that the war in the east was already won that by July 1941 he had ordered a switch in economic resources from the army to the airforce and navy—in preparation for the coming war against Britain and the USA.[27] He was not alone in this assumption of imminent success: Soviet military morale had all but collapsed and Stalin ordered the execution of any officers attempting to surrender to the Germans and the arrest of their families.[28]

By mid-October 1941 the situation for Stalin was dire and peace-feelers were sent out via the Bulgarian ambassador in Moscow while Stalin prepared to evacuate the city. Hitler's subsequent intervention to demand an attack upon the Ukraine, rather than OKH's preference for taking Moscow in 1941, may have been a mistake. But success in either field of operations would not necessarily have achieved victory over the Soviet Union because Stalin and the Communist Party leadership, unlike most of Hitler's other political opponents, *appeared* unwilling to surrender under any conditions. For example, the winter of 1941–2 marked the beginning of the battle of Leningrad. German and Finnish armies had originally attacked in summer clothes, and, like the British in the Crimea a century earlier (and in every other war since), had assumed that the war would be over by Christmas. It was not, and they surrounded the city and proceeded to starve and shell its inhabitants, but thirty months later, in January 1944, the siege was lifted by the Red Army. By then 630,000 Russian civilians had died of the cold and hunger and with them a further 200,000 killed by the Germans (Hodgson 1995: 234–5).[29] As Hitler admitted: 'one cannot beat the Russian with operational successes . . . because he simply does not acknowledge defeat' (quoted in Geyer 1986: 591).

After the German offensive on Moscow also ground to a halt, General Brauchitsch, who had replaced Fritsch in 1938, was replaced by Hitler as Commander-in-Chief of the Army in December 1941. From this point, Hitler became the supreme strategic leader, convinced that only he could win back the initiative. As General Jodl, chief of the OKW operations staff who served him, noted:

The man who succeeded in occupying Norway before the very eyes of the British fleet with its maritime supremacy, and who with numerically inferior forces brought down the feared military power of France like a house of cards in a campaign of forty days, was no longer willing, after these successes, to listen to military advisers who had previously warned him against such overextensions of his military power. From that time on, he required of them nothing more than the technical support necessary to implement his decisions, and the smooth functioning of the military organization to carry them out. (quoted in Craig 1986: 492)

But Hitler made two related strategic errors. First, he made little use of the anticommunist feelings common amongst the local population, which could have been decisive at this time. Secondly, he insisted on the wider military conquest of Soviet space at the expense of concentrating on the political objectives of under-mining the Soviet system. Both of these allowed Stalin to turn a war of ideology into the Great Patriotic War; not a novel war between communism and fascism but a traditional war between German and Russian. The *Wehrmacht*, having delayed the attack on Moscow and Leningrad too long, then compounded the error by continuing the assaults under atrocious winter conditions with a rapidly depleting stock of soldiers and armour. By March 1942 German losses amounted to over 1 million soldiers and the sixteen armoured divisions had only 140 opera-tional tanks left between them. In June 1942, when the *Wehrmacht* planned to move south to capture the oilfields of the Caucasus, centred around Baku, the total strength of the Soviet forces was almost 500 divisions, against which the German army in the east could muster barely 165 (Magenheimer 1998: 75–125, 142).[30] Worse was to come, for the Germans then split the attacking force equally between Army Group B under von Weichs attacking Stalingrad, and Army Group A, under List, attacking the Caucasus and Baku. Neither section had suf-ficient strength to take its respective targets and both failed. Yet Hitler refused to accept the position and withdraw to organize a strong defensive line, opting instead for the continued assault upon Stalingrad. As November progressed and the Soviet army began organizing a winter offensive, local German intelligence reported the information to Hitler, but he preferred that provided by the central intelligence unit, which proved to be wrong. Thus Hitler left the German Sixth Army in Stalingrad, and 225,000 of the original 250,000 German troops were lost, 110,000 as POWs (Magenheimer 1998: 160–7).

When it came to securing lightening victories by breaking the will of his oppo-nents, Hitler was indeed undoubtedly brilliant, but this was the limit of his genius—once his victim refused to cower before him, he had no solution, politi-cal or military, to the problem. Hence, when first Britain and then the Soviet Union did not sue for peace when the situation was dire, Hitler was unable to develop a coherent strategy. In fact, Hitler's attack upon the Soviet Union *had* paralysed Stalin temporarily: he did not address the Soviet people for two weeks and contemporaries noted his ashen and shaken face. In a speech in May 1945 Stalin even thanked the Soviet people for *not* dismissing him at the time—though quite how they could have done it is unclear; but Hitler never knew this (Overy 1995: 257). The only 'strategic' solution for Hitler was greater violence—and this simply induced the Soviets to even greater counter-violence. As Geyer (1986: 593) concludes: 'The challenge of total war was to calibrate the increase of violence to the decline of the enemy's resolve. The unpremeditated outcome of the German practice of war was to escalate force and terror to the point that it stiffened the resistance of old enemies and created new ones.'

It was in the Soviet Union that the problem of 'escalatory war' was most clearly present: the barbarism of the German invaders stiffened a Soviet defence that had nowhere else to go. Even for those not motivated by a hatred for the Nazis or a desire for revenge, the alternatives to fighting were dubious. Desertion was punishable not just by personal retribution (around 400,000 men were sent to penal battalions) but by family punishment, and the actions of the *Wehrmacht* demonstrated that surrender was probably more lethal than continuing to fight.[31] The consequence of this rising barbarism was to initiate a staunch defence by the Red Army and, as Bartov suggests, to propel every German soldier into a situation where morality simply did not matter: 'This does not mean that every individual German soldier was a committed National Socialist; rather, it is to say that the vast majority of troops internalized the distorted Nazi presentation of reality, and consequently felt that they had no alternative but to fight to the death' (Bartov 1991: 144).

Hitler's apparent confusion in the Soviet campaign, then, was not just a sign of his inability to develop a coherent strategy, because he never had one. His approach was always to engineer competition between his subordinates as his pseudo-Darwinian beliefs required and because previously it had worked. More damaging still, Hitler's inability to compromise or limit his ambition to the goals that his advisers thought were achievable, given Germany's resources, ensured that over time the coalition against Germany grew ever stronger. In July 1940 only Britain stood between him and the domination of Western Europe; seventeen months later, in December 1941, the two greatest military powers on earth stood between him and domination of the earth, and his policy of 'escalatory war' never provided a level of benefits that outweighed the disadvantages incurred (Geyer 1986: 578). But Hitler had little of the military genius he was credited with; he was a motivator not an organizer.[32] Indeed, the closer Hitler got to moving from the former to the latter, the more problematic became his actions, and a qualitatively different light now grew over Hitler. If the Jewish Bolsheviks of the Soviet Union, the *Untermensch* of subhumans, could defeat the greatest race on earth, how valid was the Nazi argument after all? It is noticeable that, although the Nazi leadership tried to protect Hitler from the failures of the *Wehrmacht*, this became an increasingly difficult task as the defeats multiplied and as Hitler's influence upon the *Wehrmacht* and its strategy and tactics became more obvious. Hence, Hitler's errors piled one upon the other in quick succession: he reinforced Tunisia with troops that could not have altered the situation; and he declared war on the USA. On 7 December 1941 the Japanese attacked Pearl Harbour, much to Hitler's glee, since he had been trying to get Japan to divert American interests towards the Pacific and away from the Atlantic for months. Four days later, and quite unnecessarily—since there was no German–Japanese pact—Hitler declared war on the USA. It was the case that Hitler had always intended to attack the USA, but this was for a future date, when the Soviet Union had been conquered and in alliance with—or through control over—Great Britain (Craig 1986: 493; Burleigh 1997: 342, 343). However, the difference between Hitler's ultimate ambitions and his strategic skill at the time was becoming ever more visible. By this time, as Jodl wrote while awaiting trial at Nuremberg after the war: 'activity as a strategist was essentially ended. From then on, he intervened more and more frequently in operational decisions, often down to matters of tactical detail, in order to impose with unbending will what he thought the generals simply refused to comprehend; that one had to stand or fall, that each voluntary step backwards was an evil in itself' (quoted in Craig 1986: 497). Perhaps more importantly, given the failure in the East, General Warlimont suggested that Hitler was ignorant of 'the relative strengths of two sides: the factors of time and space' (quoted in Overy 1995: 274). Even when it was patently obvious that a successful conquest was unlikely—but a defeat was also unlikely—Hitler would not countenance the advice of his subordinates to stabilize the eastward expansion of the Reich and exploit the anti-communism of the non-Russian and even Russian population. Goebbels and Field Marshall von Manstein both tried to persuade Hitler that an 'Eastern proclamation' should be made, prohibiting any further attacks on, or derogation of, the conquered peoples of the East, in favour of a new policy of 'partnership'. Hitler refused to sign or issue it and demanded a military victory before any apparent 'reconciliation' with Stalin or anti-communist forces would be countenanced. Any such moves, in Hitler's opinion, would be perceived as signs of weakness and defeat. More particularly, since Hitler had identified the slavs and Russians as inferior beings, how could he admit he had been wrong all along and strike up a partnership with them?

The result was the Kursk offensive in July 1943, which involved half of all Soviet armour and almost two-thirds of German armour. The subsequent battle eliminated between 15 and 20 per cent of the German armour, and, while it did not ensure that the Soviet Union could destroy Germany at will, it certainly terminated any hope that Hitler might have had for another successful military invasion. The Soviet Union had now sustained total casualties of almost five million and had lost more soldiers in two months than the USA and Britain sustained in the entire war (Overy 1995: 212). But it still managed to deploy 166 divisions for its summer offensive in 1944—against a German line held by just forty-two divisions. By then Hitler had rejected all calls to make a strategic withdrawal. Thus von Manstein demanded a shortening of the German lines to the Bug–Dniester line; von Kleist demanded an evacuation of Crimea; while Jodl recommended a retreat to a line joining Riga and Odessa. All three were rejected and no divisions were released for buttressing the defences in the west; on the contrary between July 1943 and April 1944 twenty-three divisions were moved from the west to the east—but it was never enough (Magenheimer 1998: 242–3). Of the 380,000 German troops deployed against the initial Soviet attack in the summer of 1944, 300,000 were either killed or captured. Within six weeks a further 100,000 troops had been lost in Poland and Byelorussia and 180,000 more defending Romania in August. By comparison, about 400,000 losses were sustained on the Western front between D-Day and the end of September 1944 (Magenheimer 1998: 253–5, 258).

Whatever the numbers, the cost was enormous and Hitler's mythical invincibility died with them. While Hitler interfered with military decisions at an increasing rate, the opposite was the case for most of the other political leaders of the war. Stalin played a smaller and smaller role in operational decisions as the war progressed, Roosevelt never pretended he had any expertise in the field, while Churchill *thought* he had a lot to offer his chiefs of staff but—following his record at Gallipoli and in Norway—if they collectively disagreed with him, he seldom overruled them (Overy 1995: 258–67).

Soon the Red Army would be at the gates of Berlin to inaugurate communism amongst the workers of Berlin—the very scenario that Hitler had invaded the Soviet Union to prevent. But what had happened to the fabled German working class? Had it also been devoured by carnivorous sheep?

War in Germany

The fate of those German workers left to run the economy has long been an enigma to many. There were certainly material benefits to be had for compliance, and the banning of trade unions (replaced by the German Labour Front (DAF), which grew to twenty million members) effectively terminated all hope of any collective resistance. This in itself generated support for Hitler from the business élite (defined as the top 5 per cent of incomes), who saw their share of national income between 1929 and 1941 rise by 20 per cent, while the equivalent American élite saw their share fall by 15 per cent over the same period (Hobsbawm 1994: 129). But, for the workers, unemployment was no longer likely, paid holidays sponsored through the Nazi 'Strength through Joy' organization became commonplace, and the prospect of owning a Volkswagen, a people's car, through the popular 'save five marks a week' scheme, appeared attractive to many—even if only SS officers and the Nazi élite ever got to drive one along Hitler's new autobahns before or during the war.[33]

Though they were usually spared the worst excesses meted out to slave workers,[34] German workers were still under the apparent scrutiny of the Gestapo, but Hitler himself appears to have been considered as above reproach on the shop floor. Indeed, Hitler's appearance at the helm coincided not just with the elimination of most workers' economic fears but also with the acquisition of new pride in German identity. This became manifest both through the foreign policy success of the Führer and through the appearance of a new underclass of foreign workers and slaves who, at last, took the worst labour from the German workers and who served under their authority. Individual advancement through the new German identity, not collective resistance through the old one, was what the Nazis offered, and, by and large, the German workers seemed to have dropped the latter in favour of the former (Peukert 1987a). By 1944 there were seven million foreign workers (mainly slaves) in Germany, making up 20 per cent of the entire workforce.

There were strikes, go-slows, and productivity problems amongst the German working class under Nazi control, but, as Bartov (1994: 45) concludes: 'this domestic tension rarely transformed itself into political resistance . . . and the regime . . . does not seem to have been seriously threatened by the working class at any time.' On the contrary:

the mass of Germany's population became involved in one way or another in the war, and a growing proportion of its men young, middle aged, and old, workers, bourgeois, and aristocrats, nazis and former socialists and communists, were recruited and sent to the front, turning miraculously into Europe's toughest and most determined troops, mostly fighting with extraordinary cohesion almost until the bitter end. For, throughout the war, combat morale amongst the Wehrmacht generally remained extremely high, mutinies were almost unknown, and an excellent system of manpower organization, draconian punishment, and extensive indoctrination combined to hold combat units tightly together, while a series of astonishing victories made it easier to withstand even greater defeats in the hope of fortune's wheel turning once more in Germany's favour. (Bartov 1994: 46)

However, the losses incurred in the east against the much underrated armed forces of the Soviet Union meant that by the end of 1941 many of the workers previously exempt from military service were called up. Yet the *Wehrmacht*'s ordinary troops remained amongst the regime's strongest supporters and their morale was consistently higher than that of the German civilians back home. Public support for Hitler, as measured by the SD, remained buoyant until the summer of 1942 and thereafter dropped in line with each German defeat and withdrawal. By July 1944 the reports were stopped, since even their collection had become counterproductive (Berghahn 1987: 173). Amongst the troops, though, it was not until March 1945 that morale wavered, and research amongst captured *Wehrmacht* soldiers consistently showed around two-thirds strongly committed to and supportive of Hitler. They were, as Goebbels noted from Allied sources: 'fighting like savage fanatics . . . our prisoners still maintain the view that Germany must definitely win the war . . . [they] have an almost mystical faith in Hitler. This is the reason why we are still on our feet and fighting' (quoted in Bartov 1994: 52). As late as December 1944 Hitler still assumed that the Allies would fall out amongst themselves to give Germany a breathing space: 'Never has there been such a coalition. Ultra-capitalistic states on the one hand, ultra-Marxist states on the other. On the one hand a dying Empire, Britain; on the other hand a colony bent on that inheritance, the United States . . . Even now they are at loggerheads' (quoted in Neillands 1995: 44). Such optimism appeared to run right through the German forces, who, almost until the end, assumed that they would soon join the Americans and the British against the Soviet Union.

Indeed, rather than support for the Nazis decreasing amongst the *Wehrmacht* as the war continued, the opposite seems to have been true, as the ranks were filled with those previously influenced by their membership of the Hitler Youth (which had achieved 38 per cent density by 1933) and by the Nazification of the German educational system. By the beginning of the war the Hitler Youth had around seven million members—over 80 per cent density—and directly after the war twice as many Germans under the age of 19 still held Hitler in high regard as did those over the age of 19 (Kershaw 1994: 209–10). In contrast, by 1943 still only a quarter of the German population were members of the Nazi party, with the highest proportions amongst the medical and educational professions (Berghahn

1987: 136). As those members of the military involved in plotting Hitler's death came to realize, no body of troops anywhere could be expected to support the assassination, let alone help in its execution, and only Hitler's death would begin to dissolve the Hitler myth.

That myth combined an array of fragments; it kept the selfless Führer from his selfish henchmen; it secured to him alone all responsibility for Germany's economic miracle; it rendered him the arbiter of justice against 'fanatics', like Rohm; it encouraged his supporters to assume that any 'excess' was carried out without his knowledge; it imbued him with infallible judgement in political and military matters; and, finally, it projected him as the only bulwark against Bolshevism and Judaism. However 'mythical' the myth was, it was critically important for welding the German population to the Führer and for encouraging Hitler to live in and through his *alter ego* (Kershaw 1994: 198–209).

On 25 July 1943 Mussolini was deposed in a bloodless *coup*—an impossibility in Germany, where no constitutional mechanism existed for replacing Hitler. Few people were admitted to Hitler's presence and the leadership was, in any case, radically split but generally subservient to him. Rees argues that, when so many of the *Wehrmacht*, and not just the Gestapo and the SS, had participated in atrocities in the east (and, again, research has yet to point to *any* military unit that was not involved in atrocities in the east), the prospect of suing for surrender did not look particularly enticing (Rees 1997: 210–11). Whether the participants were driven by assumptions about their personal oath of loyalty to the Führer, or they genuinely believed that those they had murdered were subhumans, the retribution of their enemies would undoubtedly be harsh and the *Wehrmacht* knew it. As Graf von Kielmansegg, a German officer, answered his own rhetorical question: 'What did the German soldier fight for and, one has to ask, against what? For me this is the decisive reason: all those who had been in Russia at least knew what Germany could expect if Bolshevism came to Germany . . . If it had only been England and France, we would have stopped earlier in a simplified manner. Not against Russia' (quoted in Rees 1997: 224). Not that the German civilian population was vehemently protesting against the Nazis or the influx of slave labourers; on the contrary, 'the Germans', concludes Geyer, 'not only experienced it [the benefits of racism] but by and large liked it' (quoted in Rees 1997: 220). And those who protested could expect little support from the mass of the population.

Hans and Sophie Scholl, students at Munich University and members of the resistance group called 'White Rose', were executed on 22 February 1943, four days after they had distributed leaflets calling for their fellow students to rise up against Hitler. Sophie assumed that her death would initiate an uprising, writing as she awaited her execution: 'What we have written and said is in the minds of all of you, but you lack the courage to say it aloud' (quoted in Hodgson 1995: 211). But she could not have been more wrong. Instead, her actions provoked a pro-Nazi demonstration, and, three days later, a packed auditorium cheered a speech by Jakob Schmied, a Nazi student leader, deploring their treachery (Fest

1997: 199). Probably more typical was Johhanes Zahn, who, though a member of the *Wehrmacht*, was no lover of Hitler, but what could he do? 'Fight them? I wouldn't have risked it . . . the majority decided . . . shut up and see that nothing happens to you' (quoted in Rees 1997: 235). In fact, there is only one recorded instance of a protest by Germans on behalf of Jews after Hitler's accession to power, and this occurred in 1943 when the last remaining Jews openly living in Berlin (around 4,000 survived by being hidden by their 'Aryan' friends) were deported to Auschwitz (Berghahn 1987: 171). The last 2,000 to be rounded up were married to non-Jewish Germans, and, when these people protested for ten days outside the Rosenstrasse holding centre, Goebbels ordered the release of their spouses (Hodgson 1995: 211). There is no record of any punishment being meted out to the protesters (nor to those who protested against the euthanasia programme)—in acute contrast to the popular claims of coercion as the reason for the lack of resistance.[35]

Many Germans argued that the Casablanca declaration of 24 January 1943, in which the Allies insisted on an unconditional surrender, removed from the Germans the face-saving mechanism for a ceasefire. Of course, a major cause of the Second World War was the assumption—vigorously promoted by Hitler—that the German army had surrendered in the First World War for no apparent reason—except the betrayal of communists and Jews in Berlin. Thus, from the Allied perspective, to accept a conditional surrender by the Germans before the Allies had even reached German soil was simply reconstructing the situation of 1918. From the German perspective, the surrender of November 1918 had been a national dishonour of epic proportions, and, even against the Western Allies, the *Wehrmacht* fought with astonishing tenacity, without any real fear that falling into the hands of these allies would render them open to unparalleled acts of bestial revenge. But they were certain that a repetition of 1918 would render the German army open to everlasting shame: it would have humiliated Hitler and dishonoured the country; neither of these possibilities could be countenanced. The demand for an unconditional surrender may have persuaded the Germans to fight on in a hopeless situation in the Second World War, but at least their ultimate defeat could not be laid at the door of betrayal again, thereby prompting an excuse for a Third World War. On the contrary, the declaration undermined some of the conspirators within Germany who were attempting to assassinate Hitler, for now his death might be to no avail (Fest 1997: 210–11).

Hitler's health rapidly deteriorated from 1943, and he became increasingly irritable, increasingly isolated, and decreasingly successful. He no longer visited the front after September 1943, he visited no bombed German city, his hands shook, and his gait and appearance became that of an old man. But he remained in control, at least of the military situation, if not the domestic political situation, which no longer appeared to interest him. The failed assassination attempt in July 1944 merely increased his distrust of the military élite and encouraged him to interfere more disastrously with the development of new tanks, the V1 and V2 rockets, and the new Messerschmitt ME262 jet fighter.[36] On all three

counts Hitler demanded that designs for fast defensive weapons be reconstructed for slower offensive weapons and the result was merely to delay their
eventual production until it was too late (Kershaw 1991: 172, 174). But these
were minor tactical errors in an altogether flawed strategy: the Germans could
not defeat the British, because the Channel, the RAF, and American support got
in the way; and they could not defeat the Soviets, because the Soviets would not
give up. In effect, the Soviets used Hitler's secret weapon against his army: if it
was a battle of wills, the Germans could not win it unless the Soviet system collapsed—and Stalin was willing to sacrifice vast numbers of his soldiers to prevent this. Hitler could possibly have reached a compromise with some of the
conquered populations, but this ran directly counter to his identification of such
people as inferior beings.

D-Day saw the beginning of the end in the west, as one million soldiers,
170,000 vehicles, and 500,000 tons of *matériel* were landed in just two weeks. On
22 June four Soviet army groups pierced the thin German defensive line between
the Minsk and the Beresins rivers, marking the beginning of the end in the east.
Hitler may have boasted that he welcomed this final showdown, but
Stauffenberg, who saw him the day after D-Day, reported that he seemed in a
daze, trembling and pushing maps aimlessly around a table (Fest 1997: 238). He
insisted on his soldiers defending every yard of territory to the death and on taking the offensive wherever possible—a policy that, in Overy's (1995: 275) cutting
phrase, was 'more Custer than Clausewitz'.

The significance of this phrase became palpably clear thereafter. In almost five
years between 1 September 1939 and 20 July 1944, 2.8 million German soldiers
and civilians died. Between 20 July 1944—by which time most Germans seemed
to assume that the war was already lost—and 8 May 1945, 4.8 million died. Put
another way, before 20 July 1944, on average, 1,588 Germans died every week;
after 20 July 1944 this number multiplied tenfold to 16,641 per day (Fest 1997: 3,
4). And, as the German Reich reeled under the Allied hammer blows from the
west and the east, Hitler ordered the SS to destroy whatever was left of German
infrastructure.

Within a few weeks of 20 July, 5,000 Germans were to commit suicide or die at
the hands of German firing squads after a bomb placed by Count von
Stauffenberg failed to kill Hitler. The overwhelming response of the *Wehrmacht*
was of disgust at the betrayal, not frustration at the failure. Part of the reason for
the limited popularity of the plotters was the deeply ingrained sense of duty
amongst the German officers. In fact, it was so deep that many of those who were
involved in the various assassination attempts refused to defend themselves or
resist arrest by the Gestapo or the SS, since this too would have been dishonourable (Fest 1997: 293).[37] Not one German officer who had not previously been
involved in the plot joined the plotters—even when it looked as if Hitler was
indeed dead. Despite this the plotters were not the 'very small clique of ambitious
officers' that Hitler suspected. Initially he had intended to broadcast show trials,
in Stalinist style, to demonstrate their unpopularity and weakness, but ten days

after the trials started, on 7 August 1944, the broadcasts were stopped after the defendants began using the trials to denounce the crimes of the regime and to reveal the size of disaffection within the army and the country. The prosecutor, Roland Freisler, as well as some of the 'defence' lawyers, made much of the heavenly providence that had saved Hitler's life.[38] Almost all those brought before the court were quickly convicted and immediately hanged in the Plötensee prison from meat hooks, in accordance with Hitler's wishes that they be 'strung up like butchered cattle'. All their executions were filmed so that he could watch them die at his own leisure. The land and possessions of all those found guilty were confiscated and their families imprisoned in concentration camps (Fest 1997: 292–323). In September 1944, and again in early April 1945, further papers and the diaries of Admiral Canaris, chief of OKW military intelligence and implicated in the Stauffenberg plot, were discovered. They revealed a far greater network of conspirators than Hitler had discovered and he was outraged at the 'betrayal', but the conspirators were too few, too weak, and too late.

Of all the organizations, institutions, social classes, statuses, and ideologies available to resist Hitler, not one proved capable of mobilizing against him or providing a powerful enough body of ideals to check him. Certainly there were resisters who were social democrats, communists, or Christians, but none of these ideologies prevailed upon the mass or even a large number of adherents to resist. Only individual conscience was strong enough to prevail. Not that all the plotters against him were moral zealots—far from it. As Fest concludes, there was no common thread that kept the conspirators together. Some despised his attack upon the Jews, others reviled his contempt for German honour, while others simply insisted that his actions were not in the interests of the country (Fest 1997: 325–7). What is also the case is that the military authorities were also deeply culpable; even those who considered Hitler's and the SS's actions criminal still clung to the notion that they were held in place by a code of honour and a personal oath. But, since honour was something inestimably lightweight when measured against the butchered millions of enemy soldiers and civilians, we should be strongly sceptical of such rationalizing. The military supported Hitler and prospered under him; they knew what was happening and even those who did not participate in criminal activity sustained it by their inaction against it. Even when Stauffenberg's bomb appeared to have released them from their personal oaths, and provided a way to regain their military honour, the mass of soldiers chose not to choose the opportunity. But had they done so there is little evidence that the mass of the civilian population would have supported them. As Crew (1994a: 27) asserts: 'Many ordinary Germans actively participated in the construction of Nazi rule, not because they had been converted to Nazi ideology, but because, under Nazism, the satisfaction of quite ordinary needs and desires could contribute to the extension and reproduction of Nazi power.' Loyalty to Hitler by the people of Germany, by its armed forces, and by its leadership remained solid right until the very last few days in April 1945, when both Göring and Himmler unsuccessfully attempted to take control. On 30 April 1945, just about the same time that Soviet soldiers were raising the Red Flag over the Reichstag building in Berlin, Hitler shot himself.

Analysis

It should be clear that Hitler's leadership rested on a great deal more than the threat of being cut in two, either by him or by his entourage. Controlling the largest part of Europe could not have been achieved without the willing or unwilling connivance of vast numbers of people, across the social-class spectrum and across the religious and ethnic divide. Hitler's leadership resided in the voluntary support of millions. It should also be clear that this voluntarism was buttressed by the ever-present danger of imprisonment, torture, and death for many other millions. Whether Jews, gypsies, communists, Red Army commissars, Red Army soldiers, political opponents, gays, the disabled, or the mentally ill, all were fodder for the grisly machines of extermination. And here lies the irony: Hitler did not succeed, in so far as he did, just because he was an individual willing to undertake or legitimate *any* activity in the pursuit of his aims; he succeeded because millions of others, primarily but not only Germans, *wanted* to help him. And for that we must look to the four arts of leadership.

The Philosophical Arts: Identity

Hitler's leadership was critically bound up with the construction of a German identity grounded in the shame of the past and the honour of the future. That identity was firmly rooted in mythical accounts of responsibility for German failure, which absolved the 'true' Aryan population from any blame and which cast all responsibility onto the 'other'. Whatever the falsehoods involved in this construction, there is little doubt that it served as a powerful motivator for personal and professional loyalty to Hitler. Moreover, that identity drew as deeply on a mythical past as it did upon a mythical future and the Janus-like result operated more strongly that any of its main rivals—the communists who devalued German history and looked only to the future, the social democrats who looked favourably only on the present, and the conservatives who just looked backwards.

Hitler's personal identity operated in a complex weave with that of the Nazi party, the *Wehrmacht* and ultimately the German population, for, although he came to represent all the groups when they were successful, he simultaneously managed to distance himself from the actions of the Nazi party and the *Wehrmacht* when such actions were deemed failures or mistakes.

Hitler had constructed a new German identity from the ashes of 1918 and Versailles that, however mythical in its justifications and rationalizations of history, appealed to a large number of Germans. Moreover, one did not have to identify with the Nazis or with Hitler's new Germany; it was enough to identify with the benefits the regime offered for the regime to survive. Hitler did not need a population of fanatics; he simply needed a population that either supported his reconstructed German identity or was unwilling to challenge it. This, surely, is the lesson: the mobilization of a society or an organization does not depend upon a consensual identity; rather it rests on an identifiable solidarity. In other words, the construction of a system that allowed individuals to construe a common enemy was sufficient to ensure their alignment within a common identity; as a German in Hitler's Germany, you did not need to be a Nazi to support the Nazi state.

Fortunately, Hitler was too riddled with pseudo-Darwinian racism to recognize this. Hence the possibility of securing a compromise with the Soviet Union in 1942 or mobilizing the vast numbers of Soviet citizens against the Communist Party through some form of partnership never appealed to him. Surely a Darwinian battle for survival was the only way of resolving such a conflict between populations that Hitler painted as racially and morally at opposite ends of the evolutionary spectrum? If it was, Hitler played a large part in embodying and bringing about precisely what befell one of his heroes: Wagner's Siegfried, whose death in *Götterdämmerung* (The Twilight of the Gods)—fittingly 'stabbed in the back'—led to the destruction of Valhalla itself. As Siegfried's wife, Brünnhilde, prepares to light Siegfried's funeral pyre, she sings her penultimate lines, to bring destruction on everything and everyone:

> For the end of the gods is nigh.
> Thus do I throw this torch
> At Valhalla's vaulting towers.

The Fine Arts: Strategic Vision

Hitler's personal vision eventually became that of a 'messiah', sent to rescue a fallen nation through an indomitable will to power. That personal vision was transparently clear for anyone who cared to read *Mein Kampf* or listen to his speeches: he was going to rid the world of bolshevism and Jews and he was going to erect a German empire across Europe that would last for a thousand years. But that will to power, while it secured the beginnings of a German empire, was unable and unwilling to compromise under any circumstances about anything of significance, and, as a consequence, all the territorial gains that Hitler's armies made were thrown away when his unflinching focus was transformed into tunnel vision; that is when the abyss looked into him.

The Martial Arts: Organizational Tactics

Tactically, Hitler made some astonishingly bold moves and some incredibly rash decisions. He dominated the Polish army and the Jewish population by using the tactics of martial and civilian *blitzkriegs*. There was little that was sophisticated about either of these assaults, but then Hitler never was a subtle tactician. On the other hand, he managed to neutralize the internal opposition of the social democrats, the communists, and the trade unions by learning early on that legitimacy has significant advantages. When Hitler took power legally, he completely wrong-footed this internal opposition, whose only contingency plan involved a revolt against an illegal seizure of power.

But perhaps his most significant tactic was used against France, for he inverted the superior military power of the French army. That is to say, he encouraged them to maintain their 'impregnable' *Maginot* line with its thinly dispersed screens of tanks and simply concentrated his forces against them. Ironically, it was this same tactic that exposed his western flank when he concentrated his armoured defences around Calais, allowing the Allies to occupy Normandy with relatively light casualties.

What Hitler also failed to understand was the importance of a controlled retreat, a compromise, and an acceptance of limited gains. All of these may have perpetuated his regime, but he adopted none of them with any real intent.

The Performing Arts: Persuasive Communication

That Hitler ultimately failed, on the other hand, can be traced, in part, to the fear that he engendered in others. As we have seen many times, all leaders make mistakes. But a critical difference between success and failure lies in the extent to which subordinates can compensate for the errors of their leaders—and in Hitler's case this was progressively delimited as the war continued. His subordinates could have saved Germany from catastrophe, but he denied them the freedom of manœuvre to execute the necessary changes and they were too cowed to wrest it from him. In short he had persuaded them that he was invincible and that anyone who resisted would be destroyed. Neither of these was true but many believed them to be true, and that is the critical point.

But it should always be remembered that the German population as a whole never voted for Hitler nor did a majority, but a majority voted *against* democracy and *for* some kind of authoritarian dictatorship. Those Germans who resisted him were never able to organize sufficient numbers and resources to topple him and that, in itself, is an indictment of complicity. Hitler's leadership was morally shallow but practically deep, it insinuated itself right into the heart of the population, and it left those with the courage to stand up and be counted to count only on being alone. Sophie Scholl thought that her deeply held convictions and personal sacrifice would be sufficient example to lead the German students in a rebellion against tyranny; she was wrong, because she misunderstood the depth of Hitler's leadership and he convicted and sacrificed her as an example of how wrong she was. Her (un)persuasive communication revealed only how persuasive Hitler had been.

Notes

1. Ironically Hitler usually referred to the British as the English, but, amongst all the nationalities making up the United Kingdom, the English have probably the least

claim to a definitive ethnic identity. Indeed, one consequence of the wars in the twentieth century has been that the very idea of a British identity has been cast into doubt,
as the empire collapsed, Europe arose, and the various elements of the United
Kingdom showed clear signs of imminent separation, with Scottish and Welsh devolution and some degree of independence returning to Northern Ireland. But the identity of all these groups has long been a contested arena. Historically, linguistically,
and ethnically, the component parts of the 'Celtic fringe' have little in common, other
than being 'not-English'. And Daniel Defoe's albeit satirical *The True-Born Englishman*, with its eighteenth-century account of the ethnically diverse origins of the
English—'a mongrel half-bred race', as he describes it—casts doubt upon all those
who suggest there was a time when English identity was both clear and ethnically
'pure'. The force of Defoe's dissent draws its vitriol from a denial of clear boundaries
between groups, for Sahlins is surely right to suggest that 'National identity, like ethnic or communal identity, is contingent and relational: it is defined by the social and
territorial boundaries drawn to distinguish the collective self and its implicit negation, the other' (Sahlins 1989: 271, quoted in Colley 1992: 5–6).

2. The monument was sometimes used as target practice for the roving Allied fighter
   pilots.

3. Many of the *Freikorps* wore swastikas as armbands and death's head (*totenkopf*) cap
   badges, both traditional right-wing symbols and both taken up by the SS (*Schutz
   Staffel* (protection squad)]. Death's-head badges were worn by Hitler's *Leibstandarte* SS guards in the 1930s before the *Totenkopfverbande* concentration-camp
   guards adopted it. Further back in time, the Prussian Lieb-Husaren (royal bodyguard) wore black uniforms and death's-head badges in memory of Frederick
   William I. Thus the SS claimed links back into 'German' history. The badges were
   also prominent at Waterloo (Bishop 1999*b*: 40–3).

4. At the cost of thirteen *Freikorps* deaths, the Spartacists, suffering 100 dead, were
   destroyed (Craig 1981: 396–408). Crucially the two Spartacists leaders, Karl
   Liebknecht and Rosa Luxemburg, who were captured during the fighting, were subsequently murdered.

5. *Schutz Staffel* (protection squad), originally the personal bodyguard of Hitler in the
   1920s.

6. The concept of 'Aryan' nations had been constructed only in 1898 (Hobsbawm 1994:
   118). The original concept of the 'Aryan' derived from the work of Friedrich Müller,
   a nineteenth-century philologist, who argued that a specific form of Indo-European
   language—the Aryan language—had developed, but this had nothing to do with
   racial concerns, still less with the 'Germans' (see Williamson 1996: 30).

7. By 1934, for example, the Nazi propaganda unit in Munich employed 14,000 people
   (Berghahn 1987: 137).

8. The SS oath, taken by the new *Waffen* SS after basic training, was as follows:

   > I swear to thee, Adolf Hitler,
   > As Führer and Chancellor of the German Reich
   > Loyalty and bravery.
   > I vow to thee and to the superiors whom thou shall appoint
   > Obedience unto death
   > So help me God.

9. In 1936 the *Adolf Hitler Schule* system was inaugurated to train future leaders from
   the ranks of those within the Hitler Youth. Boys between 12 and 18 attended a two-

week selection camp and then followed a curriculum heavily slanted towards physical education (five PE sessions to every one and a half academic sessions) (Bishop 1999c: 19).

10. By 1937 the *Lebensborn* (Fountain of Life Association) project was launched with the intention of improving the German 'race' through selected breeding. Young women, deemed to be physically perfect, were encouraged to attend one of the 13 *Lebensborn* centres to be impregnated by volunteer SS soldiers. The project was not limited to such experiments: around 200,000 blond and blue-eyed children were kidnapped from occupied Europe, especially Poland, and sent to assessment centres in Germany, where they were either 'Germanicized' through German foster parents or, if rejected, enslaved or murdered (Bishop 1999d: 44).

11. Allianz, a German insurance company, insured several Nazi buildings and institutions, including: Auschwitz, Dachau, and Berchtesgaden. Bertelsmann, the third largest media group in the world and current owners of Random House publishers, published Nazi propaganda during the war. Daimler-Benz (now called Daimler-Chrysler), the builder of Mercedes cars, Krupp, a major arms manufacturer, and Siemens all used slave labour. Degussa—currently Germany's largest precious metal company—also processed the dental gold from the extermination camps, while its subsidiary, Degesch, made Zyklon B, the gas used to murder the camp inmates. Deutsche Bank, then called the German Bank and Discount Company, provided financial cedits to Degesch and to the companies that built Auschwitz, and it was also involved in the forced sale of Jewish property. Deutsche Bank, along with Dresdner Bank—which bought gold looted from concentration-camp victims—face an $18 billion joint lawsuit in New York brought by 10,000 holocaust victims or relatives. Dresdner Bank, known as the SS Bank during the war (three board members were SS officers (Goldin 1998: 28)), bought six tons of gold from the Nazi regime between 1942 and 1944 and sold it for a profit of 2.4 million Swiss francs at the time. Between 274 and 324 kilograms of this gold came from camp victims—an estimated £1.9 million in 1999 prices (Traynor 1999a: 15). The Dresdner Bank acquired the British merchant bank, Kleinwort Benson, in 1995 and is funding the new building for the Ministry of Defence in London (*Observer*, 26 Feb. 1999). IG Farben, broken up after the war into BASF and Hoechst and Bayer, made cyanide tablets. Volkswagen, founded with Hitler's help, used slave labour to manufacture the Volkswagen beetle and the V1 rocket (Glaister 1998: 2–3). In October 1998 Gerhard Schröder, the German Chancellor, negotiated with German companies to provide a final settlement for the ex-slave labourers. This followed two large Swiss banks agreeing to pay £750 million to settle outstanding demands by Jewish survivors with claims on the gold stolen by the Nazis and hidden in Switzerland. Volkswagen has already agreed to provide £7 million for its ex-slaves, as has Siemens. The German banks face a claim for £4 billion and Dagussa a similarly large claim that could cripple it. Since 1950 Germany has paid out £40 billion in war reparations (*Guardian,* 5 Feb. 1999). French businesses are also being investigated for their part in assisting the expropriation and transportation of French Jews. The French state railway, SNCF, is being sued for running more than 3,000 trains to move 75,000 French Jews to Germany and Poland—only 2,400 returned. Six French banks are being sued for administering the removal of Jewish assets, and French art galleries and museums are being sued for the 2,000 paintings still not returned to their original Jewish owners (Henley 1999). In March 1999 the *Observer* newspaper alleged that Barclays Bank French subsidiary

provided full cooperation with the Nazi occupiers, volunteering the names of Jewish staff and investing money stolen from French Jews in German industry (*Observer*, 28 Mar. 1999).

12. In October 1998 Gerhart Reigner claimed in his book, *Ne jamais désespérer* (Never Lose Hope) that the then pontiff, Pope Pius XII, was made aware of the 'final solution' in March 1942, but this is denied by the Vatican (*Guardian*, 10 Oct. 1998).

13. The Law for the Prevention of Hereditarily Diseased Offspring oversaw the sterilization of those diagnosed as suffering from: schizophrenia, hereditary deafness, hereditary epilepsy, manic depression, Huntington's chorea, chronic alcoholism, and extreme physical malformation. In 1934 32,268 sterilizations took place and by the following year double this number were operated on. In 1935 German bishops ruled that, since marriage was primarily oriented towards procreation, those who had been sterilized should not marry. Protests by Catholics soon persuaded the bishops that they were wrong (Welch 1995: 68–9).

14. Kershaw (1991: 103) puts the figure at 400,000.

15. The professionalism of the Gestapo was also questionable: most of the personnel in the early years were ex-police officers not fervent Nazis, let alone members of the SS. In 1939 only 3,000 of the 20,000 members of the Gestapo were in the SS, and, although the proportion increased with the duration of the war, their technical and forensic skills became subordinated to their allegiance to the Führer. By the end of the war the Gestapo may well have been populated by criminals rather than criminologists, but with that went a decline of efficiency and a rise in bureaucratic confusion (Mallmann and Paul 1994: 166–89).

16. Hitler was usually uninterested in sport—except when it might prove a vehicle for demonstrating Nazi superiority. Hence his manifest embarrassment by Jessie Owens at the 1936 Berlin Olympics and when Norway beat Germany at football on 7 August 1936 in the same stadium. When Germany played Austria in April 1938—just a week before the unification—the German team was ordered to play 'beautiful, unaggressive football': the Austrian side won 2–0 after two penalty decisions were mysteriously awarded by the referee. Gerhard Fuchs and Julian Hirsch, two national stars, were among 300 Jewish players who 'disappeared' from the footballing scene following a ban on all Jewish players from 1933 imposed by the German Football Board (Connolly 1999).

17. Of course, it could be argued that Baldwin, then Prime Minister, was simply responding to the public mood of pacifism, but his election pledge in the election of 1935 was to rearm not to disarm. Nevertheless, the bitter memories of the trenches in 1914–18, the traditional fear of the Treasury that the defence budget was squandering precious resources (though some defence spending would clearly have reduced the mass unemployment of the time), and the quasi-isolationist philosophy of the élite, all inhibited the necessary response at the time—as indeed did the memories of Verdun and an unlimited belief in the impregnability of the Maginot Line on the part of the French. The appeasement process reached its apotheosis under Chamberlain, convinced by his 'experts' that any future war would involve mass air bombing in which a sixty-day assault would leave 600,000 dead and twice as many wounded. In fact, actual deaths in Britain due to air attack numbered about a tenth of this. Chamberlain's appeasement philosophy, rooted in economic incentives, may have been appropriate for a weak and unpopular Weimar government, but it was wholly inappropriate for a strong and popular Nazi government (Kagan 1997: 376).

18. The SS also became a quasi-independent state within a state: it ran forty businesses and 150 factories, it 'paid' for the 'final solution', and it financed thirty-eight *waffen* SS divisions. By 1942 the SS was Europe's leading mineral water distributor and on 7 April 1945 the US Army discovered a mine at Merkers full of stolen valuables hidden by the Nazis: the gold alone was valued at $241,113,302 ($35 an ounce) (Goldin 1998: 34).

19. Ironically, it was only when Hitler shifted from politics to war that the limits of his strategic skill began to show (Craig 1986: 493).

20. Germans allowed themselves 2,300 calories a day, Poles were allowed 900, and Jews 183 (Hodgson 1995: 210).

21. The recent discovery of Himmler's diaries for 1941–2 have reignited the debate about the timing of the decision concerning the 'final solution', with some arguing that the decision may have been taken much earlier in 1941 (see Traynor 1999c).

22. About 30,000 Ukrainians volunteered for a special division of the SS. Of these 8,400 were imprisoned by the British at the end of the war and, despite Stalin's demands, were not handed back. About 1.3 million Ukrainians were rounded up and sent as slave labourers to Germany. About 25,000 of these were given asylum in Britain at the end of the war (*Observer*, 20 Sept. 1998, 20). On 16 March 1999 over 500 veterans of the original 140,000 Latvian *Waffen* SS marched through Riga, the Latvian capital, to 'commemorate' their role in the Second World War. 95% of Latvia's 70,000 Jews were murdered during the war (*Guardian*, 17 Mar. 1999).

23. Hans Münch, an SS doctor in the Hygiene Institute with Josef Mengele at Auschwitz, who, like almost half his profession, had been in the Nazi party since 1939, constructed a rationale for gassing and 'experimenting' on prisoners worthy of his overlord's warped logic. Since epidemics of typhus, typhoid, and dysentery existed, gassing people was the 'logical conclusion, it was the only way to prevent the whole camp from being destroyed. If they hadn't been gassed they would have died terrible deaths from the epidemics' (quoted in *Der Spiegel*, 28 Sept. 1998; trans. by Sandra Smith, *Observer*, 24 Oct. 1998). That the camp was *designed* to gas Jews and the epidemics were a direct consequence of the appalling conditions seems not to register with Münch. Even his experimentation on prisoners is rationalized as a humane act: after all, he argues, was he not saving people from the gas chamber by conducting experiments on them? In fact Münch refused to take part in the selections for execution, but, far from being disciplined for this, he was promoted six months later to Untersturmführer (2nd Lieutenant).

24. Magenheimer (1998: 21, 26) suggests that the British resistance to Hitler stemmed not just from an anti-Nazi policy but also from an anti-German policy. In the words of Sir Robert Vansittart, chief adviser to the British Foreign Secretary, 'the German Reich and the Reich concept have been the curse of the world for 75 years, and if we do not destroy it this time, we will never do it. The enemy is the German Reich and not only Nazism.'

25. The German armaments industry was extraordinarily slow in mobilizing for war: a general mobilization was not called until the autumn of 1940, and not until the spring of 1943, after the Battle of Stalingrad, were women drafted into the weapons factories.

26. Overall German tank production increased from 5,520 in 1943 to 8,001 in 1944. Despite all the air attacks, it has been suggested that no more than 12% of the total weight of bombs fell on industrial areas. Only by the spring of 1945 had half the

armaments, one-third of the steel, and almost all oil production been rendered ineffective (Magenheimer 1998: 225).

27. The diversion denuded the *Wehrmacht* without supplying the necessary resources to the German navy or airforce. For example, Admiral Dönitz insisted that he required a force of 300 submarines for the Atlantic, with 100–150 on constant patrol to ensure success against the Allied convoys; by 1942 there were seldom more than fifty available. In the *Luftwaffe* the problem was not just a shortage of supply but an over-commitment to offensive bombers when defensive fighters were critical. In 1942, at the highpoint of German offensive action, the ratio of defensive to offensive aircraft stood at 1:1; by 1944 the ratio had not altered (Magenheimer 1998: 132–4).

28. By 1 April 1942 3.6 million Soviet soldiers had surrendered to the *Wehrmacht*, and Stalin, fearing Hitler would exploit anti-communist feelings amongst these POWs and recruit an army against the Soviet Union, had 330,000 NKVD (Commissariat for Internal Affairs—the forerunner of the KGB) troops in 'special formations' with orders to execute anyone suspected of entertaining pro-German sympathies.

29. In fact, Soviet casualty figures for the war as a whole are the most unreliable of all. Gorbachev claimed in 1990 that there had been 8.5 million military casualties and 18.5 million civilian casualties. Magenheimer (1998: 271–4) suggests this overall total of 27 million is probably about right, though Erickson (1994) suggests that they may have been as high as 50 million, while Overy (1997: p. xvi) suggests between 43 million and 47 million.

30. Even in 1941 Hitler underestimated the strength of the Soviet arms production capability and overestimated that of the Germans; in that year the Soviet Union produced 24,500 tanks and 33,000 pieces of artillery, while the Germans produced 11,000 tanks and 7,800 pieces of artillery (Magenheimer 1998: 139).

31. Only about 1.8 million of the 5.7 million Soviet prisoners taken by the Germans survived the war (excluding the 2 million Soviet citizens executed directly), while the corresponding figures for German POW deaths was 1 million of the 3 million captured. Only 4% of Western POWs died in German captivity (Erickson 1994: 19; Burleigh 1997: 324; Rees 1997: 196).

32. Hitler's disinclination for organizational responsibility led him to refuse the post of party chair in 1921 (see Kershaw 1998: 156).

33. The autobahns, Europe's first multiple-lane highways, are often seen as Hitler's greatest pre-war contribution to German development. In fact they were planned under the Weimar Republic and the first stretch, between Cologne and Bonn, was completed in 1932—the year before Hitler rose to power. Only 3,000 of the planned 11,000 km were completed before 1939 (Bishop 1999e: 48).

34. 70% of the Volkswagen factory were slaves—a form of labour that the Germans had initially used in the First World War (Berghahn 1987: 50; Hodgson 1995: 202). Between 7 million and 10 million slave workers (90% were Slavs, mainly Poles, Ukrainians, and Russians) survived the war and under the post-war agreements were eligible to claim for their imprisonment and damages to their health but not for the absence of earnings. About £35 billion was paid by the German government under this scheme between 1945 and 1998, but the sums were often small. For example, Zofia Koscik, a Ukrainian slave worker now living in Poland, was paid £143 for three years' slavery in Germany from a German–Polish reconciliation fund (*Guardian*, 13 Jan. 1999). Ten Czech women were paid £3,340 each in 1999 by Siemens in compensation for their slave labour in Ravensbruck (*Guardian*, 20 July 1999). Hans

Mommsen was given access to the archives of Volkswagen and established that 10,000 (66%) of Volkswagen workers were foreign slaves by 1942, mainly producing arms at Wolfsburg. In July 1998 Volkswagen, which had already paid £9 million to Holocaust research charities, agreed to compensate former slave workers from a 'private aid fund' (*Guardian*, 8 July 1998, 13). In May 1999 a documentary screened by the German public-service broadcaster, ARD, claimed that between 350 and 400 babies of slave labourers were starved of food and medicines when they were forcibly separated from their mothers and sent to a home at Rühen near Wolsburg (*Guardian*, 6 May 1999).

35. There were also many efforts by Jews and other prisoners to resist their captors, most significantly through the Warsaw ghetto rising in April 1943, and in Treblinka and Sorbibor camps in August and October of the same year. Even the crematoria in Auschwitz were blown up in 1944 by the inmates. But when the Russians liberated the camp in January 1945, only 7,000 people remained alive. In the six buildings that had not been destroyed by the Germans, the Russians found 836,255 women's dresses. When American troops liberated Dachau in April 1945, all 500 SS guards were executed within an hour (Hodgson 1995: 214–16).

36. Hitler's fascination with the V1 and V2 'revenge weapons' was considered by Speer as a 'massive blunder'. Speer was well aware that anti-aircraft weapons were more important—but also that the conventional AAA (anti-aircraft artillery) was grossly wasteful (on average it took 16,000 shots to down an Allied aircraft and by 1944 1.1 million people were deployed on the German AAA defences). However, the development of anti-aircraft rockets was subordinated to the production of V1s and V2s. Even the diversion of resources to fighter production over AAA production would have been more effective for the Germans. For example, the Schweinfurt raid by 291 American bombers on 14 October 1943 led to eighty-two losses; only eleven of these were shot down by AAA, the rest were hit by fighter aircraft (Magenheimer 1998: 230–2).

37. The Allied response to the conspirators, both in its overtures for peace and its requests for help, was similarly stymied by notions of honour. Not only did the Allies refuse to help; they even helped the Gestapo by broadcasting a list of conspirators after Stauffenberg's failed bomb attempt and, once the war was over, insisted on banning several books written by German resisters. The list broadcast by the British did not contain Rommel's name and it is not clear that Rommel was ever directly involved with the conspiracies (probably because he had never espoused shock or shame at the activities of the Nazi state), but he was clearly unhappy with Hitler's handling of the war. Rommel had been gravely injured on 17 July 1944 in an air attack on his car, but, despite there being no evidence against him, he was 'persuaded' to commit suicide on 14 October. This was after being given the choice by the authorities between suicide and a state trial that would inevitably harm his family (Fest 1997: 312–13). The Allies even kept some resisters in prison longer than some confirmed Nazis. As the American camp commandant informed General Gersdorff, a conspirator against Hitler, who had complained that his sentence was lengthier than that of General Engel, a man loyal to Hitler—

General Engel has demonstrated throughout his military career that he always carries out his orders. He will not engage in any resistance to us in civilian life either, and therefore he poses no threat. You, on the other hand, have shown that you follow your own conscience on occasion and consequently might not obey our orders under certain circumstances. People like you . . . are therefore dangerous to us. For this reason, you will remain in custody.   (quoted in Fest 1997: 323–4)

38. Presumably this was not the same heavenly providence that was responsible for Freisler being the only person killed when an Allied bomb fell on the courthouse on 3 February 1945.

9

Martin Luther King's 'Dream Speech': The Rhetoric of Social Leadership

The world will little note, nor long remember what we say here, but it can never forget what they did here.

(Abraham Lincoln in his Gettysburg Address 19 November 1863)

Leadership as Rhetorical Performance

When Lincoln spoke at the burial ground for the Union dead at Gettysburg, a mere 272 words ensured that the costliest battle of the war was transformed from a catastrophic bloodbath that changed little, to a complete verbal reconstruction of American history, identity, and purpose (Wills 1992).[1] This chapter looks, amongst other things, at the significance of rhetoric to leadership by focusing upon Martin Luther King and in particular on his 'Dream Speech', allegedly the greatest speech of the twentieth century, exactly 100 years after what was, apparently, the greatest speech of the nineteenth century.

Edward Everett, a renowned orator, had already spent over two hours relaying the details of the battle and its significance in the main commemoration before Lincoln spoke. But his style of peroration was 'made obsolete within half an hour of the time when it was spoken' (Wills 1992: 148)[2] by the following:

Fellow-countrymen—Four score and seven years ago our fathers brought forth on this continent a new nation, conceived in Liberty, and dedicated to the proposition that all men are created equal.

Now we are engaged in a great civil war, testing whether that nation, or any nation so conceived and so dedicated, can long endure. We are met on a great battlefield of that war. We have come to dedicate a portion of that field, as a final resting-place for those who here gave their lives that that nation might live. It is altogether fit and proper that we should do this.

But, in a larger sense, we cannot dedicate—we cannot consecrate—we cannot hallow this ground. The brave men, living and dead, who struggled here, have consecrated it, far above our poor power to add or detract. The world will little note, nor long remember, what we say here, but it can never forget what they did here. It is for us, the living, rather, to be dedicated here to the unfinished work which they who fought here have thus far so nobly advanced. It is rather for us to be here dedicated to the great task remaining before us—that from these honoured dead we take increased devotion to that cause for which they gave the last full measure of devotion—that we here highly resolve that these dead shall not have died in vain—that this nation, under God, shall have a new birth of freedom—and that government of the people, by the people, for the people, shall not perish from the earth.

In fact, Lincoln's invitation to speak was an afterthought, and he was just asked to deliver 'a few words'. His speech lasted barely three minutes and was delivered to somewhere between 10,000 and 20,000 people. The site of the speech was the unfinished cemetery at Gettysburg, which was laid out in semi-circular fashion to ensure that no regiment or state took priority over another. Lincoln, having talked with the designer and seen the plan before hand, was well aware of the resonance this would create with the end of his opening sentence: 'the proposition that all men are created equal.' Lincoln was not an impromptu speaker; he crafted his words on paper and vocalized them extraordinarily carefully. As a keen student of the theatre, especially Shakespeare, he was well aware of the significance of rhythm and sound. For writing itself, he had only the highest praise, for 'its utility may be conceived by the reflection that to *it* we owe everything which distinguishes us from savages. Take it from us, and the Bible, all history, all science, all government, all commerce, and nearly all social intercourse, go with it' (quoted in Wills 1992: 154). Thus in his speech no names are mentioned, nor are any regiments or states, or battles; even Gettysburg, slavery, and the Union are absent. Instead, Lincoln lifted the audience beyond their visceral concerns of the time to a different place, where ideals were forged not bodies butchered. In Wills's (1992: 37) apt phrase: 'The nightmare realities [were] etherealized in the crucible of his language.'

In particular, what Lincoln managed to bring off was a reinterpretation of the origins of the Union, from one where the Constitution supported slavery to one where all men were equal. In this 'he performed one of the most daring acts of open-air sleight-of-hand ever witnessed by the unsuspecting' (Wills 1992: 38). While thousands of men risked their very lives in an effort to settle the question of American identity, Lincoln, in effect, had settled the issue by refounding the United States on a new basis in a mere 272 words. Not that the sleight of hand went unnoticed at the time—but the notice was unable to repel the new image. As Wills (1992: 147) concludes: 'for most people now, the Declaration means what Lincoln told us it means, as a way of correcting the Constitution itself without overthrowing it.' How did Lincoln achieve this, and what was this sleight of hand? He was, after all, and at best, equivocal about racial equality. But he was adamant that democracy was the best political system for the Union and unswerving in his belief that, if slavery—or any other individual 'right'—threatened the democratic Union, it must be removed by whatever force necessary, including a military act. For Lincoln, emancipation was a military necessity more than a political preference (Wills 1992: 142–3). Thus, although the 'founding fathers' had not intended to prioritize democracy above the other principles, Lincoln's actions in suspending *habeas corpus* during the war—but allowing the 1864 election to continue—effectively subordinated individual freedom to majority rule (Kleinfeld 1997: 24–7). Lincoln's Gettysburg address similarly reconstructed the Declaration of Independence into a document equivalent in status to the Constitution, thereby elevating equality into a critical—and new— principle, because the word equality is not in the pre-war Constitution or the original Bill of Rights. As a result of the 'Civil War amendments', the Thirteenth, Fourteenth, and Fifteenth, black Americans became citizens, slavery was abolished, suffrage was confirmed for all, and, for the first time, the word 'equal' entered the Constitution (Kleinfeld 1997: 28–30). Whether Lincoln became convinced that equality was a critical principle is still debated and it seems more likely that adoption of the principle served—in a Machiavellian way—his larger purpose of saving the Union.

Wills's persuasive rendering of accounts suggests that Lincoln, like Pericles before him, focused on the present and the future, not on the past. He kept the dead anonymous to deepen the passion of mourning by refusing to give vent to it. He kept the scene universal by resisting the urge to provide details. He used a number of antitheses drawn from the ancient Greek rhetorical heritage: the fallen 'gave' rather than 'lost' their lives—an act of voluntary sacrifice for the sake of an ideal not an act of involuntary folly for the sake of a hill. The speech is as much about birth as it is about death, and the task left by the dead, can only—and therefore must—be completed by the living. Thus the death of thousands is rendered not a colossal waste but the necessary sacrifice for the new nation to be born. Lincoln's speech 'is economical, taut and interconnected, like the machinery he tested and developed for battle. Words were weapons, for him, even though he meant them to be weapons of peace in the midst of war' (Wills 1992: 174).

In what follows I begin by briefly considering the significance of speech and language and go on to describe the origins and guidelines established by the ancient Greeks (and to a lesser extent Romans) in the art of rhetoric. Aristotle's model of rhetoric is then explored, reconstructed, and used to examine recent examples of rhetoric, in particular an analysis of Martin Luther's 'Dream Speech'.

Talk, talk

How important is talk to leadership? How important is speech-making to leadership? The answer to the former question must be critical. The answer to the latter might be less so. Since almost 75 per cent of management time is ostensibly involved in conversation, we may assume that most management is secured through talk and therefore most leadership is too (Stewart 1967). But what is less clear is what kind of conversations managers and leaders have. Strauss suggests that social order at any level (from family life through hospital discipline to international relations) is unthinkable without negotiations; indeed his thesis is that order itself is better conceptualized as 'negotiated order' in so far as some form of negotiation is always critical to organization (Strauss 1978: p. ix).

Conversational analysis, in which the significance of turn-taking and sense-making are of primary importance, has long been predicated on the assumption that talk is the medium through which action is facilitated and organization made possible: talk constitutes the world. This is in sharp contrast to approaches that treat human action as the consequence of structures and talk as the neutral vehicle for the transmission of information. With the structural approach we might consider leadership as the necessary result of externally determining structures: critical situations bring forth dynamic leaders. With the action approach, particularly in its ethnomethodological forms, talk instantiates structure: that is to say that instances of talk and action constitute structures, they make structures exist, they do not occur because of structures. Here the talk of people constitutes a situation as critical. There is, therefore, no iron cage of bureaucracy, or steel structure of social class, existing outside individuals and coercing them to act in particular ways; there are, instead, the talk and action of individuals who create and reproduce or constitute an organization or society in a particular way. Of course, the members of such an organization or society may *believe* themselves to be coerced by external rules and regulations, and, if their talk and actions reproduce this assumption, then the organizational or social status quo will continue—but they have it within their power to stop this (see Boden 1994; Burr 1995; also Fairclough 1992).

Most of the approach of conversational analysis is, as the title implies, limited to conversation. This also implies that turn-taking, turn-making, and the sequencing of interactions are vital in the construction of the organization. As Boden argues, the focus on conversation does not mean that such an approach is limited to an arena of partial significance, not just because so much of organizational work occurs in and through talk, but because the decisions about what to do, where to go, and when to act are themselves construed through dialogue:

Rather than being the exciting 'tilt points' and 'critical moments' of common parlance, actual decision making is a diffuse incremental affair. Organizational members create decisions *from within* and discover their sequential elements, collaborative stages, and even functional parts *as they go along* . . . As real time phenomena, *decisions* are, in fact, largely invisible, whereas *decision making* can be located in the fine laminations of actions and reactions that build, from one moment to another, into the organization. (Boden 1994: 21, 22)

However, speech-making seems a rather distinct and very small element of talk and appears to involve none of the turn-talking interaction beloved of conversational analysis. Yet, when successful speeches are analysed, they tend not to be monologues but asymmetric dialogues: the listeners tend not to listen in stony silence but to become involved in the speech—they clap, shout, nod, shake their heads, walk out, stand up, whistle, and many other things beside. So perhaps speeches are not a qualitatively unique form of talk after all, but merely a form of asymmetric conversation, and part of the success of a speech may indeed lie in the ability of the speaker to engage the listeners in a 'conversation'. This is especially clear in listening to—as opposed to reading—Martin Luther King's 'Dream Speech', because the audience is dynamically interactive with King, they answer his rhetorical questions, and, in the light of black religious traditions, they engage with rather than simply listen to his words.

The exact importance of speech-making to leadership is more difficult to assess: talk may be crucial to leaders and organizations, but are speeches vital or primarily symbolic, involving little more than a ritual? Some leaders (for example General Haig) hardly ever spoke to their troops, while others (for instance, General Patton) appear to have done the opposite. There may be many people employed by global corporations who have never heard their CEO or Chairperson speak live but may nevertheless have read his or her words or watched the corporate video or seen him or her on the news media occasionally. In some leadership positions, particularly political ones where speech-making is the *sine qua non* of their existence, a hefty majority of support in the democratic body of representatives may actually mean that the speeches of the leader are not necessarily crucial to political success—but they may be intended for domestic consumption through the news media. However, there are occasions when a speech does appear to make a considerable difference to the outcome of the situation. Most memorably these are at times of apparent danger or worry or promise—the rallying cry of the commander in battle; the captain's talk before a sporting match; the call for calm to a political demonstration under physical attack; the CEO's speech to the AGM explaining the catastrophic results or the union leader's demand for strike action at a mass rally in support of a victimized colleague. Typically, these are the situations where a speech of quality and power can appear to swing the mood of the listeners in one direction or another—though, of course, it is impossible to establish this with any certainty. The size of the group of listeners need not be large: a parent's appeal to a daughter or son not to undertake a specific course of action may succeed or fail through the quality of the debate; or the words used by an irate consumer may—or may not—persuade a shopkeeper to refund the money. Moreover, a 'speech' may consist of a single sentence that persuades just one person to change his or her current action, which, in turn, may encourage others. The subsequent effect may be equivalent to a social avalanche, but the origin of this may, as in its natural equivalent, be a very small movement by a single flake of snow or a single individual.

The precise role of language is, of course, subject to considerable debate. Realist assumptions portray language as reflective of the world; it merely describes whatever is 'real' or at least tries to get as close to reality as possible. Thus science is an incremental search for the truth about the world and, the closer the language mirrors that truth, the clearer the picture we have of it. On the other hand, a variety of alternative approaches (postmodernist, poststructuralist, constructivist, and so on) suggest that language is not a reflector of the world but a constructor of it. In these approaches the language constitutes reality because the world is knowable only through language and because that knowledge is necessarily constrained by the limits of language (see Boden 1994; Burr 1995; Grint and Woolgar 1997). In effect, whatever the reality is (and it is not necessary to assume that there is no reality beyond the language but just that we cannot gain access to it except through language), our version of it is simultaneously brought into view by, and possibly obscured through, language. For example, it is not physically possible to construct a model of human behaviour that has a unique template for each individual—we simply cannot wander round with four billion human types in our heads. Consequently we develop stereotypes, based on socially acquired knowledge about others, and operate on this basis. Naturally the stereotypes are often erroneous and/or unhelpful, but it seems that we are stuck with them and cannot refine them down to the point of individual differences. Thus language operates to help us recognize others but at the same time constrains our interpretations of them.

Equally significant here, language is not merely a mechanism for describing reality, or what we take to be reality, by constituting the world in particular ways; it is also a mechanism for changing the world, and for leaders this is of fundamental import. As Austin (1962) argues, language is also performative—that is, it acts to bring things into existence. It does this either in the sense that, for example, the phrase 'black hole' brings into existence a phenomenon that appears to explain a previously unknown phenomenon or a previously inexplicable series of data. Or it is performative in the sense that language operates to bring some act or process to fruition—'stop reading this!' It is also the case that language is performative in the sense that it can mobilize different constituencies. For instance, Potter and Reicher suggest that the term 'community' provided different performative functions for the various groups involved in the St Paul's riot in Bristol, England, in 1981. For some it was a close-knit 'community', for others it was a 'community' relations problem, for others it was a problem of the Black 'community' (Potter and Reicher 1987).

This raises another issue to do with language: it is necessarily social. Hence, when Martin Luther King Jr. talks of the 'black population', he is not merely describing his account of a group of people, but also mobilizing an array of related ideas and concepts. In effect the term constitutes a particular 'reality', it performs in a particular way and has particular effects, most notably it legitimates some action and expression and delegitimates others (Deetz 1992).

This kind of dispute over the 'same' term is reflected in the disputes over the civil-rights movement in the USA. In the direct footsteps of Lincoln, while King sought to wrestle the traditions of the USA to support the civil-rights movement, his opponents attempted to demonstrate how the very 'same' traditions explained why civil rights should not be extended to black Americans. In effect, the 'same' traditions embody different communities, they mobilize oppositional political formations by claiming sovereignty over apparently identical symbols, myths, and traditions. But before we consider this, let us return to the origins of the debate about speeches by considering what is often regarded as one of the most effective manuals for speakers of all time: Aristotle's *The Art of Rhetoric*.

The Art of Rhetoric

The Origins of The Art of Rhetoric

Formally, and formerly, the act of speaking, especially public speaking, was the subject of immense scholarly interest and advice. In its earliest form, 'rhetoric', from the Greek *rhâtür* (speaker in the assembly), was the art of using speech to persuade. It is not coincidental that the art of rhetoric and the rule of democracy were coeval. As Lawson-Tancred suggests, when political rule is through naked force, or inherited tradition, there is little need to *persuade* the people of one's right to rule, though in fact ancient Greek society held oratorical skills almost as high as military prowess (Lawson-Tancred 1991: 3). The origins of rhetorical skill appear to lie in Syracuse, a Greek colonial city, and the skill moved rapidly throughout Greek society, where the political and the legal system depended upon rhetorical skill. By the time of the Peloponnesian War (431–404 BC), professional teachers of rhetoric and speech-writers (*logographoi*) had appeared, and training in rhetoric had become commonplace. Classical theoreticians (Georgias, Plato, Aristotle, and Cicero) were very divided in their debates about the nature of rhetoric, in particular whether it was an essential part of life or a sleight of hand (Wardy 1996). A considerable amount of work hinged around the word *eikos*—'probable', 'plausible', or 'likely'—and it is this notional gap between the truth and the representation of the truth that so bedevilled the dispute on the respectability of rhetoric.

Georgias had originally argued that rhetoric, the art of persuasion in which emotion and power were influential features, was an inevitable element of all human life. For Plato, the use of rhetoric—as an act of manipulative persuasion—was both inferior to, and subversive of, philosophy, in particular the dialectical questioning method used by Socrates to establish truth through reason and rational debate. In effect, the battle in its extreme formulation—which prefigured the current debates between modernism and postmodernism—was balanced around whether the truth was objectively persuasive or whether rhetoric was persuasively objective.

Plato was vehemently opposed to democracy and regarded the teaching of rhetoric as a dangerous malpractice. It was, for him, the mischievous tool of the demagogue: it enslaved the masses; it pleased rather than benefited the mob, for it provided even the worst political leaders with the technical skill to manipulate the masses in whatever direction they chose (Wardy 1996: 8; Grint 1997b). For Plato, the direction was crucial, and rhetorical skill should always be subordinated to the direction, and not vice versa. But for Georgias, the Athenian right to free speech and the rule of democracy (for male citizens at least) made rhetoric a principle skill for all to master. It was a skill that could be used for good or evil, it did not embody any values in and of itself. Of course, heroic deeds were also important—but without their recording in rhetoric they were soon lost to history. In contrast, Plato's representation of Socrates suggests that the teacher of philosophical dialectic did not pretend to know the answers—as he suggests rhetoricians did—but merely taught the techniques for understanding, to attain knowledge for its own sake, and increase his or her own knowledge in the dialectical process with the student (Wardy 1996: 54, 70). Whatever the results of the battle in any theoretical sense, in the hands of Aristotle, the construction of rules for rhetoric became formalized, and these rules changed little between Cicero and the late eighteenth and early nineteenth centuries, when the formal teaching of rhetoric as a university subject generally fell from favour.

It is ironic, or in Wardy's phrase 'deeply provocative, almost shocking', that Aristotle (384–322 BC), the erstwhile student of Plato and enemy of 'rhetoric', did not also fall from favour after he had completed a major text on rhetoric. In fact, Aristotle had four explanations for this apparent betrayal (Wardy 1996: 108).

First, he still maintained that, since truth and justice were stronger than lies and injustice, then 'false' rhetoric would not be able to overturn the former. Truth and justice, then, had a 'natural advantage' (Wardy 1996: 110). Secondly, his arch opponent and intellectual competitor, Isocrates, had developed a very successful school based on the study of rhetoric—which shaded Aristotle's school with its pulling power—and, with the decline of Athenian democracy, the utility of persuasion took on a different meaning. Indeed, Protagoras, a contemporary of Socrates, and held by many at the time to have been the greatest public speaker of the time, was held to 'enchant' or 'bewitch' his audience with his voice—a point that would presumably run directly counter to the kind of critically rational audience that Plato professed to encourage. For Aristotle, the reality that rhetoric was *already* being taught meant that he now had a duty to educate people about the tricks that rhetoricians would use to persuade them of falsehoods.

Thirdly, Aristotle argued that rhetoric could be studied, but only in the context of its philosophical foundations and formations. Rhetoric, at the hands of Aristotle, was to become not the pragmatic bag of tricks he associated with its Isocratic version, but with the scientific roots of knowledge that Aristotle inherited from Plato and Socrates. In an Athenian environment in particular, where legal attack upon one's character and actions could arise from any citizen, and where juries became increasingly adept at convicting citizens from the richer echelons of Athenian society, the ability to defend oneself through rhetorical skill rapidly became a requirement of political survival, rather than just a useful resource for many leaders. Aristotle, thus, sought to set the study of rhetoric both with an *episteme*—a field of theoretical speculation—and a *techne*—a related set of practical concepts. In effect, Aristotle's version of rhetoric was to be both philosophical *and* to have clear, and related, practical consequences.

Fourthly, although Plato was adamant that rhetoric persuaded through emotion not reason—and hence his dislike of it—Aristotle suggested that one could appeal to the listeners' emotions if, but only if, the intent and effect were to enable them to see the rationality of the argument. Manipulative rousing of the emotions was wrong, but using empathy to explain why a course of action should be taken was respectable.

Unfortunately for Aristotle, his efforts had a limited effect in their time, not through any lack of skill on his part but because within five years of his death the great Athenian experiment in democracy had been plunged into darkness with the rise of the tyrant Demetrius (an ex-pupil of Aristotle). The subsequent restructuring of the legal system meant the requirements for rhetorical skill were marginal at best. Not until around 50 BC and Cicero's (106–43 BC) *Orator,* the Roman equivalent of *The Rhetoric,* does rhetoric return to centre stage in the Western world, where it remained until the early part of the third century AD— and the beginning of the end of the Roman world.

Unpacking The Art of Rhetoric

Aristotle, reflecting the common Greek assumption that there were three kinds of most things, divided forms of rhetoric into three: 'forensic'- legal speeches of the prosecution and defence; 'deliberative'- political advice; and 'epideictic'— speeches praising or blaming someone or thing (Wardy 1996: 26). He also argued that persuasiveness depended upon three criteria: personal character, emotional appeal, and logical proof. In turn, these three operated in a triangle of effectiveness, as illustrated in Fig. 9.1.

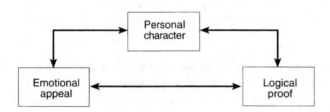

Fig. 9.1. Aristotle's model of rhetoric

In fact, the first two (personal character and emotional appeal) are often difficult to separate and the third (logical proof) is seldom as effective as Aristotle maintains; if logical proof was effective, we would probably spend little time analysing the forms of speech and more time on the content. Unfortunately, self-evident facts that speak for themselves seem few and far between in the context that we are concerned with. This does not mean that appeals to rationality, to the 'truth', and to the 'facts' are irrelevant; far from it, they are crucial elements of persuasion; but they are not in and of themselves sufficient to persuade others on each and very occasion. This is most blatantly clear when scientific 'experts' disagree on the 'facts', such as in the BSE case in the UK (see Grint 1997*a*). But its practical utility lies in the recognition that (*a*) facts do not speak for themselves and (*b*) what appears a rational argument for one person maybe be subordinated to a different rationality for another. For instance, it may be irrational to resist the introduction of new technology at work, since, ultimately, the organization will become uncompetitive and vanish. However, workers may believe that by the time the company collapses they will have retired, or they regard the threat of closure as just another management trick to exploit them or whatever. Rationality is important then, and it would be rather foolish to forgo a rational explanation for why your followers should continue to follow you, but that does not mean followers are necessarily swayed by rational argument. In some local contexts the power of rational accounts may increase—for example, within a scientific community—but in other contexts it may be less relevant.

Personal character—especially perceived as that which engenders trust and enables the audience to identify with the speaker—is, however, deemed to be relevant by most authorities on the topic. Shakespeare's *Henry V* provides one such fictional identification when the King speaks to his troops on the eve of the Battle of Agincourt:

> That he which hath no stomach to this fight,
> Let him depart; his passport shall be made,
> And crowns for convoy put into his purse:
> We would not die in that man's company
> That fears his fellow ship to die with us . . .
> We few, we happy few, we band of brothers;
> For he to-day that sheds his blood with me
> Shall be my brother; be he ne'er so vile.
>
> (*Henry V*, Act IV, Sc.ii)

Personal character also has to demonstrate a set of ideals that appear to be deeply and steadfastly held. Mrs Thatcher, for all that she never achieved the support of the majority of the British electorate, nevertheless manifested precisely this indomitable spirit throughout her period of office. As she said just after the war in the Falklands: 'When we started out, there were waverers and the faint hearts; the people who thought that Britain could no longer seize the initiative for herself, the people who thought we could no longer do the great things which we once did . . . Well they were wrong.'[3]

The emotional appeal, which Aristotle thought was necessary to persuade an audience to change its mind, leads Huczynski (1993) to assess Lewin's Unfreeze-Change-Refreeze model. In fact, Huczynski suggests that much of this approach was originally developed—after Aristotle—by John Wesley in the eighteenth century as a method of religious conversion. Aristotle, Wesley, Lewin, and more recently Adey, Shayer, and Yates, all argue that change requires some initial form of disequilibrium, or cognitive conflict, to occur in the minds of the target audience with regards to previously held beliefs. In effect, assumed 'truths' have to be shown to be false or of limited utility (Adey *et al.* 1991). But there must also be a clear alternative to prevent the original beliefs becoming even more rigidly adhered to. For Wesley, the disequilibrium was generated by forcing listeners to choose—immediately—between damnation or salvation; for modern gurus the choice will probably be between imminent organizational failure and unbeliev-able financial success. Both approaches utilize a degree of fear and there are clear traces of the kind of method used by cult leaders to disorient their potential fol-lowers' critical faculties. This intense level of anxiety is then extended long enough to disable the critical intellectual faculties for the 'conversion' to occur. General Patton's approach to his troops on the eve of D-Day appeared to repro-duce this. Rather than delivering a speech that concentrated on the logical issues at hand (that many of his listeners were about to be maimed or killed), he con-centrated on their emotional responses:

Men, this stuff we hear about America wanting to stay out of the war—not wanting to fight—is a lot of bull-shit. Americans love to fight—traditionally! All real Americans love the sting and clash of battle . . . You men are veterans, or you would not be here. You are ready! A man, to continue breathing, must be alert at all times. If not, sometime some German sonofabitch, will sneak up behind him and beat him to death with a sockful of shit. [The troops roared their approval.] There are four hundred neatly marked graves somewhere in Sicily, all because ONE MAN went to sleep on his job [pause]. But they are GERMAN graves for we caught the bastards asleep before they did . . . Why by God, I actu-ally pity those poor sons-of-bitches we are going up against [howls of delight and clap-ping]. (quoted in D'Este 1996: 602–3)

Since, by all accounts, Patton achieved immense popularity with his own troops (in distinct contrast to his unpopularity with just about everybody else), we may assume that Patton's ability to motivate his troops, to get them to change their mind and to persuade them to fight and quite possibly die, seems closely associ-ated with his rhetorical abilities.[4] What particularly seems to have impressed Patton's troops was his absolute conviction that he knew best, that he knew the solution to their immediate problem, but that he also knew what would happen if they did not follow his orders. In short, Patton generates a high level of dis-comfort and then offers the possibility of reducing this—if and only if—they fol-low his prescription:

Sure we all want to go home. We want this thing over with. But you can't win a war lying down . . . The shortest way home is through Berlin! Why if a man is lying down in a shell hole, if he just stays there all the day the Boche will get to him eventually, and probably get him first! . . . We will win this war, but we will win it only by fighting and by showing guts [pause]. There is one great thing you men will be able to say when you get home. You may thank God for it. Thank God that, at least thirty years from now, when you are sitting around the fireside with your grandson on your knee and he asks 'what did you do in the great World War II?', you won't have to say, 'I shovelled shit in Louisiana'. (quoted in D'Este 1996: 604–5)

Aristotle might have supported Patton's personal display of energy as another element of personal character and an essential precondition for leadership—either by appearing to speak without notes or by developing an active lifestyle. At first sight, quite how Ronald Reagan got away with this latter element is difficult to comprehend, but his acting skills may have displaced the necessity of action.

Reagan was a master of 'playing' to the audience, with a formidable memory for data, at least until he became President, which may be why his lapses in memory seemed so bizarre (De Groot 1995). His rise to national prominence as a politician can be mapped through his articulation of the 'moral majority's' antipathy towards the student protests in Californian universities in the late 1960s. De Groot insists that the vast majority of California's population had no time for the student rebellion that spread onto the campuses of Berkeley in particular in the late 1960s, and Reagan was able to increase and maintain his popularity by concentrating attention on 'the small minority of beatniks, radicals and filthy speech activists (who) have brought shame to . . . a great university' (quoted in De Groot 1995: 32). The very word 'Berkeley' seems to have been enough for Reagan to secure spontaneous applause from his audience and his tough stance only increased his popularity at the expense of the students. His ability to capture public prejudice against the students was remarkable. For example, in a remark that was repeated endlessly he suggested that he had seen a group of protesters who 'were carrying signs that said "Make Love not War". The only trouble was they didn't look like they were capable of doing either. His hair was cut like Tarzan, and he acted like Jane, and he smelled like Cheetah' (quoted in De Groot 1995: 33).

There were three golden rules of rhetoric that Reagan always remembered. First, conversational plain speaking or the 'small talk' that dominates informal social gatherings is probably inadequate to generate the kinds of interest necessary to persuade people of something. But this does not mean that one needs to wax lyrical with sophisticated sentences. On the contrary, Reagan's political success coincided with what the *San Diego Union*, a conservative popular paper, called his ability 'to speak common sense. Common sense may be "simplistic", as the liberals like to call it. But the people understand it. And they can't act unless they understand the issues' (quoted De Groot 1995: 33).

Secondly, it is not necessary to be rhetorically gifted to achieve success; it is possible to 'act out' a speech, and, as long as it is delivered properly, it can work. With enough acting skill—and a good speech-writer (Peggy Noonan)—Reagan could bring off memorable speeches, or at least phrases. On the day of the Challenger space-shuttle disaster, Reagan used allegory, or figurative speech—one of the most important devices with which to construct a good speech—in his words about the crew to the American people: 'We will never forget them, nor the last time we saw them, this morning, as they prepared for the journey and waved goodbye and "slipped the surly bonds of earth" to "touch the face of God".'[5]

Thirdly, the utility of a phrase or story does not depend on its validity. For example, several of Reagan's claims about student drug taking, black violence, and the communist infiltration of the university faculty were without foundation—but their effects were achieved before this could be established. More recently, during the Gulf War, the claims about the existence of Iraqi tanks on the Saudi border, and of Iraqi troops throwing Kuwaiti babies from their incubators, were subsequently shown to be false—but only after they had galvanized Western opinion into supporting the war efforts of the Allied forces.

Reagan probably became more famous, not for his ability to deliver a good speech but for his tendency to forget where he was in the middle of a speech, or whether he had authorized certain dubious actions by his subordinates, or when he was simply repeating himself. But repetition is not always an error; indeed, it remains a fundamental technique of speech making. This is not so much in the format adopted *ad nauseum* by Mrs Thatcher ('No, no, no!'), but in the rather more subtle technique known to the Greeks as *anadiplosis* (double back)—the repetition of the words or phrase used at the end of one sentence, line, or clause at the beginning or end of the next. Lincoln's resounding example in his 1863 Gettysburg Address—'Government of the people, by the people, for the people'—is probably amongst the most famous and effective. His four-hour-long speech, 'The monstrous injustice of slavery' speech, delivered during an election campaign on 16 October 1854, prefigures his fondness for this technique with six consecutive sentences starting with 'Let us'. One hundred and forty years later Nelson Mandela's 'Let freedom reign' speech reproduces the same technique and phrasing towards the end, where five of the final eight sentences begin with 'let', and seventeen of forty sentences start with 'We'.

Churchill, long regarded as the man who mobilized the English language for war, provided many of the speeches that allegedly persuaded the British to fight on, when all around them the situation looked extremely bleak (Warner 1994). His post-Dunkirk speech on 4 June 1940 is a classic example of anadiplosis:

We shall go on to the end, we shall fight in France, we shall fight on the seas and oceans, we shall fight with growing confidence and strength in the air, we shall defend our island, whatever the cost may be, we shall fight on the beaches, we shall fight on the landing grounds, we shall fight in the fields and in the streets, we shall fight in the hills; we shall never surrender.

Yet the delivery of the speech itself was curiously flat and monotone. 'Strength in the air' was delivered in a rising and relatively vigorous tone, but 'we shall defend our island' sounds as though he has just ordered a pizza over the phone, and hardly appears likely to invigorate a nation. Similarly 'we shall fight on the beaches' starts to sound excited, but by the time he has reached 'the streets' and 'the fields' most of his listeners have probably nipped out for a cup of coffee.[6]

Often, the most memorable phrases do not so much involve conventional repetition as the reconstruction and inversion of the repetition. Again derived from the Greek original *chiasmus* (word inversion), this usually involves a reversal of the word order in the second of two parallel phrases for its effect, such as Kennedy's: 'Ask not what your country can do for you; ask what you can do for your country.' The effect of this is best assessed by contrasting it to the rather dour and awkward original version that had read: 'We do not campaign stressing what our country is going to do for us as a people. We stress what we can do for our country, all of us.'

Like Reagan's, many of John F. Kennedy's speeches were written by a professional speech-writer—Theodore Sorenson. George Bush also used one—Peggy

Noonan—whose work with Reagan we have already noted. However, while Reagan was an actor of some skill and Kennedy was a speaker of some skill, Bush was neither. According to Lawson (1996), this double (in)competence persuaded senior Republicans to use Peggy Noonan's writing skills to pep up his style— hence his most famous lines: 'The Congress will push me to raise taxes, and I'll say no, and they'll push and I'll say no, and they'll push again. And all I can say to them is, read my lips: no new taxes!' Whatever the disutility of the speech in the long term—as a hostage to fortune that partially sealed Bush's re-election fate— the phrasing nevertheless reveals what Atkinson (1984) calls a classic 'clap- trap'—that is, a linguistic device, supported by non-verbal cues, for when the audience should expect a significant comment and clap immediately afterwards. Atkinson points to two particularly powerful claptraps: TPCs (Two Part Contrasts) and LOTs (Lists of Three).[7] According to Atkinson, TPCs (equivalent to antithesis) account for about one-third of all successful claptraps. Perhaps George Orwell's *Animal Farm* embodies one of the most famous ones: 'All ani- mals are equal, but some are more equal than others.'

But why should a TPC be so effective? One argument might be that it mirrors the binary nature of our language: that, for example, we recognize 'day' only by knowing what 'night' looks like; that we can be 'good' only by understanding the word 'bad'. This structuralist argument—in which the utility of the word is derived from its relationship to other words—is, of course, an important element of the TPC. But there may be more to it than this.

Another suggestion is that it replicates the concept of irony, a concept derived from the Greek word for 'dissembler'—*eiün*. In Plato's hands irony is used— through Socrates—to demonstrate the naïvety of those around him, but in the hands of the Roman rhetoricians, especially Cicero and Quintilian, it became a form of discourse in which the meaning was the contrary of the words (Cuddon 1979: 336–8). Moreover, used here, irony implies the sense of an incongruity between what is expected and what is experienced. The idea of expectations is critical here, because without the expectation the experience cannot be adjudged. Many of the most significant literary works have been constructed within this framework, in which either the ideals espoused by dominant groups are ridiculed through ironic exaggeration, or the words or behaviour or situation of an indi- vidual imply the opposite of that person's assumption. The use of irony is so com- mon in literature that it needs only to be said that Dante, Chaucer, Shakespeare, Voltaire, and Swift used it at length for its prevalence to be recognized.

These methodological tools of ideal comparison and irony have a greater sig- nificance in the construction of memory. In this case, the irony of particular situ- ations appears to impress itself more vividly than most other experiences. Fussell's (1975) reconstruction of the memory of the First World War is a case in point here, most notably because the war had started in an expectation of inno- cence—where glory and the public schools' cry of 'Play up! Play up! And play the game' echoed more a sporting competition with a few bloody noses than the mass destruction soon to be wrought. The rush to enlist on all sides seems grossly incongruous with our own knowledge of what happened to most of these volunteers, but it can be explained if the expectations of the participants are accepted.

The thoughts of Haig, on the eve of the Battle of the Somme, clearly demonstrate the power of irony: 'The wire has never been cut so well nor the artillery preparation so thorough' (quoted in Fussell 1975: 29). The next day 57,000 British troops were killed or wounded in the worst disaster to befall the British army—primarily because the wire had not been cut and because the artillery proved ineffective in the extreme. Indeed, not only did Haig's account of 1 July 1916 to *The Times* bear absolutely no resemblance to the local truth,[8] but, when the British failure of 1916 was compared to the 'success' of the German offensive in the spring of 1918, the result was the same. As Fussell (1975: 17) laments: 'they [the Germans] were engaged in demonstrating the most ironic point of all, namely, that successful attack ruins troops. In this way it was just like defeat.'

This construction of irony pervades many features of everyday life: we try to avoid talking of how well our cars are running—just in case we provoke the god of irony into disabling the clutch; we try to avoid talking about aged relatives—just in case the god of irony strikes them dead the next morning; we write the car off—on the day after we cleaned it for the first time in months; the old soldier who survives forty years of combat and is knocked down by a car on the first day of his retirement; the school where the children of the psychiatrists are the most unbalanced and insecure of the entire class, and so on. What occurs here, then, is the generation of expectation that, as a direct consequence of a preceding event, a subsequent event is most unlikely. Indeed the opposite of what happens is expected, and it is the paradox of this contrast that both generates the irony and maintains it in one's memory.

What might be considered the ironic disintegration of many of our recent leaders has occurred along similar lines: Mrs Thatcher, having warned the British population for so long about the 'enemy within' (trade unionists, miners, communists, and so on), is cut down by her own side, not 'the enemy'. General Patton, feared by the Germans as the greatest Allied commander and responsible for orchestrating thousands of deaths on the battlefield, is almost relieved of command for slapping a soldier, and ultimately killed not by a bullet or a shell but by a piece of bad driving by an American soldier. Gandhi, the arch-proponent of non-violence, is ruthlessly gunned down by a fellow Hindu. Of course, irony also operates at a larger scale: more people died of influenza than from battlefield wounds in the First World War; entire rail networks are brought to a standstill by 'leaves on the track'; and so on.

In contrast, the second most effective claptrap (15 per cent of successful claptraps) is not a pair of contrasting words or ideas but a List of Three (LOT). Atkinson argues that it is especially effective when the first part has a rising intonation and the third part a falling one. Churchill provides several examples: 'never in the field of human conflict was so much owed by so many to so few', or his equivalently memorable 'This is not the end. It is not even the beginning of the end. But it is, perhaps, the end of the beginning.' Note that sometimes an LOF (List of Four) may work. When Churchill took over from Chamberlain as British Prime Minister on 13 May 1940, he said to the House of Commons: 'I have nothing to offer but blood, toil, tears and sweat.' But it remains less well known than either of his previously mentioned LOTs, even though one of his biographers, Robert Rhodes James, says that the effect was electrifying and Churchill withdrew from the chamber, saying to one of his aides: 'That got the SODS, didn't it!' (quoted in MacArthur 1993: 185).

But why should a list of three appear so much more powerful than a list of two or four or more? After all, if language is structured along binary opposites, then we should expect the more powerful rhetorical device to remain locked into the dual rather than the triple format. However, Fussell (1975: 125–35) argues that the number three has a history that is as long as language. Pythagoras thought three was the perfect number. Aristotle, of course, was adamant that a large proportion of the categories he dealt with in rhetoric comprised three forms. There were three forms of friendship (based on interest, pleasure, and contemplation); three factors of speech (speaker, subject, and listener); three types of rhetorical speech (deliberative, forensic, and display); three ages (youth, prime, and old age); three methods of persuasion (logic, emotion, and character); three effects of fortune (birth, wealth, and power); and three virtues of good oratory (clarity, decoration, and propriety). Greek religion divided the world into three: the sky, the earth, and the underworld. Neptune carried a three-pronged spear (as did the devil), while Pluto had a three-headed dog. Faith, hope, and charity are the three Christian virtues, while the world, the flesh, and the devil are the three enemies, to say nothing of the 'holy trinity' or the three wise men, or of Jesus being rejected three times by Judas. In fact, many fairy tales and romantic tales are premised upon this same triple structure; either in the structure of the narrative—the fall, the ordeal, and the redemption—or in terms of the triadic construction of the narrative. In other words, the significance of the third character or event is that it resolves or terminates the problem: the third of the three little pigs; the third of Goldilocks's tests (the bed) in the house of the three bears; and so on. Many jokes are premised upon this same approach—'there were three men: an Englishman, an Irishman and a Scotsman . . .'; even bank pin numbers are predicated on three attempts before the card is withdrawn by the ATM; many national flags have three colours in them; and, as they say, 'third time lucky'.[9]

So significant is the rhetorical construction and delivery of the speech that many would agree with the old adage that it is not what you say but how you say it that counts. As Huczynski (1993: 262) notes: 'spellbinding oratory and the guru's 'charisma' were not the result of supernatural powers, but involved mastering a relatively small number of powerful technical skills such as the creation of TPCs and LOTs.'

Of course, rhetoric may not be enough on its own, and there were few leaders more adept at stage managing events than Adolf Hitler. Sporting events were no exception to the thirst for power and the 1936 Berlin Olympics proved an ideal backdrop to Hitler's pretensions. Robert Mitchell, then a member of the British water polo team, recounts how:

When we started a game—particularly if Hitler was there—the other teams would all line up in the water and give the Nazi salute; and we sort of stood there and lounged against the goal post at the other end, and tried to look as lounging as possible . . . [but at the end of the Olympics] the lights were going down and the Olympic flame went out and then there was utter silence and utter darkness and it really was most impressive and then they started 'Zeig Heil' and that was when 100,000 people were going 'Zeig Heil, Zeig Heil' and I literally had to put my hand in my pocket—literally—to stop myself being hypnotized into doing it with them, it was absolutely hypnotic.   (quoted in BBC 1 1995)

Some measure of Hitler's own rhetorical skill (enhanced as it was by elocution and public-speaking lessons (Larsen 1976) can be gauged by watching any of his speeches; even non-German speakers can be awed at the tone and terror of the invective. This might sound paradoxical: how can a listener who cannot understand the language of the speaker nevertheless experience some kind of emotional response to it? If Mehrabian's (1968) research is valid, then this is actually not such a paradox, for it suggests that only 8 per cent of listeners' attention focuses upon *what* is being said, while *how* it is said accounts for 50 per cent, and what the speaker looks like accounts for the remaining 42 per cent. We do not have to accept the apparently objective division of 'effects' to note that there may well be something of significance in what Mehrabian claims.

Our review of speech making generates considerable support for Aristotle's emphasis on the personal character and emotional appeal of the speaker, and there obviously is a place for logical proofs, but it does not appear to be sufficient to analyse the power and effectiveness of a speech by these three criteria alone. Aristotle suggests that speeches can be distinguished by speaker, auditor, and subject matter. It would not be beyond Aristotle's wit to have recognized the role of the situation in the effectiveness—or otherwise—of speeches. Indeed, much of his (and Plato's) original antipathy to rhetorical skills was rooted in a recognition that under dire circumstances a skilful rhetorician could have enormous control over his or her audience—hence the distaste for rhetoric linked to the swaying of the democratic 'mob'. In fact, as already mentioned, Aristotle suggests that there are (only) three forms of context: deliberative, forensic, and display. Implicitly, then, Aristotle extends the analysis beyond the character of the speaker to the context, but his distaste for teaching rhetoric as an assembly of skills divorced from its philosophical examination seems to dissuade him from analysing its utility more overtly.

Aristotle is also rather limiting in his focus upon emotional appeal as the main technique for influencing listeners. We have noted above that many of the techniques—which were indeed known to Aristotle—are not necessarily grounded in emotional appeals. For example, the rhythm of a speech or the sophisticated use of metaphor or chiasmus or irony appears to secure its effects not through emotion but through its appeal to the intellect.

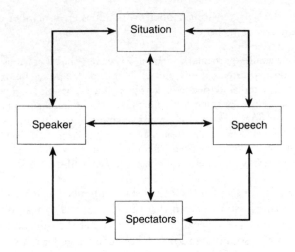

Fig. 9.2. The Immutable 4S Model of speech making

We can summarize the position so far by suggesting that the original triangle suggested by Aristotle to analyse speeches (character, emotion, logic) might usefully be reconstructed as shown in Fig. 9.2. Instead of the emotional issues being separated from the individual and the speaker, we can suggest that they are more usefully seen as a consequence of both. A successful speech cannot be determined by attending to the speech act alone but also warrants a review of its speaker, the situation, and the 'spectators' (those who witness it first hand or second hand through another medium). These cover Aristotle's framework but widen it to include areas not considered significant by him. This is as much because Aristotle concentrated in *The Rhetoric* on the speech act itself, and probably because the contextual and collective aspects of a successful speech are a recognition of contemporary concerns for the irredeemably social nature of language and organization.

In this alternative model, the Immutable 4S Model, the spectators include the immediate listeners and the processes through which a speech reaches beyond the immediate to others in different places and times. After all, a stunning speech by a popular leader in a desperate situation is not going to be remembered if no one bothers to record it, or take it down in written form, or relate it in verbal form for memorizing. The alternative diagram suggests that, even with a good speech, a critical situation, and receptive spectators, an unpopular speaker may not succeed. Likewise, a popular speaker, good speech, and supportive spectators—but a situation without any form of apparent crisis—is unlikely to mobilize the listeners to some form of action. In effect, any single problematic element may well bring the whole show down.

Remodelling Aristotle

But this all seems too mechanical: can the provision of all four elements guarantee an effective speech? I doubt it. First, because nothing can be guaranteed in management or life—as chaos theory has clearly demonstrated (see Grint 1997*a*). Secondly, because mass media research since Lazarsfeld's pioneering 1944 work has for a long time overturned the postulated mechanical link between speaker, message, and receiver. It simply is not the case that the message-sender can control the interpretative effort involved in understanding a message. There may well be opinion-formers to mediate between sender and receiver of the message, but there is a larger form of mediation involved—the interpretative effort involved in this. By that I mean that we can adopt this new model only if we can be certain what the individual is like, whether the spectators are in a receptive mood, what the situation is, what a good speech is, and what the requisite skills are.

As an illustration we could consider whether the skill of making jokes or a sophisticated use of metaphor is appropriate to a speech. It *may* be, but if one or two influential members of your audience are not amused by your first ice-cracking joke, then you could be in trouble; but the same joke to the next group may work perfectly. The problem is how can we read the group to know whether specific techniques of speech making will work? We can probably make a good guess *after* the event—but that is usually a little late. Similarly how do we know—for certain—that the situation is as grave or as good as we think? We might think a crisis has arrived, but, again, if powerful voices are ranged against your 'panic' analysis, then you may be unable to persuade your audience that radical action is necessary. Finally, we might acknowledge that some leaders or speakers are sometimes successful and that their style tends to work with specific situations: Churchill's bellicosity was fine for war but not for peace. Hence he was not popular before the Second World War, was then Prime Minister between 1940 and 1945, but failed to gain reappointment in the 1945 election because the war was over. But how then did he return to power between 1951 and 1955?

It should be self-evident that our immutable model is fixed to a very changeable foundation. In fact the whole structure itself exists as a *mobilizer* rather than as a(n) *(im)mobilizer*. It *can* perform certain actions for us but it *may* not. It *can* bring off a speech but it *may* not. In short, we should concentrate not on what the situation *is* but on what the audience is persuaded it is; not on what the individual *is* but on how the individual performs on the day; not on what skills and techniques are guaranteed to work but on what works in the performance. And who evaluates all this? Well the listeners certainly—but not just the immediate listeners, because there are many who may be persuaded at a subsequent date. Opinion leaders certainly, and they operate across a range of organizations, members of the speaker's own organization, media editors, politicians, and so on. The consequence is that, although we can be relatively clear that the four elements are important, we cannot be sure that any speech will work, and we cannot control

where or how the speech will travel after it has been given. It may be sunk without trace, it may embody a phrase that *becomes* memorable rather than *is* memorable. In sum, the entire arena within which this phenomenon occurs is an
inventive arena—it has to be made to happen and does not simply happen
because of the power of the elements. It has, in effect, to be brought off by all
those involved and not just by the speaker. This brings us to the alternative
Mutable 5S Model shown in Fig. 9.3.

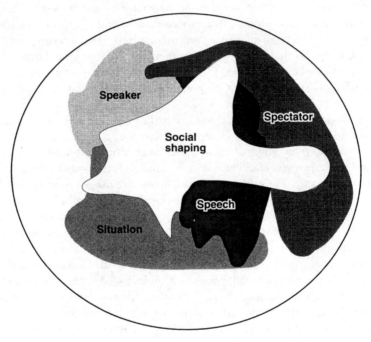

Fig. 9.3. The Mutable 5S Model of speech making

In the Mutable 5S Model, the seamless links between the speech, the speaker,
the situation, and the spectators are represented by the asymmetric forms.
Whereas the 4S model implies a clear boundary between them, this model recon-
structs the active roles of individuals and groups in socially shaping the contents
and boundaries, rather than merely responding to them. For example, a speaker
may persuade the spectators that a crisis is at hand, that the speaker is a good and
honourable leader, that spectators are able to make a difference to the situation,
and that the speech marks a milestone in their collective journey. All of these
issues, then, are negotiated not given, and the negotiated nature of the boundaries means that we cannot determine their form in advance.

Under this model the ambiguity of the outcome, represented by the central core
of 'social shaping', also reminds us of the essentially indeterminate nature of

organizational processes. However, acknowledging that it is impossible to guarantee anything here, the ability of speakers to develop a network of supporters who are able to offer powerful readings of the speech may enable the speaker to secure his or her general intention. Hence, popular presidents, with strong support in the media, are more likely to get their version of events to stick than unpopular ones without media support. In this case, the shift is decidedly one that moves beyond the individual speaker to the social and collective forms of organization that generate persuasive interpretations of the message. In short, speeches are the product not of gifted individuals but of an entire corpus of supporters, human and non-human, who between them render oppositional accounts of the speech illegitimate or at least less legitimate than their own version. Speeches, therefore, are contested processes not merely objective events. They are contingent but not arbitrary—speeches do not mean anything the listener likes but neither do they necessarily mean exactly what the speaker intends. They are constituted into existence not merely rolled out. They are, in sum, 'brought off' not just 'delivered'.

In the final section I want to draw the threads of the discussion on talk and rhetoric together by using Martin Luther King's 1963 'Dream Speech' as a case study. It should go without saying—but often does not—that this is one (my) reading of the speech, and therefore one interpretation and not a definitive or objective assessment. This reflection on the part of the analyst is important because otherwise the fifth S, the social shaping, may appear to be a neutral gloss rather than the active shaping, constructing, and constituting of the speech that it actually is. In other words, although there is no section marked 'social shaping' in the next section, this is because the social shaping is an undeniable element of all the other elements.

Martin Luther King's 'Dream Speech'

Martin Luther King fits most people's criteria for a charismatic leader. He remains the only black American honoured by a national holiday and his 'Dream Speech', in Gardner's words, is generally recognized as one of the greatest, if not *the* greatest, of the twentieth century. President Kennedy congratulated him immediately it was finished and the *New York Times* reported that 'it will be a long time before [Washington] forgets the melodious and melancholy voice of Rev. Dr. Martin Luther King Jr., crying out his dreams to the multitude . . . Dr. King touched all the themes of the day, only better than anybody else' (Gardner 1996: 215). What was the multitude crying out for?

The Situation

The legal position of blacks in the USA, especially in the south, below the Mason Dixon line that divided Maryland from Pennsylvania—very roughly the north from the south—was radically changed by the Emancipation Proclamation of

1863, the Fourteenth Amendment of 1868, and the Fifteenth Amendment of 1870. These freed remaining slaves in the south, provided due process and equal protection before the law, and extended the suffrage to all (male) citizens. The Civil War had been fought to save the Union rather than to end slavery; it resulted in both, but it did not instigate equal citizenship. When the south rejected the Fourteenth Amendment, it was divided into five military districts and ruled by Union generals. In the 1860s and early 1870s, as the Reconstruction of the south took shape, the newly enfranchised black men began to participate and stand for local and state elections, and in 1875 the Civil Rights Bill was enacted to provide 'equal enjoyment' of public accommodation and other facilities. In some parts of the south (primarily South Carolina), schools and public places were partially desegregated. However, the withdrawal of federal troops in 1877 freed the south to undermine all the legislation and, as a political minority without substantial economic power and without land or credit, black Americans remained rooted in a sharecropping economy and rapidly began to lose ground under the racist 'Jim Crow' system.[10] By the end of the nineteenth century most of the legislative gains had been lost (Cook 1998: 14–17). Particularly in the south, poverty remained endemic, and a raft of methods was introduced to disenfranchise black voters. Within the next fifty years almost 3,500 lynchings of blacks occurred, with the vast majority carried out by southern whites. In 1883 the Supreme Court found the 1875 Civil Rights Bill unconstitutional, and the *Plessy* v. *Ferguson* case of 1896—which held that 'separate but equal' was a legitimate approach to race[11]— accepted the legal segregation of most aspects of life, as long as the facilities were 'equal'. Literacy and property tests as well as various spurious requirements, many of which were 'justified' by the *zeitgeist* of scientific racism at the time (see Grint 1994), ensured that by the turn of the century the vast majority of southern blacks were effectively disenfranchised and legally treated as second-class citizens. As Fox Piven and Cloward conclude, until the Second World War 'the structure of coercion and of socialization was so formidable that defiance could not be contemplated' (Fox Piven and Cloward 1977: 189).

Yet this did not inhibit defiance by many blacks, known and unknown, but it did ensure that those who resisted took enormous personal risks. What it also encouraged was the realization that only certain forms of action were likely to change the situation. Personal risk taking may be admirable but it was hardly likely, in and of itself, to generate the kind of collective response that might overturn Jim Crow. When manifestations of the 'strange fruit' hanging from southern trees became an every other day occurrence in the 1880s, the risks for resistance were obvious and terrifying (Dubovoy 1997: 21). While the black population, particularly in the south, owned almost nothing and remained without substantial support from any section of the white community, the kind of resource mobilization open to leaders is self-evidently limited. The question was: how could the mass be mobilized? For black Americans the answer historically has been through organization at the grass roots, but to get to this point requires the organization of words, the mobilization of rhetoric.

The nineteenth-century history of black mobilization against slavery and against segregation, not surprisingly then, is one of public communicators and local organization. The ranks of the former category are limited only by the degree to which their actions have themselves been recorded. If black men and women gave rousing speeches to mobilize slave resistance but the speeches were neither written down, nor passed on through oral testimony, then we have no knowledge of them. For those early black leaders of whom we do have evidence, Frederick Douglass (1817–1895) probably stands out as the first celebrated national orator. The son of the only literate slave of the 600 on Colonel Lloyd's plantation, Douglass escaped slavery in 1838 to live in Massachusetts (slavery was abolished in five northern states by 1787). After being asked to speak spontaneously at an anti-slavery rally in 1841, Douglass emerged as a brilliant public speaker and, through his own newspaper, *North Star*, dedicated himself to the abolition of slavery and the construction of civil rights for the black population and for women. His own autobiographies, *Narrative of the Life of Frederick Douglass* and *My Bondage and my Freedom*, remain the most popular of all slave and ex-slave autobiographies.

Black women also featured strongly in the nineteenth-century resistance, and again it was primarily through their speeches and writings that the likes of Ida B. Wells (1862–1931) and Mary Church Terrell (1863–1954) led the black communities towards freedom. Harriet Tubman (1820–1913) was one of the few leaders not noted for rhetorical skills: her leadership involved constructing and running the 'underground railway', which, in eighteen military-style expeditions during the 1850s, spirited slaves (around 300 in total) from the south to the north. Once the civil war had broken out, Tubman joined the Union side as a scout, helping to free more than 750 slaves in one campaign alone. Sojourner Truth (1797–1883), one of the most prominent black women at the time, unlike most of the black leaders of either gender, was illiterate. A deeply religious woman—as indeed most of the black leaders were—Sojourner Truth had escaped slavery and spent much of her life touring the country and speaking against slavery. Her entries within the *Penguin Book of Historic Speeches* cover two speeches: 'A'n't I a woman?' and 'I have a right to have just as much as a man' (MacArthur 1996). Her illiteracy demonstrates an important point about the nature of rhetoric and reality: since she did not write her speeches down, we have only other people's accounts of what she said, how she spoke, and what the effects were. The version quoted by MacArthur reads as though it was spoken by someone out of a cartoon set in the deepest part of the south, the dialect is so strong—yet inconsistent (in fact Truth came from New York State and her first language was Dutch (Painter 1996: 7)): 'Dat man ober dar say dat womin needs to be helped into carriages, and lifted over ditches, and to hab de best place everywhar. Nobody eber helps me into carriages, or ober mud-puddles, or gibs me any best place. And a'n't I a woman?' (MacArthur 1996: 433). This was based on an account of Truth's speech, originally delivered at a Women's Rights Convention in Akron, Ohio, in 1851, and 'remembered' by Frances Dana Gage, a renowned (white) feminist writer of the period. Gage's version was in response to an account of Truth's life entitled 'Sojourner Truth: the Libyan Sybil' in *Atlantic Monthly* by Harriet Beecher Stowe in April 1863.[12] Stowe was already a famous author but not an active feminist or abolitionist; at this time Sojourner Truth was still a relatively obscure black abolitionist and feminist. Gage's account of Truth's Akron speech was published in the New York *Independent* and related how Truth had spoken against a background of racism and misogyny in the meeting and how the previous feeble public speakers had been taught a rhetorical lesson in both how to speak and how to persuade. Truth had persuaded particularly through the use of the now memorable 'And a'n't I a woman?', repeated four times in just 23 sentences, and through the pity she had induced when she told the audience that she had borne and lost thirteen children. As one might expect, Truth left the audience stunned. But Painter's (1996) reconstruction of the speech based on the account by Marius Robinson in the Salem newspaper, the *Anti-Slavery Bugle* on 7 June 1851, less than a week after the speech had been delivered (as opposed to the dozen years it had taken Gage to 'remember' it), suggests a quite different perspective. In this account (the official proceedings of the convention omitted any reference to Truth), Truth did not storm the meeting, was not heckled by racists or misogynists, did not speak in strong dialect, did not use the phrase 'And a'n't I a woman?', and did not leave the others in the room stunned by her performance. Painter suggests that Gage had her own reasons for reconstructing the speech as she did, though Painter herself admits that we will never know precisely what Truth said, nor how she said it. And this is the point: the rhetorical nature of leadership is necessarily dependent upon reconstruction and reproduction by others for its effects and perpetual existence. Truth only became a black leader and a notable speaker because her actions and speeches were reproduced by others— but precisely what actually occurred, we may never know.

A year after Gage and Stowe had brought Truth to national importance, Truth visited President Lincoln. In Truth's own account she said to Lincoln that she had never heard of him before he became President, to which he allegedly replied, 'I had heard of you many times before that' (quoted in Painter 1996: 206). Some time later, an alternative account, published by Truth's friend Lucy Colman, who was present at the meeting, suggests that Lincoln was (typically) less than civil towards Truth, called her 'Aunty' (a name used by contemporary whites for their black washerwoman), and made no comment about her fame.

Lincoln was certainly not a champion of the black population, even if he did emancipate them (his preference was to 'repatriate' them to Africa and the West Indies). But, as we saw at the beginning of this chapter, Lincoln was a brilliant orator and does seem to have changed the way many Americans perceived of themselves and their individual and collective identity. For Lincoln, there was a world of difference between ending slavery and accepting blacks as equals; for blacks like Booker T. Washington, the only way to close the distance between the two was to demonstrate that blacks were 'worthy' of white respect through self-education and self-help. Washington's Tuskegee Institute in Alabama was designed to induce blacks to accept white values; this way a thriving black community could develop that would not threaten white society—and therefore not increase the ever-present possibility of violence and lynchings.

W. E. B. Du Bois, originally a supporter of Washington, was influential in establishing the alternative National Association for the Advancement of Coloured People (NAACP) in 1909 (as was King's maternal grandfather—the Revd A. D. Williams), which insisted on both a more confrontational stance in the courts and its own paper, but also on alliances with progressive whites.[13] Eventually Du Bois adopted an isolationist stance and left the NAACP. Some limited support came from the unions, especially the United Mineworkers of America, the United Auto Workers, and the Food, Tobacco, Agricultural, and Allied Workers Union, but beyond these three little could be relied upon.[14] The Communist Party of the United States did provide some support, but by the cold-war era such support usually proved counterproductive. Elsewhere, in mainstream politics, President Roosevelt—in contrast to Eleanor—was never really interested in the plight of black Americans—particularly if showing interest meant undermining his democratic white support in the south. The unravelling of the racist legislation really began during the Second World War. After 1940 the Supreme Court upheld the right of blacks to eat in unsegregated dining cars on the interstate railways and to vote in southern primary elections as well as to enrol in public institutions of higher education (Fox Piven and Cloward 1977). In 1941 A. Philip Randolph, the founder-leader of the Brotherhood of Sleeping Car Porters, forced President Roosevelt to prevent racial discrimination in the employment practices of the federal and defence industries by threatening a march of 100,000 people on Washington. And he did the same in 1947 when President Truman ordered a peacetime draft. By 1948 the armed forces had been desegregated and the Democratic Party had included civil-rights amendments in its platform. However, the outbreak of war in Korea and the onslaught of McCarthyism soon ensured that the problem returned to its classification as a 'southern problem' rather than an American issue.

One is sometimes tempted to assume that Martin Luther King single-handedly initiated, led, and secured the vote for the millions of blacks in the USA, especially in the south, disenfranchised for the most part by the time of the First World War. As the conservative groups like the NAACP persisted in their evolutionary moves towards civil rights, King's own Southern Christian Leadership Conference (SCLC) took the mantle of leadership and forced the federal establishment to coerce the southern states into concession after concession until the Civil Rights bills of 1965 and after. This version of events ensures that King's charismatic character explains most, if not all, of the events that followed. Gardner (1996) does not take this extreme line but is adamant that leaders make a significant difference to the unfolding of events. In his terms, such charismatic individuals have a story or central message (which they must personally embody) that generates an account of why the followers are in the position they find themselves in and what they must do to change it. They also have a strong

relationship with their followers and are powerfully supported by an organizational form.[15]

But there were also many black Americans at the time who suggested that
King's claim, that the Montgomery bus boycott had produced 'the new Negro',
was little short of a fabrication. Roy Wilkins, the head of the rival NAACP, suggested that 'The Negro of 1956 who stands on his own two feet is not a new
Negro; he is the grandson of the great grandson of the men who hated slavery. By
his own hands, through his own struggles, in his own organized groups—of
churches, fraternal societies, the NAACP and others—he has fought his way to
the place where he now stands' (quoted in Cook 1998: 39). Of these institutions
probably the most important were the black evangelical churches.

The opposite approach reduces the role of the individual to marginal significance, and with it charisma. Fox Piven and Cloward, for example, suggest that
protest movements are shaped by institutional conditions, and not by the purpo-
sive efforts of leaders and organizers. The limitations are large and unyielding.
'Yet within these boundaries created by these limitations, some latitude for pur-
posive effort remains' (Fox Piven and Cloward 1977: 37). Furthermore, 'The civil
rights movement was not, then, the fundamental cause of this political transformation; the fundamental cause was economic change, and the political forces set
in motion by economic change' (Fox Piven and Cloward 1977: 252). In other
words, Martin Luther King Jr., may have made a little difference to the actual
process and result, but the major cause was the structure of the economy.

Either way, whether the charismatic King or structural forces were responsible
for the acquisition of civil rights, the actions of the rest of the population are
deemed irrelevant. But this can survive as an explanatory account only if we
choose to ignore or forget the preceding period of protest or the simultaneous
protest of thousands of people, most, but certainly not all, black or African
Americans.

Fairclough's account of the developments in what appears to be a typical small
hamlet, Lebeau, Louisiana, in 1950 should be a warning against such a memory
lapse (A. Fairclough 1996). Lebeau, as was normal for the time, had no black voters, and in June Alvin Jones, a local leader of a group affiliated to the NAACP, led
five blacks to register their vote in the parish court house. All six were beaten up
by the police on duty there. An FBI investigation found no evidence of any beatings, and, when three black men filed suit against the registrar of voters, one of
them was shot dead by the deputy sheriff; the other two fled the area. However,
black persistence paid off and three years later blacks began to vote for the first
time since their disenfranchisement fifty years earlier. This action occurred
before the famous desegregation of schools ruling, handed down by the Supreme
Court in *Brown* v. *Board of Education* 1954, and before the Montgomery bus
boycott began. Indeed, despite its dubious status, Louisiana had witnessed several other breakthroughs before King or the civil-rights movement appeared.
The first attempt to desegregate schools had occurred in the 1930s through the
NAACP, and it was the same organization that sponsored the development of

black lawyers to fight Jim Crow practices in the courts. For example, in 1940 the New Orleans branch of the NAACP boycotted a concert because the auditorium was segregated; in 1943 all twenty-four black passengers on a New Orleans bus were arrested after a fracas when a uniformed black soldier was ordered to vacate the front seat.[16]

The war forced President Roosevelt to instigate a new Committee on Fair Employment Practice after the demand for labour mushroomed in the defence industries, and in 1941–2, spurred on by the examples of union 'sit-downs' and Gandhi's non-violent resistance, a group of black and white activists began planning a campaign of civil disobedience to secure racial equality and founded the Congress of Racial Equality (CORE). This began its first sit-in at a segregated restaurant in Chicago in 1942. The war clearly played an important part in radicalizing a large section of the black population: between 1940 and 1945 NAACP membership rose 20 per cent to 450,000, and the number of registered black voters in the south rose from 3 to 12 per cent (R. Cook 1998: 75, 81). Relatedly, equal pay was won by black teachers after an eight-year campaign in 1948, the same year that desegregation of the military began; and in 1953 blacks boycotted Baton Rouge city buses in a protest against laws that required them to stand even when 'white' seats were empty. Such protests, individual and collective, had occurred sporadically during the war, but, in Fairclough's words, 'the *struggle* for civil rights became the civil rights *movement* after 1955'. It was, then, the preceding fifteen years of action by individuals, by the Church, by the Communist Party, by labour unions, and by NAACP activists that weakened the white supremacists sufficiently enough for open defiance to become a possibility from 1955 onwards. Edgar Nixon, for example, President of the Montgomery NAACP and leader of the Brotherhood of Sleeping Car Porters, was instrumental in increasing the registration of black voters in Alabama from 25,000 in 1940 to 600,000 by 1948 (J. White 1996: 47). In Guerin's conclusion: 'The labor movement gave Black people the opportunity to do things that the civil rights movement gave (them) the right to do' (quoted in J. White 1996: 45).

Nixon was also involved in bailing Rosa Parks (née McCauley), a seamstress who was arrested and convicted for refusing to vacate her seat for a white passenger on a Montgomery bus. The segregation laws at the time required Rosa to pay at the front of the bus, get off, re-enter at the rear, sit only in the 'coloured' section, and vacate her seat should any white not have a seat. Rosa was the daughter of a teacher and the great-granddaughter of an indentured Irish labourer who had married a black slave after the civil war. Rosa had been educated at a private school for black children in Montgomery with white teachers— who were shunned by their white neighbours. In 1932 Rosa McCauley married Raymond Parks, a barber from Montgomery and an active member of the NAACP. Rosa Parks subsequently became a leader of the Montgomery Voters League, secretary of the local chapter of the NAACP, and headed the NAACP Youth Council. She had attended the Highlander School in Tennessee that trained future black leaders, but the arrest was not part of a strategy to secure a likely martyr. However, it was immediately clear to all involved that Parks was an ideal candidate for the task—unlike Claudette Colvin, a pregnant 15 year old, who had physically resisted arrest for the same 'offence' nine months earlier (Garrow 1986: 15). 'I had no idea', Parks said later, 'when I refused to give up my seat on that Montgomery bus that my small action would help to put an end to the segregation laws in the South' (quoted in Dubovoy 1997: 94). Lula Farmer, wife of a CORE founder James Farmer, told him immediately that this was 'precisely the spark that you've been working and hoping for, for years'. Other local Montgomery black leaders agreed that the arrest of someone as respectable as Parks provided an ideal test case to take the segregation laws to the courts.

Montgomery, an Alabama city that had very recently started to unravel some of the Jim Crow practices, had just voted into public office Clyde Sellers, a hardline segregationist. Nixon, along with the local Women's Political Council, organized a one-day bus boycott against Montgomery City Lines following the distribution of 40,000 leaflets within twenty-four hours of Parks's arrest. The boycott, called for four days later, was virtually 100 per cent effective, and Nixon was involved in securing King's agreement first to lead an extended boycott and then the Montgomery Improvement Association (MIA). In fact King was not the obvious candidate and several other existing local leaders were possible options. Yet all these led a particular interest group and none—except King—was sufficiently independent to hold together the disparate amalgam of groups and individuals.

The inaugural meeting attracted 4,000 blacks (around 8 per cent of the black population)[17] and, according to Fred Gay, the MIA's lawyer, 'there was an electricity in the air. Such a feeling of unity, success and enthusiasm had never been before in the city of Montgomery, certainly never demonstrated by African Americans' (quoted in R. Cook 1998: 102). The initial MIA demands were mild and did not extend to the end of segregation. Eventually, the MIA filed a civil case in the federal court to test the legality of Alabama's bus-segregation ordinance, rather than await the outcome of an appeal against the state conviction of Rosa Parks. (A similar appeal on the part of Viola White had been awaiting judicial review for ten years.) The bombing of Nixon's and King's homes at this time failed to deter either one of them, nor the rest of the protesters—but it did marginalize those moderates on either side. However, non-violence remained an important part of the strategy for two main reasons: to maintain solidarity amongst the black community, and to minimize the excuse for white violence. King, though interested in the Gandhian ideas of non-violence propagated by some leading northern black activists like Bayard Rustin, and having heard a lecture on Gandhi in 1950, was already committed to the strategy, as much for religious as for theoretical or pragmatic reasons. In 1956 the dual strategy of local protest and legal action prevailed: the federal court, followed by the Supreme Court, rendered the action of the Montgomery bus company illegal.

In February 1960, shortly after the election of a Democrat President, the policy of forcing local state authorities into confrontation with the federal authorities increased dramatically when black students across the south began sit-ins within segregated food stores. Although sit-ins had been attempted in 1958 and 1959, the sit-in that started the flood of grass-root action occurred in Greensboro, North Carolina. There, four black students, with links to the local NAACP but without their blessing, decided to start their own protest by sitting down at a whites-only counter in the Woolworth store. Despite protests, they remained there all day and returned the following day along with hundreds of black and white student supporters. By April, seventy-eight sit-ins had occurred and 2,000 protesters had been arrested. The sit-ins spread to Atlanta, and King formed the Southern Christian Leadership Conference (SCLC) to support the students. 'Support' is a significant word here, because, despite the actions of the SCLC—and the disquiet of the much larger NAACP, whose more middle-class supporters were not enamoured of such direct action—there was little control involved. The students' own body, the Student Non-violent Coordinating Committee (SNCC), appeared to do very little coordinating, because it primarily involved spontaneous action (Fox Piven and Cloward 1977: 222–3). In fact, the radicals' dismissal of the NAACP was probably overdone. A. Fairclough (1996: 22) certainly concludes that 'Southern whites tried to destroy the NAACP not because the organization was ineffective, but because its combination of courtroom action, political pressure and popular mobilization was proving all *too* effective'. However, in this period King's own role was very much restricted to one of media spokesperson, rather than popular leader, of the emerging civil-rights movement (Ling 1998: 18).

At this time the movement depended critically on personal risk taking, to the extent that as many as a quarter of all black students in the mainly black colleges in the southern states seem to have been directly involved in the protests—despite the constant threat of arrest, and worse. Only 11 per cent reported that nothing untoward had happened to them as a consequence of their involvement. In effect, 50,000 people, most of them black, were involved in the sit-in protests and over 3,600 spent some time in jail for their actions in the first twelve months of the protest (Fox Piven and Cloward 1977: 222–4).

The SCLC's increasingly confrontational stance was in contrast to that of the rival black organizations, such as the NAACP and the National Baptist Convention, whose incremental and institutional approach has persisted for many years. Indeed, initially, King had been careful to minimize antagonizing the NAACP by retaining control over local activists and by establishing that the removal of hate could not be achieved by hate, only by love. Mass action compromised both aspects: he could not control it and it was likely to end in violence. However, the student sit-ins of 1960 showed King that a more direct approach—though still non-violent—might achieve quicker and better results. Gradually King and many other local and national leaders came to recognize that the most successful route forward was one in which local activism generated the incentive for federal intervention. Indeed, at one point King said that 'It is no exaggeration to say that the President could give segregation its death blow through a stroke of the pen' (quoted in R. Cook 1998: 121). However, while King's focus was at this federal level, the mission could be accomplished only on the backs of literally thousands of (primarily) black activists and leaders at the local level. In fact, it is Cook's claim precisely that, although King was critical to the civil-rights campaign, it was never possible for him to achieve anything alone (R. Cook 1998). It was, therefore, these people, as much as national leaders like King, who forced the federal authorities to act. The situation, then, was not one where King had to begin from the beginning but one where decades of struggle by ordinary people across the southern states laid the groundwork both for his personal role and also for the collective effort to continue. In short, the civil-rights situation was already a collective phenomenon and not the construction of any single individual; it required 'deep' leadership to be effective in any sense of the word.

In 1961 the Congress of Racial Equality (CRE), which had already been deeply involved in the sit-in protests, began sending 'freedom riders' to the south to force the federal authorities to act against segregation on the federally controlled bus and train terminals. In December 1961, eight of the nine SNCC freedom riders travelling to Albany, having survived several attacks by white mobs, were arrested for breaking segregation rules. Within a few days first 500 and then 1,000 others were jailed, for Christmas, for protesting against the arrests, including King. In August 1962 another 1,000 were imprisoned; the protest had moved from actions by a few dedicated militants to actions by large numbers of 'ordinary' people prepared to face the penalty for their actions (Fox Piven and Cloward 1977: 236–8). Despite—or rather because of—the level of violence deployed against the freedom riders by southern racists, the federal authorities were again forced to act to end the segregated terminal facilities. It was this that Bob Moses called the requirement for 'annealing'—heating the (political) temperature until the (federal) body became malleable (R. Cook 1998: 165).

In late 1961 a SNCC freedom ride to Albany, Georgia, had resulted in hundreds of arrests and King was invited by a local black leader to help, though SNCC activists insisted that King's presence would undermine the confidence of the local black population to solve their own problems. Where organizers like Ella Baker resented the authoritarian leadership of the NAACP and the patriarchy of the SCLC, she also disputed the utility of charismatics like King and praised the participatory practices of the SNCC, for 'This inclination towards group-centred leadership, rather than towards a leader-centred group pattern of organization, was refreshing indeed to those of the older group who bear the scars of the battle, the frustrations and the disillusionment that comes when the prophetic leader turns out to have heavy feet of clay' (quoted in R. Cook 1998: 154). Or, in the rather more succinct words of Bob Moses, responding to the praise heaped on King: 'Don't you think we need a lot of leaders?' (quoted in R. Cook 1998: 155). After all, had not King himself asserted that 'leadership never ascends from the pew to the pulpit, but . . . invariably descends from the pulpit to the pew' (quoted in R. Cook 1998: 238).

In the event, King's presence secured an agreement by the city government to set up a meeting to discuss segregation—but as soon as King had left town, the city governors refused to honour their agreement. When King returned the following year, Pritchett, the police chief, ensured that no attacks on the protesters occurred and King was himself forced to tour the city asking the local black youth, frustrated by the inaction of the governors, to desist their sporadic rioting. It was, in R. Cook's (1998: 128) view, 'the first major defeat of his career as a civil rights leader'. It was also a lesson for all the civil-rights groups—a major campaign had to be rooted in a pre-existing network of support if it was to have any chance of success; simply parachuting national leaders into trouble spots would not work.

The civil-rights campaign then, paradoxically perhaps, was indebted to its most bigoted opponents for their public proclamations and behaviour, which often appear to have shamed the establishment into pro-rights action. For example, the Birmingham Police Commissioner, Eugene 'Bull' Connor, was credited by John F. Kennedy with doing as much to help the movement as Abraham Lincoln (Gardner 1996: 212). Birmingham had been targeted by the SCLC (Project C (confrontation)) because of its reactionary status, because—in contrast to Albany—the SCLC already had a strong base there, and because the white community was split. When the protests began, on 2 April 1963, thirty-five protesters had been arrested within three days. Within four days a further forty five had been arrested, and the following week a further fifty were imprisoned, including King—who was already looking for a dramatic gesture to turn the spotlight on the city. Once in prison he wrote his famous 'Letter from Birmingham City Jail', a biting attack upon his liberal critics, especially those disconcerted by the radical use of non-violent tactics as a method of ensuring rapid change. His intention was, he claimed, 'to create such a crisis and foster a tension that a community which has constantly refused to negotiate is forced to confront the issue' (Ling 1998: 18). In short, and ironically given his stance, King had to make his opponents violently attack him. But with even Bull Connor then refusing to play the part of a violent racist chief of police, the protest began to falter—until James Bevel instigated a children's march. By 2 May, 959 of 6,000 children had been arrested and TV pictures of police dogs attacking children flashed around the nation and the world. By 10 May, over 3,000 people had been arrested and widespread violence had become a daily occurrence. Robert Kennedy, embarrassed by the media, was reluctantly forced to send federal marshals to restore order, and he began the political process to have segregation on interstate buses made illegal, forcing Commissioner Connor and Governor Wallace to back down and release the prisoners.[18] The following month President Kennedy, unable to quell the continuing protests throughout the country (there were almost 1,500 demonstrations and 20,000 arrests in the summer of 1963), including the north, requested that Congress enact a comprehensive civil-rights bill (Fox Piven and Cloward 1977: 243–5; R. Cook 1998: 130–3).

It is important to remember that events in the USA were also affected by the decolonization and independence movements in Africa and Asia. As King's

'Letter from Birmingham City Jail' made clear: 'We have waited for more than 340 years for our constitutional and God-given rights. The nations of Asia and Africa are moving with jet-like speed toward the goal of political independence and we still creep at horse and buggy pace toward the gaining of a cup of coffee at a lunch counter' (quoted in W. A. Jackson 1996: 112). It was this increasing distance between the American dream and the American reality that generated the fertile soil for the 'Dream Speech'.

The immediate origins of the speech lay not in the 340th anniversary of America's pilgrim fathers missing the opportunity to inaugurate a republic based upon racial equality, but in the 100th anniversary of the Civil War that had, in theory, provided a second opportunity for the same thing. The decision to commemorate the Civil War had been taken by President Eisenhower in 1957 and the consequent US Civil War Centennial Commission (USCC) was given three and a half years to organize a variety of events. In 1959 Eisenhower, speaking at the funeral of Walter W. Williams, who claimed to have fought in the Civil War, suggested that 'the wounds of the deep and bitter dispute which once divided our nation have long since healed' (quoted in R. Cook 1998: 1). The following period witnessed another conflict, this time over the meaning of the war, with southern whites insistent that it represented the failed but heroic struggle for independence, while blacks spoke of it as the war to end slavery and northern whites regarded it as a war to maintain the Union. Thus the first major event to be commemorated was the confederate victory at Bull Run, while the second was the Emancipation Proclamation (1863). When New Jersey sent Madeleine Williams, a black delegate, to the USCC meeting at Fort Sumpter, Charleston, the municipal segregation laws prevented her from being accommodated in the same hotel as all the other delegates. As the northern delegates pulled out of the meeting, the newly elected John F. Kennedy insisted that, as a federally sponsored body, the USCC would have to ensure equal treatment and the meeting was moved to the naval base.

But the speech itself developed from the call for a 'March on Washington for Jobs and Freedom', which had first been made in November 1962, by Randolph, now a veteran civil-rights activist. It received short shrift from a divided and uncertain black leadership. However, the events of 1963 changed the perception of what could be achieved through direct action and protest. Thus on 28 August 1963, at the Lincoln Memorial, and in front of up to 250,000 people, Martin Luther King delivered what is conventionally regarded as one of the greatest speeches of the twentieth century. He did not finish writing the speech until 04.00 that morning and it was the culmination of the 'March on Washington for Jobs and Freedom', itself part of the wider 'Free by '63' campaign for justice and equality by American blacks.

The Speaker

Martin Luther King Jr. was born Michael King Jr. in Atlanta in 1929. At the age of five his father, an important Baptist minister, changed both their names to incorporate the Lutheran namesake. King Jr. excelled at school and took a first degree in Divinity from Crozier Theological Seminary, Pennsylvania, and a doctorate in sociology in 1955 from Boston University. Apparently an articulate speaker, he accepted his first post as minister of the Dexter Avenue Baptist Church in Montgomery, Alabama, the year before completing his doctorate—which was also the year when Rosa Parks was arrested.

King seems to have been chosen to lead the boycott against the Montgomery buses because he was educated and articulate, his parish was relatively well off, and he should, therefore, have drawn the more conservative elements into the struggle. He was also a newcomer, without the political baggage that other existing leaders carried that might have split the protest and deterred the possible leaders from taking risks that they felt unacceptable. In effect, he could aggregate a greater and more heterogeneous network of support than any other potential leader at the time.

He does not appear to have thrust himself forward as leader of the Montgomery Improvement Association (MIA) but, having found himself at the centre of the storm, believed that it was his calling, rather than a fortuitous situation. On 27 January 1956, just as the bus boycott was ending its second week, King recounts how he had decided to give up the leadership of the MIA. He had received over forty telephoned threats and, at midnight, another one had given him three days to leave or die. He knew that the cause was right, but that was not enough to keep him there: he had a wife, a new daughter and his own fears to contend with, and he was looking for a face-saving escape route. He prayed for guidance saying:

I think the cause that we represent is right. But Lord I must confess that I'm weak now. I'm faltering. I'm losing my courage. And I can't let the people see me like this because if they see me weak and losing my courage, they will begin to get weak ... And it seemed to me at that moment that I heard an inner voice saying to me, 'Martin Luther, stand up for righteousness. Stand up for justice. Stand up for truth. And lo I will be with you, even until the end of the world.' ... Almost at once my fears began to go. My uncertainty disappeared. (quoted in Garrow 1993: 58)

We have already seen the significance of this kind of belief in destiny in the likes of Hitler, Nelson, and Nightingale, and from this point on everything appeared to drive King to lead from the front. And each time fear or anxiety threatened to overwhelm him, he recalled his 'conversation with God in the kitchen', and re-established his certainty and equanimity. He was the first person arrested by the authorities and was convicted of breaking a 1921 statute against boycotts. He urged the adoption of non-violent direct action in Gandhian form (satyagraha) and certainly embodied this in his personal life, at one point dropping his hands when physically attacked at a conference in December 1961—despite his previous experience of being stabbed. For King, non-violence was not simply a utilitarian tactic to resist oppression; it was also the philosophical glue that could unite his disparate followers together.

In 1957 King made the front cover of *Time* magazine and, as leader of the SCLC, visited Nkrumah in Ghana and Nehru in India, as well as President Eisenhower and Vice-President Nixon. But he had little faith in any of the existing alternative strategies for change: traditional black nationalism and Marxism were simply too limited in their appeal for him. And he was increasingly disenchanted by a liberal capitalism that was 'always in danger of inspiring men to be more concerned about making a living than making a life' (quoted in Carson 1996: 117).

King joined his father as co-pastor of the Ebenezer Baptist Church in Atlanta in 1960 and began to agitate against all forms of segregation and discrimination, but his farewell sermon to his Montgomery congregation clearly revealed his assumption that fate was driving him rather than him driving fate: 'I can't stop now. History has thrust something upon me which I cannot turn away from' (quoted in Gardner 1996: 210). Georgia State Police certainly tried to stop him almost as soon as he arrived, jailing him for a technicality (driving with an out-of-state licence). However, telephone calls from John F. Kennedy to King's wife, Coretta, and from Robert Kennedy to the presiding judge, ensured King's quick release. Gardner calls these calls 'acts of kindness', but the knife-edged presidential election that followed—and the significance of the black vote in securing John F. Kennedy's success—implies that the Kennedys were more politically motivated than 'kind' (Fox Piven and Cloward 1977: 225–6; R. Cook 1998: 120).

The year of the 'Dream Speech' was certainly a busy one for King, who campaigned tirelessly up and down the country, making on average a speech every day of the year and travelling about 750 miles on each of these days (Gardner 1996: 212). King obviously intended to make a historically significant speech at the Lincoln memorial and the context could hardly have been more auspicious—it was, after all, the largest single peaceful protest gathering in the history of the USA. Indeed, King had previously told a friend that he intended to give 'a sort of Gettysburg Address', and he seems to have fulfilled this aim, mingling images of Jefferson, Lincoln, and Jesus in quick succession (quoted in Miller and Lewis 1996: 155).

The critical rhetorical form that pervades the entire speech is an antithesis between what should be and what is—but to get to the promised land King asserts that his followers must pass through an ordeal of violence, in the typical structure of virtually all romantic quests. Indeed, the title and backbone of the speech are the dream: the promise, the fall, the ordeal, and the redemption. This is crucially rooted not in the ideology of black Americans but in that of the founding fathers of the Constitution. Thus the legitimacy of the black calls for *freedom*, *justice*, and *equality* (LOT) can be denied by the whites only if the latter deny their own heritage (or deny that black Americans are not legitimate people in some way). Hence the metaphorical 'check' (cheque) that black Americans had come to cash is a 'promissory note': it had already been earned by black Americans; it was not a charitable donation by white America.

The Spectators

The march on Washington was organized by six disparate black groups under the umbrella of the Council for United Civil Rights Leadership, which had raised $800,000 to help local groups advertise and mobilize (Garrow 1993: 275–6). The march was facilitated, rather than (as was more usual) inhibited, by the Justice Department and the local police. President Kennedy endorsed the idea on 17 July, after the Council assured him there would be no violence. By August, four white representative leaders were added to the march's organizing committee to ensure multi-racial support. The collective leadership then spent the run-up to the march on the television and in the media addressing the concerns of the marchers, with King denying that the march wanted an end to discrimination and insisting that equality was the goal (Garrow 1993: 280–1).

Lilley and Platt's analysis of the civil-rights movement, and the leadership of Martin Luther King suggests that he represented a markedly heterogeneous figure to the followers of the movement. For instance, using 621 letters sent by correspondents to King, Lilley and Platt claim that the writers regarded him as one of (at least) four different characters—as a black leader, as a Christian leader, as a non-violent leader, or as a democratic leader. Nor does this division map 'naturally' onto the background of the writer—for example, not all black writers regarded him as first and foremost a black leader. As Lilley and Platt (1997: 330) argue:

he bore several meanings simultaneously for both Black and white participants in the movement . . . Correspondents saw in King and his efforts multiple conceptions of his leadership and performances . . . King seems aware of his multiple public meanings for he once confided, 'I am conscious of two Martin Luther Kings . . . The Martin Luther King that the people talk about seems to be somebody foreign to me.'

One critical implication of this is that a social movement need not be rooted in a consensus to achieve an effective solidarity—there was no consensus about what King represented, but there did appear to be an effective solidarity within the civil rights movement. In Kertzer's words, rituals can construct 'solidarity without consensus . . . since what often underlies people's political allegiances is their social identification with a group rather than their sharing of beliefs with other members' (Kertzer 1988, quoted in Lilley and Platt 1997: 332). Another way of explaining King's successful retention of this heterogeneous support network might be to suggest that the very ambiguity of his message allowed different groups to read different things into his messages and proceed on that basis (see Donellon *et al.* 1986). Indeed, it was precisely because King operated at the indeterminate centre, as a bridge between black and white, between conservative, liberal, and radical, that he managed to retain such a grip on the imagination of the country. He was a 'conservative militant' (R. Cook 1998: 6).

There is, of course, a fine line between constructive ambiguity and a blurred vision. Leaders cannot afford to be completely indiscriminate in their calls to action; they cannot, in effect, be all things to all people. But Kertzer's distinction between solidarity and consensus provides the boundary line: King need not depend upon consensus amongst his followers and certainly could not guarantee this amongst the members of the other groups present on the day (Kertzer 1988). However, providing he could generate solidarity, and he did this by switching the focus of his 'dream', or his interpretative repertoires, to 'perform' different communities—black, civil rights, democrat, and Christian—he could remain optimistic (Potter and Wetherell 1987). This ability to recruit such a diverse group of supporters does not mean that the message was anodyne or that it ignored the critical issues of race and inequality; far from it—though Gardner (1996: 212) curiously calls King's approach 'colour-blind'. Of course, we should remember that the speech was not delivered just to the 210,000–250,000 in the audience (25 per cent of whom were white), but also to millions watching it live on TV across the nation.

The Speech

I am happy to join with you today in what will go down in history as the greatest demonstration for freedom in the history of our nation.

Five score years ago, a great American, in whose symbolic shadow we stand, signed the Emancipation Proclamation. This momentous decree came as a great beacon light of hope to millions of Negro slaves who had been seared in the flames of withering injustice. It came as a joyous daybreak to end the long night of captivity.

But one hundred years later, we must face the tragic fact that the Negro is still not free. One hundred years later, the life of the Negro is still sadly crippled by the manacles of segregation and the chains of discrimination. One hundred years later, the Negro lives on a lonely island of poverty in the midst of a vast ocean of material prosperity. One hundred years later, the Negro is still languished in the corners of American society and finds himself an exile in his own land. So we have come here today to dramatize an appalling condition.

In a sense we have come to our nation's capital to cash a check. When the architects of our republic wrote the magnificent words of the Constitution and the Declaration of Independence, they were signing a promissory note to which every American was to fall heir. This note was a promise that all men would be guaranteed the unalienable rights of life, liberty, and the pursuit of happiness.

It is obvious today that America has defaulted on this promissory note insofar as her citizens of color are concerned. Instead of honoring this sacred obligation, America has given the Negro people a bad check; a check which has come back marked 'insufficient funds'. But we refuse to believe that the bank of justice is bankrupt. We refuse to believe that there are insufficient funds in the great vaults of opportunity of this nation. So we have come to cash this check—a check that will give us upon demand the riches of freedom and the security of justice. We have also come to this hallowed spot to remind America of the fierce urgency *of now*. This is no time to engage in the luxury of cooling off or to take the tranquilizing drug of gradualism.

Now is the time to make real the promises of Democracy.

Now is the time to rise from the dark and desolate valley of segregation to the sunlit path of racial justice.

Now is the time to open the doors of opportunity to all of God's children.

Now is the time to lift our nation from the quicksands of racial injustice to the solid rock of brotherhood.

It would be fatal for the nation to overlook the urgency of the moment and to underestimate the determination of the Negro. This sweltering summer of the Negro's legitimate discontent will not pass until there is an invigorating autumn of freedom and equality. Nineteen sixty-three is not an end, but a beginning. Those who hope that the Negro needed to blow off steam and will now be content will have a rude awakening if the nation returns to business as usual. There will be neither rest nor tranquility in America until the Negro is granted his citizenship rights. The whirlwinds of revolt will continue to shake the foundations of our nation until the bright day of justice emerges.

But there is something that I must say to my people who stand on the warm threshold which leads into the palace of justice. In the process of gaining our rightful place we must not be guilty of wrongful deeds. Let us not seek to satisfy our thirst for freedom by drinking from the cup of bitterness and hatred. We must forever conduct our struggle on the high plane of dignity and discipline. We must not allow our creative protest to degenerate into physical violence. Again and again we must rise to the majestic heights of meeting physical force with soul force. The marvelous new militancy which has engulfed the Negro community must not lead us to a distrust of all white people, for many of our white brothers, as evidenced by their presence here today, have come to realize that their destiny is tied up with our destiny and their freedom is inextricably bound to our freedom. We cannot walk alone.

And as we walk, we must make the pledge that we shall march ahead. We cannot turn back. There are those who are asking the devotees of civil rights, 'When will you be satisfied?' We can never be satisfied as long as the Negro is the victim of the unspeakable horrors of police brutality. We can never be satisfied as long as our bodies, heavy with the fatigue of travel, cannot gain lodging in the motels of the highways and the hotels of the cities. We cannot be satisfied as long as the Negro's basic mobility is from a smaller ghetto to a larger one. We can never be satisfied as long as a Negro in Mississippi cannot vote and a Negro in New York believes he has nothing for which to vote. No, no, we are not satisfied, and we will not be satisfied until justice rolls down like waters and righteousness like a mighty stream.

I am not unmindful that some of you have come here out of great trials and tribulations. Some of you have come fresh from narrow jail cells. Some of you have come from areas where your quest for freedom left you battered by the storms of persecution and staggered by the winds of police brutality. You have been the veterans of creative suffering. Continue to work with the faith that unearned suffering is redemptive.

Go back to Mississippi, go back to Alabama, go back to South Carolina, go back to Georgia, go back to Louisiana, go back to the slums and ghettos of our northern cities, knowing that somehow this situation can and will be changed. Let us not wallow in the valley of despair.

I say to you today, my friends, that in spite of the difficulties and frustrations of the moment I still have a dream. It is a dream deeply rooted in the American dream.

I have a dream that one day this nation will rise up and live out the true meaning of its creed: 'We hold these truths to be self-evident; that all men are created equal.'

I have a dream that one day on the red hills of Georgia the sons of former slaves and the sons of former slave-owners will be able to sit down together at the table of brotherhood.

I have a dream that one day even the state of Mississippi, a desert state sweltering with the heat of injustice and oppression, will be transformed into an oasis of freedom and justice.

I have a dream that my four little children will one day live in a nation where they will not be judged by the color of their skin but by the content of their character.

I have a dream today.

I have a dream that one day the state of Alabama, whose governor's lips are presently dripping with the words of interposition and nullification, will be transformed into a situation where little black boys and black girls will be able to join hands with little white boys and white girls and walk together as sisters and brothers.

I have a dream today.

I have a dream that one day every valley shall be exalted, every hill and mountain shall be made low, the rough places will be made plains, and the crooked places will be made straight, and the glory of the Lord shall be revealed, and all flesh shall see it together.

This is our hope. This is the faith with which I return to the South. With this faith we will be able to hew out of the mountain of despair a stone of hope. With this faith we will be able to transform the jangling discords of our nation into a beautiful symphony of brotherhood. With this faith we will be able to work together, to pray together, to struggle together, to go to jail together, to stand up for freedom together, knowing that we will be free one day.

This will be the day when all of God's children will be able to sing with new meaning

> My country, 'tis of thee,
> Sweet land of liberty,
>   Of thee I sing:
> Land where my fathers died,
> Land of the pilgrims' pride,
> From every mountainside
>   Let freedom ring.

And if America is to be a great nation this must become true.
So let freedom ring from the prodigious hilltops of New Hampshire.
Let freedom ring from the mighty mountains of New York.
Let freedom ring from the heightening Alleghenies of Pennsylvania!
Let freedom ring from the snowcapped Rockies of Colorado!
Let freedom ring from the curvacious peaks of California!
But not only that; let freedom ring from Stone Mountain of Georgia!
Let freedom ring from Lookout Mountain of Tennessee!
Let freedom ring from every hill and molehill of Mississippi.
From every mountainside, let freedom ring.

When we let freedom ring, when we let it ring from every village and every hamlet, from every state and every city, we will be able to speed up that day when all of God's children, black men and white men, Jews and Gentiles, Protestants and Catholics, will be able to join hands and sing in the words of the old Negro spiritual, 'Free at last, free at last. Thank God almighty, we are free at last!'

King was supposed to have prepared his speech by the previous day so that the mass media could secure advance copies, and other members of the leadership could evaluate—and if necessary veto—the contents. However, since he had not finished the speech this proved impossible, though the ideas underlying the dream had been delivered on two earlier occasions in his speech at Birmingham in April and Detroit in June (Garrow 1993: 283). As King recalled:

The previous June, following a peaceful assembly of thousands of people through the streets of downtown Detroit, Michigan, I had delivered a speech in Cobo Hall, in which I used the phrase 'I have a dream.' I had used it many times before, and I just felt that I wanted to use it here. I don't know why. I hadn't thought about it before the speech. (quoted in Carson 1999: 223)

Certainly King's speech resonates with the symbols of American power and the American dream: the speech carefully draws into play the geography of all the states, and a huge network of non-human elements: the Emancipation Proclamation, the Constitution, the Declaration of Independence, the Washington Monument, the Lincoln Memorial, the bank of justice, a cup of bitterness, motels of the highways, hotels of the cities, jail cells, valleys of despair, red hills of Georgia, the table of brotherhood, the prodigious hilltops of New Hampshire, the storms of persecution, the winds of police brutality, and numerous other elements. All these are held in place through King's rhetoric; he stands at the symbolic centre of the nation, but even the molehills of Mississippi play their part in the network of the journey towards the promised land. Geertz (1983) suggests that the positioning of events is critical to their influence—the closer one is to the centre of power the more likely it is that one's actions are associated with critical significance.

A radically condensed version of King's speech might be something like this:

It's been a hundred years since we were promised freedom and we still haven't got it. This state of affairs cannot continue. We must not sink to violent tactics but we want freedom now. This isn't just a black problem, it's an American problem. I have a dream that one day we will achieve our rights. Everyone go home and keep up the good work.

This has all the parsimony beloved of some approaches to social science—it says the bare minimum and gets the message across without wasting words. Why, it takes barely fifteen seconds to say it, while King took about seventeen minutes (he had been allotted only eight). The point is the condensed version is about as stimulating as sensory deprivation, or (in tune with the skill of rhetoric) it is like a tree trying to keep a dog from gnawing its bark away (simile), or it is a pile of rubbish (metaphor), or it fails because it has no structure, style, or subtlety (LOT), or it fails because its desirable limits limit its desirability (TPC). This does not mean that succinct speeches invariably fail. Patton's speech to the 761st 'Black Panther' Tank Battalion (the first black tank battalion to fight in the US Army) on the eve of Normandy is seven sentences long, but it ends with a call to action that is completely missing from the condensed 'Dream Speech' above: 'If you want me you can always find me in the lead tank' (quoted in MacArthur 1996: 220).

Nor am I suggesting that the rhetorical devices deployed are essentially related to the speaker; on the contrary, just as language is necessarily a social process, so too is the successful bringing-off of a speech. Unless King can generate an array of resonances within his audience, unless he can draw them into the network of images, symbols, and narratives that he is trying to evoke, the speech will fail. But whether it fails or not cannot be judged by King himself but only by his audience, his spectators. That audience need not necessarily be those physically present— they may reject his call. But, if a more powerful voice considers the speech a success, and reproduces an account of the speech to that effect, then the historical record may indeed show the speech to have been a success. This obviously requires considerable resources, but the manipulation of historical records is hardly a unique or novel affair, nor one limited to the imagination of George Orwell or Stalin.

The Promise

After the scene-setting introduction, the speech starts with a direct echo of Lincoln's Gettysburg opening ('Four score and seven years ago our fathers brought forth on this continent a new nation . . .'—which, of course, itself reflects the four score and ten years that represent the human lifespan in Psalm 90): 'Five score years ago, a great American . . .' and this also sets the historical root of the speech firmly in American and not European history. The Emancipation Proclamation was 'a great beacon light of hope to millions of Negro slaves who had been seared in the flames of withering injustice'. Note how this early sentence already alerts us to the skill with which King weaves his 'dream' from the multiple threads of the Bible, American history, democracy, and slavery. The promise is not just an easy way into the main content of the speech; it is quintessential, because it generates the expectations that follow. However, the promise has yet to be fulfilled, and the consequences of the fall from grace form the substance of the second part of the speech. The promise also replicates the Christian promise of future redemption, and the rhythm and interaction of the speech are clearly rooted in black American religious sermons, which King was obviously well placed to exploit.

The Fall

The second section begins with a clear relocation of the reality back into the past of slavery: 'one hundred years later, the life of the Negro is still sadly crippled by the manacles of segregation and the chains of discrimination.' Although replete with symbolism, simile, and metaphor, this particular section introduces a metonym, the substitution of a word referring to an attribute for the thing that is meant: manacles = slavery/inequality. Moreover, although not evident from the printed text, this line's rhythm is clearly spoken as a rhyme.

'One hundred years later [note the *anadiplosis*/repetition], the Negro lives on a lonely island of poverty in the midst of a vast ocean of material prosperity.' Here antithesis, the juxtaposition of contrasting ideas, phrases, or words to produce an effect of balance, is conjoined to a powerful metaphor, or non-literal resemblance. And this geographic metaphor, wrapped into an antithetical structure, continues in the next line, for 'the Negro . . . finds himself an exile in his own land'.

Two sentences later King introduces the idea of a cheque that the black population has come to cash in the American bank of justice and constructs his second LOT: 'This note was a promise that all men would be guaranteed the unalienable rights of *life*, *liberty*, and the *pursuit of happiness*.' A paragraph further on King develops one of his rare alliterations and begins the third and main section of the speech: the 'ordeal'.

The Ordeal

To get from the fall back—or rather forward—to the promise classically involves a necessary degree of suffering through a 'proving' ordeal, and King is clear that there is no easy path: '*Now* is the time to rise from the dark and desolate valley of segregation to the sunlit path of racial justice.' This is an important limit, because the overuse of alliteration can quickly resemble the announcer in a music hall.

At the concluding line of his four-line *anadiplosis*, initiated by 'Now is the time,' he goes on to say that 'It would be fatal for the nation to overlook the urgency of the moment and to underestimate the determination of the Negro.' Here King combines both a list of three (LOT) and an antithesis (TPC): 'overlook' contrasts with 'underestimate', 'urgency' reflects 'determination', while 'moment' and 'Negro' complete the triad.

Another technique is used in the following line: 'This sweltering summer of the Negro's legitimate discontent will not pass until there is an invigorating autumn of freedom and equality.' This is a clever inversion of 'Now is the Winter of our discontent | Made glorious summer by this Sun of York' (*Richard III*, Act I, Sc. i; see Miller and Lewis 1996: 160). But one of the noisiest responses of applause from the audience is reserved for the line: 'Let us not seek to satisfy our thirst for freedom by drinking from the cup of bitterness and hatred'. This clever conjunction of metaphors also encapsulates the Christian myth of the poisoned chalice.

King then widens the appeal of his dream beyond the black community, both because the dream cannot be achieved without the support of the white community and because the white dream can itself be achieved only through the American dream—which talks not of races or colours but of the nation. Thus in a presaging of Jesse Jackson's subsequent rainbow coalition approach to Democrat politics, King's words encompass a whole rainbow of communities: 'The marvelous new militancy which has engulfed the Negro community must not lead us to a distrust of all white people, for many of our white brothers, as evidenced by their presence here today, have come to realize that their destiny is tied up with our destiny and their freedom is inextricably bound to our freedom. We cannot walk alone.'

This section is dominated by *anadiplosis*. Four consecutive sentences in the early part start with '*Now* is the time'; the next paragraph but one is full of 'we must' or 'we must not'; the following paragraph is littered with 'we cannot' or 'we can never'; this is followed by 'Go back' in the paragraph before the eight paragraphs that start with 'I have a dream'; and the ten sentences towards the end that begin with 'Let freedom ring . . .'. Each of these elements is itself replete with rhetorical forms. Take, for example, this one:

[1] We can never be satisfied as long as the Negro is the victim of the unspeakable horrors of police brutality. [2] We can never be satisfied as long as our bodies, heavy with the fatigue of travel, cannot gain lodgings in the motels of the highways and the hotels of the cities. [3] We cannot be satisfied as long as the Negro's basic mobility is from a smaller ghetto to a larger one. [4] We can never be satisfied as long as a Negro in Mississippi cannot vote and a Negro in New York believes he has nothing for which to vote.

In this section each sentence embodies the antithetical structure that mirrors the entire speech: the promise denied; the dream unfulfilled; the promised land vanished. It also manages a biblical reference in sentence (2) to Mary and Joseph, who were refused lodgings in Bethlehem at the birth of Jesus, as well as representing black Americans' metaphorical journey in time from slavery to freedom. Additionally, it is clearly confronting a significant practical problem for black Americans in the difficulty involved in gaining accommodation. Sentence (3) gains its effect by deluding the listener into assuming a different ending: 'from a small ghetto to a large cosmopolitan city' would be a traditional TPC, but King breaks the rule to achieve the effect by halving the contrast and cementing each half to the same base (small ghetto/large ghetto). Sentence (4) provides an example of *chiasmus* (word inversion) in which the more conventional ending 'and a Negro in New York believes he has nothing to vote for' is replaced with a word inversion to finish off the second phrase in the same order as the first. A second example of *chiasmus* occurs two sentences later, when King begins the next section of his speech with : 'I am not unmindful . . .' and the sentence is completed with the al*literation*: 'trials and tribulations'. But the very next sentence is just as creative: 'Some of you have come fresh from narrow jail cells.' The contrast here, between 'fresh' and 'narrow', is not only an unusual one but suggests an antithetical image where 'fresh' implies open spaces and clean air, while 'narrow' suggests enclosure and fetid air. Yet this unfortunate beginning is turned by King, through biblical images, into a necessary ordeal: 'Some of you have come from areas where your quest for freedom left you battered by the storms of persecution and staggered by the winds of police brutality. You have been veterans of creative suffering. Continue to work with the faith that unearned suffering is redemptive.'

The Redemption

The final section is itself an extended excursion on redemption, and moves from the suffering of the ordeal back to the promise embodied in the first part. This is the most famous element and encapsulates King's vision of the future. It begins with a call to action rather than an acceptance of fatalism: 'Go back to Mississippi, go back to Alabama, go back to South Carolina, go back to Georgia, go back to Louisiana, go back to the slums and ghettos of our northern cities, knowing that somehow this situation can and will be changed. Let us not wallow in the valley of despair.' The call receives rapturous applause and two aspects of it are significant. First, King tells his audience that there is indeed light at the end of the tunnel and that the disparity between the promise and the reality can be transcended. However, the second aspect is just as important: King does not tell them that he has the solution to their problems and they can leave it to him to resolve; on the contrary, King has virtually nothing to say on what practical steps need to be taken to secure success. Instead his dream remains at this level—there is a better future but exactly which road gets there remains ambiguous. This, surely, is the greatest irony of what is traditionally regarded as the greatest speech of the twentieth century: the followers are not told what to do, only that they *must* keep going and that they *will* succeed. Why the ambiguity? Why does not King tell them what needs to be done? Surely this would mark out a great leader from a great speech?

Two counter-arguments are worth considering here. Heifetz's *Leadership Without Easy Answers* combines a novel and an old theme. The novel theme is about forcing subordinates to reflect upon their influence in the achievement of goals. The old theme is about the difference between situations that require mechanistic responses—which he calls 'technical' issues (often called 'management' elsewhere to distinguish it from 'leadership')—and those that require 'adaptive' responses (often called 'leadership' elsewhere). In so far as Heifetz also distinguishes between the exercise of 'authority' and the exercise of 'leadership'—sometimes labelled power derived from formal role and power derived from informal role—Heifetz also hinges his ideas on a distinction familiar to Weber and many others since. Hence, for Heifetz, the critical issue is whether people have the ability and skill or whatever to intervene in situations that are not routine and in which the answer cannot be derived from previous experience. Part of the role of the leader in such situations is to reflect the problem-solving back onto the followers. In sum, the leader must not take on the mantle of magician him or herself. I have no doubt that the refusal of leaders to own the problem is simultaneously the best way to create organizational learning and responsibility—and the best way for leaders to make themselves unpopular with followers whose expectations are premised upon more traditional notions of leadership. Storr, for example, notes how 'gurus'—such as Bhagwan Shree Rajneesh, Jim Jones, and Shoko Asahara—appear to own the problem of purpose and provide meaning for their followers in a way that galvanizes their physical and mental power as well as enervating their critical moral faculties (Storr 1996). In this context, King's speech galvanizes his followers but forces them to go back to their homes to carry on the work. In other words, King refuses to own the problem because he recognizes that he alone cannot solve it. Civil rights cannot be secured by an individual but only through mass social action.

The second point about King's apparent 'lacuna' is that the avoidance of specific commands or actions allows his followers and supporters to determine not just what they should do in their own local contexts but also what King's message actually means. In other words, the very ambiguity of King's speech enables a variety of interpretations to occur within the body of supporters, which ensures the collective effort is maintained. Had King spoken of the actions required just of black people; then the problem would have remained a black problem; had he spoken of the issue as one just for Christians or civil-rights activists, then, again, the problem would have been restricted to them. That our leaders are less solid than we think, and that we followers are significant in their construction, is the essence of Lilley and Platt's account of Martin Luther King discussed above.

Halfway through the section 'I have a dream . . .' that forms the main body of the text, King again switches to the TPC structure: 'I have a dream that one day even the state of Mississippi, a desert state sweltering with the heat of injustice and oppression, will be transformed into an oasis of freedom and justice.' Here, the traditional contrast would end with 'an oasis of justice and freedom' to mirror the first section, but the reversal allows the last word to remain as 'justice'. This is a call not simply for what ought to be in a theoretical future, but for what already exists—albeit in theory. This is followed by a TPC that secures another bout of applause: 'I have a dream that my four little children will one day live in a nation where they will not be judged by the color of their skin but by the content of their character.' It would have been quicker to finish the sentence after the word 'skin' but the addition of the second section turns an everyday statement into a memorable phrase.

Again and again King refers back to biblical scenes, but they are relocated in the present material conditions: 'I have a dream that one day every valley shall be exalted, every hill and mountain shall be made low, the rough places will be made plains, and the crooked places will be made straight . . .'. This fundamentally Christian imagery of equality through inversion, however, while it will not be realized overnight, starts here and now. Thus he refers to being able to 'hew out of the mountain of despair a stone of hope', and the contrast between the mountain and the stone does not deny that they are both made from the same material: the American dream.

The last element of the redemption section of the speech, in which 'let freedom ring' is repeated ten times, is actually closely styled on a speech by the black pastor Archibald Carey given in 1952 (see Miller and Lewis 1996: 157). But the effect of the *anadiplosis* remains a powerful one, ending with a carefully crafted reference to freedom ringing from the most racist of states, even every 'molehill in Mississippi'—one of the lowest points both geographically, and for King politically, in the USA.

Finally King ends—as you might have expected—with a triple listing of opposites, followed by a triple *anadiplosis*: 'we will be able to speed up that day when all of God's children, black men and white men, Jews and Gentiles, Protestants and Catholics, will be able to join hands and sing in the words of the old Negro spiritual, 'Free at last, free at last. Thank God almighty, we are free at last!'

In R. Cook's (1998: 137) words: 'For one fleeting moment his vision of an integrated, beloved community appeared to be an attainable reality in America.' Or, in Garrow's (1993: 284) words: 'Although he did not know it, the speech had been the rhetorical achievement of a lifetime, the clarion call that conveyed the moral power of the movement's cause to the millions who had watched the whole live national network coverage.' Three weeks later a bomb in Birmingham killed four black children.

After the Speech

The next two years seemed to presage the unravelling of the racist lobby: first, in 1963, King was made *Time* magazine's 'Man of the Year', and one year on he was awarded the Nobel Peace Prize. President Johnson signed the first of several Civil Rights Acts on 2 July 1964, which guaranteed the right to vote for all citizens, and in November Johnson was elected with 65 per cent of the popular vote.[19] But, as the long-awaited 'freedom' failed to deliver anything like the 'dream', and as violence against the black population continued, movements to the left of King began to shed doubt on the utility of non-violence. Securing political rights through the vote had been arduous but possible; securing economic rights began to prove arduous and impossible. Malcolm X (until his assassination in 1965), within Elijah Muhammad's Nation of Islam, and the Black Panther leaders, Eldridge Cleaver, and SNCC's Stokely Carmichael, all attacked King, and he was torn between the constitutional path he had pursued for so long and the more radical demands of those seeking violent confrontation. Yet, as Carson concludes in his review of the rival approaches, black power militancy of the late 1960s was either readily suppressed or transformed into configurations that did not threaten to dominate political and economic élites. After Malcolm X had left the Nation of Islam to form his own Organization of African-American Unity, even he began making overtures to King about the importance of unity (Carson 1996: 116–17, 120).

Moreover, as King's interests swung outwards and northwards to consider the problems of Vietnam and of poverty in the northern cities like Chicago—much to the consternation of the FBI—many of his followers appeared more concerned with day-to-day survival on the streets of the USA. By 1968 King was still moving left, while many blacks were moving towards a black nationalist or separatist line pursued by Stokely Carmichael and Malcolm X, and many radical whites were leaving the field altogether to concentrate on Vietnam. It was a clear crossroads for King, because the civil-rights movement that he had done so much to help was unravelling, but it is not clear which road he would have taken, though his increasing attacks upon capitalism and the war made him few new friends. On 3 April, in support of striking sanitation workers in Memphis, he spoke fatefully of what the future held:

I don't know what will happen now. We've got some difficult days ahead. But it doesn't matter with me now. Because I've been to the mountaintop . . . and I've seen the promised land. I may not get there with you. But I want you to know tonight, that we, as a people, will get to the promised land. And I'm happy tonight. I'm not worried about anything. I'm not fearing any man. (quoted in Gardner 1996: 218)

The following day, 4 April 1968, King was assassinated. Six days later Congress passed the new Civil Rights Act. Two months after this Robert F. Kennedy was also assassinated.

Conclusion

By 1965, although many Americans regarded King as *the* leader of the civil-rights movement, there were several who did not. He was the leader of the SCLC, but this was only one of several organizations within the civil-rights umbrella. Moreover, just as other charismatics have tended to enervate as well as invigorate some of their followers, so too King was criticized because of his style. As Forman insists, many local activists regarded King's presence as counterproductive to the civil-rights movement: 'A strong people's movement was in progress, the people were feeling their own strength grow. I knew much harm could be done by inter-jecting the Messiah complex—people would feel that only a particular individual could save them and would not move on their own to fight racism and exploita-tion' (Foreman 1972: 255; quoted in R. Cook 1998: 7). This is important because not only does it demonstrate the contested nature of King's contribution and sig-nificance but it suggests that leadership of a movement like the US civil-rights movement cannot be explained solely by the actions of formal or visible leaders. As R. Cook (1998: 7) summarizes the evidence: 'the civil rights movement drew most of its strength from local people and community institutions.' For Cook, although this is an important caveat for the 'great-man' theory of history, King was still *primus inter pares*, and it is still the case that grass-roots activists and local leaders could not, in and of themselves, have removed *de jure* segregation from the southern USA in the 1960s.

Analysis

The Philosophical Arts: Identity

For most blacks and whites in the 1960s, Martin Luther King was the movement's chief figurehead. 'Instantly recognizable by dint of his frequent media appear-ances, the SCLC President symbolized more than any other leader the ongoing search for integration. He did so by speaking to blacks and whites alike in lan-guage which both races could understand and by articulating what was for many Americans a compelling vision of an inclusive but national community tolerant of diversity and intolerant of prejudice and poverty' (R. Cook 1998: 218.) Once again we should note that the gap between King's personal identity and the col-lective identity he tried to lead was minimal: he embodied them both.

This heterogeneous movement was not held together by a consensus on King's personal identity but by a solidarity with the ideal community identity formed by the founders of the USA, and the ambiguity of this ideal allowed a great diversity of support to remain united. We should also recall that identity is not configured

wholly through words or even just through humans, for the civil-rights movement drew heavily upon the iconography of American history: the documents of
the Constitution, the memorials to liberation and liberators. Hence the identity
that King constructs looks both forward and back: back to the sea of promises
and forward to the promised land.

The Fine Arts: Strategic Vision

King clearly had an engaging vision for securing black civil rights, which we
might call a 'concrete' utopia. That is, it was utopian in that such permanent
rights had been unsuccessfully sought for most of the twentieth century, but it
was also concrete in its realism—for whites had already secured civil rights.
What King did was lead the way to the achievable political 'utopia'. However,
once the legislative changes had been secured, King was faced with a much more
difficult dream: economic equality. This was, and remains, an 'abstract' utopia,
for few communities have ever achieved or even sought anything like this, and
King's developing vision never established what the vision would actually look
like nor how it could be achieved.

Ling (1998: 19) suggests that King had 'never been a master strategist' and little that King 'led' was initiated by him, so dependent was he upon local activists.
His last great struggle, the Poor People's Campaign of 1968, aimed at establishing radical social change, was launched against the federal government not
against recalcitrant local states or cities, but the Washington target was both distant and the immediate goals moving. Moreover, the campaign had no local traditions or networks to build on, and its demise following King's assassination is
testament both to his own personal following and to the limits that even he had
to face. R. Cook (1998: 218) is also clear that King would not have been able to
spearhead the destruction of the legal segregation system in the south without the
actions of the grass-root supporters. But this is to conflate strategy with execution and, while the two are obviously related, it is inevitably the case that leaders
are dependent upon followers for the achievement—or attempted achievement—of strategies.

The Martial Arts: Organizational Tactics

There were few cases in King's lifetime when he could dominate his opponents
through the use of superior resources, because he almost never acquired them.
But there were some occasions when he took a conscious decision not to pull his
followers into a battle of attrition with his opponents, and this tactic of withdrawal is an important element of the leader's armoury if he or she is to minimize
unnecessary damage to his or her followers or resources. For example, on 9
March 1965 King had led a group of marchers across the Edmund Pettus bridge
on the way to Montgomery but had halted the march and ordered his followers
to go no further after a prior negotiation with the authorities. Several leaders of

the SNCC who knew nothing of King's secret negotiations were appalled at his 'surrender', but he had prevented further bloodshed and avoided breaking the federal law. The latter was crucial, because within five days President Johnson informed the country that he was sending a voting rights bill to Congress (R. Cook 1998: 147). This utilization of the legal system to advance civil rights was a classic form of neutralization by King, for he managed to restrict the legal powers of the various state authorities by juxtaposing them against the more powerful federal courts.

But King's greatest exploitation of the martial-arts approach to organizational tactics was in inverting the resources of his opponents, for much of his success was premised directly upon the contradiction of his philosophy of non-violence. That is to say, only where the opponents of civil rights engaged in violent attacks upon the peaceful protesters did the media become interested and the federal government appear worried. Paradoxically, therefore, King had to persuade his opponents to engage in the kinds of activities that he publicly stated as reprehensible: he needed them to fight him when he had already publicly stated that the protests would be peaceful. Only that way, only by using the greater resources of his opponents against themselves, could he ever hope to be successful, because, ironically, neither violent protest nor peaceful protest seemed to work; the protesters had to be peaceful but the authorities had to be violent.

The Performing Arts: Persuasive Communication

Ultimately, however, King's greatest 'art' was the art of persuasive communication. He certainly had no riches or material rewards to offer his supporters—but he did have an honourable goal. To achieve the vision of civil rights, the local movements and activists had to be connected together and had to be mobilized into bringing the federal government into play. Like the media, the federal government was generally uninterested in local events that did not involve King or widespread violence, and it remains the case that King's role was more akin to talking from the top of an iceberg of invisible local activists rather than a role that actively mobilized the local population. Thus Charles Payne's review of the Mississippi activists suggests that 'the issues that were invisible to the media and to the current generation of Black activists are still almost as invisible to scholars' (Payne 1995, quoted in Ling 1998: 18). Nevertheless, King managed to ensure that the images flashed across the world's TV screens were consistently those of unarmed and peaceful protesters, often children or students, being brutally beaten by armed police or soldiers. 'King's ability to operate at the interface of Black and white culture contributed to his effectiveness as a communicator of Black objectives to white Americans' (R. Cook 1998: 218). And it was this embodiment and mobilization of the American dream in his speeches that made his message so formidable and probably explains why he was shot.[20]

Finally we should reiterate the technical and performative skill that King used in his role on the stage of his struggles. His oratory was enormously skilful, but it was not the result of any 'magic'. Instead it was a skill that had been honed for decades and the 'Dream Speech' used almost all the known technical devices that have been around for several millennia. It was also a performance that crowned the greatest ever peaceful protest in US history in which every conceivable stage prop and symbol were deployed to maximum effect.

Notes

1. The Battle of Gettysburg cost both sides around 23,000 dead (Brogan 1986: 347).
2. As Mike Harper has suggested, it may be that Lincoln's radically short speech was designed to deter the newspaper editors from their conventional 'editing', since the entire text could be transmitted on the new telegraph system without alteration (personal communication, 1998).
3. Speech to a rally of Conservative Women, 3 July 1982.
4. Amongst other things (see D'Este 1996).
5. From 'The future doesn't belong to the faint hearted', 28 Jan. 1986, in MacArthur (1993: 448–9). The lines come from 'High Flight (An Airman's Ecstasy)' by John Gillespie Magee, a fighter pilot killed in 1941.
6. The speech can be heard on Peter Hill's 1996 collection *Great Political Speeches*, (London: Hodder Headline Audio Books).
7. See Huczynski's (1993) useful review.
8. Haig said: 'the general situation was favourable . . . effective, nay substantial progress . . . everything has gone well . . . there is every reason to be sanguine about the result' (quoted in Fussell 1975: 88).
9. Readers may be pleased to note that not all cultures are enamoured of threes: some Native Americans regard four as a sacred number, while the Japanese regard four as unlucky, since its pronunciation resembles the word for death (Versluis 1994: 83–4).
10. The origin of 'Jim Crow' is unknown.
11. R. Cook (1998: 24) calls this 'one of the basest fictions ever peddled by the American legal system'.
12. Harriet Beecher Stowe was the author of the fantastically successful *Uncle Tom's Cabin*.
13. In March 1999 the National Civil Rights Movement (NCRM) was launched in Britain—based directly on the NAACP.
14. In 1910, 75% of all US blacks lived in rural areas and 90% lived in the south. However, the decline and mechanization of southern agriculture, in conjunction with the increased industrial development of the north, meant that by 1940 roughly a quarter of the black population lived outside the south, and by 1965 this had increased to half. By 1960 only 40% of the remaining blacks in the south lived in rural areas.
15. Gardner (1996) also posits expertise as central, but this is not clearly displayed in any of the so-called direct leaders (leading from actions rather than influencing through ideas/writings) he discusses.
16. The Second World War had led some black Americans to adopt a double V sign: Vs for Victories abroad and at home.
17. Blacks formed 37% of Montgomery's total population, 8% of its voters, and two-thirds of the bus passengers.

18. King's popularity with CBS had led southern racists to call it the Coloured Broadcasting System (R. Cook 1998: 220).
19. President Kennedy, who had tried to use King's speech to demonstrate widespread support for his Civil Rights Bill, had been assassinated in November 1963.
20. In September 1998 Coretta King filed a suit against Loyd Jowers, a former Memphis restaurateur, in an attempt to establish whether the FBI was involved in a conspiracy to murder her husband (Honigsbaum 1998: 18).

10

The End of Leadership?

Thou seekest disciples? Thou seekest ciphers.

(Friedrich W. Nietzsche, quoted in Harter (1995: 30))

In this final chapter I want to draw the threads of the central arguments together by considering some of the more significant implications for leadership today. I do this by considering the four main arts in sequence before turning to the final conclusion: the end of leadership.

The Who Question and Philosophical Arts: Constructing Identity and the Construction of Truth

Leadership is closely related to movement—that is, getting a body of followers to move in one direction or another—and it is obvious that much of the contemporary world of organizations is grounded in the cash nexus as a mobilizer. But we also know that money has severe limitations as a mobilizer of followers: it may induce them to go to work, for example, but it may not make them work when they are there. It may encourage them to join the army or the nursing profession, but it is seldom sufficient to ensure such followers are prepared to risk their lives for the sake of a wage. There are some cases: a few of the nurses in the Crimea seem to have enrolled for money, but most went because of their religious faith. The demands of the mutineers were heavily weighted with wage claims, but many were also concerned with unpopular officers and with rights to leave in harbour, and so on. By and large, the majority of the radical risk-taking by followers in this review of leadership has been associated with mobilizers other than money: it is not Virgin's monetary compensation that draws people to work there but the identity of the organization as an exciting and innovative company; it was not the lure of gold that attracted recruits to Hitler's SS but the opportunity to join an élite, and an élitist, organization that struck fear in friend and foe; it was not the lure of prize money that encouraged Nelson's crew to 'turn-over' with him because Nelson was not interested in it—he was after glory; and it certainly was not the opportunity to make a fortune that led the civil-rights activists to stage sit-ins and organize 'freedom-rides', because they almost always resulted in violent assaults and imprisonment. In sum, although money may act as a basic mobilizer for followers, it seldom operates at the extreme edge, where success depends upon the willingness to take personal risks.

That kind of mobilization is often—though clearly not always—associated with the identity of the follower or leader or organization: who are they, and who are we? These are the kinds of questions posed by such philosophical arts. Equally important, that very identity appears not to be 'discovered' or allowed to reveal itself by the leader, but to be superimposed upon or constructed through a body of followers.

For example, we have seen how Hitler's construction of the new German 'Aryan' identity is premised upon several wholly invented myths: that the Treaty of Versailles was unparalleled in its gratuitous shaming of a nation; that left-wing Jewish leaders were wholly responsible for the defeat of the Germany army in 1918; and that the Aryan nation of Germans was both objectively superior to any other 'race' and had the right to achieve and maintain its control over the rest of the world with whatever means were deemed necessary. That none of this was 'true' is irrelevant, because Hitler used his power to make it 'true'. He persuaded ordinary—and probably hitherto perfectly decent—Germans to carry out indescribably disgusting acts of murder on the grounds that their targets were not humans at all. And even if we assume that only the fanatics of the Nazi party, the SA, and the SS were actually prepared to die for such an identity, this does not mean that the identity construction was relevant only to these groups. Far from it, the old, the conservatives, the rural-dweller, the unemployed, the young, women, industrialists, workers, and a whole host of other groups could find sufficient association within the Nazi 'brand' to satisfy themselves that the regime should at best receive their support, and at worst not be undermined by any actions they might take. In effect, Hitler invented a German identity that mobilized the fanatics and immobilized the sceptics.

At the opposite end of the moral spectrum, Martin Luther King operated in a similar way. His ambiguous messages and complex character enabled the construction of an identity that allowed many disparate groups and individuals to see him and the civil-rights movement as worthy of their support. And just as Lincoln had reconstructed American identity a century beforehand at Gettysburg, so King's 'Dream Speech' evoked an image of social unity that has rarely been painted before or since. That King's own role may well have been exaggerated is less relevant than the impact he had on the development of a new identity.

Elsewhere we have seen how Earl Spencer's identification of the mutineers as political revolutionaries undermined their chances of appearing as loyal but unhappy sailors; how Laker was identified with 'cheap' not 'economical' air flights; how Nelson embodied the military hero in his actions, dress, and (self-written) battle accounts; how the British press moved the nation to support Florence Nightingale's demands for decent medical care for its soldiers, only to switch midstream and demand indecent revenge upon the Indian 'mutineers', thereby scuppering Nightingale's long-term plans almost overnight; how Ford became identified as a trustworthy and honest common man because of, not despite, his manifest ignorance and naïvety; how Ford combined a Peace Ship to save the world with a mission to save Ford and ended up persuading the American population that he had saved the government rather than the other way round; how Frere's rendering of Zulu intentions as essentially aggressive, militaristic, and uncivilized ensured imperial support for the destruction of an entire culture; and how the British army's identification of their African auxiliaries as second rate led them to arm, train, and lead them so poorly that they almost inevitably failed to stand firm against the Zulu attack at Isandhlwana. On the other side, Cetshwayo's perpetuation of the Zulu army in age-related not regional regiments effectively constructed a solidaristic identity for his soldiers that was so effective it dominated southern Africa for many years.

Yet none of the identities we have discussed was written in the hearts of the people involved, as if it was a stick of Blackpool rock with a name through the core. Each and every one was invented from a motley mass of historical, mythical, social, and metaphorical flotsam and jetsam and imposed upon a population so successfully than many people thought of themselves as little more than identical pieces of candy ready and willing to be sacrificed for the good of the great community that they had come to believe was 'truly' theirs. In sum, perhaps we should summarize this issue thus: the success of leaders is dependent upon the extent to which they can construct and articulate an identity that pushes followers further than money can pull them.

But the confidence to do this is related to the certainty that leaders have in their own identity. For example, it is noticeable that many of the leaders discussed believed themselves fated or destined to achieve particular things. Nightingale certainly believed God had chosen her for a particular role—and the requirements of that role induced her to abandon her life of relative idleness and luxury to give herself to saving the poor bloody infantry of the British army. But it also inhibited her from seeking the very publicity that might have achieved much more than she did. Martin Luther King felt similarly destined to sacrifice himself for the disadvantaged, though he was clearly less reticent about seeking the limelight—if he thought that was how to achieve his goal. Nelson was similarly assured of a glorious future—at least until 1805—by the words of a West Indian fortune-teller and, just like General Patton and Hitler, the right of certainty was radically translated into the certainty of right.

The What Question and Fine Arts: Strategic Vision and the Invention of Leadership

All of the leaders in this book generated a clear and relatively simple answer to the what question: what do you want to achieve? The Zulus wanted to protect their interests—so did the British troops facing them. Nightingale wanted to save 'her' soldiers from unnecessary death, while the British army wanted to save itself from unnecessary expenditure and outside interference. The mutineers wanted justice and decent wages and conditions, but the Admiralty wanted loyal and subordinate sailors. Laker wanted to become financially successful by branding a new market, while Branson wanted to become financially successful by marketing a new brand. Ford wanted to revolutionize American transport, Nelson wanted to secure British domination of the seas, Hitler wanted to inaugurate a new German empire in a world without Jews or communists, and King wanted to secure civil rights and social advancement for his fellow black Americans. In their visions they were all relatively innovative and relatively consistent. They all also embodied their social visions in their personal visions, so that it became difficult to distinguish the one from the other: Ford from mass-produced cars, Nelson from naval victories, Hitler from systematic murder, and King from the civil-rights movement.

But there were some consistencies that undermined the visions. Henry Ford became besotted with his Model T as the strategic and long-term solution to American family transport needs long after GM had shown that consumers were captured by fashion and conspicuous consumption not perfected technology.

Hitler's consistent application of the principle of pseudo-Darwinian survival facilitated the drive across Europe, but the opportunity to seal the eastern border and integrate the territory won by 1942 was cast away by his overarching principle of racial superiority. Yet his acquisition of the Chancellory was achieved through an opportunist acceptance that the legitimate acquisition of power did not inhibit him from an illegitimate subsequent deployment of that same power. In effect, the political opportunism that rendered his early leadership so successful was sacrificed to the military desire for uncompromising victory.

Nelson was inconsistent in his approach to regulations—he broke and kept them at will—but the successful outcome of this inconsistency is both the cause and effect of his leadership skill. King's strategic inconsistency is perhaps best manifest in the way his short-term strategy of inducing violent attacks against the civil-rights activists was directly contrary to his long-term strategy of securing progress through peaceful means. Again, it is not the inconsistency in itself that is the issue here, but the point that only the inconsistency appears to work: either a wholly non-violent strategy or a wholly violent strategy would probably have failed, but the ironic cementing of the two differentiated elements together generated a paradoxical package that opened up the opportunity for radical social change.

In the naval mutinies the Spithead sailors successfully managed to combine opportunistic control over captured officers and ships with long-term commitment to naval authority in an explosive compound. But the same technique by their Nore compatriots failed, because they were unwilling to extend that paradox to the point where a violent attack upon the authorities was possibly the only means of maintaining a relatively equal relationship with the Admiralty. For its part, it was the Admiralty's own inconsistent combination of short-term appeals to partnership and long-term objectives of sectional violence and revenge that set the explosive compound alight and blew the mutineers apart. In short, the Admiralty changed the rules of the game, while the mutineers were still rehearsing the moves that had won in the previous event.

Finally, the Zulus' frail chances to maintain their independence were probably lost when Cetshwayo prevented his army from advancing across the border into Natal just after Isandhlwana. This was a consistent strategy, because he wished to demonstrate that the Zulu attacks were wholly defensive. But the British strategic inconsistency—they were invading Zululand just to protect Natal—proved superior, because they were undeterred from doing whatever they felt necessary to destroy the Zulu nation.

We can summarize this paradox thus: leadership success is dependent upon the extent to which leaders are sufficiently and inventively inconsistent to wrong-foot their more consistent opponents. Here we can see just how important leaders' inventiveness is: if they are unable to imagine utopias that attract their supporters, they will fail; but if the utopias are abstract rather than concrete, unrealistic rather than realistic, then that very utopia may turn into a dystopia, the vision into a nightmare, creation into destruction.

The How Question and Martial Arts: Organizational Tactics and the Indeterminacy of Leadership

The third lesson that can be drawn from the review relates to the how question: how are we going to achieve the strategic vision that reflects our identity? This is always a difficult question for leaders to answer, because leadership is indeterminate and because organizations are indeterminate. That is to say, not just that the effect of leadership cannot be precisely determined either in advance or after the event, but, more importantly, that what happened need not have happened, for other possibilities, however small, were always open. One need only consider the likelihood of one's own life to ponder on this. The chance that a particular sperm meets a particular egg in a specific set of circumstances is a likelihood that no self-respecting gambler would bet on. To assume further, just to get to this point requires a similar set of unlikely circumstances coalescing through thousands of human generations to produce the current population of the world requires a mathematical model beyond my conception—no pun intended! Working backwards through time, we may need only a slight variation in decision-making by a few individuals to generate a different future. If that is the case, then life is far more indeterminate than we perhaps believe, and this means that the significance of leadership is critical, because even relatively small decisions may make crucial differences to the construction—rather than the more determinate phrase 'unfolding'—of the future.

Of course, the consequence of this is that leaders who are wrong (and like everyone else leaders always err sometimes)—but convinced they are right—tend to expose their organizations and followers to higher and higher levels of risk. For example, Hitler's 'miraculous' invasions of Poland and France persuaded not just Hitler but many of his military advisers that he was a gifted strategist. His early military success laid the groundwork for his subsequent failure, but—and this is the point here—this need not have happened. Hitler's advisers put

themselves in the shoes of Hitler's opponents and rationally assessed the likelihood of a successful occupation of Germany's demilitarized areas, the
Sudetenland, and Austria, as well as the invasion of Poland, France, and Russia.
On each case they suggested he was wrong but each time—except the last—he
proved them wrong. But the point is that Hitler's advisers knew his actions were
not determinate—they were not foreordained to succeed and only did so because
the Allies proved unable or unwilling to generate sufficient political will and
organizational skill to resist. In effect, Hitler invented the future. Primarily this
future was secured through the deployment of a variety of organizational tactics
that mirror the martial arts. For instance, he adopted dominating tactics against
the Polish forces and against the Jews, both of whom were markedly weaker than
their German opponents. But Hitler neutralized the internal opposition of the
political left and the trade-union movement by remaining within the law because
he could not dominate them in 1933. An even greater success was achieved
against the French and British forces in 1940 by inverting their marginally superior forces against them, for, as long as they spread their defences thinly along the
whole of the 'impregnable' French defences, the German *Blitzkrieg* could generate an unstoppable charge all the way to Paris.

However, once the will and the skill of the German forces had been developed,
a series of undetermined errors allowed the Allies to succeed, and each of those
errors can be routed straight back to the German leadership. In almost all cases
the *Wehrmacht* fought with great determination and some considerable success
to hold their ground—so it was not the case that the German soldiers and junior
officers were at fault in their tactical decisions; rather it was the strategic incompetence of their superior officers in general, and Hitler in particular, that undermined their chances. This issue can be condensed as follows: all leaders err, but
the most successful leaders are those who lead an organization that is empowered
to compensate for his or her errors. The examples of this are manifold but I shall
just select a few for illustrative purposes.

In the Crimea the army medical leadership's incompetence was not compen-
sated for by the subordinate officers, because this was an organizational difficulty
of immense complexity. But Nightingale succeeded because she was not within a
military strait-jacket and because her followers in Britain were able to balance
her hesitancy about publicity by their own influence over the newspapers and
public opinion. Indeed, Nightingale inverted the army's resources against it—the
longer she waited for their acceptance of her position, the longer the army
demonstrated its own incompetence. Once she had returned, however, the opposite happened, for her tight grip on her supporters and her own strategy effectively undermined her own aims.

Laker's errors could never be properly offset by his subordinates, because they
were unwilling to point them out to him or because he would not listen. Branson,
on the other hand, tends to leave most of the decision-making to his subordinates—though he remains extremely visible as the leader of Virgin. Moreover
Branson's greatest successes have been achieved where he has encouraged a

stronger opponent to lash out at him and then used the courts and his own personal popularity to win the subsequent court case. In an economic battle of attrition with British Airways, a small airline like Virgin Atlantic cannot hope to secure victory—as Laker found to his cost. In such circumstances, the weaker opponent has to outwit the larger and has to *use* the resources of the stronger against that organization, and not simply try to *avoid* being crushed by it.

In Henry Ford's case his success almost always correlates with a shared decision-making, and the greater the personal control and visible leadership he exerted the less successful became the business. Many of his 'victories' were achieved through dominating his opponents—or even family and colleagues—but the consequence was often that Ford was allowed to make decisions that many knew were erroneous but none chose to point out to him. Ford, like many leaders, always wanted to be seen to be in control, to be visibly present at the front, but such a tactic often undermines the confidence of subordinates to lead informally in the absence of the formal leader.

One can go further than this to consider when visibility is essential and when its manifest absence might be preferable. For example, in the short term any situation that is successfully interpreted as a crisis might provide a suitable environment for a visible display of leadership. For example, Richard Parker trying to secure a peaceful termination of the Nore mutiny or Lieutenant Chard leading the foray to secure a water barrel in front of Rorke's Drift. But leaders cannot be in all places at all times, and therefore must generate a support network that ensures the requisite actions are undertaken without their presence in the long term. In this form we might consider Branson's determination that the staff of Virgin Atlantic appear as keen on customer service when he is not around as when he is. Or take Henry Ford's determination to generate an organization that adhered as closely to his engineering standards as it possibly could. In this case Ford's only solution to the problem of leadership-at-a-distance was to eliminate the human operatives wherever possible and replace them with machines. Unfortunately for Ford, this quest for determinacy proved as elusive as all the others we have considered. And even when it appeared that Ford was achieving conformance to engineering standards, it was almost always at the expense of sales and profits. His customers did not want the perfect Model T; they wanted what he would not give them: novelty, change, progress, and conspicuous consumption—they wanted to be visible.

The related utility of networking also appears critical to the ascension of individuals to positions of power. Nelson would probably not have had the opportunities he had to demonstrate his skill and courage if his uncle had not happened to be Comptroller of the Navy and on the Admiralty Board. Again this is not to say that Nelson's career was mapped out in advance, but whatever can constrain the chaos of space and time in a favourable direction can but help. And the Battle of the Nile is a clear example where that indeterminacy can work in favour of one leader and against another. For had Napoleon not dispossessed the French ships of many sailors, and had the captain of the *Guerrier* anchored a few more metres towards land, Captain Foley's *Goliath* would not have been able to get landward of the French line and proceed to attack the French with impunity because none of the French landward guns had been run out for action. In this case, the undoubted bravery and skill of the French officers and crews could not compensate for the errors of their leaders. In contrast, Nelson's devolved organizational tactics usually—though not always—ensured that any errors on his part would not necessarily jeopardize the success of the operation, while the inventiveness of his subordinates was corralled to good effect.

Moreover, the simple size of the relative groups is an inadequate basis to consider their likely success. Rather more successful and useful is an assessment that considers the strength of the various links between the elements—be they human or non-human. The French had larger ships and larger guns, but their firing rate was much slower and their officers and sailors far less experienced than their British counterparts. Hence it was the stronger links between the British ships, guns, sails, sailors, and officers that prevailed over the weaker links of their French adversaries. When this was clear to Nelson he attempted to dominate his enemies, but when the outcome was less certain he transcended their greater strength either by neutralizing a significant proportion through cutting the line— as at Trafalgar—or he inverted his opponents' resources—as at the Nile, where their 'impregnable' landward side lulled them into defeat.

On many occasions in this trail through leadership we have seen not just how a weaker organization can overcome a stronger but also how an organization that appears virtually impotent can transcend that weakness and turn the strength of its opponent or competitor against it. For example, Martin Luther King's non-violent strategy was not just a consequence of the Christian pacifism that prevailed amongst his organization; it was also a recognition that the forces stacked against the securement of black civil rights were enormous. Where the very real intimidation of individuals did not deter resistance, the powers of the local states simply seemed impenetrable and the federal state disinterested. But linking these two was the very bridge to success. By 'forcing' the racist local authorities to react publicly and violently to their peaceful demands for change, the civil-rights activists coerced the federal authorities to take action against the local authorities. It was not that peaceful protest worked, because very often it did not; it was only when the activists drew the local authorities into manifestly overt and politically embarrassing violent attacks upon unarmed protesters that the federal state stepped in. By the time the racist local authorities realized what was happening and began to develop more sophisticated counter-tactics, it was too late, because, whatever local police officers thought about the organization to undermine the civil-rights movement, they were unable or unwilling to intervene.

In effect, thinking about organizational tactics as different forms of martial art encourages us to move away from the assumptions, in karate or boxing, for example, that the leader who accumulates the greater resources will, in most cases, be successful. By reconsidering the utility of aikido we can better appreciate how the greater resources of an opponent can be neutralized to even out the contest or even swing the resource balance in a different direction. And by considering the metaphor of T'ai Chi we can perceive how the resources of an opponent can be utilized to undermine the opponent.

But such tactics cannot be achieved by dint of the leader's inventive adoption of various martial arts, for only followers can secure the strategic vision through such organizational tactics, and only the followers are usually close enough to recognize when the leader's strategy or tactics are misaligned. This turns the study of leadership on its head, for now we should concern ourselves with a different aspect, not just how inventive the leader is but how inventive the followers are. Thus the success of leaders is critically dependent upon the extent to which followers' competence can compensate for leaders' incompetence.

The Why Question: Persuasive Communication and the Irony of Leadership

My final art but penultimate concern is communications, and we should be clear from the start that leadership is not a science but an art; it is a performance not a recipe; it is an invention not a discovery. If it was a science, we could reduce the essence down to a parsimonious set of rules and apply the result with confidence. Unfortunately this is not the case.

Let us start with Martin Luther King, perhaps the greatest communicator of this century. If I read his speech to a group of people, I doubt very much whether I would get to the end without somebody walking out or throwing something at me. Nor is it clear that anyone can read a biography of him—or anyone else—and hope to reproduce the events. If this tells us nothing else, it should tell us that communication involves more than the speaker, more than the leader. It was certainly the case for Martin Luther King, for one individual—no matter how good an orator—could not change the system. That required hundreds and thousands of local people, activists and ordinary citizens, blacks and whites, to take a stand—and a great personal risk—to galvanize their fellow citizens into taking action. For the most part that action has remained invisible, and the temptation is to read the movement for civil rights as the direct consequence of Martin Luther King's leadership. And here lies a double lesson for leadership. On the one hand, successful leaders tend to be those who become or remain very 'visible', either through personal appearances or more likely through the media or through gossip, myth, and stories. It is surely not coincidental that some of our most notable leaders—Julius Caesar, Alexander the Great, and Nelson, for example—just happen to have written their own history or to have secured close control over what was written about them.

On the other hand, there is more to leadership than being visible, stealing or procuring whatever glory or success is available, and denying responsibility for whatever failures occur. Indeed, one might argue that invisibility is as significant as visibility in precisely the same conjunction that sees indeterminacy made determinate. By this I mean that one measure of success might be the extent to which followers execute leaders' wishes when leaders are not present or at least not visible. At one extreme we might consider the influence of religious leaders such as Jesus Christ and Muhammad. In both cases one need not be a true 'believer' to recognize that their authority extends well beyond their own mortal lives and often out of sight of any religious office whose role is to police the believers in the true faith.

Those invisible sinews of leadership are, of course, supplemented by the leader's performative communications. In the case of Nelson, his direct control over his subordinate officers and sailors certainly operated through visibility, for his love of ostentatious uniforms and medals, and preference for taking very public risks, made him both a well-known public figure and a target for his enemies. But at sea Nelson could not hope to be visible to more than a small minority of his own ship's company and his influence over the fleet had, therefore, to operate along invisible lines. And where his communications were visible to the fleet—for instance, in the signal flags that he used—it is worth pondering again what the target audience of his communications was. 'Close with the enemy' and 'England expects . . .' are hardly likely to have instituted radical changes in battle tactics, nor would they have necessarily made much difference to the sailors as they approached the Franco-Spanish fleet at Trafalgar. On the contrary, if anything, such signals seem to have annoyed several of his captains for their patronizing tone: after all, they knew what to do. So what were the flags for? They certainly make more sense if we consider them as communications back to England for the history-writers to make the most of—as they most surely did. In short, Nelson was painfully aware of the importance of actively constructing the narrative of events and not simply allowing someone else to write them as he or she saw fit.

The same goes for the great proportion of leaders we have considered—the military leaders, for example, worried by what the reporters will say about them, but who use military security as the excuse for denying them access to the battlefields. Or the business and political leaders who threaten to file suit against anyone they deem to have besmirched their (allegedly) good character. Indeed, the entire system of 'official secrets' is often of greater use in protecting the reputations of the existing or recent political élite than in ensuring the safety of the nation. Controlling information, therefore, becomes a *sine qua non* of leadership—without it how would we mere mortal followers believe in our leaders?

To this end, leadership might be considered as a talisman held by the wearer to ward off evil and induce good luck. Many people, and perhaps a majority of soldiers in war, take refuge in a talisman of some description: a rabbit's foot, a St Christopher, a cross, or a lucky coin. Or perhaps they engage in 'lucky' rituals, like the English footballer Paul Ince, who always puts his shirt on in the tunnel as he approaches the ground and not in the dressing room. Or they 'touch wood' every time they suggest their family is well or their car has not broken down. Whatever the ritual or talisman, to non-believers the ritual is a meaningless charade, and its futility can be ascertained by those crumpled bodies lying in heaps still clutching their lucky mascots or bibles. But the point is that, where the talisman fails, the wearer does not complain, because all such failures are dead—and if they are not dead they are 'lucky' not to be so—hence the talisman worked. For those who live, the talisman clearly worked and the charm will continue to be worn in the knowledge that it works. We might consider just how close leadership is to this, for we can never be sure whether it works—but only a brave individual goes over the top without one. And if the leader fails us, well we get another, rather than risk anything worse. Thus the belief in leadership continues apace, not necessarily because it works but because we assume it must and cannot conceive of a system where there are no leaders, where we are simply left to our own devices, to perform on our own.

In effect, then, leadership is a performance, an inventive display, and we can summarize this by suggesting that successful leadership depends upon the extent to which leaders 'perform' the words and deeds conventionally associated with leaders—but it also requires followers to believe in the performance.

The End of Leadership?

Finally, what is the end of leadership? I do not imply by this that we can do without leadership, but we probably could do without leaders. That is to say, that it may well be a requirement of all human organizations that some individual or group takes responsibility for ensuring its direction is one that secures the interests of the members. But this is a long way from saying that we need leaders—if that implies a group that are clearly and permanently distinguished from the rest. All too often in this review it seems that the errors of leaders are commonplace, but what distinguishes a successful from a failed leader is whether the subordinates can and will save the organization from the mistakes of its leaders.

Ironically, it might also be the case that many of our problems stem not from what our leaders do but from what we the followers let them get away with. It is therefore important to note that the power of leaders rests not in themselves, as possessions, but on their followers, as a network of relationships. Just as leadership is indeterminate, one of the ways that leaders persuade their followers to obey them or follow them is by suggesting that leaders can determine the future, that what is negotiable is actually non-negotiable. The dereliction of followers' responsibility is not simply something that can be laid at the feet of failed leaders. It fits all too often on the shoulders of those who silently followed without resisting, of those who refused to speak out against their own leaders and whose inaction allowed the leaders to proclaim that, since none was against them, all must be for them. The unreflective genuflection of followers before leaders is as much responsible for leaders' errors as anything they do.

We are left with a dilemma: leadership is an indeterminate skill that masquerades as a determinate skill. In other words, leaders tend to operate on the premiss—which is usually false—that what they do can determine the future of their organization, but we know this is seldom if ever the case. And, because it is manifestly erroneous, we are left with a paradox: the most successful leaders appear to be those who cultivate the least compliant followers, for when leaders err—and they always do—the leader with compliant followers will fail. But leaders who make mistakes that can be resolved by their subordinates are more likely to succeed. We can go further than this to argue that the trick of leadership—and the real invention—is to develop followers who privately resolve the problems leaders have caused or cannot resolve, but publicly deny their intervention. This is not to suggest that such a situation ought to result in the replacement of the leader, because the new leader will undoubtedly find him or herself in similar situations.

Thus leadership reverts to its talismanic origins: it performs a ritual that followers appear to require. Whether it actually works miracles or not is irrelevant, because, as long as followers believe they need leaders, leaders will be necessary. The problem, therefore, is to develop an organizational culture that prevents the leader from believing that his or her position of responsibility is a reason for omnipotence.

Perhaps we can conclude by comparing differing images of leadership. The conventional approach has been to suggest that leaders are 'at the top of the tree', the 'top dog', who through some Darwinist battle have fought their way to the 'top of the pile'. Such a leader is the font of all wisdom and deserves the riches and glory that go with 'high office'. Note that all these imply not just a lofty position but standing on something—that something is usually the bodies of followers who are likely to be metaphorically or literally 'wasted' as and when 'the situation' requires. Or, as the organizational jungle joke goes: when leaders look down from the top of the tree in the jungle, all they see is their organization staffed by monkeys. When followers look up at their leaders from their position at the bottom, all they see is bums. The history of the world is full of such leaders, whose errors of judgement and refusal to listen to the good advice of their followers have left millions of followers as physical, emotional, or economic casualties.

In contrast, the approach I am suggesting here conceives of leaders as responsible to their followers, as 'in front' but not 'on top'; as 'pulling' followers after them, not 'pushing' them in front; and as 'sharing the way' not just 'showing the way'. This is not because such an approach is more liberal or more humane or more 'progressive'—though all of these things may be valuable—but because only leaders who recognize their fallibility and operate on that basis are likely to succeed in the long run. It is followers that save leaders and therefore make them. This does not mean that leaders are irrelevant, but it does mean that no scientific or systemic approach is going to produce the error-free leader. However, if we abandon the infinite quest for scientific certainty and seek out the philosophical, fine, martial, and performing arts, we might go some way to resolving that most perennial of human questions: what is leadership?

References

Abercrombie, N., Hill, S., and Turner, B. S. (1980), *The Dominant Ideology Thesis* (London: Tavistock).

Ackroyd, S., and Crowdy, P. A. (1990), 'Can Culture be Managed? Working with Raw Materials: The Case of the English Slaughtermen', *Personnel Review*, 19/5: 3–12.

Adey, P., Shayer, M., and Yates, C. (1991), *Better Learning: A Report from the Cognitive Acceleration through Science Education (CASE) Project* (King's College, London).

Allen, J. (1992), 'Fordism and Modern Industry' in J. Allen, P. Braham, and P. Lewis, (eds.) *Political and Economic Forms of Modernity* (Cambridge: Polity Press).

Anderson, B. (1991), *Imagined Communities: Reflections on the Origin and Spread of Nationalism* (London: Verso).

Arnold, H., and Faurote, F. (1915), *Ford's Method and the Ford Shops* (New York: Engineering Magazine Company).

Atkinson, J. M. (1984), *Our Masters' Voices* (London: Routledge).

Audain, C. (1998), *Florence Nightingale* (Internet Website: http://www.wcottlan.edu/1riddle/women/nitegale.htm).

Austin, J. L. (1962), *How to Do Things with Words* (London: Oxford University Press).

Bald, J. (1991), 'Naval Regulations, *c.*1530', *History Today*, 41 (June).

Baly, M. (1997), *Florence Nightingale and the Nursing Legacy* (London: Whurr Publishers).

Banks, H. (1982), *The Rise and Fall of Freddie Laker* (London: Faber & Faber).

Barth, F. (1969) (ed.), *Ethnic Groups and Boundaries* (Oslo: Universitetsforlaget).

Bartov, O. (1991), *Hitler's Army: Soldiers, Nazis and the War in the Third Reich* (Oxford: Oxford University Press).

—— (1994), 'The Missing Years: German Workers, German Soldiers', in Crew (1994*b*).

Batchelor, R. (1994), *Henry Ford: Mass Production, Modernism and Design* (Manchester: Manchester University Press).

Bates, S. (1998), 'All Finished on the Western Front', *Guardian*, 11 Nov., 2–3.

BBC1 (1995), 'Sporting Fever', in *People's Century* (London: BBC Books).

BBC2 (1997), 'Trouble at the Top: Freddie's Back', 28 June.

Beatty, W. (1999), 'The Death of Lord Nelson 1805', in King and Hattendorf (1999).

Beeston, R. (1999), 'Divers Reveal Nelson's Blast from the Past', *The Times*, 28 June.

Berghahn, V. R. (1987), *Modern Germany* (Cambridge: Cambridge University Press).

Bessel, R. (1987*a*), 'Political Violence and the Nazi Seizure of Power', in Bessel (1987*b*).

—— (1987*b*) (ed.), *Life in the Third Reich* (Oxford: Oxford University Press).

Bethune, J. D. (1999), 'The Battle of Cape St. Vincent', in King and Hattendorf (1999).

Bishop. C. (1999*a*), 'The Holocaust', *Hitler's Third Reich* I. i. 8–16.

—— (1999*b*), 'Nazi Symbols', *Hitler's Third Reich* I. i. 40–3.

—— (1999*c*), 'Eugenics, Motherhood and the SS', *Hitler's Third Reich* I. i. 19.

—— (1999*d*), 'Adolf Hitler Schule', *Hitler's Third Reich* I. i. 44.

—— (1999*e*), 'Autobahn', *Hitler's Third Reich* I. i. 48.

Blackhurst, C. (1998), 'At the Court of King Richard', *Management Today* (April), 39–44.

Bloch, E. (1986), *The Principle of Hope* (Oxford: Oxford University Press).

Boden, D. (1994), *The Business of Talk* (Cambridge: Polity Press).

Böhme, H. (1978), *An Introduction to the Social and Economic History of Germany* (Oxford: Blackwell).

Boreham, P. (1983), 'Indetermination: Professional Knowledge, Organization and Control', *Sociological Review*, 31/4: 693–718.

Bowden, S. M. (1991), 'Demand and Supply Constraints in the Inter–War UK Car Industry: Did the Manufacturers Get it Right?', *Business History*, 33/2: 241–67.

Boyes, E. (1997), '*Virgin* Flies in Face of Convention', *Advertising Age*, 68/3: 4.

Bracher, K. D. (1973) *The German Dictatorship* (Harmondsworth: Penguin).

Branson, R. (1998), *Losing My Virginity* (London: Virgin).

Briggs, A. (1994), *A Social History of England* (London: BCA).

Brindle, D. (1999), 'Nurses Snuff Nightingale Image', *Guardian*, 27 Apr.

Broers, M. (1998), 'The Empire behind the Lines', *History Today*, 48/1: 20–6.

Brogan, H. (1986) *The Pelican History of the United States of America* (Harmondsworth: Pelican.)

Brown, M. (1998), *Richard Branson: The Authorized Biography* (London: Headline).

Brown, R. (1991), *Society and Economy in Modern Britain 1700–1850* (London: Routledge).

Browning, C. R. (1994), 'One Day in Jozefow: Initiation to Mass Murder', in Crew (1994).

Brummer, A., and Cowe, R. (1998), 'Living off Hot Air', *Guardian*, 10 Sept., 4.

Bullock, A. (1962), *Hitler: A Study in Tyranny* (Harmondsworth: Penguin).

Burleigh, M. (1997), 'Nazi Europe: What if Nazi Germany had Defeated the Soviet Union?', in N. Ferguson (ed.), *Virtual History: Alternatives and Counterfactuals* (London: Picador).

Burr, V. (1995), *An Introduction to Social Constructionism* (London: Routledge).

Burroughs, P. (1994), 'An Unreformed Army 1815–1868', in Chandler and Beckett (1994).

Callan, K., and Warshaw, M. (1996), 'The Best Business Schools for Entrepreneurs', *Success* (Sept.), 29–33.

Campbell-Smith, D. (1986), *Struggle for Take-Off: The British Airways Story* (Sevenoaks, Kent: Coronet Books).

Carr, W. (1987), 'Nazi Policy against the Jews', in Bessel (1987*b*).

Carson, C. (1996), 'African–American Political Thoughts', in B. Ward and T. Badger (eds.), *The Making of Martin Luther King and the Civil Rights Movement* (London: Macmillan).

—— (1999) (ed.), *The Autobiography of Martin Luther King, Jr.* (London: Little, Brown & Co.).

Chandler, D. (1994), 'The Great Captain General 1702–1714' in Chandler and Beckett (1994).

—— and Beckett, I. (1994) (eds.), *The Oxford Illustrated History of the British Army* (Oxford: Oxford University Press)

Cherfas, T. (1997*a*), 'Hot Nights in the Batteries' in Kerr (1997*b*).

—— (1997*b*), 'War and Peace', in Kerr (1997*b*).

Church, R. (1994), *The Rise and Decline of the British Motor Industry* (London: Macmillan).

Clausewitz, C. Von. (1976), *On War* (Princeton: Princeton University Press).

Cochrane, T. (1999), 'The Audacious Cruise of the *Speedy*', in King and Hattendorf (1999).

Cohen, A. P. (1985), *The Symbolic Construction of Community* (London: Tavistock).

Cohen, I. B. (1984), 'Florence Nightingale', *Scientific American*, 250: 128–37.

Colley, L. (1994), *Britons: Forging the Nation 1707–1837* (London: Pimlico).

—— (1999), 'This Country is Not So Special', *New Statesman*, 1 May, 19–21.

Connolly, K. (1999), 'Much More than a Game', *Guardian*, 20 July.

Cook, E. T. (1913), *The Life of Florence Nightingale*, 2 vols. (London: Macmillan).

Cook, R. (1998), *Sweet Land of Liberty: The African–American Struggle for Civil Rights in the Twentieth Century* (London: Longman).

Cooley, C. H. (1922), *Human Nature and the Social Order* (New York: Scribners).

Craig, G. A. (1981), *Germany 1866–1945* (Oxford: Oxford University Press).

—— (1986), 'The Political Leader as Strategist', in P. Paret (ed.), *Makers of Modern Strategy: From Machiavelli to the Nuclear Age* (Oxford: Oxford University Press).

Crew, D. F. (1994a) 'General Introduction', in Crew (1994b).

—— (1994b), (ed.) *Nazism and German Society 1933–1945* (London: Routledge).

Cuddon, J. A. (1979), *A Dictionary of Literary Terms* (Harmondsworth: Penguin).

Darwin, B. (1979) (ed.), *The Oxford Dictionary of Quotations* (London: Book Club Associates).

Davis, W. (1998), 'The Rubber Industry's Biological Nightmare', *Fortune*, 136/2: 32–9.

Dearlove, D. (1998), *Business the Richard Branson Way* (Oxford: Capstone Publishing Ltd.).

Deetz, S. A. (1992), *Democracy in an Age of Corporate Colonization* (Albany, NY: State University of New York Press).

Denoyelle, P., and Larréché, J.-C. (1995), *Virgin Atlantic Airways: Ten Years After* (INSEAD, Fontainebleau: INSEAD Case Study).

D'Este, C. (1996), *A Genius for War: A Life of General George S. Patton* (London: HarperCollins).

De Groot, G. (1995), 'Reagan's Rise', *History Today*, 45/9: 31–6.

Dillman, G. A. (1992), *Kyushu Jitsu* (Reading, Pa.: Dillman Karate International Books).

Dillon, W. H. (1999), 'Commence the Work of Destruction: The Glorious First of June 1794' in King and Hattendorf (1999).

Donellon, A., Gray, B., and Bougon, M. (1986), 'Communication, Meaning and Organized Action', *Administrative Science Quarterly*, 31: 43–55.

Donoho, R, (1996), 'Say it Ain't So', *Successful Meeting*, 45: 10.

Doray, B. (1988), *From Taylorism to Fordism: A Rational Madness* (London: Free Association Books).

Dore, R. (1989), 'Where Are We Now? Musings of an Evolutionist', *Work, Employment and Society*, 3/4: 425–46.

Douglas, M. (1966), *Purity and Danger* (London: Routledge & Kegan Paul).

Doward, J. (1999), 'Dell Vaults to No. 1 in PCs', *Guardian*, 15 Aug.

Downer, L. (1996), 'Branson's American Invasion', *Fortune*, 134/11: 11–16.

Dubovoy, S. (1997), *Civil Rights Leaders* (New York: Facts on File, Incs).

Durey, M. (1998), 'The Fate of the Rebels after 1798', *History Today*, 48/6: 21–7.

Eastwick, R. (1999), 'The Fortune of War 1799', in King and Hattendorf (1999).

Edwards, D. (1978), *The Soldiers' Revolt* (Nottingham: Spokesman).

Edwards, R. (1979), *Contested Terrain: The Transformation of the Workplace in the Twentieth Century* (London: Heinemann).

Edwards, W. E. (1925), *Notes on British History, Part IV, 1783 to 1901* (London: Rivingtons).

Elias, N. (1989), *Studien über die Deutschen* (Frankfurt: Suhrkamp).

Ellis, J. (1993), *The Social History of the Machine Gun* (London: Pimlico).

Erickson, J. (1994), 'Disquiet on the Eastern Front', *The Times Higher*, 1 July, 18–19.

Esdaile, C. J. (1995), *The Wars of Napoleon* (Harlow: Longman).

—— (1998), 'Popular Resistance in Napoleonic Europe', *History Today*, 48/2: 37–44.

Fairclough, A. (1996), 'The Civil Rights Movement in Louisiana, 1939–54', in B. Ward, and T. Badger (eds.), *The Making of Martin Luther King and the Civil Rights Movement* (London: Macmillan).

Fairclough, N. (1992), *Discourse and Social Change* (Cambridge: Polity Press).

Faith, N. (1998), *Mayday: The Perils of the Waves* (London: Channel 4 Books).

Fest, J. (1974), *Hitler* (London: Weidenfeld & Nicolson).

—— (1997), *Plotting Hitler's Death* (London: Phoenix).

Finch, J. (1999), 'Dell and IBM Sign $16bn Pact', *Guardian*, 6 Mar.

Flink, J. (1988), *The Automobile Age* (Cambridge, Mass.: MIT Press).

Flitton, D. (1998), *Case Yellow*, Discovery TV, 3 Mar.

Ford, H. (1926), *Today and Tomorrow* (London: Heinemann).

—— (1991), *Ford on Management: Harnessing the American Spirit* (Oxford: Basil Blackwell).

Foreman, J. (1972), *The Making of Black Revolutionaries* (New York: Macmillan).

Foucault, M. (1980), *Power/Knowledge* (Brighton: Harvester).

—— (1983), 'The Subject and the Power' in H. L. Dreyfus, and P. Rabinow (eds.), *Michel Foucault* (Chicago: University of Chicago Press).

—— (1986), 'Afterword', in H. L. Dreyfus and P. Rabinow (eds.), *Michel Foucault: Beyond Structuralism and Hermeneutics* (Chicago: Chicago University Press).

Fox Piven, F., and Cloward, R. A. (1977), *Poor People's Movements: Why They Succeed and How They Fail* (Oxford: Blackwell).

Frew, G. (1998), 'At the Court of the Virgin King', *Oxford Times Weekend*, 2 Oct.

Furtado, P. (1993), *Depression and Dictatorship* (London: Hamlyn).

Fussell, P. (1975), *The Great War and Modern Memory* (Oxford: Oxford University Press).

Gardiner, J., and Wenborn, N. (1995) (eds.), *The History Today Companion to British History* (London: Collins & Brown).

Gardner, H. (1996), *Leading Minds: An Anatomy of Leadership* (London: HarperCollins).

Garrow, D. J. (1993), *Bearing the Cross: Martin Luther King, Jr. and the Southern Christian Leadership Conference* (London: Vintage Books).

Gartman, D. (1979), 'The Assembly Line and Capitalist Control at Ford', in A. Zimbalist (ed.), *Case Studies on the Labor Process* (New York: Monthly Review Press).

Gatrell, V. A. C. (1994), *The Hanging Tree: Execution and the English People 1770–1868* (Oxford: Oxford University Press).

Geary, D. (1998), 'Who Voted for the Nazis?', *History Today*, 40/10: 8–17.

Geertz, C. (1983), 'Centers, Kings and Charisma: Reflections on the Symbols of Power', in C. Geertz, *Local Knowledge* (New York: Basic Books).

Gellately, R. (1991), *The Gestapo and German Society* (Oxford: Oxford University Press).

Gergen, K. J. (1992), 'Organization Theory in the Postmodern Era', in M. Reed and M. Hughes (eds.), *Rethinking Organization: New Directions in Organization Theory and Analysis* (London: Sage).

George, C. S. (1972), *The History of Management Thought* (Englewood Cliffs, NJ: Prentice-Hall).

Geyer, M. (1986), 'German Strategy in the Age of Machine Warfare, 1914–1945', in P. Paret (ed.), *Makers of Modern Strategy: From Machiavelli to the Nuclear Age* (Oxford: Oxford University Press).

—— (1987), 'The Nazi State Reconsidered', in Bessel (1987*b*).

Gilmour, I. (1993), *Riot, Risings and Revolution: Governance and Violence in Eighteenth Century England* (London: Pimlico).

Glaister, D. (1998), 'Shadow of Shame', *Guardian*, 22 Dec.

Glover, M. (1997), *Rorke's Drift* (Ware: Wordsworth Editions).

Golby, J. M. (1986), (ed.) *Culture and Society in Britain 1850–1890* (Oxford: Oxford University Press).

Gold, M. (1997), 'The Doomed City', in Kerr (1997*b*).

Goldhagen, D. J. (1996), *Hitler's Willing Executioners: Ordinary Germans and the Holocaust* (London: Little, Brown & Co.).

—— (1997), *Hitler's Willing Executioners: Ordinary Germans and the Holocaust* (London: Little, Brown & Co.).

Goldie, S. M. (1997), *Florence Nightingale: Letters from the Crimea* (Manchester: Mandolin).

Goldin, M. (1998), 'Financing the SS', *History Today*, 48/6: 28–34.

Gordon, T., and Greenspan, D. (1994), 'The Management of Chaotic Systems', *Technological Forecasting and Social Change*, 47: 49–62.

Grabsky, P. (1993), *The Great Commanders* (London: Boxtree).

Green, J. (1979) *Famous Last Words* (London: Pan).

Grint, K. (1991), *The Sociology of Work* (Cambridge: Polity Press).

—— (1994) 'Reengineering History: Social Resonances and Business Process Reengineering', *Organization: The Interdisciplinary Journal of Organization, Theory and Society*, 1/1: 179–202.

—— (1995), *Management: A Sociological Introduction* (Cambridge: Polity Press).

—— (1997*a*), *Fuzzy Management* (Oxford: Oxford University Press).

—— (1997*b*) (ed.), *Leadership: Classical, Contemporary and Critical Approaches* (Oxford: Oxford University Press).

—— (1998*a*), *The Sociology of Work*, 2nd edn. (Cambridge: Polity Press).

—— (1998*b*), 'Determining the Indeterminacies of Change Leadership', *Management Decision*, 36/8: 503–8.

—— and Woolgar, S. (1997), *The Machine at Work* (Cambridge: Polity Press).

Guttridge, L. F. (1992), *Mutiny: A History of Naval Insurrection* (Shepperton, UK: Ian Allen).

Guy, A. J. (1994), 'The Army of the Georges, 1714–1783' in Chandler and Beckett (1994).

Hall, Simon (1998), 'Beowulf: New Light on the Dark Ages', *History Today*, 48/12: 4–5.

Hall, Stuart (1998), 'Who Remembers the Fate of the *Lancastria*?', *Guardian*, 26 Jan. 3.

Harman, C. (1982), *The Lost Revolution: Germany 1918–1923* (London: Bookmarks).

Harper, K. (1999), 'Virgin Gains at BA's Expense', *Guardian*, 26 May.

—— and Bates, S. (1999), 'BA Fined £4 million for Illegal Trading', *Guardian*, 15 July.

Harter, J. (1995), *Thoughts on Leadership* (Chicago: Forbes/Triumph Books).

Harvey, A. D. (1998), 'Napoleon—the Myth', *History Today*, 48/1: 27–32.

Heifetz, R. A. (1994), *Leadership Without Easy Answers* (Cambridge, Mass.: Belknap Press).

Hellen, N. (1997), 'How Freud could have Saved Us from Hitler', *Independent*, 12 Nov.

Henley, J. (1999), 'Holocaust Cable to the Pope', *Guardian*, 10 Oct.

Herbert, U. (1987), 'Good Times, Bad Times: Memories of the Third Reich', in Bessel (1987*b*).

Hibbert, C. (1995), *Nelson: A Personal History* (Harmondsworth: Penguin).

Hill, E. J. M. (1998), *Florence Nightingale* (Internet website: http://www.kume. edu/service/clendening/florence/introduction.html).

Hobsbawm, E. (1994), *Age of Extremes: The Short Twentieth Century* (London: Michael Joseph).

Hodgson, G. (1995), *People's Century: From the Dawn of the Century to the Start of the Cold War* (London: BBC Books).

Honigsbaum, M. (1998), 'Widow Calls on Judge to Decide who Killed Martin Luther King', *Observer*, 27 Sept.

Hooper, J. (1999), 'Nazi Slave Labourers Agree to Payout', *Guardian*, 15 Dec.

Hounsell, D. (1984), *From the American System to Mass Production* (Baltimore: John Hopkins University Press).

Howard, T. (1997), 'Charisma and History: The Case of Münster, Westphalia, 1534–1535' (Internet paper on http://www.lib.virginia.edu/journals/EH/EH35/howard 1.html).

Huczynski, A. A. (1993*)*, *Management Gurus: What Makes Them and How to Become One* (London: Routledge).

Hunt, J. (1996), 'Using your Defects to Best Effect', *Director* (Feb.), 81–2.

Huxley, A. (1936), 'Notes on Propaganda', *Harper's Magazine*, 174: 36.

In Business (1999), 'Virgin Invests More in its Cola' (Apr.).

Jabri, V. (1996), *Discourses on Violence: Conflict Analysis Reconsidered* (Manchester: Manchester University Press).

Jackson, T. (1995), *Virgin King: Inside Richard Branson's Business Empire* (London: HarperCollins).

Jackson, W. A. (1996), 'White Liberal Intellectuals and Civil Rights', in B. Ward and T. Badger (eds.), *The Making of Martin Luther King and the Civil Rights Movement* (London: Macmillan).

James, C. L. R. (1980), *The Black Jacobins* (London: Allison & Busby).

James, L. (1997), *Raj: The Making and Unmaking of British India* (London: Abacus).

James, S. (1999), *The Ancient Celts: Ancient People or Modern Invention?* (London: British Museum Press).

Jenkins, R. (1996), *Social Identities* (London: Routledge).

Johnson, J. E. (1996), *Florence Nightingale* (Internet web site: http://miso.wwa.com/~jej/nightin.htm).

Kagan, D. (1997), *On the Origins of War* (London: Pimlico).

Kast, F. E., and Rosenzweig, J. E. (1970), *Organization and Management: A Systems Approach* (New York: McGraw-Hill).

Keegan, J. (1976), *The Face of Battle* (Harmondsworth: Penguin).

—— (1993*a*), *A History of Warfare* (London: Hutchinson).

—— (1993*b*), *Battle at Sea: From Man-Of-War to Submarine* (London: Pimlico).

Keeley, L. H. (1996), *War before Civilization* (Oxford: Oxford University Press).

Keitner, C. (1997), 'Power and Identity in Nationalist Conflicts', *Oxford International Review*, 8/2: 11–18.

Kelly, J. (1999), 'Feminist, Rebel and the Ideal Role Model', *Daily Mail*, 28 Apr.

Kendall, W. (1975), *The Labour Movement in Europe* (London: Allen Lane).

Kerr, P. (1997*a*), 'Valleys of Death', in Kerr (1997*b*).

—— (1997b), (ed.) *The Crimean War* (London: Boxtree).

Kershaw, I. (1983), *Popular Opinion and Political Dissent in the Third Reich 1933–1945* (Oxford: Oxford University Press).

—— (1991), *Hitler* (London: Longman).

—— (1994), 'The "Hitler Myth": Image and Reality in the Third Reich', in Crew (1994b).

—— (1998), *Hitler 1889–1936: Hubris* (London: Penguin).

Kertzer, D. (1988), *Ritual, Politics and Power* (New Haven, Conn.: Yale University Press).

Kets de Vries, M. (1996), 'Leaders Who Make a Difference', *European Management Journal*, 14/5: 486–93.

King, D., and Hattendorf, J. B. (1999), (eds.) *Every Man Will Do His Duty: An Anthology of Firsthand Accounts from the Age of Nelson* (New York: Henry Holt & Co.).

Kirk, R. (1997), 'Panzer', *Sky History*, 8 Mar.

Kleinfeld, J. (1997), 'The Union Lincoln Made', *History Today*, 47/11: 24–30.

Knight, I. (1995), *The Anatomy of the Zulu Army: From Shaka to Cetshwayo 1818–1879* (London: Greenhill Books).

—— (1998), *Great Zulu Battles 1838–1906* (London: Arms & Armour Press).

Kouzes, J. M., and Posner, B. Z. (1987), *The Leadership Challenge* (London: Jossey-Bass).

Laband, J., and Knight, I. (1997), *The War Correspondents: The Anglo-Zulu War* (Stroud: Bramley Books).

Lacey, R. (1986), *Ford* (London: Heinemann).

Laker (1977), 'Sir Freddie Laker' (Official Laker Airways Internet web page: http://www.lakerair.com/lakerbio/lakerbio.html).

Langbein, H. (1994), *Against All Hope: Resistance in the Nazi Concentration Camps 1938–1945* (London: Constable).

Larsen, E. (1976), *Weimar Witness* (London: Bachman & Turner).

Latour, B. (1986), 'The Powers of Association', in J. Law (ed.), *Power, Action and Belief* (London: Routledge).

Lavery, B. (1989), *Nelson's Navy: The Ships, Men and Organization 1793–1815* (London: Conway Maritime Press).

Lawson, M. (1996), 'The Art of Political Speaking', *Guardian*, 18 Sept.

Lawson-Tancred, H. (1991), 'Introduction', in Aristotle, *The Art of Rhetoric* (Harmondsworth: Penguin).

Lazarsfeld, P. F. (1944), *The People's Choice* (New York: Columbia University Press).

Lazonick, W. (1991), *Business Organization and the Myth of the Market Economy* (Cambridge: Cambridge University Press).

Lennon, P. (1999), 'The Attack that Never Was', *Guardian*, 17 Apr.

Levy, D. (1994), 'Chaos Theory and Strategy: Theory, Application, and Managerial Implications', *Strategic Management Journal*, 15: 167–78.

Lewchuck, W. (1987), *American Technology and the British Vehicle Industry* (Cambridge: Cambridge University Press).

Lewis, H. B. (1971), *Shame and Guilt in Neurosis* (New York: International Universities Press).

Lilley, S. J., and Platt, G. M. (1997), 'Correspondents' Images of Martin Luther King, Jr: An Interpretive Theory of Movement Leadership', in Grint (1997b).

Ling, P. (1998), 'Martin Luther King's Half-Forgotten Dream', *History Today*, 48/4: 17–22.

Lister, D. (1999), 'Cola War Proves Costly for Branson', *Evening Standard*, 17 Mar.

Littler, C. (1982), *The Development of the Labour Process in Britain, Japan and the USA* (London: Heinemann).

Lyon, D. (1996), *Sea Battles in Close Up: The Age of Nelson* (Shepperton, Surrey: Ian Allen Publishing).

MacArthur, B. (1993), *The Penguin Book of Twentieth Century Speeches* (Harmondsworth: Penguin).

—— (1996), *The Penguin Book of Historic Speeches* (Harmondsworth: Penguin).

McDonald, C. J. (1998), *Florence Nightingale* (Internet web site: http://www.dnai.com/~borneo/nightingale/cv.htm).

McGregor, D. (1984), 'Theory X and Theory Y', in D. Pugh (ed.), *Organization Theory* (Harmondsworth: Penguin).

Machiavelli, N. (1981), *The Prince* (Harmondsworth: Penguin).

—— (1997), *The Prince*, in Grint (1997*b*).

Magenheimer, H. (1998), *Hitler's War: Germany's Key Strategic Decisions 1940–1945* (London: Arms & Armour).

Malcolm, N. (1999), *Kosovo: A Short History* (London: Papermac).

Mallmann, K. M., and Paul, G. (1994), 'Omniscient, Omnipotent, and Omnipresent? Gestapo, Society and Resistance', in Crew (1994*b*).

Mann, M. (1986), *The Sources of Social Power*, i (Cambridge: Cambridge University Press).

Manwaring, G. E., and Dobrée, B. (1937), *The Floating Republic: An Account of the Mutinies at Spithead and the Nore in 1797* (London: Penguin).

Marsh, H. (1997), 'Can Branson Stretch to US?', *Marketing*, 3 Apr.

Marx, K. (1954), *Capital*, i (London: Lawrence & Wishart).

Matthew, H. C. G. (1986), 'The Liberal Age', in Morgan (1986).

Mazur, L. (1996) 'Follow the Leader', *Marketing Focus*, 29 Feb.

Mehrabian, A. (1968), 'Communication without Words', *Psychology Today*, 2: 53–5.

Millar, S. (1999), 'The Last Flight of Zulu Delta 576', *Guardian*, 27 May.

Miller, K. D., and Lewis, E. M. (1996), 'Touchstones, Authorities and Marian Anderson: The Making of "I Have a Dream" ', in B. Ward and T. Badger (eds.), *The Making of Martin Luther King* (Basingstoke: Macmillan).

Monteath, P. (1998), 'The Führer's Decision', *History Today*, 48/9: 4–6.

Morales, R. (1994), *Flexible Production: Restructuring of the International Automobile Industry* (Cambridge: Polity Press).

Morgan, J., and Cruz, C. (1997), 'In the Wake of Henry Ford's "craziness" ', *Purchasing*, 14 Aug. 3–6.

Morgan, K. O. (1986) (ed.), *The Oxford Illustrated History of Britain* (Oxford: Oxford University Press).

Morris, D. R. (1994), *The Washing of the Spears: A History of the Rise of the Zulu Nation under Shaka and its Fall in the Zulu War of 1879* (London: Pimlico).

Morrocco, J. D. (1996), 'BA defends pact with American', *Aviation Week and Space Technology*, 145: 3.

Mulvihill, M. (1997), 'Troubled Waters', in Kerr (1997*b*).

Murray, W. A. (1995*a*), 'Towards World War 1871–1914', in Parker (1995).

—— (1995*b*), 'The Industrialization of War 1815–71' in Parker (1995).

Nagle, J. (1999), 'Mad Dickey's Amusement 1798–1800', in King and Hattendorf (1999).

Neale, J. (1985), *The Cutlass and the Lash: Mutiny and Discipline in Nelson's Navy* (London: Pluto Press).

Neillands, R. (1995), *The Conquest of the Reich* (London: Orion).

Nightingale, F. (1858), *Mortality of the British Army during the Russian War* (London).

Noakes, J. (1987), 'Social Outcasts in the Third Reich', in Bessel (1987*b*).

Noble, D. F. (1977), *America by Design: Science, Technology and the Rise of Corporate Capitalism* (Oxford: Oxford University Press).

Northouse, P. G. (1997), *Leadership: Theory and Practice* (London: Sage).

Norton-Taylor, R. (1998), 'Churchill Planned to Drench Germany in Gas', *Guardian,* 2 Nov.

Overy, R. (1995), *Why the Allies Won* (London: Jonathan Cape).

—— (1997), *Russia's War* (London: Allen Lane).

Painter, N. I. (1996), *Sojourner Truth: A Life, A Symbol* (New York: W. W. Norton).

Palmer, A.W. (1963), *A Dictionary of Modern History* (Harmondsworth: Penguin).

Parker, G. (1995) (ed.), *The Cambridge Illustrated History of Warfare* (Cambridge: Cambridge University Press).

Payne, C. (1995), *I've Got the Light of Freedom: The Organizing Tradition and the Mississippi Freedom Struggle* (Berkeley and Los Angeles: University of California Press).

Pears, I. (1997), 'The Gentleman and the Hero: Wellington and Napoleon in the Nineteenth Century', in Grint (1997*b*).

Peddie, J. (1994), *The Roman War Machine* (Stroud: Alan Sutton).

Perkin, H. (1972), *The Origins of Modern English Society 1780–1880* (London: Routledge & Kegan Paul).

Peukert, D. J. K. (1987*a*), *Inside Nazi Germany: Conformity, Opposition and Racism in Everyday Life* (London: Yale University Press).

—— (1987*b*), 'Youth in the Third Reich', in Bessel (1987*b*).

Pine, L. (1997), 'Nazism in the Classroom', *History Today,* 47/3: 22–7.

Pino, R. (1999), *Corporate Aikido* (New York: McGraw-Hill).

Pocock, T. (1994), *Horatio Nelson* (London: Pimlico).

Pope, D. (1997), *Life in Nelson's Navy* (London: Chatham Publishing).

—— (1998), *The Black Ship* (New York: Owl Books).

Pope, S. (1998), *Hornblower's Navy: Life at Sea in the Age of Nelson* (London: Orion Media).

Potter, J., and Reicher, S. (1987), 'Discourses of Community and Conflict', *British Journal of Social Psychology,* 26: 25–40.

—— and Wetherell, M. (1987), *Discourse and Social Psychology* (London: Sage).

Poulsen, C. (1984), *The English Rebels* (London: Journeyman Press).

Putnam, L. L., Phillips, N., and Chapman, P. (1996), 'Metaphors of Communication in Organization', in S. R. Clegg, C. Hardy, and W. R. Nord (eds.), *Handbook of Organizational Studies* (London: Sage).

Pye, G. (1997*a*), 'Sisters of Mercy', in Kerr (1997*b*).

—— (1997*b*), 'A Real Russian Winter', in Kerr (1997*b*).

Rapport, M. (1998), 'Napoleon's Rise to Power', *History Today,* 48/1: 12–19.

Rees, L. (1997), *The Nazis: A Warning from History* (London: BBC).

Rhodes-James, R. (1998), *A Spirit Undaunted* (New York: Little Brown).

Richardson, W. (1999), 'In the King's Service, 1793–1794', in King and Hattendorf (1999).

Roberts, A. (1997), 'Hitler's England: What if Germany had Invaded Britain in May 1940?', in P. Paret (ed.), *Makers of Modern Strategy: From Machiavelli to the Nuclear Age* (Oxford: Oxford University Press).

Robinson, W. (1999), 'The Battle of Trafalgar 1805', in King and Hattendorf (1999).

Rodger, N. A. M. (1986), *The Wooden World: An Anatomy of the Georgian Navy* (London: Fontana).

Rosenbaum, R. (1998), *Explaining Hitler* (London: Macmillan).

Sadowski, Y. (1998), 'What Really Makes the World Go to War', *Guardian*, 1 Aug.

Sage, H. (1997), 'Branson Risks Brand with *Virgin* Ventures', *Marketing Week*, 19/43: 26.

Sahlins, P. (1989), *Boundaries: The Making of France and Spain in the Pyrenees* (Berkeley and Los Angeles: University of California Press).

Sampson, A. (1984), *Empires of the Sky: The Politics, Contests and Cartels of World Airlines* (London: Hodder & Stoughton).

Santosuosso, A. (1997), *Soldiers, Citizens and the Symbols of War* (Oxford: Westview).

Sargant Florence, P. (1961), *The Logic of British and American Industry* (London: Routledge & Kegan Paul).

Scheff, T. (1994), 'A Theory of Ethnic Nationalism', in C. Calhoun (ed.), *Social Theory and the Politics of Identity* (Oxford: Blackwell).

Schom, A. (1992), *Trafalgar: Countdown to Battle, 1803–1805* (Harmondsworth: Penguin).

Schwartz, M., and Fish, A. (1998), *Business History*, 40/3: 48–71.

Serrin, W. (1974), *The Company and the Union* (New York: Vintage Books).

Sheff, D. (1997), 'The Interview: Richard Branson', *Forbes*, 24 Feb.

Sherif, M. (1967), *Group Conflict and Co-operation* (London: Routledge & Kegan Paul).

Shils, E. (1963), 'Charisma, Order and Status', *American Sociological Review*, 30: 199–213.

Small, H. (1998), *Florence Nightingale: Avenging Angel* (London: Constable).

Smith, G. (1979), *Democracy in Western Germany* (London: Heinemann Educational Books).

Spiers, E. (1994), 'The Late Victorian Army 1868–1914', in Chandler and Beckett (1994).

Steinweis, A. (1995), 'Hitler and Carlyle's "Historical Greatness" ', *History Today*, 45/6: 33–8.

Stewart, R. (1967), *Managers and their Jobs* (Maidenhead: McGraw-Hill).

Storr, A. (1996), *Feet of Clay: A Study of Gurus* (London: HarperCollins).

Strachey, L. (1920), *Eminent Victorians* (London: Chatto & Windus).

Strauss, A. (1978), *Negotiations: Varieties, Processes, Contexts and Social Order* (London: Jossey-Bass).

Summers, A. (1988), *Angels and Citizens: British Women as Military Nurses 1854–1914* (London: Routledge & Kegan Paul).

Swan, J. (1992), 'Apocalypse at Münster', in R. Cowley (ed.), *Experience of War* (London: W. W. Norton & Co.).

Taylor, A. J. (1972), *Laissez-Faire and State Intervention in Nineteenth Century Britain* (London: Macmillan).

Temple Patterson, A. (1968), *The Naval Mutiny at Spithead 1797* (Portsmouth: Portsmouth City Council).

Thiétart, A., and Forgues, B. (1995), 'Chaos Theory and Organization', *Organization Science*, 6/1: 19–31.

Thomas, H. (1997), *The Slave Trade: The History of the Atlantic Slave Trade 1440–1870* (London: Picador).

Tracy, N. (1998a) (ed.), *The Naval Chronicle: The Contemporary Record of the Royal Navy at War*, i: *1793–1798* (London: Chatham Publishing).

—— (1998b) (ed.), *The Naval Chronicle: The Contemporary Record of the Royal Navy at War*, ii: *1799–1804* (London: Chatham Publishing).

Traynor, I. (1999a), 'German Bank Sold Gold from Death Camps', *Guardian*, 30 Jan.

—— (1999b), 'German Firms to Pay £1 Billion to Slave Victims', *Guardian*, 17 Feb.

—— (1999c), 'Chronicles of Death Foretold', *Guardian*, 5 May.

Trollope, J. (1994), *Britannia's Daughters: Women of the British Empire* (London: Pimlico).

Troup, F. (1975), *South Africa: An Historical Introduction* (Harmondsworth: Penguin).

Veranov, M. (1997), *Third Reich at War* (London: Robinson).

Versluis, A. (1994), *Native American Traditions* (Shaftesbury: Element Books).

Vicinus, M., and Nergaard, B. (1990) (eds.), *Ever Yours, Florence Nightingale* (Cambridge, Mass.: Harvard University Press).

Wardy, R. (1996), *The Birth of Rhetoric: Georgias, Plato and their Successors* (London: Routledge).

Warner, M. (1994), 'Home: Our Famous Island Race', Reith Lecture, BBC2, Mar.

Weber, M. (1970), 'Politics as a Vocation', in H. H. Gerth and C. Wright Mills (eds.), *From Max Weber* (London: Routledge & Kegan Paul).

—— (1978), *Economy and Society* (Berkeley and Los Angeles: University of California Press).

Welch, D. (1995), *The Third Reich: Politics and Propaganda* (London: Routledge).

Wheeler, J. S. (1999), *The Making of a World Power* (Stroud: Sutton).

Whisler, T. R. (1999), *The British Motor Industry, 1954–94* (Oxford: Oxford University Press).

White, C. (1995), 'The Immortal Memory', in C. White (ed.), *The Nelson Companion* (Stroud: Sutton).

—— (1998), *1797: Nelson's Year of Destiny* (Stroud: Sutton).

White, J. (1996), 'Nixon *Was* the One: Edgar Daniel Nixon, the MIA and the Montgomery Bus Boycott', in B. Ward and T. Badger (eds.), *The Making of Martin Luther King and the Civil Rights Movement* (London: Macmillan).

White, R. P., Hodgson, P., and Crainer, S. (1996), *The Future of Leadership: A White Water Revolution* (London: Ashridge/Pitman Publishing).

Wilke, G. (1987), 'Village Life in Nazi Germany', in Bessel (1987b).

Williams, K., Haslam, C., and Williams, J. (1992), 'Ford Versus "Fordism": The Beginning of Mass Production?', *Work, Employment and Society*, 6/4: 517–55.

—— —— —— Adcroft, A., and Johal, S. (1993), 'The Myth of the Line: Ford's Production of the Model T at Highland Park, 1909–16', *Business History*, 36/3: 66–87.

Williamson, G. (1996), *The SS: Hitler's Instrument of Terror* (Leicester: Sidgwick & Jackson).

Wills, G. (1992), *Lincoln at Gettysburg: The Words that Remade America* (New York: Touchstone).

Willis, J., and Turnock, R. (1998), 'The Veil of Tears', *Guardian*, 17 Aug.

Wilson, J. M. (1996), 'Henry Ford: A Just-in-Time Pioneer', *Production and Inventory Management Journal* (second quarter), 26–31.

Winston, B. (1997), 'Triumph of the Will', *History Today*, 47/1: 24–8.

Winter, D. (1996a), 'Feisty Ford', *Ward's Auto-World*, 32/5: 63–5.

—— (1996b), 'The Mass-Production Revolution', *Ward's Auto-World*, 32/5: 101–2.

Womack, J. P., Jones, D. T., and Roos, D. (1990), *The Machine that Changed the World* (New York: Rawson Associates).

Wood, W. J. (1984), *Leaders and Battles: The Art of Military Leadership* (Novato, Calif.: Presidio Press).

Woodham-Smith, C. (1982), *Florence Nightingale* (London: Constable & Co, Ltd.).

Woolgar, S. (1983), 'Irony in the Social Study of Science', in K. Knorr-Cetina and M. J. Mulkay (eds.), *Science Observed: Perspectives on the Social Study of Science* (London: Sage).

Wright, P. (1996), *Managerial Leadership* (London: Routledge).

Young, P., and Jesser, P. (1997), *The Media and the Military: From the Crimea to Desert Strike* (London: Macmillan).

Zoia, D. E. (1996), 'Global Roots Run Deep', *Ward's Auto-World*, 32/5: 160.

Index

Lightning Source UK Ltd.
Milton Keynes UK
UKOW03f0058190913

217467UK00001B/15/P

*This book has been printed digitally and produced in a standard specification
in order to ensure its continuing availability*

OXFORD
UNIVERSITY PRESS

Great Clarendon Street, Oxford OX2 6DP
United Kingdom

Oxford University Press is a department of the University of Oxford.
It furthers the University's objective of excellence in research, scholarship,
and education by publishing worldwide.
Oxford is a registered trade mark of Oxford University Press in the UK
and in certain other countries

British Library Cataloguing in Publication Data
Data available

Library of Congress Cataloging in Publication Data
Data available

ISBN 978-0-19-924489-8

The Arts of Leadership

KEITH GRINT

OXFORD
UNIVERSITY PRESS

THE ARTS OF LEADERSHIP